商务印书馆（成都）有限责任公司出品

商学导论

第 7 版，双语教学版

〔美〕威廉·普赖德　罗伯特·休斯　杰克·卡普尔　著
孔小磊　译注

商务印书馆
2025年·北京

Introduction to Business, 7th Edition

William M. Pride　　*Robert J. Hughes*　　*Jack R. Kapoor*

978-0-357-71794-3

Cengage
200 Pier 4 Boulevard
Boston, MA 02210
USA

Brief Contents 简要目录

Contents 目录

Chapter 2: Global Business 31

全球商务

PART 2 Business Ownership and Entrepreneurship 46

企业所有权和企业家精神

PART 3 Management and Organization 90 管理和组织

Chapter 5: Understanding the Management Process 91 管理过程

Chapter 7: Producing Quality Goods and Services 134 提供优质商品和服务

PART 4 Human Resources 160

人力资源

Chapter 8: Attracting and Retaining the Best Employees 161

吸引和留住最优秀的员工

Chapter 9: Motivating and Satisfying Employees 186

激励和提高员工的满意度

PART 5 Marketing 210 市场营销

Chapter 10: Building Customer Relationships Through Effective Marketing 211 通过有效的市场营销建立客户关系

Chapter 15: Mastering Financial Management 359

掌握财务管理

Acknowledgments 致谢

The quality of this book and its supplements program has been helped immensely by the insightful and rich comments of a special set of instructors. Their thoughtful and helpful comments had real impact in shaping the final product. We wish to thank:

Ken Anglin, *Minnesota State University, Mankato*
Ellen A. Benowitz, *Mercer County Community College*
Michael Bento, *Owens Community College*
Laura Bulas, *Central Community College, NE*
Brennan Carr, *Long Beach City College*
Paul Coakley, *The Community College of Baltimore County*
Jean Condon, *Mid-Plains Community College*
Mary Cooke, *Surry Community College*
Dean Danielson, *San Joaquin Delta College*
Gary Donnelly, *Casper College*
Karen Edwards, *Chemeketa Community College*
Donna K. Fisher, *Georgia Southern University*
Mark Fox, *Indiana University South Bend*
Connie Golden, *Lakeland Community College*
Karen Gore, *Ivy Tech Community College—Evansville*
John Guess, *Delgado Community College*
Tom Hendricks, *Oakland Community College*
Robert James, *Macomb Community College*
Eileen Kearney, *Montgomery Community College*
Mary Beth Klinger, *College of Southern Maryland*
Natasha Lindsey, *University of North Alabama*
Emilio Lopez, *Dallas College*
Robert Lupton, *Central Washington University*
John Mago, *Anoka Ramsey Community College*
Pamela G. McElligott, *St. Louis Community College Meramec*
Myke McMullen, *Long Beach City College*
Carol Miller, *Community College of Denver*
Diane Minger, *Dallas College*
Jaideep Motwani, *Grand Valley State*
Mark Nagel, *Normandale Community College*
Dyan Pease, *Sacramento City College*
Jeffrey D. Penley, *Catawba Valley Community College*
Angela J. Rabatin, *Prince George's Community College*
Anthony Racka, *Oakland Community College—Auburn Hills Campus*
Dwight Riley, *Dallas College*
Carol Rowey, *Community College of Rhode Island*
Christy Shell, *Houston Community College*
Cindy Simerly, *Lakeland Community College*
Yolanda I. Smith, *Northern Virginia Community College*
Gail South, *Montgomery College*
Rieann Spence-Gale, *Northern Virginia Comm. College—Alexandria Campus*
Kurt Stanberry, *University of Houston, Downtown*
John Striebich, *Monroe Community College*
Keith Taylor, *Lansing Community College*
Tricia Troyer, *Waubonsee Community College*
Leo Trudel, *University of Maine - Fort Kent*
Anne Williams, *Gateway Community College*
Kevin Wortley, *Dallas College*

We want to thank the following people for their professional and technical assistance: Gwyn Walters, Klarisa Posada, Ashley Nguyen, Kelsey Reddick, Brenda Aram, Theresa Kapoor, David Pierce, Kathryn Thumme, Karen Tucker, Dave Kapoor, Susan Fant, and Jeff Penley.

Many talented professionals at Cengage Learning have contributed to the development of *Foundations of Business, 7e*. We are especially grateful to Erin Joyner, Thais Alencar, Joe Sabatino, Heather Thompson, Clara Kuhlman, Allie Janneck, Stephanie Hall, Megan Guiliani, Angela Sheehan, Sara Greenwood, Hannah May, Amanda Ryan, Tony Winslow, Cara Suriyamongkol, and Nick Perez. Their inspiration, patience, support, and friendship are invaluable.

W. M. P.
R. J. H.
J. R. K.

About the Authors 作者介绍

William M. Pride
Texas A&M University

William M. Pride is Professor of Marketing at Mays Business School, Texas A&M University. He received his PhD from Louisiana State University. He is the author of Cengage Learning's *Marketing*, 20th edition, a market leader. Dr. Pride's research interests are in advertising, promotion, and distribution channels.

Dr. Pride's research articles have appeared in major journals in the fields of advertising and marketing, such as *Journal of Marketing, Journal of Marketing Research, Journal of the Academy of Marketing Science*, and the *Journal of Advertising*. Dr. Pride is a member of the American Marketing Association, Academy of Marketing Science, Society for Marketing Advances, and the Marketing Management Association. Dr. Pride has taught Principles of Marketing and other marketing courses for more than 45 years at both the undergraduate and graduate levels.

Robert J. Hughes
Dallas College - Richland Campus

Robert J. Hughes (EdD, University of North Texas) specializes in business administration and college instruction. He has taught Introduction to Business for more than 35 years both on campus and online for Richland College—one of seven campuses that are part of the Dallas College System. In addition to *Business* and *Foundations of Business*, published by Cengage Learning, he has authored college textbooks in personal finance and business mathematics; served as a content consultant for two popular national television series, *It's Strictly Business* and *Dollars & Sense: Personal Finance for the 21st Century*, and is the lead author for a business math project utilizing computer-assisted instruction funded by the ALEKS Corporation. He is also active in many academic and professional organizations and has served as a consultant and investment advisor to individuals, businesses, and charitable organizations. Dr. Hughes is the recipient of three different Teaching in Excellence Awards at Richland College. According to Dr. Hughes, after 35 years of teaching Introduction to Business, the course is still exciting: "There's nothing quite like the thrill of seeing students succeed, especially in a course like Introduction to Business, which provides the foundation for not only academic courses, but also life in the real world."

Jack R. Kapoor
College of DuPage

Jack R. Kapoor (EdD, Northern Illinois University) has been a Professor of Business and Economics in the Business and Technology Division at the College of DuPage, where he has taught Introduction to Business, Marketing, Management, Economics, and Personal Finance since 1969. He previously taught at Illinois Institute of Technology's Stuart School of Management, San Francisco State University's School of World Business, and other colleges. Professor Kapoor was awarded the Business and Services Division's Outstanding Professor Award for 1999–2000. He served as an Assistant National Bank Examiner for the U.S. Treasury Department and as an international trade consultant to Bolting Manufacturing Co., Ltd., Mumbai, India.

Dr. Kapoor is known internationally as a coauthor of several textbooks in Business and Personal Finance, including Business MindTap (Cengage Learning), has served as a content consultant for two popular national television series, *Dollars & Sense: Personal Finance for the 21st Century* and *The Business File: An Introduction to Business*, and developed two full-length audio courses in business and personal finance. He has been quoted in many national newspapers and magazines, including *USA Today, U.S. News & World Report*, the *Chicago Sun-Times, Crain's Small Business*, the *Chicago Tribune*, and other publications.

Dr. Kapoor has traveled around the world and has studied business practices in capitalist, socialist, and communist countries.

PART 1
The Environment of Business
商业环境

Chapter 1
Ethics and Social Responsibility in Business

Chapter 2
Global Business

In this part of *Introduction to Business*, we discuss ethical and social responsibility issues that affect business firms and our society. Then we explore the increasing importance of international business.

Chapter 1

Ethics and Social Responsibility in Business

商业伦理与社会责任

Why Should You Care?

Business ethics and social responsibility issues have become extremely relevant in today's business world. Business schools teach business ethics to prepare managers to be more responsible. Corporations are developing ethics and social responsibility programs to help meet these needs in the workplace.

Learning Objectives

Once you complete this chapter, you will be able to:

1-1 Define *business ethics.*

1-2 Identify the types of ethical concerns that arise in the business world.

1-3 Discuss the factors that affect the level of ethical behavior in organizations.

1-4 Explain how organizations can encourage ethical decision making in business.

1-5 Describe how our current views on the social responsibility of business have evolved.

1-6 List the responsibilities businesses have to the public, especially with regard to consumer rights and public health.

1-7 Analyze how present employment practices are being used to counteract past abuses.

1-8 Describe the major environmental issues and businesses' response to them.

1-9 Identify the steps a business must take to implement a program of social responsibility.

Inside Business 商业透视：美国普渡制药的营销策略加剧了阿片类药物危机

Marketing Tactics at Purdue Fueled the Opioid Crisis

The opioid crisis has killed more than 450,000 people in the United States since 1999 largely due to illegal and misleading marketing. Purdue Pharma LP, a privately held pharmaceutical company, reached an $8.34 billion settlement for its marketing and distribution of OxyContin, an addictive painkiller, after years of state and federal investigations. Purdue is not the only company implicated in the crisis. Manufacturer Johnson & Johnson and distributors McKesson, Cardinal Health, and AmerisourceBergen have also faced legal action.

Ethical misconduct at Purdue included illegal kickbacks, funding pain treatment groups, misrepresentations made to the Drug Enforcement Administration (DEA), and marketing messages that minimized the addictive nature of OxyContin. The drugmaker used marketing data to target physicians who were the highest opioid prescribers as well as physicians in states with lighter prescription regulations. After compiling detailed prescriber profiles, Purdue would attempt to influence the physicians' prescribing patterns. In two instances, Purdue paid doctors to influence them to write more opioid prescriptions. Additionally, the company made false claims about the safety of the product.

Purdue's unethical and illegal actions had a direct impact on society, fueling the opioid crisis and a culture of corruption throughout its supply chain. Purdue has since made changes in leadership, operations, governance, and oversight to keep the company in compliance with the law. Purdue's owners, the Sackler family, created an image of philanthropy and avoided being publicly tied to the opioid crisis. Now, many prominent institutions will no longer accept donations from the family. However, neither the Sackler family nor top Purdue executives will face prison time as a result of the settlement.[1]

Did you know?

Purdue Pharma's corporate values are integrity, courage, innovation, and collaboration.

Obviously, organizations want to be seen as responsible corporate citizens and recognize the need to harmonize their operations with environmental demands and other social concerns. However, as shown in the opening vignette, not all firms have adopted a mindset that includes social responsibility and ethics in their strategies, decisions, and activities. Some managers still regard such business programs as a poor investment, in which the cost is not worth the return. Other managers—indeed, most managers—view the cost of these programs as a necessary business expense, similar to wages or rent.

Most managers today are finding ways to balance an agenda of socially responsible activities with the drive to generate profits. This also happens to be a good way for organizations to demonstrate their values and to attract like-minded employees, customers, and shareholders. In a highly competitive global business environment, an increasing number of companies are seeking to set themselves apart by developing a reputation for ethical and socially responsible behavior.

We begin this chapter by defining *business ethics* and examining ethical issues. Next, we look at the standards of behavior in organizations and how ethical behavior can be encouraged. We then turn to the topic of social responsibility. We explore the evolution of the idea of social responsibility, compare and contrast two present-day models of social responsibility, and present arguments for and against increasing the social responsibility of business. We then explore business responsibilities toward the public. Next, we discuss how social responsibility in business has affected employment practices and environmental concerns. Finally, we consider the commitment and planning that go into a firm's program of social responsibility.

商业伦理的定义

1-1 Business Ethics Defined

Learning Objective

1-1 Define *business ethics.*

Ethics is the study of right and wrong and of the morality of the choices individuals make. An ethical decision or action is one that is "right" according to some standard of behavior. When there is strong consensus regarding a particular unethical action, society may demand laws to prohibit it. **Business ethics** is the application of moral standards to business situations. Recent court cases involving unethical behavior have helped make business ethics a matter of public concern. In one such case, concert promoter Billy McFarland was convicted of fraud, sentenced to six years in prison, and ordered to pay millions in restitution for bilking concert goers and investors of the Fyre Festival. Concert goers, who had paid as much as $100,000 to attend, were led to expect to hobnob with celebrities and models while enjoying lavish accommodations and popular bands, but found nothing of the kind when they arrived. McFarland also faces numerous lawsuits related to the ill-fated festival, and several celebrities who endorsed it on social media were fined.[2] While all unethical business actions do not result in fines and jail time, they do harm others by eroding trust in business decisions and decision makers. Regardless of their legality, all business decisions can be judged as right or wrong.

✓ Concept Check

- What is meant by business ethics?
- How do business ethics differ from personal ethics?

商业中的伦理问题

1-2 Ethical Issues in Business

Learning Objective

1-2 Identify the types of ethical concerns that arise in the business world.

Ethical issues often arise out of a business's relationships with investors, customers, employees, creditors, suppliers, or competitors. Each of these stakeholder groups has specific concerns and usually exerts pressure on the organization's managers. Investors, for example, want management to make sensible financial decisions that will boost sales, profits, and returns on their investments. Customers expect a firm's products to be safe, reliable, and reasonably priced. Employees demand to be treated fairly in hiring, promotion, and compensation decisions. Creditors require accounts to be paid on time and the accounting information furnished by the firm to be accurate. Competitors expect the firm's competitive practices to be fair and honest. Chick-fil-A, for example, sued 17 chicken suppliers, including Tyson Foods, Perdue Farms, and Pilgrim's Pride, accusing them of price-fixing—colluding to keep the prices it pays for poultry artificially high. The fast-food restaurant chain contends that the suppliers engaged in anticompetitive behavior by conspiring to share confidential bidding and pricing information in order to sustain higher chicken prices, resulting in consumers paying more for inferior chicken. A court will have to resolve the dispute.[3]

Businesspeople face ethical issues every day, and some of these issues can be difficult to assess. Although some types of issues arise infrequently, others occur regularly. Let's take a closer look at several ethical issues.

公平和诚实

1-2a Fairness and Honesty

Fairness and honesty in business are two important ethical concerns. Besides obeying all laws and regulations, businesspeople are expected to refrain from knowingly deceiving, misrepresenting, or intimidating others. The consequences of failing to do so can be expensive. For example, NeuroMetrix, Inc., paid more than $4 million to settle Federal Trade Commission (FTC) charges that it deceptively promoted its Quell electrical nerve stimulation device. The commission claimed the company misled customers when it falsely touted the device as "clinically proven" and "Food and Drug Administration (FDA) cleared" for treating pain, when it was neither. In addition to the fine, the company and its marketers were ordered not to make any further false or misleading claims about the product.[4]

伦理
ethics the study of right and wrong and of the morality of the choices individuals make

商业伦理
business ethics the application of moral standards to business situations

If consumers feel they have been deceived or that companies have been unfair, they will take their business elsewhere and may even ask regulators to intervene. For instance, the Securities and Exchange Commission (SEC) charged the stock-trading app Robinhood with giving customers misleading information about the actual costs of trading with the app and failing to obtain the best reasonably available terms to execute their orders. The SEC blamed the app for depriving customers of $34 million in total. Robinhood paid $65 million to settle the case and updated its procedures to ensure that it executes the best trades possible for its users.[5]

组织关系

1-2b Organizational Relationships

Businesspeople may be tempted to place their personal welfare above the welfare of others or the welfare of the organization. As an example, Kristin M. Lapree was convicted of misappropriating more than $700,000 of funds while she worked as the business manager of Wisconsin-based Rettler Corporation. She was sentenced to six years in prison and ordered to pay restitution.[6] Aside from the legality of such actions, they may threaten the livelihood of employees and the business itself and harm relations with customers, suppliers, and others.

Relationships among co-workers often create ethical problems. Unethical behavior in these areas includes taking credit for others' ideas or work, not meeting one's commitments in a mutual agreement, and pressuring others to behave unethically. Managers and executives have even more power to pressure others due to their ability to provide rewards and sanctions. Consider Wells Fargo, which suffered incalculable damage to its reputation after investigators revealed that managers had pressured employees to achieve unrealistic sales quotas, which led many bank employees to open fake accounts for customers without their knowledge. The company ultimately paid billions of dollars to settle criminal and civil charges; several of its executives also face charges as a result of the scandal.[7] The Global Business Ethics Survey reported that 22 percent of workers around the world say

Ethics violations Ethics violations can be more than humiliating. Ethics violators sometimes go to prison, pay large fines, lose their jobs, lose their families, and pay expensive legal fees.

they feel pressured to compromise their organization's ethics guidelines and policies, or to break the law; in North America, that value is 31 percent.[8]

One issue related to fairness and honesty is **plagiarism**—knowingly taking someone else's words, ideas, or other original material without acknowledging the source. When exposed, the consequences of plagiarism can be grave. For example, the U.S. Army War College rescinded the master's degree that it had awarded U.S. Senator John Walsh after an academic review by the college determined that Walsh had copied significant parts of his final paper from other sources. Walsh withdrew from his reelection campaign soon after the scandal.[9]

When misconduct occurs in business, investors also suffer. Investors and owners must be able to trust that companies are acting in their best interests and reporting their activities truthfully. They have the right to expect that all actions by a firm contribute toward a return on their investment. Two issues that raise flags for investors are executive compensation packages that are out of line with performance and the conflict of interest that may occur when a chief executive officer also sits on the board of directors—the group that oversees the CEO. In recent years, investors have protested high executive compensation, particularly when those executives do not generate strong profits for the owners. Shareholders have voted against executive compensation packages at a number of companies, including Electronic Arts, Ameriprise, Disney, and more.[10] Activist investors have also protested companies whose CEOs also sit on the board of directors, which can result in a conflict of interest when the CEO's performance is under review.

利益冲突

1-2c Conflicts of Interest

A **conflict of interest** results when businesspeople take advantage of a situation for their own personal interest rather than for the employer's interest. Examples of situations involving conflicts of interest generally involve an employee who has divided loyalties, such as a manager who is dating a subordinate, an employee with a close relative who works for a competitor, a purchasing manager who chooses to do business with another firm in which he is an investor, or a firm that advises clients without informing them that it has a relationship with some of the products it recommends. Even the appearance of a conflict of interest can jeopardize a businessperson's credibility. As an example, Louis DeJoy came under fire for failing to divest his ownership shares of XPO Logistics—where he previously served as CEO and chairman—when he was appointed Postmaster General by then President Donald Trump. His continued equity stake in XPO, a transportation and logistics firm that has million-dollar contracts with the U.S. Postal Service, created a conflict of interest for him when making shipping decisions for the federal agency. After the backlash, DeJoy agreed to sell his XPO stock.[11] In such cases, consumers and taxpayers have the right to know whether the head of a major government agency may be favoring certain contractors over others in order to benefit financially.

Conflicts of interest may occur when payments and gifts make their way into business deals. Although bribes—gifts, favors, or payments offered with the intent of influencing an outcome—are often part of business negotiations overseas, it is illegal for American businesspersons and companies to use bribes in the United States or abroad. Defending against bribery charges can be costly and affect future business negotiations. A wise rule to remember is that anything given to a person that might unfairly influence that person's business decision is a bribe, and all bribes are unethical.

剽窃

plagiarism knowingly taking someone else's words, ideas, or other original material without acknowledging the source

利益冲突

conflict of interest when businesspeople take advantage of a situation for their own personal interest rather than for the employer's interest

At Procter & Gamble (P&G), all employees are obligated to act solely in the best interests of the company. P&G defines a conflict of interest as when an employee has a personal relationship or financial or other interest that could interfere with this obligation, or when employees use their position with the company for personal gain. The company requires employees to disclose all potential conflicts of interest and to take prompt actions to eliminate a conflict when the company asks them to do so. Generally, P&G prohibits employees from receiving gifts, entertainment, or other gratuities from people with whom the company does business because doing so could imply an obligation on the part of the company and potentially pose a conflict of interest.[12]

沟通

1-2d Communications

Business communications, especially advertising, can present ethical questions. False and misleading advertising is illegal and unethical, and it can infuriate customers. For example, angry consumers filed suit against the Folger Coffee Company, arguing that 30.5 ounce canisters of Folgers ground coffee claim to contain enough to make 240 servings, but actually hold just 173 servings when prepared according to the instructions on the canister. Disgruntled consumers have filed similar lawsuits against other coffee makers.[13] In another example, the Federal Trade Commission fined Williams-Sonoma $1 million and ordered the retailer to stop claiming that some products sold in Williams-Sonoma and Pottery Barn stores are "Made in USA," when they contained significant imported components.[14] Sponsors of advertisements aimed at children must be especially careful to avoid misleading messages. Advertisers of health-related products also must take precautions to guard against deception when using such descriptive terms as *low fat, fat free,* and *light.* In fact, the Federal Trade Commission has issued guidelines on the use of these labels.

✓ Concept Check

- What are the different types of ethical concerns that may arise in the business world?
- Explain and give an example of how advertising can present ethical questions.

Entrepreneurial Success

创业成功：与社交媒体建立健康的关系

Building a Healthy Relationship with Social Media

Social media has long been criticized for its negative impact on society. For example, algorithms are often designed to manipulate users to stay on social networks as long as possible. It has also had immeasurable implications for data privacy. But despite these downfalls, social media still holds value for entrepreneurs as a source of inspiration, tools, insights, and community. With just a few simple changes, entrepreneurs can build a healthier relationship with social media.

For startups, establishing a brand on social media is critical, and an opportunity exists for creative, thoughtful engagement. However, it's important to be in control of your tech environment. Many apps allow users to reduce their screen time. A tool called Mailbrew rounds up social feeds and email newsletters into a single daily digest, and an app called Freedom blocks distracting apps on desktop and mobile devices to help users be more productive. Utilizing such resources can help you become the master of your devices.

Entrepreneurs can also set a positive example for their team members by promoting work-life balance and setting clear parameters for "on" and "off" times. Many entrepreneurs work around the clock, so it can be challenging to step away from the laptop and call it a day. But, by protecting off hours, entrepreneurs can cultivate a more productive work environment. In the end, unplugging can be positive for mental health and help people replenish their energy.

It's up to the next generation of business owners to disrupt the social media cycle. Rather than calling it quits, entrepreneurs can redefine their connection with their devices and build a healthier relationship with social media.

Sources: Based on information in Aytekin Tank, "How Entrepreneurs Can Harness The Power of Social Media for Good," *Entrepreneur*, October 22, 2020; Adi Robertson, "Telling People to Delete Facebook Won't Fix the Internet," *The Verge*, September 4, 2020.

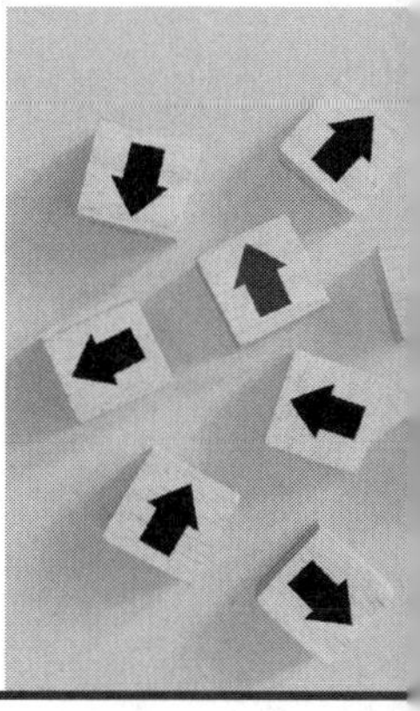

影响伦理行为的因素

1-3 Factors Affecting Ethical Behavior

Learning Objective

1-3 Discuss the factors that affect the level of ethical behavior in organizations.

Is it possible for an individual with strong moral values to make ethically questionable decisions in a business setting? What factors affect a person's inclination to make either ethical or unethical decisions in a business organization? Although the answers to these questions are not entirely clear, three general sets of factors do appear to influence the standards of behavior in an organization.[15] As shown in Figure 1-1, these include individual factors, social factors, and opportunities.

影响伦理的个体因素

1-3a Individual Factors Affecting Ethics

Several factors influence an individual's ethical choices and behavior in an organization, including personal knowledge, values, and goals. How much an individual knows about an issue is one factor. A decision maker with a greater amount of knowledge regarding a situation may take steps to avoid ethical problems, whereas a less-informed person may unknowingly make choices that could lead to ethical problems. Individuals' moral values and central, value-related attitudes also clearly influence their business behavior and choices. Most organizations do not try to change an employee's personal ethics but instead strive to hire people with good character and values that complement their own. The actions of specific individuals in scandal-plagued companies, such as Wells Fargo, Volkswagen, Theranos, Turing Pharmaceuticals, and Enron, often raise questions about individuals' personal character and integrity. Finally, most people join organizations to accomplish personal goals. The types of personal goals an individual aspires to and how they choose to pursue them have a significant impact on that individual's behavior in an organization.

影响伦理的社会因素

1-3b Social Factors Affecting Ethics

Many social factors can affect ethical behavior within a firm, including cultural norms, actions and decisions of co-workers, values and attitudes of "significant others," and the use of the internet. A person's behavior in the workplace, to some degree, is determined by cultural norms, and these social factors vary from one culture to another. For example, in some countries it is acceptable and ethical for customs agents to receive gratuities for performing ordinary, legal tasks that are a part of their jobs, whereas in other countries these practices would be viewed as unethical and perhaps illegal. The actions and decisions of co-workers may also shape a person's sense of business ethics. For example, if your co-workers peruse YouTube and Instagram on company time and at company expense, you might come to view that behavior as acceptable and ethical because everyone does it. The moral values and attitudes of "significant others"—spouses, friends, and relatives,

Figure 1-1 Factors That Affect the Level of Ethical Behavior in an Organization

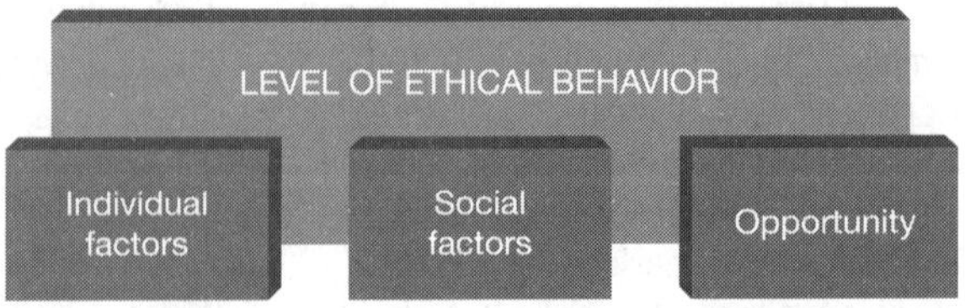

Source: Based on O. C. Ferrell and Larry Gresham, "A Contingency Framework for Understanding Ethical Decision Making in Marketing," *Journal of Marketing* (Summer 1985), 89.

for instance—also can affect an employee's perception of what is ethical and unethical behavior in the workplace.

The internet also presents challenges for firms whose employees enjoy easy access through convenient high-speed connections at work. An employee's behavior online can be viewed as offensive to co-workers and possibly lead to lawsuits against the firm if employees engage in unethical behavior on controversial websites not related to their job. Moreover, if an employee posts controversial content on social media using their employer's email, Instagram, or Twitter* account, that content may run counter to the company's core values and reflect negatively on the company. Interestingly, one recent survey of employees found that most workers assume that their use of technology at work will be monitored. A large majority of employees approved of most monitoring methods such as monitoring faxes and email, tracking Web use, and even recording telephone calls.

机会是影响伦理的因素

1-3c Opportunity as a Factor Affecting Ethics

Several factors related to opportunity affect ethics in an organization. *Opportunity* refers to the amount of freedom an organization affords an employee to behave unethically if he or she makes that choice. If the employee is rewarded in some way for an unethical choice—receiving praise or a bonus, for example—or fails to suffer any kind of consequence, he or she is more likely to make that same choice in the future. In some organizations, certain company policies and procedures reduce the opportunity to be unethical. For example, at some fast-food restaurants, one employee takes your order and receives your payment, and another fills the order. This procedure reduces the opportunity to be unethical because the person handling the money is not dispensing the product, and the person giving out the product is not handling the money.

The existence of codes of ethics and other policies on ethics, as well as the importance management places on these policies are other elements of opportunity (codes of ethics are discussed in more detail in the next section). The degree of enforcement of company policies, procedures, and ethical codes is a major force affecting opportunity. When employees see that violations are dealt with consistently and firmly, they are less likely to act unethically knowing that doing so will bring repercussions.

Now that we have considered some of the factors believed to influence the level of ethical behavior in the workplace, let us explore what can be done to encourage ethical behavior and to discourage unethical behavior.

✓ Concept Check

- Describe several individual factors that influence the level of ethical behavior in an organization.
- Explain several social factors that affect ethics in an organization.
- How does opportunity influence the level of ethical behavior in the workplace?

鼓励符合伦理的行为

1-4 Encouraging Ethical Behavior

Most authorities agree that there is room for improvement in business ethics. A more problematic question is: Can business be made more ethical in the real world? The majority opinion on this issue suggests that government, trade associations, and individual firms indeed can promote acceptable levels of ethical behavior.

Learning Objective

1-4 Explain how organizations can encourage ethical decision making in business.

政府在鼓励伦理行为方面的作用

1-4a Government's Role in Encouraging Ethics

The government can encourage ethical behavior in business by enacting more stringent regulations and laws. One example is the landmark **Sarbanes-Oxley Act of 2002**, which provides sweeping legal protection for those who report corporate misconduct. Among other things, the law deals with corporate responsibility,

2002 年萨班斯 – 奥克斯利法案
Sarbanes-Oxley Act of 2002 provides sweeping legal protection for employees who report corporate misconduct

* 编者注：Twitter 于 2023 年 7 月更名为 X。

Sarbanes-Oxley Act The Sarbanes-Oxley Act of 2002 includes tough provisions to deter and punish corporate and accounting fraud and corruption. The legislation passed with unanimous support.

conflicts of interest, and corporate accountability. However, rules require enforcement, and the unethical businessperson frequently seems to "slip something by" without getting caught. Increased regulation may help, but it cannot solve the entire ethics problem.

行业协会在鼓励伦理行为方面的作用

1-4b Trade Associations' Role in Encouraging Ethics

Trade associations can and often do provide ethical guidelines for their members. These organizations, which operate within particular industries, are in an excellent position to exert pressure on members to stop engaging in questionable business practices that may harm all firms in the industry. For example, a pharmaceutical trade group adopted a new set of guidelines intended to end the extravagant dinners and expensive gifts sales representatives often give to physicians to persuade them to prescribe a particular medicine. However, enforcement and authority vary from association to association. Because trade associations exist for the benefit of their members, harsh measures may be self-defeating. Trade associations must also ensure that their codes do not contain provisions that may run afoul of antitrust laws.

公司在鼓励伦理行为方面的作用

1-4c Individual Companies' Role in Encouraging Ethics

Enforced codes of ethics are perhaps the most effective way to encourage ethical behavior within organizations. A **code of ethics** is a written guide to acceptable and ethical behavior as defined by an organization; it outlines uniform policies, standards, and punishments for violations. Because a code of ethics informs employees what is expected of them and what will happen if they violate the rules, it can go a long way toward encouraging ethical behavior. However, codes cannot possibly cover every situation. Companies also must create an environment in which employees recognize the importance of complying with the written code. Managers must provide direction by fostering communication, actively modeling and encouraging ethical decision making, and training employees to make ethical decisions. However, codes that are not enforced are likely to be viewed as lip service by employees and other stakeholders. Figure 1-2 offers snippets of some of the guiding principles behind well-known companies' codes of ethics.

伦理准则
code of ethics a guide to acceptable and ethical behavior as defined by the organization

Figure 1-2 Defining Acceptable Behavior at Starbucks, Nike, and Apple

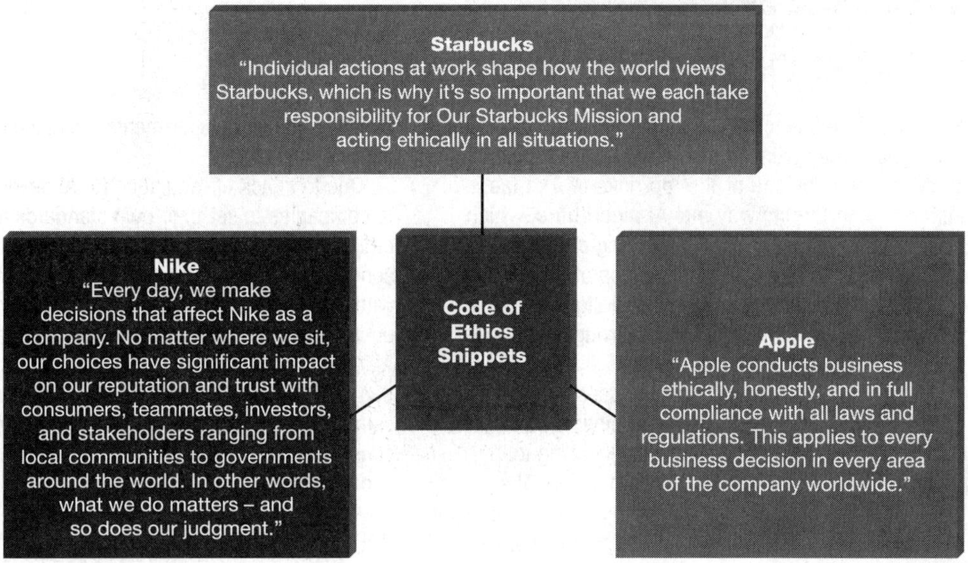

Sources: Starbucks, "Business Ethics and Compliance: Standards of Business Conduct"; Nike, "Inside the Lines: The NIKE Code of Ethics"; Apple, "Business Conduct: The Way We Do Business Worldwide".

Beginning in the 1980s, an increasing number of organizations created and implemented ethics codes. Today, about 95 percent of *Fortune* 1000 firms have a formal code of ethics or conduct. For example, the ethics code of Starbucks defines the firm's mission and values and includes provisions relating to policies and procedures; laws and regulations; relationships with customers, suppliers, competitors, and the community; conflicts of interest; handling of proprietary information; and more. Starbucks' code also details how employees can express concerns or find guidance in ambiguous situations and even provides a graphical decision-making framework that employees can apply to difficult decisions.[16]

In the wake of a number of corporate scandals and the Sarbanes-Oxley Act, many large companies now have created a new executive position, the chief ethics (or compliance) officer. Assigning an ethics officer who guides ethical conduct provides employees someone to consult if they are not sure of the right thing to do. An ethics officer meets with employees and top management to provide ethical advice, establishes and maintains an anonymous confidential service to answer questions about ethical issues, and takes action on ethics code violations.

Sometimes even employees who want to act ethically may find it difficult to do so. Unethical practices can become ingrained in an organization. Employees with high personal ethics may then take a controversial step called *whistle-blowing*. **Whistle-blowing** is informing the press or government officials about unethical practices within an organization. Consider Teresa Ross, who brought a lawsuit against Group Health Cooperative (GHC, now Kaiser Foundation Health Plan's Washington subsidiary) under the False Claims Act, which permits whistle-blowers to sue companies they believe have defrauded the government. Ross, who worked as Director of Risk Adjustment Services for the healthcare firm, believed that GHC was defrauding Medicare by inflating or altering patients' diagnoses in order to receive

举报
whistle-blowing informing the press or government officials about unethical practices within one's organization

Exploring Careers

职业探索：首席伦理官的兴起

The Rise of the Chief Ethics Officer

With artificial intelligence (AI) applications spreading throughout the business world, executives now rank ethics issues as one of the top risks of AI. Bias, for instance, can find its way into AI algorithms, which can lead to discrimination. This mounting concern has contributed to the rise of the chief ethics officer. Ethics officers are executives who provide oversight to guide the organization through legal and ethical standards.

Though the role does not have a set job description like other C-suite roles, some companies are looking to the chief ethics officer to ensure AI algorithms are fair and unbiased. AI has been integrated into a variety of functions, from recruiting and contact tracing to facial recognition and email marketing. Candidates for the chief ethics officer role may have a background in business law and human resources, though some tech departments are hiring dedicated AI ethics officers.

Due to a lack of regulation for AI development, it's up to companies to set their own standards and policies. The ethics officer can assess risks, create a code of ethics, conduct internal training programs, ensure compliance with regulations, monitor ongoing ethical conduct, and act on violations of the company's ethics code. In addition to AI, other tech issues to consider are privacy, data collection, and security. The chief ethics officer can play a critical part in eliminating bias, guarding against unintended consequences, and holding individuals and organizations accountable.

Sources: Based on information in "Rise of the Chief Ethics Officer," *Forbes*, March 27, 2019; Geoff Nudelman, "20 Minutes With: Hypergiant Industries' Chief Ethics Officer Will Griffin on Diversity and Ethics in Technology," *Barron's*, September 7, 2020; Merve Hickok, "What Does an AI Ethicist Do? A Guide for the Why, the What, and the How," *Medium*, April 27, 2020.

higher payments. The company eventually settled the case with the Department of Justice for \$6.3 million. Ross was awarded about \$1.5 million for blowing the whistle.[17]

Whistle-blowing, however, can have serious repercussions for employees: Those who "blow the whistle" may face retaliation and sometimes even lose their jobs. The Sarbanes-Oxley Act of 2002 protects whistle-blowers who report corporate misconduct. Any executive who retaliates against a whistle-blower can be held criminally liable and imprisoned for up to ten years. Federal employees who report misconduct are likewise protected by the Whistleblower Protection Act of 1989.

When companies set up anonymous hotlines to advise employees who are unsure how to handle ethically questionable situations, employees actually may be more likely to engage in whistle-blowing. When firms instead create an environment that educates employees and nurtures ethical behavior, fewer ethical problems arise. Ultimately, the need for whistle-blowing is greatly reduced.

It is difficult for an organization to develop ethics codes, programs, and procedures to deal with all relationships and every situation. Michael Josephson, an expert on workplace ethics, says, "The objective of such programs is to establish a business culture in which it's easier to do the right thing than the wrong thing, and where concerned co-workers and vigilant supervisors repress illegal or improper conduct that can potentially endanger or embarrass the company."[18] When no company policies or procedures exist or apply, a quick test to determine if a behavior is ethical is to see if others—co-workers, customers, and suppliers—approve of it. Ethical decisions will always withstand scrutiny. Openness and communication about choices will often build trust and strengthen business relationships. Table 1-1 provides some general guidelines for making ethical decisions.

✓ Concept Check

- How can the government encourage the ethical behavior of organizations?
- What is the role of trade associations in encouraging ethics?
- What is whistle-blowing? Who protects the whistle-blowers?

Table 1-1 Guidelines for Making Ethical Decisions

1. Listen and learn	Recognize the problem or decision-making opportunity that confronts your company, team, or unit. Don't argue, criticize, or defend yourself—keep listening and reviewing until you are sure that you understand others.
2. Identify the ethical issues	Examine how co-workers and consumers are affected by the situation or decision at hand. Examine how you feel about the situation, and attempt to understand the viewpoint of those involved in the decision or in the consequences of the decision.
3. Create and analyze options	Try to put aside strong feelings such as anger or a desire for power and prestige and come up with as many alternatives as possible before developing an analysis. Ask everyone involved for ideas about which options offer the best long-term results for you and the company. Then decide which option will increase your self-respect even if, in the long run, things don't work out the way you hope they will.
4. Identify the best option from your point of view	Consider it and test it against some established criteria, such as respect, understanding, caring, fairness, honesty, and openness.
5. Explain your decision and resolve any differences that arise	This may require neutral arbitration from a trusted manager or taking "time out" to reconsider, consult, or exchange written proposals before a decision is reached.

Source: Based on information in Tom Rusk with D. Patrick Miller, "Doing the Right Thing," *Sky* (Delta Airlines), August 1993, 18–22.

社会责任

1-5 Social Responsibility

Learning Objective

1-5 Describe how our current views on the social responsibility of business have evolved.

社会责任

social responsibility the recognition that business activities have an impact on society and the consideration of that impact in business decision making

Social responsibility is the recognition that business activities have an impact on society and the consideration of that impact in business decision making. Alphabet and its subsidiary Google, for example, have pledged to donate $14.5 million to support initiatives to combat racial injustice, inequity, and violence, including grants to the Center for Policing Equity and Equal Justice Initiative.[19] Obviously, social responsibility costs money. It is perhaps not so obvious—except in isolated cases—that social responsibility is also good business. Many companies contribute resources, knowledge, and products as well as money to help neighbors and others during times of crisis. For example, Procter & Gamble's orange Loads of Hope trucks are a welcome sight during disaster relief efforts. Residents in disaster areas can drop off loads of dirty laundry at the mobile laundromats, and volunteers use Tide products and high-efficiency machines to wash, dry, and even fold their clothes. Thus far, the program has helped nearly 48,000 families and brought a sense of normalcy and hope back to survivors so that they can focus on more pressing matters.[20] Efforts like these bring positive associations for brands that can help them stand out in a competitive market. Customers eventually find out which firms act responsibly and which do not. Just as easily as they can purchase a product made by a company that is socially responsible, they can choose against buying from the firm that is not.

Social responsibility is good business. Natural disasters create opportunities for companies to engage in socially responsible behavior. Procter & Gamble's Loads of Hope program takes in disaster survivors' dirty laundry and returns it to them clean and folded, allowing them to deal with more important problems.

Even small businesses can develop social responsibility programs. For example, P. Terry's, which operates 19 fast-food hamburger stands in Central Texas, donates 100 percent of its profits from one day each quarter to a local charity. The company, which has donated more than $1 million to local nonprofits, lets customers know about upcoming charity days through its social media accounts.[21] In general, people are more likely to want to work for and buy from such organizations.

Table 1-2 10 Best Corporate Citizens

1.	Owens Corning
2.	Citi
3.	General Mills
4.	Cisco
5.	HP
6.	Intel
7.	Ecolab
8.	General Motors
9.	Hess
10.	Accenture

Source: "100 Best Corporate Citizens of 2020," *3BL Media*, https://100best.3blmedia.com/ (accessed January 21, 2021).

Increasingly, companies large and small are striving to be good corporate citizens. **Corporate citizenship** is adopting a strategic approach to fulfilling economic, ethical, environmental, and social responsibilities. This requires balancing the needs, desires, and demands of a diverse group of stakeholders including investors, employees, customers, regulators, competitors, neighborhoods and communities, and social activists. Consider Chris Kempczinski, president and CEO of McDonald's, who views the company's role in society as going beyond feeding Big Macs to customers: "What we realized is that for 65 years, McDonald's purpose has been to both feed and foster communities. To our franchisees, suppliers and employees, the words 'billions served' aren't just about the burgers and fries we serve, but the tens of thousands of communities around the world that we serve." One way the company does that is through its longtime sponsorship of Ronald McDonald House Charities, which helps support the families of sick and injured children during treatment.[22] Table 1-2 lists the best corporate citizens as evaluated by 3BL Media.

企业社会责任的演变

1-5a The Evolution of Social Responsibility in Business

Business is far from perfect in many respects, but its record of social responsibility today is much better than that in past decades. In fact, present demands for social responsibility have their roots in outraged reactions to the abusive business practices of the early 1900s.

During the first quarter of the 20th century, businesses were free to operate pretty much as they chose. Government protection of workers and consumers was minimal. As a result, people either accepted what business had to offer or they did without. Working conditions often were deplorable by today's standards. The average workweek in most industries exceeded 60 hours, no minimum-wage law existed, and employee benefits were almost nonexistent. Workplaces were crowded and unsafe, and industrial accidents were the rule rather than the exception. To improve working conditions, employees organized and joined labor unions. During the early 1900s, however, businesses—with the help of government—were able to use court orders, brute force, and even the few existing antitrust laws to defeat union attempts to improve working conditions.

During this period, consumers generally were subject to the doctrine of **caveat emptor**, a Latin phrase meaning "let the buyer beware." In other words, "what you see is what you get," and if it is not what you expected, too bad. Although victims of unscrupulous business practices could take legal action, going to court was very expensive, and consumers rarely won their cases. Moreover, no consumer groups or government agencies existed to publicize their consumers' grievances or to hold sellers accountable for their actions.

Before the 1930s, most people believed that competition and the action of the marketplace would, in time, correct abuses. Government, therefore, became involved in day-to-day business activities only in cases of obvious abuse of the free-market system. Six of the most important business-related federal laws passed between 1887 and 1914 are described in Table 1-3. As you can see, these laws were aimed more at encouraging competition than at correcting abuses, although two of them did deal with the purity of food and drug products.

The collapse of the stock market on October 29, 1929, triggered the Great Depression. Factory production fell by almost half, and up to 25 percent of the nation's workforce was unemployed. Public pressure soon mounted for the government to "do something" about the economy and about worsening social conditions. Soon after Franklin D. Roosevelt became president in 1933, he instituted programs to restore the economy and improve social conditions. The government passed laws to correct what many viewed as the monopolistic abuses of big business, and provided various social services for individuals. These massive federal programs became the foundation for increased government involvement in the dealings between business and society.

企业公民

corporate citizenship adopting a strategic approach to fulfilling economic, ethical, environmental, and social responsibilities

买者自慎

caveat emptor a Latin phrase meaning "let the buyer beware"

Table 1-3 Early Government Regulations That Affected American Business

Government Regulation	Major Provisions
Interstate Commerce Act (1887)	First federal act to regulate business practices; provided regulation of railroads and shipping rates
Sherman Antitrust Act (1890)	Prevented monopolies or mergers where competition was endangered
Pure Food and Drug Act (1906)	Established limited supervision of interstate sales of food and drugs
Meat Inspection Act (1906)	Provided for limited supervision of interstate sales of meat and meat products
Federal Trade Commission Act (1914)	Created the Federal Trade Commission to investigate illegal trade practices
Clayton Antitrust Act (1914)	Eliminated many forms of price discrimination that gave large businesses a competitive advantage over smaller firms

As government involvement has increased, so has everyone's awareness of the social responsibility of business. Today's business owners are concerned about the return on their investment, but at the same time most of them demand ethical behavior from employees. In addition, employees demand better working conditions, and consumers want safe, reliable products. Various advocacy groups echo these concerns and also call for careful consideration of the Earth's delicate ecological balance. Therefore, managers must operate in a complex business environment—one in which they are just as responsible for their managerial actions as for their actions as individual citizens. Interestingly, today's high-tech and internet-based firms fare relatively well when it comes to environmental issues, worker conditions, animal testing, and charitable donations.

社会责任的两种观点

1-5b Two Views of Social Responsibility

Government regulation and public awareness are *external* forces that have increased the social responsibility of business. However, business decisions are made within the firm—there, social responsibility begins with the attitude of management. Two contrasting philosophies, or models, define the range of management attitudes toward social responsibility.

According to the traditional concept of business, a firm exists to produce quality goods and services, earn a reasonable profit, and provide jobs. In line with this concept, the **economic model of social responsibility** holds that society will benefit most when business is left alone to produce and market profitable products that society needs. The economic model has its origins in the 18th century, when businesses were owned primarily by entrepreneurs or owner-managers. Competition was vigorous among small firms, and short-run profits and survival were the primary concerns. To the manager who adopts this traditional attitude, social responsibility is someone else's job. After all, stockholders invest in a corporation to earn a return on their investment, not because the firm is socially responsible, and the firm is legally obligated to act in the economic interest of its stockholders. Moreover, profitable firms pay federal, state, and local taxes that are used to meet the needs of society. Thus, managers who concentrate on profit believe that they fulfill their social responsibility indirectly through the taxes paid by their firms. As a result, social responsibility becomes the problem of the government, various environmental groups, charitable foundations, and similar organizations.

In contrast, some managers believe that they have a responsibility not only to stockholders but also to customers, employees, suppliers, and the general public. This broader view is referred to as the **socioeconomic model of social responsibility**, which places emphasis not only on profits but also on the impact of business decisions on society.

社会责任的经济模式
economic model of social responsibility the view that society will benefit most when business is left alone to produce and market profitable products that society needs

社会责任的社会经济模式
socioeconomic model of social responsibility the concept that business should emphasize not only profits but also the impact of its decisions on society

Recently, increasing numbers of managers and firms have adopted the socioeconomic model, and they have done so for at least three reasons. First, business is dominated by the corporate form of ownership, and the corporation is a creation of society. If a corporation does not perform as a good citizen, society can and will demand changes. Second, many firms have begun to take pride in their social responsibility records, among them Starbucks, HP, Colgate-Palmolive, and Coca-Cola. Of course, many other corporations are much more socially responsible today than they were ten years ago. Third, many businesspeople believe that it is in their best interest to take the initiative in this area. The alternative may be legal action brought against the firm by some special-interest group; in such a situation, the firm may lose control of its activities.

社会责任的利弊

1-5c The Pros and Cons of Social Responsibility

Business owners, managers, customers, and government officials have debated the pros and cons of the economic and socioeconomic models for years. Each side seems to have four major arguments to reinforce its viewpoint.

Proponents of the socioeconomic model maintain that a business must do more than simply seek profits. To support their position, they offer the following arguments:

1. Because business is a part of our society, it cannot ignore social issues.
2. Business has the technical, financial, and managerial resources needed to tackle today's complex social issues.
3. By helping resolve social issues, business can create a more stable environment for long-term profitability.
4. Socially responsible decision making by firms can prevent increased government intervention, which would force businesses to do what they fail to do voluntarily.

These arguments are based on the assumption that a business has a responsibility not only to its stockholders but also to its customers, employees, suppliers, and the general public.

Opponents of the socioeconomic model argue that business should do what it does best: earn a profit by manufacturing and marketing products that people want. Those who support this position argue as follows:

1. Business managers are responsible primarily to stockholders, so management must be concerned with providing a return on owners' investments.
2. Corporate time, money, and talent should be used to maximize profits, not to solve society's problems.
3. Social problems affect society in general, so individual businesses should not be expected to solve these problems.
4. Social issues are the responsibility of government officials who are elected for that purpose and who are accountable to the voters for their decisions.

These arguments obviously are based on the assumption that the primary objective of business is to earn profits and that government and social institutions should deal with social problems.

Today, few firms are either purely economic or purely socioeconomic in outlook; most have chosen some middle ground between the two extremes. However, our society generally seems to want—and even to expect—some degree of social responsibility from business. Thus, within this middle ground, businesses are leaning toward the socioeconomic view. In the next several sections, we look at some results of this movement in four specific areas: the public, employment practices, the environment, and implementation of social responsibility programs.

✓ Concept Check

- What is social responsibility? How can business be socially responsible?
- Outline the historical evolution of business social responsibility.
- Explain two views on the social responsibility of business.
- What are the arguments for and against increased social responsibility?

企业的公共责任

1-6 Public Responsibilities of Business

In recent years, more businesses have adopted the idea that they have basic responsibilities to the public, particularly to consumers and public health.

Learning Objective

1-6 List the responsibilities businesses have to the public, especially with regard to consumer rights and public health.

消费者权益保护

1-6a Consumerism

Consumerism consists of all activities undertaken to protect the rights of consumers. The fundamental issues pursued by the consumer movement fall into three categories: environmental protection, product performance and safety, and information disclosure. Although consumerism has been with us to some extent since the early 19th century, the consumer movement became stronger in the 1960s. It was then that President John F. Kennedy declared that the consumer was entitled to a new "Bill of Rights."

The Basic Rights of Consumers President Kennedy's Consumer Bill of Rights asserted that consumers have a right to safety, to be informed, to choose, and to be heard. Two additional rights added since 1975 are the right to consumer education and the right to courteous service. These six rights are the basis of much of the consumer-oriented legislation passed during the last 55 years. These rights also provide an effective outline of the objectives and accomplishments of the consumer movement.

The consumers' right to safety means that the products they purchase must be safe for their intended use, must include thorough and explicit directions for proper use, and must be tested by the manufacturer to ensure product quality and reliability. Federal agencies, such as the Food and Drug Administration and the Consumer Product Safety Commission, have the power to force businesses that make or sell defective products to take corrective actions such as offering refunds, recalling defective products, issuing public warnings, and reimbursing consumers—all of which can be expensive. Moreover, consumers and the government have been winning an increasing number of product-liability lawsuits against sellers of defective products. The amount of the awards in these suits has been increasing steadily. For example, a Florida man won $41.1 million when he sued R.J. Reynolds Tobacco Company and Phillip Morris USA, claiming that for decades they had concealed the hazards of smoking, which led him to develop severe COPD.[23] Yet another major reason for improving product safety is consumers' demand for safe products. People simply will stop buying a product they believe is unsafe or unreliable.

消费者权益保护
consumerism all activities undertaken to protect the rights of consumers

The right to safety The Consumer Bill of Rights asserts buyers' basic rights. The right to safety means that products must be safe for their intended use and tested by the producer to ensure product quality and safety.

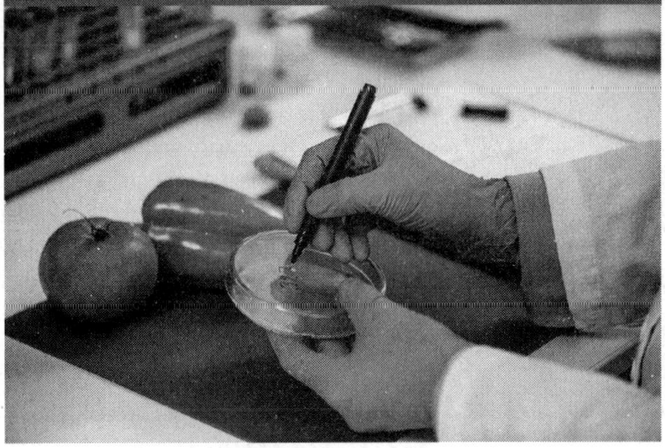

The right to be informed means that consumers must have access to complete information about a product before they buy it. Detailed information about ingredients and nutrition must be provided on food containers, information about fabrics and laundering methods must be attached to clothing, and lenders must disclose the true cost of borrowing the money they make available to customers who purchase merchandise on credit. In addition, manufacturers must inform consumers about the potential dangers of using their products. Manufacturers that fail to provide such information can be held responsible for personal injuries suffered because of their products. For example, Maytag provides customers with a lengthy booklet that describes how they should use their new washing machines. Sometimes such warnings seem excessive, but they are necessary if user injuries (and resulting lawsuits) are to be avoided.

The right to choose means that consumers must have a choice of products, offered by different manufacturers and sellers, to satisfy a particular need. The government has done its part by encouraging competition through antitrust legislation. The greater the competition, the greater is the choice available to consumers. Competition and the resulting freedom of choice provide additional benefits for customers by reducing prices. For example, when personal computers were introduced, they cost more than $5,000. Thanks to intense competition and technological advancements, personal computers today can be purchased for less than $500.

The right to be heard means that someone will listen and take appropriate action when customers complain. In fact, management began to listen to consumers after World War II, when competition between businesses that manufactured and sold consumer goods increased. One way that firms gained a competitive edge was to listen to consumers and provide the products they said they wanted and needed. Today, businesses are listening even more attentively, and many larger firms have consumer relations departments that can be contacted easily via email and social media. Other groups listen, too. Most large cities and some states have consumer affairs offices to act on citizens' complaints.

In 1975, President Gerald Ford added to the Consumer Bill of Rights *the right to consumer education,* which entitles people to be fully informed about their rights as consumers. In 1994, President Bill Clinton added a sixth right, *the right to service,* which entitles consumers to convenience, courtesy, and responsiveness from manufacturers and sellers of consumer products.

Ethics and Social Responsibility

商业伦理与社会责任：谷歌被控违反反垄断法

Google Sued for Antitrust Violations

Google, the world's largest search engine and one of the largest companies in the United States, faces a series of lawsuits centered around anticompetitive behavior. The Department of Justice and 11 state attorneys general filed a lawsuit against the company to prevent it from using anticompetitive practices to maintain its monopolies in the search and search advertising markets. Anticompetitive behavior negatively affects both consumers and competitors. Among other things, stifling competition inhibits innovation and reduces the options available to consumers.

Complaints against the tech giant include entering into exclusionary agreements that prohibit preinstallation of competing search services and using monopoly profits to pay for preferential treatment for its products. Google has responded to the lawsuit, saying it believes there is nothing wrong with its business agreements. A separate case from more than 30 states alleges Google uses its general search monopoly to discriminate against vertical search companies like Yelp and Kayak. A third lawsuit from a smaller group of states alleges Google uses its position in the advertising marketplace to create unfair conditions for advertisers and publishers, taking in a higher percentage of online ad spending.

Though on a surface level it may seem Google is being targeted for being successful, the accusations made against the company are serious. The distinction between competitive behavior and anticompetitive behavior is that being competitive relates to efforts taken to become the best while being anticompetitive relates to suppressing the competition. Antitrust laws are intended to promote competition and protect consumers. Lawsuits such as the ones Google faces stand to reshape the tech industry.

Sources: Based on information in Department of Justice, "Justice Department Sues Monopolist Google For Violating Antitrust Laws," October 20, 2020; Gilad Edelman, "Google's Antitrust Cases: A Guide for the Perplexed," *Wired*, December 18, 2020; Federal Trade Commission, "Guide to Antitrust Laws".

Major Consumerism Forces The major forces in consumerism are individual consumer advocates and organizations, consumer education programs, and consumer laws. Consumer advocates take it upon themselves to protect the rights of consumers. They band together into consumer organizations, either independently or under government sponsorship. They write letters and advocate for stricter legislation concerning practices that may harm consumers. In Europe, for example, some consumer groups have complained to regulators that Amazon's Prime membership service is difficult to cancel, manipulating users into sticking with a plan they no longer want. Public Citizen, a consumer group in the United States, has made a similar complaint to the Federal Trade Commission.[24] Some consumer advocates and organizations encourage consumers to boycott products and businesses to which they have objections.

Educating consumers to make wiser purchasing decisions is perhaps one of the most far-reaching aspects of consumerism. Increasingly, consumer education is becoming a part of high school and college curricula and adult education programs. These programs cover many topics—for instance, what major factors should be considered when buying specific products, such as insurance, real estate, automobiles, appliances and furniture, clothes, and food; the provisions of certain consumer-protection laws; and the sources of information that can help individuals become knowledgeable consumers.

Major advances in consumerism have come through federal legislation. Some laws enacted in the last 60 years to protect your rights as a consumer are listed and described in Table 1-4.

Most businesspeople now realize that they ignore consumer issues only at their own peril. Managers know that improper handling of consumer complaints can result in lost sales, bad publicity, and lawsuits.

公共健康

1-6b Public Health

Many people believe that businesses have a basic responsibility to contribute to the general well-being of the public, starting with ensuring that their products do not harm anyone. Beyond this basic responsibility, however, there is disagreement as to how far businesses' responsibility to public health should extend, especially about issues such as obesity, smoking, heart disease, alcohol use, and even smartphone use while driving. These issues are not black and white, but exploring them can help us find balance among the desires and demands of various stakeholders.

Obesity has become a major public health topic in recent years, with more than one-third of adult Americans being categorized as obese. Other countries are experiencing similar trends. People who are obese or significantly overweight face higher rates of diabetes, strokes, heart disease, and some types of cancer, and the swelling numbers of these illnesses place a great burden on the healthcare system, the costs of which are borne by society. Public health advocates have called for companies—particularly those that market sugary drinks and fast food—to modify their products or at least their advertising in an effort to reduce the consumption of these products, which have been shown to contribute to rising rates of obesity. Perhaps as a result, some producers of these products have suffered losses and are responding with new ideas and products. Coca-Cola, for example, discontinued hundreds of brands, including some with higher levels of sugar, such as Odwalla. In recent years, the beverage giant has introduced or acquired new beverage brands such as Fairlife milk, Simply juices, and Topo Chic mineral waters that have less sugar and/or provide health benefits.[25] Other companies, including Panera and Starbucks, are posting the calories in their offerings right on their menus and apps to help people make better choices.

Another major public health topic facing business relates to smoking and tobacco products. The relationship between smoking—even secondhand smoke—and cancer has been well documented, but some consumers still demand to buy cigarettes and tobacco

Table 1-4 Major Federal Legislation Protecting Consumers Since 1960

Legislation	Major Provisions
Federal Hazardous Substances Labeling Act (1960)	Required warning labels on household chemicals if they were highly toxic
Kefauver-Harris Drug Amendments (1962)	Established testing practices for drugs and required manufacturers to label drugs with generic names in addition to trade names
Cigarette Labeling Act (1965)	Required manufacturers to place standard warning labels on all cigarette packages and advertising
Fair Packaging and Labeling Act (1966)	Called for all products sold across state lines to be labeled with net weight, ingredients, and manufacturer's name and address
Motor Vehicle Safety Act (1966)	Established standards for safer cars
Truth in Lending Act (1968)	Required lenders and credit merchants to disclose the full cost of finance charges in both dollars and annual percentage rates
Credit Card Liability Act (1970)	Limited credit card holder's liability to $50 per card and stopped credit card companies from issuing unsolicited cards Required credit bureaus to provide credit reports to consumers regarding their own credit files; also provided for correction of incorrect information
Consumer Product Safety Commission Act (1972)	Established an abbreviated procedure for registering certain generic drugs
Fair Credit Billing Act (1974)	Amended the Truth in Lending Act to enable consumers to challenge billing errors
Equal Credit Opportunity Act (1974)	Provided equal credit opportunities for all individuals regardless of sex or marital status Provided for minimum disclosure standards for written consumer-product warranties for products that cost more than $15
Amendments to the Equal Credit Opportunity Act (1976, 1994)	Prevented discrimination based on race, creed, color, religion, age, and income when granting credit
Fair Debt Collection Practices Act (1977)	Outlawed abusive collection practices by third parties
Nutrition Labeling and Education Act (1990)	Required the Food and Drug Administration to review current food labeling and packaging focusing on nutrition label content, label format, ingredient labeling, food descriptors and standards, and health messages
Telephone Consumer Protection Act (1991)	Prohibited the use of automated dialing and prerecorded voice calling equipment to make calls or deliver messages
Consumer Credit Reporting Reform Act (1997)	Placed more responsibility for accurate credit data on credit issuers; required creditors to verify that disputed data are accurate and to notify a consumer before reinstating the data
Children's Online Privacy Protection Act (2000)	Placed parents in control over what information is collected online from their children younger than 13 years; required commercial website operators to maintain the confidentiality, security, and integrity of personal information collected from children
Do Not Call Implementation Act (2003)	Directed the FCC and the FTC to coordinate so that their rules are consistent regarding telemarketing call practices including the Do Not Call Registry and other lists, as well as call abandonment
Credit Card Accountability, Responsibility, and Disclosure Act (2009)	Provided the most sweeping changes in credit card protections since the Truth in Lending Act of 1968
Dodd-Frank Wall Street Reform and Consumer Protection Act of 2010	Promoted the financial stability of the United States by improving accountability and responsibility in the financial system; established a new Consumer Financial Protection Agency to regulate home mortgages, car loans, and credit cards; became Public Law on July 21, 2010

products. While most people agree that businesses should not knowingly sell products that harm customers, what should they do when consumers continue to demand those products? CVS Health earned significant publicity several years ago when it announced that it would stop selling cigarettes in its stores, even though it lost $2 billion in revenue from doing so.[26] In recent years, the rise of vaping has further compounded the issue. Marketers of e-cigarettes and vaping products insist that their products are safer than cigarettes and even tout them as a method to stop smoking. Health advocates, however, say they are still harmful, and worry that the vapors—which often come in flavors such as bubblegum and pina colada—may be especially attractive to minors. Some cities have banned e-cigarettes along with conventional ones, and federal regulators are studying the devices to determine whether further regulation is needed.

One growing concern is the use of smartphones and smartphone apps while driving. Should cell phone service providers take steps to prevent customers from texting and using apps that distract from driving or merely advise them to refrain from these activities? AT&T launched its "It Can Wait" promotion campaign to ask customers to avoid texting while driving, and more than 38 million users pledged not to. The cell phone service provider asked customers to use the hashtag #X to alert their friends and followers that they are about to be unreachable on social media because they are driving.[27] There are other issues businesses face with regard to public health, including labeling products that contain genetically modified organisms (GMOs), making questionable claims about the health benefits of supplements and ingredients, where and how to provide affordable housing for the homeless, and many more.

✓ Concept Check

- Describe the six basic rights of consumers.
- What are the major forces in consumerism today?
- What are some of the federal laws enacted in the last 60 years to protect your rights as a consumer?
- What are some of the issues businesses must consider with regard to public health?

对员工的责任
1-7 Responsibilities to Employees

Learning Objective

1-7 Analyze how present employment practices are being used to counteract past abuses.

Everyone should have the opportunity to land a job for which they are qualified and to be rewarded on the basis of ability and performance. This is a fundamental issue for Americans, and it also makes good business sense. Yet, over the years, this opportunity has been denied to members of various racial, religious, political, national, and other underrepresented groups, and members of these groups are often singled out for unfavorable treatment in the workplace.

The federal government responded to the outcry of minority groups during the 1960s and 1970s by passing a number of laws forbidding discrimination in the workplace. Yet, more than 50 years after passage of the Civil Rights Act of 1964, abuses still exist. An example is the disparity in income levels for Whites, Blacks, Hispanics, and Asians, as illustrated in Figure 1-3. Lower incomes and higher unemployment rates also characterize Native Americans, people with disabilities, and women. Responsible managers have instituted a number of programs to counteract the results of discrimination.

平权行动计划
1-7a Affirmative Action Programs

An **affirmative action program** is a plan designed to increase the number of employees from underrepresented groups at all levels within an organization. Employers with federal contracts of more than $50,000 per year must have written affirmative action plans. The objective of such programs is to ensure that members of underrepresented groups are represented within the organization in approximately the same proportion as in the surrounding community. If 25 percent of the electricians in a geographic area in which a company is located are Black, then approximately 25 percent of the electricians it employs also should be Black. Affirmative action plans encompass all areas of human resources management: recruiting, hiring, training, promotion, and pay.

平权行动计划
affirmative action program a plan designed to increase the number of employees from underrepresented groups at all levels within an organization

Unfortunately, affirmative action programs have been plagued by two problems. The first involves quotas. In the beginning, many firms pledged to recruit and hire a

Figure 1-3 Comparative Income Levels

Real Median Household Income by Race and Hispanic Origin: 1967 to 2019

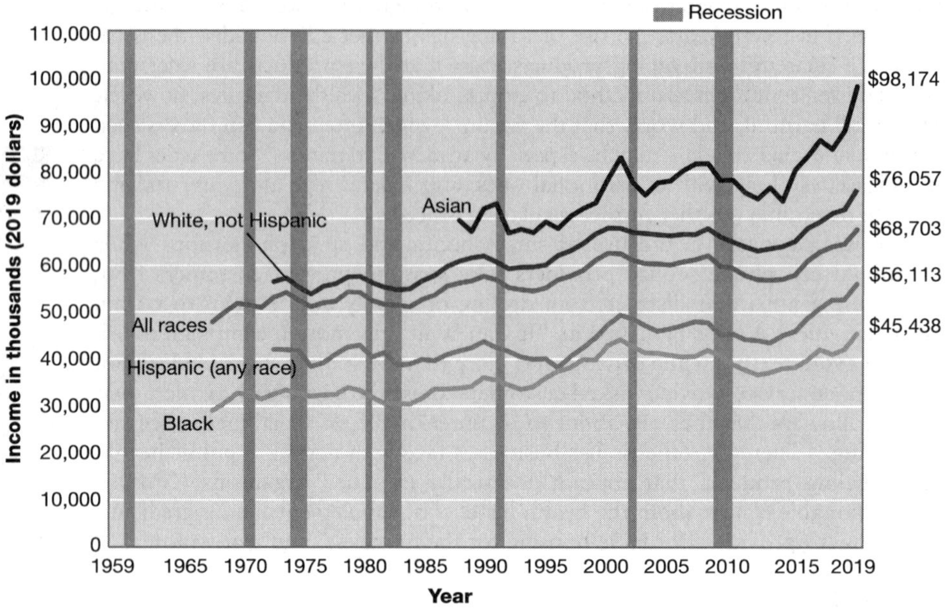

Note: The data for 2017 and beyond reflect the implementation of an updated processing system. The data for 2013 and beyond reflect the implementation of the redesigned income questions. The data points are placed at the midpoints of the respective years. Median household income data are not available prior to 1967.

Source: U.S. Census Bureau, Current Population Survey, 1968 to 2020 Annual Social and Economic Supplements.

certain number of people from underrepresented groups by a specific date. To achieve this goal, they were forced to consider only applicants from underrepresented groups for job openings; if they hired nonminority workers, they would be defeating their own purpose. However, the courts have ruled that such quotas are unconstitutional even though their purpose is commendable. They are, in fact, a form of discrimination called *reverse discrimination.*

平等就业机会委员会
Equal Employment Opportunity Commission (EEOC) a government agency with the power to investigate complaints of employment discrimination and the power to sue firms that practice it

The second problem is that although most such programs have been reasonably successful, not all businesspeople are in favor of affirmative action programs. Managers not committed to these programs can "play the game" and still discriminate against workers. To help solve this problem, Congress created (and later strengthened) the **Equal Employment Opportunity Commission (EEOC)**, a government agency with the power to investigate complaints of employment discrimination and sue firms that practice it.

Workplace diversity A company with a diverse workforce benefits in a number of ways.

The threat of legal action has persuaded some corporations to amend their hiring and promotional policies, but the discrepancy between men's and women's salaries still exists, as illustrated in Figure 1-4. For more than 60 years, women have consistently earned only about 80 cents for each dollar earned by men.

长期失业者培训计划

1-7b Training Programs for the Hard-Core Unemployed

For some firms, social responsibility extends far beyond placing a help-wanted advertisement in the local newspaper. These firms have assumed the task of helping

Figure 1-4 Relative Earning of Male and Female Workers

The ratio of women's to men's annual full-time earnings was 80% in 2019, up from 74% first reached in 1996.

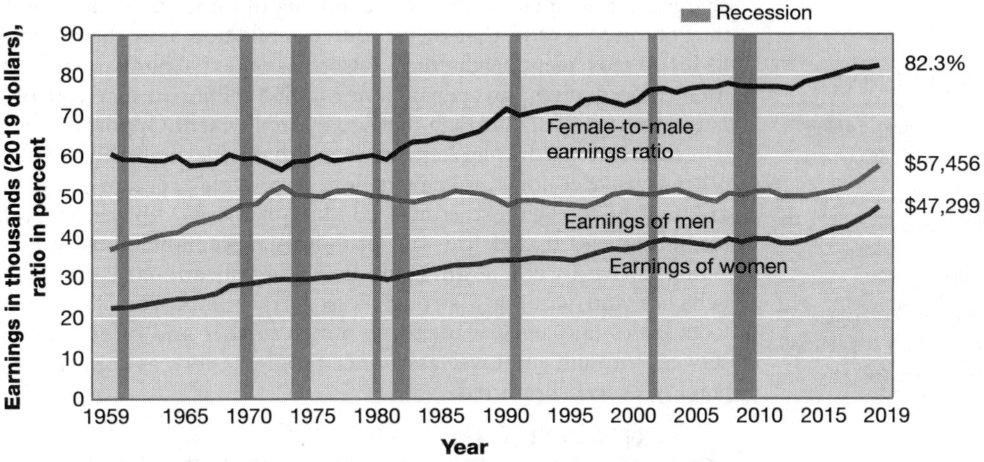

Note: The data for 2017 and beyond reflect the implementation of the redesigned income questions. The data for 2013 and beyond reflect the implementation of the redesigned income questions. The data points are placed at the midpoints of the respective years. Data on earnings of full-time, year-round workers are not readily available before 1960. Data are for people aged 14 and older for years prior to 1980.

Source: U.S. Census Bureau, Current Population Survey, 1961 to 2020 Annual Social and Economic Supplements.

the **hard-core unemployed**, workers with little education or vocational training and a long history of unemployment. These individuals may not have gained employable skills and education due to disabilities, systemic racism, economic factors, or personal issues. For example, Midas Hospitality, a hotel development and management firm, teamed up with the Boone Center, Inc., a vocational training facility for adults with intellectual and developmental disabilities, to create a program to prepare students for hotel housekeeping jobs in the St. Louis area.[28] In the past, such workers often were turned down routinely by personnel managers, even for the most menial jobs.

减少性骚扰和虐待行为的计划

1-7c Programs to Reduce Sexual Harassment and Abusive Behavior

Another hot button issue in the workplace is addressing sexual harassment, bullying, and other abusive behaviors. The Workplace Bullying Institute (WBI) defines bullying in the workplace as repeated work sabotage; verbal abuse; and/or abusive conduct that is threatening, humiliating, or intimidating. The stress of bullying can result in physical and mental health issues that can ultimately cost employers many hours of lost worker productivity as well as lower morale and higher turnover. The WBI has found that 19 percent of respondents to a survey have suffered abusive conduct at work; 19 percent say they have witnessed it in the workplace.[29] Other researchers have found much higher rates of bullying. Moreover, research by the WBI suggests that half of victims do not report their bullying out of fear of further harassment because their bully is in a position of power.[30] Even football players can be subject to bullying in the workplace: Former Miami Dolphins tackle Jonathan Martin left the team because he felt he could not continue to do his job in the face of repeated bullying from other teammates.[31]

When bullying takes on sexual overtones, it becomes sexual harassment, which the U.S. Equal Employment Opportunity Commission defines as unwelcome sexual advances, requests for sexual favors, and other verbal or physical harassment of a physical nature. Unlike bullying, sexual harassment is illegal.[32] It can also result in poor morale, high turnover, and expensive lawsuits. For example, two women filed

长期失业者
hard-core unemployed workers with little education or vocational training and a long history of unemployment

a $500 million class-action lawsuit against McDonald's, claiming that the sexual harassment they endured at corporate-owned restaurants in Florida created a "hostile work environment" for all women working in those stores. In addition to those charges, the women claimed the company did not act to stop the harassment when they reported it, and that they endured retaliation after their complaints.[33] With the #MeToo movement heightening awareness of sexual harassment in the workplace, it's no surprise that employers paid a record $68 million to survivors of workplace sexual harassment in 2019 through the Equal Employment Opportunity Commission.[34]

To create a workplace environment that stifles bullying, sexual harassment, and other abusive conduct, managers need to provide programs, much like the ones that are used to foster more ethical conduct in the workplace. In addition to creating formal policies that define and prohibit unacceptable abusive conduct, companies should strive to create an antibullying organizational culture by modeling good behavior and sending a strong message that improper conduct will be punished. Companies may even want to go a step further and offer training and additional services through employee assistance programs such as counseling to ensure that all employees feel supported.[35]

✓ Concept Check

- What is an affirmative action program? What is its purpose?
- Why did Congress create (and later strengthen) the Equal Employment Opportunity Commission?
- How can businesses reduce sexual harassment and abusive behavior at the workplace?

对环境的责任

1-8 Responsibilities to the Environment

Learning Objective

1-8 Describe the major environmental issues and businesses' response to them.

According to a report published by the U.S. Sentencing Commission, the most common federal offense committed by organizations is not fraud or money laundering but environmental crime. Environmental offenses made up nearly a third of all crimes committed by organizations, followed by fraud at 21 percent and food/drug crimes at 12.2 percent. Seventy percent of the environmental crimes were water-related, 16.7 percent affected wildlife, 8.3 percent involved hazardous materials, and 5 percent were air-related.[36]

A growing social consciousness by the public and some business managers, fostered by government legislation, has led to major efforts to reduce environmental pollution, conserve natural resources, and reverse some of the worst damage caused by past negligence in this area.

环境问题

1-8a Environmental Issues

A significant environmental issue is the amount of waste produced by businesses and society. For example, by some estimates, the United States throws out one-third of all the food produced, and grocery stores are responsible for as much as 10 percent of that. One reason for the large amount of grocery waste is consumer expectations: Consumers bypass fruits and vegetables that do not appear to be perfect, so supermarkets discard any produce that doesn't meet that expectation, even when that produce is otherwise safe and healthy.[37] The disposal problem has grown over the past few years because modern technology has continued to produce increasing amounts of chemical and radioactive waste. U.S. manufacturers produce an estimated 40 to 60 million tons of contaminated oil, solvents, acids, and sludge each year. Service businesses, utility companies, hospitals, and other industries also dump vast amounts of wastes into the environment. While companies today strive to reduce waste from operations as much as possible, much still winds up in landfills. A shortage of landfills, owing to stricter regulations, makes garbage disposal a serious problem in some areas. Incinerators help to solve the landfill-shortage problem, but they bring with them their own problems. They reduce the amount of garbage and also leave tons of ash to be buried—ash that often has a higher concentration of toxicity than the original garbage. Increasingly, plastic waste winds up in the ocean, where it accumulates into huge "garbage patches" or breaks down into microplastics that harm marine life.

Another major environmental issue is **pollution**, the contamination of water, air, or land through the actions of people in an industrialized society. Pollution harms water and air quality, threatens human and animal health, degrades habitats, and contributes to climate change. Among the serious threats to people posed by pollutants are respiratory irritation, asthma, cancer, kidney and liver damage, anemia, and heart failure. Businesspeople harm the environment when they unwittingly—or knowingly—dump hazardous chemicals and waste in unapproved ways. For example, Bernhard Schulte Shipmanagement was fined $1.75 million for improperly discharging a ship's bilge waste water into Hawaiian waters and failing to log the discharge as required by law. The Singapore-based company must also implement an environmental compliance plan for all of its vessels operating in U.S. waters.[38] For decades, environmentalists have been warning us about the dangers of industrial pollution. Unfortunately, business and government leaders either ignored the problem or were not concerned about it until pollution became a threat to life and health in America.

环境立法的影响

1-8b Effects of Environmental Legislation

As in other areas of concern to our society, legislation and regulations play a crucial role in pollution control. The laws outlined in Table 1-5 reflect the scope of current environmental legislation: laws to promote clean air, clean water, and even quiet work and living environments. Of major importance was the creation of the Environmental Protection Agency (EPA), the federal agency charged with enforcing laws designed to protect the environment.

污染

pollution the contamination of water, air, or land through the actions of people in an industrialized society

Table 1-5 Summary of Major Environmental Laws

Legislation	Major Provisions
National Environmental Policy Act (1970)	Established the Environmental Protection Agency (EPA) to enforce federal laws that involve the environment
Clean Air Act Amendment (1970)	Provided stringent automotive, aircraft, and factory emission standards
Water Quality Improvement Act (1970)	Strengthened existing water pollution regulations and provided for large monetary fines against violators
Resource Recovery Act (1970)	Enlarged the solid-waste disposal program and provided for enforcement by the EPA
Water Pollution Control Act Amendment (1972)	Established standards for cleaning navigable streams and lakes and eliminating all harmful waste disposal by 1985
Noise Control Act (1972)	Established standards for major sources of noise and required the EPA to advise the Federal Aviation Administration on standards for airplanes
Clean Air Act Amendment (1977)	Established new deadlines for cleaning up polluted areas; also required review of existing air quality standards
Resource Conservation and Recovery Act (1984)	Amended the original 1976 act and required federal regulation of potentially dangerous solid-waste disposal
Clean Air Act Amendment (1987)	Established a national air quality standard for ozone
Oil Pollution Act (1990)	Expanded the nation's oil spill prevention and response activities; also established the Oil Spill Liability Trust Fund
Clean Air Act Amendments (1990)	Required that motor vehicles be equipped with onboard systems to control about 90% of refueling vapors
Food Quality Protection Act (1996)	Amended the Federal Insecticide, Fungicide and Rodenticide Act and the Federal Food Drug and Cosmetic Act; the requirements included a new safety standard—reasonable certainty of no harm—that must be applied to all pesticides used on foods
American Recovery and Reinvestment Act (2009)	Provided $7.22 billion to the EPA to protect and promote "green" jobs and a healthier environment

Pollution Oil spills can have long-lasting effects on our wildlife and other natural resources. As our population and businesses expand, the need to reduce pollution at its source becomes more important.

When they are aware of a pollution problem, many firms are proactive in addressing it rather than wait to be cited by the EPA. Other owners and managers, however, take the position that environmental standards are too strict. (Loosely translated, this means that compliance with present standards is too expensive.) Consequently, it often has been necessary for the EPA to take legal action to force firms to install antipollution equipment and to clean up waste storage areas. Americold Logistics, for example, was fined $41,500 for illegally leaking pollutants into a creek and violating its Washington state industrial stormwater permit, among other EPA charges. The company, which promptly acknowledged and acted to resolve the issues, agreed to develop and implement plans to reduce pollutants leaving its food warehouse facility.[39]

Experience has shown that the combination of environmental legislation, voluntary compliance, and EPA action can succeed in restoring the environment and keeping it clean. However, much still remains to be done.

企业对环境问题的回应
1-8c Business Response to Environmental Concerns

回收利用
recycling converting used materials into new products or components for new products in order to prevent their unnecessary disposal

One of the most effective ways that companies can reduce their impact on the environment is to reduce waste from operations and other activities. Identifying and eliminating inefficiencies in production and operations is where most firms begin that process. Finding alternative uses for waste is another. For example, leftover food from supermarkets and restaurants is often donated to local food banks or sold to farmers who feed it to livestock. Most companies strive to recycle as much as possible. **Recycling** involves converting used materials into new products or components for new products in order to prevent their unnecessary disposal. Companies can recycle waste paper, glass, rubber, metals, some plastic packaging, and other materials so that they or their components can be reprocessed into new products and kept out of landfills. As an example, Madewell gives customers $20 toward a new pair of Madewell jeans when they bring in worn-out or out-of-style jeans of any brand. The clothing company donates the used denim to the Cotton's Blue Jeans Go Green program, which turns it into insulation for homes, preventing 529 tons of waste from going into a landfill thus far.[40]

Reducing dependence on fossil fuels Today's businesses (and consumers) are more open to alternative sources of energy because they are concerned about the negative impact of conventional energy sources.

Another way businesses strive to be more environmentally conscious is through the use of "greener" forms of power to counter their use of huge quantities of energy during operations and other activities. Companies can audit their operations to identify places where more efficient and environmentally friendly products can be used to save energy, such as using LED light bulbs—which reduce heat as well as power use—and even natural sunlight to light workplaces. Many companies are turning to alternative forms of power generation,

Sustaining the Planet

保护地球：可持续发展有利可图吗

Is Sustainability Profitable?

Sustainability has taken the spotlight as environmental consciousness grows among consumers, business professionals, and investors. Though sustainability was once an afterthought for many organizations, more than ever shoppers are looking for products and brands that align with their values. Long story short: sustainability leads to profitability.

In the not-too-distant past, it was difficult to convince investors that sustainability and profitability were linked. Now, with many companies aligning executive bonuses with sustainability targets, there's a growing consensus that environmental, social, and governance practices are strategic priorities. This shift has caused businesses to evaluate their supply chains, from materials to transportation, to find opportunities to limit their environmental impact. Environmental goals often include water reduction, zero waste to landfill, and lowering carbon energy use. Additionally, companies can focus on making products more durable, reusable, repairable, and recyclable.

Investors, who now see that the future is green, often have specific environmental expectations and put pressure on companies to evolve. Many organizations have reaped the benefits of leading with sustainability. According to *The Wall Street Journal*, the most sustainably managed companies in the world include Sony (hardware), Philips (medical equipment), Cisco Systems (hardware), Merck (biotechnology and pharmaceuticals), and Iberdrola (electric utilities and power generators). These organizations have all prioritized environmental concerns while maintaining high profits, showing that sustainability can play a critical role in an organization's future success.

Sources: Based on information in Dieter Holger and Olivia Bugault, "CEOs Increasingly See Sustainability as Path to Profitability," *The Wall Street Journal*, October 12, 2020; Fabiana Negrin Ochoa, Dieter Holger, Maitane Sardon, and Catherine Lindsay, "The 100 Most Sustainably Managed Companies in the World," *The Wall Street Journal*, October 13, 2020.

including solar and wind power which do not rely on diminishing sources of fossil fuels. New Belgium Brewing in Fort Collins, Colorado, became the first company to be 100 percent powered by the wind, but many other companies have followed suit. A number of Fortune 500 businesses, including Google, Apple, Starbucks, Cisco, and Bank of America, get 100 percent of their electricity from renewable energy sources such as wind and solar.[41]

Recognizing public demand for greater environmental responsibility, more and more firms are adopting environmentally friendly practices and products that are less harmful to the environment. **Green marketing** is the process of creating, making, delivering, and promoting products that are environmentally safe. It may include making modifications to products, manufacturing processes, packaging, and/or promotion activities to make or deliver products that are better for the environment. Chipotle Mexican Grill, for example, built its reputation as a green marketer by abiding by its "Cultivate a Better World" mission, which requires using real ingredients that "are responsibly sourced and classically cooked with people, animals and the environment in mind." To live by that mission, the company strives to use only natural animal products (treated humanely and fed a vegetarian diet that does not include growth hormones or antibiotics), organic ingredients, and where possible, local sources. It also educates consumers and other stakeholders about its efforts through a Real Foodprint tracker on its app as well as a regularly released Sustainability Report that details its sustainability goals and progress in reaching them. It is significant that Chipotle has not yet achieved all its sustainability goals, but its mission guides the firm in all decision making and activities.[42]

Recognizing that consumers increasingly prefer to purchase from businesses that make recycling, green energy, and sustainability a strategic priority, companies are increasingly touting their green efforts. However, green marketers must take care to ensure that their claims are backed by evidence that shows a significant

绿色营销

green marketing the process of creating, making, delivering, and promoting products that are environmentally safe

environmental benefit and does not mislead consumers or they may run afoul of the Federal Trade Commission.[43] Companies that take their green marketing efforts too far, without relevance or support for their environmental claims risk being labeled guilty of *green washing*.

As we have seen, more businesses are trying harder to make their activities and products sustainable going forward, but what about cleaning up past environmental messes—oil spills, improperly stored industrial wastes, polluting emissions, and more—that harm the environment today? Many business leaders offer one answer: Use tax money to clean up the environment and to keep it clean. They reason that business is not the only source of pollution, so business should not be forced to absorb the entire cost of the cleanup. Environmentalists disagree. They believe that the cost of proper treatment and disposal of industrial wastes is an expense of doing business. In either case, consumers ultimately will bear a large part of the cost—either as taxes or in the form of higher prices for goods and services.

✓ Concept Check

- What are the major environmental issues facing society today?
- Summarize major provisions of federal environmental laws enacted since 1970.
- What is businesses' response to environmental concerns?

实施社会责任计划

1-9 Implementing a Program of Social Responsibility

Learning Objective

1-9 Identify the steps a business must take to implement a program of social responsibility

A firm's decision to be socially responsible is a step in the right direction—but only the first step. The business then must develop and implement a program to reach this goal. The program will be affected by the firm's size, financial resources, past record in the area of social responsibility, and competition. Above all, however, the program must have the firm's total commitment or it will fail.

An effective program for ethics and social responsibility requires time, money, and organization. In most cases, developing and implementing such a program will require four steps: securing the commitment of top executives, planning, appointing a director, and preparing a social audit.

高层管理人员的承诺

1-9a Commitment of Top Executives

Without the support of top executives, any program will soon falter and become ineffective. At CitiGroup, the board of directors maintains the Ethics, Conduct, and Culture Committee, which oversees the financial conglomerate's ethics and compliance program.[44] As evidence of their commitment to social responsibility, top managers should develop a policy statement that outlines key areas of concern. Such statements set a tone of positive support and later will serve as a guide for other employees as they become involved in the program.

规划

1-9b Planning

Next, a committee of managers should be appointed to plan the program. Whatever form their plan takes, it should deal with each of the issues described in the top managers' policy statement. If necessary, outside consultants can be hired to help develop the plan.

委任董事

1-9c Appointment of a Director

After the social responsibility plan is established, a top-level executive should be appointed to implement the organization's plan. This individual should be charged with recommending specific policies and helping individual departments to understand and live up to the social responsibilities the firm has assumed. Depending on the size of the firm, the director may require a staff to handle the program on a day-to-day basis. For example, at Cisco, Tae Yoo, Senior Vice President of Corporate Affairs, administers the technology giant's corporate social responsibility program, including applying its resources to facilitate problem solving that has positive impacts on people, society, and the Earth.[45]

社会审计

1-9d The Social Audit

At specified intervals, the program director should prepare a social audit for the firm. A **social audit** is a comprehensive report of what an organization has done and is doing with regard to social issues that affect it. This document provides the information the firm needs to evaluate and revise its social responsibility program. Typical subject areas include human resources, community involvement, the quality and safety of products, business practices, and efforts to reduce pollution and improve the environment. The information included in a social audit should be as accurate and as quantitative as possible, and the audit should reveal both positive and negative aspects of the program. Caesars Entertainment, which operates casinos, evaluates its corporate citizenship efforts annually and then issues a report describing its performance for a variety of stakeholders including employees, investors, and the media. Caesars' Corporate Citizenship Report details its performance in meeting goals in the areas of responsible gaming, employee development, environmental stewardship, and community investment.[46]

Today, many companies listen to concerned individuals within and outside the company. For example, the Citi Ethics Line listens to and acts on concerns expressed by employees and others about possible violations of company policies, laws, or regulations, such as improper or unethical business practices, as well as health, safety, and environmental issues. Employees are encouraged to communicate their concerns, as well as ask questions about ethical issues. The Ethics Line is available to all Citi employees, as well as concerned individuals outside the company.

社会审计
social audit a comprehensive report of what an organization has done and is doing with regard to social issues that affect it

✓ Concept Check

- What steps must a business take to implement a program of social responsibility?
- What is the social audit? Who should prepare a social audit for the firm?

Discussion Questions 讨论题

1. When a company acts in an ethically questionable manner, what types of problems are caused for the organization and its customers?
2. What factors affect ethical behavior and choices? How can businesses use this knowledge to further ethical behavior in their organizations?
3. How can employees take an ethical stand regarding a business decision when their superior already has taken a different position?
4. How can businesses encourage employees to make ethical choices?
5. Overall, would it be more profitable for a business to follow the economic model or the socioeconomic model of social responsibility?
6. Why should business take on the task of training the hard-core unemployed?
7. To what extent should the blame for vehicular air pollution be shared by manufacturers, consumers, and government?
8. Why is there so much government regulation involving social responsibility issues? Should there be less?

Case 1 案例 1：全食超市的全食交易保障

Inside Whole Trade at Whole Foods

Whole Foods Market, a natural supermarket chain, was founded in Austin, Texas, in 1980. At the time, the market for natural, unprocessed foods was small, but the company soon expanded to new cities as demand grew. Now, the grocer can be found in 500 locations across North America and the United Kingdom. Since the beginning, responsible sourcing has been a core component of Whole Foods' business. This stakeholder orientation focuses on the needs of its customers, its employees, its communities, and people at every level of its supply chain.

The Whole Trade Guarantee is Whole Foods' ethical trading program. It supports ethical trade, proper working conditions, and environmental protection in the production of the products it sells. Products with this label meet rigorous quality standards and come from certified farms that have a history of positive impacts on their employees, supply chain partners, communities, and the environment. Through the program, Whole Foods provides funds to the farms they work with to support various community initiatives such as community centers, medical services, and dental care. Programs such as Whole Trade support Whole Foods' mission to nourish both people and the planet.

Whole Foods has often been called "Whole Paycheck" because of the more expensive price tags on its products. However, Whole Foods believes that, as a responsible buyer, it has a duty to monitor its impact on the environment and individuals throughout the supply chain. Pressure from retailers to lower costs can lead to farm owners exploiting workers to deliver products cheaply. One of Whole Foods' goals is to provide its shoppers with affordable, sustainable food that also supports farmers and farmworkers.

Beyond creating win–win partnerships with its suppliers, Whole Foods ultimately views customers as its most important stakeholder. To differentiate itself from its competitors, Whole Foods emphasizes the quality of its products over price. The company has a variety of quality standards to ensure its customers get the best, including standards for its meat, eggs, seafood, supplements, beauty products, and household cleaners. In addition, Whole Foods bans more than 100 ingredients such as high-fructose corn syrup.

Employees at Whole Foods are another top priority. Full-time team members are offered comprehensive health insurance. The company also provides its team members with career and learning development, volunteer programs through the Whole Planet Foundation, and team member assistance plans. In addition to competitive pay, the company also offers 401(k) plans and health savings accounts, discounts, and paid time off.

All of these efforts combined help Whole Foods earn profits, which in turn creates value for its shareholders. Profits are essential for any business to survive, and Whole Foods believes it has a responsibility to its parent company, Amazon, to use its capital in the best way possible to achieve the best results possible. Not everyone was pleased when Amazon acquired Whole Foods in 2017 for $13.4 billion. Many employees noticed a change in working conditions such as heavier workloads and budget cuts. Amazon also sought to make Whole Foods' products more affordable by purchasing a greater number of products from national food distributors rather than local farms. Prices have since returned to pre-Amazon levels but other initiatives—such as discounts for Amazon Prime members—remain to provide customers with more value.

Whole Food's strong relationships with its supply chain partners are fostered by its Whole Trade program. This is a core strength that can be leveraged by both Whole Foods and Amazon to stand out. Though many criticized Amazon's acquisition of Whole Foods due to their cultural differences, Amazon's deep pockets and robust supply chain knowledge will surely benefit Whole Foods in the long run. By committing to ethical and sustainable trading practices, Whole Foods sets itself apart from traditional supermarkets.[47]

Questions

1. Why do you think Whole Foods wants to support the farmers and farmworkers in its supply chain?
2. Why are customers willing to pay a premium for goods at Whole Foods?
3. How does Whole Foods meet the needs of its customers?

Chapter

2

Global Business

全球商务

Learning Objectives

Once you complete this chapter, you will be able to:

2-1 Explain the economic bases for and importance of international business.

2-2 Explore the methods by which a firm can organize for and enter into international markets.

Why Should You Care?

Free trade—are you for or against it? Most economists support free-trade policies, but public support can be lukewarm, and certain groups are adamantly opposed, contending that "trade harms large segments of U.S. workers," "degrades the environment," and "exploits the poor."

Inside Business 商业透视：星巴克走向全球以实现增长

Starbucks Goes Global for Growth

Starbucks, the world's largest coffeehouse chain, has more stores internationally than it does in the United States as a result of putting global expansion at the center of its growth strategy. Domestically, Starbucks has slowed new store openings and closed locations deemed redundant in dense metro areas in order to put the company in a more profitable position. While Starbucks tackles changing consumer behavior in the United States, other countries present valuable growth opportunities.

An aggressive push into China, Starbucks' fastest-growing market, has been successful for the company. According to Starbucks China CEO and chairperson Belinda Wong, at one point in time, Starbucks opened a new store in China every 15 hours. The company announced plans to invest $150 million in a roasting plant in China, deepening its commitment to building the Starbucks brand throughout Asia. The company's only other non-U.S. roasting facility is in Amsterdam to support Europe.

To penetrate China's coffee market, the coffeehouse chain focused on rolling out innovation even faster than in the United States. For example, to appeal to local tastes, the menu in China includes a variety of tea-based beverages as well as exclusive drink categories. Additionally, Starbucks rolled out delivery in Beijing and Shanghai and 11 other cities in China before it expanded delivery in the United States. The Asia-Pacific market accounts for approximately half of Starbucks' global new store growth.[1]

Did you know?

Starbucks has 32,000 stores across more than 80 markets.

Like Starbucks, many companies, large and small, do business around the world. Did you know that only 31 percent of the Coca-Cola Company's sales come from North America? Asia-Pacific and Latin American markets generate 14 percent and 11 percent, respectively, of the revenues of the beverage giant.[2] Even small businesses can find great success in global markets. One such company is Combustion Associates of Corona, California, a small business founded by husband-and-wife immigrants from Bangladesh. The company designs, manufactures, and exports large power generators to developing countries.[3] Whether they buy or sell products across national borders, these companies are all contributing to the volume of international trade that is fueling the global economy.

Theoretically, international trade is every bit as logical and worthwhile as interstate trade between, say, California and Washington. Yet, nations tend to restrict the import of certain goods for a variety of reasons. For example, the United States restricted the import of Mexican fresh tomatoes because they were undercutting price levels of domestic fresh tomatoes. Despite such restrictions, international trade has increased almost steadily since World War II. Many of the industrialized nations have signed trade agreements intended to reduce problems in international business and to help less-developed nations participate in world trade. Individual firms around the world have seized the opportunity to compete in foreign markets by exporting products and increasing foreign production, as well as by other means.

In this chapter, we describe international trade in terms of modern specialization, whereby each country trades the surplus goods and services it produces most efficiently for products its citizens and organizations need.

Entrepreneurial Success

创业成功：阿里巴巴通过提供指导助力企业家

Alibaba Provides Guidance to Help Entrepreneurs

Alibaba, one of the world's largest e-commerce companies, invests in Hong Kong and Taiwan-based entrepreneurs through its not-for-profit arm, the Alibaba Entrepreneurs Fund. In addition to investment capital, Alibaba provides guidance to help individuals scale their businesses, making use of Alibaba's tools and resources. The e-commerce giant aims to build Hong Kong's start-up ecosystem by fueling entrepreneurship and innovation.

According to a survey conducted by Alibaba and KPMG, corporate executives benefit from collaborating with start-ups because it helps keep them up to date on the latest innovations. Entrepreneurs develop new ideas, find solutions that address society's needs, diversify the economy, and create upward mobility. Lynk, one of the businesses Alibaba has invested in, is the first-ever Software-as-a-Service platform built on an expert network. The service allows businesses to easily connect with a diverse set of 840,000 advisors rather than hiring experts in-house. The company has raised more than $30 million in capital.

By supporting the entrepreneurial landscape in China, Alibaba's marketplace and other platforms will benefit. The Alibaba Entrepreneurs Fund follows a venture capitalist model, except profits from the company's venture investments are returned to the fund for reinvestment, ensuring capital is always available. Independent professionals with start-up experience evaluate and select the entrepreneurs that will receive funding and strategic guidance from Alibaba's network of business leaders. The not-for-profit looks for innovative start-ups in the big data, cleantech, e-commerce, fintech, and logistics sectors, among others. Alibaba then leverages its resources to help the entrepreneurs grow their businesses.

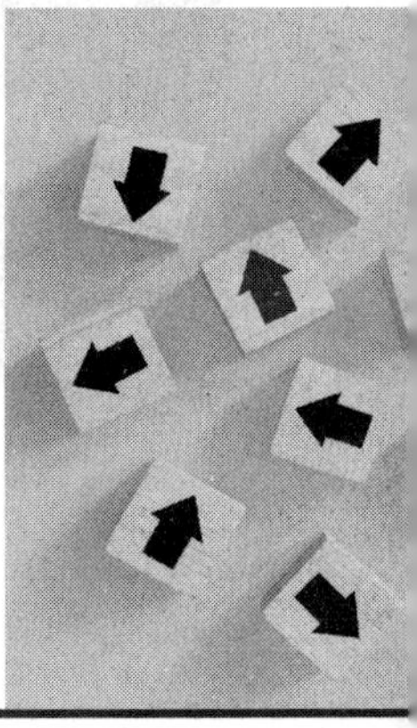

Sources: Based on information in "Alibaba Hong Kong Entrepreneurs Fund Launches JUMPSTARTER 2021 Global Pitch Competition," *Business Wire*, July 28, 2020; Alibaba Entrepreneurs Fund, "Transforming Hong Kong Through Entrepreneurship"; Catherine Shu, "Lynk, a 'Knowledge -as-a-Service' Platform with More Than 840,000 Experts, Raises $24 Million," *TechCrunch*, January 27, 2021.

国际商务基础

2-1 The Basis for International Business

Learning Objective

2-1 Explain the economic bases for and importance of international business.

International business encompasses all business activities that involve exchanges across national boundaries. Thus, a firm is engaged in international business when it buys some portion of its input from, or sells some portion of its output to, an organization located in a foreign country. (A small retail store may sell goods produced in some other country. However, because it purchases these goods from American distributors, it is not engaged in international trade.)

绝对优势和比较优势

2-1a Absolute and Comparative Advantage

Some countries are better equipped than others to produce particular goods or services. The reason may be a country's natural resources, its labor supply, or even customs or a historical accident. In such cases, it would be advantageous for a country to specialize in the production of such products so that it can produce them most efficiently. The country could use what it needed of these products and then trade the surplus for products it could not produce efficiently on its own. Saudi Arabia thus has specialized in the production of crude oil and petroleum products; South Africa, in diamonds; and Australia, in wool. Each of these countries is said to have an absolute advantage with regard to a particular product. An **absolute advantage** is the ability to produce a specific product more efficiently than any other nation.

国际商务
international business all business activities that involve exchanges across national boundaries

绝对优势
absolute advantage the ability to produce a specific product more efficiently than any other nation

A U.S. absolute advantage. The United States has long specialized in the production of wheat. Because of its specific geography and climate, the United States enjoys an absolute advantage—the ability to produce wheat more efficiently than countries in other parts of the world.

One country may have an absolute advantage with regard to several products, whereas another country may have no absolute advantage at all. Yet it is still worthwhile for these two countries to specialize and trade with each other. To see why this is so, imagine that you are the president of a successful manufacturing firm and that you can accurately type 90 words per minute. Your assistant can type 80 words per minute but would run the business poorly. Thus, you have an absolute advantage over your assistant in both typing and managing. However, you cannot afford to type your own letters because your time is better spent in managing the business. That is, you have a comparative advantage in managing. A **comparative advantage** is the ability to produce a specific product more efficiently than any other product. Your assistant, on the other hand, has a comparative advantage in clerical duties because he or she can do that better than managing the business. Thus, you spend your time managing, and you leave the document preparation to your assistant. Overall, the business is run as efficiently as possible because you are each working in accordance with your own comparative advantage.

The same is true for nations. Goods and services are produced more efficiently when each country specializes in the products for which it has a comparative advantage. Moreover, by definition, every country has a comparative advantage in some product. The United States has many comparative advantages—in research and development, high-technology industries, and identifying new markets, for instance.

进出口

2-1b Exporting and Importing

Suppose that the United States specializes in producing corn. It then will produce a surplus of corn, but perhaps it will have a shortage of wine. France, on the other hand, specializes in producing wine but experiences a shortage of corn. To satisfy both needs—for corn and for wine—the two countries should trade with each other. The United States should export corn and import wine. France should export wine and import corn.

Exporting is selling and shipping raw materials or products to other nations. The Boeing Company, for example, exports its airplanes to a number of countries for use by their airlines. On a smaller scale, the Liriope Factory, a small Louisiana nursery, has expanded the customer base for its ground cover plants by exporting to European markets.[4] Figure 2-1 shows selected top merchandise-exporting states in the United States.

Importing is purchasing raw materials or products in other nations and bringing them into one's own country. Thus, buyers for Macy's department stores may purchase rugs in India or raincoats in England and have them shipped back to the United States for resale.

贸易差额

2-1c Balance of Trade

Importing and exporting are the principal activities in international trade. They give rise to an important concept called the *balance of trade*. A nation's **balance of trade** is the total value of its exports minus the total value of its imports over

比较优势
comparative advantage the ability to produce a specific product more efficiently than any other product

出口
exporting selling and shipping raw materials or products to other nations

进口
importing purchasing raw materials or products in other nations and bringing them into one's own country

贸易差额
balance of trade the total value of a nation's exports minus the total value of its imports over a specified period of time

Figure 2-1 Selected Top Exporting States

Texas and California account for about one-third of all U.S. exports.

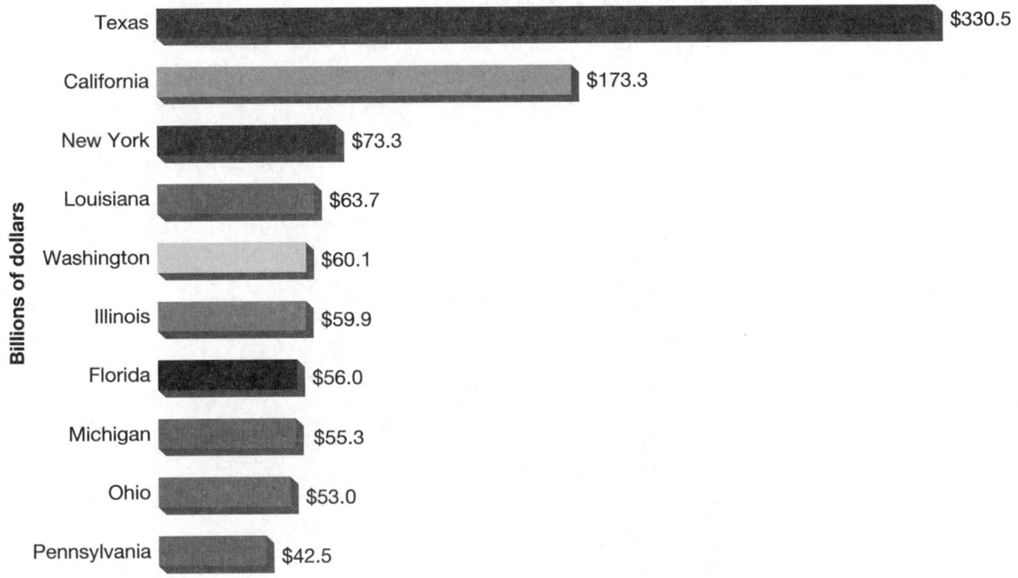

Source: Daniel Workman, "America's Top 20 Export States," *World's Top Exports*, March 2020.

a specified period of time. If a country imports more than it exports, its balance of trade is negative and is said to be *unfavorable*. On the other hand, when a country exports more than it imports, it is said to have a *favorable* balance of trade.

In 2020, the United States imported $2,810.6 billion worth of goods and services and exported $2,131.9 billion worth. It thus had a trade deficit of $678.7 billion.[5] A **trade deficit** is a negative balance of trade (refer to Figure 2-2). However, the United States has consistently enjoyed a large and rapidly growing surplus in services, such as computer and banking services. For example, in 2020, the United States imported $460.1 billion worth of services and exported $697.1 billion worth, thus creating a favorable balance of $237 billion.[6]

贸易逆差
trade deficit a negative balance of trade

U.S. exports. U.S. aircraft and spacecraft products represent the third largest U.S. exports.

Figure 2-2 U.S. International Trade in Goods and Services

If a country imports more goods than it exports, the balance of trade is negative, as it was in the United States from 2000 to 2020.

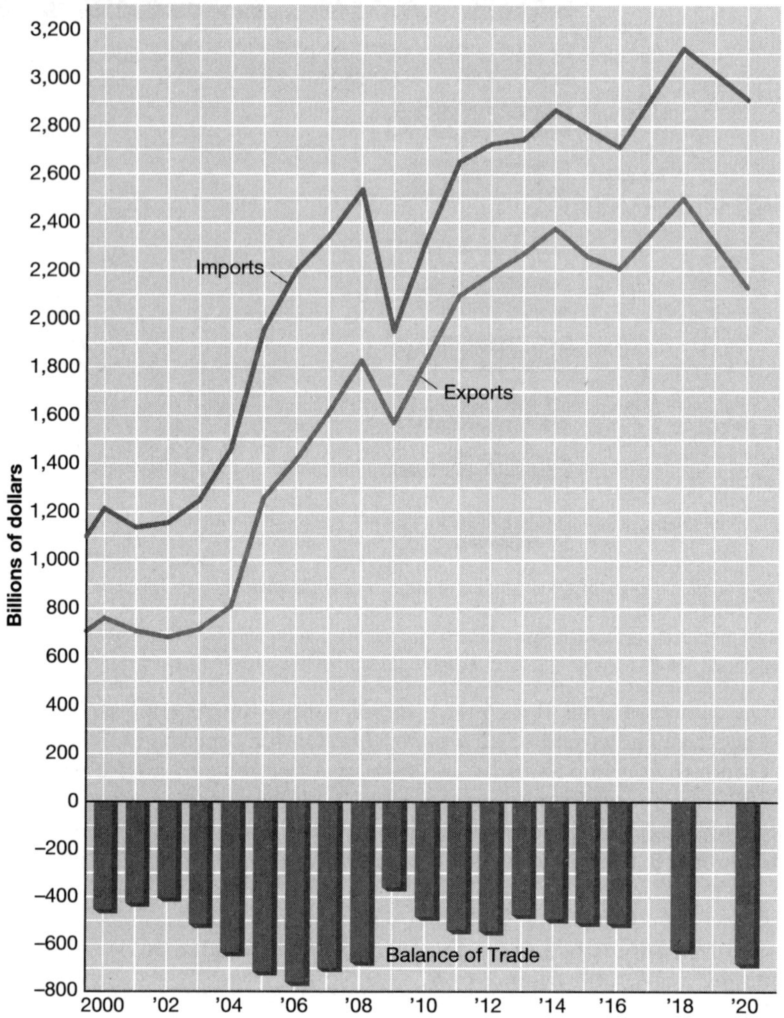

Sources: U.S. Department of Commerce, International Trade Administration; U.S. Bureau of Economic Analysis, "U.S. International Trade in Goods and Services, December 2020," February 5, 2021; U.S. Bureau of Economic Analysis, "U.S. International Trade in Goods and Services, December 2018," March 6, 2019.

Question: *Are trade deficits bad?*

Answer: It's complicated. A negative balance of trade is often viewed as unfavorable because the country must export money to pay for its excess imports. However, trade deficits also mean that consumers at home have the benefit of a wider variety of products at competitive prices. Consider the iPhone, which is manufactured in China. If it were to be made in the United States, it likely would retail for $2,000, but lower supply and labor costs overseas mean that Apple can sell most models for less than $1,000, or twice as many.[7] These lower prices also help stifle the threat of inflation. In the long run, though, trade deficits give rise to sending more jobs overseas where costs are often significantly lower, thereby resulting in less job creation at home. This is indeed what is happening in the United States.

A nation's **balance of payments** is the total flow of money into a country minus the total flow of money out of that country over a specified period of time. Balance of payments, therefore, is a much broader concept than balance of trade. It includes imports and exports, of course. However, it also includes investments, money spent by foreign tourists, payments by foreign governments, aid to foreign governments, and all other receipts and payments. A continual deficit in a nation's balance of payments (a negative balance) can cause other nations to lose confidence in that nation's economy. Alternatively, a persistent surplus may indicate that the country encourages exports but limits imports by imposing trade restrictions.

国际贸易的经济展望
2-1d The Economic Outlook for Trade

International trade is a major growth vehicle for the United States. More than 40 million full- and part-time jobs, or about one out of every five jobs in the United States, depend on international trade. The percentage of American jobs tied to global trade has doubled since 1992, growing from 10.4 percent to 20.2 percent.[8] In 2018, for the first time, the U.S. exports exceeded $2.5 trillion, up from $25 billion in 1960.[9] Many other countries have experienced similar growth. This dramatic increase in trade volume over the past 60 years has been one of the most important factors in the rise of living standards around the world. During this time, exports have become increasingly important to the U.S. economy. Exports as a percentage of U.S. GDP have increased steadily since 1970, except during recessions. Table 2-1 shows U.S. exports and imports for selected world areas in 2020, and Table 2-2 shows the value of U.S. merchandise exports to, and imports from, each of the nation's eight major trading partners. Note that Canada and Mexico are our best partners for our exports; China and Mexico, for imports.

Although the worldwide recessions of 1991, 2001–2002, and 2008–2009 slowed the rate of growth, and the global COVID-19 pandemic economic crisis caused the sharpest decline in more than 75 years, globalization is a reality of our time. In the United States, international trade now accounts for over one-fourth of gross domestic product (GDP). As trade barriers decrease, new competitors enter the global marketplace, creating more choices for consumers and new opportunities for job seekers. Looking ahead, the International Monetary Fund (IMF), an international bank with 190 member nations, expected global growth to continue, albeit more slowly as world economies recover from the pandemic and social unrest. The IMF

Table 2-1 U.S. Exports and Imports of Goods for Selected World Areas in 2020 in Billions of Dollars

Selected World Area*	Exports	Imports
North America	$468	$596
Europe	$332	$577
Euro Area	$213	$368
European Union	$232	$415
Pacific Rim	$376	$825
South/Central America	$130	$91
Africa	$22	$24
OPEC	$35	$19
Other Countries	$74	$209

*Countries may be included in more than one area grouping.

Source: U.S. Department of Commerce, Bureau of Economic Analysis, "Monthly U.S International Trade in Goods, December 2020".

国际收支
balance of payments the total flow of money into a country minus the total flow of money out of that country over a specified period of time

Table 2-2 **Top Trading Partners: Value of U.S. Merchandise Exports and Imports of Goods, 2020**

Rank	Country	Exports ($ billions)	Imports ($ billions)	Total Trade ($ billions)	Percent of Total Trade
1	China	124.6	435.4	560.1	14.9
2	Mexico	212.7	325.4	538.1	14.3
3	Canada	255.4	270.4	525.8	14.0
4	Japan	64.1	119.5	183.6	4.9
5	Germany	57.8	115.1	172.9	4.6
6	Korea, South	51.2	76.0	127.2	3.4
7	United Kingdom	59.0	50.2	109.2	2.9
8	Switzerland	18.0	74.8	92.8	2.5

Source: U.S. Department of Commerce, Census Bureau, "Top Trading Partners".

expected the world economic growth to be 5.5 percent and 4.2 percent in 2021 and 2022, respectively,[10] although the lingering economic effects of the COVID-19 pandemic may reduce that. Let's take a quick look at trade with some major nations and regions.

Canada and Western Europe Due in part to sharing a border and language, the economic relationship between the United States and Canada is one of the most efficient, most integrated, and most dynamic in the world. Together, the two nations generated 703.8 billion in bilateral trade in 2019—almost $2 billion a day, or $23,000 every second.[11] The nearly 450 million residents of the European Union make its member countries attractive trading partners, generating an estimated trade in goods of more than $658 billion in 2020.[12] Most other advanced economies, including Norway, Sweden, Switzerland, and the United Kingdom, are also major importers to and buyers of exports from the United States. Thanks in part to stability, similar per capita incomes, and growing economies, these relationships are likely to endure.

International expansion. Uber continues its globalization efforts by offering its services in more than 10,000 cities worldwide.

Mexico and Latin America Mexico, another leading trading partner, represents a tremendous opportunity for businesses looking for new markets. Latin America is home to 10 Free Trade Area countries and more than 650 million consumers. In addition to Mexico, these countries include Chile, Colombia, Peru, and the six countries of the Dominican Republic-Central America FTA or "CAFTA-DR" (Costa Rica, The Dominican Republic, El Salvador, Guatemala, Honduras, and Nicaragua). U.S. trade in goods with Central and South American nations added up to $221 billion a year in 2020[13] and is expected to grow as trade barriers among the nations ease.

Technology and Innovation

技术与创新：Spotify 谋求全球主导地位

Spotify Makes a Play for Global Dominance

Spotify, a Swedish digital music, podcast, and video streaming service, has more than 354 million users in 93 markets. Although the company controls about one-third of the global music-streaming market, it faces steep competition for consumer dollars against Pandora, Apple Music, YouTube Music, Tidal, and Amazon Music, among others. To grow its market share, Spotify is eyeing global expansion.

Spotify sees international growth as an opportunity to stay ahead of the streaming competition. Russia, one of Spotify's latest markets, is the fastest-growing market for music. In addition, Spotify expanded to Albania, Belarus, Bosnia and Herzegovina, Croatia, Kazakhstan, Kosovo, Moldavia, Montenegro, North Macedonia, Serbia, Slovenia, and Ukraine. In each market, Spotify works with local distributors and establishes local partnerships to offer a local experience on a global platform.

Spotify follows a freemium pricing strategy, meaning it offers free entry-level access, hoping to convert free users into premium subscribers. Its premium service eliminates advertisements and allows users to download music, skip an unlimited number of songs, and access Spotify's full library of music. This pricing strategy is not unique, however, as many of its competitors, including Pandora and Amazon Music, also offer free versions of their platforms.

To increase revenue, leadership at Spotify says it will increase subscription prices in mature markets where it offers more value than it did previously. The company has been busy developing and releasing original and exclusive content in 16 markets to differentiate the platform from competitors. Spotify's goal is to solidify its dominance in the audio streaming market while increasing earnings from active subscribers.

Sources: Based on information in Spotify, "Company Info"; David Trainer, "It Sounds Like Spotify Is In Trouble," *Forbes*, October 13, 2020; Kenneth Li, Supantha Mukherjee, "Spotify Expands to Russia and 12 Other Countries," *Reuters*, July 14, 2020; Sarah Perez, "Spotify CEO Says Company Will 'Further Expand Price Increases'," *TechCrunch*, October 29, 2020.

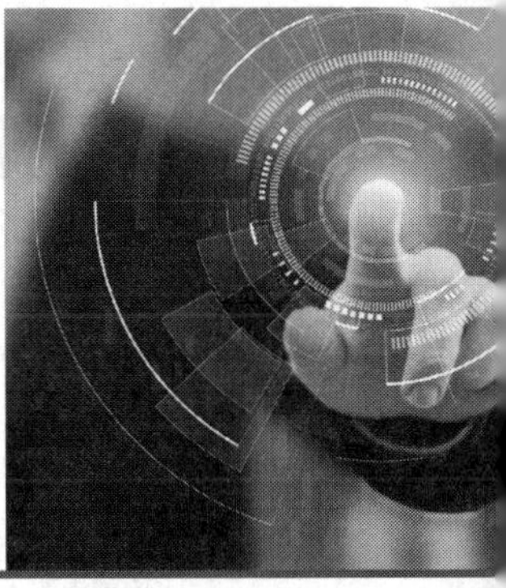

Asia Japan is the world's third largest economy and the United States' fourth largest trading partner. China's emergence as a global economic power has been among the most dramatic economic developments of recent decades. Indeed, China has grown to be the world's second largest economy, and the United States shares more than half a trillion dollars in annual bilateral trade. Also, as the emerging middle class in India, buys U.S. products, it means jobs and income for the U.S. middle class. With a market of over 1.35 billion of the world's consumers and per capita incomes expected to grow, India's vast market promises U.S. companies continued strong demand for goods and services.

Africa Sub-Saharan Africa is home to 1.1 billion people in 46 countries with immense natural resources that offer great trade potential. U.S. trade to and from Africa has tripled over the past decade, and U.S. exports of goods to this region now exceed $22 billion.[14] Although some of these nations have experienced conflict and stagnating economies, Ghana, Rwanda, Ethiopia, and others have experienced dramatic economic growth in recent years. Companies are increasingly looking for opportunities in these growing economies, whose residents are younger than average and have growing disposable incomes.

Middle East/North Africa Some of the countries of the Middle East and North Africa (MENA)—particularly Egypt and Saudi Arabia—have become important trading partners to the United States. Although political instability in the region has been a challenge to developing long-term relationships, the vast natural resources and growing per capita incomes make the region desirable to companies.

✓ Concept Check

- Why do firms engage in international trade?
- What is the difference between an absolute advantage and a comparative advantage?
- What is the difference between balance of trade and balance of payments?
- Which nations are the principal trading partners of the United States?

进入国际商务的方式

2-2 Methods of Entering International Business

Learning Objective

2-2 Explore the methods by which a firm can organize for and enter into international markets.

A firm that has decided to enter international markets can do so in several ways. These different approaches require varying degrees of involvement, investment, and risk. Typically, a firm begins its international operations at the simplest level. Then, depending on its goals, it may progress to higher levels of involvement. Table 2-3 describes the steps in entering international markets.

出口

2-2a Exporting

Exporting can be a relatively low-risk method of expanding operations by entering foreign markets. As an example, the Canadian firm LED Roadway Lighting Ltd. manufactures energy-efficient road lighting products that can help cities and utilities meet their goals to cut costs and reduce their climate footprint. To expand its business beyond Canada, the company began exporting its products to customers

Table 2-3 Steps in Entering International Markets

Step	Activity	Marketing Tasks
1	Identify exportable products	Identify key selling features Identify needs that they satisfy Identify the selling constraints that are imposed
2	Identify key foreign markets for the products	Determine who the customers are Pinpoint what and when they will buy Do market research Establish priority, or "target," countries
3	Analyze how to sell in each priority market (methods will be affected by product characteristics and unique features of country/market)	Locate available government and private-sector resources Determine service and backup sales requirements
4	Set export prices and payment terms, methods, and techniques	Establish methods of export pricing Establish sales terms, quotations, invoices, and conditions of sale Determine methods of international payments, secured and unsecured
5	Estimate resource requirements and returns	Estimate financial requirements Estimate human resources requirements (full- or part-time export department or operation) Estimate plant production capacity Determine necessary product adaptations
6	Establish overseas distribution network	Determine distribution agreement and other key marketing decisions (price, repair policies, returns, territory, performance, and termination). Know your customer (use U.S. Department of Commerce international marketing services)
7	Determine shipping, traffic, and documentation procedures and requirements	Determine methods of shipment (air or ocean freight, truck, rail) Finalize containerization Obtain validated export license Follow export-administration documentation procedures
8	Promote, sell, and be paid	Use international media, communications, advertising, trade shows, and exhibitions Determine the need for overseas travel (when, where, and how often?) Initiate customer follow-up procedures
9	Continuously analyze current marketing, economic, and political situations	Recognize changing factors influencing marketing strategies Constantly reevaluate

Source: U.S. Department of Commerce, International Trade Administration, Washington, DC.

in Caribbean nations, where high power rates allow customers to quickly realize savings from using LED lighting products. LED Roadway Lighting continues to look for new export opportunities such as the United Kingdom.[15] Exporting opens up several levels of involvement to exporting firms.

At the most basic level, the exporting firm may sell its products outright to an *export-import merchant*, which is a type of wholesaler specializing in international trade. This merchant assumes all the risks of product ownership, distribution, and sale. It may even purchase the goods in the producer's home country and assume responsibility for exporting the goods. An important and practical issue for domestic firms dealing with foreign customers is securing payment. Figure 2-3 depicts a simplified version of the process. This is a two-sided issue that reflects the mutual concern rightly felt by both parties to the trade deal: The exporter would like to be paid before shipping the merchandise, whereas the importer obviously would prefer to know that it has received the shipment before releasing any funds. Neither side wants to take the risk of fulfilling its part of the deal only to discover later that the other side has not. The result would lead to legal costs and complex, lengthy dealings that would waste everyone's resources. This mutual level of mistrust, in fact, makes good business sense and has been around since the beginning of trade centuries ago. The solution then was the same as it still is today—for both parties to use a mutually trusted go-between who can ensure that the payment is held until the merchandise is in fact delivered according to the terms of the trade contract. The go-between representatives employed by the importer and exporter are still, as they were in the past, the local domestic banks involved in international business.

Alternatively, the exporting firm may ship its products to an *export-import agent*, which arranges the sale of the products to foreign intermediaries for a commission or fee. The agent is an independent firm—like other agents—that sells and may perform other marketing functions for the exporter. The exporter, however, retains title to the products during shipment and until they are sold.

An exporting firm also may establish its own *sales offices*, or *branches*, in foreign countries. These installations are international extensions of the firm's distribution system. They represent a deeper involvement in international business than the other exporting techniques we have discussed—and thus they carry a greater risk. The exporting firm maintains control over sales, and it gains both experience in and knowledge of foreign markets. Eventually, the firm also may develop its own sales force to operate in conjunction with foreign sales offices.

Figure 2-3 Exporting to International Markets

After signing contracts, the importer will ask its local bank to issue a *letter of credit* for the funds needed to pay for the merchandise. The transporter of the merchandise provides the exporter evidence of the shipment via a *bill of lading*. The exporter signs over title to the merchandise and issues a *draft* from its bank, which orders the importer's bank to pay for the merchandise.

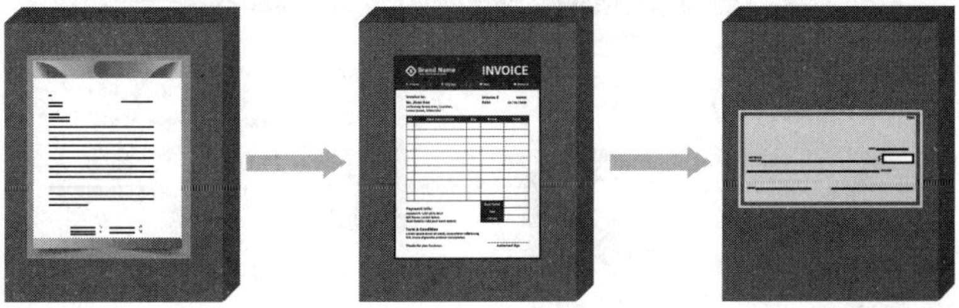

Another option is via a **trading company**, which provides a link between buyers and sellers in different countries. A trading company, as its name implies, is not involved in manufacturing or owning assets related to manufacturing. It buys products in one country at the lowest price consistent with quality and sells to buyers in another country. An important function of trading companies is taking title to products and performing all the activities necessary to move the products from the domestic country to a foreign country. For example, large grain-trading companies operating out of home offices both in the United States and overseas control a major portion of the world's trade in basic food commodities. These trading companies sell homogeneous agricultural commodities that can be stored and moved rapidly in response to market conditions.

In the early 1990s, many developing nations had major restrictions on converting domestic currency into foreign currency. Therefore, companies that wanted to export had to resort to barter agreements with importers. **Countertrade** is essentially an international barter transaction in which goods and services are exchanged for different goods and services. As an example, Iran has purchased rice and other imports from India with payment in crude oil.[16] Countertrade is still used today, particularly for trade with countries that have difficult relations with the home nation.

许可和特许经营

2-2b Licensing and Franchising

Licensing and franchising represent slightly more complex arrangements for international trade. **Licensing** is a contractual agreement in which one firm permits another to produce and market its product and to use its brand name in return for a royalty or other compensation. For example, Yoplait yogurt is a French yogurt licensed for production in the United States. The Yoplait brand maintains an appealing French image, and in return, the U.S. producer pays the French firm a percentage of its income from sales of the product.

Licensing is especially advantageous for small manufacturers wanting to launch a well-known domestic brand internationally. For example, Swedish-owned Electrolux licenses many of its products to firms in India, China, and many other countries. Licensing thus provides a simple method for expanding into a foreign market with virtually no investment. On the other hand, if the licensee does not maintain the licensor's product standards, the product's reputation may be damaged.

贸易公司
trading company provides a link between buyers and sellers in different countries

对等贸易
countertrade an international barter transaction

许可
licensing a contractual agreement in which one firm permits another to produce and market its product and to use its brand name in return for a royalty or other compensation

Another possible disadvantage is that a licensing arrangement may not provide the original producer with any foreign marketing experience.

Franchising is similar to licensing in that it is a contractual arrangement for an individual or organization to operate facilities, typically stores, on behalf of another. As we shall see in Chapter 4, a franchisor, such as KFC, allows a franchisee to use the franchisor's brand name and methods of doing business in its own stores in exchange for fees and royalties. This arrangement can enable a popular brand to expand into overseas markets with relatively little investment. Consider that consumers around the world can get donuts, muffins, bagels, and coffee at 3,200 Dunkin' restaurants in 36 countries, in addition to 8,500 restaurants in the United States.[17]

合同制造

2-2c Contract Manufacturing

Companies that want a little more control over their products and are willing to take on a greater degree of risk may engage in contract manufacturing. **Contract manufacturing** occurs when one firm employs another business—often in another country—to manufacture its products or product components to the domestic firm's specifications. The resulting product typically carries the domestic firm's name. In fact, many U.S. companies use contract manufacturing to take advantage of lower labor costs in other countries, which can help lower the prices of their products to consumers. Contract manufacturing is used far more often than you might guess, and it is common in the electronics, automotive, and fashion industries, among others. Consider Swedish fast-fashion retailer H&M, which contracts with hundreds of different companies in 40 countries to produce its trendy clothing. Recently, the firm has begun identifying the company, country, and even factory producing each item of clothing for interested consumers and stakeholders.[18]

Indeed, **outsourcing**, the contracting of manufacturing and/or other activities to overseas companies that specialize in those activities and can offer them at a lower cost, has become very common in recent years. Many companies have achieved significant cost savings from outsourcing manufacturing to countries such as India, Bangladesh, Vietnam, and the Philippines, where labor costs and taxes are significantly lower than in the United States. In most cases, these savings are passed on to shareholders and to consumers in the form of lower prices. However, outsourcing is controversial because it has resulted in the loss of American manufacturing jobs and higher unemployment in manufacturing sectors.

合同制造
contract manufacturing an arrangement in which one firm contracts with another business, often in another country, to manufacture products or product components to its specifications

外包
outsourcing an arrangement in which one firm contracts manufacturing or other activities to a firm in another country that specializes in those activities and can offer them at a lower cost than domestic firms

战略联盟
strategic alliance a partnership formed to create competitive advantage on a worldwide basis

合资企业和联盟

2-2d Joint Ventures and Alliances

A *joint venture* is a partnership formed to achieve a specific goal or to operate for a specific period of time. A joint venture with an established firm in a foreign country provides immediate market knowledge and access, reduced risk, and control over product attributes. However, joint-venture agreements established across national borders can become extremely complex. As a result, joint-venture agreements generally require a very high level of commitment from all the parties involved. A joint venture may be used to produce and market an existing product in a foreign nation or to develop an entirely new product. For example, New York-based Pfizer, one of the world's leading pharmaceutical companies, entered into a joint venture with BioNTech, a German biotechnology company, to create and distribute a vaccine for the COVID-19 virus.[19]

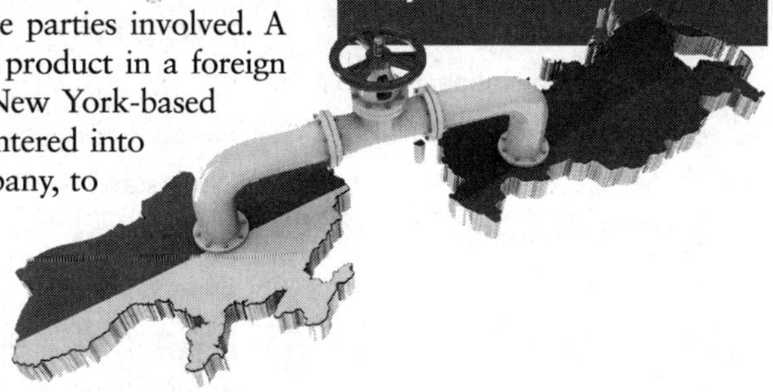

Joint venture. Large pipelines can involve multiple countries. They can be organized based on the use of joint ventures.

A **strategic alliance**, a more recent form of international business structure, is a partnership formed to create competitive advantage on a worldwide basis. Strategic alliances are very similar to joint ventures. The number of strategic alliances is growing at an estimated rate of about 20 percent per year. In fact, in the automobile and computer industries, strategic alliances are becoming the predominant means of competing. International competition is so fierce and the costs of competing on a global basis are so high that few firms have all the resources needed to do it alone. Thus, individual firms that lack the internal resources essential for international success may seek to collaborate with other companies. An example of such an alliance is the agreement between Honda and General Motors to collaborate to make electric vehicles using technologies from both firms.[20]

直接投资

2-2e **Direct Investment**

At a still deeper level of involvement in international business, a firm may invest directly in its own facilities, that is, its own production and marketing facilities in one or more foreign nations. This *direct investment* provides complete control over operations, but it carries a greater risk than the joint venture. The firm is really establishing a subsidiary in a foreign country. Most firms do so only after they have engaged in simpler levels of international trade and acquired some knowledge of the host country's markets.

Direct investment may take either of two forms. In the first, the company builds or purchases manufacturing and other facilities in a foreign country. It uses these facilities to produce its own established products and to market them in that country and perhaps in neighboring countries. Firms such as General Motors, Dow Chemical, and Colgate-Palmolive are multinational companies with worldwide manufacturing facilities.

A second form of direct investment in international business is the purchase of an existing firm in a foreign country under an arrangement that allows it to operate independently of the parent company. When Sony Corporation (a Japanese firm) decided to enter the motion picture business in the United States, it chose to purchase Columbia Pictures Entertainment, Inc., rather than start a new motion picture studio from scratch.

✓ Concept Check

- List the most common methods of entering international business.
- Two methods of engaging in international business may be categorized as either direct or indirect. How would you classify each of the methods described in this chapter? Why?
- In what ways is a multinational corporation different from a large corporation that does business in several countries?

跨国公司

multinational corporation a firm that operates on a worldwide scale without ties to any specific nation or region

跨国公司

2-2f **Multinational Firms**

A **multinational corporation** is a firm that operates on a worldwide scale without ties to any specific nation or region. The multinational firm represents the highest level of involvement in international business. It is equally "at home" in most countries of the world. In fact, as far as the operations of the multinational enterprise are concerned, national boundaries exist only on maps. It is, however, organized under the laws of its home country. Table 2-4 shows the ten largest foreign and U.S. public multinational companies; the ranking is based on a composite score reflecting each company's best three out of four rankings for sales, profits, assets, and market value.

Table 2-4 The Ten Largest Foreign and U.S. Multinational Corporations

Rank	Company	Business	Country	Revenue ($ millions)
1	Walmart	General Merchandise	United States	523,964
2	Sinopec	Energy	China	407,009
3	State Grid	Power Grids	China	383,906
4	China National Petroleum	Energy	China	379,130
5	Royal Dutch Shell	Energy	Netherlands	352,106
6	Saudi Aramco	Petroleum	Saudi Arabia	329,784
7	Volkswagen	Automobiles	Germany	282,760
8	BP	Energy	United Kingdom	282,616
9	Amazon	Internet and Retail	United States	280,522
10	Toyota	Automobiles	Japan	275,288

Source: "Global 500," *Fortune*.

Discussion Questions 讨论题

1. When should a firm consider expanding from strictly domestic trade to international trade? When should it consider becoming further involved in international trade? What factors might affect the firm's decisions in each case?
2. Some politicians think tariffs will reduce their countries' trade deficits. Are they correct?
3. What effects might the devaluation of a nation's currency have on its business firms, its consumers, and the debts it owes to other nations?
4. Should imports to the United States be curtailed, by 20 percent or so, to eliminate our trade deficit? What might happen if this were done?
5. When the U.S. dollar is strong relative to other nations' currencies, what is the effect on imports and exports?

Case 2 案例 2：本田的战略就是电动化且令人振奋

Honda's Strategy Is Electrifying

Honda Motor Company, a Japan-based multinational motorcycle manufacturer, was founded by Soichiro Honda in 1937. Honda, a Japanese engineer and innovator, built Honda Motor Company from the ground up. The automotive manufacturer, which started with 12 employees retrofitting bicycles with engines, has grown to more than 218,000 employees producing 19 million motorcycles, nearly 5 million automobiles, and more than 5 million power products every year. Today, Honda continues to innovate as the automotive market accelerates its transition to electric and hybrid technology.

Soichiro Honda always had an interest in vehicles. He founded Tokai Seiki (Eastern Sea Precision Machine Company) to make piston rings. Though he won a contract with Toyota, he lost the contract when it became evident that quality was lacking. He visited Toyota factories across Japan to learn more about quality control and perfect his product. Eventually, he created acceptable pistons using an auto-mated process that could employ unskilled war-time laborers. At the start of World War II, Tokai Seiki was placed under the control of the Ministry of Commerce and Industry, and Honda was demoted at his own company. After the war, Honda sold what remained of Tokai Seiki to Toyota and used the profits to open the Honda Technical Research Institute.

With just a dozen employees in 1946, the company built and sold motorized bicycles using the former Imperial Army's generator engines. Demand was high, and the Honda Technical Research Institute soon ran out of stock. The com-pany set out to make its own engine. Honda liquidated his business and used the money to incorporate Honda Motor Company. Its first complete motorcycle, the Honda 1949 D-Type, was just the start. The company grew to become the largest manufacturer of motorcycles by 1964.

In 1959, Honda Motor Company expanded into North America, opening its first overseas subsidiary in Los Angeles. Around this time, Honda opened Honda R&D Co., Ltd. to independently focus on research and development. Over the next several decades, Honda Motor Company continued to expand its product lines as well as operations and exports, opening its first overseas production facility in Belgium and becoming the first Japanese car manufacturer to open a pro-duction facility in the United States. Honda is now a house-hold name with a reputation for producing quality cars and motorcycles.

Though Honda Motor Company is the world's largest man-ufacturer of internal combustion engines, it has had its sights set on new mobility for decades. In 2002, the company offered customers in the United States and Japan the Honda FCX, a fuel-cell powered car. Regulatory change and shifting con-sumer behavior in Europe have accelerated Honda's long-term electrification plans for the region, a strategy the company calls "Electric Vision." These changes have pushed Honda to introduce electrified powertrains for all of its European main-stream models several years ahead of schedule. Additionally, the company's advanced two-motor hybrid technology seen in the Honda Jazz hatchback and CR-V Hybrid has been met with acclaim across Europe. In a traditional hybrid model, an electric motor assists the car's engine, but in the Jazz hybrid electric vehicle, an electric engine assists the motor.

In the United States, on the other hand, Honda has a long road ahead to an electric future. Honda phased out the Clarity EV, its only all-electric car in the U.S. market at the time, leaving its fuel-cell and plug-in hybrid models. Buyers were unimpressed with its 89-mile driving range. In contrast, both the Chevy Bolt EV and Tesla Model 3 travel around 240 miles. To focus on the next generation of products, Honda partnered with rival General Motors (GM) to create two new all-electric vehicles using GM's proprietary Ultium battery and hands-free driver-assist technology wrapped in Honda's design. Strategic alliances such as this allow com-panies to pool resources, combine scale and manufacturing efficiencies, and create a competitive advantage.

By 2030, the majority of Honda's cars will be electric, zero-emission vehicles. Though there is still much progress to be made in the United States, Honda is quickly bringing its Electric Vision strategy to life in Europe. Additionally, Honda stands to greatly benefit from its strategic partnership with GM. Honda Motor Company's long history and its reputation for quality show that Honda is a company that knows how to innovate and adapt.[21]

Questions

1. How did Honda Motor Company build its reputation for producing quality cars and motorcycles?
2. What are the advantages of Honda's strategic alliance with GM?
3. How is Honda adapting to regulatory change and shifting consumer behavior in Europe?

PART 2
Business Ownership and Entrepreneurship
企业所有权和企业家精神

Chapter 3
Choosing a Form of Business Ownership

Chapter 4
Small Business, Entrepreneurship, and Franchises

In this part, we examine two very practical aspects of business: The most popular (and most important) forms of legal ownership business owners choose. In addition, because the majority of businesses are small, we look at specific issues related to small business.

Chapter

3

Choosing a Form of Business Ownership

选择企业的所有权形式

Learning Objectives

Once you complete this chapter, you will be able to:

3-1 Describe the advantages and disadvantages of sole proprietorships.

3-2 Explain the different types of partners and the importance of partnership agreements.

3-3 Describe the advantages and disadvantages of partnerships.

3-4 Summarize how a corporation is formed.

3-5 Describe the advantages and disadvantages of a corporation.

Why Should You Care?

There's a good chance that during your lifetime you will work for a business or start a business. With this fact in mind, the material in this chapter can help you understand how and why businesses are organized.

Inside Business 商业透视：亚马逊通过收购自动驾驶汽车公司来加速扩张

Amazon Accelerates with Autonomous Vehicle Acquisition

You recognize the corporate name Amazon, but do you know how successful the company is today? The online retailer was founded by Jeff Bezos and began operations in 1995. The new company used its early success selling books to expand and become one of the largest retailers in the world. Today, Amazon generates over $350 billion in annual revenues, and 2020 profits soared during the COVID-19 pandemic when people used its website to buy just about everything they needed including groceries, cleaning supplies, clothing, toilet paper, and other essential items. And yet, even though it is one of the most successful companies in the world, it doesn't pay dividends to stockholders. Why? The simple answer is that Amazon reinvests its profits to improve its current operations *and* buy other companies that fit with Amazon's strategic plans to grow and expand.

In many cases, the companies that Amazon invests in or buys are smaller start-up companies that have developed software or new technology that has the potential to become extremely valuable as the world becomes more dependent on automation and technology. For example, it invested in start-ups Aurora (self-driving cars) and Rivian (electric trucks). Now Amazon is expanding and investing even more money in automotive technology with its acquisition of Zoox for $1.3 billion. What makes this an attractive acquisition for Amazon is Zoox's current projects to develop a self-driving, ride-hailing vehicle from the ground up that is controlled by its own proprietary software and artificial intelligence (AI). According to many experts, autonomous cars coupled with ride hailing ("robotaxis" or driverless taxis) could be the way people get from place to place in the future.

The acquisition makes sense: Amazon invested to acquire Zoox's state-of-the art technology and experimental versions of a protype robotaxi, while Zoox gets financial backing from Amazon. Amazon's current focus is not to implement the technology on its logistics operations for delivering packages, but rather to use the technology to enter a new market that is different from online retailing. If Zoox and its robotaxi are successful, it would pit Amazon against ride-sharing giants Uber and Lyft as well as Waymo—an autonomous driving start-up subsidiary of Alphabet, the parent company of Google.

When robotaxis begin to serve major cities in the United States, Amazon and Zoox could lead the market. Unlike other robotaxis in development, Zoox's four-wheel vehicle is bi-directional—meaning it can drive both forward and backward as well as side to side—and it can reach speeds up to 75 mph. By combining their strengths, Zoox and Amazon stand a good chance to create a successful autonomous ride-hailing service.[1]

Did you know?

Amazon invested billions in start-ups Aurora, Rivian, and Zoox to create autonomous driving vehicles, electric trucks, and robotaxis.

Just for a moment, think about how business is defined.

> *"Business is the organized effort of individuals to produce and sell for a profit, the goods and services that satisfy society's needs."*

A company like Amazon must make many decisions in order to grow and expand. While most people have bought something online using Amazon, the company wasn't always a large, successful company. For Jeff Bezos and the people who started Amazon, one of the most important decisions they had to make was choosing a form of ownership. Options included sole proprietorship, partnership, corporation, or special forms of ownership that will meet a company's special needs. Amazon chose the corporate form of ownership because it provided a number of advantages compared to other forms of business ownership.

We begin this chapter by describing the three common forms of business ownership: sole proprietorships, partnerships, and corporations. We discuss how these types of businesses are formed and note the advantages and disadvantages of each.

独资企业

3-1 Sole Proprietorships

Learning Objective

3-1 Describe the advantages and disadvantages of sole proprietorships.

A **sole proprietorship** is a business that is owned (and usually operated) by one person. Although a few sole proprietorships are large and have many employees, most are small. Some of today's largest corporations, including Walmart, JCPenney, and Procter & Gamble Company, started out as tiny—and in many cases, struggling—sole proprietorships.

Often entrepreneurs with a promising idea choose the sole proprietorship form of ownership. Way back in 1886, Samuel Curtis Johnson sold wood parquet flooring in Racine, Wisconsin. His business—a sole proprietorship—was successful selling floors, but he became much more successful selling floor wax—an idea he got after many customers asked what the best way was to protect their new parquet floor and at the same time maintain the shiny new look. Their questions inspired Mr. Johnson to create his first batch of floor wax. Some would say, why is this important? After all, this was 1886. Fast forward: Today, Mr. Johnson's small sole proprietorship business has grown and expanded to become a global company with annual revenues in excess of $10 billion and more than 13,000 employees. The SC Johnson Company still sells floor wax, but its product line now includes Windex glass cleaner, Pledge furniture polish, Ziploc food storage bags, Off insect repellant, Kiwi shoe polish, and many other consumer and professional products. See the Chapter 3 case at the end of the chapter for more about SC Johnson.[2]

Figure 3-1 shows that there are approximately 26.4 million sole proprietorships in the United States. They account for 72 percent of the country's business firms. Although the most popular form of ownership when compared with partnerships and corporations, they rank last in total sales revenues. As shown in Figure 3-2, sole proprietorships account for about $1.5 trillion, or about 4 percent of total annual sales.

Sole proprietorships are most common in retailing, service, and agriculture. Thus, the small, clothing boutique, appliance-repair shop down the street, and independent farmer are likely to be sole proprietorships.

Figure 3-1 Relative Percentages of Sole Proprietorships, Partnerships, and Corporations in the United States

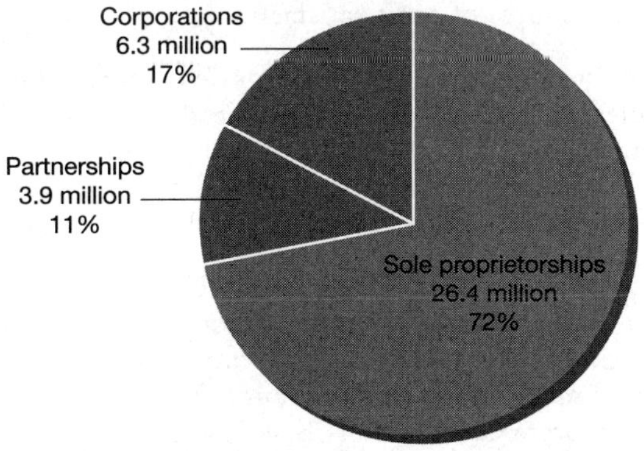

Source: "Statistics of Income," The Internal Revenue Service website.

独资企业
sole proprietorship a business that is owned (and usually operated) by one person

Figure 3-2 Total Sales Receipts of Sole Proprietorships, Partnerships, and Corporations in the United States

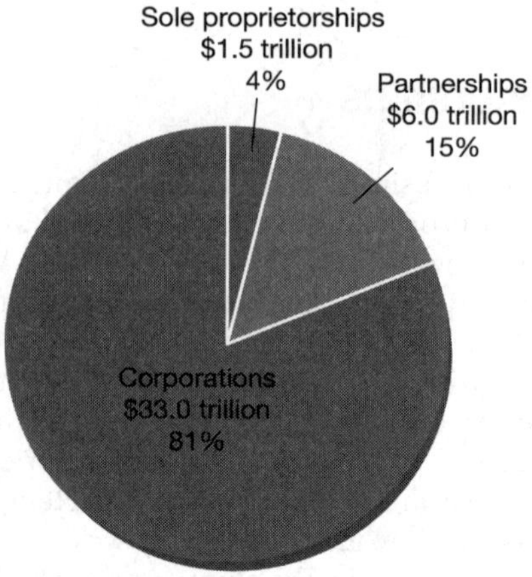

Source: "Statistics of Income," The Internal Revenue Service website.

独资企业的优势

3-1a Advantages of Sole Proprietorships

Most of the advantages of sole proprietorships arise from the two main characteristics of this form of ownership: simplicity and individual control.

Ease of Start-Up and Closure Sole proprietorship is the simplest way to start a business. A sole proprietorship can be, and most often is, established without the services of an attorney. The legal requirements often are limited to registering the name of the business and obtaining any necessary licenses or permits.

If the enterprise does not succeed, the firm can be closed as easily as it was opened. Creditors must be paid, of course, but generally, the owner of a sole proprietorship does not have to go through any legal procedure before hanging up an "Out of Business" sign.

Pride of Ownership Successful sole proprietors are often very proud of their accomplishments—and rightfully so. In almost every case, the owner deserves a great deal of credit for solving the day-to-day problems associated with operating a sole proprietorship business. Unfortunately, the reverse is also true. When the business fails, it is often the sole proprietor who is to blame.

Retention of All Profits Because all profits become the personal earnings of the owner, the owner has a strong incentive to succeed. This direct financial reward attracts many entrepreneurs to the sole proprietorship form of business and, if the business succeeds, is a source of great satisfaction.

No Special Taxes Profits earned by a sole proprietorship are taxed as the personal income of the owner. As a result, a sole proprietor must report business profit or loss and certain other financial information for a business on the Internal Revenue Service's Schedule C, which becomes part of their personal income tax return. They must also make estimated quarterly tax payments to the federal government.

Flexibility of Being Your Own Boss Sole proprietors are completely free to make decisions about the firm's operations. Without asking or waiting for anyone's approval, sole proprietors can move a shop's location, open a new store, or close an old one. And they can make an immediate change in business hours. The manager of a store in a large corporate chain such as Best Buy Company may have to seek the approval of numerous managers and company officials before making such changes.

Going out of business hurts! There are many reasons why businesses—especially sole proprietors and partnerships—fail. Lack of money, poor management, bad location, poor product selection, and many other factors can cause a business to close the doors. Regardless of the reason, it always hurts those who have invested their time, money, and effort to start a business.

独资企业的劣势
3-1b Disadvantages of Sole Proprietorships

The disadvantages of a sole proprietorship stem from the fact that these businesses are owned by one person. Some capable sole proprietors experience no problems. Individuals who start out with few management skills and little money are most at risk for failure.

Unlimited Liability **Unlimited liability** is a legal concept that holds a business owner personally responsible for all the debts of the business. There is legally no difference between the debts of the business and the debts of the proprietor. If the business fails, or if the business is involved in a lawsuit and loses, the owner's personal property—including savings and other assets—can be seized (and sold if necessary) to pay creditors.

Unlimited liability is perhaps the major factor that tends to discourage would-be entrepreneurs with substantial personal wealth from using the sole proprietor form of business organization. Unlimited liability is also a reason why many sole proprietors switch to the corporate form of ownership or some other type of business organization that limits their personal liability once their businesses become successful.

Lack of Continuity Legally, the sole proprietor *is* the business. If the owner retires, is declared legally incompetent, or dies, the business essentially ceases to exist. In many cases, however—especially when the business is a profitable enterprise—the owner may sell the business or the owner's heirs may take it over and either sell it or continue to operate it. The business also can suffer if the sole proprietor becomes ill and cannot work for an extended period of time. If the owner, for example, has a heart attack, there is often no one who can step in and manage the business. An illness can be devastating if the sole proprietor's personal skills are what determine if the business is a success or a failure.

Lack of Money Banks, suppliers, and other lenders usually are unwilling to lend large sums of money to sole proprietorships. Only one person—the sole proprietor—can be held responsible for repaying such loans, and the assets of most sole proprietors usually are limited. Moreover, these assets may have been used already as security or collateral for personal borrowing (a home mortgage or car loan) or for short-term credit from suppliers. Lenders also worry about the lack of continuity of sole proprietorships: Who will repay a loan if the sole proprietor dies?

无限责任
unlimited liability a legal concept that holds a business owner personally responsible for all the debts of the business

Finally, many lenders are concerned about the large number of sole proprietorships that fail—a topic discussed in Chapter 4.

The limited ability to borrow money can prevent a sole proprietorship from growing. It is the main reason that many business owners, when in need of relatively large amounts of capital, change from a sole proprietorship to a partnership or the corporate form of ownership.

Limited Management Skills The sole proprietor is often the sole manager—in addition to being the only salesperson, buyer, accountant, and, on occasion, janitor. Even the most experienced business owners are unlikely to have expertise in all these areas. Unless they obtain the necessary expertise by hiring employees, assistants, or consultants, the business can suffer in the areas in which the owner is less knowledgeable. For the many sole proprietors who cannot afford to hire the help they need, there just are not enough hours in the day to do everything that needs to be done.

Difficulty in Hiring Employees The sole proprietor may find it hard to attract and keep competent help. Potential employees may feel that there is no room for advancement in a firm whose owner assumes all managerial responsibilities. And when those who *are* hired are ready to take on added responsibility, they may find that the only way to do so is to quit a sole proprietorship business and go to work for a larger firm or start their own business. The lure of higher salaries and increased benefits also may cause existing employees to change jobs.

✓ Concept Check

- What is a sole proprietorship?
- What are the advantages of a sole proprietorship?
- What are the disadvantages of a sole proprietorship?

超越独资企业

3-1c Beyond the Sole Proprietorship

Like many others, you may decide that the major disadvantage of a sole proprietorship is the limited amount that one person can do in a workday. One way to reduce the effect of this disadvantage (and retain many of the advantages) is to form a partnership and have more than one owner.

Ethics and Social Responsibility

商业伦理与社会责任：美国运通如何帮助小企业

How American Express Helps Small Businesses

During the COVID-19 pandemic, one thing became clear: regular customers are necessary for small businesses to survive. Knowing this, American Express, the company that started Small Business Saturday—an initiative to encourage customers to shop at small businesses—committed more than $200 million to launch its largest global "shop small" campaign to date. In addition, the credit card company pledged $10 million to support Black-owned small businesses during the pandemic.

According to research conducted by American Express, many small businesses were in danger of failing. As many as 25 percent of small business owners stopped paying themselves a salary during the pandemic in order to remain open. The research data also showed having regular customers return would help small businesses recover and at the same time help local communities. For this reason, American Express developed a program to provide incentives to encourage customers to shop small. The credit card company offered customers $5 back if they spent $10 or more at eligible small businesses, an offer that could be redeemed up to ten times.

It's important for small businesses to survive and grow because they bring value to their communities beyond the goods and services they sell. According to American Express, for every dollar spent at small businesses, $0.67 stays in the local community. American Express's long-running history of supporting "shop small" campaigns and small business owners demonstrates that it views small businesses as the lifeblood of the U.S. economy.

Sources: Based on information in Alexandra Pastore, "American Express Launches Its Largest Global Shop Small Campaign," *WWD*, June 29, 2020; Daily Flash TV, "American Express Help Small Business | Walter Frye | DailyFlashTV," *YouTube*, July 5, 2020; Robert Hackett, "AmEx Will Give You up to $50 If You Shop at Small Businesses," *Fortune*, June 29, 2020.

合伙企业
3-2 Partnerships

A person who would not think of starting and running a sole proprietorship business alone may enthusiastically seize the opportunity to form a business partnership. The U.S. Uniform Partnership Act defines a **partnership** as a voluntary association of two or more persons to act as co-owners of a business for profit. Way back in 1837, William Procter and James Gamble—two sole proprietors—formed a partnership called Procter & Gamble (P&G). Their partnership combined the talents of each man and helped the new partnership business compete with 14 other soap and candle makers in Cincinnati, Ohio. Eventually, in 1890, P&G incorporated to raise additional capital for expansion that allowed the company to become a global giant. Today, P&G brands are known worldwide and include Pantene, Gillette, Tide, Crest, and many more that people use every day.[3]

As shown in Figures 3-1 and 3-2, there are approximately 3.9 million partnerships in the United States, and this type of ownership accounts for about $6 trillion in sales receipts each year. Note, however, that this form of ownership is much less common than the sole proprietorship or the corporation. In fact, as shown in Figure 3-1, partnerships represent only about 11 percent of all American businesses. Although there is no legal maximum on the number of partners a partnership may have, most have only two. Regardless of the number of people involved, a partnership often represents a pooling of special managerial skills and talents; at other times, it is the result of a sole proprietor taking on a partner for the purpose of obtaining more capital.

Learning Objective

3-2 Explain the different types of partners and the importance of partnership agreements.

合伙人的类型
3-2a Types of Partners

All partners are not necessarily equal. Some may be active in running the business, whereas others may have a limited role.

合伙企业
partnership a voluntary association of two or more persons to act as co-owners of a business for profit

General Partners A **general partner** is a person who assumes full or shared responsibility for operating a business. General partners are active in day-to-day business operations, and each partner can enter into contracts on behalf of the other partners. They also assume unlimited liability for all debts, including business debts incurred by any other general partner without their knowledge or consent. To avoid future liability, a general partner who withdraws from the partnership must give notice to creditors, customers, and suppliers.

Limited Partners A **limited partner** is a person who invests money in a business but who has no management responsibility or liability for losses beyond their investment in the partnership. Typically, the general partner or partners collect management fees and receive a percentage of profits. Limited partners receive a portion of profits and tax benefits. Limited partnerships, for example, may be formed to finance real estate, oil and gas, motion picture, and other business ventures.

Because of potential liability problems, special rules apply to limited partnerships. These rules are intended to protect customers and creditors who deal with limited partnerships. For example, prospective partners in a limited partnership must file a formal declaration, usually with the secretary of state, that describes the essential details of the partnership and the liability status of each partner involved in the business. At least one general partner must be responsible for the debts of the limited partnership. Also, some states require the name of a limited partnership to include the term "limited partnership" or the abbreviation "LP."

普通合伙人
general partner a person who assumes full or shared responsibility for operating a business

有限合伙人
limited partner a person who invests money in a business but has no management responsibility or liability for losses beyond the amount they invested in the partnership

合伙协议

3-2b The Partnership Agreement

Articles of partnership refers to an agreement listing and explaining the terms of the partnership. Although both oral and written partnership agreements are legal and can be enforced in the courts, a written agreement has an obvious advantage. It is not subject to lapses of memory. Although the people involved in a partnership can draft their own agreement, most experts recommend consulting an attorney. Figure 3-3 shows a typical partnership agreement. The partnership agreement should state:

- The names of the people involved and the address of the business;
- What the nature of the business is;
- What each partner's duties will be;
- The investment each partner will make;
- How much salary each partner receives and how profits or losses will be divided; and
- What happens if a partner wants to dissolve the partnership or dies.

When entering into a partnership agreement, partners would be wise to let a neutral third party—a consultant, an accountant, a lawyer, or a mutual friend—assist with any disputes that might arise.

✓ Concept Check

- How does a sole proprietorship differ from a partnership?
- Explain the difference between a general partner and a limited partner.
- Describe the issues that should be included in a partnership agreement.

Figure 3-3 Articles of Partnership

The articles of partnership is a written or oral agreement that lists and explains the terms of a partnership.

PARTNERSHIP AGREEMENT

Names of partners — This agreement, made June 20, 2022, between Penelope Wolfburg of 783A South Street, Hazelton, Idaho, and Ingrid Swenson of RR 5, Box 96, Hazelton, Idaho.

Nature, name, and address of business — 1. The above named persons have this day formed a partnership that shall operate under the name of W-S Jewelers, located at 85 Broad Street, Hazelton, Idaho 83335, and shall engage in jewelry sales and repairs.

Duration of partnership — 2. The duration of this agreement will be for a term of fifteen (15) years, beginning June 20, 2022, or for a shorter period if agreed upon in writing by both partners.

Contribution of capital — 3. The initial investment by each partner will be as follows: Penelope Wolfburg, assets and liabilities of Wolfburg's Jewelry Store, valued at a capital investment of $40,000; Ingrid Swenson, cash of $20,000. These investments are partnership property.

Duties of each partner — 4. Each partner will give her time, skill, and attention to the operation of this partnership and will engage in no other business enterprise unless permission is granted in writing by the other partner.

Salaries, withdrawals, and distribution of profits — 5. The salary for each partner will be as follows: Penelope Wolfburg, $40,000 per year; Ingrid Swenson, $30,000 per year. Neither partner may withdraw cash or other assets from the business without express permission in writing from the other partner. All profits and losses of the business will be shared as follows: Penelope Wolfburg, 60 percent; Ingrid Swenson, 40 percent.

Termination — 6. Upon the dissolution of the partnership due to termination of this agreement, or to written permission by each of the partners, or to the death or incapacitation of one or both partners, a new contract may be entered into by the partners or the sole continuing partner has the option to purchase the other partner's interest in the business at a price that shall not exceed the balance in the terminating partner's capital account. The payment shall be made in cash in equal quarterly installments from the date of termination.

7. At the conclusion of this contract, unless it is agreed by both partners to continue the operation of the business under a new contract, the assets of the partnership, after the liabilities are paid, will be divided in proportion to the balance in each partner's capital account on that date.

Signatures — *Penelope Wolfburg* / Penelope Wolfburg — *Ingrid Swenson* / Ingrid Swenson

Date — *June 20, 2022* / Date — *June 20, 2022* / Date

Source: Adapted from Goldman and Sigismond, *Cengage Advantage Books: Business Law 9E*.

合伙企业的优势和劣势

3-3 Advantages and Disadvantages of Partnerships

Learning Objective

3-3 Describe the advantages and disadvantages of partnerships.

When compared to sole proprietorships and corporations, partnerships are the least popular form of business ownership. Still there are situations when forming a partnership makes perfect sense.

合伙企业的优势

3-3a Advantages of Partnerships

Before you make a decision to form a partnership, all the people involved should consider both the advantages and disadvantages of a partnership. Partnerships have many advantages. The most important are described below.

Ease of Start-Up Partnerships are relatively easy to form. As with a sole proprietorship, the legal requirements often are limited to registering the name of the business and obtaining any necessary licenses or permits. It may not even be necessary to prepare written articles of partnership, although doing so is generally a good idea.

Availability of Capital and Credit Because partners can pool their funds, a partnership usually has more capital available than a sole proprietorship does. This additional capital, coupled with the general partners' unlimited liability and combined management skills, may encourage banks and suppliers to extend more credit or approve larger loans to a partnership than to a sole proprietor. Still, partnerships have found it hard to get long-term financing simply because lenders worry about the possibility of management disagreements and lack of continuity.

Personal Interest General partners are very concerned with the operation of the firm—perhaps even more so than sole proprietors. After all, they are responsible for the actions of all other general partners, as well as for their own. The pride of ownership from solving the day-to-day problems of operating a business—with the help of another person(s)—is a strong motivating force and often makes all the people involved in the partnership work harder to become more successful.

Combined Business Skills and Knowledge Partners often have complementary skills. The weakness of one partner—in manufacturing, for example—may be offset by another partner's strength in that area. Moreover, the ability to discuss important decisions with another concerned individual often relieves some pressure and leads to more effective decision making.

Retention of Profits As in a sole proprietorship, all profits belong to the owners of the partnership. The partners share directly in the financial rewards and therefore are highly motivated to do their best to make the firm succeed. As noted earlier, the partnership agreement should state how much profit or loss each partner receives or is responsible for.

No Special Taxes Although a partnership pays no income tax, the Internal Revenue Service requires partnerships to file an annual information return that states the receipts and expenses for the partnership and the amount of profit or loss. The partnership return must also list the names of all partners involved in the business and their share of the partnership's profit or loss. Then all partners are required to report their share of profit (or loss) from the partnership on their individual tax returns. Ultimately each partner's share of the partnership profit is taxed in the same way a sole proprietor is taxed.

When a business is successful, it's a great source of pride for the owners. Small business owners will tell you that it takes a lot of hard work to create a successful business. It also takes money, good management skills, the ability to overcome problems, and in some cases luck. And yet, when a business is successful, there's a great deal of pride in what they've accomplished.

合伙企业的劣势

3-3b Disadvantages of Partnerships

Although partnerships have many advantages when compared with sole proprietorships and corporations, they also have some disadvantages, which anyone thinking of forming a partnership should consider.

Unlimited Liability As we have noted, each *general* partner has unlimited liability for all debts of the business. Each partner is legally and personally responsible for the debts, taxes, and actions of any other partner conducting partnership business, even if that partner did not incur those debts or do anything wrong. General partners thus run the risk of having to use their personal assets to pay creditors. *Limited* partners, however, risk only their original investment.

Today, many states allow partners to form a *limited liability partnership* (LLP), in which a partner may have limited liability protection from legal action resulting from the malpractice or negligence of the other partners. Many states that allow LLPs restrict this type of ownership to certain types of professionals such as accountants, architects, attorneys, and similar professionals. (Note the difference between a limited partnership and an LLP. A limited partnership must have at least one general partner that has unlimited liability. On the other hand, all partners in an LLP may have limited liability *for the malpractice and negligence of the other partners*.)

Management Disagreements What happens to a partnership if one of the partners brings a spouse or a relative into the business? What happens if a partner wants to withdraw more money from the business? Notice that each of these situations—and for that matter, most of the other problems that can develop in a partnership—involves one partner doing something that disturbs the other partner(s). This human factor is especially important because business partners—with egos, ambitions, and money on the line—are especially susceptible to friction. When partners begin to disagree about decisions, policies, or ethics, distrust may build and get worse as time passes. In these situations, it may become impossible to operate the business successfully.

Lack of Continuity Partnerships are terminated if any one of the general partners withdraws from the business, is declared legally incompetent, or dies. However, the remaining partners can purchase that partner's ownership share. For example, the partnership agreement may permit surviving partners to continue the business after buying a deceased partner's interest from the estate. However, if the partnership loses an owner whose specific management or technical skills cannot be replaced, it is not likely to survive.

Frozen Investment It is easy to invest money in a partnership, but it is sometimes quite difficult to get it out. This is the case, for example, when remaining partners are unwilling to buy the share of the business that belongs to a partner who retires. To avoid such difficulties, the partnership agreement should include some procedure for buying out a partner.

In some cases, a partner must find someone outside the firm to buy their share. How easy or difficult it is to find an outsider depends on how successful the business is and how willing existing partners are to accept a new partner.

超越合伙企业

3-3c Beyond the Partnership

The main advantages of a partnership over a sole proprietorship are increased availability of capital and credit and the combined business skills and knowledge of the partners. However, some of the basic disadvantages of the sole proprietorship also plague the general partnership. A third form of business ownership, the corporation, overcomes many of these disadvantages.

✓ Concept Check

- What are the advantages of a partnership?
- What are the disadvantages of a partnership?

公司

3-4 Corporations

Learning Objective

3-4 Summarize how a corporation is formed.

Recognize the name Ray Kroc? Maybe not the name, but there's a good chance you have purchased some fast food from McDonalds. Here's the story: Back in 1954, Ray Kroc was selling Multimixers malt machines when he met two brothers, Dick and Mac McDonald, who were running a fast-food restaurant that served burgers, fries, and beverages. The McDonald brothers were looking for an agent to help grow their business. Kroc saw an opportunity and founded the McDonald's System, Inc., a predecessor to today's McDonald's Corporation. Kroc's goal was to build a restaurant system that would be famous for providing food of consistently high quality that tasted the same in Alaska as it did in Alabama.

While Kroc and the executives of McDonald's had to make many decisions, one very important decision was to incorporate the business. While they could have chosen other forms of business ownership, the decision to incorporate enabled the company to attract investors and raise additional capital for expansion that eventually allowed it to become a global giant. Today, McDonald's has more than 38,000 locations in more than 100 countries around the globe.[4]

While not all sole proprietorships and partnerships become corporations, there are reasons why business owners choose the corporate form of ownership. Let's begin with a definition of a corporation. Perhaps the best definition of a corporation was given by Chief Justice John Marshall in a famous Supreme Court decision in 1819. A corporation, he said, "is an artificial person, invisible, intangible, and existing only in contemplation of the law." In other words, a **corporation** (sometimes referred to as a *regular* or a *C corporation*) is an artificial person, created by law, with most of the legal rights of a real person. These include:

- The right to start and operate a business.
- The right to buy or sell property.
- The right to borrow money.
- The right to sue or be sued.
- The right to enter into binding contracts.

公司

corporation (sometimes referred to as a *regular* or a *C corporation*) an artificial person, created by law, with most of the legal rights of a real person

Unlike a real person, however, a corporation exists only on paper. There are approximately 6.3 million corporations in the United States. They comprise about 17 percent of all businesses, but they account for 81 percent of sales revenues (refer to Figures 3-1 and 3-2).

公司所有权
3-4a Corporate Ownership

The shares of ownership of a corporation are called **stock**. Once a corporation has been formed, it may sell its stock to individuals or other companies that want to invest in the corporation. It also may issue stock as a reward to key employees or as a return to investors in place of cash payments. The people who own a corporation's stock—and thus own part of the corporation—are called **stockholders**.

A **closed corporation** (sometimes referred to as a private corporation) is a corporation whose stock is owned by relatively few people and is not sold to the general public. As an example, Mars—the company famous for M&Ms, Snickers, Dove, Milky Way, Twix, and other food products—is a privately held, family-owned, closed corporation. Although many people think that a closed corporation is a small company, there are exceptions. Mars, for example, has annual sales of more than $37 billion, employs more than 130,000 associates worldwide, and operates in 80 different countries.[5]

An **open corporation** (sometimes referred to as a public corporation) is one whose stock can be bought and sold by any individual. Examples of open corporations include General Electric, Microsoft, Apple, and Nike.

成立公司
3-4b Forming a Corporation

Although you may think that incorporating a business guarantees success, it does not. There is no special magic about placing the word *Incorporated* or the abbreviation *Inc.* after the name of a business. Unfortunately, like sole proprietorships or partnerships, corporations can go broke. The decision to incorporate a business, therefore, should be made only after carefully considering whether the corporate form of ownership suits your needs better than the sole proprietorship or partnership forms. To help you to decide if the corporate form of organization is the right choice, you may want to visit the library. You can also use an internet search engine and enter the term "business incorporation" for useful websites.

股票
stock the shares of ownership of a corporation

股东
stockholder a person who owns a corporation's stock

股份不公开公司
closed corporation (sometimes referred to as a private corporation) a corporation whose stock is owned by relatively few people and is not sold to the general public

股份公开公司
open corporation (sometimes referred to as a public corporation) a corporation whose stock can be bought and sold by any individual

Ronald McDonald stops in Bangkok, Thailand, to talk with a customer. When McDonald's opened the first store in 1954, no one—even Ray Kroc, one of the founders of McDonald's—would have dreamed that today the restaurant chain would have more than 38,000 locations in more than 100 different countries around the globe. Part of the reason why the founders chose to incorporate the business was the ability to raise capital that could be used for expansion.

If you decide the corporate form is the best form of ownership for you and your business, most experts recommend obtaining legal advice from an attorney who has helped other clients form a corporation to make sure all legal requirements are met. While it may be possible to incorporate a business without legal help, it is well to keep in mind the old saying, "A man who acts as his own attorney has a fool for a client." Table 3-1 lists some aspects of starting and running a business that may require legal help.

Where to Incorporate A business is allowed to incorporate in any state that it chooses. Most small- and medium-sized businesses are incorporated in the state where they do the most business. The founders of larger corporations or of those that will do business nationwide often compare the benefits that various states provide to corporations. The decision on where to incorporate usually is based on two factors: (1) the cost of incorporating in one state compared with the cost in another state and (2) the advantages and disadvantages of each state's corporate laws and tax structure. Some states are more hospitable than others, and some offer fewer restrictions, lower taxes, and other benefits to attract new firms. Delaware, Nevada, and Wyoming are often chosen by corporations that do business in more than one state because of their corporation-friendly laws and pro-business climate.[6]

An incorporated business is called a **domestic corporation** in the state in which it is incorporated. In all other states where it does business, it is called a **foreign corporation**. Home Depot is incorporated in Delaware, where it is a domestic corporation. In the remaining 49 states, Home Depot is a foreign corporation. Home Depot must register in all states where it does business and may be required to pay taxes and annual fees to each state. A corporation chartered by a foreign government and conducting business in the United States is an **alien corporation**. Royal Dutch Shell, Toyota, Nestlé, and Samsung Corporation are examples of alien corporations.

The Corporate Charter Once a home state has been chosen, the incorporator(s) submits *articles of incorporation* to the secretary of state or appropriate state authority. When the articles of incorporation are approved, they become a contract, often called the corporate charter, between a corporation and the state in which the state recognizes the formation of the artificial person that is the corporation. Usually, the articles of incorporation include the following information:

- The firm's name and address;
- The incorporators' names and addresses;
- The purpose of the corporation;

Table 3-1 Ten Aspects of Business That May Require Legal Help

1. Choosing either the sole proprietorship, partnership, corporate, or some special form of business ownership
2. Constructing a partnership agreement
3. Incorporating a business
4. Registering a corporation's stock
5. Obtaining a trademark, patent, or copyright
6. Filing for licenses or permits at the local, state, and federal levels
7. Purchasing an existing business or real estate
8. Creating valid contracts
9. Hiring employees and independent contractors
10. Extending credit and collecting debts

本州公司
domestic corporation a corporation in the state in which it is incorporated

外来公司
foreign corporation a corporation in any state in which it does business except the one in which it is incorporated

外国公司
alien corporation a corporation chartered by a foreign government and conducting business in the United States

- The maximum amount of stock and types of stock to be issued;
- The length of time the corporation is to exist; and
- The name and address of the corporation's registered agent.

Before making a decision to organize your business as a corporation, you may want to consider two additional areas: stockholders' rights and the importance of the organizational meeting.

Stockholders' Rights Even if you own a single share of stock, you're legally a part owner of the corporation. There are two basic types of stock. Owners of **common stock** may vote on corporate matters. Generally, an owner of common stock has one vote for each share owned. However, any claims of common stockholders on profits, dividends, and assets of the corporation are paid after the claims of others. The owners of **preferred stock** usually have no voting rights, but their claims on dividends are paid before those of common stockholders. Although some large corporations may issue both common and preferred stock, smaller corporations generally issue only common stock.

Perhaps the most important right of owners of both common and preferred stock is to share in the profit earned by the corporation through the payment of dividends. A **dividend** is a distribution of earnings to the stockholders of a corporation. Other rights include receiving information about the corporation, voting on changes to the corporate charter, and attending the corporation's annual stockholders' meeting, where they may exercise their right to vote.

Because common stockholders usually live all over the nation, very few may actually attend a corporation's annual meeting. Instead, they vote by proxy. A **proxy** is a legal form listing issues to be decided at a stockholders' meeting and enabling stockholders to transfer their voting rights to some other individual or individuals. A stockholder can register a vote and transfer voting rights simply by signing and returning the proxy form. Today, most corporations also allow stockholders to exercise their right to vote by proxy by accessing the internet or using a toll-free phone number.

Organizational Meeting As the last step in forming a corporation, the incorporators and original stockholders meet to adopt corporate bylaws and elect their first board of directors. (Later, directors will be elected or reelected at the corporation's annual meetings by the firm's stockholders.) The board members are directly responsible to the stockholders for the way they operate the firm.

公司结构

3-4c Corporate Structure

The organizational structure of most corporations is more complicated than that of a sole proprietorship or partnership. In a corporation, both the board of directors and the corporate officers are involved in management.

Board of Directors As an artificial person, a corporation can act only through its directors, who represent the corporation's stockholders. The **board of directors** is the top governing body of a corporation and is elected by the stockholders. In theory, then, the stockholders are able to control the activities of the entire corporation through its directors because they are the group that elects the board of directors (refer to Figure 3-4).

普通股
common stock the most basic form of corporate ownership and whose owners may vote on corporate policies

优先股
preferred stock stock owned by individuals or firms who usually do not have voting rights but whose claims on dividends are paid before those of common-stock owners

股息
dividend a distribution of earnings to the stockholders of a corporation

委托书
proxy a legal form listing issues to be decided at a stockholders' meeting and enabling stockholders to transfer their voting rights to some other individual or individuals

董事会
board of directors the top governing body of a corporation, the members of which are elected by the stockholders

Figure 3-4 Hierarchy of Corporate Structure

Stockholders exercise a great deal of influence through their right to elect the board of directors.

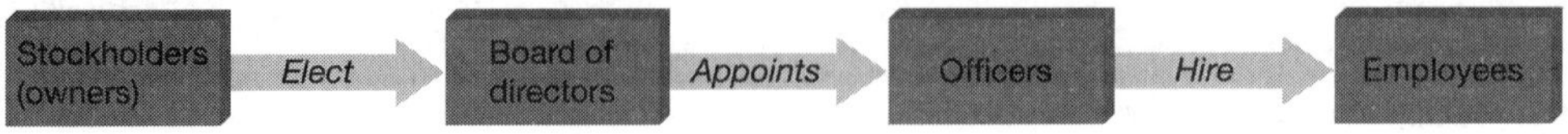

Board members can be chosen from within the corporation or from outside it. *Note:* For a small corporation, only one director is required in many states, although you can choose to have more. In larger corporations, directors who are elected from within the corporation are usually its top managers—the president and executive vice presidents, for example. Those elected from outside the corporation generally are experienced managers or entrepreneurs with proven leadership ability and/or specific talents the organization seems to need. In smaller corporations, majority stockholders usually serve as board members.

The major responsibilities of the board of directors are to set company goals and develop general plans (or strategies) for meeting those goals. The board is also responsible for the firm's overall operation and appointing corporate officers.

Corporate Officers **Corporate officers** are appointed by the board of directors. Although a small corporation may not have all of the following officers, the chairperson of the board, president, executive vice presidents, corporate secretary, and treasurer are all corporate officers. They help the board make plans, carry out strategies established by the board, hire employees, and manage day-to-day business activities. Periodically (usually each month), they report to the board of directors. And at the annual meeting, the directors report to the stockholders.

✓ Concept Check

- Explain the difference between an open corporation and a closed corporation.
- How is a domestic corporation different from a foreign corporation and an alien corporation?
- Outline the incorporation process, and describe the basic corporate structure.
- What rights do stockholders have?

公司的优势和劣势

3-5 Advantages and Disadvantages of Corporations

Learning Objective

3-5 Describe the advantages and disadvantages of a corporation.

When Warren Buffett started his first partnership more than 60 years ago, he never dreamed he would wind up putting together a wildly diverse collection of businesses under one corporate umbrella. It all started when Buffett set up a series of partnerships with family and friends to pool cash for buying big blocks of stock in companies he had researched. Not all of the companies Buffett chose paid off, but many were so successful that Buffett quickly earned a worldwide reputation for his ability to pick just the "right" company. Today, Berkshire Hathaway now owns more than 60 different companies, brings in more than $250 billion in annual revenue, and employs 390,000 people.

Although Warren Buffett started with partnerships, he eventually chose the corporate form of ownership because it provided a number of advantages when compared to a partnership or the other forms of business ownership.

公司的优势

3-5a Advantages of Corporations

Limited Liability **Limited liability** is a feature of corporate ownership that limits each owner's financial liability to the amount of money that they have paid for the corporation's stock. This feature arises from the fact that the corporation is itself a legal person, separate from its owners. If a corporation fails or is involved in a lawsuit and loses, creditors have a claim only on the corporation's assets. Because it overcomes the problem of unlimited liability connected with sole proprietorships and general partnerships, limited liability is one of the chief reasons why entrepreneurs often choose the corporate form of organization. For example, Ford Motor Company and Tesla are both incorporated because of the limited liability protection provided by the corporate form of ownership. The limited liability protection is often referred to as the "corporate veil," and protects the personal assets of investors, executives, and employees in case a corporation is sued.

Ease of Raising Capital The corporation is one of the most effective forms of business ownership for raising capital. Like sole proprietorships and partnerships, corporations can borrow from lending institutions. However, they also can raise additional sums of money by selling stock. In fact, the amount of capital that can

公司高管
corporate officers the chairperson of the board, president, executive vice presidents, corporate secretary, treasurer, and any other top executive appointed by the board of directors

有限责任
limited liability a feature of corporate ownership that limits each owner's financial liability to the amount of money that they have paid for the corporation's stock

be raised by selling stock can be staggering. Snowflake, a company that provides a cloud-based data platform that enables customers to consolidate and share data to improve decision making, raised more than $3 billion by selling stock in late 2020.[7] Money from an initial public offering (IPO) can be used by a corporation for expansion, to repay debt, or for any valid reason. While not all IPOs are as large as Snowflake's, individuals are more willing to invest in corporations than in other forms of business because of limited liability, and they can generally sell their stock easily—hopefully for a profit.

Ease of Transfer of Ownership Accessing a brokerage firm website or a telephone call to a stockbroker is all that is required to sell stock in a public corporation. Willing buyers are available for most stocks at the current market price. Ownership is transferred when the sale is made, and practically no restrictions apply to the sale and purchase of stock issued by a public corporation.

Perpetual Life Since it is essentially a legal "person," a corporation exists independently of its owners and survives them. The withdrawal, death, or incompetence of a key executive or owner does not cause the corporation to be terminated. Kellogg's was originally founded in 1906 and is one of the world's largest cereal manufacturers, even though its original founder, W. K. Kellogg, has been dead for decades.

Specialized Management Typically, corporations are able to recruit more skilled, knowledgeable, and talented managers than proprietorships and partnerships. Both Google and Apple can attract employees with the best talent and skills in the industry because people want to work for successful companies that have a history of developing new ideas or services. Corporations—especially those in high-demand industries—also pay larger salaries, offer excellent employee benefits, and are large enough to offer considerable opportunity for employee advancement. Within the corporate structure, administration, human resources, finance, marketing, distribution, and manufacturing are placed in the charge of experts in these fields.

Airbnb sold stock to investors and raised $3.5 billion. On Wall Street, the term initial public offering (IPO) is used to describe a company's first public stock offering. Airbnb—a company that uses an online platform or mobile device to match property owners with guests for vacation rentals—was one of the largest IPOs in recent history. Investors who bought shares in the Airbnb IPO believed the company would increase revenues and profits *and* its stock would increase in value.

Sustaining the Planet

保护地球：具有可持续发展意识的企业着眼于 B 型企业认证

Sustainable-Minded Businesses Eye B Corp Certification

Companies that balance profit with purpose look to B Corp certification to demonstrate their commitment to social responsibility and sustainability. Certified B Corporations voluntarily meet high standards for social and environmental performance, public transparency, and legal accountability. The first 82 B Corps were certified in 2007. Now, there are more than 3,500 across 70 countries.

B Corps use profit for social and environmental good, such as reducing inequality, building strong communities, and creating high-quality jobs. They must meet a minimum B Impact Assessment score that measures each company's impact on employees, customers, community, and the environment. To maintain public transparency, companies must make their scores and information about their full assessment available to the public.

Initially, the group of Certified B Corporations was largely made up of small businesses but now includes major corporations such as food product company Danone North America. Other well-known B Corps include Patagonia Works and New Belgium Brewing. Meeting the rigorous standards of certification can be costly. In the United States, B Corps are required to reincorporate into a benefit corporation or amend their articles of incorporation to legally solidify their commitment. With more and more companies dedicating time and resources to meet B Corp standards, it's clear that many business leaders no longer believe that companies exist only to maximize stockholder profit.

Sources: Based on information in Sarah Shearman, "Purpose over Profit: Are B-Corps the Future of Sustainable Business?" *Reuters*; Certified B Corporation, "About B Corps"; Benefit Corporation, "Why Is Benefit Corp Right for Me?"

公司的劣势

3-5b Disadvantages of Corporations

Like its advantages, many of a corporation's disadvantages stem from its legal definition as an artificial person or legal entity. The most serious disadvantages are described in the following text. Also refer to Table 3-2 for a comparison of some of the advantages and disadvantages of a sole proprietorship, general partnership, and corporation.

Difficulty and Expense of Formation The costs of incorporating, in terms of both time and money, often discourage many business owners from forming corporations. For even a small business, the use of an attorney is usually necessary to complete the legal forms that are submitted to the secretary of state. Application fees, attorney's fees, registration costs associated with selling stock, and other

Table 3-2 Some Advantages and Disadvantages of a Sole Proprietorship, Partnership, and Corporation

	Sole Proprietorship	General Partnership	Regular C Corporation
Protecting against liability for debts	Difficult	Difficult	Easy
Raising money	Difficult	Difficult	Easy
Ownership transfer	Difficult	Difficult	Easy
Preserving continuity	Difficult	Difficult	Easy
Government regulations	Few	Few	Many
Formation	Easy	Easy	Difficult
Income taxation	Once	Once	Twice

organizational costs can amount to thousands of dollars. Before deciding to incorporate a small business, you may want to review the material in the section "Forming a Corporation" earlier in this chapter.

Oprah gets the red-carpet treatment! While most people recognize Oprah Winfrey as a talk-show host, she is also an accomplished actor, author, television executive, *and* businessperson. She has starred in movies, produced Broadway shows, written best-selling books, founded *O Magazine* and Harpo Productions, and is recognized as a philanthropist who supports many diverse charitable causes. Today, many people believe she has used her talents and business skills to become one of the most influential people in the twenty-first century.

Government Regulation and Increased Paperwork A corporation must register and meet various government standards before it can sell its stock to the public. Then it must file many reports on its business operations and finances with local, state, and federal governments. In addition, the corporation must make periodic reports to its stockholders. To prepare all the necessary reports, even small corporations often need the help of an attorney, certified public accountant, and other professionals on a regular basis. In addition, a corporation's activities are often restricted by law to those spelled out in its corporate charter.

Conflict Within the Corporation Because a large corporation may employ thousands of employees, some conflict is inevitable. For example, the pressure to increase sales revenue, reduce expenses, and increase profits often leads to increased stress and tension for both managers and employees in all types of business ownership. This is especially true when a corporation operates in a competitive industry, attempts to develop and market new products, or must downsize the workforce to reduce employee salary expense. Consider what happened in early 2020 when non-essential businesses were closed because of the COVID-19 pandemic. Managers had to make hard decisions that affected employees. Do we lay off workers and, if so, which ones? They also had to make decisions about how to pay expenses when there were no sales during the closures. Even when businesses began to reopen, they had to make decisions about which stores to reopen, which ones to permanently close, and how to keep employees and customers safe. Decisions of this type are always hard and create stress and conflict for everyone involved.

Double Taxation Corporations must pay a tax on their profits. In addition, stockholders must pay a personal income tax on profits received as dividends. Corporate profits thus are taxed twice—once as corporate income and a second time as the personal income of stockholders. *Note:* Both the S corporation and the limited liability company (LLC) discussed in the next section eliminate the disadvantage of double taxation and are a primary reason why business owners choose these special types of business ownership.

✓ Concept Check

- What are the advantages of a corporation?
- What are the disadvantages of a corporation?

Lack of Secrecy Because open corporations are required to submit detailed reports to government agencies and to stockholders, they cannot keep all of their operations confidential. Competitors can study these corporate reports and then use the information to compete more effectively. In effect, every public corporation has to share some of its secrets about its management, finances, and other business activities with its competitors.

Discussion Questions 讨论题

1. If you were to start a business, which ownership form would you choose? What factors might affect your choice?
2. Why might an investor choose to become a partner in a limited partnership instead of purchasing the stock of an open corporation?
3. Discuss the following statement: "Corporations are not really run by their owners."

Case 3 案例 3：这是庄臣公司的家族事务

It's a Family Affair at SC Johnson

SC Johnson, a multi-billion-dollar family-owned business, is a multinational manufacturer of household and professional products. Windex, Pledge, Drano, Scrubbing Bubbles, and Shout are just a few brands included in SC Johnson's product portfolio. Today, Fisk Johnson is a fifth-generation family member and CEO for the privately-held company, which was founded in 1886.

It all started because of an entrepreneur named Samuel Curtis Johnson, a parquet floor salesman in Racine, Wisconsin. He traveled around Wisconsin and surrounding states selling flooring to contractors and returned home on weekends to perform managerial duties. He noted that his customers would often ask how to care for their new flooring, and, recognizing that a high-quality floor cleaning product was missing from the market, he set out to create the perfect product to meet his customers' needs. The end result was Johnson's Prepared Wax. Initially, he gave a can of wax to customers with their flooring orders, but demand grew beyond the customers that purchased his parquet flooring. By 1898, sales of Johnson's floor-care products exceeded flooring sales.

Now, SC Johnson is one of the oldest family-owned businesses in the United States. In the company's more than 130-year history, its owners have never taken the company public unlike competitors Unilever and Procter & Gamble. Being privately held offers many advantages. For instance, privately held companies are not required to reveal financial results to the public. According to Fisk Johnson, the financial reports that public companies must file with the government and Wall Street are a great source of information on competitors. Being privately owned also allows the company to remain true to its values rather than answer to shareholders and investors.

Another key to SC Johnson's success is investing in research and development (R&D). The SC Johnson Research Tower, its former hub for R&D, operated from 1950 to 1982 and gave birth to brands such as Raid, Glade, Off!, and Pledge. As the company's product line continued to grow, the company's R&D efforts outgrew the Research Tower facility, and the department moved to a larger facility. Today, one of the key factors for the company's R&D efforts is how each ingredient in a product will impact people and the environment. SC Johnson's Greenlist program, for example, assures customers the company has evaluated the ingredients that go into its products. The goal—to protect human health and the environment—looks at hazard and risk in a four-step evaluation process that reviews the following criteria: (1) chronic human health hazards, (2) long-term environmental hazards, (3) acute risks to human and environmental health, and (4) other potential effects. If an ingredient is flagged as potentially hazardous, SC Johnson will then determine what concentration of the ingredient is appropriate for use before the final product is approved to begin the manufacturing process. In some cases, ingredients or even products are rejected. For example, the company has banned 200 unique raw materials and more than 2,400 fragrance materials.

According to CEO Johnson, remaining private allows the company to prioritize people over profit. Because SC Johnson believes employees should be treated with integrity, respect, and fairness, the company has earned a reputation for being a great place to work. The company has also received recognition for diversity and inclusion, scoring a perfect 100 percent on the 2020 Corporate Equality Index from the Human Rights Campaign. Beyond its own employees, SC Johnson is committed to strengthening communities around the world. For example, through the company's 20 Days of Giving campaign, it donated $400,000 to organizations in communities where it operates to support economic and social mobility in underserved areas. And during the COVID-19 pandemic, SC Johnson donated $10 million to support public needs and individuals on the front lines.

SC Johnson is also finding new ways to support the environment by reducing plastic packaging to eliminate waste. In 2020, SC Johnson joined the Coalition of Action on Plastic Waste alongside Coca-Cola, Walmart, Pepsi, and others. The goal of the coalition is to develop a circular approach to plastic use in the consumer goods industry. SC Johnson aims to make 100 percent of its plastic packaging recyclable, reusable, or compostable.

Samuel Curtis Johnson's floor wax laid the foundation for a thriving private company and family business. Stockholders and industry analysts often exert pressure on public companies to improve financial performance, but SC Johnson has the freedom to make the best decisions for customers, employees, and the environment, even if it comes at the expense of short-term profits. In this way, SC Johnson looks to the future while honoring its past.[8]

Discussion Questions

1. SC Johnson has a long history of developing consumer and household products. How has research and development enabled the company to develop new products that are consumer safe and environmentally friendly?
2. SC Johnson competes with Unilever, Procter & Gamble, and other large corporations that have stockholders and yet, SC Johnson has chosen to remain a private, family business. What are the advantages of management's decision to remain private? Are there disadvantages of this type of private ownership?
3. Back in 1886, Samuel Curtis Johnson started a small business; today that business is a large, successful *private* corporation. How does being private impact customers, employees, and the environment?

Chapter 4

Small Business, Entrepreneurship, and Franchises

小企业、企业家精神和特许经营

Why Should You Care?

America's small businesses drive the U.S. economy. Small businesses represent 99.9 percent of all employer firms, and there is a good probability that you will work for a small business or perhaps even start your own business. This chapter can help you become a good employee or a successful entrepreneur.

Learning Objectives

Once you complete this chapter, you will be able to:

4-1 Recognize the importance of small businesses to the U.S. economy.

4-2 Describe the kinds of people who start small businesses.

4-3 Describe the advantages and disadvantages of operating a small business.

4-4 Examine common reasons for small-business failure.

4-5 Discuss the importance of a business plan.

4-6 Explore franchising, including its types, growth, and advantages and disadvantages.

4-7 Describe methods entrepreneurs can use to finance their small business.

Inside Business 商业透视：塔可贝尔成为一家增长最快的特许经营商

Taco Bell Becomes One of the Fastest Growing Franchises

Taco Bell was founded in 1962 in Downey, California. Two years later, a retired Los Angeles policeman, Kermit Becky, became Taco Bell's first franchisee. Now, Taco Bell is a subsidiary of Yum! Brands Inc. alongside KFC and Pizza Hut. With more than 7,400 restaurants in 30 countries, Taco Bell is one of the fastest-growing franchises. The company is prioritizing international expansion, experimenting with new restaurant concepts, and focusing on menu innovation to support growth.

Much of the company's rapid growth can be attributed to international expansion. In the past, Taco Bell was slow to expand outside of the United States, but that is beginning to change. The company operates more than 500 stores internationally with plans to build 600 restaurants in India alone over the next decade. Other notable countries of growth include the United Kingdom, Thailand, and Australia. According to Liz Williams, president of Taco Bell International, the Mexican food category is becoming increasingly popular around the world. "It's becoming much more well-known and picking up a lot of energy in terms of consumer pull," Williams told *Restaurant Business*.

To succeed in other countries, Taco Bell is leaning into its Cantina concept, which was first introduced in the United States. Now, the experiential Cantina restaurants—which feature an urban restaurant design and serve alcoholic beverages—are one of Taco Bell's key growth strategies. In addition to the Cantina concept, Taco Bell is testing a Go Mobile restaurant in the United States that is built around digital transactions. The stores are much smaller than the chain's traditional footprint and feature a double drive-through lane with a dedicated pick-up option for app users.

Lastly, Taco Bell has revamped its menu to streamline the restaurant experience and make room for fresh and innovative menu items, including plant-based offerings. This, along with Taco Bell's focus on international franchises and adapting to a new era of fast-food culture, has contributed to the company's recent growth. Taco Bell's goal is to become a $20 billion brand with 10,000 restaurants around the world before 2030.[1]

Did you know?

Taco Bell serves more than 40 million customers each week in the United States.

Most businesses start small and those that survive usually stay small. However, businesses like Taco Bell provide a solid foundation for our economy—as employers, as suppliers and purchasers of goods and services, and as taxpayers. Small enterprise spans the gamut from corner newspaper vending to the development of robotic technologies and flying taxis. The owners of small businesses sell gasoline, flowers, and coffee to go. They publish magazines, haul freight, teach languages, and program computers. They make wines, movies, and high-fashion clothes. They build new homes and restore old ones. They fix appliances, recycle metals, and sell used cars. They drive cabs and fly planes. They make us well when we are ill, and they sell us the products of corporate giants. In fact, 74 percent of real estate, rental, and leasing industries; 61 percent of the businesses in the leisure and hospitality services; and 86 percent of the construction industries are dominated by small businesses.

In this chapter, we look closely at this important business sector—beginning with a definition of small business, the importance of small businesses in our economy, and a description of industries that often attract small businesses. Next, we provide a profile of the kinds of people who start small businesses. We also present the advantages and disadvantages of smallness in business and consider why small businesses may fail. We examine the importance and components of a business plan. We then discuss the pros and cons of franchising, an approach to small-business ownership that has become very popular in the last 60 years.

小企业：简介

4-1 Small Business: a Profile

Learning Objective

4-1 Recognize the importance of small businesses to the U.S. economy.

The **Small Business Administration (SBA)**, created by Congress in 1953 to assist, counsel, and protect the interests of small businesses in the United States, defines a **small business** as "an independent business having fewer than 500 employees."[2] This is probably consistent with how you think of small businesses in your community. Consider the small independent coffee shop down the street, which probably has fewer than ten part-time employees and sells about $215,000 worth of coffee and pastries a year. Compare that to Starbucks, which has more than 32,000 locations worldwide and generates billions of dollars in revenue.[3] However, the SBA categorically defines smallness on the basis of the particular industry in which a business operates. Table 4-1 presents a sample of the SBA's "smallness" guidelines for various industries. Thus, number of employees and/or sales revenue may dictate size in a particular industry, and "small businesses" with more than 500 employees may still be viewed as small in some industries. On the other hand, 81 percent of small businesses have no employees at all, just the owner (the SBA refers to these as "nonemployers").[4] The SBA periodically revises and simplifies its small-business size regulations.

A business with annual sales in millions of dollars may not seem very small. However, for many firms, profit is only a small percentage of total sales. Consider an independent restaurant that brings in sales of $5 million in a year: once it has paid for ingredients and supplies, the wages of cooks and servers, as well as rent, utilities, taxes, and advertising and accounting expenses, the firm may earn only $50,000 or $60,000. Indeed, most small firms have annual sales well below the maximum limits in the SBA guidelines.

Table 4-1 Industry Group-Size Standards

Small-business size standards are usually stated in number of employees or average annual sales. The SBA has established two widely used size standards—500 employees for most manufacturing and mining industries and $7.5 million in average annual sales for many nonmanufacturing industries. In the United States, 99.9 percent of all businesses are considered small.

Industry Group	Size Standard
Manufacturing, mining industries	500–1,500 employees
Wholesale trade	100–250 employees
Agriculture	$750,000
Retail trade, barber shops, beauty salons	$7.5 million
General and heavy construction (except dredging)	$36.5 million
Dredging	$27.5 million
Special trade contractors	$15 million
Travel agencies, tour operators	$20.5 million
Department stores	$32.5 million
Discount stores	$29.5 million
Furniture stores	$20.5 million

Source: U.S. Small Business Administration, "Table of Small Business Size Standards Matched to North American Industry Classification System Codes".

小企业管理局

Small Business Administration (SBA) a government agency that assists, counsels, and protects the interests of small businesses in the United States

小企业

small business an independent business with fewer than 500 employees, depending on its industry

小企业群体
4-1a The Small-Business Sector

In the United States, it typically takes less than a week and $600 to establish a business as a legal entity. The steps include registering the name of the business, applying for tax IDs, and setting up unemployment and workers' compensation insurance. In Japan, however, a typical entrepreneur spends more than $3,500 and 11 days to follow eight different procedures.

A surprising number of Americans take advantage of their freedom to start a business. There are, in fact, about 31.7 million businesses in this country. Only 20,139 of these employ more than 500 workers—enough to be considered large.[5]

Interest in owning or starting a small business has never been greater than it is today. During the last decade, the number of small businesses in the United States has increased 49 percent. However, about two-thirds of businesses launched between 1994 and 2018 survived at least two years. A little less than half survived five years or longer and just one-third of firms survived ten years or longer.[6] The makeup of the small-business sector thus is constantly changing. Despite the high failure rate, many small businesses succeed modestly. Some, like Apple Computer, Inc., are extremely successful—to the point where they can no longer be considered small.

小企业在我们经济中的重要性
4-1b The Importance of Small Business in Our Economy

Small businesses are vital to the U.S. economy. For example, small businesses:

- represent 99.9 percent of all employer firms;
- employ about half of all private-sector employees;
- pay 40 percent of total U.S. private payroll;
- have generated 65 percent of net new jobs over the past 20 years; and
- made up 97.5 percent of all exporters and produced 32 percent of known export value.[7]

This country's economic history abounds with stories of ambitious entrepreneurs who turned their ideas into business dynasties. The Ford Motor Company started as a one-man operation with an innovative method for industrial production. L.L.Bean, Inc., can trace its beginnings to a basement shop in Freeport, Maine. Dell Computer started in Michael Dell's dorm room, while HP started in a California garage. Indeed, every year since 1963, the president of the United States has proclaimed National Small Business Week to recognize the contributions of small businesses to the economic well-being of America. Let's examine these a little closer.

Providing Technical Innovation Invention and innovation are part of the foundations of our economy. The increases in productivity that have characterized the past 200 years of our history are all rooted in one principal source: new ways to do a job with less effort for less money. Studies show that the incidence of innovation among small-business workers is significantly higher than among workers in large businesses. One such example is Colorado Springs-based Braxton Technologies, LLC, which provides hardware, software, and support services for satellites for defense and aerospace industry customers. The company recently received the prestigious Tibbitts Award from the SBA for excellence in innovation and research.[8]

According to the U.S. Office of Management and Budget, more than half the major technological advances of the 20th century originated with individual inventors and small companies. Even just a sampling of those innovations is remarkable:

- Air-conditioning
- Airplanes
- Automatic transmission
- FM radio

The future of diagnostics. QuantuMDx is a technology developer with a focus on delivering innovative diagnostic solutions to address global health inequality. The company, co-founded by CEO Elaine Warburton, is privately owned with a strong commercial and humanitarian focus.

- Heart valves
- Helicopters
- Instant cameras
- Insulin
- Jet engines
- Penicillin
- Personal computers, and
- Power steering.

Perhaps even more remarkable—and important—is that many of these inventions sparked major new U.S. industries or contributed to an established industry by adding some valuable service.

Providing Employment Small firms traditionally have added more than their share of new jobs to the economy. Between 2000 and 2019, small businesses were responsible for 10.5 million net new jobs; in comparison, large companies created 5.6 million net new jobs.[9] In recent years, seven out of the ten industries that added the most new jobs were small-business-dominated industries such as business services, leisure and hospitality services, and special trade contractors. Small firms hire a larger proportion of employees who are younger workers, older workers, women, and workers who prefer to work part time. Moreover, it is small businesses that provide two-thirds of workers with their first jobs and initial on-the-job training in basic skills. According to the SBA, small businesses represent 99.9 percent of all employers, employ nearly half of the private sector workforce, and provide about two-thirds of the net new jobs added to our economy.

Providing Competition Small businesses challenge larger, established firms in many ways, causing them to become more efficient and more responsive to consumer needs. Consider Andy Dunn and Brian Spaly, who became frustrated at their inability to find pants that fit well, so they decided to design and sell their own. They launched Bonobos as a direct-to-consumer men's pants company, filling online orders out of Dunn's apartment. By focusing "maniacally" on the customer experience and offering innovative products, they quickly grew Bonobos into a million-dollar brand and expanded into men's and later women's apparel. Bonobos became one of the first internet companies to open brick-and-mortar stores, and ultimately was acquired by giant Walmart.[10] A small business cannot, of course, compete with a large firm in all respects. However, a number of small firms, each competing in its own particular area and its own particular way, together have the desired competitive effect. Thus, several small janitorial companies together add up to reasonable competition for the no-longer-small ServiceMaster.

Filling Needs of Society and Other Businesses Small firms also provide a variety of goods and services to consumers, to each other, and to much larger firms. General Motors relies on more than 32,000 companies for parts and supplies and depends on more than 11,000 independent dealers to sell its automobiles and trucks. Large firms generally buy parts and assemblies from smaller firms for one very good reason: It is less expensive than manufacturing the parts in their own factories. This lower cost eventually is reflected in the price that consumers pay for their products.

It is clear that small businesses are a vital part of our economy and that, as consumers and as members of the labor force, we all benefit enormously from their existence. Now let us look at the situation from the viewpoint of the owners of small businesses.

吸引小企业的行业

4-1c Industries That Attract Small Businesses

Some industries, such as auto manufacturing, require huge investments in machinery and equipment. Businesses in such industries are big from the day they are started—if an entrepreneur or group of entrepreneurs can gather the capital required to start one. By contrast, a number of other industries require only a low initial investment and some special skills or knowledge. It is these industries that tend to attract new businesses. Growing industries, such as outpatient-care facilities, are attractive because of their profit potential. However, knowledgeable entrepreneurs choose areas with which they are familiar, and these are most often the more established industries. The various kinds of businesses generally fall into three broad categories of industry: distribution, service, and production.

Distribution Industries This category includes retailing, wholesaling, transportation, and communications—industries concerned with the movement of goods from producers to consumers. Distribution industries account for approximately 33 percent of all small businesses. Of these, almost three-quarters are involved in retailing, that is, the sale of goods directly to consumers. Clothing and jewelry stores, pet shops, bookstores, and grocery stores, for example, are all retailing firms. Slightly less than one-quarter of the small distribution firms are wholesalers. Wholesalers purchase products in quantity from manufacturers and then resell them to retailers.

Service Industries This category accounts for more than 48 percent of all small businesses. Of these, about three-quarters provide such nonfinancial services as medical and dental care; watch, shoe, and TV repairs; haircutting and styling; restaurant meals; and dry cleaning. About 8 percent of the small service firms offer financial services, such as accounting, insurance, real estate, and investment counseling. An increasing number of self-employed Americans are running service businesses from home.

Production Industries This last category includes the construction, mining, and manufacturing industries. Only about 19 percent of all small businesses are in this group, mainly because these industries require relatively large initial investments. Small firms that do venture into production generally make parts and subassemblies for larger manufacturing firms or supply special skills to larger construction firms.

✓ Concept Check

- What information would you need to determine whether a particular business is small according to SBA guidelines?
- Describe four contributions of small business to the American economy.
- Distinguish among service industries, distribution industries, and production industries.

Exploring Careers

职业探索：给有抱负的企业家一些建议

Tips for Aspiring Entrepreneurs

Becoming an entrepreneur can be rewarding, but it can be incredibly difficult to start and grow a business. Entrepreneurs who risk time, money, and effort to start and operate a business often do so in an attempt to bring a new idea to the market. However, it's not always about who is the first but rather who is the best. Today, the best businesses deliver the most value to consumers who have more power and choice than ever before.

It's not enough for business owners to create a product. Successful products solve a problem. Entrepreneurs often rely on professional experience to identify shortcomings in an industry. For example, Zoom's founder and CEO Eric Yuan was once the vice president of engineering for Cisco's Webex video conferencing business. He wasn't happy with the company's service, which often cut in and out and lacked various modern features. His calls to update the platform were ignored, so he left in 2010 to build and launch Zoom, a cloud-based video-conferencing tool of the future that prioritized customer needs. Today, Zoom is valued at nearly $100 billion.

Entrepreneurs should establish an authentic relationship with consumers. Brands have a compelling story to tell, and entrepreneurs should consider being the ones to tell that story. Many of the world's most successful entrepreneurs, such as Bill Gates (Microsoft), Oprah Winfrey (Harpo), Jeff Bezos (Amazon), Elon Musk (Tesla), Jack Ma (Alibaba), and Mark Zuckerberg (Facebook), are charismatic leaders. It's not necessary to become a full-fledged celebrity CEO, but a willingness to step into the spotlight to communicate with consumers can help individuals root for both the company and the entrepreneur behind it.

Original ideas often turn out to be not-so-original. This is because the market and cultural forces that inspire one entrepreneur are likely influencing another entrepreneur at the same time. For instance, rival ride-hailing companies Uber and Lyft were founded just a few years apart. The startup landscape can be incredibly competitive with multiple companies introducing similar products simultaneously. Entrepreneurs should consider how they can use their competitive advantage to solve problems in a way that delivers value to consumers.

Sources: Based on information in Emily Heyward, "So You Want to Be an Entrepreneur?" *Harvard Business Review*, July 23, 2020; Samantha Murphy Kelly, "Zoom's Massive 'Overnight Success' Actually Took Nine Years," *CNN*, March 27, 2020.

小企业中的人：企业家

4-2 The People in Small Businesses: The Entrepreneurs

Learning Objective

4-2 Describe the kinds of people who start small businesses.

We define entrepreneurs as people who risk their time, effort, and money to start and operate a business. As we've already shown, the entrepreneurial spirit is alive and well in the United States. Small businesses typically are managed by the people who started and own them, at least in their first years. Most of these people have held jobs with other firms and still could be so employed if they wanted. Yet owners of small businesses would rather take the risk of starting and operating their own firms, even if the money they make is less than the salaries they otherwise might earn. Researchers have suggested a variety of personal factors as reasons why people go into business for themselves. Let's take a look at them.

企业家的特点

4-2a Characteristics of Entrepreneurs

Entrepreneurial spirit is the desire to create a new business. For example, Madeline Haydon saw that dairy-free coffee creamer options were limited and recognized an opportunity to introduce creamer products to satisfy consumers who are diabetic, lactose-intolerant, or simply want a plant-based product without artificial or genetically modified ingredients. Although she was warned not to proceed by

Sweet success. Mikaila Ulmer started a lemonade stand when she was just four years old to help her overcome a fear of bees, using her grandmother's recipe for honey-sweetened flaxseed lemonade. Now a teenager, Ulmer's Me & the Bees lemonade is sold in 1,500 stores and brings in millions of dollars in sales, some of which Ulmer's company donates to organizations working to save imperiled honeybee populations.

advisors with experience in the food industry, she started her company Nutpods and introduced dairy-free flavored and unsweetened creamers. Her customers loved the creamy products so much that Amazon named Nutpods its Small Business of the Year.[11]

Figure 4-1 lists some common reasons entrepreneurs give for wanting to start their own business. A majority say they simply have "had enough" of working and earning a profit for someone else. Others lost their jobs for some reason or saw them outsourced to another country and decided to start the business they had always wanted. Still others may have had an idea for a new product or a new way to sell an existing product, or the opportunity to go into business arose suddenly, perhaps as a result of a hobby. Christian Bok started Renova Medical Wear after seeing how hard it was for his mother to get dressed while recovering from surgery. His company now designs and makes dignified

Figure 4-1 What Motivates Entrepreneurs?

Entrepreneurs have many reasons for wanting to start a business, but these are the most common reasons.

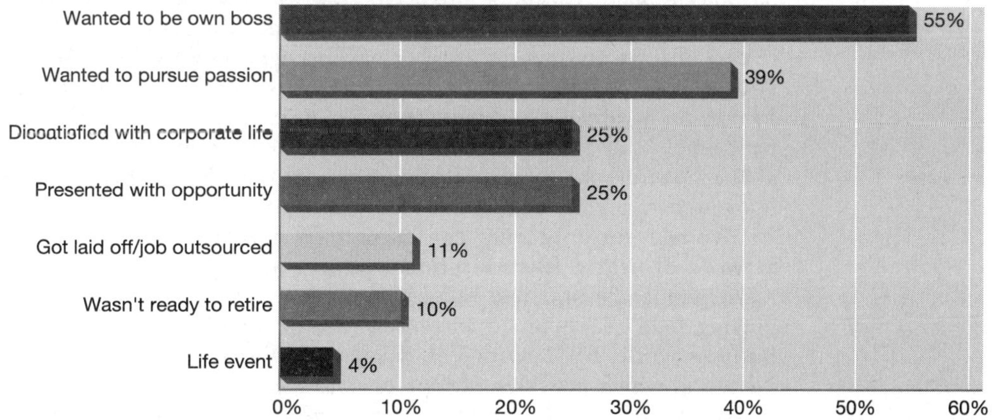

Source: Small Business Trends Alliance survey, "Small Business Trends 2020," Guidant Financial.

and comfortable adaptive clothing for postsurgical patients to help make their recovery less stressful.[12]

In some people, the motivation to start a business develops slowly as they gain the knowledge and ability required for success as a business owner. Knowledge and ability—especially management ability—are probably the most important factors involved. A new firm is very much built around the entrepreneur. The owner must be able to manage the firm's finances, its personnel (if there are any employees), and its day-to-day operations. They must handle sales, advertising, purchasing, pricing, and a variety of other business functions. The knowledge and ability to do so are acquired most often through experience working for other firms in the same area of business.

Other factors that may influence a person to start a small business include

- independence;
- a desire to determine one's own destiny;
- a willingness to find and accept a challenge;
- family background (in particular, researchers think that people whose families have been in business, successfully or not, are most apt to start and run their own businesses); and
- age (those who start their own businesses also tend to cluster around certain ages—more than 70 percent are between 24 and 44 years of age).

女性小企业主

4-2b **Women as Small-Business Owners**

According to American Express's *State of Women-Owned Business Report,* women today are starting 1,800 businesses *a day!* There are now nearly 13 million women-owned businesses (defined as being at least 51 percent owned, operated, and controlled by one or more women) that generate $1.9 trillion in revenues and provide jobs for 9.4 million workers. Although women make up 51 percent of the U.S. population, they own 42 percent of all businesses, up from 4.6 percent in 1972. The number of businesses owned by women of color has grown even more dramatically, and they now account for 50 percent of all women-owned businesses.[13] Of course, not all of these businesses are small, but most started out that way. Kendra Scott, for example, began designing jewelry in a guest bedroom after her first child was born. After 20 years of hard work, she grew her jewelry and home goods company to a $1 billion brand with more than 90 stores as well as an online shop.[14] About half of all small businesses are based out of the owner's home, and a majority of these are owned by women.

A significant number of women choose to start their own business because they have been unable to find a job, need a job with sufficient flexibility to allow them to care for family members, want to supplement their families' income, and/or want to capitalize on an opportunity they have recognized.[15] Consider Staci Pompey, who bought a sewing machine and launched a store on Etsy, an e-commerce site that focuses on handmade and vintage goods, to sell face masks during the COVID-19 pandemic. Aside from providing a much-needed product for consumers concerned about the virus, she generated significant extra income for her family while staying home to care for her children.[16]

Women entrepreneurs can turn to Women's Business Centers (WBCs), a network of nearly 100 educational centers throughout the United States. WBCs assist women in starting and growing small businesses and seek to "level the playing field" for women entrepreneurs, who still face unique obstacles in the business world. SBA's Office of Women's Business Ownership oversees the WBC Network, which provides entrepreneurs, especially women who are economically or socially disadvantaged, comprehensive training and counseling on business topics in several languages.[17]

Entrepreneurial Success

创业成功：完美契合——一个青少年如何与TOMS的创始人达成交易

A Perfect Fit: How a Teen Landed a Deal with the Founder of TOMS

At the age of 15, Carson Grill was already running his own business. With the help of his father Jason Grill, Carson co-founded Touch Up Cup, a company selling paint storage containers. The father-son duo identified a problem and invented the solution. They came up with the idea for their product when they were painting their house. They opened old cans of paint to find rusty, clumpy, smelly paint. Carson invented the Touch Up Cup as a way to store a small amount of paint. The 13-ounce polypropylene container, which features a stainless-steel mixing ball for easy mixing, allows the paint to be saved for more than ten years.

Before its big break on ABC's *Shark Tank*, the product was already available online and in 4,000 retail locations, bringing in $220,000 in sales over two years. Carson, a long-time fan of the show, watched old episodes to perfect his pitch for the investors, upgraded the company's website to prepare for a rush of visitors, and ramped up inventory.

Carson already has four patents to his name: one utility patent for the Touch Up Cup and three design patents for additional storage products. Carson's knowledge of the business and entrepreneurial spirit caught the eye of several of the sharks, but it was guest shark Blake Mycoskie, the founder of TOMS, that had the winning offer. Mycoskie is a social entrepreneur, author, and philanthropist. The Grills accepted an offer from Mycoskie for a $175,000 investment for 17.5 percent equity.

The exposure alone from the Touch Up Cup's *Shark Tank* deal boosted company sales. The show led to thousands of new sales and opened the door for talks with major retailers. The company projected that the following year would bring $2 million in sales. Carson's entrepreneurial mind won't stop there. Next, he aims to make his food-saving products, called Fresh Line Keepers, just as successful.

Sources: Based on information in Taylor Locke, "'Shark Tank': How This 15-Year-Old Landed a 6-Figure Deal With the Founder of Toms," *CNBC*; Touch Up Cup, "About Us"; Liz Engel, "Cincinnati's 'Shark Tank' Teen Has Big Plans for 2021," *Cincinnati Business Courier*, December 23, 2020.

青少年小企业主

4-2c Teenagers as Small-Business Owners

Entrepreneurship among teens is also growing. Still, teen entrepreneurs face unique pressures in juggling their schoolwork, social life, and startup workload. Additionally, they may encounter difficulties with the legalities of starting and financing a business if their state requires company executives to be over age 18; further, banks often require applicants for credit or loans to be over 18. Some teen entrepreneurs ultimately quit school to run promising startups, whereas others quit or cut back on their business activities. Sisters Caroline Bercaw and Isabel Bercaw founded Da Bomb Bath Bombs before they were officially teenagers in Minneapolis, Minnesota. They made their bath bombs stand out by making them out of gentle ingredients and including a prize in the center. By the time they were 14 and 15 years old, their products were in 30 local stores; a year later, they were making 20,000 bath bombs a month in the basement of their home for national distribution. When discount chain Target asked the teens to supply 1,800 stores, they had to scale up quickly, so they enlisted their mom as chief executive. Today their business generates $20 million in revenue.[18]

移民企业家

4-2d Immigrants as Entrepreneurs

Jerry was born in China's Taiwan . His father died when he was very young, and his mother moved the family to the United States a few years later. Jerry learned English quickly and did well in school. While at Stanford University, he began creating websites as a hobby, including one about other websites that he called "Jerry's Guide to the World Wide Web." Within months, Jerry's Guide generated so much traffic that it became a burden for the computer infrastructure at Stanford; university officials requested he find another host. The name of the website was later changed to Yahoo! Jerry—whose full name is Jerry Yang—co-founded Yahoo with David Filo; they incorporated, obtained venture capital, and began hiring employees. At one point, the

Bath bombs are da bomb. Carline Bercaw and Isabel Bercaw turned their love of using and creating fun bath bombs into a $20 million family business when they were still teens.

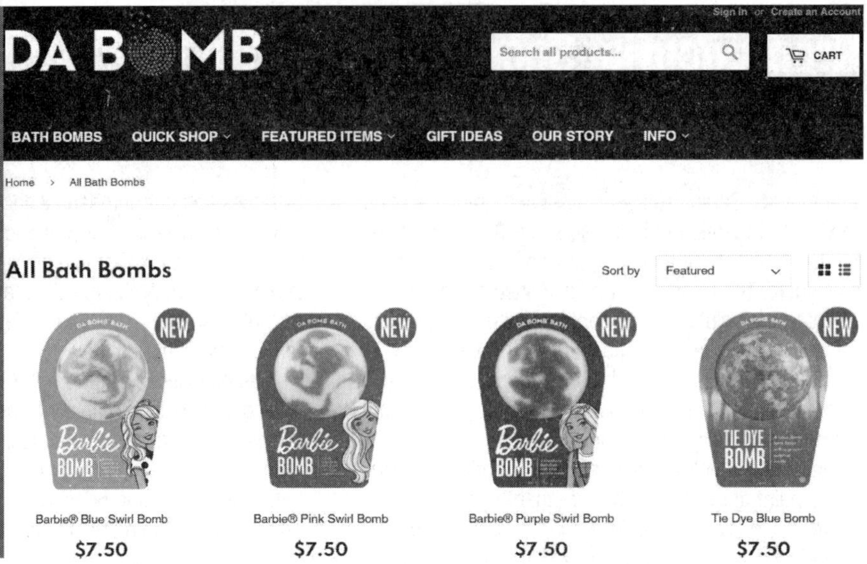

value of Yahoo peaked at more than $100 billion, and the personal wealth of Jerry Yang exceeds $2 billion today, though he is no longer with the company he founded.[19]

Jerry Yang's story is far from unique. More than half of U.S. startups that became billion-dollar companies have an immigrant founder or top executive, including Uber, Warby Parker, Slack, Stripe, Credit Karma, Discord, Eventbrite, Evernote, Zoom, Peloton, and ZocDoc. Moreover, it is estimated that immigrants are responsible for a quarter of invention and entrepreneurship in the United States.[20] Entrepreneurship has been growing among immigrants like Jerry Yang. The SBA estimates that one out of every six American businesses with employees is owned by an immigrant.[21]

✓ Concept Check

- What kinds of factors encourage people to start new businesses?
- What kinds of people start businesses?

小的利与弊

4-3 The Pros and Cons of Smallness

Learning Objective

4-3 Describe the advantages and disadvantages of operating a small business.

Do most owners of small businesses dream that their firms will grow into giant corporations—managed by professionals—while they serve only on the board of directors? Or would they rather stay small, in a firm where they have the opportunity (and the responsibility) to do everything that needs to be done? The answers depend on the personal characteristics and motivations of the individual owners. For many, the advantages of remaining small far outweigh the disadvantages.

小企业的优势

4-3a Advantages of Small Businesses

Small-business owners with limited resources often must struggle to enter competitive new markets. They also have to deal with increasing international competition. However, they enjoy several unique advantages.

Personal Relationships with Customers and Employees For those who like dealing with people, small business is the place to be. The owners of retail shops get to know many of their customers by name and deal with them on a personal basis. Through such relationships, small-business owners often become involved in the social, cultural, and political life of the community. Relationships between owner-managers and employees also tend to be closer in smaller businesses. In many cases, the owner is a friend and counselor as well as the boss.

These personal relationships provide an important business advantage. The personal service small businesses offer to customers is a major competitive weapon—one that larger firms try to match but often cannot. In addition, close relationships with employees often help the small-business owner to keep effective workers who might earn more with a larger firm.

Ability to Adapt to Change Being their own boss, small-business owner-managers do not need anyone's permission to adapt to change. An owner may add or discontinue merchandise or services, change store hours, and experiment with various price strategies in response to changes in market conditions. And through personal relationships with customers, the owners of small businesses quickly become aware of changes in people's needs and interests, as well as in the activities of competing firms. Although the COVID-19 pandemic devastated small businesses and caused many to fail, others blossomed by adapting in creative ways. As an example, Atlanta entrepreneur Eric Levitan had started Vivo to provide strength-training workouts in communities for adults 55 and over after observing his parents struggle with mobility and aging challenges. When the pandemic made in-person classes impossible, he pivoted and began offering classes via Zoom with a live instructor. Although Vivo is still quite small, the pandemic in fact expanded his potential market to older adults around the world.[22]

Simplified Record Keeping Many small firms need only a simple set of records. Record keeping might consist of a checkbook, a cash-receipts journal in which to record all sales, and a cash-disbursements journal in which to record all amounts paid out. More often, entrepreneurs today use software designed for small-business finances or outsource bookkeeping and personnel tasks to other small businesses that are experts in them. Obviously, small-business owners must maintain sufficient records to allow for producing and filing accurate tax returns.

Independence Small-business owners do not have to punch in and out, compete for vacation times, take orders from superiors, or worry about being fired or laid off. They are the masters of their own destinies—at least with regard to employment. For many people, this is the prime advantage of owning a small business.

Additional Advantages Small-business owners also enjoy all the advantages of sole proprietorships, which were discussed in Chapter 3. These include being able to keep all profits, the ease and low cost of going into business and (if necessary) going out of business, and being able to keep proprietary information private.

Getting personal. For those who like dealing with people, small business is the place to be. Here a business owner provides personalized service to a happy customer.

小企业的劣势

4-3b Disadvantages of Small Businesses

Personal contacts with customers, closer relationships with employees, being your own boss, less cumbersome record-keeping chores, and independence are the bright side of small business. In contrast, the dark side reflects problems unique to these firms.

Risk of Failure As we have noted, small businesses (especially new ones) run a heavy risk of going out of business—only about 50 percent survive at least five years. Even older, well-established small firms can be hit hard by an economic downturn if they do not have the financial resources to weather an extended difficult period.

Limited Potential Small businesses that survive do so with varying degrees of success. Many are simply the means of making a living for owners and their families. The owner may have some technical skill—as a hair stylist or electrician, for example—and may have started a business to put this skill to work. Such a business is unlikely to grow into big business. In addition, employees' potential for advancement is limited.

Limited Ability to Raise Capital Small businesses typically have a limited ability to obtain capital. Most small-business financing (64 percent) comes out of the owner's pocket or from family savings. Business loans from lending institutions provide only about one-sixth of the capital required by small businesses. A surprising amount of financing comes from personal credit cards (9 percent).[23] About half of all new firms begin with less than $30,000 in total capital, according to Census Bureau and Federal Reserve surveys. In fact, almost 36 percent of new firms begin with less than

Technology and Innovation

技术与创新：新冠肺炎挑战美国创新

COVID-19 Challenges American Innovation

Hundreds of thousands of small businesses closed permanently as a result of the COVID-19 pandemic. It's estimated that 110,000 businesses in the restaurant industry alone closed permanently due to the global crisis and resulting recession. When fewer small businesses exist, there is less innovation and entrepreneurship, two elements that characterize the United States.

The percentage of firms with fewer than 100 employees has been declining since the 1980s, a trend accelerated by the pandemic. Larger businesses had more resources to fight the pandemic. The number of bankruptcy filings among public companies was far below the numbers reached during the Global Recession. Simply put, small businesses have fewer financial resources available to them. Bank loans are the top source of outside financing for small businesses, yet 70 percent of senior loan officers reported to the Federal Reserve that they were tightening lending standards for small firms during the COVID-19 crisis. Though many small businesses benefited from the government's Paycheck Protection Program, for some the funds came too late and for others, the funds didn't stretch far enough. Large, public companies, on the other hand, had ready access to capital markets for funding.

Though life began to return to normal for many individuals in the year following the pandemic, the damage done to small businesses is likely to have long-lasting effects. Small businesses that grow to become larger firms significantly contribute to job growth for the U.S. economy. But, with so many businesses now closed for good, there are fewer companies that will grow to become major employers, slowing the speed of economic recovery. Additionally, with fewer small businesses, larger firms have less competition and therefore less motivation to innovate. This also means there will be fewer small firms for acquisition, which is a significant way large companies expand and improve their product offerings.

The pandemic changed the dynamics of business in America. Many small businesses, which had fewer financial resources than large firms, suffered disproportionately. Though many business owners were able to adapt to survive, a significant portion were not. This decrease in entrepreneurship will have a lasting effect on American innovation.

Sources: Based on information in Justin Lahart, "Covid Is Crushing Small Businesses. That's Bad News for American Innovation," *The Wall Street Journal*, October 9, 2020; Carolina Gonzalez, "Restaurant Closings Top 110,000 with Industry in 'Free Fall'," *Bloomberg*, December 7, 2020.

$20,000, usually provided by the owner or family members and friends.[24] According to the SBA, average capital for starting a new business is $80,000.

Although every person who considers starting a small business should be aware of the hazards and pitfalls we have noted, a well-conceived business plan may help to avoid the risk of failure. The U.S. government is also dedicated to helping small businesses make it. It expresses this aim most actively through the SBA.

✓ Concept Check

- What are the major advantages of smallness in business?
- What are the major disadvantages of smallness?

为什么有些企业家和小企业会失败

4-4 Why Some Entrepreneurs and Small Businesses Fail

Learning Objective

4-4 Examine common reasons for small-business failure.

Every day, and in every part of the country, people open new businesses. Table 4-2 shows the number of businesses that opened and the number of business that closed in a year. Although many businesses fail, others thrive due to well-conceived ideas developed by entrepreneurs with the expertise, resources, and determination to make their businesses succeed. As these well-prepared entrepreneurs pursue their individual goals, our society benefits in many ways from their work and creativity.

The reality is that small businesses are prone to failure. Funding, management, and planning are the key ingredients in the survival of a small business, and the lack of these are the most common reasons for failure. Businesses can experience a number of money-related problems. It may take several years before a business begins to show a profit. Entrepreneurs need to have not only the capital to open a business but also the money to operate it in its possibly lengthy start-up phase. One cash flow obstacle often leads to others. Moreover, a series of cash flow predicaments usually ends in a business failure. This scenario is played out all too often by small and not-so-small start-up internet firms that fail to meet their financial backers' expectations and so are denied a second wave of investment dollars to continue their drive to establish a profitable online firm.

Starting a small business also requires much more than optimism and a good idea. Many entrepreneurs lack the management skills required to run a business successfully. Money, time, personnel, and inventory all need to be managed effectively if a small business is to succeed. Even businesses that survive may have trouble expanding. Frequently, entrepreneurs with successful small businesses make the mistake of overexpansion. Fast growth often results in dramatic changes in a business. Thus, the entrepreneur must plan carefully and adjust competently to new and potentially disruptive situations.

✓ Concept Check

- What are the major causes of small-business failure?
- Do these causes also apply to larger businesses?

Table 4-2 U.S. Employer Business Start-ups and Closures

	New (In Thousands)	Closures (In Thousands)
2016	433	400
2015	414	396
2014	404	392
2013	404	367
2012	409	362
2011	398	404
2010	385	417
2009	406	486
2008	488	471

Source: U.S. Small Business Administration, Office of Advocacy, "Frequently Asked Questions," September 2019.

商业计划的重要性

4-5 The Importance of a Business Plan

Learning Objective

4-5 Discuss the importance of a business plan.

Lack of planning can be as deadly as lack of money to a new small business. Planning is important to any business, large or small, and never should be overlooked or taken lightly. A **business plan** is a carefully constructed guide for the person starting a business. Jeff Bezos drafted a business plan for an online bookseller while on a cross-country road trip. It helped him convince family members and friends to invest in what would become Amazon, now a $1.7 trillion company.[25]

Consider the business plan a tool with three basic purposes: communication, management, and planning. As a communication tool, a business plan serves as a concise document that potential investors can examine to see if they would like to invest or assist in financing a new venture. It shows whether a business has the potential to make a profit. As a management tool, the business plan helps track, monitor, and evaluate the progress. The business plan is a living document; it is modified as the entrepreneur gains knowledge and experience. It also serves to establish timelines and milestones and allows comparison of growth projections against actual accomplishments. Finally, as a planning tool, the business plan guides a businessperson through the various phases of business. For example, the plan helps to identify obstacles to avoid and to establish alternatives.

Table 4-3 lists the 12 sections that a business plan should include. Each section is further explained at the end of each of the six major parts in this textbook. The goal of each of these end-of-the-part exercises is to help businesspeople create their own business plans. When constructing a business plan, the entrepreneur should strive to keep it easy to read, uncluttered, and complete. Like other busy executives, officials of financial institutions do not have the time to wade through pages of extraneous data. The business plan should answer the four questions banking officials and investors are most interested in: (1) What exactly is the nature and mission of the new venture? (2) Why is this new enterprise a good idea? (3) What are the businessperson's goals? (4) How much will the new venture cost?

The great amount of time and consideration that should go into creating a business plan probably will end up saving time later. For example, Sharon Burch, who was running a computer software business while earning a degree in business administration, had to write a business plan as part of one of her courses. Burch has said, "I wish I'd taken the class before I started my business. I see a lot of things I could have done differently. But it has helped me since because I've been using the business plan as a guide for my business." Accuracy and realistic expectations are crucial to an effective business plan. It is unethical to deceive loan officers, and it is unwise to deceive yourself.

✓ Concept Check

- Why is a business plan important?
- What are the major components of a business plan? Why should an individual develop a business plan?

商业计划书
business plan a carefully constructed guide for the person starting a business

Table 4-3 Components of a Business Plan

1.	*Introduction.* Basic information such as the name, address, and phone number of the business; the date the plan was issued; and a statement of confidentiality to keep important information away from potential competitors.
2.	*Executive Summary.* A one- to two-page overview of the entire business plan, including a justification why the business will succeed.
3.	*Benefits to the Community.* Information on how the business will have an impact on economic development, community development, and human development.
4.	*Company and Industry.* The background of the company, choice of the legal business form, information on the products or services to be offered, and examination of the potential customers, current competitors, and the business's future.
5.	*Management Team.* Discussion of skills, talents, and job descriptions of management team, managerial compensation, management training needs, and professional assistance requirements.
6.	*Manufacturing and Operations Plan.* Discussion of facilities needed, space requirements, capital equipment, labor force, inventory control, and purchasing requirement.
7.	*Labor Force.* Discussion of the quality of skilled workers available and the training, compensation, and motivation of workers.
8.	*Marketing Plan.* Discussion of markets, market trends, competition, market share, pricing, promotion, distribution, and service policy.
9.	*Financial Plan.* Summary of the investment needed, sales and cash flow forecasts, breakeven analysis, and sources of funding.
10.	*Exit Strategy.* Discussion of a succession plan or going public. Who will take over the business?
11.	*Critical Risks and Assumptions.* Evaluation of the weaknesses of the business and how the company plans to deal with these and other business problems.
12.	*Appendix.* Supplementary information crucial to the plan, such as résumés of owners and principal managers, advertising samples, organization chart, and any related information.

Source: From HATTEN, *Small Business Management*, 5E.

特许经营

4-6 Franchising

Although many entrepreneurs choose to start a business from scratch, others have found a different path to success. Entrepreneurs can purchase an existing business from an owner looking to move on. Another option is acquiring a **franchise**, a license to operate an individually owned business as if it were part of a chain of outlets or stores. Often, the business itself is also called a *franchise*. Among the most familiar franchises are McDonald's, Kumon, Planet Fitness, ACE Hardware, and KFC. Many other franchises carry familiar names; this method of doing business has become very popular in the last 60 years or so. It can be an attractive means of starting and operating a small business.

Learning Objective

4-6 Explore franchising, including its types, growth, and advantages and disadvantages.

特许经营权
franchise a license to operate an individually owned business as though it were part of a chain of outlets or stores

特许经营
franchising the actual granting of a franchise

特许方
franchisor an individual or organization granting a franchise

加盟商
franchisee a person or organization purchasing a franchise

什么是特许经营

4-6a What Is Franchising?

Franchising is the actual granting of a franchise. A **franchisor** is an individual or organization granting a franchise. A **franchisee** is a person or organization purchasing a franchise. The franchisor supplies a known and advertised business name, management skills, the required training and materials, and a method of doing business. The franchisee supplies labor and capital, operates the franchised business, and agrees to abide by the provisions of the franchise agreement. Table 4-4 lists the basic franchisee rights and obligations that would be covered in a typical franchise agreement.

Table 4-4 Basic Rights and Obligations Delineated in a Franchise Agreement

Franchisee rights include:
1. Use of trademarks, trade names, and patents of the franchisor;
2. Use of the brand image and the design and decor of the premises developed by the franchisor;
3. Use of the franchisor's secret methods;
4. Use of the franchisor's copyrighted materials;
5. Use of recipes, formulae, specifications, processes, and methods of manufacture developed by the franchisor;
6. Conducting the franchised business upon or from the agreed premises strictly in accordance with the franchisor's methods and subject to the franchisor's directions;
7. Guidelines established by the franchisor regarding exclusive territorial rights; and
8. Rights to obtain supplies from nominated suppliers at special prices.
Franchisee obligations include:
1. To carry on the business franchised and no other business upon the approved and nominated premises;
2. To observe certain minimum operating hours;
3. To pay a franchise fee;
4. To follow the accounting system laid down by the franchisor;
5. Not to advertise without prior approval of the advertisements by the franchisor;
6. To use and display such point-of-sale advertising materials as the franchisor stipulates;
7. To maintain the premises in good, clean, and sanitary condition and to redecorate when required to do so by the franchisor;
8. To maintain the widest possible insurance coverage;
9. To permit the franchisor's staff to enter the premises to inspect and see if the franchisor's standards are being maintained;
10. To purchase goods or products from the franchisor or its designated suppliers;
11. To train the staff in the franchisor's methods to ensure that they are neatly and appropriately clothed; and
12. Not to assign the franchise contract without the franchisor's consent.

Source: Office of Entrepreneurship Education Resources.

特许经营的发展

4-6b The Growth of Franchising

Franchising, which began in the United States around the time of the Civil War, was originally used by large firms, such as the Singer Sewing Company, to distribute their products. Franchising has been increasing steadily in popularity since the early 1900s, primarily for service stations and car dealerships; however, growth has escalated since the mid-1970s. The proliferation of franchises generally has paralleled the expansion of the fast-food industry. Of course, franchising is not limited to fast foods. Hair salons, tanning parlors, and dentists and lawyers are participating in franchising arrangements in growing numbers. Franchised health clubs, pest exterminators, and campgrounds are already widespread, as are franchised tax preparers and travel agencies. The real estate industry also has experienced a rapid increase in franchising. Franchising is also growing outside the United States.

The growth of franchising. Franchising is designed to provide a tested formula for success, along with ongoing advice and training. The franchisor, such as McDonald's or Panda Express, supplies a known and advertised business name, management skills, the required training and materials, and a method of doing business. Franchising, however, is not a guarantee of success for either franchisees or franchisors.

Moreover, franchising is attracting more women and people of color than ever before. As an example, Michelle Lewis quit her full-time job to open a store through the Painting with a Twist franchise, which offers customers the ability to socialize while creating art. When her store became successful, she opened two more stores in the Detroit area with her sister, and now oversees 30 employees.[26] Unlike starting a business from scratch, franchising can offer franchisees from underrepresented groups greater access to business connections and support. Indeed, many franchisors such as Wendy's, McDonald's, Burger King, and Church's Chicken have special corporate programs to attract underrepresented groups and women as franchisees. Just as important, successful women and underrepresented franchisees are willing to get involved by offering advice and guidance to new franchisees. Herman Petty, the first Black McDonald's franchisee, says that the company provided significant help while he worked to establish his first store in 1968. In turn, Petty traveled to help other Black franchisees, eventually organizing a support group, the National Black McDonald's Operators Association, to help Black franchisees in other areas. Today, members of this association own McDonald's restaurants throughout the United States, South Africa, and the Caribbean.[27]

特许经营的类型

4-6c Types of Franchising

Franchising arrangements fall into three general categories. In the first approach, a manufacturer authorizes a number of retail stores to sell a certain brand-name item. This type of franchising arrangement, one of the oldest, is prevalent in sales of passenger cars and trucks, farm equipment, shoes, paint, earth-moving equipment, and petroleum. About 90 percent of all gasoline is sold through franchised, independent retail service stations, and franchised dealers handle virtually all sales of new cars and trucks.

In the second type of franchising arrangement, a producer licenses distributors to sell a given product to retailers. This arrangement is common in the soft drink industry. National manufacturers of soft drink syrups—the Coca-Cola Company and PepsiCo—franchise independent bottlers who then serve retailers.

Sustaining the Planet

保护地球：了解 Oxi Fresh 的特许经营增长

Inside Oxi Fresh's Franchise Growth

Oxi Fresh Carpet Cleaning uses innovative, environmentally friendly products to offer greener carpet cleaning services. The Denver-based company's cleaning method requires only two gallons of water per home compared to the 40 to 50 gallons many other steam cleaners require. With 450 locations in the United States and Canada, the company has been ranked as one of the top growth franchises by *Entrepreneur*.

Oxi Fresh's history is characterized by rapid expansion. It was founded in 2006 by Jonathan Barnett with a single location. Barnett, who owned an International Basketball League franchise called the Colorado Crossover, used his experience with franchising and his experience in carpet cleaning to open the first Oxi Fresh location. Within just six months, Barnett grew the company to 17 locations in five states. In 2014, the company expanded outside of the United States for the first time as it entered Canada. Today, the company has completed more than one million cleanings across its 450 locations.

In addition to growth, Oxi Fresh has been recognized for franchisee satisfaction. The company focuses on providing its franchisees with the tools they need to succeed, such as training materials, an easy-to-use online scheduling tool, business management systems, and email marketing. For example, the company uses a customer relationship management (CRM) system that helps franchisees to manage schedules, track return on investment for marketing investments, complete payroll, and manage customers. Additionally, the company hosts a national convention to connect with franchisees and share best practices.

The home services franchise category as a whole is experiencing significant gains, which demonstrates the strength of the industry. Oxi Fresh has found there is increasing demand for greener carpet cleaning services. In addition to selling a more sustainable product, Oxi Fresh contributes in other ways to sustaining the planet. Every time a customer books a carpet cleaning service through Oxi Fresh's online scheduler, the company makes a donation to Water.org, a nonprofit that is fighting the global water crisis. As one of the greenest carpet cleaning franchises in the United States, Oxi Fresh is poised for growth.

Sources: Based on information in "Oxi Fresh Carpet Cleaning Poised for Enormous Growth in 2021," *Yahoo! Finance*, February 25, 2021; "Oxi Fresh Carpet Cleaning Ranked as Top Growth Franchise by Entrepreneur Magazine," *Franchising.com*, September 23, 2020; Oxi Fresh Carpet Cleaning, "History"; Annie Pilon, "In the Spotlight: Oxi Fresh Clears the Air About What Sets It Apart from other Carpet Cleaners," *Small Business Trends*, May 22, 2019.

In a third form of franchising, a franchisor supplies brand names, techniques, or other services rather than a complete product. Although the franchisor may provide certain production and distribution services, its primary role is the careful development and control of marketing strategies. This approach to franchising, which is the most typical today, is used by Orange Therapy, Hampton Inn, 7-Eleven Inc., Anytime Fitness, Denny's Inc., Pizza Hut Inc., Dunkin', and Subway, to name but a few.

Dual-branded franchises, in which two franchisors offer their products together, are a new small-business trend. FAT Brands, for example, has been opening co-branded Fatburger and Buffalo's Express stores.[28]

特许经营的优势

4-6d Advantages of Franchising

Franchising plays a vital role in our economy. Why? Because franchising offers advantages to both the franchisor and the franchisee.

To the Franchisor The franchisor gains fast and well-controlled distribution of its products without incurring the high cost of constructing and operating its own outlets. The franchisor thus has more capital available to expand production and to use for advertising. At the same time, it can ensure, through the franchise agreement, that outlets are maintained and operated according to its own standards. The franchisor also benefits from the fact that the franchisee—a sole proprietor in

The Peterbrooke Chocolatier story. Peterbrooke Chocolatier has been making gelato and handmade treats like chocolate sushi rolls and seasonal chocolate molds for nearly 40 years. Since then, the firm has grown from a small Jacksonville, Florida, shop into an award-winning company. Franchises are now located throughout the Southeastern United States.

most cases—is likely to be highly motivated to succeed. The success of the franchise means more sales, which translate into higher royalties for the franchisor.

To the Franchisee The franchisee gets the opportunity to start a business with limited capital and to make use of the business experience of others. Moreover, an outlet with a nationally advertised name, such as Dunkin', McDonald's, or Great Clips, has guaranteed customers as soon as it opens. If business problems arise, the franchisor gives the franchisee guidance and advice. This counseling is primarily responsible for the high degree of success enjoyed by franchises. In most cases, the franchisee does not pay for such help. As an example, Taco Bell provides franchisees with classroom and on-the-job training, proprietary software, online and toll-free support, and an intranet for franchisees.[29]

The franchisee also receives materials to use in local advertising and can take part in national promotional campaigns sponsored by the franchisor. McDonald's and its franchisees, for example, are among the nation's top 30 advertisers. Finally, the franchisee may be able to minimize the cost of advertising, supplies, and various business necessities by purchasing them in cooperation with other franchisees.

特许经营的劣势
4-6e Disadvantages of Franchising

The main disadvantage of franchising affects the franchisee, and it arises because the franchisor retains a great deal of control. The franchisor's contract can dictate every aspect of the business: decor, design of employee uniforms, types of signs, required menu items, and all the details of business operations. All Burger King french fries taste the same because all Burger King franchisees have to make them the same way.

Disputes over franchise contracts are the cause of many lawsuits. In one case, a group of U.S. franchisees of Canadian fast-food restaurant chain Tim Hortons sued the franchisor, alleging the company charged them unfairly high prices on food and supplies required to operate their restaurants after it had received rebates from those suppliers. The lawsuit also contends that Tim Hortons's parent company owns the suppliers that the franchisees are required to use, further enriching the company at the franchisees' expense.[30] In another case, H&R Block filed suit against a former franchisee for flouting a noncompete agreement and continuing to use the H&R Block brand after his franchise agreement had been terminated due to his failure to pay royalties.[31]

Even success can cause problems. Sometimes a franchise is so successful that the franchisor opens its own outlet nearby, in direct competition—although franchisees may fight back. For example, a court ruled that Burger King could not enter into direct competition with a franchisee because the contract was not specific on the issue. A spokesperson for one franchisor contends that the company "gives no geographical protection" to its franchise holders and thus is free to move in on them.

Franchise holders pay for their security, usually with a onetime franchise fee and continuing royalty and advertising fees, collected as a percentage of sales. For example, a Subway franchisee pays an initial franchise fee of $15,000 and fee of 12.5 percent of gross sales (8 percent royalty and 4.5 percent advertising fees). In some fields, franchise agreements are not uniform. One franchisee may pay more than another for the same services.

Franchise operators work hard. They often put in 10- and 12-hour days, six days a week. The International Franchise Association advises prospective franchise purchasers to investigate before investing and to approach buying a franchise cautiously. Franchises vary widely in approach as well as in products. Some, such as Dunkin' and Baskin-Robbins, require long hours. Others, such as Great Clips and SportClips hair salons, are more appropriate for those who do not want to spend so many hours at their stores.

✓ Concept Check

- Explain the relationships among a franchise, the franchisor, and the franchisee.
- Describe the three general categories of franchising arrangements.
- Cite one major benefit of franchising for the franchisor. Cite one major benefit of franchising for the franchisee.

小企业融资

4-7 Financing the Small Business

Learning Objective

4-7 Describe methods entrepreneurs can use to finance their small business.

After deciding whether to start from scratch or purchase an existing business or franchise, an entrepreneur must determine how to finance the startup. As mentioned earlier, most entrepreneurs start their businesses using their own personal savings and assets (Figure 4-2). Many borrow from friends and family members, even though that could lead to friction in relationships down the road. Others max out their credit cards. Some firms are able to secure grants from government or nonprofit sources, but these are usually for relatively small amounts and often require complex application processes. Beyond these resources, an entrepreneur generally has two sources of funding: debt and equity.

Figure 4-2 Sources of Capital for Entrepreneurs

Small businesses get financing from various sources; the most important is personal savings.

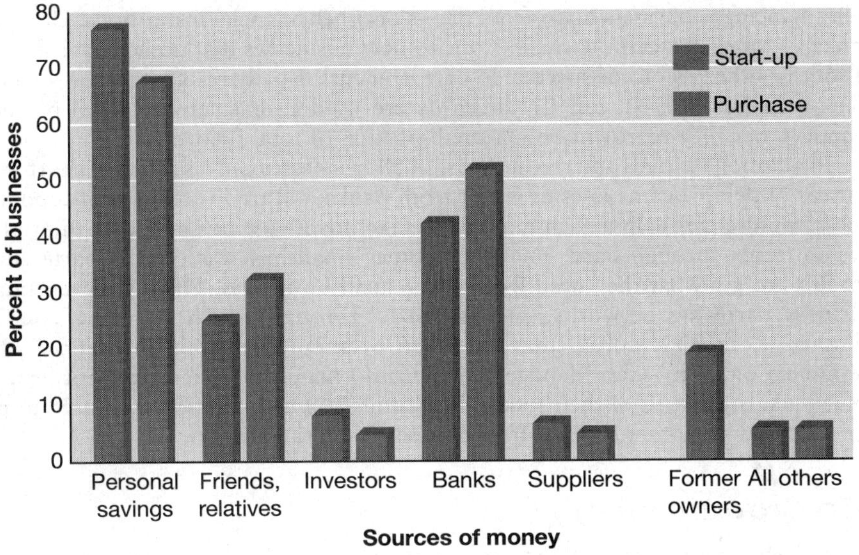

Source: Data developed and provided by the National Federation of Independent Business Foundation and sponsored by the American Express Travel Related Services Company, Inc.

股权融资
4-7a Equity Financing

Equity financing involves raising funds by promising investors a share of future profits and an ownership stake in the business. Other than equity financing through family and friends, entrepreneurs often seek out **venture capital**—money that is invested in small (and sometimes struggling) firms that have the potential to become successful. In many cases, only a lack of capital keeps these firms from rapid and solid growth. The organizations that invest in these promising firms expect that their investments will grow with the firms and become quite profitable. Consider Serena Ventures, which strives to invest in startups that "are changing the world with their ideas and products." Founded by tennis ace Serena Williams, the firm focuses its resources on startups founded by people of color, women, and younger entrepreneurs who often face extra challenges raising funds. Among Serena Ventures' investment success stories are Tonal, Billie, Olly, Propel, and Noom.[32] A small business with a track record of success can also pursue *angel investors*, private individuals who invest money in exchange for ownership in the company. The angel investor at some point hopes to sell their ownership stake for a profit.

Venture and angel capital are a relatively small part of business financing. While the average venture capital investment has increased significantly in recent years, the smallest firms still have difficulty obtaining venture capital, especially those owned by women and people of color. To help such businesses, the Small Business Administration licenses, regulates, and provides financial assistance to **small-business investment companies (SBICs),** which are privately owned firms that provide venture capital to small enterprises that meet their investment standards. Firms such as Apple, Costco, Whole Foods, FedEx, Intel, and Staples all received financing through SBICs during their initial growth period. The 314 SBICs are intended to be profit-making organizations. The aid that SBA offers allows them to invest in small businesses that otherwise would not attract venture capital. Since Congress created the program in 1958, SBICs have been providing financing for more than 166,000 small businesses for a total of about $67 billion.[33]

风险投资
venture capital money that is invested in small (and sometimes struggling) firms that have the potential to become successful

小企业投资公司
small-business investment companies (SBICs) privately owned firms that provide venture capital to small enterprises that meet their investment standards

债务融资
4-7b Debt Financing

Small-business founders also use *debt financing*, which requires the entrepreneur to repay the invested amount at a later date. One of the most common sources of debt financing is business loans from banks or other financial institutions. However, banks are often reluctant to make loans to new businesses that do not have a credit history or other record of success, so entrepreneurs usually resort to other financial sources in the early stages. Credit cards are used extensively by small-business founders, but they represent only a small portion of total financing.

In addition to loans and credit cards, small businesses can also turn to short-term sources of debt, such as lines of credit from banks and trade credit from suppliers. These sources can help a firm expand to take advantage of new opportunities or stretch to get through hard times. Sometimes small-business owners barter their products to get what they need from other small businesses. There are even small-business bartering networks, such as BizX, through which members conduct transactions in BizX dollars that they earn by supplying goods and services. For example, Commonwealth Management, a California property management firm, let some tenants pay part of their rent in BizX dollars, which the firm then used to pay for janitorial and other services from businesses on the platform.[34]

众筹
4-7c Crowdfunding

A relatively new source of financing is *crowdfunding* through online sites such as Kickstarter and Indiegogo. In crowdfunding, entrepreneurs post descriptions of their project or business and then invite people to contribute. Contributors typically get a reward based on their contribution level; however, some crowdfunding sites work more like loans (debt financing) while others operate more like venture capitalists, with backers getting a small ownership share for their investment (equity financing). A sampling of projects on Kickstarter include fundraising campaigns by musical artists, filmmakers, app developers, and a variety of inventors. It is estimated that crowdfunding raised an annual $17.2 billion in the United States and is expected to grow to $300 billion globally by 2025.[35] Because business owners from underrepresented groups face greater financing challenges, they are increasingly turning to crowdfunding sources to grow their businesses. As an example, David Favela, who founded Border X Brewing, raised $200,000 in equity financing through crowdfunding sources.[36]

✓ Concept Check

- How can an entrepreneur finance a startup?
- What is the difference between debt and equity financing?

Discussion Questions 讨论题

1. What industries seem to be most attractive to entrepreneurs? Why do you think that is?
2. How do entrepreneurs differ from other people? What kinds of things motivate them?
3. What benefits do small businesses provide our economy? Given all these benefits, should society do more to protect them?
4. What are the most common reasons that small businesses fail? What steps should entrepreneurs take to protect their firms from failure?
5. Are the so-called advantages of small business really advantages? Wouldn't every small-business owner like their business to grow into a large firm?
6. What is the role of the business plan?

Case 4 案例 4：最成功企业家的特质

Traits of the Most Successful Entrepreneurs

When one hears the word entrepreneur, many faces come to mind. Elon Musk, Sara Blakely, Warren Buffet, Martha Stewart, Bill Gates, and Daymond John are just a few that might spring to mind. There are a variety of traits that characterize entrepreneurs such as having an entrepreneurial spirit, being independent, and embracing failure. An entrepreneurial spirit is a mindset that embraces innovation and continuous improvement. Being an entrepreneur also requires the desire to work hard, take risks, and pursue one's passions.

Entrepreneurs have the ability to identify gaps in the market. That was the case with entrepreneur Vera Wang. Wang started working for *Vogue* magazine at the age of 22 and became the fashion editor by 23. Later, she was the design director for Ralph Lauren, a luxury American fashion company. With extensive experience in the fashion industry, she recognized an opportunity to introduce sophisticated, dramatic, feminine, and modern bridal gown designs. She opened her own boutique which quickly became popular, attracting celebrity clients such as Kate Hudson and Victoria Beckham. Wang, who continues to design iconic wedding dresses, has a net worth of $650 million.

Entrepreneurs think creatively and bring new perspectives to the table. This can be seen with Google's co-founders Sergey Brin and Larry Page. The two worked on a research project at Stanford University called BackRub. They created a search tool that ranked websites based on the number of backlinks they had (i.e., links to websites from other websites). At the time, existing search engines ranked websites based on how many times a search term appeared on the page. This advanced algorithm led to Google. Within its first five years, Google had more than 18 million searches a day.

Successful entrepreneurs have a desire to pursue their passions. Mark Zuckerberg, for example, developed a love for programming at an early age. When he was 12, he created a messaging platform he called Zucknet for inter-office communication at his dad's business. Microsoft even tried to recruit Zuckerberg as a result of his Synapse music player, but he declined so he could attend college. While in college, Zuckerberg developed several programs including CourseMatch, FaceMash, and Facebook. Facebook now has nearly 3 billion users.

Entrepreneurs have to be willing to work hard. Mark Cuban, an American entrepreneur, television personality, and the owner of the NBA's Dallas Mavericks, has an estimated worth of $4.3 billion. Cuban showed a willingness to work hard from a young age, selling garbage bags at the age of 12 so that he could afford basketball shoes. After college, Cuban founded MicroSolutions, which he later sold for $6 million. Cuban says he worked 20-hour-days and didn't take a vacation for seven years. Not long after, Cuban co-founded Broadcast.com, an online streaming audio service that was acquired by Yahoo for $5.7 billion in stock.

Entrepreneurs are risk-takers. Bill Gates, the founder of Microsoft, took a big risk when he was a student at Harvard University. When the world's first personal computer kit, the Altair, was created, Gates and his friend Paul Allen contacted the manufacturer about having written a computer language for the microcomputer. In reality, they were far from ready. When the president of the company returned Gates' phone call, he and Allen worked day and night to convert BASIC, a popular mainframe computer programming language, for use on the personal computer.

There are millions of entrepreneurs in the United States alone, but having an entrepreneurial spirit is not enough to guarantee success. Unfortunately, there is no perfect formula. But having the right mindset and traits can go a long way. Do you think you have what it takes?[37]

Questions

1. Describe what it means to have an entrepreneurial spirit. Use one of the entrepreneurs mentioned as an example.
2. Why is it important to be able to identify gaps in the market?
3. Aside from the traits discussed here, what other personal factors do you think contribute to entrepreneurial success?

PART 3
Management and Organization

管理和组织

This part of the book deals with the organization—the "thing" that is a business. We begin with a discussion of the management functions involved in developing and operating a business. Next, we analyze the organization's elements and structure. Then we consider a firm's operations that are related to the production of goods and services.

Chapter

5

Understanding the Management Process

管理过程

Learning Objectives

Once you complete this chapter, you will be able to:

5-1 Define management.

5-2 Describe the four basic management functions: planning, organizing, leading and motivating, and controlling.

5-3 Distinguish among the various kinds of managers in terms of both level and area of management.

5-4 Recognize the key management skills of successful managers.

5-5 Identify the different types of leadership.

5-6 Discuss the steps in the managerial decision-making process.

Why Should You Care?

Most of the people who read this chapter will advance upward and become managers. Thus, an overview of the field of management is essential.

Inside Business 商业透视：亲力亲为的投资者质疑 Twitter 的放手式管理

Hands-On Investors Question Twitter's Hands-Off Management

Jack Dorsey, a technology entrepreneur, is the co-founder and CEO of Twitter, a social networking service, as well as the founder and CEO of Square, a mobile payment company. Dorsey is known for being a hands-off leader. According to current and former employees, Dorsey is slow to act and tends to delegate major decisions. Investors, unsure if Dorsey could dedicate enough time to Twitter due to his split responsibilities and arms-length leadership style, launched an evaluation of the company's management performance.

Elliott Management Corp., which took a sizeable stake in Twitter, has a reputation as one of Wall Street's toughest activist investors. Elliott Management raised questions about Dorsey's management abilities after Dorsey decided to work remotely from Africa while still leading both of his companies. To appease investors, Twitter appointed two new board members, committed to $2 billion in share buybacks, and formed a committee to study Twitter's leadership. After months of evaluation, the board committee recommended that Twitter's management structure remain in place but suggested changes to the board structure to allow investors to have more authority.

Though the initial investigation is complete, the board committee will continue to evaluate Twitter's management performance ongoing. When Dorsey was questioned about his time management at an annual shareholder's meeting, he said, "To me, this is not a function of time, it's a function of prioritization." Dorsey maintains that he is able to focus on the most important challenges his companies face.[1]

Did You Know?

Jack Dorsey is the only person to be the CEO of two public companies with market valuations greater than $5 billion.

The leadership burdens that confront Jack Dorsey as the chief executive of Twitter illustrate that management can be one of the most challenging yet rewarding professions available today. Depending on its size, a firm may employ a number of specialized managers who are responsible for particular areas of management, such as marketing, finance, and operations. That same organization also includes managers at several levels within the firm.

In this chapter, we define *management* and describe the four basic management functions of planning, organizing, leading and motivating, and controlling. Then we focus on the types of managers with respect to levels of responsibility and areas of expertise. Next, we focus on the skills of effective managers and the different roles managers must play. Finally, we examine several styles of leadership and explore the process by which managers make decisions.

什么是管理
5-1 What Is Management?

Learning Objective

5-1 Define management.

Management is the process of coordinating people and other resources to achieve the goals of an organization. As we know, most organizations make use of four kinds of resources: material, human, financial, and informational (refer to Figure 5-1).

管理
management the process of coordinating people and other resources to achieve the goals of an organization

Material resources are the tangible, physical resources an organization uses. For example, General Motors uses steel, glass, and fiberglass to produce cars and trucks on complex machine-driven assembly lines. A college or university uses books, classroom buildings, desks, and computers to educate students. However, the Mayo Clinic uses operating room equipment, diagnostic machines, and laboratory tests to provide healthcare.

Figure 5-1 The Four Main Resources of Management

Managers coordinate an organization's resources to achieve the organization's goals.

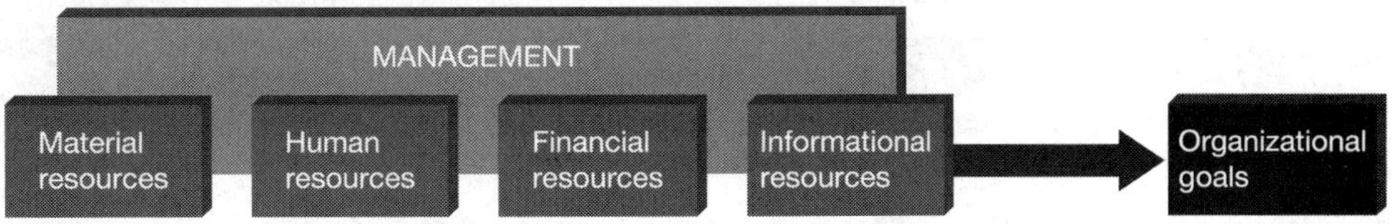

Perhaps the most important resources of any organization are its *human resources*—people. In fact, some firms live by the philosophy that employees are their most important assets. Some managers believe that the way employees are developed and managed has more impact on an organization than other vital components such as marketing, financial decisions, production, or technology. Research supports this belief. It shows that prioritizing human resources and working to ensure that employees are happy can greatly affect productivity and customer relationships.

Financial resources are the funds an organization uses to meet its obligations to investors and creditors. A 7-Eleven convenience store obtains money from customers at the checkout counter and uses a portion to pay its employees and suppliers. Your college obtains money in the form of tuition, income from endowments, and state and federal grants. It uses the money to pay bills, insurance premiums, and salaries.

Increasingly, organizations are finding that they cannot afford to ignore *information*. External environmental conditions—the economy, consumer markets, technology, politics, and cultural forces—are all changing so rapidly that a business must adapt to survive. To adapt to change, the business must gather information about competitors and changes to the industry in order to learn from the failures and successes of others.

It is important to realize that the four types of resources described earlier are only general categories. Within each category are hundreds or thousands of more specific resources. It is this complex mix of specific resources—which varies between companies and industries—that managers must coordinate to produce goods and services.

Another way to look at management is in terms of the different functions managers perform, which are planning, organizing, leading and motivating employees, and controlling. We look at each of these management functions in the next section.

✓ Concept Check

- What is management?
- What are the four kinds of resources?

基本的管理职能

5-2 Basic Management Functions

Learning Objective

5-2 Describe the four basic management functions: planning, organizing, leading and motivating, and controlling.

Management functions do not occur according to some rigid, preset timetable. Managers do not plan in January, organize in February, lead and motivate in March, and control in April. At any given time, managers may engage in a number of functions simultaneously. However, each function tends to lead naturally to others. Figure 5-2 provides a visual framework for a more detailed discussion of the four basic management functions. How well managers perform these key functions determines whether a business is successful.

计划

5-2a Planning

Planning, in its simplest form, is establishing organizational goals and deciding how to accomplish them. It is often referred to as the "first" management function because all other management functions depend on planning.

计划

planning establishing organizational goals and deciding how to accomplish them

Figure 5-2 The Management Process

Note that management is not a step-by-step procedure but a process with a feedback loop that represents a flow.

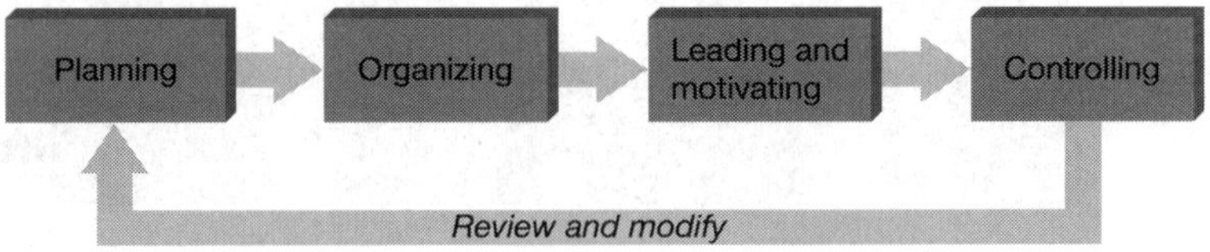

Organizations such as Starbucks, Amazon, and Nike base the planning process on a mission statement. An organization's **mission** is a statement of the basic purpose that makes that organization different from others. Starbucks' mission statement, for example, is "to inspire and nurture the human spirit—one person, one cup, and one neighborhood at a time."[2] Amazon's mission is "to be Earth's most customer-centric company."[3] Nike's mission is "to bring inspiration and innovation to every athlete in the world."[4] Once an organization has decided on its mission, the next step is strategic planning.

使命
mission a statement of the basic purpose that makes an organization different from others

战略规划过程
strategic planning process the establishment of an organization's major goals and objectives and the allocation of resources to achieve them

长期目标
goal an end result that an organization is expected to achieve over a one- to ten-year period

短期目标
objective a specific statement detailing what an organization intends to accomplish over a shorter period of time

Strategic Planning Process The **strategic planning process** involves establishing an organization's major goals and objectives and allocating resources to achieve them. Top management is responsible for strategic planning, although customers, products, competitors, and company resources all factor into the process.

In today's rapidly changing business environment, constant internal or external changes may necessitate changes in a company's goals, mission, or strategy. Consider that many firms had to shelve plans to open new stores and instead close or modify operations at existing ones in response to the COVID-19 pandemic. The timeline for strategic plans is generally one to two years, but can be much longer. Strategic plans should be flexible and include action items, such as outlining how plans will be implemented.

Establishing Goals and Objectives A **goal** is an end result that an organization is expected to achieve over a one- to ten-year period. An **objective** is a specific

Human resources. Superior human resources management can set a firm apart. Do you have a great business plan or product? A competitor can easily copy both. Great employees, however, are much harder to duplicate. That's why being able to attract, train, and retain talented workers can give a firm a competitive advantage over its rivals.

statement detailing what the organization intends to accomplish over a shorter period of time.

Goals and objectives can involve a variety of factors, such as sales, company growth, costs, customer satisfaction, and employee morale. Although a small manufacturer may focus primarily on sales objectives for the next six months, a large firm may be more interested in goals that will drive the firm for several years. Verizon, for example, launched a "responsible business plan" called Citizen Verizon, which included a goal to become fully carbon neutral by 2035 by reducing emissions, implementing more renewable energy, and purchasing carbon offsets.[5] Finally, goals are set at every level of an organization. Every member of an organization—the president of the company, the head of a department, and an operating employee at the lowest level—has a set of goals that they hope to achieve.

It is likely that some conflicts will arise among levels within the organization, but goals must be made consistent across an organization. A production department, for example, may have a goal of minimizing costs. One way to do this is to produce only one type of product. Marketing may have a goal of maximizing sales, which might be achieved by offering a wide range of products and options. As part of goal-setting, the manager responsible for *both* departments must strike a balance between conflicting goals. This balancing process is called *optimization.*

The optimization of conflicting goals requires insight and ability. Faced with the marketing-versus-production conflict just described, most managers would find a middle ground through offering a moderately diverse product line featuring only the most popular products. Such a compromise would be best for the whole organization.

SWOT Analysis **SWOT analysis** is the identification and evaluation of a firm's strengths, weaknesses, opportunities, and threats. Strengths and weaknesses are internal factors that affect a company's capabilities. Strengths refer to a firm's favorable characteristics and core competencies. **Core competencies** are approaches and processes that a company performs well that may give it an advantage over its competitors. These core competencies may help the firm attract financial and human resources that increase the firm's capacity to produce products that satisfy customers. Weaknesses refer to internal limitations a company faces in developing or implementing plans. At times, managers have difficulty identifying and understanding the negative effects of weaknesses in their organizations.

External opportunities and threats exist independently of the firm. Opportunities refer to favorable conditions in the environment that could benefit the organization if properly exploited. Threats, on the other hand, are conditions or barriers that may prevent the firm from reaching its objectives. Opportunities and threats can stem from many sources within the business environment. Because environmental factors vary between firms and industries, threats for some firms may be opportunities for others. Examples of strengths, weaknesses, opportunities, and threats are shown in Figure 5-3.

Types of Plans Once goals and objectives have been set for the organization, managers must develop plans for achieving them. A **plan** is an outline of the actions by which an organization intends to accomplish its goals and objectives. The organization develops several types of plans, as shown in Figure 5-4.

An organization's **strategic plan** is its broadest plan, developed as a guide during the strategic planning process for major policy setting and decision making. Strategic plans are set by the board of directors and top management and are generally designed to achieve the organization's long-term goals. Thus, a firm's strategic plan defines what business the company is in or wants to be in and the kind of company it is or wants to be. For example, Tesla, headed by Elon Musk, crafted a strategic plan to first develop and introduce a viable electric performance car and then to follow with a well-made model for the luxury car market.

SWOT 分析
SWOT analysis the identification and evaluation of a firm's strengths, weaknesses, opportunities, and threats

核心竞争力
core competencies approaches and processes that a company performs well that may give it an advantage over its competitors

计划
plan an outline of the actions by which an organization intends to accomplish its goals and objectives

战略规划
strategic plan an organization's broadest plan, developed as a guide for major policy setting and decision making

Figure 5-3 Elements and Examples of SWOT Analysis

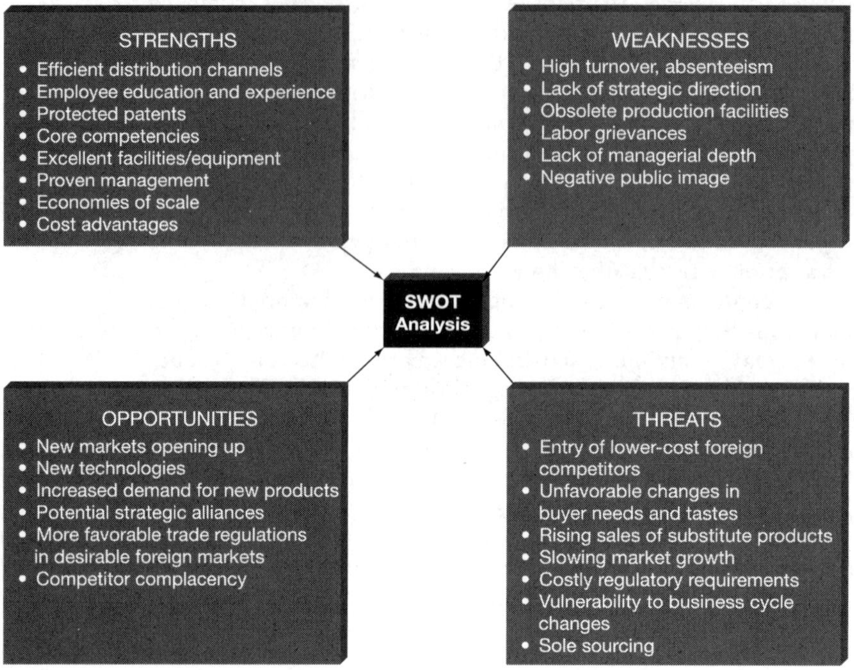

The company's first venture, the Tesla Roadster, fulfilled the first part of the plan, and its well-received Model S satisfied the second. These successes enabled Tesla to generate funds and brand recognition to launch the final part of its strategic plan to introduce a mass-market $35,000 electric vehicle, the Model 3, which had a lengthy waiting list to purchase years in advance of its introduction. Customer satisfaction with and enthusiasm for these vehicles along with Musk's charisma and showmanship fueled demand for even more electric vehicle types—including the Cybertruck pickup and a semi. Tesla is now executing a new strategic plan that involves using Tesla-branded batteries and solar technology to power not only electric cars but households, cities, and more with new products such as autonomous vehicles.[6]

In addition to strategic plans, most organizations also employ several narrower kinds of plans. A **tactical plan** is a smaller-scale plan developed to implement a strategy. Most tactical plans cover a one- to three-year period. If a strategic plan will take five years to complete, the firm may develop five tactical plans, one covering each year. Tactical plans may be updated periodically as dictated by conditions and experience. Their more limited scope permits them to be changed more easily than strategies. For example, as part of its strategic plan to slash costs, AT&T's COO John Stankey launched several tactical plans to restructure some aspects of the telecommunications conglomerate, streamline operations, lay off employees, and improve energy efficiency. Stankey expects these one- to three-year plans to yield millions of dollars in savings and help the firm achieve its profit margin goals.[7]

An **operational plan** is a type of plan designed to implement tactical plans. Operational plans are usually established for one year or less and deal with how to accomplish the organization's specific objectives.

战术计划
tactical plan a smaller-scale plan developed to implement a strategy

运营计划
operational plan a type of plan designed to implement tactical plans

Figure 5-4 Types of Plans

Managers develop and rely on several types of plans.

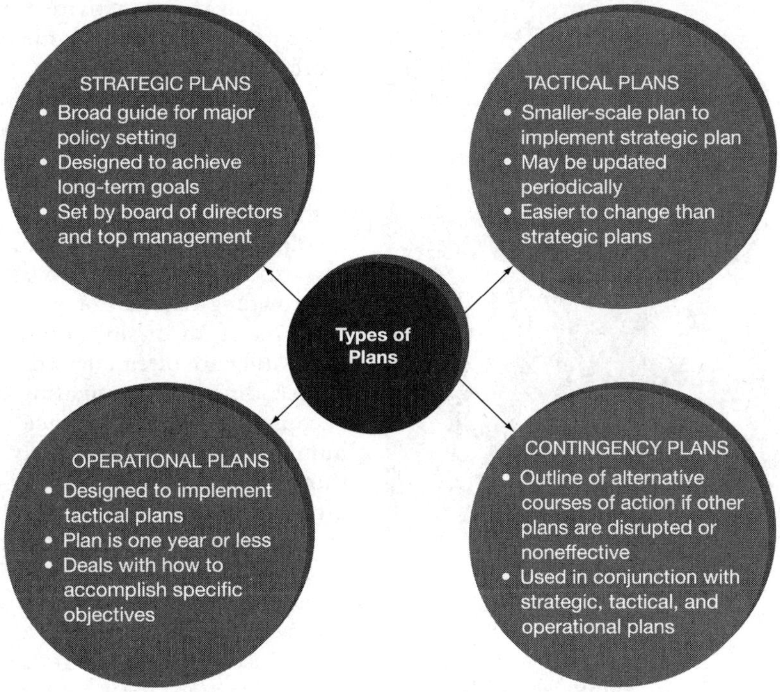

Regardless of how hard managers try, sometimes business activities do not go as planned. Today, most corporations also develop contingency plans along with strategies, tactical plans, and operational plans. A **contingency plan** is a plan that outlines alternative courses of action that may be taken if an organization's other plans are disrupted or become ineffective. Contingency plans may address disruptions caused by natural disasters, pandemics, criminal or ethical misconduct, hacking, political instability, or other unexpected activities. Also known as crisis plans, contingency plans can help halt the escalation of a disruptive situation and thereby minimize further harm to people, resources, or reputations. H-E-B, a Texas-based supermarket chain, has crisis plans and emergency management teams to help weather hurricanes and other disasters so that it can continue to serve its customers and support its employees. These initiatives also helped the company keep its supply chains moving during the COVID-19 pandemic.[8] Despite their usefulness, about one third of companies lack a crisis plan, and those that do have contingency plans often fail to update or practice for them, thereby limiting their value in a crisis.[9]

组织

5-2b Organizing the Enterprise

After goal-setting and planning, the manager's second major function is organization. **Organizing** is the grouping of resources and activities to accomplish some end result in an efficient and effective manner. Consider the case of an inventor who creates a new product and goes into business to sell it. At first, the inventor will do everything—purchase raw materials, make the product, advertise it, sell it, and keep business records. Eventually, as business grows, the inventor will need help. To begin with, the inventor might hire a professional sales representative and a part-time bookkeeper. Later, it also might be necessary to hire sales staff, people to assist with production, and an accountant. As new

应急计划
contingency plan a plan that outlines alternative courses of action that may be taken if an organization's other plans are disrupted or become ineffective

组织
organizing the grouping of resources and activities to accomplish some end result in an efficient and effective manner

personnel are hired, the inventor must decide what each person will do, to whom each person will report, and how each person can best take part in the organization's activities. We discuss these and other facets of the organizing function in much more detail in Chapter 6.

Encouraging employees is part of motivating them. Organizations employ numerous motivational messages. There are considerable differences among people regarding the factors and messages that motivate them.

领导
leading the process of influencing people to work toward a common goal

激励
motivating the process of providing reasons for people to work in the best interests of an organization

指导
directing the combined processes of leading and motivating

控制
controlling the process of evaluating and regulating ongoing activities to ensure that goals are achieved

领导和激励

5-2c Leading and Motivating

The leading and motivating function is concerned with an organization's human resources. Specifically, **leading** is the process of influencing people to work toward a common goal. **Motivating** is the process of providing reasons for people to work in the best interests of an organization. Together, leading and motivating are often referred to as **directing**.

Leading and motivating are critical activities because of the importance of an organization's human resources. Obviously, different people do things for different reasons—that is, they have different *motivations*. Some are interested primarily in earning as much money as they can. Others may be spurred on by opportunities to get promoted. Part of a manager's job, then, is to determine what factors motivate workers and to try to provide those incentives to encourage effective performance. Many people choose to work at Cisco because of its reputation for treating its employees well (it has been on *Fortune's* Best Companies to Work For list for more than two decades), and they want to be part of a major information technology company with strong growth potential. In addition to a competitive compensation plan and bonuses, Cisco provides generous benefits—such as tuition reimbursement, flexible work options, subsidized childcare, onsite fitness and medical facilities, and lengthy maternity and paternity leave and support—and strives to create fun workspaces.[10] A lot of research has been done on both motivation and leadership. As you will see in Chapter 9, research on motivation has yielded very useful information. However, research on leadership has been less successful. Despite decades of study, no one has discovered a general set of personal traits or characteristics that makes a good leader. Later in this chapter, we discuss leadership in more detail.

控制正在进行的活动

5-2d Controlling Ongoing Activities

Controlling is the process of evaluating and regulating ongoing activities to ensure that goals are achieved. The control function includes three steps (refer to Figure 5-5). The first is *setting standards* against which performance can be compared. The second is *measuring actual performance* and comparing it with the standard. The third is *taking corrective action* as necessary. Notice that the control function is circular in nature. The steps in the control function must be repeated periodically until the goal is achieved. For example, suppose that Southwest Airlines establishes a goal of increasing profits by 12 percent. Southwest's management will monitor its profit on a monthly basis to ensure success. After three months, if profit has increased by 3 percent, management may assume that plans are effective. In this case, no action will likely be taken. However, if profit has increased by only 1 percent, some corrective action will be needed to get the firm on track. The action that is required depends on the reason for the less-than-expected increase.

Figure 5-5 The Control Function

The control function includes three steps: setting standards, measuring actual performance, and taking corrective action.

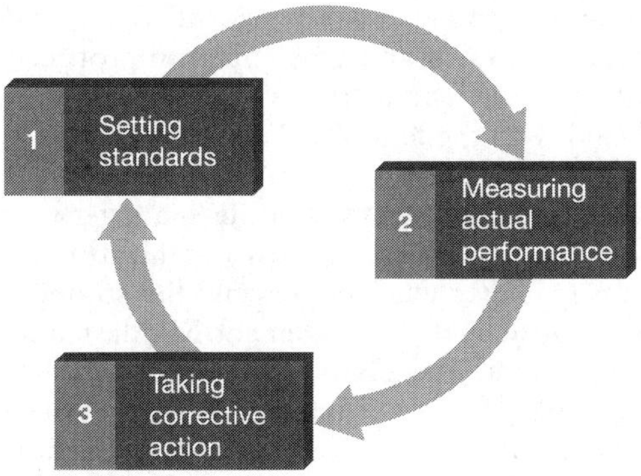

✓ Concept Check

- Why is planning sometimes referred to as the "first" management function?
- What is a plan? Differentiate among the major types of plans.
- What kind of motivations do different employees have?
- What are the three steps of controlling?

管理者的类型

5-3 Kinds of Managers

Learning Objective

5-3 Distinguish among the various kinds of managers in terms of both level and area of management.

Managers can be classified in two ways: according to their level within an organization and according to their area of management. In this section, we use both perspectives to explore the various types of managers.

管理层级

5-3a Levels of Management

For the moment, think of an organization as a three-story structure (as illustrated in Figure 5-6). Each story corresponds to one of the three general levels of management: top managers, middle managers, and first-line managers.

Top Managers A **top manager** is an upper-level executive who guides and controls an organization's overall fortunes. Top managers represent the smallest of the three groups. In terms of planning, they are generally responsible for developing the

Figure 5-6 Management Levels Found in Most Companies

The coordinated effort of all three levels of managers is required to implement the goals of any company.

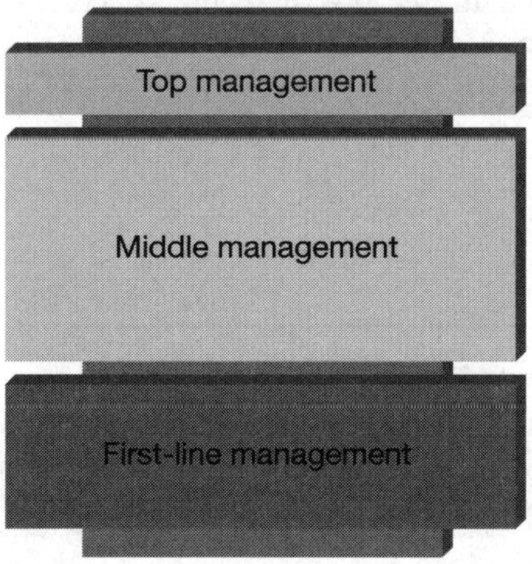

高层管理者
top manager an upper-level executive who guides and controls the overall fortunes of an organization

organization's mission. They also determine the firm's strategy. It takes years of hard work, long hours, and perseverance; talent; and no small share of good luck to reach the ranks of top management in large companies. Common job titles associated with top managers are president, vice president, chief executive officer (CEO), and chief operating officer (COO). These are often referred to as the "C-suite" because so many of the titles begin with the letter "C."

Middle Managers Middle managers make up the largest group of managers in most organizations. A **middle manager** is a manager who implements the strategy and major policies developed by top management. Middle managers develop tactical and operational plans, and they coordinate and supervise the activities of first-line managers. Titles at the middle-management level include division manager, department head, plant manager, and operations manager.

First-Line Managers A **first-line manager** is a manager who coordinates and supervises the activities of operating employees. First-line managers spend most of their time working with and motivating their employees, answering questions, and solving day-to-day problems. Most first-line managers are former operating employees who were promoted into management. Many of today's middle and top managers began their management careers on this first management level. Common titles for first-line managers include office manager, supervisor, and foreman.

管理专业化的几个领域

5-3b Areas of Management Specialization

Organizational structure can also be divided into areas of management specialization (refer to Figure 5-7). The most common areas are finance, operations, marketing, human resources, and administration. Depending on its mission, goals, and objectives, an organization may include other areas as well—research and development (R&D), for example.

Financial Managers A **financial manager** is primarily responsible for an organization's financial resources. Accounting and investment are specialized areas within financial management. Because financing affects the operation of the entire firm, many CEOs and presidents of large companies are people who were first trained as financial managers.

Top manager. As the first Black woman CEO of a Fortune 500 company, Rosalind Brewer is certainly on a roll. Brewer began her journey to success by working as a research technician for a paper manufacturer for 22 years. Frustrated by the lack of control she had in research and development there, she transferred to administration, where she moved up to the role of president for manufacturing and global operations. From there, she joined Walmart as a regional vice president in 2006, then eventually became president of Walmart East. Of course, she didn't just stop there. In 2012, she became the president and CEO of Sam's Club. Then in 2017, she migrated to the role of COO for Starbucks, earning herself a spot in *Fortune* magazine as one of the 50 Most Powerful Women in Business. Today, she is the CEO of Walgreens where she continues to be a powerhouse in the business world.

中层管理者
middle manager a manager who implements the strategy and major policies developed by top management

一线管理者
first-line manager a manager who coordinates and supervises the activities of operating employees

财务经理
financial manager a manager who is primarily responsible for an organization's financial resources

Figure 5-7 Areas of Management Specialization

Other areas may have to be added, depending on the nature of the firm and the industry.

Harnessing the cooperation of an organization's specialized managers. Imagine the managers of different departments as a team of horses. If they—and their employees—don't all work together and pull in the same direction, the organization won't get to the destination it is trying to reach.

Operations Managers An **operations manager** manages the systems that convert resources into goods and services. Traditionally, operations management has been equated with manufacturing—the production of goods. However, in recent years, many of the techniques and procedures of operations management have been applied to the production of services and to a variety of nonbusiness activities. As with financial management, operations management has produced a large percentage of today's company CEOs and presidents.

Marketing Managers A **marketing manager** is responsible for facilitating the exchange of products between an organization and its customers or clients. Specific areas within marketing are marketing research, product management, advertising, promotion, sales, and distribution. A sizable number of today's company presidents have risen from marketing management.

Human Resources Managers A **human resources manager** is charged with managing an organization's human resources programs. This individual engages in human resources planning; designs systems for hiring, training, and evaluating the performance of employees; and ensures that the organization follows government regulations concerning employment practices. There are many technological tools to help human resources managers. For example, Workday, Inc. produces a suite of software and tools for human resources departments, including a program to streamline the recruiting and hiring process and tools that help HR managers collect and process information.

Administrative Managers An **administrative manager** (also called a *general manager*) is not associated with any specific functional area but provides overall administrative guidance and leadership. Hospital administrators are an example of administrative managers. They do not specialize in operations, finance, marketing, or human resources management but instead coordinate the activities of specialized managers in all these areas. In many respects, most top managers are really administrative managers.

Whatever their level and specialization in the organization, successful managers generally exhibit certain key skills and are able to play a variety of managerial roles. However, as we shall see, some skills are likely to be more critical at one level of management than at another.

✓ Concept Check

- Describe the three levels of management.
- Identify the various areas of management specialization and describe the responsibilities of each.

运营经理
operations manager a manager who manages the systems that convert resources into goods and services

营销经理
marketing manager a manager who is responsible for facilitating the exchange of products between an organization and its customers or clients

人力资源经理
human resources manager a person charged with managing an organization's human resources programs

行政经理
administrative manager a manager who is not associated with any specific functional area but who provides overall administrative guidance and leadership

Ethics and Social Responsibility

商业伦理与社会责任：Everlane的完全透明承诺失败了

Radical Transparency at Everlane Goes Bust

Everlane, a direct-to-consumer clothing company, promised radical transparency. The company said it would reveal pricing markups, its clothing suppliers, and its ecological impact. But now, current and former employees say Everlane's ethical image was an illusion. Employees accuse Everlane of union-busting, racism, and of selling a false ethical image to the world.

With Everlane's corporate culture under the microscope, Michael Preysman, founder and CEO, launched an internal investigation that confirmed many of the complaints. Investigators found that new hires felt unwelcome, that leaders used inappropriate terms when referring to people of color, that there was no procedure for submitting harassment and discrimination claims, and more. In response, Preysman expressed the desire to revisit the company's code of ethics. Additionally, the company committed to several diversity initiatives such as hiring a Black board member, diversifying the senior leadership team, and introducing anti-racism training.

To top it off, Everlane's commitments to ethical labor and sustainability have attracted criticism as well. Brand ratings platform Good on You gave Everlane a "not good enough" overall rating for failing to adequately track greenhouse gas emissions, reduce water use, and guarantee living wages. Consumers and employees are increasingly attracted to companies that share their values. When a company such as Everlane fails to deliver on its promises, its stakeholders lose trust in the organization. Everlane's management will have to redefine what it means to be radically transparent and recommit to living out the firm's values.

Sources: Based on information in Jessica Testa, Vanessa Friedman, and Elizabeth Paton, "Everlane's Promise of 'Radical Transparency' Unravels," *The New York Times*, July 26, 2020; Kaley Roshitsh, "Everlane, Reformation Respond to Callouts in Remake Transparency Report," *WWD*, December 9, 2020; Elizabeth Segran, "Everlane Is the Latest Company to Come Under Fire for a Toxic Workplace," *Fast Company*, January 8, 2020.

成功管理者的关键技能

5-4 Key Skills of Successful Managers

Learning Objective

5-4 Recognize the key management skills of successful managers.

As shown in Figure 5-8, managers need a variety of skills, including conceptual, analytic, interpersonal, technical, and communication skills.

概念技能

5-4a Conceptual Skills

Conceptual skills involve the ability to think in abstract terms. Conceptual skills allow a manager to see the "big picture" and understand how the various parts of an organization or idea can fit together. Consider Jeff Bezos, who founded and led Amazon for many years (he now serves as its executive chair). Despite media and investor criticism during the many years Amazon operated in the red, Bezos never lost sight of his vision of an internet commerce site where people could shop quickly and easily. His strict long-term focus on the customer ensured that Amazon would eventually fulfill that vision. Conceptual skills are useful in a wide range of situations, including the optimization of goals described earlier.

分析技能

5-4b Analytic Skills

Employers expect managers to use **analytic skills** to identify problems correctly, generate reasonable alternatives, and select the "best" alternatives to solve problems. Top-level managers especially need these skills because they must discern the important issues from the less important ones, as well as recognize the underlying reasons for different situations. Soon after Mary Barra became the CEO of General Motors, she faced a crisis related to defective ignition switches in some GM vehicles,

概念技能
conceptual skills the ability to think in abstract terms

分析技能
analytic skills the ability to identify problems correctly, generate reasonable alternatives, and select the "best" alternatives to solve problems

Figure 5-8 Key Skills of Successful Managers

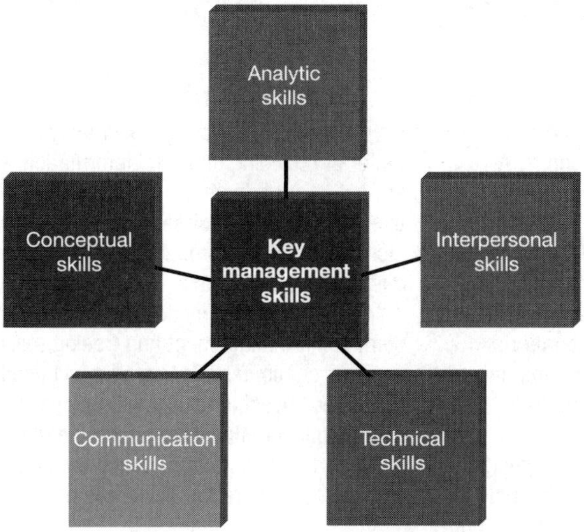

which ultimately caused hundreds of deaths and injuries. She quickly established a crisis team and launched an independent investigation. After analyzing the situation, she chose to fire a number of employees who she felt failed to act; and she had GM apologize for the faulty switches, set up a multimillion-dollar victim's compensation fund, and pay out millions of dollars to settle claims related to the scandal. After determining that General Motors' "toxic culture" had prevented employees from speaking up about the faulty ignition switches before they caused harm, she set about changing that culture. She began that process by modeling the behaviors she wanted to see. She also applied her analytic skills to turning around the automaker by taking actions such as selling an underperforming division and investing in new automotive technologies.[11] Managers who use these skills not only address a situation but also correct the initial event or problem that caused it to occur. Thus, these skills are vital to running a business efficiently and logically.

人际交往技能

5-4c Interpersonal Skills

Interpersonal skills, also known as soft skills or people skills, involve the ability to deal effectively with other people, both inside and outside an organization. Examples of interpersonal skills are the ability to listen to and build relationships with people, understand their needs and motives, and show genuine compassion. Conflict resolution, patience, and diplomacy are also useful skills for today's leaders.

技术技能

5-4d Technical Skills

Technical skills involve specific skills needed to accomplish a specialized activity. For example, engineers and machinists need technical skills to do their jobs. First-line managers (and, to a lesser extent, middle managers) need to understand the technical skills relevant to the activities they manage in order to train subordinates, answer questions, and provide guidance, even though the managers may not perform the technical tasks themselves. In general, top managers do not rely on technical skills as heavily as managers at other levels. Still, understanding the technical side of a business is an aid to effective management at every level.

人际交往技能
interpersonal skills the ability to deal effectively with other people

技术技能
technical skills specific skills needed to accomplish a specialized activity

Technology and Innovation 技术与创新：人工智能会取代管理者吗

Will AI Replace Managers?

Artificial intelligence (AI) involves computers performing tasks that traditionally require human intelligence. AI has a broad set of applications, from AI-enabled inventory-tracking robots to AI-powered customer service chats. Hilton, for example, uses AI to simplify its recruiting process. This has caused many people to question if the technology will bring more management-free organizations. While AI can perform many managerial duties, it's more likely that humans and AI will exist side-by-side for many years to come.

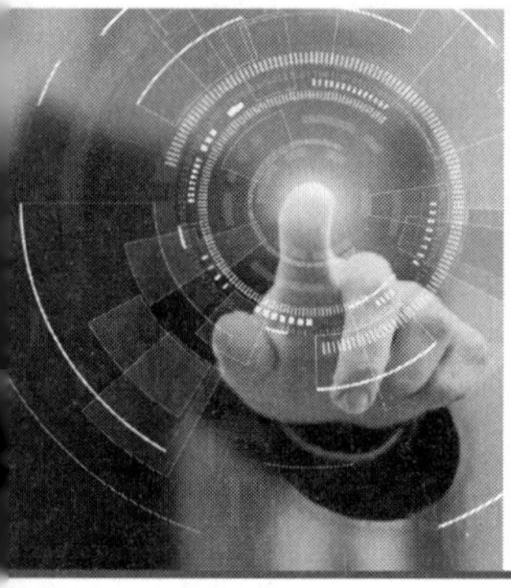

AI may influence organizational design that fosters innovation and experimentation. In the future, managers may no longer be expected to perform administrative tasks but rather focus on their human skills such as creativity and innovation, things AI hasn't mastered. Managers would have more time to build relationships with their employees. According to a study by Oracle and Future Workplace, employees think robots are better at providing unbiased information while managers are better at understanding feelings. By taking administrative tasks away and streamlining processes, AI stands to increase employee productivity and allow organizations to operate at a faster pace.

AI isn't replacing managers just yet. Rather, AI is supplementing management and freeing managers to focus on more critical tasks. Managers will need to balance resources, invest in reskilling employees, and advance new models of education, creating pathways to continuous learning. Leaders must embrace the challenges AI brings to properly prepare the workforce of tomorrow.

Sources: Based on information in Martin Fleming, "AI Is Changing Work—and Leaders Need to Adapt," *Harvard Business Review*, March 24, 2020; Dan Schawbel, "How Artificial Intelligence Is Redefining the Role of Manager," *World Economic Forum*, November 15, 2019; Joe McKendrick, "Artificial Intelligence May Bring More Management-Free Organizations," *Forbes*, June 8, 2020.

沟通技能

5-4e Communication Skills

Communication skills, both oral and written, involve the ability to speak, listen, and write effectively. Managers need both oral and written communication skills. Because a large part of a manager's day is spent conversing with others, the ability to speak *and* listen is critical. Oral communication skills are used when a manager makes sales presentations, conducts interviews, and holds press conferences. Written communication skills are important because a manager's ability to prepare letters, emails, memos, sales reports, and other written documents may spell the difference between success and failure. Computers, smartphones, and other high-tech devices make communication in today's businesses easier and faster. To manage an organization effectively and to stay informed, it is very important that managers understand how to use and maximize the potential of digital communication devices.

✓ Concept Check

- What are the key skills that successful managers should have?
- For each skill, provide two reasons why a successful manager should have that skill.

沟通技能
communication skills the ability to speak, listen, and write effectively

Learning Objective

5-5 Identify the different types of leadership.

领导力

5-5 Leadership

Leadership has been defined broadly as the ability to influence others. Leadership is different from management in that a leader strives for voluntary cooperation, whereas a manager may have to depend on coercion to change employee behavior.

领导力
leadership the ability to influence others

正式领导和非正式领导

5-5a Formal and Informal Leadership

Some experts make distinctions between formal leadership and informal leadership. Formal leaders have legitimate power of position. They have *authority* within an organization to influence others to work toward the organization's objectives.

Informal leaders usually have no such authority and may or may not exert their influence in support of the organization. Both formal and informal leaders make use of several kinds of power, including the ability to grant rewards or impose punishments, the possession of expert knowledge, and personal attraction or charisma. Informal leaders who identify with the organization's goals are a valuable asset to any organization. However, a business can be greatly hampered by informal leaders who turn work groups against management.

How good are your managerial skills? To be successful, managers must master and simultaneously utilize a number of skills. These include technical skills that aid with specialized work, conceptual skills that foster abstract thinking, and interpersonal skills to help manage and motivate employees. Which of these skills will you need to work on as you build your career?

领导风格

5-5b Styles of Leadership

For many years, finding a consensus on the most important leadership traits was difficult. Leadership was viewed as a combination of personality traits, such as self-confidence, concern for people, intelligence, and dependability. In recent years, the emphasis has been on styles of leadership. Several styles have emerged, including autocratic, participative, laissez-faire, transformational, transactional, and charismatic.

Autocratic leadership, also called authoritative leadership, is a hands-on, task-oriented leadership style. These leaders make decisions unilaterally, with little concern for employee opinions or knowledge. Employees are told exactly what is expected from them and given specific guidelines, rules, and regulations on how to achieve their tasks. Strict compliance is expected.

Participative leadership, which involves all members of a team identifying essential goals and developing strategies to reach those goals, is common in today's business organizations. Participative leaders consult workers before making decisions and make final decisions based on their support, though they retain final authority for decision making. This helps workers understand which goals are important and fosters a sense of ownership and commitment to reach them. Communication is open up and down the hierarchy. Coaching, collaborating, and negotiating are important skills for participative leaders.

Laissez-faire leadership, also known as free-rein leadership, is a hands-off leadership style. These leaders provide general direction along with tools and resources and then delegate responsibility and decision making to subordinates. As long as employees are satisfying expectations, these leaders expect them to apply their own skills and knowledge to furthering the goals of the organization. Warren Buffett, CEO and chief investor of Berkshire Hathaway, is a famously laissez-faire leader.

Transformational leadership recognizes that today's competitive landscape requires challenging the status quo with new ideas. These leaders promote communication and transparency with high expectations while providing support and recognition to subordinates. Many of the industry disruptors of recent years, including Google's Larry Page and Dollar Shave Club's Michael Dubin, provided transformational leadership to develop new business models.

Transactional leadership is a leadership style that emphasizes structure, monitoring employee performance, and using rewards and punishments to motivate subordinates to achieve organizational goals. These leaders tend to focus on the chain of command, productivity, and efficiency. They generally try to be considerate of subordinates because doing so can improve productivity. Transactional leadership is especially common in sports teams though it is often found in business organizations as well.

Finally, **charismatic leadership** is personality dependent. These leaders influence, inspire, and motivate employees to perform due to their own innate charm

专制型领导
autocratic leadership task-oriented leadership style in which workers are told what to do and how to accomplish it without having a say in the decision-making process

参与型领导
participative leadership leadership style in which all members of a team are involved in identifying essential goals and developing strategies to reach those goals

自由放任型领导
laissez-faire leadership a hands-off leadership style that provides direction, tools, and resources to employees while delegating responsibility and decision-making authority to them

变革型领导
transformational leadership leadership style that focuses on transforming organizations and industries

交易型领导
transactional leadership leadership style that emphasizes structure, performance and productivity, and reward systems

魅力型领导
charismatic leadership personality-dependent leadership style

Exploring Careers

职业探索：根据谷歌的研究，优秀管理者具备的主要特质

Top Traits of Good Managers, According to Google

Having great managers and leaders can improve productivity and employee retention. Google conducted research to discover what makes the perfect manager with the goal of training its leaders to develop those qualities and behaviors. The tech giant was able to successfully identify a series of traits that good managers should have.

Google found that good leaders are also good coaches and use problems as teaching moments. Rather than micromanage employees, great managers empower their teams and give them the freedom to explore their ideas and take risks. At the same time, leaders should create a psychologically safe environment where employees feel free from embarrassment or punishment for making mistakes and asking questions.

Good managers are productive and results-oriented, but, perhaps more importantly, they are good communicators who show empathy. They support the success of their team members, but they aren't afraid to provide constructive criticism. Great managers, being results-oriented, have a vision for the team's future as well as the technical skills necessary to advise the team. Google also found that managers shouldn't just lead—they should collaborate. Finally, good managers are decisive and commit to their decisions.

While it may be challenging to hire a manager that exhibits all of these characteristics and behaviors, Google has been able to train its leaders and use this knowledge to improve employee retention, satisfaction, and performance. Ten years of research have paid off.

Sources: Based on information in Justin Bariso, "10 Traits of a 'Perfect' Boss, According to Research by Google," *Business Insider*, August 1, 2020; Poppy Noor, "Google Released Research on What Makes a Good Boss - Do You Agree?" *The Guardian*, October 21, 2019; "Learn About Google's Manager Research," re:Work.

Playing multiple leadership roles. Elon Musk, co-founder and CEO of Tesla, provides leadership in product design, engineering, and global manufacturing. At Space X, he oversees the development of rockets and spacecraft. At Neuralink, he provides top level leadership aimed at developing ultra-high bandwidth brain-machine interfaces to connect the human brain to computers. His leadership at The Boring Company focuses on providing low-cost tunneling technology for use in urban transportation.

and personality. They tend to be idealistic and forward-thinking and model behavior that reflects their high expectations. Oprah Winfrey and the late Steve Jobs are well-known examples of charismatic leaders who inspired their subordinates to perform very well in competitive industries.

哪种领导风格最好

5-5c Which Leadership Style Is the Best?

Today, most management experts agree that no "best" managerial leadership style exists. Each of the styles described—autocratic, participative, laissez-faire, transformational, transactional, and charismatic—has advantages and disadvantages. For example, participative leadership can motivate employees to work effectively because they have a sense of ownership in decision making. However, the decision-making process in participative leadership takes time that subordinates could be devoting to the work itself. In a similar vein, autocratic leaders can be very effective during times of crisis. However, outside of such times, their leadership can stifle the creativity of subordinates that could otherwise benefit the organization.

Although hundreds of research studies have been conducted to prove which leadership style is best, there are no definite conclusions. Each of the leadership styles can be highly effective in the right situation. The *most* effective style depends on the right balance between interaction among employees, characteristics of the work situation, and the manager's personality.

Concept Check

- Describe the major leadership styles.
- Which one is best?

制定管理决策

5-6 Managerial Decision Making

Learning Objective

5-6 Discuss the steps in the managerial decision-making process.

Decision making is the act of choosing one alternative from a set of alternatives.[12] In ordinary situations, decisions are made casually and informally. We encounter a problem, mull it over, settle on a solution, and go on. Managers, however, require a more systematic method for solving complex problems. As shown in Figure 5-9, the managerial decision-making process involves four steps: (1) identifying the problem or opportunity, (2) generating alternatives, (3) selecting an alternative, and (4) implementing and evaluating the solution.

识别问题或机会

5-6a Identifying the Problem or Opportunity

A **problem** is the discrepancy between an actual condition and a desired condition—the difference between what is occurring and what one wishes would occur. For example, a marketing manager at Campbell Soup Company has a problem if sales revenues for its Pepperidge Farm Goldfish crackers are declining (the actual condition). To solve this problem, the marketing manager must take steps to increase sales revenues (desired condition). Most people consider a problem to be "negative," but a problem also can be "positive." Some problems can be viewed as "opportunities." Consider the success of plant-based meat alternatives such as Beyond Meat and Impossible Foods, which highlighted a surprising market—consumers increasingly willing to try meat alternatives to be healthier and kinder to the environment. Although meat producers could have viewed these new competitors as a threat, Tyson, Perdue, Hormel, and others saw an opportunity to reach these consumers. Hormel introduced a plant-based ground meat product, while Nestlé introduced the Awesome Burger. Tyson and Perdue both launched part meat, part plant products such as "chicken" nuggets.[13]

Although accurate identification of a problem is essential before it can be solved or turned into an opportunity, this stage of decision making creates many difficulties for managers. Sometimes managers' preconceptions of the problem prevent them from seeing the actual situation. They produce an answer before the proper question has been asked, leading them to focus on insignificant issues. Also, managers may mistakenly analyze problems in terms of symptoms rather than underlying causes.

Effective managers learn to look ahead so that they are prepared when decisions must be made. They clarify situations and examine the causes of problems, asking whether the presence or absence of certain variables alters a situation. Finally, they consider how individual behaviors and values affect the way problems or opportunities are defined.

Figure 5-9 Major Steps in the Managerial Decision-Making Process

Managers require a systematic method for solving problems in a variety of situations.

制定决策
decision making the act of choosing one alternative from a set of alternatives

问题
problem the discrepancy between an actual condition and a desired condition

Entrepreneurial Success

创业成功：杰夫·贝佐斯做高风险决策的秘诀

Jeff Bezos Reveals His Secret to Making High-Stakes Decisions

Managers are faced with making tough decisions on a daily basis, but every leader has their own style of decision making. Jeff Bezos, founder and executive chairman of Amazon, says his secret is to make a small number of high-quality decisions and to plan three years out.

Bezos believes executives shouldn't be making thousands of decisions each day. Instead, they should make fewer, better decisions. One key, he says, to making the right choices quickly is determining if a decision is a one-way door or a two-way door. One-way door decisions are irreversible and highly consequential, so you do not want to make the decision quickly. Two-way door decisions, on the other hand, can be reversed and adjusted, so employees and managers don't need to spend as much time analyzing outcomes.

Another way to speed up decision making is to escalate controversial decisions to senior managers. When teams are gridlocked, making a decision can feel like going to war. Rather than allowing junior employees to argue and become demoralized, senior leaders can make the call after hearing various points of view. Leaders can respectfully disagree and challenge decisions, but at the end of the day, Bezos says everyone needs to agree to disagree and wholly commit to the final decision.

Bezos's philosophy on making high-stakes decisions is supported in Amazon's leadership principle "bias for action," which speaks to the importance of speed in making decisions and taking action. Whether you're managing a huge company like Amazon or a small start-up, it can be nearly impossible to have enough time to consider all information when it comes to decision making. Bezos believes his decision-making style is his key to success.

Sources: Based on information in Buster Benson, "Ex-Amazon Manager: Jeff Bezos Is 'Obsessed' with This Decision-Making Style—'It's His Key to Success,'" *CNBC*, November 14, 2019; Amazon, "Leadership Principles"; Jeff Bezos, "Jeff Bezos: Here's How I Make Amazon's Highest-Stakes Decisions," *Fast Company*, November 23, 2020.

产生备选方案

5-6b Generating Alternatives

After a problem has been defined, the next task is to generate alternatives. The more important the decision, the more attention must be devoted to this stage. Managers should be open to fresh, innovative ideas as well as obvious answers.

Certain techniques can aid in the generation of creative alternatives. Brainstorming, commonly used in group discussions, encourages participants to produce many new ideas. During brainstorming, other group members are not permitted to criticize or ridicule. Another approach, developed by the U.S. Navy, is called "Blast! Then Refine." Group members tackle a recurring problem by erasing all previous solutions and procedures. The group then reevaluates its original objectives, modifies them if necessary, and devises new solutions. Other techniques—including trial and error—are also useful in this stage of decision making.

选择备选方案

5-6c Selecting an Alternative

Final decisions are influenced by a number of considerations, including financial constraints, human and informational resources, time limits, legal obstacles, and political factors. Managers must select the alternative that will be most effective and practical.

At times, two or more alternatives or some combination of alternatives will be equally appropriate. Managers may choose solutions to problems on several levels. The word *satisfice* describes solutions that are only adequate and not ideal. When lacking time or information, managers often make decisions that "satisfice." Whenever possible, managers should try to investigate alternatives carefully and select the ideal solution.

实施和评估解决方案

5-6d Implementing and Evaluating the Solution

Implementation of a decision requires time, planning, preparation of personnel, and evaluation of results. Managers usually deal with unforeseen consequences even when they have carefully considered the alternatives.

The final step in managerial decision making entails evaluating a decision's effectiveness. If the alternative that was chosen removes the difference between the actual condition and the desired condition, the decision is considered effective. If the problem still exists, managers may select one of the following choices:

- Decide to give the chosen alternative more time to work.
- Adopt a different alternative.
- Start the problem identification process all over again.

Managers should be aware that failure to evaluate decisions adequately may have negative consequences.

✓ Concept Check

- Describe the major steps in the managerial decision-making process.
- Why does a manager need to evaluate the solution and look for problems after a solution has been implemented?

Discussion Questions 讨论题

1. Define the word *manager* without using the word *management* in your definition.
2. Does a healthy firm (one that is doing well) have to worry about effective management? Explain.
3. What might be the mission of a neighborhood restaurant? Of the Salvation Army? What might be reasonable objectives for these organizations?
4. What are the major elements of SWOT analysis?
5. How do a strategic plan, a tactical plan, and an operational plan differ? What do they all have in common?
6. Should all firms have contingency plans? Why or why not?
7. Why are leadership and motivation necessary in a business in which people are paid for their work?
8. Compare and contrast the major styles of leadership.
9. According to this chapter, the leadership style that is most effective depends on interaction among the employees, characteristics of the work situation, and the manager's personality. Do you agree or disagree? Explain your answer.
10. Do you think that people are really as important to an organization as this chapter seems to indicate?
11. Discuss what happens during each of the four steps of the managerial decision-making process.

Case 5 案例5：特斯拉——从初创公司到华尔街宠儿

Tesla: From Start-Up to Wall Street Darling

Tesla is one of the most valuable car makers in the world. The company, which also makes energy generation products, has a reputation for industry-disrupting innovation, but Tesla wasn't an overnight success. Tesla was founded by engineers Martin Eberhard and Marc Tarpenning in 2003, the same year General Motors discontinued its EV1, citing a lack of demand for electric vehicles (EVs). They sold their e-book business to start Tesla and build a greener car—a high-end performance EV for wealthy car enthusiasts.

Elon Musk joined the company in 2004 with an investment of $30 million and became the chair of the board of directors. The company's plan was to focus its efforts on lithiumion batteries, which were cheaper and more powerful than the batteries used in previous EVs. They planned to create a high-margin, high-performance sports car to get away from the stigma surrounding EVs at the time and use the revenue to fund a more affordable car in the long run. Another core goal was to achieve economies of scale to bring down the cost per unit.

Tesla spent many years testing and designing components and prototypes of what would become the Roadster. The company wanted to reduce the complexity in manufacturing, but costs spiraled out of control as the company customized more and more parts. Eberhard resigned as CEO in 2007 and was replaced by Ze'ev Drori, who pushed the company forward to finalize the long-awaited Roadsters. Eberhard and Tarpenning broke all ties with Tesla around the same time Roadsters finally went into production; they later suggested they had been forced out.

The next year, Eberhard sued both Tesla and Elon Musk, alleging Eberhard's leadership had been wrongly blamed for the company's early financial and operational struggles. Eberhard said Musk unfairly took credit for the Roadster. Musk offered Eberhard a small severance package, but Tesla rescinded the package after Eberhard created a blog post discussing Tesla employees. Tesla denied Eberhard's allegations, and he eventually dropped his lawsuit.

In 2008, Musk took the reins as CEO and made several big moves to save the company, including cutting 25 percent of the workforce, selling a 10 percent stake to Daimler AG, and borrowing $465 million from the U.S. government. Though only 2,450 Roadsters were made, they demonstrated that EVs could have a longer driving range and reach high speeds, making EVs more appealing to the mass market. Tesla's 2010 initial public offering (IPO) raised $226 million, showing that investors had confidence in the EV revolution.

With one successful vehicle under its belt, Tesla decided to go after the wider market with the Model S, the world's first premium all-electric sedan, in 2012 and the Model X, the safest SUV ever tested, in 2015. Both vehicles had impressive acceleration times and driving ranges, but the high cost of lithium-ion batteries was still weighing on the company. To reduce costs, Tesla brought battery cell production in-house with the creation of Gigafactory 1 outside of Sparks, Nevada. The cost of battery cells declined through economies of scale and the reduction of waste, making the vehicles more affordable for consumers.

Next, Tesla began to focus on the energy side of its business, introducing Solar Roof solar tiles and the Powerwall home battery. The company changed its name from Tesla Motors to Tesla, Inc. in 2017, to represent the company's shift from a car manufacturer to a sustainable energy solution company. The automaker's energy solutions enable homeowners, businesses, and utilities to manage renewable energy generation, storage, and consumption.

Tesla introduced the Model 3 in 2017, which was considered to be its first car for the masses. By 2018, the Model 3 had become the number-one selling plug-in car in the world, passing the Nissan Leaf by 2,000 units. In 2019, the company achieved Musk's goal of creating a more affordable EV for the broader market when it released a base model of the Model 3 at a price point of $35,000 for a limited time. Tesla continued to target the consumer market with its first compact crossover, the Model Y, and a new kind of pickup truck, the Cybertruck, in 2019. In addition to capturing more of the consumer market, Tesla is investing in heavy-duty trucks with Tesla Semi, an electric semitrailer truck that is designed to be far less expensive per mile than traditional semi-trucks. The truck accelerates faster and drives uphill faster than a traditional semi and includes advanced safety features.

Tesla, which has fumbled when it comes to setting expectations and meeting deadlines, will need to streamline its operations to be a contender in the mass car market. Investors continue to bet on the automaker with its stock reaching record highs. In fact, Tesla became the most valuable automaker in the world based on market value. The company's mission is to accelerate the world's transition to sustainable energy. Working to cover more forms of transport greatly expands Tesla's footprint in the automotive industry and improves the carbon footprint of the transportation industry as a whole.[14]

Questions

1. What strengths have contributed to Tesla's success?
2. Tesla planned to create a high-margin, high-performance sports car and use the revenue to fund a more affordable car in the long run. Was this plan successful? Why or why not?
3. How does Tesla live up to its mission?

Chapter

6

Creating a Flexible Organization

创建柔性组织

Learning Objectives

Once you complete this chapter, you will be able to:

6-1 Define an organization.

6-2 Explain why job specialization is important.

6-3 Identify the various bases for departmentalization.

6-4 Describe how decentralization follows from delegation.

6-5 Explore how the span of management describes an organization.

6-6 Identify four forms of organizational structure.

6-7 Examine the types, development, and uses of teams.

6-8 Describe how committees and task forces are used.

6-9 Explain the functions of the informal organization and the grapevine in a business.

Why Should You Care?

To operate a successful business, those in charge must create an organization that operates efficiently and is able to attract employees.

Inside Business 商业透视：可口可乐推出重组计划

Coca-Cola Shakes It Up with a Reorganization Plan

The Coca-Cola Company, the world's largest soft drink company, announced plans to offer voluntary severance packages to about 4,000 of its most recently hired employees as it reorganizes its business segments and reorients its beverage strategy. Organizations often restructure to gain efficiencies and save money; however, reorganizations are costly upfront. Coca-Cola's severance program alone is expected to cost the company anywhere from $350 million to $550 million.

Under its previous structure, the beverage giant had 17 business units under four geographical departments, as well as Global Ventures and Bottling Investments. Now, Coca-Cola moves to nine new operating units under four geographical departments. This transition will combine regional and local execution in order to rapidly scale ideas and fuel innovation. Coca-Cola says the new structure is more streamlined and allows for interconnectivity and consistency, eliminating duplicated resources.

Coca-Cola also eliminated several brands to slim down its portfolio, including Tab, Zico, and Odwalla. The strategic structure shake-up serves to reinforce Coca-Cola's leadership in five product categories that the company believes have the strongest consumer opportunities: Coca-Cola; sparkling flavors; hydration, sports, coffee, and tea; nutrition, juice, milk, and plant; and emerging categories. Operating leaders will report to the president and chief operating officer while global category leads will report to the chief marketing officer. Coca-Cola recognizes that the market is fast-changing and expects this shift will drive future growth.[1]

Did You Know?

The Coca-Cola Company offers 500 brands in more than 200 countries and territories.

To survive and to grow, companies like Coca-Cola must constantly look for ways to improve their methods of doing business. Managers at Coca-Cola, like those at many organizations, maintain an organizational structure that best supports the achievement of company goals and the creation of innovative products that foster long-term customer relationships. When firms are organized, or reorganized, the focus is sometimes on achieving low operating costs. Other firms, such as L.L.Bean, emphasize providing high-quality products to ensure customer satisfaction. The issue of a firm's organizational structure is important because it can influence performance.

We begin this chapter by examining the business organization—what it is and how it functions in today's business environment. Next, we focus one by one on five characteristics that shape an organization's structure. We discuss job specialization within a company, the grouping of jobs into manageable units or departments, the delegation of power from management to workers, the span of management, and establishment of a chain of command. Then we step back for an overall view of organizational structure, the use and development of teams, and how committees and task forces are used. Finally, we look at the network of social interactions—the informal organization—that operates within the formal business structure.

组织
organization a group of two or more people working together to achieve a common set of goals

什么是组织

6-1 What Is an Organization?

Learning Objective

6-1 Define an organization.

We used the term *organization* throughout Chapter 5 without really defining it, mainly because its everyday meaning is close to its business meaning. Here, however, let us agree that an **organization** is a group of two or more people working together to achieve a common set of goals. A neighborhood dry cleaner owned and operated by a husband-and-wife team is an organization. IBM and Home Depot, which employ thousands of workers worldwide, are also organizations. Although each corporation's organizational structure is more complex than the dry-cleaning establishment, all must be organized to achieve their goals.

An inventor who goes into business to produce and market a new invention hires people, decides what each will do, determines who will report to whom, and so on. These activities are the essence of organizing, or structuring, the organization. An organization chart helps illustrate the shape of an organization.

An **organization chart** is a diagram that represents the positions and relationships within an organization. An example of an organization chart is shown in Figure 6-1. Each rectangle represents a particular position or person in the organization. At the top is the president, next are the vice presidents, and so on. The solid vertical lines connecting each level of the hierarchy indicate who is in the chain of command. The **chain of command** is the line of authority that extends from the highest to the lowest levels of the organization. You can see that each vice president reports directly to the president. Similarly, the plant managers, regional sales managers, and accounting department manager report to the vice presidents. An organization's chain of command can be short or long. A small local restaurant may have a very short chain of command consisting of the owner at the top and employees below. Large multinational corporations, on the other hand, may have very long chains of command. No matter what the length of the chain of command, organizations must ensure that communication along the chain is clear. Not everyone

组织结构图
organization chart a diagram that represents the positions and relationships within an organization
指挥链
chain of command the line of authority that extends from the highest to the lowest levels of an organization

Entrepreneurial Success

创业成功：Mikaila Ulmer 创立一个拯救蜜蜂的企业

Mikaila Ulmer Builds a Business to Save the Bees

Mikaila Ulmer started her business, Me & the Bees Lemonade, at just four years of age. A fear of bees quickly turned to fascination as she learned that honeybees are vital pollinators, yet they are dying at record rates. With her great-grandmother's flaxseed lemonade recipe in hand, Ulmer decided to sell honey-sweetened lemonade and donate a percentage of the profits to organizations fighting to save the honeybees. An appearance on ABC's Shark Tank landed Ulmer a $60,000 deal with investor Daymond John. Now, after ten years of business, her flaxseed lemonade company has grown into a national brand with products sold in 1,500 stores, including Whole Foods, Wegmans, and The Fresh Market.

Me & the Bees Lemonade's growth from a lemonade stand to a national brand required numerous organizational changes. In the company's early days, Ulmer hand-pressed lemonade in her kitchen and learned business basics from her dad. As her company grew, Ulmer hired individuals to handle day-to-day business tasks, such as accounting and distribution, while Ulmer attends school, manages the team, travels for speaking engagements, and focuses on the overall business strategy. She believes that finding the right people for your business and seeking out guidance is critical for success.

One day, Ulmer—who was named one of *Time* magazine's 30 most influential teens in America—would like to become an investor herself. Me & the Bees Lemonade expanded its product mix to include lip balm made with beeswax and is continuing to establish new partnerships with major grocery stores. One thing is certain: this social entrepreneur is just getting started.

Sources: Based on information in Me & the Bees, "Meet Mikaila CEO Me & the Bees Lemonade FB #shemeansbusiness," YouTube, April 19, 2018; "Me & the Bees Lemonade: Teen Entrepreneur Shares Inspiring Story," *Today,* November 30, 2020; AJ Horch, "Me & the Bees Lemonade Founder Started Her Empire at 4 Years Old. Her Motto: 'Dream Like a Kid'," *CNBC,* February 26, 2020; Addie Broyles, "Balancing Keynotes and Homework: A Day in the Life of the 15-Year-Old Me and the Bees Founder," *Austin American-Statesman,* December 13, 2019.

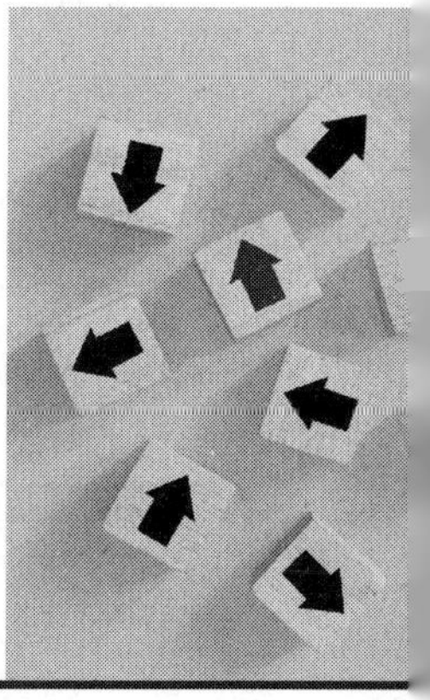

Figure 6-1 A Typical Corporate Organization Chart

A company's organization chart depicts the positions and relationships within the organization and shows the managerial chains of command.

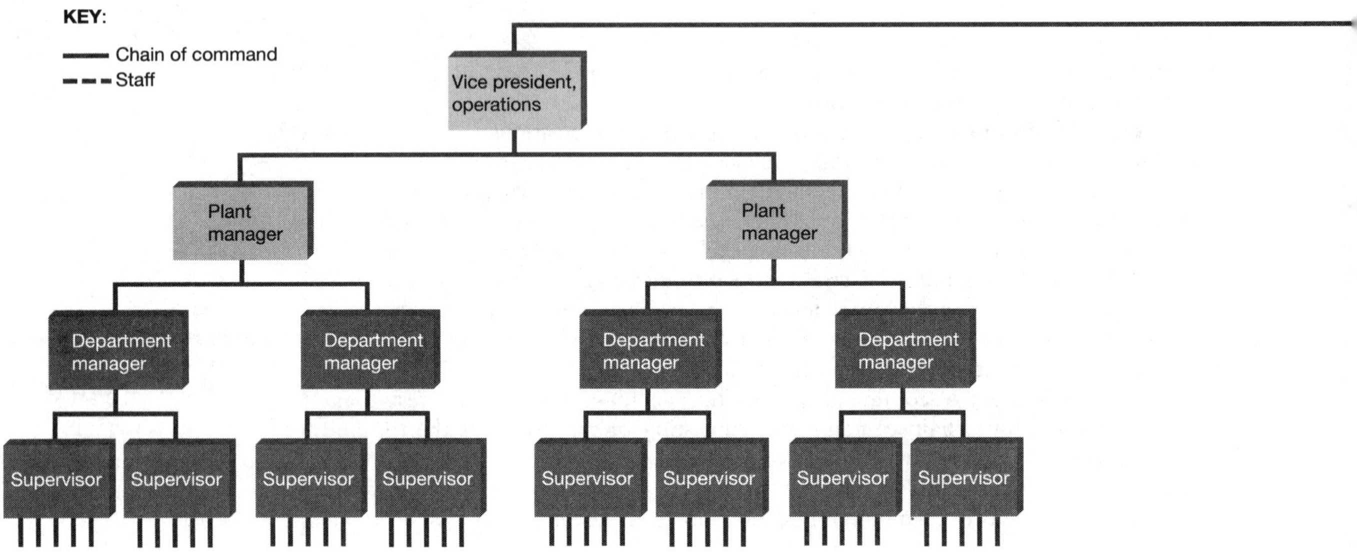

who works for an organization is part of the direct chain of command. In the chart these positions are represented by broken lines, as you can see with the directors of legal services, public affairs, and human resources. Instead, they hold *advisory*, or *staff*, positions. This difference will be examined later in the chapter when we discuss line-and-staff positions.

Most smaller organizations find organization charts useful. They clarify positions and relationships for everyone in the organization, and they help managers to track growth and change in the organizational structure. However, many large organizations, such as ExxonMobil, Kellogg's, and Procter & Gamble (P&G), do not maintain complete, detailed charts. There are two reasons for this. First, it is difficult to chart even a few dozen positions accurately, much less the thousands that characterize larger firms. Second, larger organizations are almost always changing parts of their structure. An organization chart would be outdated before it was completed. Increasingly, technology can help even large and complicated organizations implement up-to-date organization charts.

When a firm is founded, management must decide how to organize the firm. These decisions focus on job design, departmentalization, delegation, span of management, and chain of command. In the next several sections, we discuss major issues associated with these dimensions.

✓ Concept Check

- How do large and small organizations use organization charts differently?
- Identify the major considerations when organizing a business.

岗位设计
job design structuring the tasks and activities required to accomplish a firm's objectives into specific jobs so as to foster productivity and employee satisfaction

Learning Objective

6-2 Explain why job specialization is important.

岗位设计

6-2 Job Design

The next set of decisions in creating a flexible organization is **job design**, which involves structuring the tasks and activities required to accomplish a firm's objectives into specific jobs so as to foster productivity and employee satisfaction. Job specialization is an often-used approach.

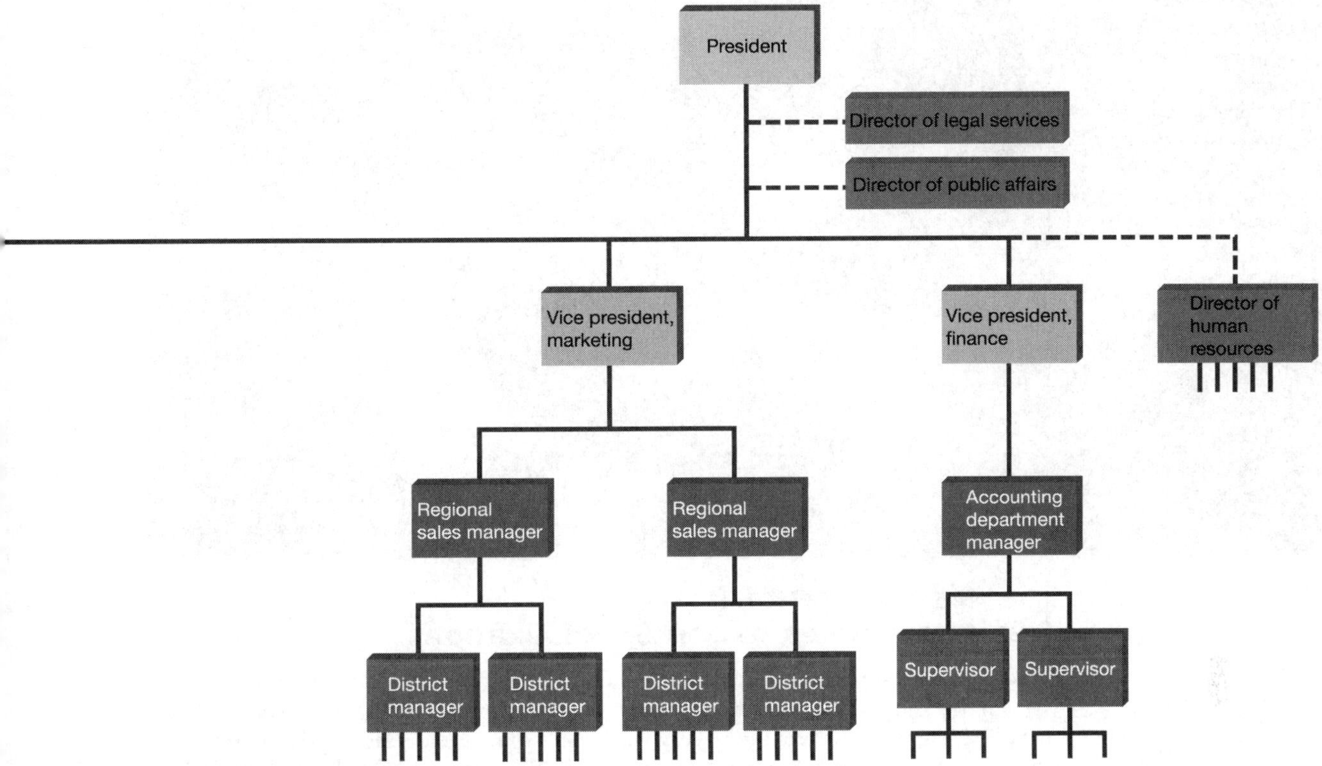

岗位专业化
6-2a Job Specialization

We define *specialization* as the separation of a manufacturing process into distinct tasks and the assignment of different tasks to different people. Here we are extending that concept to *all* the activities performed within an organization. Thus, **job specialization** is the separation of all organizational activities into distinct tasks and the assignment of different tasks to different people. Adam Smith, the 18th-century economist whose theories gave rise to capitalism, was the first to emphasize the power of specialization in his book, *The Wealth of Nations.* According to Smith, the various tasks in a particular pin factory were arranged so that one worker drew the wire for the pins, another straightened the wire, a third cut it, a fourth ground the point, and a fifth attached the head. Smith claimed that 10 men were able to produce 48,000 pins per day. Before specialization, they could produce only 200 pins per day because each worker had to perform all five tasks!

For a number of reasons, some job specialization is necessary in every organization because the "job" of most organizations is too large for one person to handle. In a firm such as Ford Motor Company, thousands of people are needed to manufacture automobiles. Others are needed to sell the cars, control the firm's finances, and so on. Second, when a worker has to learn one specific, highly specialized task, that individual can learn it quickly and perform it efficiently. Third, a worker repeating the same job does not lose time changing operations, as the pin workers did when producing complete pins. Fourth, the more specialized the job, the easier it is to design specialized equipment. And finally, the more specialized the job, the easier the job training.

Unfortunately, specialization can have negative consequences. The most significant drawback is the boredom and dissatisfaction employees may feel when repeating the same job. Bored employees may be absent from work frequently, not put much effort into their work, and even sabotage the company's efforts to produce quality products.

岗位专业化
job specialization the separation of all organizational activities into distinct tasks and the assignment of different tasks to different people

Specialization has its drawbacks. This employee has a specialized job that includes stitching a component of shoes. Specialization is efficient for the firm, but it can leave employees bored and dissatisfied. What do you think a firm can do to offset these problems?

岗位专业化的替代方案
6-2b Alternatives to Job Specialization

To combat these problems, managers often turn to job rotation. **Job rotation** is the systematic shifting of employees from one job to another. For example, a worker may be assigned a different job every week for a four-week period and then return to the first job in the fifth week. Job rotation provides a variety of tasks so that workers are less likely to become bored and dissatisfied. Intel, for instance, encourages job rotation as a means of sharing ideas, perspectives, and best practices across the company. Job rotation helps workers stay interested in their jobs, develop new skills, and identify new roles where they may want to focus their energies in the future.

Two other approaches to job design—job enlargement and job enrichment—also can provide solutions to the problems caused by job specialization. These topics, along with other methods used to motivate employees, are discussed in Chapter 9.

✓ Concept Check

- What are the positive and negative effects of specialization?
- What are three ways to reduce the negative effects of specialization?

部门化
6-3 Departmentalization

Learning Objective

6-3 Identify the various bases for departmentalization.

After jobs are designed, they must be grouped together into "working units," or departments. This process is called **departmentalization**, which is the process of grouping jobs into manageable units. Today, the most common bases for organizing a business into effective departments are by function, by product, by location, and by customer.

按职能部门化
6-3a By Function

Departmentalization by function groups jobs that relate to the same organizational activity. Under this scheme, all marketing personnel are grouped together in the marketing department, all production personnel in the production department, and so on.

Most smaller and newer organizations departmentalize by function. Supervision is simplified because everyone is involved in the same activities and coordination is easy. The disadvantages of this method of grouping jobs are that it can lead to slow decision making and it tends to emphasize the department over the organization as a whole.

岗位轮换
job rotation the systematic shifting of employees from one job to another

部门化
departmentalization the process of grouping jobs into manageable units

按职能部门化
departmentalization by function grouping jobs that relate to the same organizational activity

按产品部门化

6-3b By Product

Departmentalization by product groups activities related to a particular good or service. P&G, for instance, has divisions for product sectors: baby and feminine care, beauty, fabric and home care, grooming, healthcare and family care, and P&G ventures.[2] This approach is used often by older and larger firms that produce and sell a variety of products. Each department handles its own marketing, production, financial management, and human resources activities.

Departmentalization by product makes decision making easier and provides for the integration of all activities associated with each product. However, it causes some duplication of specialized activities—such as finance—between departments. Moreover, the emphasis is placed on the product rather than on the whole organization.

How is this firm organized? These call center employees are organized by their function. Some organizations are structured in other ways. For example, if your university has more than one campus, they are organized by location but also by function such as by their business, social sciences, and math departments. Your school also might be organized by customer such as by undergraduate, graduate, and continuing education students.

按区域部门化

6-3c By Location

Departmentalization by location groups activities according to the defined geographic area in which they are performed. Departmental areas may range from whole countries (for international firms) to regions within countries (for national firms) to areas of several city blocks (for police departments organized into precincts). For example, Ford has divisions for the Americas, Europe, Asia Pacific and Africa, and China. Departmentalization by location allows the organization to respond readily to the unique demands or requirements of different locations. Nevertheless, a large administrative staff and an elaborate control system may be needed to coordinate operations across many locations.

按顾客部门化

6-3d By Customer

Departmentalization by customer groups activities according to the needs of various customer populations. The advantage of this approach is that it allows the firm to deal efficiently with unique customers or customer groups. For example, an aircraft maker might have a department for government customers and one for corporate customers because their needs are different. The biggest drawback is that a larger-than-usual administrative staff is needed.

部门化的多种组合

6-3e Combinations of Bases

Many organizations use a combination of departmentalization bases. Toyota, for instance, is reorganizing by product and location. It has product divisions such as R&D and Engineering, Compact Car Company, Mid-size Vehicle Company, CV Company, Lexus International Company, Power Train Company, and Connected Company, as well as divisions based on location.[3]

Take a moment to examine Figure 6-2. Notice that departmentalization by customer is used to organize New-Wave Fashions, Inc., into three major divisions: Men's, Women's, and Children's clothing. Then functional departmentalization is used to distinguish the firm's production and marketing activities. Finally, location is used to organize the firm's marketing efforts.

按产品部门化
departmentalization by product grouping activities related to a particular product or service

按区域部门化
departmentalization by location grouping activities according to the defined geographic area in which they are performed

按客户部门化
departmentalization by customer grouping activities according to the needs of various customer populations

Technology and Innovation

技术与创新：苹果公司的组织结构如何支持创新

How Apple's Organizational Structure Supports Innovation

Apple's fast-paced, non-stop innovation has greatly contributed to the company's success. This has been enabled by Apple's functional organizational model. When former CEO Steve Jobs returned to the company in 1996, Apple's conventional structure was divided into business units, and each division was run by general managers. However, the decentralized structure often led to conflict among managers and hindered innovation. In a single day, Jobs laid off all the general managers.

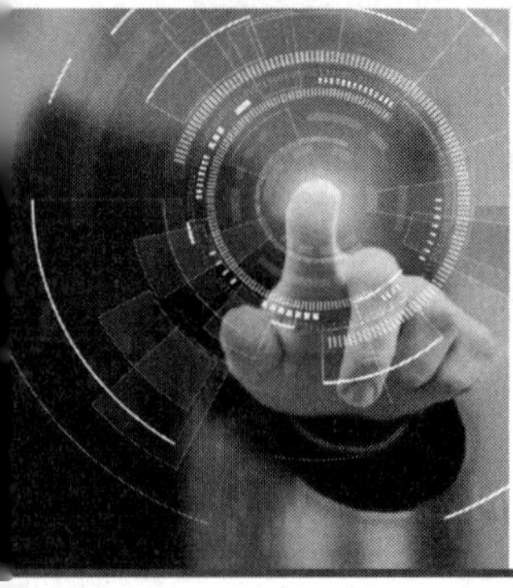

The new structure at Apple combined the functional departments of the business units into one functional organization to align expertise with decision rights. This structure still exists at Apple today even though the company is far more complex than it was in the late 1990s. Aside from Apple's current CEO Tim Cook, the tech giant operates without conventional general managers. Many business experts believe that when firms grow from small start-up to large and complex businesses, they must move from a functional to a multidivisional structure to prevent congestion when it comes to decision making. Apple, however, requires a structure that centers around functional expertise due to its rapid product development and high rates of disruption in the markets in which it competes.

From Apple's point of view, allowing technical experts to make important decisions rather than general managers increases the quality of those decisions and decreases the chances that cost targets will take over the decision-making process. When it comes to introducing a new product or a new feature, Apple is able to strike a balance between cost and the value added to the user experience by aligning expertise with decision rights.

Sources: Based on information in Joel M. Podolny and Morten T. Hansen, "How Apple Is Organized for Innovation," *Harvard Business Review,* November–December 2020; Jonny Evans, "The Apple University Guide to Effective Business Management," *Computer World,* October 23, 2020.

Figure 6-2 Multibase Departmentalization for New-Wave Fashions, Inc.

Most firms use more than one basis for departmentalization to improve efficiency and to avoid overlapping positions.

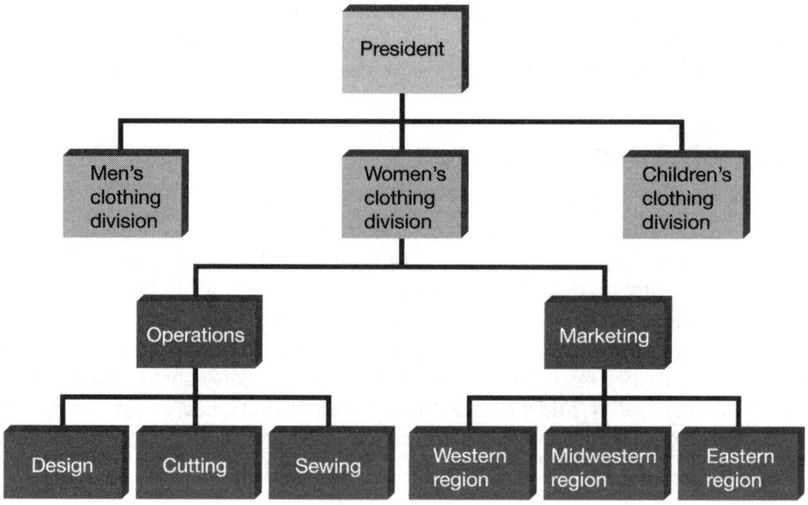

✓ Concept Check

- What are the four most common bases for departmentalization?
- Give an example of each.

授权、分权和集权

6-4 Delegation, Decentralization, and Centralization

Learning Objective

6-4 Describe how decentralization follows from delegation.

The third major step in the organizing process is to distribute power in the organization. **Delegation** assigns work and power to other workers. The degree of centralization or decentralization of authority is determined by the overall pattern of delegation within the organization.

授权

6-4a Delegation of Authority

Because no manager can do everything, delegation is vital to completion of a manager's work. Delegation is also important in developing the skills and abilities of subordinates. It allows those who are being groomed for higher-level positions to play increasingly important roles in decision making.

Steps in Delegation The delegation process generally involves three steps (refer to Figure 6-3). First, the manager must *assign responsibility*. **Responsibility** is the duty to do a job or perform a task. In most job settings, a manager simply gives the worker a job to do. Typical job assignments might range from preparing a report on the status of a new quality control program to being put in charge of a task force. Second, the manager must *grant authority*. **Authority** is the power, within the organization, to accomplish an assigned job or task. This might include the power to obtain specific information, order supplies, authorize relevant expenditures, or make certain decisions. Finally, the manager must *create accountability*. **Accountability** is the obligation of a worker to accomplish an assigned job or task.

Note that accountability is created but it cannot be delegated. Suppose that you are an operations manager for Target and are responsible for performing a specific task. You, in turn, delegate this task to someone else. You nonetheless remain accountable to your immediate supervisor for getting the task done properly. If the other person fails to complete the assignment, you—not the person to whom you delegated the task—will be held accountable.

Barriers to Delegation For several reasons, managers may be unwilling to delegate work. This may be because the manager does not trust the employee to complete the task, or because the manager fears the employee will perform exceptionally and attract the notice of higher-level managers. Finally, some managers do not delegate because they are disorganized and they are not able to plan and assign work effectively.

Figure 6-3 Steps in the Delegation Process

To be successful, a manager must learn how to delegate. No one can do everything alone.

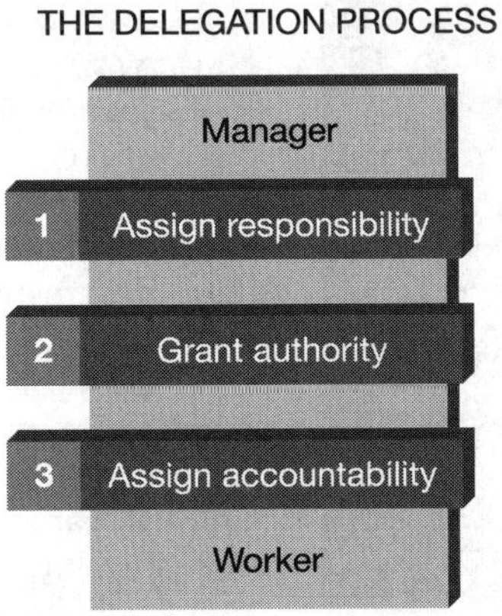

授权
delegation assigning part of a manager's work and power to other workers

责任
responsibility the duty to do a job or perform a task

权力
authority the power, within an organization, to accomplish an assigned job or task

问责制
accountability the obligation of a worker to accomplish an assigned job or task

Ethics and Social Responsibility

商业伦理与社会责任：高层管理人员迫于压力将变通规则

Top Managers Feel Pressure to Bend the Rules

Occasionally, employees may feel pressure to compromise on their organization's ethics standards, which can contribute to a decline in the company's overall reputation and performance. According to the Ethics & Compliance Initiative's Global Business Ethics Survey, top managers are twice as likely to experience this type of pressure.

Pressure to bend the rules can be caused by factors such as meeting performance goals, trying to save one's job, or attempting to advance one's career or financial interests.

The survey shows that employees higher up in the organizational chart are most at risk for feeling pressure to bend the rules in the workplace. The survey also revealed that when top management shows a strong commitment to both ethical leadership and organizational values, the employees they oversee are three times less likely to experience pressure. Leaders need to understand the importance of their role in managing employees and should be trained on the skills necessary to demonstrate support for organizational ethics and values to subordinates.

Understanding risk factors can help organizations be proactive in addressing potential conflicts before they arise. To reduce workplace pressures, firms can commit to ethical leadership and shared values while building an ethics-focused organizational culture. Building a strong ethics and compliance program that holds employees accountable for their mistakes can be critical in maintaining strong ethics health.

Sources: Based on information in "Global Business Ethics Survey: Top Managers Twice as Likely to Experience Pressure to Bend the Rules in Organizations," *Yahoo Finance,* August 31, 2020; Ethics and Compliance Initiative, "Global Business Ethics Survey: Pressure in the Workplace," 2020; Jaclyn Jaeger, "Survey: Weak Leadership Contributes to Employee Pressure to Bend Rules," *Compliance Week,* August 21, 2020.

分权组织
decentralized organization an organization in which management consciously attempts to spread authority widely across various organization levels

分权

6-4b Decentralization of Authority

The pattern of delegation throughout an organization determines the extent to which that organization is decentralized or centralized. In a **decentralized organization**, management consciously attempts to spread authority widely across various organization levels. A **centralized organization**, on the other hand, systematically works to concentrate authority at the upper levels. For example, shipping companies like UPS tend to be centralized, with shipping dispatches coordinated by upper management. Large organizations may have characteristics of both decentralized and centralized organizations. Berkshire Hathaway is a highly decentralized conglomerate corporation that owns more than 80 companies. Though the CEOs of each subsidiary company report directly to Berkshire Hathaway's CEO Warren Buffett, they are trusted, given nearly complete autonomy, and encouraged to plan for the long term as long as they do so in accordance with Berkshire Hathaway's ethical code. Such strict decentralization is unusual, particularly in such a huge parent company, but it helped Warren Buffett, the founder, build a $500 billion company.[4]

Delegate, delegate, delegate. The industrialist Andrew Carnegie once said, "No person will make a great business who wants to do it all himself or get all the credit." Delegating gives employees different tasks to do, which can enrich and enlarge their jobs. It also enables both employees and their superiors to learn new skills required for higher-level positions.

A number of factors can influence the extent to which a firm is decentralized. One is the external environment in which the firm operates. The more complex and unpredictable this environment, the more likely it is that top management will let lower-level managers make important decisions because lower-level managers are closer to the issues and the customers. Another factor is the nature of the decision itself. The riskier or more important the decisions that have to be made, the greater is the tendency to centralize decision making. A third factor is the abilities of lower-level managers. If these managers do not have strong decision-making skills, top managers will be reluctant to decentralize. Finally, a firm that has practiced centralization or decentralization is likely to maintain that same posture in the future.

In principle, neither decentralization nor centralization is right. What works for one organization may or may not work for another. Every organization must assess its own situation and choose the level of centralization or decentralization that will work best.

✓ Concept Check

- Identify and describe the three steps in the delegation process.
- Differentiate decentralized organization and centralized organization.

管理范围

6-5 The Span of Management

Learning Objective

6-5 Explore how the span of management describes an organization.

The fourth major step in organizing a business is establishing the **span of management** **(or span of control)**, which is the number of workers who report directly to one manager. Hundreds of years of research has shown that there is no perfect ratio of subordinates to managers. More recently, theorists have focused on the width of the span of management. This issue is complicated because the span of management may change by department within the same organization. A highly mechanized factory where all operations are standardized may allow for a wide span of management. An advertising agency, where new problems and opportunities arise every day and where teamwork is a constant necessity, will have a much narrower span of management.

管理范围的大小

6-5a Wide and Narrow Spans of Management

A *wide* span of management exists when a manager has a larger number of subordinates. A *narrow* span exists when the manager has only a few subordinates. Several factors determine the span that is best for a particular manager (refer to Figure 6-4). Generally, the span of management may be wide

Figure 6-4 The Span of Management

Several criteria determine whether a firm uses a wide span of management, in which a number of workers report to one manager, or a narrow span, in which a manager supervises only a few workers.

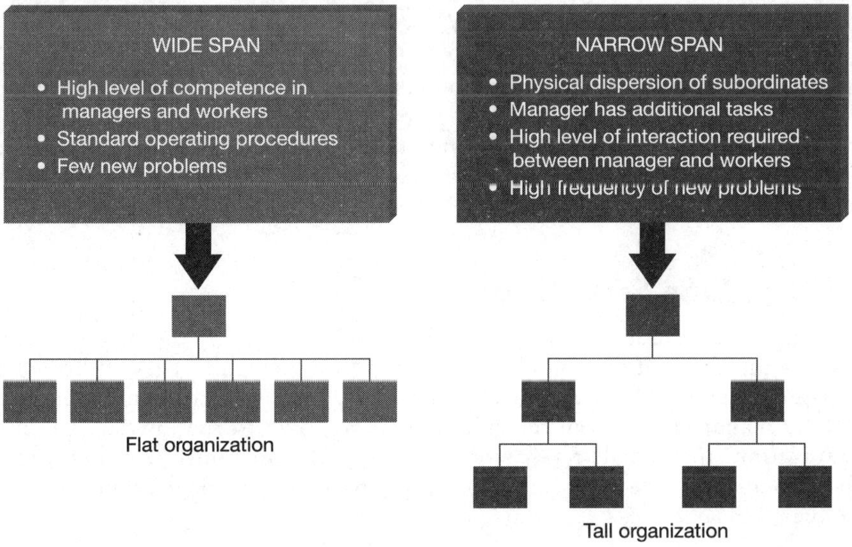

集权组织
centralized organization an organization that systematically works to concentrate authority at the upper levels of the organization

管理范围（或控制范围）
span of management (or span of control) the number of workers who report directly to one manager

Narrow versus wide spans of management: Which is better? The manager in the middle of the photo supervises only a handful of employees. Consequently, she has a narrow span of management. Companies are constantly searching for the ideal number of employees their supervisors should manage.

when (1) the manager and the subordinates are very competent, (2) the organization has a well-established set of standard operating procedures, and (3) few new problems are expected to arise. The span should be narrow when (1) workers are physically located far from one another, (2) the manager has much work to do in addition to supervising workers, (3) a great deal of interaction is required between supervisor and workers, and (4) new problems arise frequently.

组织高度

6-5b Organizational Height

The span of management has an obvious impact on relations between managers and workers. It has a more subtle, but equally important, impact on the height of the organization. **Organizational height** is the number of layers, or levels, of management in a firm. The span of management plays a direct role in determining the height of the organization (refer to Figure 6-4). If the span of management is wide, fewer levels are needed, and the organization is *flat*. If the span of management is narrow, more levels are needed, and the resulting organization is *tall*.

In a tall organization, administrative costs are higher because more managers are needed. Communication may become distorted because information has to pass up and down through more levels. When companies are cutting costs, one option is to decrease organizational height in order to reduce related administrative expenses. For example, Infosys, an India-based information technology firm, flattened its five-tiered structure into two layers in order to speed up decision making, achieve greater flexibility, eliminate redundancies among management positions, and reduce costs.[5] Although flat organizations avoid these problems, their managers may perform more administrative duties simply because there are fewer managers. Wide spans of management also may require managers to spend considerably more time supervising and working with subordinates.

✓ Concept Check

- Describe the two spans of management.
- What are problems associated with each one?

组织结构的形式

6-6 Forms of Organizational Structure

Learning Objective

6-6 Identify four forms of organizational structure.

Up to this point, we have focused our attention on the major characteristics of organizational structure. In many ways, this is like discussing the parts of a jigsaw puzzle one by one. It is now time to put the puzzle together. We will next discuss four basic forms of organizational structure: line, line-and-staff, matrix, and virtual.

直线结构

6-6a The Line Structure

The simplest and oldest form of organizational structure is the **line structure**, in which the chain of command goes directly from person to person throughout the organization. Thus, a straight line could be drawn down through the levels of management, from the chief executive down to the lowest level in the organization. In a small retail store, for example, an hourly employee might report to an assistant manager, who reports to a store manager, who reports to the owner.

组织高度
organizational height the number of layers, or levels, of management in a firm

直线结构
line structure an organizational structure in which the chain of command goes directly from person to person throughout the organization

Managers within a line structure, called **line managers**, make decisions and give orders to subordinates to achieve the organization's goals. A line structure's simplicity and clear chain of command allow line managers to make decisions quickly with direct accountability because the decision maker only has one supervisor to report to.

The downside of a line structure is that line managers are responsible for many activities, and therefore must have a wide range of knowledge about all of them. While this may not be a problem for small organizations with a lower volume of activities, in a larger organization, activities are more numerous and complex, thus making it more difficult for line managers to fully understand what they oversee. Therefore, line managers in a larger organization would have a hard time making an educated decision without expert advice from outside sources. As a result, line structures are not very effective in medium- or large-sized organizations, but are very popular in small organizations.

直线与职能结构

6-6b The Line-and-Staff Structure

A **line-and-staff structure** not only utilizes the chain of command from a line structure but also provides line managers with specialists, called staff managers. Therefore, this structure works much better for medium- and large-sized organizations than line management alone. **Staff managers** provide support, advice, and expertise to line managers, thus eliminating the major drawback of line structures. Staff managers are not part of the chain of command like line managers are, but they do have authority over their assistants (refer to Figure 6-5).

Both line and staff managers are needed for effective management, but the two positions differ in important ways. Most importantly, line managers have *line authority*, which means that they can make decisions and issue directives relating to the organization's goals. Staff managers seldom have this kind of authority. Instead, they usually have either advisory authority or functional authority. *Advisory authority* is the expectation that line managers will consult the appropriate staff manager when making decisions. *Functional authority* is a

Figure 6-5 Line and Staff Managers

A line manager has direct responsibility for achieving the company's goals and is in the direct chain of command. A staff manager supports and advises the line managers.

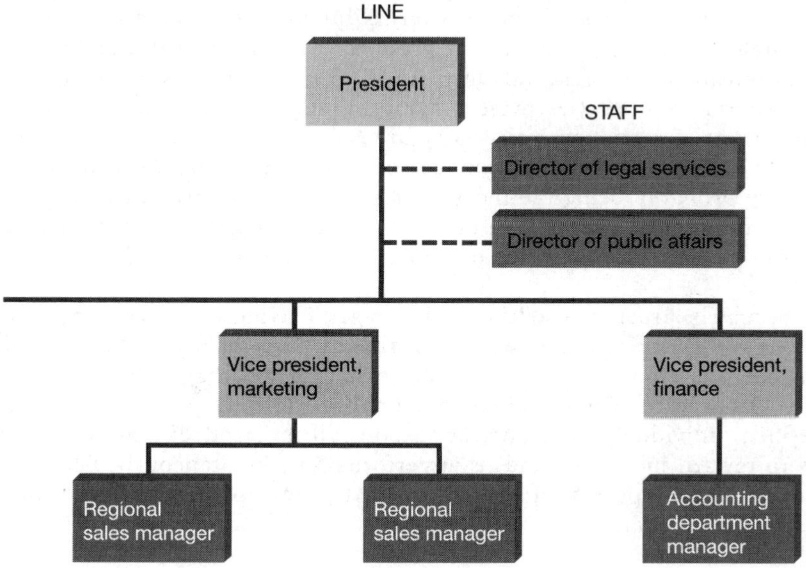

部门经理
line managers managers who make decisions and give orders to subordinates to achieve the organization's goals

直线与职能结构
line-and-staff structure an organizational structure that utilizes the chain of command from a line structure in combination with the assistance of staff managers

职能管理者
staff managers managers who provide support, advice, and expertise to line managers

Line-and-staff organization structure. Ronald McDonald occupies a staff position and does not have direct authority over other employees at McDonald's. Holger Beeck, the CEO of McDonald's Germany, does have direct authority over other McDonald's employees and thus occupies a line position.

stronger form. It is the authority of staff managers to make decisions and issue directives about their areas of expertise. For example, a legal adviser for Nike can decide whether to retain a particular clause in a contract but cannot decide product pricing.

Staff managers in a line-and-staff structure tend to have more access to information than line managers. This means that line managers must rely on the staff managers for information. This is usually not an issue, unless staff managers make a wrong decision and there is no one else to catch their mistake.[6] For a variety of reasons, conflict between line managers and staff managers is fairly common in business. Staff managers often have more formal education and sometimes are younger (and perhaps more ambitious) than line managers. Line managers may perceive staff managers as a threat to their own authority and thus may resent them. For their part, staff managers may become annoyed or angry if their expert recommendations are not adopted by line management.

Fortunately, there are several ways to minimize the likelihood of such conflict. One way is to integrate line and staff managers into one team. Another is to ensure that the areas of responsibility of line and staff managers are clearly defined. Finally, line and staff managers both can be held accountable for the results of their activities.

矩阵结构

6-6c The Matrix Structure

The **matrix structure** combines vertical and horizontal lines of authority, forming a matrix shape in the organizational chart. The matrix structure occurs when product departmentalization is superimposed on a functionally departmentalized organization. In a matrix organization, authority flows both down and across, and individuals report to more than one superior at the same time.

To understand the structure of a matrix organization, consider the usual functional arrangement, with people working in departments such as engineering, finance, and marketing. Now suppose that we assign people from these departments to a special group that is working on a new project as a team—a cross-functional team. A **cross-functional team** consists of individuals with varying specialties, expertise, and skills who are brought together to achieve a common task. Frequently, cross-functional teams are charged with the responsibility of developing new products. The manager in charge of a team is usually called a *project manager.* Any individual who is working with the team reports to *both* the project manager and the individual's superior in the functional department (refer to Figure 6-6).

Matrix structures offer advantages over other organizational forms, added flexibility probably being the most obvious one. The matrix structure can also increase productivity, raise morale, and nurture creativity and innovation. In addition, employees experience personal development through doing a variety of jobs.

The matrix structure also has disadvantages. Having employees report to more than one supervisor can cause confusion about who is in charge. Like committees, teams may take longer to resolve problems and issues than individuals working alone. Other difficulties include personality clashes, poor communication, undefined individual roles, unclear responsibilities, and difficulties in finding ways to reward individual and team performance simultaneously. Because more managers and support staff may be needed, a matrix structure may be more expensive to maintain.

矩阵结构
matrix structure an organizational structure that combines vertical and horizontal lines of authority, usually by superimposing product departmentalization on a functionally departmentalized organization

跨职能团队
cross-functional team a team of individuals with varying specialties, expertise, and skills who are brought together to achieve a common task

Figure 6-6 A Matrix Structure

A matrix is usually the result of combining product departmentalization with function departmentalization. It is a complex structure in which employees have more than one supervisor.

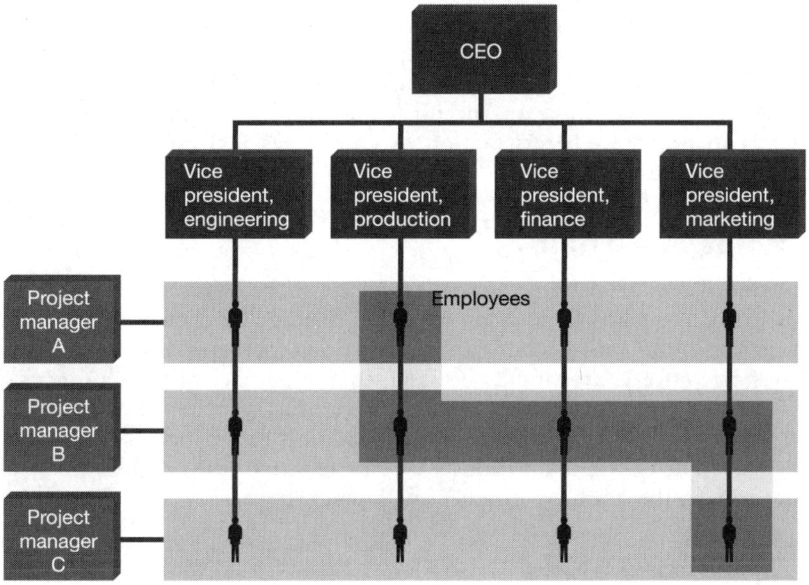

Source: Ricky W. Griffin, *Fundamentals of Management*, 9th ed. Copyright © 2019, p. 157 by Cengage, Boston, MA. Adapted with permission.

虚拟结构

6-6d The Virtual Structure

In a **virtual structure** (sometimes called a *network organization*), administration is the primary function performed, and other functions such as engineering, production, marketing, and finance are contracted out to other organizations. Such structures may be temporary, such as a group of individuals and companies collaborating to develop and distribute a feature film. Organizational members often operate in different locations, and they communicate and share work via video and software tools. Frequently, a virtual organization does not manufacture the products it sells. This type of organization has a few permanent employees consisting of top management and hourly clerical workers. Leased facilities and equipment, as well as temporary workers, are increased or decreased as the organization's needs change. Thus, there is limited formal structure associated with a virtual organization.

An obvious strength of a virtual structure is flexibility that allows the organization to adjust quickly to changes. Virtual structures consist of a lot of teams working together, rather than relying on one centralized leader. One noteworthy benefit is that firms with a virtual structure are more likely to survive the loss of an important member. Some of the challenges faced by managers in network-structured organizations include controlling the quality of work performed by other organizations, low morale and high turnover among hourly workers, and a lack of a clear hierarchy.

虚拟结构
virtual structure an organizational structure in which administration is the primary function, and most other functions are contracted out to other firms

✓ Concept Check

- Describe four forms of organizational structure.
- Give an example of each form.

团队和团队合作
6-7 Teams and Teamwork

Learning Objective

6-7 Examine the types, development, and uses of teams.

The concepts of teams and teamwork may be most commonly associated with sports, but they are also integral parts of business organizations. The use of teams is popular because it encourages employees to participate more fully in business decisions. The growing number of companies organizing their workforces into teams reflects an effort to increase employee productivity and creativity because team members are working on specific goals and are given greater autonomy. This leads to greater job satisfaction as employees feel more involved in the management process.[7]

什么是团队
6-7a What Is a Team?

In a business organization, a **team** is two or more workers collaborating to achieve a shared mission, goal, or work product. In particular, team members share responsibility and accountability, and their performance is measured by their collective effort. A team may be assigned any number of tasks or goals, from development of a new product to selling that product. A team can also be created to identify or solve a problem that an organization is experiencing. Teamwork may seem like a simple concept, but teams are a microcosm of the organization, and any complications in the work environment will affect the team.

团队类型
6-7b Types of Teams

Businesses may have several types of teams to achieve different purposes, including problem-solving teams, self-managed teams, cross-functional teams, and virtual teams. Regardless of type, all team members must collaborate to bring their respective skills, knowledge, and resources to fulfill the team's shared purpose.

Problem-Solving Teams The most common type of team in business organizations is the **problem-solving team**. It is generally used temporarily to bring knowledgeable employees together to tackle a specific problem. Once the problem is solved, the team typically is disbanded.

Self-Managed Work Teams **Self-managed teams** are groups of employees with the authority and skills to manage themselves. Experts suggest that workers on self-managed teams are more motivated and satisfied because they have greater task variety and job control. On many work teams, members are cross trained to perform everyone else's jobs and rotate through all the jobs for which the team is responsible. In a traditional business structure, management is responsible for hiring and firing employees, establishing budgets, purchasing supplies, conducting performance reviews, and taking corrective action. When self-managed teams are in place, they take over some or all of these management functions. The major advantages and disadvantages of self-managed teams are detailed in Figure 6-7.

Figure 6-7 Advantages and Disadvantages of Self-Managed Teams

While self-managed teams provide advantages, managers must recognize their disadvantages.

ADVANTAGES	DISADVANTAGES
• Boosts employee morale	• Additional training costs
• Increases productivity	• Teams may be disorganized
• Aids innovation	• Conflicts may arise
• Reduces employee boredom	• Leadership role may be unclear

团队
team two or more workers collaborating to achieve a shared mission, goal, or work product

问题解决团队
problem-solving team a team of knowledgeable employees brought together to tackle a specific problem

自我管理团队
self-managed teams groups of employees with the authority and skills to manage themselves

Cross-Functional Teams Earlier, we discussed how matrix structures often rely on cross-functional teams of individuals with varying specialties, expertise, and skills that are brought together to achieve a common task. For example, a purchasing agent might create a cross-functional team to gain insight into useful purchases for the company. Ideally, a cross-functional team consists of a group of people with complementary skill sets and perspectives to enable the group to solve problems effectively and efficiently. Cross-functional team projects may be temporary, in which case the team is disbanded once the mission is accomplished, or they may be permanent.

These teams often are empowered to make major decisions. When a cross-functional team is employed, prospective team members may receive special training because effective teamwork can require different skills. For cross-functional teams to be successful, team members must be given specific information on the job each performs. The team must also develop a sense of cohesiveness and maintain good communications among its members.

Although cross-functional teams are not necessarily self-managed, most self-managed teams are cross-functional. Cross-functional teams can also be cross-divisional. The internet and digital tools have helped strengthen the communication abilities of cross-functional teams. Increasingly, the ability to work in cross-functional teams is an important skill as the world becomes more interconnected and businesses must adapt quickly to change. Major corporations such as Google, Whirlpool, and Procter & Gamble all utilize the diverse viewpoints that come out of cross-functional teams.

Virtual Teams Teams no longer have to be geographically close, thanks to sophisticated communications technology. A **virtual team** consists of members who are geographically dispersed but communicate electronically. In fact, team members may never meet in person but rely solely on email, video conferences, voice mail, and other technological interactions. Increasingly, virtual teams rely on group collaboration services such as Slack and Teams that serve as virtual offices where employees can gather to chat and share files and information. They are also likely to use video meeting services such as Skype, Webex, or GoToMeeting to have real-time direct visual interactions. In the global business environment, virtual, or remote, teams connect employees located anywhere in the world on a common task. Indeed, some virtual team members may be outside the firm, such as contract employees, freelancers, consultants, or employees from other organizations that are involved in the team's project. However, distance, time differences, and the lack of spontaneous face time can make working on virtual teams challenging. Clear communication is essential, especially among team members who have never met in person. Email, text, and chat communications, for example, can be misinterpreted. Team members need to be respectful of cultural and language differences in order to focus on the process and results.

Using technology to close time and space and get more done. Skype, email, and group chat software are allowing employees continents away from one another to work together effectively. Being able to hire the best employees from all around the globe to work virtually with one another can give a firm a competitive advantage. Virtual teams located in different time zones and on different continents can also enable a company to work on important projects 24/7.

开发和利用有效的团队

6-7c Developing and Using Effective Teams

It takes time for team members to establish individual roles, relationships, and duties in order to become an effective team. As a team matures, it passes through five stages of development, as shown in Figure 6-8.

虚拟团队

virtual team a team consisting of members who are geographically dispersed but communicate electronically

Exploring Careers

职 业 探 索 ：为虚拟职业做准备

Preparing for a Virtual Career

Thanks to advancements in technology, people can work from almost anywhere. The work-from-home trend was greatly accelerated by the COVID-19 pandemic, and it's likely to continue in the long term. As companies rely more and more on virtual teams, it's critical to prepare for the future of remote work by addressing key challenges: communication, isolation, and a lack of social opportunities.

One of the top challenges of remote work is clear communication. Relying solely on e-mail, webchat, and video conferences reduces opportunities for reading body language and asking follow up questions, which can result in things getting lost in translation. To counteract this, more frequent, higher quality, proactive communication is in order along with comprehensive documentation of virtual team discussions and tasks assigned to each individual.

To combat isolation, employees can more intentionally engage in video chat. Opting for voice-only contact allows for distraction. It can be tempting to multitask when the camera is disabled, checking smartphone notifications or perusing emails. Video conference is a good substitution for traditional face-to-face meetings and allows for better engagement than emails and phone calls alone. As Microsoft CEO Satya Nadella says, "Digital technology should not be a substitute for human connection." The social element of a traditional office job is difficult to replicate online. Carve out time in team meetings to socialize or schedule dedicated meetings to connect with teammates.

Remote work is on the rise, and it's here to stay. While working virtually offers many benefits, there are also challenges that must be addressed. Preparing properly for the remote work environment can increase productivity, improve communication, and contribute to overall happiness.

Sources: Based on information in John Seabrook, "Has the Pandemic Transformed the Office Forever?" *The New Yorker,* January 25, 2021; Jolene Risch, "5 Keys to Having a Remote Staff That's Engaged," *Entrepreneur,* January 25, 2021; Marie Prokopets, "10 Practices That Will Ensure You Succeed at Remote Work," *We Work Remotely,* August 13, 2019.

Forming In the *forming* stage, team members are introduced to one another and begin to develop a social dynamic. The members of the team are unsure about how to relate to one another, what behaviors are acceptable, and what the ground rules are for the team. Through group member interaction over time, team members become more comfortable and a group dynamic emerges.

Storming During the *storming* stage, the interaction may be volatile, and the team may lack unity. This is the stage at which goals and objectives begin to develop. Team members will brainstorm to develop ideas and plans and establish a broad-ranging agenda. It is important for team members to grow comfortable with each other so that they can contribute openly. It is unlikely that a team leader has materialized by this stage, although an informal leader may emerge. The success or failure of the ideas in the storming stage determines how long the team will take to reach the next stage.

Norming After storming and the first burst of activity, the team begins to stabilize during the *norming* stage. Each person's role within the group begins to solidify, and members recognize the roles of others. A sense of unity grows during this stage. If it has not occurred already, an identified leader will emerge. The group may remain somewhat in flux during norming and may even regress back to the storming stage if any conflict, especially over the leadership role, occurs.

Performing The fourth stage, *performing*, is when the team achieves its full potential, finally focusing on the assigned task. This stage may take a long time to develop, as team development issues can be complicated. The members of the team finally work in harmony under the established roles to accomplish the necessary goals.

Adjourning In the final stage, *adjourning*, the team is disbanded because the project is complete. Team members may be reassigned to other teams or tasks. This stage will not occur if the team is placed together for a task with no specific date of completion. For example, a marketing team may continue to develop promotional efforts for a store even after a specific promotional task has been accomplished.

团队中的角色

6-7d Roles within a Team

Within any team, each member has a role to play in helping the team attain its objectives. Each of these roles adds important dimensions to team member interactions. The group member who pushes the team toward achieving goals and objectives plays the *task-specialist role* by concentrating fully on the assigned task. In a cross-functional team, this might be the person with the most expertise relating to the current task. The *socioemotional* role is played by the individual who supports and encourages the emotional needs of the other members, placing the team members' personal needs above the task at hand. Although this may sound like an unimportant role, the socioemotional member's dedication to team cohesiveness leads to greater unity and higher productivity. Some team members play a *dual role*, which is a combination of the socioemotional and task-specialist roles. Team leaders might not always play this dual role, but the team is likely to be most successful when they do. Sometimes an individual assumes the *nonparticipant role*. This role behavior is characterized by people who do not contribute to accomplishing the task and do not provide favorable input with respect to team members' socioemotional needs. They are obviously not desirable team members to have.

团队凝聚力

6-7e Team Cohesiveness

Developing a unit from a diverse group of personalities, specialties, backgrounds, and work styles can be challenging and complicated. In a cohesive team, the members get along and are able to accomplish their tasks effectively. Team cohesiveness is affected by different factors, internal and external to the team. To assure cohesiveness, the ideal team size is generally 5 to 12. Anything larger and relationship development becomes too complicated. Anything smaller and the group may be excessively burdened, and tasks may not get completed. Jeff Bezos, founder and executive chairman of Amazon, famously believes that a team is too large if it takes more than two pizzas to feed everyone on it.[8] One of the most reliable ways to build cohesiveness within a team is through competition with other teams. When two teams are competing for a single prize or recognition, they are forced to become more goal-oriented and to put aside conflict. A favorable appraisal from an outsider may strengthen team cohesiveness. Because the team is being praised as a group, team members recognize their contribution as a unit. Teams are also more successful when goals have been agreed upon beforehand. A team that is clear about its objective will be able to focus on accomplishing it. Frequent interaction also builds team cohesiveness through increasing familiarity.

团队冲突及其解决方法

6-7f Team Conflict and How to Resolve It

Conflict occurs when a disagreement arises between two or more team members. Conflict traditionally has been viewed as negative, but it is unavoidable.

Figure 6-8 Stages of Team Development

When attempting to develop teams, managers must understand that multiple stages are generally required.

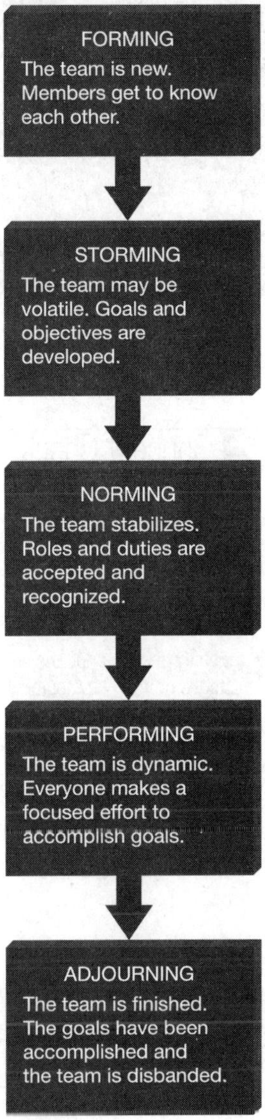

Go team, go! More companies today are using team-building exercises to help their employees figure out how to work better with one another.

If handled properly conflict can improve a team. For example, if two team members disagree about a proposition, both will spend extra time analyzing the situation closely to determine the best decision. As long as conflict is handled in a respectful and professional manner, it can improve the quality of work produced. However, if conflict turns hostile and affects the work environment, then steps must be taken to arrive at a compromise. Compromises can be difficult because neither party ends up getting everything they want. The best solution is a middle-ground alternative in which each party is satisfied to some degree. Conflict must be acknowledged before it can be dealt with or used in a constructive manner. Ignoring conflict may cause it to simmer or grow, disrupting team progress.

团队的优势和局限性
6-7g Benefits and Limitations of Teams

Understanding how teams evolve, become cohesive, and resolve conflict can help managers maximize the benefits of teams. Cohesive teams comprised of individuals with diverse skills and perspectives can achieve great creativity and innovation. They can also improve quality and response time. Teamwork can be key to reducing turnover and costs and increasing productivity, customer service, and product quality. There is also evidence that working in teams leads to higher levels of job satisfaction among employees and a harmonious work environment. Thus, an increasingly large number of companies use teams as a valuable element of their organizational structures.

However, the process of organizing teams can be stressful and time consuming, and there is no guarantee that a team will develop effectively. Obviously, teams require individuals to give up some independence in order to achieve goals, and they may have to share credit for ideas they develop within the team—even if they did most of the work. Teams can be frustrated by the unwillingness of one member to work toward team goals. If a team lacks cohesiveness and is unable to resolve conflicts, the company may experience lower productivity.

✓ Concept Check

- What are the major types of teams?
- Highlight some differences between cross-functional teams and virtual teams.
- Identify and describe the stages of team development.
- How can team conflict be reduced?
- What are some of the benefits and limitations of a team?

委员会和特别工作组
6-8 Committees and Task Forces

Learning Objective

6-8 Describe how committees and task forces are used.

In addition to teams, organizations today use several types of formal committees that may affect structure. These formal groups are typically brought together to represent members of the larger organization. An **ad hoc committee** is created for a specific short-term purpose, such as reviewing the firm's employee benefits plan or updating its diversity initiatives. Once its work is finished, the ad hoc committee disbands. A **standing committee** is a relatively permanent committee charged with performing a recurring task. A firm might establish a budget review committee, for example, to review departmental budget requests on an ongoing basis. Finally, a **task force** is a committee established to investigate a major problem or pending decision. A firm contemplating a merger with another company might form a task force to assess the pros and cons of the merger.

Committees offer some advantages over individual action. Their several members are able to bring information and knowledge to the task at hand. Furthermore, committees tend to make more accurate decisions and to transmit their results through the organization more effectively. However, committee deliberations take

临时委员会
ad hoc committee a committee created for a specific short-term purpose

常务委员会
standing committee a relatively permanent committee charged with performing some recurring task

特别工作组
task force a committee established to investigate a major problem or pending decision

longer than individual actions. In addition, unnecessary compromise may take place within the committee, or the opposite may occur, as one person dominates (and thus negates) the committee process.

> **✓ Concept Check**
> - What is the difference between a committee and a task force?
> - What are the advantages and disadvantages of using committees?

非正式组织和小道消息

6-9 The Informal Organization and the Grapevine

> **Learning Objective**
> **6-9** Explain the functions of the informal organization and the grapevine in a business.

So far, we have discussed the organization as a formal structure consisting of interrelated positions. This is the organization that is shown on an organization chart. There is another kind of organization, however, that does not appear on any chart. We define this **informal organization** as the pattern of behavior and interaction that stems from personal rather than official relationships. Embedded within every informal organization are informal groups and the notorious grapevine.

An **informal group** is created by the group members themselves to accomplish goals that may or may not be relevant to the organization. Workers may create an informal group to go bowling, form a union, get a particular manager fired or transferred, or meet for lunch. The group may last for several years or a few hours.

There is power in numbers. It's common for employees to befriend one another and form informal groups within an organization. The groups provide their members with camaraderie and information, but can create both challenges and benefits for the organization.

Informal groups can be powerful forces in organizations. They can restrict output, or they can help managers through tight spots. They can cause disagreement and conflict, or they can help to boost morale and job satisfaction. They have the power to improve or worsen employee performance and productivity. Clearly, managers should be aware of informal groups and determine how to utilize them.

The **grapevine** is the informal communications network within an organization. It is completely separate from—and sometimes much faster than—the organization's formal channels of communication. Formal communications usually follow a path that parallels the organizational chain of command. Information can be transmitted through the grapevine in any direction—up, down, diagonally, or horizontally across the organizational structure. Subordinates may pass information to their bosses, an executive may relay something to a maintenance worker, or there may be an exchange of information between people who work in totally unrelated departments. Information gleaned from the grapevine can run the gamut from the latest management decisions to gossip.

How should managers treat the grapevine? Certainly, it would be a mistake to try to eliminate it. People working together, day in and day out, are bound to communicate. A more rational approach is to recognize its existence. For example, managers should respond promptly and aggressively to inaccurate grapevine information to minimize the damage that such misinformation might do. Moreover, the grapevine can come in handy when managers are on the receiving end of important communications from the informal organization, such as when employees are expressing unhappiness with a recent action or have been recruited by a competitor.

In the next chapter, we apply these and other management concepts to an extremely important business function: the production of goods and services.

非正式组织
informal organization the pattern of behavior and interaction that stems from personal rather than official relationships

非正式团体
informal group a group created by the members themselves to accomplish goals that may or may not be relevant to an organization

小道消息
grapevine the informal communications network within an organization

> **✓ Concept Check**
> - In what ways can informal groups affect a business?
> - How is the grapevine used in a business organization?

Discussion Questions 讨论题

1. In what way do organization charts create a picture of an organization?
2. What determines the degree of specialization within an organization?
3. Describe how job rotation can be used to combat the problems caused by job specialization.
4. Why do most firms employ a combination of departmentalization bases?
5. How does a firm's top management influence its degree of centralization?
6. How is organization height related to the span of management?
7. Contrast line-and-staff and matrix forms of organizational structure.
8. Which kinds of firms would probably operate most effectively as centralized firms? As decentralized firms?
9. How do decisions concerning span of management and the use of committees affect organizational structure?
10. In what ways are team cohesiveness and team conflict related?
11. How do teams and committees differ?
12. How does the grapevine differ from formal communications within an organization?

Case 6 案例 6：Sweetgreen 坚守本源

Sweetgreen Stays True to Its Roots

Sweetgreen, a farm-to-table salad chain, combines mission and passion to build healthier communities by connecting people to real food. The company is revolutionizing the salad business. Jonathan Neman, Nicolas Jammet, and Nathaniel Ru, who met in an entrepreneurship class at Georgetown University, set out to create healthy meals made from locally sourced ingredients. After raising $300,000 from 40 investors, Sweetgreen was born in 2007.

Neman says the founders' lack of experience in the restaurant industry contributed to their success because they were able to enter it with a fresh perspective. One of their earliest challenges was learning how to lead and effectively turn problems into growth opportunities. Sweetgreen created a safe space for innovation and experimentation through its structure and goals. Managers monitor objectives and key results (OKRs). OKR is a collaborative goal-setting framework used to define and track objectives and their outcomes with measurable results. The company has a so-called learning forward document to keep track of failures and learnings from those failed endeavors.

Sweetgreen's leadership team also strives to foster a culture of gratitude. Monthly, team members write gratitude cards to employees and customers. According to Neman, "culture really does eat strategy for breakfast." Strategy shifts and products change, but a strong, unwavering organizational culture is the foundation of the company. Their leadership style is not static, but evolves as the restaurant chain grows. Today, Sweetgreen enjoys a loyal following at more than 100 locations in ten states as well as Washington, DC.

The distribution element of Sweetgreen's marketing mix is perhaps the most compelling. The company has built an entire food ecosystem that elevates Sweetgreen from fast-casual restaurant to food platform. Sweetgreen has worked to digitize its business from start to finish, and now more than half of its orders originate on the Sweetgreen app. The salad chain also has an Outpost program that offers complimentary delivery to employees of participating companies. Employees order their meals in the morning, and they are delivered to a set drop point in select office buildings in the afternoon. Additionally, blockchain—a secure digital ledger for recording information—has been integrated into the salad start-up's supply chain, allowing it to trace its fresh fruits and vegetables from farm to table. Initially, Sweetgreen used the technology to research best times for harvesting and eating produce but expanded it to improve traceability and food safety.

Sweetgreen is also known for its seasonal dishes and often works with high-profile chefs such as Nancy Silverton. For example, Sweetgreen purchased Koginut squash seeds from Row 7 Seed Company, which develops seeds for produce, and gifted the seeds to farming partners across the country. Sweetgreen purchased the resulting Koginut squash and sold it in a limited-time-only entree nationwide. The company announced the dish's arrival with a billboard in Times Square. Jammet says the company likes to "look outside the food world" to find inspiration for its promotion strategy.

The company's focus on health, wellness, and sustainable practices resonates with its core customer group: young professionals who put their money where their values are. Sweetgreen's corporate culture and marketing strategy have made its salads stand out in a category that often feels unexciting. The company has a modern supply chain, local supply chain partners, a focus on sustainability, consistent storytelling, and a popular app and loyalty program. Though it has attracted criticism for its products' high price tags, Sweetgreen pays it forward by increasing employee wages and benefits. The company, which has been valued at more than $1 billion, has experienced profitable growth. With cash from eager investors lining its pockets, Sweetgreen is poised to take off across the country.[9]

Questions

1. How has blockchain technology improve Sweetgreen's supply chain?
2. Describe the organizational culture at Sweetgreen.
3. How does management at Sweetgreen track objectives and their outcomes?

Chapter 7

Producing Quality Goods and Services

提供优质商品和服务

Why Should You Care?

Think for a moment about the products and services you bought in the past week. Those products and services could not be produced if it weren't for the production activities described in this chapter and that means consumers like you would not be able to purchase the products and services they need or want.

Learning Objectives

Once you complete this chapter, you will be able to:

7-1 Explain the nature of production.

7-2 Outline how the conversion process transforms raw materials, labor, and other resources into finished goods or services.

7-3 Discuss the importance of service businesses to consumers, other business firms, and the nation's economy.

7-4 Describe how research and development leads to new products and services.

7-5 Discuss the components involved in planning the production process.

7-6 Explain how purchasing, inventory control, scheduling, and quality control affect production.

7-7 Summarize how technology can make American firms more productive and competitive in the global marketplace.

Inside Business

商业透视：科技巨头加大研发力度

Tech Giants Double Down on R&D

Investing too many resources in research and development (R&D) activities can be risky since new ideas are unproven and may never hit the market. For technology firms, however, innovation is essential for survival. R&D spending at the five largest U.S. tech firms—Amazon, Alphabet, Microsoft, Apple, and Facebook—is on the rise. These same firms, often called "Big Tech," have the money to invest in both R&D and acquisitions that can help them improve existing operations or expand their business activities—even during an economic slowdown.

Even as far back as the Great Depression in 1929, cash-rich companies like General Electric funded R&D activities to develop new products or acquire smaller companies that could help the larger company expand and grow. Today, Big Tech is using the same proven methods to grow and expand. When the global economy slowed during the COVID-19 pandemic, these companies continued to spend heavily on R&D, hoping to emerge on the other side of the pandemic even further ahead of their competition. Each of the Big Tech companies has invested billions in research and development and acquisitions. For example, Alphabet—the parent company of Google—invested more than $20 billion in research and development each year for the last three years. In fact, total R&D spending for the five Big Tech companies exceeded $100 billion in 2020. (Note: 2020 was the latest year that complete statistics for R&D spending were available.) It is also expected that R&D spending for these same firms will continue to increase each year well into the future.

Technology giants also spend a great deal of money on acquisitions of smaller companies. In many ways, this is a form of outsourced R&D because the tech firms purchase businesses that have already done the research and laid the groundwork for new, innovative products. For example,

- Amazon acquired Selz, a start-up that equips entrepreneurs with the technology to sell products online.
- Alphabet acquired Pointy, an e-commerce hardware start-up that helps retailers list inventory online.
- Microsoft acquired CyberX, a security start-up that helps protect users from hackers.
- Apple acquired NextVR, a virtual reality streaming start-up that provides content for virtual reality headsets.
- Facebook purchased GIPHY, a technology company that provides animated images (GIFs) that users can include in text messages and social media accounts.

Though being one of the top R&D spenders does not guarantee success, the Big Tech companies will likely score many victories from their R&D investments and acquisitions. Many experts agree that investing in innovation and growing through acquisitions while smaller competitors downsize stands to further push Amazon, Alphabet, Apple, Microsoft, and Facebook ahead of other technology companies.[1]

Did you know?

Big Tech—Amazon, Alphabet, Apple, Microsoft, and Facebook—spend over $100 billion a year on research and development.

Challenges! How does a successful company continue to innovate and expand during an economic slowdown? It's a good question. And yet, for successful cash-rich Big Tech firms Amazon, Alphabet, Apple, Microsoft, and Facebook, they keep on investing in R&D and acquiring smaller companies that can fuel their growth into the future. The fact is, innovation for Big Tech companies is not an option, but an essential part of planning for future growth and expansion. Executives for these same companies would be the first to tell you that many of the topics covered in this chapter—research and development, facilities planning, purchasing, quality control, scheduling, and automation—are key factors that have enabled their businesses to grow and meet increased customer demand.

We begin this chapter with an overview of operations management—the activities required to produce goods and services that meet the needs of customers.

In this section, we also discuss the role of manufacturing in the U.S. economy, competition in the global marketplace, and careers in operations management. Next, we describe the conversion process that makes production possible and also note the growing role of services in our economy. Then we examine more closely three important aspects of operations management: developing ideas for new products, planning for production, and effectively controlling operations after production has begun. We close the chapter with a look at the productivity trends and the ways that manufacturing can be improved through automation, robotics, and technology.

什么是生产

7-1 What Is Production?

Learning Objective

7-1 Explain the nature of production.

Have you ever wondered if you could buy toilet paper and cleaning supplies the next time you went to Walmart, Target, or Walgreens? During the COVID-19 pandemic, many people faced shortages when they went to stores to buy essential products. For some consumers, the next step was to order needed products online from Amazon or other online retailers—only to receive a message that many of the same items were out of stock and there would be a delay before shipment. Shortages like these were common, and they underscore the importance of the activities described in this chapter. In fact, these products and services and millions of others like them would not exist if it weren't for production activities.

Let's begin this chapter by reviewing what an operating manager does. In Chapter 5, we described an *operations manager* as a person who manages the systems that convert resources into goods and services. This area of management is usually referred to as **operations management**, which consists of all the activities required to produce goods and services.

To produce a product or service successfully, a business must perform a number of specific activities. For example, the driving force behind the new General Motors Hummer has been to create a new kind of truck and SUV that is powered by a 1,000-horsepower electric motor. Although the 2022 model was available in late 2021, General Motors (GM) had to do a lot of research and development before the company could begin the production process. Marketing research had to determine not only if customers were willing to pay the base price—$80,000—for this all-electric vehicle (EV), but also what additional features they wanted. Marketing research also had to determine how the Hummer would compare against the competition including trucks and SUVs produced by Ford, Toyota, Nissan, Chevrolet, and GMC.

Once initial marketing research was completed, General Motors' product designers and operations managers began the process to turn the idea into reality. GM's managers couldn't just push the "start button" and immediately begin producing the new Hummer. As you will see, planning took place both *before* anything was produced and *during* the production process.

Managers were also concerned with the control of operations to ensure that the organization's goals were achieved. For a product such as the electric Hummer, control of operations involved a number of important issues, including product quality, performance standards, the amount of inventory of both raw materials and finished products, and production costs.

运营管理

operations management all the activities required to produce goods and services

大规模生产

mass production a manufacturing process that lowers the cost required to produce a large number of identical or similar products over a long period of time

分析过程

analytical process a process in operations management in which raw materials are broken into different component parts

运营管理职业

7-1a Careers in Operations Management

Although it is hard to provide information about specific career opportunities in operations management, some generalizations do apply to this management area. A basic understanding of mass production and the difference between an analytical process and a synthetic process is essential. **Mass production** is a manufacturing process that lowers the cost required to produce a large number of identical or similar products over a long period of time. An **analytical process** breaks raw materials into different component parts. For example, a barrel of crude oil refined by Marathon Oil Corporation—a Texas-based oil and energy exploration company—can be broken down into gasoline, oil, lubricants, and many other petroleum by-products. A **synthetic process** is just the opposite of the analytical one; it combines raw materials or components to create a finished product. Stanley Black & Decker uses a synthetic process when it combines plastic, steel, rechargeable batteries, and other components to produce a cordless drill.

Once you understand that operations managers are responsible for producing tangible goods or services that customers want, you must determine how you could be involved in the production process. Today's successful operations managers must:

1. Be able to motivate and lead people;
2. Understand how technology can make a manufacturer more productive;
3. Appreciate the cost-control processes that help lower production costs and improve product quality; and
4. Understand the relationship between the customer, the marketing of a product, and the production of a product.

If operations management seems like an area you might be interested in, why not do more career exploration?

合成过程
synthetic process a process in operations management in which raw materials or components are combined to create a finished product

Entrepreneurial Success

创业成功：企业家与数字化制造

Entrepreneurs and Digital Manufacturing

Manufacturing is an old industry, and U.S. employment in this industry is declining. And yet, these two factors don't mean that there aren't opportunities for today's manufacturing businesses. In fact, U.S. manufacturers produce approximately 18 percent of total global manufacturing output, and the industry is taking steps to innovate. That's where entrepreneurs come in.

A full-scale tech revolution has already begun with companies utilizing augmented reality, robots, artificial intelligence, cloud-based technology, and more. For example, 3D printing (sometimes called additive manufacturing) has been around for some time and was developed to help manufacturers create prototypes using plastics and other materials for promising ideas that often lead to production of new products. Now, entrepreneur Hanan Gothait, the CEO and founder of XJet, has developed a 3D printer that enables users to create revolutionary products in ceramic and metal. The ability to produce products in ceramic and metal creates a number of opportunities for innovative manufacturers.

In addition to 3D printing, a growing number of small start-up businesses are using new digital tools, computers, and software to change the way many items are manufactured in both small and large companies. Arculus, a German software company, has developed a "modular production platform" that uses artificial intelligence and autonomous robots to manufacture products. Using Arculus technology allows car manufacturers to change traditional assembly lines into a modular, multidimensional production system to accommodate flexible production and fluctuating demand and improve productivity. The Arculus system can also be adapted to produce other products including consumer electronics and appliances.

Often, venture capitalist firms provide needed financing to help entrepreneurs to turn an idea into new products or services. One venture capitalist firm, Playground Global, LLC, does even more than supply funding. Operating in what used to be a 70,000 square foot apricot canning factory, Playground Global now has a group of engineers, designers, and technology experts working in five world-class labs to help entrepreneurs with promising ideas create new products and services.

The bottom line: Many experts believe entrepreneurs with new ideas that are changing the way products and services are produced and the increased use of technology are pushing the manufacturing industry into a "new industrial revolution" that will continue for years.

Sources: Based on information in Trevor English, "How 3D Printing Has Changed the Manufacturing World," *Interesting Engineering*, March 22, 2020; Zac Johnson, "How to Start a Manufacturing Business," *YSF Magazine*, October 23, 2018; Sarah Goehrke, "3D Printing Entrepreneurship And Innovation: Behind The Scenes With XJet's Hanan Gothait," *Forbes*, October 23, 2019; Arculus, "About - Arculus Modular Production"; Mark Muro, "Entrepreneurs Take on Manufacturing," *Harvard Business Review*, February 22, 2016.

转化过程

7-2 The Conversion Process

Learning Objective

7-2 Outline how the conversion process transforms raw materials, labor, and other resources into finished goods or services.

The purpose of a manufacturing or a service business is to provide utility to customers. **Utility** is the ability of a good or service to satisfy a human need. Although there are four types of utilities—form, place, time, and possession—operations management focuses primarily on form utility. **Form utility** is created by people converting raw materials, finances, and information into finished products or services. The other types of utility—place, time, and possession—are discussed in Chapter 10.

But how does the conversion take place? How does Kellogg's convert corn, sugar, salt, and other ingredients; money from previous sales and stockholders' investments; production workers and managers; and economic and marketing forecasts into Frosted Flakes cereal products? How does H&R Block employ more than 3,500 full-time employees and thousands of part-time tax preparers and convert retail locations, computers and software, and advertising and promotion into tax services for its clients? They do so through the use of a conversion process like the one illustrated in Figure 7-1. As indicated by our H&R Block example, the conversion process can be used to produce services.

Figure 7-1 The Conversion Process

The conversion process converts ideas and resources into useful goods and services.

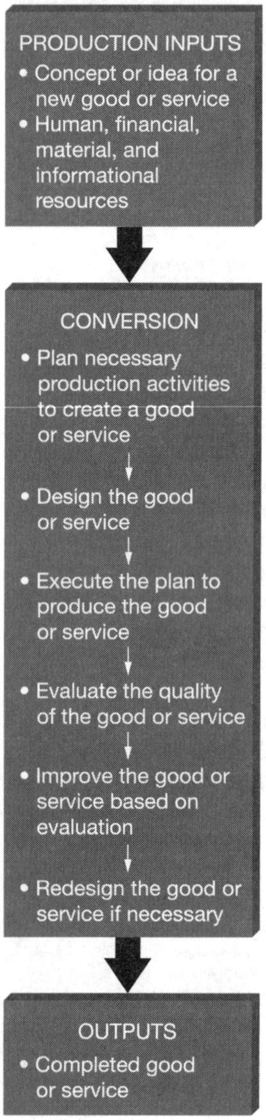

使用转化过程的生产

7-2a Production Using a Conversion Process

The conversion of resources into products and services can be described in several ways. We limit our discussion here to three: the focus, or major resource, used in the conversion process; its magnitude of change; and the number of production processes employed.

Focus or Major Resource By the *focus* of a conversion process, we mean the resource or resources that make up the major or most important *input*. The resources are financial, material, information, and people—the same resources discussed in Chapters 5. For a bank such as Citibank, financial resources are the major resource. A chemical and energy company, such as Chevron, concentrates on material resources. Your college or university is concerned primarily with information. And temporary employment services, such as Manpower, focus on the use of human resources.

Magnitude of Change The *magnitude of change* of a conversion process is the degree to which the resources are physically changed. At one extreme lie such processes as the one by which the Glad Products Company produces Glad® ClingWrap. Various chemicals in liquid or powder form are combined to produce long, thin sheets of plastic Glad ClingWrap. Here, the original resources are totally unrecognizable in the finished product. At the other extreme, Southwest Airlines produces no physical change in its original resources. The airline simply provides a service and transports people from one location to another.

Number of Production Processes A single firm may employ one production process or many. In general, larger firms that produce a variety of products or services use multiple production processes. For example, GE manufactures some of its own products, buys other merchandise from suppliers, and operates multiple divisions including a finance division, a renewable energy division, an aviation division, a healthcare division, and other divisions responsible for the products and services that customers associate with the GE name. Smaller firms, by contrast, may use one production process. For example, Advanced Architectural Stone, Inc., manufactures one basic product: building materials made from concrete.

服务的重要性日益增加

7-3 The Increasing Importance of Services

The application of the principles of operations management to the production of services has coincided with a dramatic growth in the number and diversity of service businesses. In 1900, only 28 percent of American workers were employed in service firms. By 1950, this figure had grown to 40 percent, and by the beginning of 2021, it had risen to 86 percent.[2] In fact, the American economy is now characterized as a service economy (refer to Figure 7-2). A **service economy** is one in which more effort is devoted to the production of services than to the production of goods.

规划优质服务

7-3a Planning Quality Services

Today, the managers of restaurants, laundries, real estate agencies, banks, movie theaters, airlines, travel bureaus, hospitals, and other service firms have realized that they can benefit from the experience of manufacturers. And while service firms are different from manufacturing firms, both types of businesses must complete many of the same activities in order to be successful. For example, as illustrated in the middle section of Figure 7-1, service businesses must plan, design, execute, evaluate, improve, and redesign their services in order to provide the services that their customers want.

For a service firm, planning often begins with determining who the customer is and what needs the customer has. After customer needs are identified, the next step for successful service firms is to develop a plan that will enable the firm to deliver the services that their customers want or need. For example, a swimming pool repair business must develop a business plan that includes a process for hiring and training qualified employees, obtaining necessary parts and supplies, marketing the firm's services, and creating management and accounting systems to control the firm's activities. Once the firm provides a service to a customer, successful firms evaluate the way they operate and measure customer satisfaction. And if necessary, they redesign their services to improve the customer's experience.

✓ Concept Check

- Explain how utility is related to form utility.
- In terms of focus, magnitude of change, and number, characterize the production processes used by a local pizza parlor, a dry-cleaning establishment, and a company that makes children's clothing.

Learning Objective

7-3 Discuss the importance of service businesses to consumers, other business firms, and the nation's economy.

效用
utility the ability of a good or service to satisfy a human need

形式效用
form utility utility created by people converting raw materials, finances, and information into finished products or services

服务经济
service economy an economy in which more effort is devoted to the production of services than to the production of goods

Figure 7-2 Service Industries

The growth of service firms has increased so dramatically that we now live in what is referred to as a service economy.

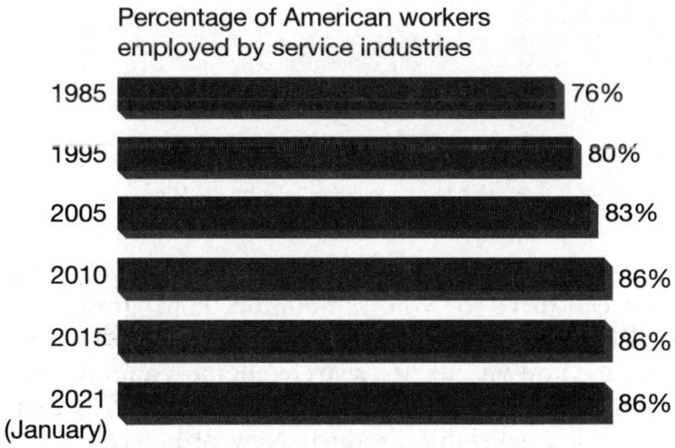

Source: "Employment by Major Industry Sector," The Bureau of Labor Statistics website.

Who answers your questions when you call a company to ask about a product or service? Answer: People who work in a company's call center. Answering questions on the phone or online queries is one-way customers obtain the answers or information they need. If a company doesn't provide good customer service, customers often post bad online reviews, tell family and friends about a company's poor customer service, or buy from another business when they make additional purchases.

评估企业的服务质量

7-3b Evaluating the Quality of a Firm's Services

The production of services is very different from the production of manufactured goods in the following five ways:

1. Service firms do not produce a product unless the customer wants or needs it.
2. Services are consumed immediately and, unlike manufactured goods, cannot be stored. For example, a hair stylist cannot store completed haircuts.
3. Services can be provided any place and are often provided when and where the customer desires the service.
4. Services are usually labor-intensive because the human resource is often the most important resource used in the production of services.
5. Services are intangible, and it is therefore more difficult to evaluate customer satisfaction.[3]

Compared with manufacturers, service firms often listen more carefully to customers and respond more quickly to the market's changing needs. For example, Maggiano's Little Italy restaurant is a chain of eating establishments owned by Brinker International. In order to continuously improve customer service, the restaurant encourages diners to complete online surveys that prompt diners to evaluate the food, atmosphere, service, and other variables. The information from the surveys is then used to fine-tune the way Maggiano's meets its customers' needs. As an incentive to complete the survey, Maggiano's gives diners a chance to win $1,000. Other restaurants often give diners free food the next time they visit a restaurant.

✓ Concept Check

- How is the production of services similar to the production of manufactured goods?
- How is the production of services different from the production of manufactured goods?
- How can service firms measure customer satisfaction?

新产品和服务从何而来

7-4 Where Do New Products and Services Come From?

Learning Objective

7-4 Describe how research and development leads to new products and services.

Question: Which of the following companies are developing an autonomous (driverless) automobile?

a. Mercedes-Benz
b. Google
c. Tesla
d. Amazon
e. Nissan

Answer: All of the companies listed above are using research and development to develop a car that can drive for you. In addition, Ford, Toyota, General Motors, and others are also working on driverless automobiles. Even more astonishing, Google—a company known for its search engine—and Amazon—the online retailer—are testing their own versions of an autonomous car that will turn each company's idea into a marketable product. New products—like an autonomous car—start with an idea. Then assuming an idea has potential, a company's research and development activities turn the idea into a reality.

研究与开发

7-4a Research and Development

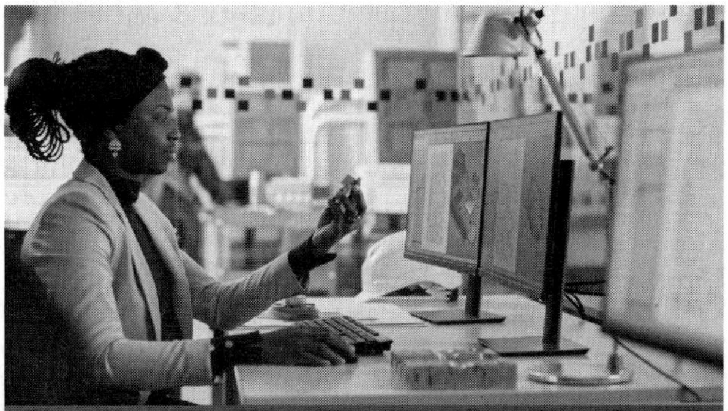

Microchips may be the most important part of a new product. In today's technological world, microchips are a major component in many products that we buy. But did you ever think about how we got microchips in the first place? The first microchips were the result of research and development activities by Robert Noyce and Jack Kilby—both engineers. Today, engineers, like the one in this photo, are using many of the same R&D activities to develop the next generation of microchips.

While the COVID-19 pandemic may have started in late 2019, it quickly spread around the globe. Increasing numbers of cases *and* deaths were reported. In many counties, emergency rooms and hospitals were full, and doctors and nurses could not keep up with the increasing number of patients. Existing vaccines didn't work on this virus, and health professionals and politicians weren't sure what they should do to combat this deadly pandemic. For many experts, the hope of a vaccine was a dream that became a reality by late 2020. Two different vaccines were developed by Moderna and a joint venture between Pfizer and BioNTech—three of the largest pharmaceutical companies in the world. Both vaccines were approved for emergency use in December 2020 by the U.S. Food and Drug Administration (FDA). While it takes much longer to develop and obtain approval for most new medicines and vaccines, the research and development activities of both firms made it happen in record time. Even though both vaccines are now available, Moderna and the joint venture between Pfizer and BioNTech continue to research ways to improve the initial vaccines to protect people from new strands of the virus. The activities that led to the creation of both vaccines generally are referred to as research and development. For our purposes, **research and development (R&D)** involves a set of activities intended to identify new ideas that have the potential to result in new goods and services.

Today, business firms use three general types of R&D activities. *Basic research* consists of activities aimed at uncovering new knowledge. The goal of basic research is scientific advancement, without regard for its potential use in the development of goods and services. *Applied research,* in contrast, consists of activities geared toward discovering new knowledge with some potential use. *Development and implementation* involves research activities undertaken specifically to put new or existing knowledge to use in producing goods and services. For many companies, R&D is a very important part of their business operations. The 3M company, for example, has always been known for its development and implementation research activities. Currently, 3M employs 8,000 researchers worldwide and has invested over $5.6 billion over the last three years to develop new products designed to make people's lives easier and safer.[4]

产品扩展和精细化

7-4b Product Extension and Refinement

If a firm sells only one product or service, when customers quit buying the product or service, the firm will die. To stay in business, the firm must, at the very least, find ways to refine or extend the want-satisfying capability of its product or service. Consider television sets. Since they were introduced in the early 1930s, television sets have been constantly *refined* so that they now provide clearer, sharper pictures with less dial adjusting. Larger televisions are now available, and prices have dropped because manufacturers are using the latest automation and technology in their production facilities. During the same time, television sets also were *extended.* There are basic flat-screen televisions without added features, and many others that include Smart Technology and Apps that can be used to access the internet and streaming services like Netflix, Hulu, and Peacock. Although it seems like LED televisions were

研究与开发
research and development (R&D) a set of activities intended to identify new ideas that have the potential to result in new goods and services

just introduced, already manufacturers like Samsung, LG, and Sony are taking the next step and developing QLED, Quantum Dots, and other technologies that will provide even better pictures on your TV screen.

For most firms, extension and refinement are expected results of their research, development, and implementation activities. Each refinement or extension results in an essentially "new" product whose sales make up for the declining sales of a product that was introduced earlier. When consumers were introduced to the original five varieties of Campbell's Soup, they discovered that these soups were of the highest quality, as well as inexpensive, and the soups were an instant success. Although one of the most successful companies at the beginning of the 1900s, Campbell's had to continue to innovate, refine, and extend its product line. To meet this need, Campbell's Soup has developed ready-to-serve products that can be popped into a microwave at work or school. As further evidence of its commitment to product extension and refinement, Campbell introduced Well Yes Soups—an entirely new gourmet soup line created with new recipes that blend traditional favorites with new vegetables and other ingredients to create new soups including Italian Style Wedding Soup, Tomato Sweet Basil Soup, and Roasted Chicken and Vegetable Soup. In fact, because of product extension, Campbell's Soup now has more than 80 soup varieties. And while it may be obvious, the goal of the company's product extension and refinement efforts is to maintain its loyal customer base and at the same time attract new customers to new and different soup products.

✓ Concept Check

- Describe how research and development leads to new products.
- What is the difference between basic research, applied research, and development and implementation?
- Explain why product extension and refinement are important.

Sustaining the Planet

保护地球：如何打造可持续和有韧性的制造业

How to Build Sustainable and Resilient Manufacturing

During the COVID-19 pandemic, many factory slowdowns or closures around the world forced manufacturers to adapt existing production methods to cope with a shortage of employees, resources, and supplies. Despite shortages and an economic slowdown, many manufacturers used technology to improve productivity and meet consumer demand for products that were in short supply. As a bonus, the unprecedented slowdown in industrial activity curbed global carbon emissions, indicating that substantial and significant change is possible when different methods and more technology are used to produce products or services.

Today, successful manufacturers are always looking for ways to improve. For example, manufacturers know that converting raw materials into finished products is both a costly and energy-intensive process. And yet, one way to reduce cost is using renewable energy. Leveraging solar energy and solar energy storage solutions, for example, can accommodate flexible demand for consumer products. Method Products, Inc., a natural cleaning products company with locations in the United States and Europe, uses multiple renewable energies. It has a wind turbine, a greenhouse, and solar panels that track the sun at its factory outside of Chicago. Method Products is also using more renewable energy in their other production facilities. Other manufacturers are evaluating not only how to conserve natural resources, but also how their products impact the environment. Nestlé, for example, uses a life cycle assessment (LCA) framework to evaluate and minimize the environmental impact of the products they manufacture.

As a result of shortages of both needed resources and finished goods and the problems manufacturers encountered during the pandemic, sustainability in manufacturing has now taken center stage. This new interest in sustainability, the digital workplace, and technology is helping all types of manufacturers to increase productivity and profitability, and to cope with an ever-changing business environment.

Sources: Blake Moret and Allie Schwertner, "Why Sustainable Manufacturing Makes Economic as Well as Ethical Sense," *World Economic Forum*, August 4, 2020; Graham Immerman, "Building a Sustainable, Resilient Industry for the Future," *Smart Industry*, June 17, 2020; Method, "Our Soap Factory".

管理者如何计划生产
7-5 How Do Managers Plan Production?

Only a few of the many ideas that are considered by a firm's research and development employees ever reach the production stage. For those ideas that do, however, the next step is planning for production. Planning for production involves three different phases: design planning, facilities planning, and operational planning (refer to Figure 7-3).

Learning Objective

7-5 Discuss the components involved in planning the production process.

设计规划
7-5a Design Planning

When the R&D staff at Samsung recommended to top management that the firm manufacture and market a "Family Hub" refrigerator, with a touch screen, Wi-Fi connectivity, and apps that allow consumers to connect with family members, provide recipe suggestions, manage their grocery lists, or even see who is at the front door, the company could not simply swing into production the next day. Instead, a great deal of time and energy had to be invested in determining what the new refrigerator would look like, where and how it would be produced, and what options would be included. These decisions are a part of design planning. **Design planning** is the development of a plan for converting an idea into an actual product or service. The major decisions involved in design planning deal with product line, required capacity, and use of technology.

Product Line A **product line** is a group of similar products that differ only in relatively minor characteristics. During the design-planning stage, a manufacturer like Samsung must determine how many different models to produce and what options to offer. Likewise, a restaurant chain such as Pizza Hut must decide how many menu items to offer.

An important issue in deciding on the product line is to balance customer preferences and production requirements. Typically, a company's marketing personnel want a "long" product line with more options to give customers greater choice. On the other hand, operations managers and production personnel generally want a "short" product line with fewer options because products are easier to produce.

Once the product line has been determined, each distinct product within the product line must be designed. **Product design** is the process of creating a set

Figure 7-3 Planning for Production

Once research and development identifies an idea that meets customer needs, three additional steps are used to convert the idea to an actual good or service.

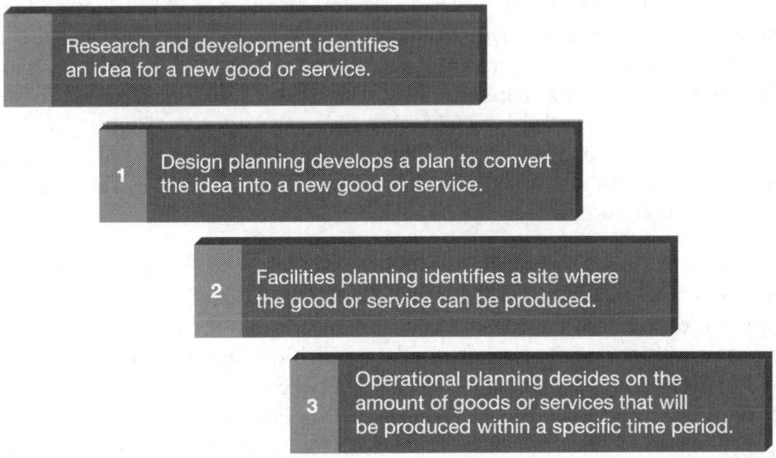

设计规划
design planning the development of a plan for converting an idea into an actual product or service

产品线
product line a group of similar products that differ only in relatively minor characteristics

产品设计
product design the process of creating a set of specifications from which a product can be produced

Appliances have come a long way since they were first created. Would you believe the first "ice boxes" had a compartment to store ice to keep food cool? Eventually, refrigerators, stoves, and washing machines evolved and now are more energy efficient and provide new features like the ones pictured in this photo. Today's successful companies, like Samsung, use a design planning process to create state-of-the-art appliances to make sure their products meet exacting specifications.

of specifications from which a product can be produced. For example, product engineers for Samsung must make sure that their new "Family Hub" refrigerator keeps food frozen in the freezer compartment. At the same time, they must make sure that lettuce and tomatoes do not freeze in the crisper section of the refrigerator. The need for a complete product design is fairly obvious; products that work cannot be manufactured without it. But services should be designed carefully as well—and *for the same reason.*

Production Capacity **Capacity** is the number of products or services that an organization can produce in a given period of time. Consider the impact of the COVID-19 pandemic on the Clorox Company. Clorox experienced increased demand for bleach and disinfecting wipes during the pandemic. To make matters worse, customers often found empty shelves in grocery stores, big discount stores, and drug stores. Online retailers including Amazon also had to delay shipments of Clorox's products. To meet demand, Clorox began to increase capacity as quickly as possible. Managers had to make decisions about what products would be made at each production facility, extend the hours each production plant would operate, and determine what else could be done to keep facilities operating at full capacity. Each management decision was made with one goal in mind: Determine the required capacity the firm needs to meet increased demand for Clorox's products.

While Clorox's capacity problems were caused by the pandemic, other firms with increased sales and future plans for expansion must often increase capacity to meet their long-term goals. For example, Mazda and Toyota agreed to share the cost of building a $2.3 billion plant in Huntsville, Alabama. The plant will assemble a Mazda SUV automobile that is new to the North American market. Toyota will produce a new crossover SUV model. Management decisions like the ones made by Clorox, Mazda, and Toyota are driven by the need to increase capacity. This, in turn, determines the size of the production facility or number of production facilities and amount of goods and services that will be produced. If a firm has too much capacity, valuable resources (plant, equipment, and money) will lie idle. If a firm has too little capacity, additional capacity may have to be added later when it is much more expensive than in the initial building stage.

Capacity means about the same thing to service businesses. For example, the capacity of a restaurant such as the Hard Rock Cafe in Nashville, Tennessee, is the number of customers it can serve at one time.

产能
capacity the number of products or services that an organization can produce in a given time

劳动密集型技术
labor-intensive technology a process in which people must do most of the work

Use of Technology During the design-planning stage, management must determine the degree to which *automation* and *technology* will be used to produce a product or service. Here, there is a trade-off between high initial costs and low operating costs (for automation) and low initial costs and high operating costs (for human labor). Ultimately, management must choose between a labor-intensive technology and a capital-intensive technology. A **labor-intensive technology** is a process in which people must do most of the work. Most construction projects, the Kansas

City Chiefs football team, and accounting firms for example, are labor-intensive. A **capital-intensive technology** is a process in which machines and equipment do most of the work. A Sony automated assembly plant is capital intensive because there are fewer workers that operate automated machinery. In many situations, people and technology are combined to create the most efficient and most cost-effective method to produce goods or services.

选址和设施规划
7-5b Site Selection and Facilities Planning

Generally, a business will choose to produce products in an existing factory as long as (1) the existing facility has enough capacity to handle increased customer demand for established products and services and any new products or services and (2) the cost of refurbishing an existing factory is less than the cost of building a new one.

After exploring the capacity of existing factories, management may decide to build a new facility. In determining where to locate production facilities, management must consider a number of variables, including the following:

- Locations of customers and suppliers;
- Quality of life for employees and management in the proposed location;
- The cost of land and building costs;
- Local and state taxes, environmental regulations, and zoning laws;
- The amount of financial support and subsidies, if any, offered by local and state governments; and
- Special requirements, such as great amounts of energy or water used in the production process.

Before making a final decision about where a proposed plant will be located and how it will be organized, two other factors—human resources and plant layout—should be examined.

Human Resources When Volvo built its new South Carolina production facility to produce automobiles, human resources managers were involved to make sure the employees needed to staff and operate the plant were available. In some cases, human resources managers must recruit workers, especially when unemployment is low and competition for qualified workers is intense. To increase the number of qualified workers at the South Carolina plant, Volvo management worked with both state and local officials to develop a 62-hour compressed manufacturing educational program that is offered at area technical schools. Upon completion of the 62-hour program, Volvo agreed to waive the one-year of manufacturing experience requirement for new employees.[5]

When a company decides to build a new facility in a foreign country, again human resources managers are involved. For example, suppose a U.S. firm like General Motors wants to lower labor costs by importing component parts from China. It has two choices. It can build its own manufacturing facility in a foreign country or it can outsource production to local firms in that country. In either case, human resources become involved in the decision. If the decision is made to build its own plant, human resources managers will have to recruit employees with the appropriate skills who are willing to relocate to a foreign country, develop training programs for local workers, or both. On the other hand, if the decision is made to outsource production to local suppliers, human resources managers must make sure that local suppliers are complying with the U.S. company's human rights policies and with all applicable national and local wage and hour laws. For General Motors, selecting suppliers in foreign countries is an important consideration. At a recent awards ceremony, General Motors recognized 116 companies representing 15 different countries with its Supplier of the Year award.[6]

资本密集型技术
capital-intensive technology a process in which machines and equipment do most of the work

Figure 7-4 Facilities Planning

The process layout is used when small batches of different products are created or when working on different parts of a product. The product layout (assembly line) is used when all products undergo the same operations in the same sequence. The fixed-position layout is used in producing a product too large to move.

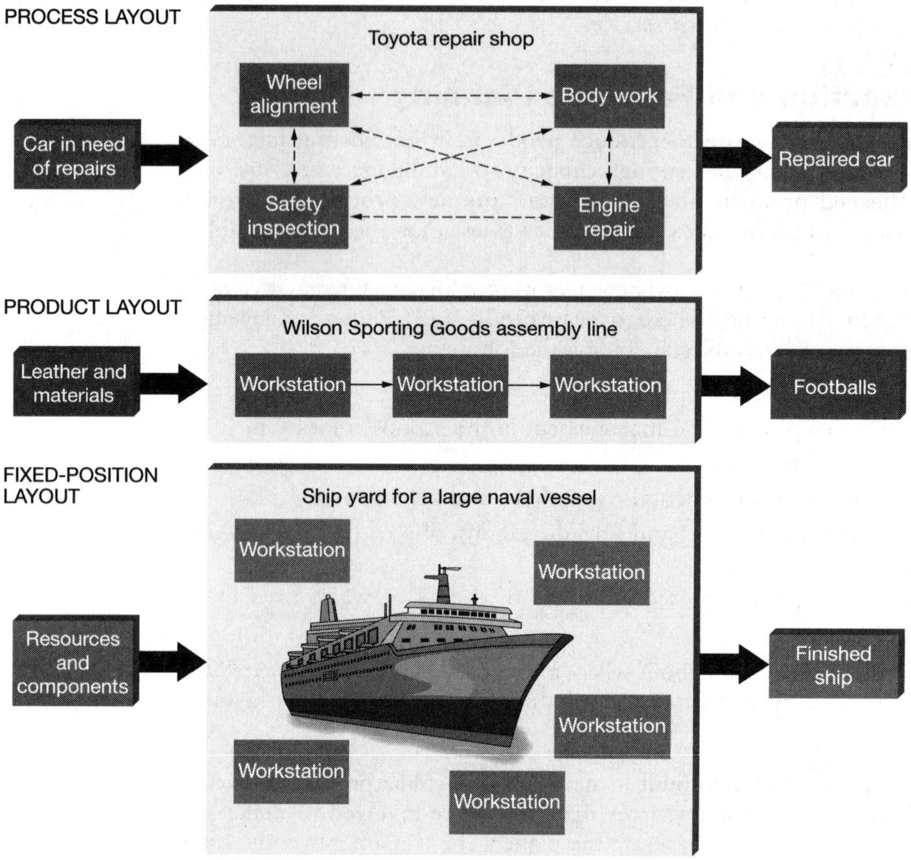

工厂布局
plant layout the arrangement of machinery, equipment, and personnel within a production facility

Plant Layout **Plant layout** is the arrangement of machinery, equipment, and personnel within a production facility. Three general types of plant layout are used (refer to Figure 7-4).

The *process layout* is used when different operations are required for creating small batches of different products or services. The facility is arranged so that each operation is performed in its own particular area. A hospital provides an example of a process layout. Specific services are located in different parts of the facility. For example, there may be areas for surgery, physical therapy, respiratory therapy, X-rays, a pharmacy, and offices for billing, accounting, insurance, and administration. If you need physical therapy, you only "visit" the department where physical therapy services are provided. Service and repair companies also use the process layout. For example, if you take your Toyota Camry for a wheel alignment, your car "visits" only the area where alignments are performed.

A *product layout* (sometimes referred to as an *assembly line*) is used when all products undergo the same operations in the same sequence. Workstations are arranged to match the sequence of operations, and work flows from station to station. An assembly line is the best example of a product layout. For example, Wilson Sporting Goods uses an assembly line process to create footballs in its Ada, Ohio, plant.

Too big to move! Ferguson Marine uses a fixed-position production layout to build both cargo freighters and naval vessels. While ships, like the one in this picture, will eventually sail the oceans of the world, during the production process it's often easier to move people, scaffolding, machinery, and parts instead of moving a large partially completed ship.

A *fixed-position layout* is used when a very large product is produced. Aircraft manufacturers, for instance, use a fixed-layout plant arrangement because of the size of its products—commercial airliners. Shipbuilders also use this type of layout because of the difficulty of moving a large product such as an ocean liner. In both examples, the product remains stationary during production, and people, parts, and equipment are moved as needed to assemble the product.

运营规划

7-5c Operational Planning

The objective of operational planning is to decide on the number of products or services each facility will produce during a specific period of time. Four steps are required.

Step 1: Selecting a Planning Horizon A **planning horizon** is simply the time period during which an operational plan will be in effect. A common planning horizon for production plans is one year. Then, before each year is up, management must plan for the next. A planning horizon of one year generally is long enough to average out seasonal increases and decreases in sales. At the same time, it is short enough for planners to adjust production to accommodate long-range sales trends.

Step 2: Estimating Market Demand The *market demand* for a product is the quantity that customers will purchase at the going price. Sales projections developed by marketing managers are the basis for market-demand estimates.

Step 3: Comparing Market Demand with Capacity The third step in operational planning is to compare the estimated market (customer) demand with the facility's capacity to produce products or services to satisfy that demand. One of three outcomes may result: Demand may exceed capacity, capacity may exceed demand, or capacity and demand may be equal. If they are equal, the facility should be operated at full capacity. However, if market demand and capacity are not equal, adjustments may be necessary.

Step 4: Adjusting Production to Meet Demand The biggest reason for changes to a firm's production schedule is changes in market (customer) demand for its products. For example, Indiana-based Berry Global Corporation produces packaging and tape and adhesive products. One particularly successful product line for Berry Global is drink cups that can be screen-printed to promote a company

规划的时间范围
planning horizon the time period during which an operational plan will be in effect

✓ Concept Check

- What are the major elements of design planning?
- Define capacity. Why is it important for a manufacturing business or a service business?
- What factors should be considered when selecting a site for a new manufacturing facility?
- What is the objective of operational planning? What four steps are used to accomplish this objective?

or its products or services.[7] If Berry Global obtains a large contract to provide promotional cups to a large drink distributor like Coca-Cola or Pepsi, the company may need to work three shifts a day, seven days a week, until the contract is fulfilled. Unfortunately, the reverse is also true. If the company's sales force does not generate new sales, there may be only enough work for the employees on one shift.

When market (customer) demand exceeds capacity, several options are available. Production of products or services may be increased by operating the facility overtime with existing personnel or by starting a second or third work shift. For manufacturers, another response is to subcontract or outsource a portion of the work to other manufacturers. If the excess demand is likely to be permanent, the firm may expand the current facility or build another facility.

What happens when capacity exceeds market (customer) demand? Again, there are several options. To reduce output temporarily, workers may be laid off or the facility may be operated on a shorter-than-normal workweek. To adjust to a permanently decreased demand, management may shift the excess capacity of a manufacturing facility to the production of other goods or services. The most radical adjustment is to eliminate the excess capacity by selling unused manufacturing facilities.

运营控制

7-6 Operations Control

Learning Objective

7-6 Explain how purchasing, inventory control, scheduling, and quality control affect production.

We have discussed the development of an idea for a product or service and the research and development and planning that translate that idea into the reality. Now we are ready to begin the production process. In this section, we examine four important areas of operations control: purchasing, inventory control, scheduling, and quality control (refer to Figure 7-5).

采购

7-6a Purchasing

Purchasing consists of all the activities involved in obtaining required materials, supplies, components (or subassemblies), and parts from other firms. Levi Strauss, for example, must purchase denim cloth, thread, and zippers before it can produce a single pair of jeans.

The objective of purchasing is to ensure that required materials are available when they are needed, in the proper amounts, and at minimum cost. Generally, the company with purchasing needs and its suppliers must develop a working relationship built on trust and reliability. In addition, many companies believe that purchasing is one area where they can promote diversity and inclusion. For example, AT&T developed a Supplier Diversity Program in 1968. Today, goals for the AT&T program include purchasing a total of 21.5 percent of all products and services from businesses owned by certified minority women, people who identify as LGBTQ+, veterans, and people with disabilities. In recent years, it

Figure 7-5 Four Aspects of Operations Control

Implementing the operations control system in any business requires the effective use of purchasing, inventory control, scheduling, and quality control.

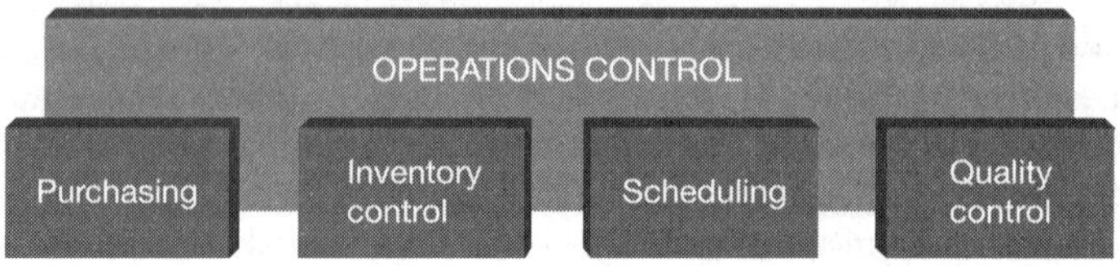

采购
purchasing all the activities involved in obtaining required materials, supplies, components, and parts from other firms

has exceeded the goal of 21.5 percent and each year purchases approximately $14 billion in merchandise and supplies from diverse businesses that obtain AT&T supplier certification.[8]

Purchasing personnel should constantly be on the lookout for new or backup suppliers, even when their needs are being met by their present suppliers, because problems such as worker strikes, equipment breakdowns, or nonessential business closures during a pandemic can cut off the flow of purchased materials from a primary supplier. Many of the product shortages that occurred during the COVID-19 pandemic were caused because manufacturers couldn't obtain needed resources from suppliers to produce products. In many cases, the inability to get resources broke the supply chain—suppliers to manufacturers to wholesalers or retailers to customers.

Gorgeous inventory! Every spring nurseries and garden centers must increase their inventory of flowering plants, shrubs, and trees that customers purchase to spruce up their yards for late spring and summer. In many cases, the supply chain for these same items includes growers, wholesalers, and retailers—different types of businesses that must maintain inventory to meet the needs of the next customer in the supply chain.

The choice of suppliers should result from careful analysis of a number of factors. The following are especially critical:

- *Price*. Comparing prices offered by different suppliers is always an essential part of selecting a supplier.
- *Quality*. Purchasing specialists always try to buy materials at a level of quality in keeping with the type of product being manufactured. The lowest acceptable quality is usually specified by product designers.
- *Reliability*. An agreement to purchase high-quality materials at a low price is the purchaser's dream. However, the dream becomes a nightmare if the supplier does not deliver.
- *Shipping costs*. The question of who pays the shipping costs should be answered before any supplier is chosen.

库存控制

7-6b Inventory Control

Can you imagine what would happen if a Coca-Cola manufacturing plant ran out of the company's familiar red-and-white aluminum cans? It would be impossible to complete the manufacturing process and ship soft drinks to retailers. Management would be forced to shut the assembly line down until the next shipment of cans arrived from a supplier. The simple fact is that shutdowns are expensive because costs such as employee wages, rent, utilities, insurance, and other expenses still must be paid.

Operations managers are concerned with three types of inventories. A *raw materials inventory* consists of materials that will become part of the product during the production process. The *work-in-process inventory* consists of partially completed products. The *finished-goods inventory* consists of completed goods. Each type of inventory also has a *holding cost,* or storage cost, and a *stock-out cost,* the cost of running out of inventory. **Inventory control** is the process of managing inventories in such a way as to minimize inventory costs, including both holding costs and potential stock-out costs.

Today, computer systems are being used to track all three types of inventory and alert managers to impending stock-outs. One of the most sophisticated methods of inventory control used today is material requirements planning. **Material requirements planning (MRP)** is a computerized system that integrates production

库存控制
inventory control the process of managing inventories in such a way as to minimize inventory costs, including both holding costs and potential stock-out costs

物料需求计划
material requirements planning (MRP) a computerized system that integrates production planning and inventory control

planning and inventory control. An MRP system answers three questions: What is needed; how much is needed; and when is it needed. One of the great advantages of an MRP system is its ability to juggle delivery schedules and lead times effectively. For a complex product such as an automobile with 30,000 or more individual parts, a manager using an MRP system can arrange both order and delivery schedules so that materials, parts, and supplies arrive when they are needed.

Because large firms can incur huge inventory costs, much attention has been devoted to inventory control. The just-in-time system used by some businesses is one result of all this attention. A **just-in-time inventory (JIT) system** is designed to ensure that materials or supplies arrive at a facility just when they are needed so that storage costs are minimized. For example, managers using a just-in-time inventory system at a Harley Davidson assembly plant determine the number of motorcycles that will be assembled in a specified time period. Then Harley Davidson purchasing personnel order just the parts needed to produce those motorcycles. In turn, suppliers deliver the parts in time or when they are needed on the assembly line. The benefits for Harley Davidson are enormous and include decreased inventory levels and a much more efficient manufacturing process that reduces costs and increases profits. While stories of large firms like Harley Davidson, Dell, and Toyota are common, smaller firms can also use JIT to reduce costs and improve profitability.

准时制库存系统
just-in-time inventory (JIT) system a system designed to ensure that materials or supplies arrive at a facility just when they are needed so that storage costs are minimized

调度
scheduling the process of ensuring that materials and other resources are at the right place at the right time

调度
7-6c Scheduling

Scheduling is the process of ensuring that materials and other resources are at the right place at the right time. As our definition implies, both place and time are important to scheduling. The *routing* of materials is the sequence of workstations that the materials will follow. Assume that Hickory White—a furniture company based in

Technology and Innovation

技术与创新：沃尔玛将库存跟踪机器人暂时搁置

Walmart Puts Inventory-Tracking Robots on the Curb

Walmart, the largest retailer in the world, ditched a multi-year, multi-million-dollar plan to introduce automated inventory-scanning robots in its stores after discovering humans achieve similar results. The move ended a contract with start-up Bossa Nova Robotics after a five-year relationship. Initially, Walmart said the Bossa Nova robots would be used in about 20 percent of its domestic stores as part of a greater push for automation.

Walmart used the machines in an effort to reduce labor costs and increase sales by reducing out-of-stock items. After testing the robots in 500 stores, however, the retailer found that humans proved to be just as, if not more, capable and effective at keeping tabs on inventory levels. As more and more consumers place orders online and then pick up merchandise at stores or ship merchandise to their homes, maintaining accurate inventory records and the actual merchandise in stores or warehouses has become increasingly important. Today, consumers expect a seamless shopping experience, and they have become spoiled by the ability to get merchandise without having to wait. This expectation makes inventory control more important than it has ever been.

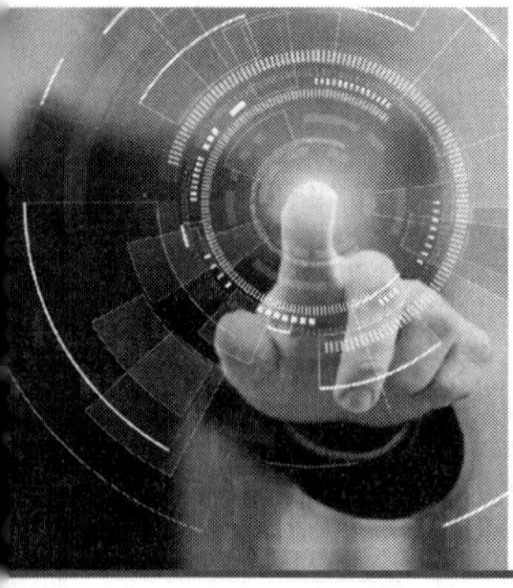

With the six-foot-tall robots out of the picture, the company is entrusting the job of inventory control once again to human employees. Industry experts project that automation will lead to millions of lost jobs, so this marks Walmart's decision as a victory for human workers. And yet, Walmart is still using automation and robots for some work in its stores including autonomous floor scrubbers. The big-box retailer is also exploring new ways to use automation and robots in its warehouses and perform other chores when automation and technology can reduce expenses and improve productivity.

Sources: Based on information in M. Corey Goldman, "Walmart Ditches Robots, Sticks With Humans for Inventory Control," *The Street*, November 3, 2020; Kenneth Garger, "Walmart Fires Inventory-Tracking Robots, Realizes Humans Work Just as Well," New York Post, November 2, 2020; Sarah Nassauer, "Walmart Scraps Plan to Have Robots Scan Shelves," The Wall Street Journal, November 2, 2020.

North Carolina—is scheduling production of an oval dining table made from cherry wood. Operations managers route the needed materials (wood, screws, packaging materials, etc.) through a series of individual workstations along an assembly line. At each workstation, a specific task is performed, and then the partially finished dining table moves to the next workstation. When routing materials, operations managers are especially concerned with the sequence of each step of the production process. For the dining table, the top and legs must be cut before the wood is finished. (If the wood were finished before being cut, the finish would be ruined, and the dining table would have to be stained again.)

When scheduling production, managers are also concerned with timing. The *timing* function specifies when the materials will arrive at each station and how long they will remain there. For the cherry dining table, it may take workers two hours to cut the table top and legs and another hour to drill the holes and assemble the table. Before packaging the dining table for shipment, it must be finished with cherry stain and allowed to dry. This last step may take as long as three days depending on weather conditions and humidity.

Regardless of whether the finished product requires a simple or complex production process, operations managers are responsible for monitoring schedules—called *follow-up*—to ensure that the work flows according to the schedule.

马尔科姆·鲍德里奇国家质量奖
Malcolm Baldrige National Quality Award an award given by the president of the United States to organizations judged to be outstanding in specific managerial tasks that lead to improved quality for both products and services

质量控制
quality control the process of ensuring that goods and services are produced in accordance with design specifications

质量控制
7-6d Quality Control

As mentioned earlier in this chapter, American business firms that compete in the competitive global marketplace have taken another look at the importance of improving quality. Today, there is even a national quality award. The **Malcolm Baldrige National Quality Award** is given by the president of the United States to organizations judged to be outstanding in specific managerial tasks that lead to improved quality for both products and services.

Quality control is the process of ensuring that goods and services are produced in accordance with design specifications. Over the years, more and more managers have realized that quality is an essential "ingredient" of the good or service being produced. This view of quality provides several benefits. Making products or completing services right the first time reduces many of the rejects and much of the rework. Also, the number of defects decreases, which causes profits to increase.

The major objective of quality control is to see that the organization lives up to the standards it has set for itself on quality. Some firms, such as Mercedes-Benz and Lexus, have built their reputations on quality. Other firms adopt a strategy of emphasizing lower prices along with reasonable (but not particularly high) quality. Today, many firms use the techniques described in Table 7-1 to gather information and statistics that can be used to improve the quality of a firm's products or services.

For a product like a Coach handbag, quality counts. Customers expect that luxury items must meet exacting specifications. After all, customers are paying "top dollar" for items like the handbags in this picture. For a luxury item, employees must inspect the product and any defect or flaw must be caught before the product leaves the company's factory.

Improving Quality Through Employee Participation One of the first steps needed to improve quality is

Table 7-1 Four Widely Used Techniques to Improve the Quality of a Firm's Products

Technique	Description
Benchmarking	A process of comparing the way a firm produces products or services to the methods used by organizations known to be leaders in an industry in order to determine the "best practices" that can be used to improve quality
Continuous Quality Improvement	Continuous improvement is a never-ending effort to eliminate problems and improve quality. Often this method involves many small changes or steps designed to improve the production process on an ongoing basis.
Statistical Process Control (SPC)	Sampling to obtain data that are plotted on control charts and graphs to see if the production process is operating as it should and to pinpoint problem areas
Statistical Quality Control (SQC)	A detailed set of specific statistical techniques used to monitor the production process to determine the acceptability of a product

employee participation. Simply put, successful firms encourage employees to accept full responsibility for the quality of their work. When Toyota, once the role model for world-class manufacturing, faced a quality crisis, the company announced a quality-improvement plan based on its famous "Toyota Way." One tenet of the Toyota Way is the need to solve problems at their source and to stop the production line if necessary to address a problem. Another tenet that enabled Toyota to resolve quality problems was the use of quality circles designated to deal with difficulties as they arise. A **quality circle** is a team of employees who meet on company time to solve problems of product quality. Quality circles have also been used successfully in companies such as IBM, Northrop Grumman Corporation, Lockheed Martin, and General Motors.

Increased effort is also being devoted to **inspection**, which is the examination of the quality of work in process. Employees perform inspections at various times during production. For example, component parts may be inspected before they become part of a finished product. In addition, finished goods may be inspected before they are shipped to customers. Items that are within design specifications continue on their way. Those that are not within design specifications are removed from production.

Total Quality Management and Six Sigma **Total quality management (TQM)** is the coordination of efforts directed at improving customer satisfaction, increasing employee participation, strengthening supplier partnerships, and facilitating an organizational atmosphere of continuous quality improvement. Although total quality management (TQM) can be used to improve the quality of a firm's products or services, it also involves other essential activities. For TQM programs to be effective, management must address each of the following components:

- *Customer satisfaction.* Increasing customer satisfaction by producing higher-quality products, providing better customer service, and showing customers that the company cares.
- *Employee participation.* Establishing policies that enable employees to contribute to decisions, develop self-managed work teams, and assume responsibility for improving the quality of products or services.
- *Strengthening supplier partnerships.* Developing good working relationships with suppliers can ensure that the right supplies and materials will be delivered on time at lower costs.
- *Continuous quality improvement.* Creating an organization based on continuous improvement has proven to be the most effective long-term approach.

质量圈
quality circle a team of employees who meet on company time to solve problems of product quality

检查
inspection the examination of the quality of work-in-process

全面质量管理
total quality management (TQM) the coordination of efforts directed at improving customer satisfaction, increasing employee participation, strengthening supplier partnerships, and facilitating an organizational atmosphere of continuous quality improvement

Although many factors influence the effectiveness of a TQM program, two issues are crucial. First, top management must make a strong commitment to a TQM program. Second, management must coordinate the above components of a TQM program so that they work in harmony with each other. Many firms including American Express, AT&T, and Motorola have used TQM to improve product quality and ultimately customer satisfaction.

Another technique that businesses may use to improve not only quality but also overall performance is Six Sigma. **Six Sigma** is a disciplined approach that relies on statistical data and improved methods to eliminate defects for a firm's products and services. Although many experts agree that Six Sigma is similar to TQM, Six Sigma often has more top-level support, much more teamwork, and a new corporate attitude or culture.[9] Today, both large and small companies can use TQM or Six Sigma to improve quality.

World Standards: The International Organization for Standardization Without a common standard of quality, customers may be at the mercy of manufacturers and suppliers. As the number of companies competing in the global marketplace has increased, so has the seriousness of this problem. To deal with the problem of standardization, the International Organization for Standardization, a nongovernmental organization with headquarters in Geneva, Switzerland, was created. The **International Organization for Standardization (ISO)** is a network of national standards institutes and similar organizations from 165 different countries that is charged with developing standards for quality products and services and environmental standards for global manufacturers and producers.[10]

Standardization is achieved through consensus agreements between national delegations representing all the economic stakeholders—suppliers, customers, and often governments. The member organization for the United States is the American National Standards Institute (ANSI) located in Washington, DC.

Although certification is not a legal requirement to conduct business globally, ISO standards are so prevalent around the globe that many customers refuse to do business with noncertified companies. As an added bonus, companies completing the certification process often discover new, cost-efficient ways to improve their existing quality-control programs.

生产计划：总结

7-6e Production Planning: A Summary

In this chapter, the activities that firms use to produce products and services have been described. Now, toward the end of the chapter, it may help to look at a table to see how all of the "pieces of the puzzle" fit together. At the top of Table 7-2, planning for production begins with research and development, design planning, site selection and facilities planning, and operational planning—all topics described in this chapter. At the bottom of Table 7-2, activities that were described in the Operations Control section (purchasing, inventory control, scheduling, and quality control) are summarized. The goal of all the planning activities in the top section and operations control activities in the bottom section is to create and produce a successful product or service. Of course, the steps for planning production and operations control should always be evaluated to determine if the firm's activities can be improved.

六西格玛
Six Sigma a disciplined approach that relies on statistical data and improved methods to eliminate defects for a firm's products and services

国际标准化组织
International Organization for Standardization (ISO) a network of national standards institutes and similar organizations from 165 different countries that is charged with developing standards for quality products and services and environmental standards for global manufacturers and producers

Table 7-2 Production Planning: A Summary

Both planning for production and operations control are necessary if a firm is to produce a successful product or service.

The Process Begins with Planning for Production
1. *Research and Development* determines if an idea for a product or service will begin the production process.
2. *Design Planning* develops a plan for producing a product or service.
3. *Site Selection and Facilities Planning* identifies a production site, a plant layout, and if human resources are available.
4. *Operational Planning* decides on the number of products or services that will be produced during a planning horizon, usually one year.
Then Four Operations Control Steps Are Used to Produce a Product or Service
1. *Purchasing* obtains required materials, supplies, parts, and needed resources from other firms.
2. *Inventory Control* ensures that materials, supplies, and parts are available when needed.
3. *Scheduling* ensures that materials and other resources are at the right place and at the right time in the production process.
4. *Quality Control* determines if the firm has lived up to the quality standards it has set for itself.
The End Result: A Successful Product or Service

✓ Concept Check

- Why is selecting a supplier important? What factors should be considered when selecting a supplier?
- What costs must be balanced and minimized through inventory control?
- Explain in what sense scheduling is a control function of operations managers.
- How can a business firm improve the quality of its products or services?

利用技术提高生产率

7-7 Improving Productivity with Technology

Learning Objective

7-7 Summarize how technology can make American firms more productive and competitive in the global marketplace.

No coverage of operations management would be complete without a discussion of productivity and technology. Productivity concerns all managers, but it is especially important to operations managers, the people who must oversee the creation of a firm's products or services. *Productivity* is defined as the average level of output per worker per hour. For example, if each worker at plant A produces 75 units per day and each worker at plant B produces only 70 units per day, the workers at plant A are more productive. If one fast-food employee serves 25 customers per hour and another serves 28 per hour, the second employee is more productive.

生产率趋势

7-7a Productivity Trends

For U.S. businesses, annual labor productivity growth rates averaged a 1.4 percent increase for the period 2007–2019.[11] More recently, the United States experienced a 2.5 percent increase in labor productivity for 2020.[12] (*Note:* At the time of publication, 2020 was the last year that actual statistics were available.) The statistics for businesses for the four calendar quarters of 2020 resemble a roller coaster ride with a slight increase in the first quarter, a huge decline in the second quarter caused by the COVID-19 pandemic, and increases in the third and fourth quarters.[13] Fortunately, as illustrated in Figure 7-6, the U.S. labor productivity growth rate has been positive every year since 1987. Unfortunately, the average growth rate has slowed for the period beginning in 2007. Based on the decline in productivity growth rates, many economists, business leaders, politicians, and government officials are quick to point out that throughout the nation, manufacturers must find ways to be more productive.

Ethics and Social Responsibility

商业伦理与社会责任：如何成为符合伦理的制造商

What It Takes to Be an Ethical Manufacturer

Ethical practices can be a core part of a manufacturing business. Companies that engage in this holistic approach to the manufacturing process, including the equitable treatment of employees and sustainable production of quality products, maintain high ethical standards to better serve all stakeholders.

One of the first benchmarks for an ethical manufacturer is the safe and equitable treatment of employees. While many safety measures are mandated by law, an ethical manufacturer goes above and beyond these requirements, never sacrificing safety for productivity. For example, Clorox, known for its namesake bleach and other consumer products, has a reputation as a company that values employees. Additionally, these organizations provide equal opportunities and fair treatment for all employees regardless of race, gender, religion, sexual orientation, ethnicity, nationality, socioeconomic status, language, abilities, age, or political beliefs.

A second benchmark for an ethical manufacturer is sustainability and concern for the environment. All production activities should be energy efficient while minimizing waste and emissions. To achieve these goals, ethical manufacturers often use alternative technologies to reduce waste of materials and natural resources. Optional certification programs exist as a form of self-regulation. For instance, in the textile industry, a Swiss group called Bluesign has established strict criteria to help textile manufacturers monitor the effect their production activities have on sustainability and the environment.

A final benchmark for ethical manufacturers is the product. At the end of the production process, ethical manufacturers provide quality products that are both safe and legal. Ethical manufacturers will often issue voluntary product recalls when safety issues are discovered after a product is sold in the marketplace. Mercedes-Benz, for example, recalled more than one million cars when it discovered an emergency call system glitch had the potential to incorrectly identify a driver's location. Product recalls like this one can be costly and damaging to a firm's reputation, but exemplify the right action that should be taken when a problem is discovered.

Ethical manufacturing is good business. Many consumers will buy from ethical manufacturers because of the way they treat their employees, their efforts to sustain the planet, and their reputation of producing quality products and services. Simply put, when consumers buy products from ethical manufacturers, they can rest easy knowing they purchased a safe item that was sustainably produced. This sense of trust fosters long-term customer relationships.

Sources: Laura Putre, "Employees Choice: The 10 Best Manufacturers to Work For," *Industry Week*, February 16, 2021; The Bluesign website; Kim Lyons, "Mercedes Recalling More Than 1 Million Vehicles Over Emergency-Call Location Error," *The Verge*; "What Is Ethical Manufacturing?" *Kangovou*, , March 20, 2017.

Figure 7-6 U.S. Productivity Growth Rates

This chart describes labor productivity growth rates for U.S. businesses for the period 1987 to 2019—the latest statistics available prior to publication.

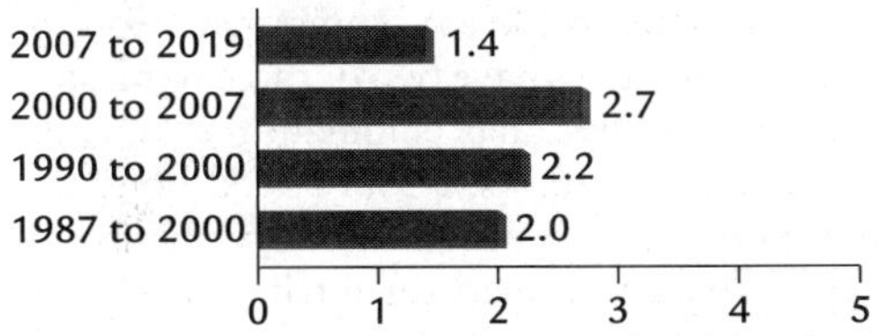

Source: Based on information in "Multifactor Productivity Trends, 2020," the Bureau of Labor Statistics website.

提升生产率
7-7b Improving Productivity Growth

Many U.S. firms are using a number of techniques to improve productivity. For example, a large number of business firms are adopting lean manufacturing to improve productivity. **Lean manufacturing** is a concept built on the idea of eliminating waste from all of the activities required to produce a product or service. Benefits of lean manufacturing include a reduction in the amount of resources required to produce a product or service, more efficient use of employee time, improved quality, and increased profits. Intel, for example, uses lean manufacturing to improve the quality of new advanced microchips. At the same time, the chip maker is able to reduce waste and defects and increase customer satisfaction. In addition to lean manufacturing, several other factors must be considered if U.S. firms are going to increase productivity *and* their ability to compete in the global marketplace. For example:

- The United States must stabilize its economy so firms will invest more money in new facilities, equipment, technology, and employee training.
- There must be more emphasis on satisfying the customer's needs and increasing customer satisfaction.
- Managers and executives must cooperate with employees to increase employee motivation and participation in the workplace.
- Businesses must examine the existing work flow in their manufacturing facilities and find ways to decrease waste and increase efficiency in the workplace.
- All government policies must be examined to ensure that unreasonable regulations that may be hindering productivity growth are eliminated.
- Increased use of automation, robotics, and computer manufacturing systems must be used to lower production costs and increase profits.

Finally, innovation and research and development efforts to create new products and services must be increased in order for U.S. firms to compete in the global marketplace. Although U.S. manufacturers spend more on research and development (R&D) than those in any other country, manufacturers' spending for R&D is increasing more rapidly in China and other countries.[14] Maintaining or increasing our level of R&D spending is essential if we are to remain competitive in the global market place.

自动化、机器人技术和计算机对生产率的影响
7-7c The Impact of Automation, Robotics, and Computers on Productivity

Automation is the total or near-total use of machines to do work. The rapid increase in automated procedures has been made possible by computer technology used in robotics and in sophisticated manufacturing systems.

Robotics **Robotics** is the creation and application of programmable machines to perform a variety of tasks by manipulating materials and tools. A recent report from PricewaterhouseCoopers (PwC) found that 59 percent of companies in the manufacturing industry are presently utilizing at least one type of production robot.[15] Robots work quickly, accurately, and steadily. Robots are especially effective in tedious, repetitive assembly-line jobs, handling heavy components or tools, working with hazardous materials, or when companies have two or three work shifts. Lincoln Electric, for example, produces robotic welders that eliminate the hot, dirty job of welding, which is key to many manufacturing tasks. As an added bonus, robotic welders are often quicker and are more precise than old-fashioned welding machines. Robots are also useful as artificial "eyes" that can inspect the quality of products as they are being processed on assembly lines or finished products before they are shipped to customers.

To date, the automotive industry has made the most extensive use of robotics, but robots also have been used to mine coal, inspect the inner surfaces of pipes, assemble computer components, clean and guard buildings at night, and even

精益生产
lean manufacturing a concept built on the idea of eliminating waste from all of the activities required to produce a product or service

自动化
automation the total or near-total use of machines to do work

机器人技术
robotics the creation and application of programmable machines to perform a variety of tasks by manipulating materials and tools

explore outer space. And robots coupled with artificial intelligence (AI) are now used to perform diagnostic procedures, provide certain kinds of patient care in hospitals, and assist doctors with robotic surgeries.

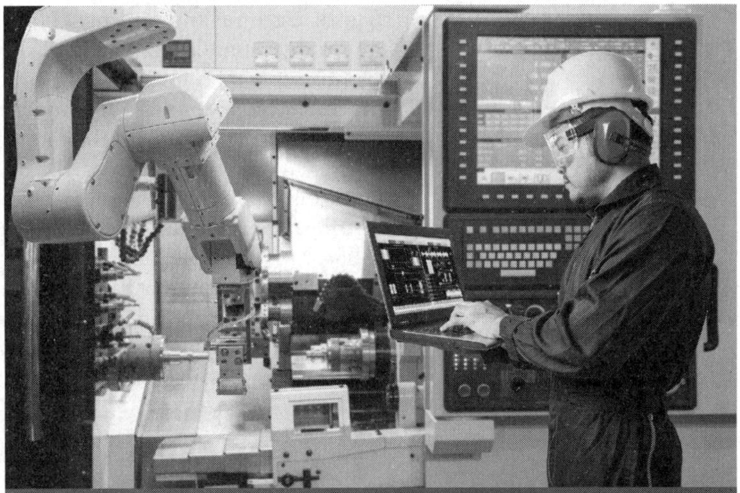

Is the robot talking to this worker or is the worker talking to the robot? It's hard to tell from the photo, but the worker is actually using a laptop computer to control a robotic arm. According to a recent PricewaterhouseCoopers (PwC) survey, 59 percent of companies in the manufacturing industry are presently utilizing at least one type of production robot to increase productivity on their assembly lines.

Computer Manufacturing Systems People are quick to point out how computers have changed their everyday lives, but most people do not realize the impact computers have had on manufacturing. In simple terms, the factory of the future has already arrived. For most manufacturers, the changeover began with the use of computer-aided design and computer-aided manufacturing. **Computer-aided design (CAD)** is the use of computers to aid in the development of products. Ford speeds up car design, Boeing designs new aircraft, and CafePress, Inc. allows you to use CAD to create custom T-shirts, drinkware, home décor, and personalized greeting cards.

Computer-aided manufacturing (CAM) is the use of software and computers to plan and control manufacturing processes. A well-designed CAM system allows manufacturers to become much more productive. Not only are a greater number of products produced, but speed and quality also increase. Using CAM systems, Toyota produces automobiles and Apple Computer creates electronic products.

If you are thinking that the next logical step is to combine the CAD and CAM computer systems, you are right. Today, the most successful manufacturers use CAD and CAM together to form a computer-integrated manufacturing system. Specifically, **computer-integrated manufacturing (CIM)** is a computer system that not only helps to design products but also controls the machinery needed to produce the finished product. For example, Sauder Woodworking—North America's leading producer of ready-to-assemble furniture—uses CIM to plan and control production of more than 40 different furniture collections for the home, including products for the home office, bedroom, kitchen, and storage.[16] Other advantages of using CIM include improved flexibility, more efficient scheduling, and higher product quality—all factors that make a production facility more competitive in today's global economy.

Flexible Manufacturing Systems Manufacturers have known for a number of years that the mass-production and traditional assembly lines used to manufacture products present a number of problems. For example, although traditional assembly lines at General Motors, Ford, Nissan, and other automobile manufacturers turn out extremely large numbers of products economically, the system requires expensive, time-consuming retooling of equipment whenever a new product is to be manufactured. This type of manufacturing is often referred to as a continuous process. **Continuous process** is a manufacturing process in which a firm produces the same product(s) over a long period of time. Now it is possible to use flexible manufacturing systems to solve such problems. A **flexible manufacturing system (FMS)** combines electronic machines and computer-integrated manufacturing in a single production system that can easily adapt to changes in the type of product being produced. Instead of having to spend large amounts of time and effort to retool the traditional mechanical equipment on an assembly line for each new product, an FMS is rearranged simply by reprogramming electronic machines. Because FMSs

计算机辅助设计
computer-aided design (CAD) the use of computers to aid in the development of products

计算机辅助制造
computer-aided manufacturing (CAM) the use of software and computers to plan and control manufacturing processes

计算机集成制造
computer-integrated manufacturing (CIM) a computer system that not only helps to design products but also controls the machinery needed to produce the finished product

连续生产过程
continuous process a manufacturing process in which a firm produces the same product(s) over a long period of time

柔性制造系统
flexible manufacturing system (FMS) a production system that combines electronic machines and computer-integrated manufacturing that can easily adapt to changes in the type of product being produced

require less time and expense to reprogram than traditional systems, manufacturers can produce smaller batches of a variety of products without raising the production cost. Flexible manufacturing is sometimes referred to as an intermittent process. An **intermittent process** is a manufacturing process in which a firm's manufacturing machines and equipment are changed to produce different products.

For most manufacturers, the driving force behind FMSs is the customer. In fact, the terms *customer-driven production* or *make to order system* are often used to describe a manufacturing system driven by customer needs and what customers want to buy. For example, advanced software and a flexible manufacturing system have enabled Dell Computer to change to a more customer-driven manufacturing process and provide customized computers for its customers. Although the costs of designing and installing an FMS such as this are high, the electronic equipment is used more frequently and efficiently than the machinery on a traditional assembly line.

可持续性和技术替代

7-7d Sustainability and Technological Displacement

Sustainability is defined as the ability to create and maintain conditions under which present and future generations can exist in productive harmony, and permit fulfilling the social, economic, and other requirements of future and present generations. While sustainability affects all aspects of a nation, its people, and the economy, the concept is especially important for manufacturers and service providers. Because of the amount of resources required to produce goods and services, these businesses must conserve resources whenever possible. As an added bonus, efforts to reduce waste and sustain the planet can often improve a firm's bottom-line profit amount.

Today, many countries around the globe produce goods and services and compete with U.S. manufacturers. And yet, U.S. producers are known for quality and innovation—especially for products that are more expensive or more complicated to manufacture. As a result, most experts agree that, because U.S. manufacturers will continue to innovate, workers who have manufacturing jobs will be highly skilled and will be able to work with robots, automation, and high-tech computerized manufacturing systems. Many workers will be faced with the choice of retraining to work with new technology or seeking jobs in other sectors of the economy. Those that don't possess high-tech skills will be unemployed. Government, business, and education will also need to cooperate in order to provide the training needed to prepare workers for new roles in an automated workplace.

The next chapter discusses many of the issues caused by technological displacement. In addition, a number of major components of human resources management are described, and we see how managers use various reward systems to boost motivation, productivity, and morale.

✓ Concept Check

- How might productivity be measured in a restaurant? In a department store? In a public school system?
- How can robotics, computer manufacturing systems, and flexible manufacturing systems help a manufacturer to produce products?

间歇过程

intermittent process a manufacturing process in which a firm's manufacturing machines and equipment are changed to produce different products

Discussion Questions 讨论题

1. Why would Rubbermaid—a successful U.S. company—need to expand and sell its products to customers in foreign countries?
2. Do certain kinds of firms need to stress particular areas of operations management? Explain.
3. Is it really necessary for service firms to engage in research and development? In planning for production and operations control?
4. How are the four areas of operations control interrelated?
5. Is operations management relevant to nonbusiness organizations such as colleges and hospitals? Why or why not?

Case 7 案例 7：丰田推动制造业变革

Toyota Drives Change in Manufacturing

Toyota is one of the world's largest automobile companies, but it faced a long road to get to this place in history. It wasn't until the company developed its original manufacturing philosophy, the Toyota Production System (TPS), that the carmaker began to thrive. This lean manufacturing approach combined with a culture built on continuously working to improve quality propelled the company to the front of the pack.

Kiichiro Toyoda founded the motor company in 1937 just two years before World War II. After the war, resources including steel and other metals were in low supply. These shortages often forced the company to modify both the product and its production process. For example, Toyota removed one of the headlamps from its Model K truck because of limited amounts of this important component. During this time, Toyota cars were low-cost vehicles with few options or accessories common in today's automobiles.

Toyota's production system, often referred to as just TPS in the automotive world, wasn't conceived until the late 1940s. The company envied the way Ford produced cars in its River Rouge plant in Michigan. One of the main differences between the two companies was that Ford stockpiled large inventories of resources and component parts for future production needs. At the time, Toyota could not afford to have so much inventory on-hand tying up its capital. Instead, Toyota began to look for ways to work around this problem. After studying the methods that American supermarkets used to control inventory, Toyota began to craft a solution based on the concepts of ordering fewer parts, but ordering more often. Using inventory practices common in U.S. supermarkets, Toyota ordered or made only enough parts to replace the ones that were used in the previous production phase. This method later became known as the just-in-time (JIT) inventory system. JIT ensures that materials arrive exactly when they are needed in order to reduce storage and holding costs. To support the JIT inventory system, the company also developed a sign-based tracking method called Kanban to track the flow of goods. Today, many experts consider Kanban to be the precursor to modern bar codes used by businesses to track parts and materials in manufacturing facilities.

TPS, JIT, and Kanban weren't Toyota's only innovations. Ford had set the standard for assembly lines, but Toyota saw room for improvement. With Ford's early production techniques, assembly lines moved continuously, which maximized efficiencies of scale but also allowed room for errors that had to be corrected later. Toyota introduced the Andon Cord, a physical rope that employees could pull to stop the assembly line and allowed workers to fix problems on the spot. The fact that employees had the power to stop the manufacturing line led to increased employee motivation to eliminate the same types of mistakes in the future. The result was a dramatic decline in the number of errors and improved quality of finished cars.

Thanks to TPS, JIT, Kanban, and the Andon Cord, Toyota built a reputation for making affordable, quality vehicles. At the same time, they were also able to produce cars quickly. Because of increased productivity, it takes only 1.6 worker-hours to produce a car, much lower than competitors. And as gas prices increased, Toyota's cheap-to-run vehicles became more appealing to U.S. consumers. By 1962, the company had produced one million cars. A decade later, that number grew to ten million.

Today, one of the secrets of Toyota's continued success is its ability to adapt the methods it has used to become one of the largest car manufacturers in order to compete in today's ever-changing business environment. For example, in some cases, it has increased inventory levels for some essential resources like microchips and electronic components needed to produce cars with the latest technological advancements. While stockpiling of some needed parts is not consistent with JIT inventory control, it was a decision that was driven by shortages of some critical parts in the last 15 to 20 years. To combat the problem of shortages, executives and managers also use a contingency planning system called RESCUE (REinforce Supply Chain Under Emergency) to provide information about potential shortages of thousands of parts supplied by a wide range of diversified suppliers. Toyota's agility in managing its inventory is a definite advantage because it prevents costly production slowdowns or temporary plant closures.

Today, Toyota has manufactured more than 250 million vehicles and shows no signs of slowing down. Because Toyota has set the benchmark for others in waste reduction, efficiency, and incremental quality improvement, companies including Caterpillar, Intel, General Motors, and a multitude of others have followed in their footsteps to increase productivity and improve quality.[17]

Discussion Questions

1. Through the years, Toyota has used TPS, JIT, Kanban, and the Andon Cord in its production plants. How have these methods enabled Toyota to improve the quality of its cars and increase the productivity of its workers?
2. Historically, Toyota has used JIT to control inventory costs, but in the last 15 to 20 years, it has begun stockpiling essential parts needed to produce cars. What factors led to this change in inventory control?
3. Today, Toyota is a recognized leader in efforts to improve product quality and increase employee productivity in the automobile industry. Do you think the same methods that Toyota uses to manufacture cars would work in other types of businesses? Explain your answer.

PART 4
Human Resources

人力资源

Chapter 8
Attracting and Retaining the Best Employees

Chapter 9
Motivating and Satisfying Employees

This part is concerned with the most important and least predictable of all resources—people. We begin by examining the human resources efforts that organizations use to hire, develop, and retain their best employees. Then we discuss employee motivation and satisfaction.

Attracting and Retaining the Best Employees

吸引和留住最优秀的员工

Learning Objectives

Once you complete this chapter, you will be able to:

8-1 Describe the major components of human resources management.

8-2 Identify the steps in human resources planning.

8-3 Discuss workplace diversity and some of the challenges and opportunities associated with it.

8-4 Explain the objectives and uses of job analysis.

8-5 Describe the processes of recruiting, selecting employees, and onboarding.

8-6 Examine decisions associated with employee compensation and benefits.

8-7 Explain the purposes and techniques of employee training and development.

8-8 Discuss performance appraisal techniques and performance feedback.

8-9 List common forms of employee turnover and explain why firms strive to minimize it.

Why Should You Care?

Being able to understand how to attract and keep the right people is crucial. Also, you can better understand your own interactions with your co-workers.

Inside Business

商业透视：Chipotle 提高员工的育儿福利

Chipotle Freshens Up Its Parental Benefits

Chipotle Mexican Grill, an American fast-casual restaurant, is known for its "food with integrity" slogan, but sometimes employees are the most important ingredient. Chipotle offers a variety of benefits to attract and retain employees, from free meals and quarterly bonuses to paid time off and education assistance. To sweeten its benefits suite, Chipotle expanded its paid parental leave program.

Chipotle now offers support center employees and eligible field employees 12 weeks of paid parental leave for birth moms and four weeks for new dads and individuals adopting children. The company also introduced a trending benefit: breastmilk shipping. With U.S. breastfeeding rates on the rise, Chipotle responded by covering the costs for nursing mothers to ship their milk during work-related trips. Additionally, through an internal employee resource group called HUSTLE (Humans Uniting to Support the Ladies' Experience), the company developed "Returnity" guidelines to help returning parents transition back to work. The guidelines highlight internal and external resources and offer advice to help parents enjoy a smooth transition.

The upgrades to Chipotle's paid parental leave benefits are part of a larger plan to enhance the company's perks. The company also implemented performance-based bonuses, expanded education programs, and began testing an unlimited paid time off policy. Marissa Andrada, chief people officer, says its upgrades to employee benefits help maximize the potential of the Chipotle workforce.[1]

Did you know?

Chipotle has more than 83,000 employees in the United States, Canada, the United Kingdom, France, and Germany.

Organizations like Chipotle know that human resources, the people who work within an organization, are *the* most important and valuable resource for a business. Without them, a firm would cease to function. For this reason, companies today spend considerable resources to attract, hire, train, and satisfy people who can help them achieve their organizational goals.

We begin our study of human resources management (HRM) with an overview of how businesses attract, retain, and develop human resources. After examining the process by which firms match their human resources needs with the supply available, we explore several dimensions of workplace diversity. Then we examine the concept of job analysis. Next, we focus on how a firm's recruiting, selection, and onboarding procedures affect a firm's success in acquiring employees. We describe forms of employee compensation, which can influence employee loyalty and productivity. Then we discuss methods of employee training, management development, and performance appraisal. We also consider types of employee turnover. Finally, we consider legislation that affects HRM practices.

人力资源管理
human resources management (HRM) all the activities involved in acquiring, maintaining, and developing an organization's human resources

人力资源管理：概述

8-1 Human Resources Management: An Overview

Learning Objective

8-1 Describe the major components of human resources management.

Organizations spend a great deal of effort to attract and utilize human resources fully. This effort is known as *human resources management*, or *staffing* and *personnel management*. **Human resources management (HRM)** consists of all the activities involved in acquiring, maintaining, and developing an organization's human resources. HRM begins with acquisition—getting people to work for the organization. The acquisition process can be very competitive, particularly for skilled employees and in fields where demand for workers exceeds supply. Next, firms must take steps to retain these valuable resources. (After all, they are the only business resources that can voluntarily leave an organization.) Finally, human resources should be developed to their full capacity.

人力资源管理活动

8-1a **HRM Activities**

Each of the three phases of HRM—acquiring, maintaining, and developing human resources—consists of related actions. Acquisition, for example, includes planning and the various activities that lead to hiring new personnel. Altogether this phase of HRM includes five separate activities:

- *Human resources planning*—determining the firm's future human resources needs
- *Job analysis*—determining the exact nature of the positions
- *Recruiting*—attracting people to apply for positions
- *Selection*—choosing and hiring the most qualified applicants
- *Onboarding*—integrating new employees into the firm

Maintaining human resources consists primarily of striving to satisfy employees and encouraging them to remain with the firm and to work effectively by using a variety of HRM programs, including the following:

- *Employee relations*—increasing employee job satisfaction through satisfaction surveys, employee communication programs, exit interviews, and fair treatment
- *Compensation*—rewarding employee effort through monetary payments
- *Benefits*—providing rewards to ensure employee well-being

The development phase of HRM is concerned with improving employees' skills and expanding their capabilities. The two important activities of this phase are:

- *Training and development*—teaching employees new skills and new jobs, and more effective ways of performing their present jobs
- *Performance appraisal*—assessing employees' current and potential performance levels

We will discuss each of these activities in more detail later in the chapter.

The power of people. Many firms believe their employees are their most important assets. However, unlike other assets such as machinery, capital, and products, employees can choose to leave an organization. Carefully designing compensation and reward packages can help a firm attract and retain valuable employees.

人力资源管理的责任
8-1b Responsibility for HRM

In general, HRM is a shared responsibility of line managers and staff HRM specialists. In very small organizations, the owner handles all or most HRM activities. As a firm grows, an owner may employ an outside party to handle some HRM functions, such as payroll and taxes, or hire a human resources manager to take over some staff responsibilities. In very large firms, such as Disney, HRM activities tend to be highly specialized, with separate groups for compensation, benefits, training and development, and other staff activities. GE, for example, has divisions and offices all over the world. Because of the size and complexity of the organization, GE has hundreds of HR managers to cover different geographic areas and departments within the firm.

Specific HRM activities are assigned to those in the best position to perform them. Human resources planning and job analysis are usually carried out by staff specialists with input from line managers. Similarly, staff experts handle recruiting and selection, although line managers are involved in hiring decisions. Staff specialists devise onboarding programs that are carried out by both staff specialists and line managers. Compensation systems (including benefits) most often are developed and administered by the HRM staff. However, line managers recommend pay increases and promotions. Training and development activities are the joint responsibility of staff and line managers. Performance appraisal is the job of the line manager, although HRM personnel design the firm's appraisal system in many organizations.

✓ Concept Check

- What are the three phases of human resources management?
- Identify the activities associated with each phase.
- How does the responsibility of HRM change with the size of a firm?

人力资源规划
8-2 Human Resources Planning

Learning Objective
8-2 Identify the steps in human resources planning.

Human resources planning is the development of strategies to meet a firm's future human resources needs. The organization's overall strategic plan is the starting point of the process. From this, human resource planners can forecast future demand for human resources. Next, the planners must determine whether the needed human resources will be available. Finally, they have to take steps to match supply with demand.

预测人力资源需求
8-2a Forecasting Human Resources Demand

Planners should base human resources demand forecasts on all relevant information available. The firm's overall strategic plan will provide information about future business ventures, new products, and projected expansions or contractions of specific product lines. Information on past staffing levels, evolving technologies, industry staffing practices, and projected economic trends also can be helpful. Technological advances are creating new opportunities in forecasting and planning for human resources demand. Increasingly, companies are using specialized software to analyze data about their employees' demographics, performance, training, and internal movements in order to make better HR decisions. Insights gained from such technology can help managers develop more cost-effective recruiting and selection strategies as well as recognize threats and opportunities.

HR managers use forecasting information to determine both the number of employees required and their qualifications. Planners use a wide range of methods to predict specific personnel needs. For example, a simple method projects personnel requirements to increase or decrease in the same proportion as sales revenue. Thus, a 30 percent increase in projected sales volume over the next two years results in a forecasted personnel increase of 30 percent for the same period. This method can be applied to specific positions and to the workforce in general. It is not, however, a very precise forecasting method. At the other end

人力资源规划
human resources planning the development of strategies to meet a firm's future human resources needs

of the spectrum are complex computer programs that perform HRM activities, such as forecasting future human resources requirements using algorithms and demographic data.

The demand for labor versus its supply: a balancing act. The supply and demand for employees with different skills is constantly shifting. In some industries, qualified workers are plentiful. In others, they are hard to find, even when the nation's unemployment rate is high.

人力资源供给预测
8-2b Forecasting Human Resources Supply

A forecast of human resources supply must take into account both the present workforce and any changes that may occur within it. For example, suppose that planners project that in five years a firm that currently employs 100 engineers will need to employ 200 engineers. Forecasting is not as simple as planning to hire 100 additional engineers. Some of the firm's current engineers will leave, move to other jobs within the firm, or be promoted. Thus, planners may project the supply of current engineers in five years at 87, which means that the firm will have to hire a total of 113 new engineers. When forecasting supply, planners should also account for the organization's existing employees to determine who can be retrained to perform required tasks.

Two useful techniques for forecasting human resources supply are the replacement chart and the skills inventory. A **replacement chart** is a list of key personnel and their possible replacements within a firm. It is important to maintain this chart to ensure that top-management positions can be filled quickly in the event of an unexpected death, resignation, or retirement. Some firms provide additional training for employees who might eventually replace top managers.

A **skills inventory** is a searchable database containing information on the skills and experience of all present employees, which can be mined to find candidates to fill available positions. For a special project, a manager may be seeking a current employee with specific information technology skills, at least six years of experience, and fluency in French. The skills inventory can quickly identify qualified employees. Skill-assessment tests, which provide the information in a skills inventory, can be administered internally or by outside vendors. Some companies, such as Halogen Software, offer customizable skills assessment and training software that allows firms to examine skills more expertly without contracting with an outside provider.

递补图
replacement chart a list of key personnel and their possible replacements within a firm

技能清单
skills inventory a computerized data bank containing information on the skills and experience of all present employees

供需匹配
8-2c Matching Supply with Demand

Once they have forecasted the supply and demand for personnel, HR planners can then devise a course of action for matching one with the other. When demand is predicted to be greater than supply, they must make plans to recruit new employees. The timing of recruitment efforts depends on the types of positions to be filled. Suppose that we expect to open another plant in five years that will need a plant manager and 25 maintenance workers, along with additional support staff. We can wait to recruit maintenance personnel. However, because the job of a plant manager is so critical, we may begin the process to fill that position immediately. If the demand excess is expected to be temporary, a firm might contract with a service that supplies temp workers. On the other hand, when the supply of employees is predicted to be greater than demand, the firm must take steps to reduce the size of its workforce, sometimes known as *rightsizing*. We will take a look at how firms can increase or reduce the size of their workforces later in this chapter.

✓ Concept Check

- How do firms forecast the demand for human resources?
- What are the techniques used to forecast human resources supply?
- How can firms match human resources supply and demand?

职场多样性

8-3 Workplace Diversity

Learning Objective

8-3 Discuss workplace diversity and some of the challenges and opportunities associated with it.

Today's workforce is highly diverse, with employees bringing a wide variety of beliefs, expectations, perspectives, and behavioral norms. Managers must be sensitive to and aware of these differences. For instance, European businesspeople may offer a kiss on the cheek as a greeting. Latin Americans tend to stand closer to people with whom they are talking than North Americans prefer. Without cultural sensitivity, job applicants who will not make eye contact during an interview may be rejected for being unapproachable, when, according to their culture, they are just being polite.

A large number of women, immigrants, and people of color have entered the U.S. workforce in recent decades. It is estimated that women make up about 47 percent of the U.S. workforce; African Americans and Hispanics each make up about 13 and 18 percent of U.S. workers, respectively.[2] Women now account for the majority of workers in the financial, education and health services, and leisure and hospitality industries. They make up 52 percent of management professional and related positions in the United States.[3]

Workplace diversity refers to the differences among people in a workforce owing to factors such as age, race, ethnicity, gender, sexual orientation, and ability. An increasingly diverse workforce requires that managers learn to supervise and motivate people who have a broad range of value systems as well as personal needs. In addition to cultural diversity, other changes have taken place as well. The high proportion of women in the workforce, combined with a new emphasis on participative parenting by men, has brought many family-related issues to the workplace. Today's more educated employees also want greater independence and flexibility, leading to improved quality of life.

Although workplace diversity presents a challenge, astute managers embrace it as an opportunity rather than a limitation. When fostered, diversity and inclusion can result in a stronger organization. Table 8-1 shows several benefits that diversity can bring to an inclusive organization, such as cost and human resources advantages. In particular, a diverse organization may gain a marketing and hiring edge because it has a greater understanding of different cultures and languages. Proper guidance and management of diversity in an organization also can improve creativity. People who embrace workplace diversity frequently are more flexible in the types of positions they will accept and are more comfortable working with diverse co-workers. Indeed, research by McKinsey & Company found that the top 25 percent of ethically and culturally diverse companies outpace the 25 percent least diverse ones by 36 percent in terms of profitability.[4]

职场多样性
workplace diversity differences among people in a workforce owing to factors such as age, race, ethnicity, gender, sexual orientation, and ability

Because workplace diversity creates challenges along with advantages, it is important for an organization's employees to understand it. To accomplish this goal, numerous U.S. firms have trained their managers to respect and support diversity

Table 8-1 Benefits of Workplace Diversity

Benefit	Description
Better use of employee talent	Companies gain a competitive advantage when they recruit, retain, and advance the best talent.
Improved understanding of the marketplace	A more diverse workforce can more easily anticipate and respond to the changing needs and desires of diverse customers.
Greater scope of understanding in leadership positions	A diverse leadership team can bring more perspectives to bear on anticipating and responding to a complex and dynamic environment.
Increased quality of team problem solving	Diverse teams can often devise more creative ideas and better solutions to problems.
Reduced costs associated with high turnover, absenteeism, and lawsuits	Flexible workplaces that satisfy and motivate employees with a variety of needs and wants help companies retain and advance the best talent.

Source: Adapted from Richard L. Daft and Dororthy Marcic, *Understanding Management,* 11th ed. (Boston, MA: Cengage, 2020), 339.

and inclusion. Diversity training programs may include recruiting, training, and mentoring women and people from underrepresented groups; training managers to view diversity positively, teaching English as a second language; and facilitating support groups for immigrants. Many companies recognize the importance of in-depth diversity training programs. A growing number of companies are publicly reporting their efforts to become more diverse and inclusive. Target, for example, releases an annual report that describes its current employee breakdown and diversity and inclusion efforts along with goals for the future.[5] More companies are also hiring diversity executives to help them reach their objectives. At Verizon, for example, Magda Yrizarry is the senior vice president and Chief Diversity Officer, which involves efforts to develop more opportunities for women, people of color, people with disabilities and neurodiversity, the LGBTQ+ community, and veterans.[6] International companies are continuously expanding their business and therefore need to meld a cohesive workforce from a labor pool with ever more diverse demographics.

Why hiring a diverse group of employees can benefit your business. Organizations that hire diverse employees benefit from their different skills and life experiences. The different points of view of these workers can help a firm find new opportunities and ways of doing things. In addition, diverse employees often have a greater understanding of diverse customers and the goods and services they prefer.

A diversity program will be successful only if it is systematic, is ongoing, and has a strong, sustained commitment from top leadership. Diversity training can improve workplace attitudes and behaviors. Even though there may be resistance in certain situations, workplace diversity is here to stay. Its impact on organizations is widespread and will continue to grow. Management must learn to overcome the obstacles and capitalize on the advantages associated with culturally diverse human resources.

✓ Concept Check

- What is workplace diversity?
- What are some of the benefits and challenges of workplace diversity?

Ethics and Social Responsibility

商业伦理与社会责任：苹果公司在种族平等问题上加倍努力

Apple Doubles Down on Racial Equity

Demand for diversity, equity, and inclusion initiatives in corporate America is on the rise. While many organizations have prioritized diversity efforts, equity remains a major issue in the workplace. Equity, which relates to equal opportunities and fair treatment, is at the center of Apple's $100 million Racial Equity and Justice Initiative (REJI).

Through REJI, Apple aims to lower systemic barriers to opportunity for communities of color by focusing on the next generation of leaders in technology. The funding will support the Propel Center in Atlanta (a global innovation and learning hub for historically Black colleges and universities), the Apple Developer Academy in Detroit (an education center for entrepreneurs, creators, and coders), and venture capital funding for 1,000 companies with diverse founders over the next 20 years. The Propel Center is a joint effort from Apple, Southern Company (an American energy company), and several community stakeholders that will support students both virtually and on-campus in Atlanta, Georgia. The Detroit-based developer academy is a collaboration with Michigan State University and will offer a 30-day introductory program as well as an extended boot camp.

In addition to REJI, Apple continues to build upon its contributions to community organizations such as community colleges, nonprofits, and other local organizations that empower the next generation. Apple's vice president of Environment, Policy, and Social Initiatives, Lisa Jackson, says "We are proud to lend our voices and resources to build new engines of opportunity that empower, inspire, and create meaningful change." In addition to REJI and community involvement, Apple has also made internal efforts to improve diversity, equity, and inclusion.

Sources: Based on information in Pavithra Mohan, "Apple Announces New Commitments to Its Racial Equity Initiative," *Fast Company*, January 12, 2021; Apple, "Apple Launches Major New Racial Equity and Justice Initiative Projects to Challenge Systemic Racism, Advance Racial Equity Nationwide," January 13, 2021.

岗位分析

8-4 Job Analysis

Learning Objective

8-4 Explain the objectives and uses of job analyses.

岗位分析
job analysis a systematic procedure for studying jobs to determine their various elements and requirements

岗位描述
job description a list of the elements that make up a particular job

岗位要求
job specification a list of the qualifications required to perform a particular job

✓ Concept Check

- What is job analysis?
- What is job specification?
- How can job specification be used to hire the right person for the job?

Managers need to understand the nature of a job before they can find the right person to do it. It would make no sense to hire new people without knowing why. **Job analysis** is a systematic procedure for studying positions to determine their various elements and requirements. Consider a clerk—in a large corporation, there may be 50 kinds of clerk positions, which may all differ in terms of activities performed, the level of proficiency required for each activity, and the set of qualifications demanded. These distinctions are the focus of job analysis.

The job analysis for a particular position typically consists of two parts—a job description and a job specification. A **job description** is a list of the elements that make up a particular job. It includes the duties to be performed, the working conditions, the responsibilities, and the tools and equipment that must be used on the job (refer to Figure 8-1). A **job specification** is a list of the qualifications required to perform a particular job, such as certain skills, abilities, education, and experience. In addition to requiring certain experience, some companies also list personality characteristics in job specifications.

The job analysis is not only the basis for recruiting and selecting new employees, but it is also used in other areas of HRM, including evaluation and the determination of equitable compensation levels.

Figure 8-1 Job Description and Job Specification

This job description explains the job of sales coordinator and lists the responsibilities of the position. The job specification is contained in the last paragraph.

CENGAGE
JOB DESCRIPTION

TITLE:	Georgia Sales Coordinator	**DATE:**	3/26/22
DEPARTMENT:	College, Sales	**GRADE:**	12
REPORTS TO:	Regional Manager	**EXEMPT/NONEXEMPT:**	Exempt

BRIEF SUMMARY:
Supervise one other Georgia-based sales representative to gain supervisory experience. Captain the four members of the outside sales rep team that are assigned to territories consisting of colleges and universities in Georgia. Oversee, coordinate, advise, and make decisions regarding Georgia sales activities. Based upon broad contact with customers across the state and communication with administrators of schools, the person will make recommendations regarding issues specific to the needs of higher education in the state of Georgia such as distance learning, conversion to the semester system, potential statewide adoptions, and faculty training.

PRINCIPAL ACCOUNTABILITIES:
1. Supervises/manages/trains one other Atlanta-based sales rep.
2. Advises two other sales reps regarding the Georgia schools in their territories.
3. Increases overall sales in Georgia as well as his or her individual sales territory.
4. Assists regional manager in planning and coordinating regional meetings and Atlanta conferences.
5. Initiates a dialogue with campus administrators, particularly in the areas of the semester conversion, distance learning, and faculty development.

DIMENSIONS:
This position will have one direct report in addition to the leadership role played within the region. Revenue most directly impacted will be within the individually assigned territory, the supervised territory, and the overall sales for the state of Georgia.

KNOWLEDGE AND SKILLS:
Must have displayed a history of consistently outstanding sales in personal territory. Must demonstrate clear teamwork and leadership skills and be willing to extend beyond the individual territory goals. Should have a clear understanding of the company's systems and product offerings in order to train and lead other sales representatives. Must have the communication skills and presence to communicate articulately with higher education administrators and to serve as a bridge between the company and higher education in the state.

Exploring Careers 职业探索：提高这些急需的技能

Sharpen These In-Demand Skills

Job hunting in a competitive job market has its challenges. To stand out as a candidate, it's important to focus on sharpening hard and soft skills that today's employers need. *Hard skills* refer to teachable abilities such as a business degree or proficiency in a foreign language while *soft skills* refer to interpersonal abilities such as teamwork and leadership. LinkedIn, the top social network for business professionals, used data from more than 20 million job listings and 660 million professional profiles to identify the most in-demand skills.

Today's most desirable hard skills relate to blockchain, cloud and distributed computing, analytical reasoning, artificial intelligence, user experience (UX) design, business analysis, affiliate marketing, sales, scientific computing, and video production. Most of these have a common thread: proficiency in emerging technologies. Without a doubt, analytical thinking and the ability to analyze data will be invaluable across industries as the business landscape evolves. The most in-demand soft skills include creativity, persuasion, collaboration, adaptability, and emotional intelligence.

Hard skills are easy to quantify and can be listed on a résumé or cover letter while soft skills can be more difficult to quantify. Instead, the ability to communicate these interpersonal abilities and characteristics during an interview is crucial. Candidates can share how they handled work challenges to show off soft skills. This is particularly important because soft skills are often key differentiators for job candidates as they are not as easily taught.

Sources: Based on information in Mara Leighton, "15 Skills LinkedIn Says Will Help You Get Hired in 2020 - and Where to Learn Them," *World Economic Forum*, September 3, 2020; Alison Doyle, "Hard Skills vs. Soft Skills: What's the Difference?" *The Balance Careers*, January 20, 2020.

招聘、筛选和入职

8-5 Recruiting, Selection, and Onboarding

Learning Objective

8-5 Describe the processes of recruiting, selecting employees, and onboarding.

In an organization with jobs waiting to be filled, HRM personnel need to (1) find candidates and (2) match the right candidate with each position. Three activities are involved: recruiting, selection, and new employee onboarding.

招聘

8-5a Recruiting

Recruiting is the process of attracting qualified job applicants. Because it is a vital link in a costly process (the cost of hiring an employee can be several thousand dollars), recruiting needs to be systematic. One goal of recruiters is to attract the "right number" of applicants, which is enough to allow a good match between applicants and open positions but not so many that matching requires a lot of time and effort. For example, if there are five open positions and five applicants, the firm has no choice. It must hire all five applicants (qualified or not). At the other extreme, if several hundred job seekers apply for the five positions, HRM personnel will spend weeks processing applications.

Recruiters may seek applicants outside the firm, within the firm, or both. The source used depends on the nature of the position, the situation within the firm, and sometimes the firm's established or traditional recruitment policies.

Organizations often start the recruiting process by considering current employees as applicants for available positions. Promoting from within provides strong motivation for current employees and helps the firm to retain quality personnel along with their experience. *Job posting*, or informing current employees of upcoming openings, is practiced by many different types of firms. It may be a

招聘
recruiting the process of attracting qualified job applicants

company policy or be required by union contract. The primary disadvantage of internal recruiting is that promoting a current employee leaves another position open. Not only does the firm still incur recruiting and selection costs, but it also must train two employees instead of one.

In many situations it may be impossible to recruit internally. For example, no current employee may be qualified to fill a new position, or the firm may be growing so rapidly that there is no time to reassign positions that open as a result of promotion or transfer. In that case, companies turn to external recruiting.

External recruiting involves attracting job applicants from outside an organization. External recruiting may include activities on college campuses and open houses, job and career fairs, soliciting recommendations from current employees, posting in newspapers, employment agencies, and online efforts. Your college or university probably has an on-campus career center where many companies engage in recruiting activities. Some firms are becoming more creative to attract younger applicants. Taco Bell has held "hiring parties" to attract applicants, offering free food and branded merchandise and holding on-the-spot job interviews.[7] Of course, the internet is a popular medium for both recruiters and job seekers. Most large organizations devote portions of their websites to job postings. Online job sites such as Monster.com, Indeed.com, and SimplyHired.com help potential employees search for positions by criteria such as location, industry, or pay.

Increasingly, social media plays a significant role in the recruiting process. Savvy companies know that their social media pages like LinkedIn, Twitter, and Instagram are among their best recruiting tools, especially for reaching digital natives like Millennials and Generation Z. A survey by the Society for Human Resources Management found that 84 percent of employers look at social media sites—most

Technology and Innovation

技术与创新：网上招聘会

Career Fairs Go Online

In-person career fairs have long been a mainstay of talent acquisition. Social distancing during the COVID-19 pandemic, however, increased demand for virtual career fairs and hiring events where recruiters and candidates interact through one-on-one chats and video calls. Though the concept is not new, the adoption of this strategic recruiting tool has risen sharply.

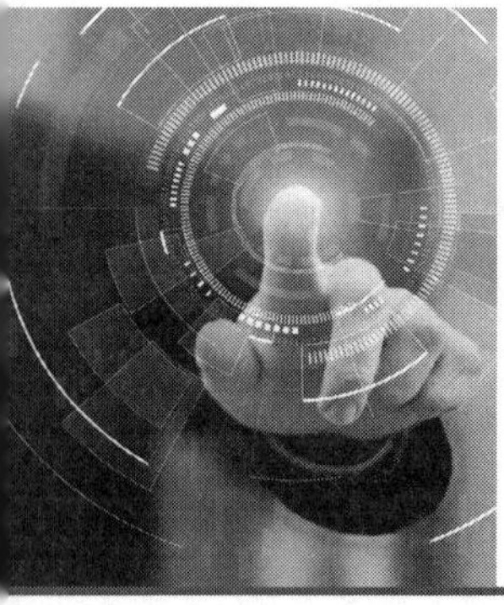

Now, in the wake of the global health crisis, it's clear that the trend toward virtual career fairs is here to stay. Both job seekers and recruiters agree that online, cloud-based hiring events are flexible and efficient. Many human resources professionals have found that virtual career fairs are easy to promote, manage, and personalize, not to mention less costly than traditional career events. In addition, organizations can easily and efficiently collect attendee data.

The growing video communications market has spelled success for many technology companies such as Brazen, a virtual hiring event and online career fair software. Brazen experienced a surge in demand from retailers, healthcare organizations, tech companies, and educational institutions. Brazen's technology has also been used by organizations to connect their laid-off and furloughed employees with other companies. The global pandemic accelerated the transition to remote work, a change that many organizations have made permanent. As more companies adopt a digital mentality, recruiting, selection, and orientation will increasingly occur online as well.

Sources: Based on information in Nicole Dienst and Kelsey Johnson, "How to Prepare for—and Land a Job—at a Virtual Career Fair," *CNBC*, August 1, 2020; Roy Maurer, "Career Fairs Go Virtual in Reaction to Pandemic," *Society for Human Resource Management*, May 18, 2020.

notably LinkedIn, Facebook, and Twitter— for recruiting purposes. The survey also found that 71 percent of companies employ social networking tools to identify and recruit applicants with specific skills, and 77 percent use social networking to raise their brand recognition.[8] Recruiters have learned that posting photos, videos, and stories about their firms humanizes them, demonstrates their culture, and depicts what it is like to work at them. Beyond posting current openings to attract today's job seekers, social recruiting can also build a following—and pool of future applicants—among those not yet in the workforce. Clearly, it is best to match the recruiting means with the kind of applicant being sought.

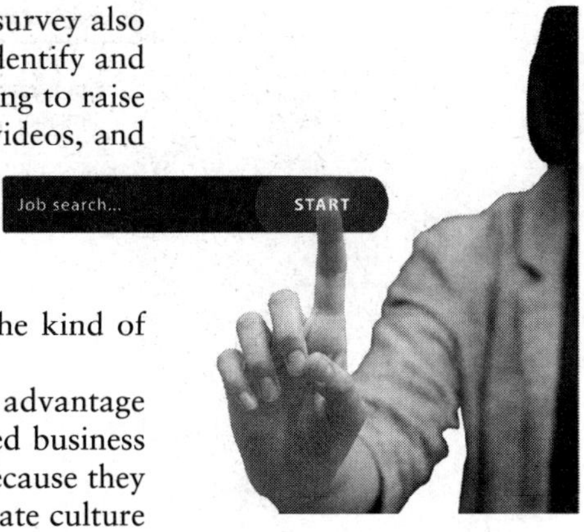

External recruiting has advantages and disadvantages. A primary advantage is that it brings people into a firm who have new perspectives and varied business backgrounds. Some firms prefer to hire recruits directly out of college because they believe that these candidates will be easier to train to fit with the corporate culture and the needs of the company. An additional benefit of hiring younger talent is that they tend to be more technologically savvy than their older counterparts, a characteristic that is highly desirable in today's workplace. A disadvantage of external recruiting is that it is often expensive, especially if private employment agencies must be used. External recruiting also may provoke resentment among present employees who wish to advance within the company.

筛选

8-5b Selection

Selection is the process of gathering information about applicants for a position and using that information to choose the most appropriate applicant. Note the use of the word *appropriate*. In selection, the idea is not to hire the person with the *most* qualifications but rather the applicant who is *most appropriate* for the job at hand—and also satisfies the firm's goals and fits into its overall culture. Line managers responsible for the position usually select applicants. However, HRM personnel usually help by developing a pool of applicants and by expediting their assessment. Common means of obtaining information about applicants' qualifications are employment applications, interviews, references, assessment centers, and social networking sites like LinkedIn and Facebook. Indeed, in many cases, social networking has changed the order in which employers receive information. Employers can peruse LinkedIn accounts, for example, to see reviews and recommendations before even interviewing a candidate. Some companies today are also showing candidates realistic job previews (RJPs)—authentic presentations that depict both positive and negative aspects of the job along with the company's culture. Presenting such realistic information about the job may weed out less interested candidates before they reach more costly steps in the selection process.

Employment Applications An employment application is useful for collecting factual information on a candidate's education, work experience, and personal history (refer to Figure 8-2). The data from applications are used for two purposes: to identify applicants who are worthy of further scrutiny and to familiarize interviewers with applicant backgrounds. Online applications are common, which helps to streamline the process and improve data-gathering capabilities for the firm. In fact, paper applications are becoming rare.

Many job candidates submit résumés, and some firms require them. A *résumé* is a one- or two-page summary of the candidate's background and qualifications. It may include a description of the type of job the applicant is seeking. A résumé may be sent to a firm to request consideration for available jobs, or it may be submitted along with an employment application.

筛选
selection the process of gathering information about applicants for a position and then using that information to choose the most appropriate applicant

Figure 8-2 Typical Employment Application

Employers use applications to collect factual information on a candidate's education, work experience, and personal history.

To improve the usefulness of information, HRM specialists ask current employees about experiences and characteristics that relate to their current jobs. These factors are included on the applications and may be weighted more heavily when evaluating new applicants' qualifications.

Employment Tests Tests administered to job candidates usually focus on aptitudes, skills, abilities, or knowledge relevant to the job. Such tests (basic computer skills tests, for example) help an employer gauge how well the applicant can perform the job. Companies may use general intelligence or personality tests, but these are seldom helpful in predicting performance. Many organizations of all sizes use predictive behavior tests, which have become more affordable with improved technology.

Interviews The interview is perhaps the most widely used selection technique because it provides an opportunity for applicants and the firm to learn more about one another. Job candidates are interviewed by at least one member of the HRM staff and by the person for whom they will be working. Candidates for higher-level jobs may meet with a department head or vice president over several interviews.

Interviewers may pose problems to test the candidate's abilities, probe employment history, and learn something about the candidate's attitudes and motivation. The candidate has a chance to find out more about the job and potential co-workers. Interviews also provide an opportunity to test the personality fit of a candidate with the organizational culture. Many organizations now conduct interviews remotely using services such as Skype, Zoom, or gotomeeting.com, only flying in the most promising candidates for face-to-face meetings.

Unfortunately, interviewing may be the stage at which discrimination begins. For example, suppose that an applicant mentions that they are the parent of small children. The interviewer may assume that the applicant will be resistant to job-related travel, even though that may not be true. In addition, interviewers may be unduly influenced by such factors as appearance. They may also ask different questions of different applicants so that it becomes impossible to compare candidates' qualifications objectively. Some of these problems can be solved through better interviewer training and by using structured interviews. In a *structured interview*, the interviewer asks only a prepared set of job-related questions. The firm also may consider using several different interviewers for each applicant, but this can be costly.

References A job candidate generally is asked to furnish the names of references—people who can verify background information and provide personal evaluations. Naturally, applicants tend to list only references who are likely to say good things. Thus, personal evaluations obtained from references may not be of much value. However, references are often contacted to verify such information as previous job responsibilities and the reason an applicant left a former job.

A job interview is similar to a first date. Like a date, interviews can occur in a variety of locations and through several formats. The purpose is to give the candidate and the company the opportunity to find out about each other. Can you think of any other selection methods that benefit *both* parties in the recruiting process?

Assessment Centers An assessment center is used primarily to select current employees for promotion to higher-level positions. Typically, a group of employees is sent to the center for a few days. While there, they participate in activities designed to simulate the management environment and to predict managerial effectiveness. Trained observers make recommendations regarding promotion possibilities. The expense of this technique limits its use.

入职培训
8-5c Onboarding

Once all information about job candidates has been collected and analyzed, the company extends a job offer. If it is accepted, the candidate becomes an employee. Soon after a candidate joins a firm, they go through the firm's onboarding program. **Onboarding** is the process of integrating new employees into the organization. It is a process that can take weeks or months and involves welcoming the new employee, helping them build relationships with managers and team members, providing training and tools to carry out their assignments, and most importantly, acclimating them to the firm's culture. One step in onboarding is **orientation**, the basic introduction of new employees to the organization. Orientation typically involves the initial hiring paperwork, supplying the employee handbook, explaining benefits, touring the facilities, and furnishing keys, logins, passwords, and the like. Larger companies may begin the onboarding process several days before new employees' first day by sending them a welcome package that includes access to an online onboarding dashboard, to help employees feel ready to get to work. Some may also assign a mentor or buddy that a new hire can shadow to learn the ropes. Strong onboarding programs also have new employees regularly check in about how they are doing so that managers can offer feedback and provide support.

入职
onboarding the process of integrating new employees into an organization

岗前介绍
orientation the basic introduction of new employees to an organization

Companies are increasingly recognizing that a strong onboarding process can boost new employee retention. One survey found that 31 percent of new hires leave within the first six months.[9] Ensuring that new hires feel welcomed and valued, and know what to do to carry out their assignments and where to go for support, makes it less likely they will leave the firm due to dissatisfaction. Keeping all employees happy is a major goal of human resources management.

✓ Concept Check

- What are the differences between internal and external recruiting?
- Under what conditions are each one of them used?
- Identify and briefly describe the types of practices and tools that are used in the selection process.
- How does onboarding help improve employee retention?

薪酬和福利

8-6 Compensation and Benefits

Learning Objective

8-6 Examine decisions associated with employee compensation and benefits.

An effective employee reward system must (1) enable employees to satisfy basic needs, (2) provide rewards comparable with those offered by other firms, (3) be distributed fairly within the organization, and (4) recognize that different people have different needs. A firm's compensation system can be structured to meet the first three of these requirements. The fourth is more difficult because it must account for many variables. Most firms offer a number of benefits that, taken together, generally help to provide for employees' varying needs.

薪酬决策

8-6a Compensation Decisions

Compensation is the payment employees receive in return for their labor. Its importance to employees is obvious. Because compensation can account for a significant percentage of a firm's operating costs, it is also an important consideration for management. Therefore, the firm's **compensation system**, the policies and strategies that determine employee compensation, must be designed carefully to provide for employees' needs while keeping labor costs within reasonable limits. For most firms, designing an effective compensation system requires three separate management decisions—wage level, wage structure, and individual wages.

Wage Level Management first must position the firm's general pay level relative to pay levels of comparable firms. Most firms choose a level near the industry average. However, a firm that is not in good financial shape may pay less than average, and large, prosperous organizations may pay more than average. Consider PayPal, which chose to give pay raises to its call center employees even though they were already being paid above market rate. CEO Dan Schulman said the pay raises helped ensure that each employee had a net disposable income of at least 20 percent. Schulman says, "You can't have passionate employees if every month they are worried about how they are going to make ends meet."[10] To determine the average pay for a job, the firm may use wage surveys. A **wage survey** is a collection of data on prevailing wage rates within an industry or a geographic area. Such surveys are compiled by industry associations, local governments, personnel associations, and (occasionally) individual firms.

Wage Structure Next, management must decide on relative pay levels for all the positions within the firm. The result of this set of decisions is called the firm's *wage structure*. The wage structure almost always is developed on the basis of a job evaluation. **Job evaluation** is the process of determining the relative worth of the various jobs within a firm. Most observers probably would agree that an administrative assistant should make more money than a custodian, but how much more?

A number of techniques may be used to evaluate jobs. The simplest is to rank all the jobs within the firm according to value. A more frequently used method is based on the job analysis. Points are allocated to each element and job requirement. For example, "college degree required" might be worth 50 points, whereas a job requiring only a high school diploma would only receive 25 points. The more points allocated, the more important the job is presumed to be (and the higher its level in the firm's wage structure).

Individual Wages Finally, the company must determine the specific payments individual employees will receive. Consider the case of two administrative assistants. Job evaluation was used to determine the level of administrative pay, but suppose that one assistant has 15 years of experience, can type 80 words per minute accurately, and can work in several computer programs, while the other

薪酬
compensation the payment employees receive in return for their labor

薪酬制度
compensation system the policies and strategies that determine employee compensation

薪资调查
wage survey a collection of data on prevailing wage rates within an industry or a geographic area

岗位评估
job evaluation the process of determining the relative worth of the various jobs within a firm

has two years of experience, can type only 55 words per minute, and knows only one computer program. In most firms, a wage range would be established (maybe $10.00 to $15.00 per hour) to reflect the range of experience and abilities, with the more qualified administrative assistant receiving the higher wage.

Two wage decisions come into play here. First, the employee's initial rate must be established. It is based on experience, other qualifications, and expected performance. Later, the employee may be given pay increases based on seniority and performance.

薪酬类型

8-6b Types of Compensation

Compensation can take a variety of forms. Most forms fall into the following categories: hourly wage, weekly or monthly salary, commissions, incentive payments, lump-sum salary increases, and profit sharing.

Hourly Wage An **hourly wage** is a specific amount of money paid for each hour worked. People who earn wages are paid their hourly wage for the first 40 hours worked in any week. Anything in excess of 40 hours is overtime, for which they are paid one-and-one-half times their hourly wage. Workers in retail and fast-food chains, on assembly lines, and in clerical positions usually are paid an hourly wage.

Weekly or Monthly Salary A **salary** is a specific amount of money paid for an employee's work during a set calendar period, regardless of the actual number of hours worked. Salaried employees receive no overtime pay, but they do not lose pay when they work less than 40 hours per week. Most professional and managerial positions are salaried.

Commissions A **commission** is a payment that is a percentage of sales revenue. Sales representatives and sales managers often are paid entirely through commissions or a combination of commissions and salary.

Incentive Payments An **incentive payment** is in addition to wages, salary, or commissions. Incentive payments are rewards for outstanding job performance. They may be distributed to all or only select employees. Some firms distribute incentive payments to all employees annually. The size of the payment depends on the firm's earnings and, at times, on the particular employee's length of service with the firm. One of the most common incentive payments is the *bonus,* a payment given beyond base pay, often at the end of the year. These payments can serve as a thank you for hard work or persevering in tough times. McDonald's, for example, gave employees at company-owned stores a bonus of 10 percent of one month's earned pay to show its appreciation of their efforts during the COVID-19 pandemic. Many of its franchisors also awarded bonuses or gift cards to their employees.[11] Firms sometimes offer incentives to team members that exceed specific sales or production goals, a practice called *gainsharing*. Some organizations reward outstanding workers individually through *merit pay*. Such incentive payments allow management to control labor costs while encouraging employees to work more efficiently.

Lump-Sum Salary Increases In traditional reward systems, an annual pay increase is spread evenly across each paycheck that year. However, some companies offer a **lump-sum salary increase**. This gives employees the option of taking the entire pay raise in one lump sum. Employees then draw their "regular" pay for the rest of the year. The lump-sum payment typically is treated as an interest-free loan that must be repaid if an employee leaves the firm during the year.

时薪
hourly wage a specific amount of money paid for each hour of work

薪金
salary a specific amount of money paid for an employee's work during a set calendar period, regardless of the actual number of hours worked

佣金
commission a payment that is a percentage of sales revenue

奖金
incentive payment a payment in addition to wages, salary, or commissions

一次性加薪
lump-sum salary increase an entire pay raise taken in one lump sum

Profit Sharing **Profit sharing** is the distribution of a percentage of a firm's profit among its employees. The idea is to motivate employees to work effectively by giving them a stake in the company's financial success. For example, every year since 1938 Hormel Foods Corporation has distributed its profits to employees in the form of dividends at the beginning of the winter holiday season. The higher the profits, the higher the dividends employees earn.[12]

缩小性别差距

8-6c Closing the Gender Gap

It is an established fact that women in the workforce are paid less than men, in spite of measures and legislation to counter this phenomenon. Analysis of median hourly compensation of both full- and part-time U.S. workers by the Pew Research Center found that women today still earn just 85 percent of what men do, although this gap has narrowed from 67 percent in 1980.[13] This gap is larger for women of color: Black women earn about 62 percent and Hispanic women about 54 percent, on average.[14] Moreover, women continue to report pay inequality and gender discrimination in the workplace. Addressing pay inequality is complicated. Studies have shown that, even after controlling for educational attainment and profession, wage gaps persist between men and women. Research suggests that factors behind the continuing wage disparity may include the idea that women are less inclined to ask for raises and that working mothers are less likely to work long hours or at specific times.

In recent decades, many states have taken steps to ensure that all workers have equal pay for comparable worth, but the issue is contentious. Critics argue that inflating salaries artificially for female-dominated occupations encourages women to keep these jobs rather than seek out higher-paying jobs. Increasingly, companies are taking steps to address the gender wage gap by conducting pay-equity analyses and publicizing the results of their investigations into their own pay gaps. Salesforce, for example, acknowledged that a review of all 17,000 employees' salaries identified gaps; the company spent nearly $9 million extra on payroll over several years to close the gap.[15] Citigroup, Starbucks, MasterCard, Facebook, Apple, Google, Intel, and Microsoft have disclosed the results of reviews of employee pay to highlight their efforts in narrowing their pay gap.[16] In any case, closing the gender gap can help companies attract and retain the best employees. Salesforce CEO Marc Benioff, for example, believes his company's efforts to close the gap helped propel it to the top of *Fortune*'s list of "Best Companies to Work For" and *People*'s list of "Companies That Care."[17]

员工福利

8-6d Employee Benefits

An **employee benefit** is a reward in addition to regular compensation that is provided indirectly to employees. Employee benefits consist mainly of services (such as health and life insurance) that are paid for partially or totally by employers, and employee expenses (such as college tuition) that employers reimburse. Currently, the average cost of these benefits in private industry is 30 percent of an employee's total compensation.[18] Thus, a person who receives a salary of $35,000 really receives total compensation of $50,000, once $15,000 in benefits (30 percent of $50,000) is factored in.

Types of Benefits Employee benefits take a variety of forms. *Pay for time not worked* covers such absences as vacation, holidays, and sick leave. *Insurance packages* may include health, life, vision, and dental insurance for employees and their families. Some firms pay the entire cost of the insurance package, and others share the cost with the employee. The costs of *pension and retirement programs* also may be borne entirely by the firm or shared with the employee.

利润分享
profit sharing the distribution of a percentage of a firm's profit among its employees

员工福利
employee benefit a reward in addition to regular compensation that is provided indirectly to employees

What job benefits are crucial to you? The benefits companies provide vary widely. Large companies are often able to offer employees more benefits than small ones. However, in small firms, employees are more likely to do a broader range of tasks and advance to higher positions more quickly.

Some benefits are required by law. For example, employers must maintain *workers' compensation insurance*, which pays medical bills for injuries that occur on the job and provides income for employees who are disabled by job-related injuries. Employers must also pay for *unemployment insurance* and contribute to each employee's federal *Social Security* account.

Other benefits employers may provide include tuition-reimbursement plans, credit union memberships, child-care services, company cafeterias, exercise rooms, and broad employee stock-option plans. Some companies offer special benefits to U.S. military reservists who are called up for active duty. Increasingly, companies offer more varied benefits to attract and retain the best employees. In the high-tech industry, competition for talented employees is so intense that many firms have adopted more extreme perks, such as free meals, extended parental leave (up to one year at Netflix), on-campus amenities like fitness and recreation, free paid days off, travel stipends, fertility assistance, and even student loan debt reimbursement.[19]

弹性福利计划
flexible benefit plan
compensation plan whereby employees receive a predetermined amount of benefit dollars to spend on a package of benefits they have selected to meet individual needs

Flexible Benefit Plans Through a **flexible benefit plan**, employees receive a predetermined amount of benefit dollars and may allocate those dollars to various categories of benefits in the way that best fits their needs. Sometimes these are known as *cafeteria plans* because employees can pick and choose what best works for them. Some flexible benefit plans offer a broad array of benefit options, including healthcare, dental care, life insurance, accidental death and dismemberment coverage for the worker and dependents, long-term disability coverage, vacation benefits, retirement savings, and dependent-care benefits. Other firms offer limited options, primarily in health and life insurance and retirement plans.

Although the cost of administering flexible plans is high, a number of organizations, including Phillips Corporation and Coca-Cola, have implemented this option. Because employees' needs are so diverse, flexible plans help firms to offer benefit packages that more specifically meet their employees' needs. Flexible plans can, in the long run, help a company contain costs because a specified amount is allocated to cover the benefits of each employee. Furthermore, organizations that offer flexible plans with many choices may be perceived as being employee-friendly. Thus, they are in a better position to attract and retain qualified employees.

✓ Concept Check

- Identify the major compensation decisions that HRM managers make.
- What are the different forms of compensation?
- What are the major types of employee benefits?
- How do flexible benefit plans work?

Entrepreneurial Success

创业成功：小企业注重更好的福利

Small Businesses Focus on Better Benefits

Working professionals have increasingly high expectations when it comes to employee benefits. From on-site child care to pet insurance, many individuals want better benefits than healthcare alone. Historically, offering competitive perks has been a challenge for small businesses and start-ups because they can be costly and time-intensive to manage. Now, a new wave of human resources (HR) providers and benefits managers such as TriNet, Zenefits, and Gusto are making better benefits a reality.

When entrepreneurs run a business, they often wear many hats such as CEO, sales manager, and HR manager. They often do not have the personal bandwidth or financial resources to offer the types of benefits that large corporations provide. However, having the right mix of benefits can be critical for retaining employees. TriNet is one cloud-based HR solution that small businesses have turned to. The company can handle everything from payroll to benefits administration and can offer the same scale that larger companies have.

According to a study by LaSalle Network, shopping for better benefits is one of the top three reasons Millennials leave their jobs. As it is, employees ages 18 to 34 are already more likely to job hop. The most desirable benefits include matching contributions to 401(k) savings programs, student loan assistance, generous paid time off, flexible working arrangements, and remote work opportunities. With competitive benefits, start-ups have a better chance of recruiting and retaining high-quality talent.

Sources: Based on information in Jessica Dickler, "Why Small Businesses Are Banking on Better Benefits," *CNBC*, January 25, 2020; Nadine El-Bawab, "More Millennials Are Demanding These Workplace Perks," *CNBC*, February 7, 2019.

培训与发展

8-7 Training and Development

Learning Objective

8-7 Explain the purposes and techniques of employee training and development.

Training and development are extremely important in helping employees succeed at their jobs and for companies to retain them. As such, they represent a major investment in human resources. For Dollar General, the importance of training is evidenced by its recent induction into *Training* magazine's "Hall of Fame" list. Dollar General has made *Training*'s "Top 125" list for nine consecutive years, distinguishing itself through its effectiveness and efficiency, number of training hours logged by employees, and survey results. Employees log nearly 1.7 million training hours annually, using a range of technologies, including mobile and online learning. The company offers nearly 12,000 courses to employees to ensure that they continue their professional development.[20] Many top managers believe that the financial and human resources invested in training and development are well worth it. Employees at all levels of a company need training and/or development about its products, specific computer programs and protocols, customer needs, company policies and codes of conduct, applicable regulations, competitors' products, and more.

Both training and development are aimed at improving employees' skills and abilities. However, the two are usually differentiated as employee training or management development. **Employee training** is the process of teaching operations and technical employees how to do their present jobs more effectively and efficiently. **Management development** is the process of preparing managers and other professionals to assume increased responsibility in both present and future positions. Thus, training and development differ in who is being taught and the purpose of the teaching. However, both are necessary for personal and organizational growth. Additionally, a number of companies encourage this growth through more informal mentorship programs. **Mentors** are older, higher-ranked employees who instruct, advise, and offer support to younger employees in the ways of the organization

员工培训
employee training the process of teaching operations and technical employees how to do their present jobs more effectively and efficiently

管理开发
management development the process of preparing managers and other professionals to assume increased responsibility in both present and future positions

导师
mentors older, higher-ranked employees who instruct, advise, and offer support to younger employees in the ways of the organization and industry

and industry. In some cases, companies use reverse mentoring by asking younger employees to advise senior staff members about technology and social media.

Companies that hope to stay competitive typically make huge commitments to employee training and development. Indeed, training accounts for about $82.5 billion of business spending in the United States.[21] Developing an effective training program involves analyzing needs, determining the best methods, and developing an evaluation system to gauge effectiveness. Some employers require workers to attain certifications targeted to their field to help them gain and maintain the specific skills they need. There are many different employee training methods, including internet-based training. Internet training is growing in popularity as it can result in significant cost, travel, and time savings.

培训需求分析

8-7a Analysis of Training Needs

When thinking about developing a training program, managers first must determine if training is actually needed and, if so, what types of training needs exist. Training needs can vary considerably. For example, some employees may need to improve their technical skills, while others need training on organizational procedures. Training also may focus on business ethics, product information, or customer service. Because training is expensive, it is critical that the correct training needs be identified. Employers may find that sometimes employees need motivation more than they need training.

培训与发展的方法

8-7b Training and Development Methods

A number of methods are available for employee training and management development. Most of these methods can be applied to both training and management development.

- *On-the-job methods*. The trainee learns by doing the work under the supervision of an experienced employee.
- *Simulations*. The work situation is simulated in a separate area so that learning takes place away from the day-to-day pressures of work.
- *Classroom teaching and lectures*. Instructors present concepts and illustrations through a variety of techniques.
- *Conferences and seminars*. Experts and learners come together to discuss problems and exchange ideas.
- *Role-playing*. Participants act out others' roles in order to better understand them (primarily a management development tool).
- *e-Learning*. Participants train by watching videos of lectures or how-to guides, playing "games" that simulate work situations, or taking online quizzes to demonstrate their proficiency in a topic.

What job training methods have you experienced, and how effective were they? Organizations train employees using a variety of methods and locations. Depending on the type of business, the training may take just a few hours or more than a year.

培训与发展评估

8-7c Evaluation of Training and Development

Training and development are expensive because the training itself can be costly and employees are not working at full productivity while they are receiving training, costing the firm further revenue. To ensure that training and development are as cost-effective as possible, the managers responsible should evaluate the company's efforts periodically.

✓ Concept Check

- What is the difference between employee training and management development?
- What are the primary training and development methods used by firms?

In order to set benchmarks and gauge program effectiveness, managers should develop measurable objectives before the training starts. For example, a measurable object would be that, after receiving training, a new employee will be able to produce a report using a specified format and be able to correctly identify 20 critical terms related to the field. The results of training evaluations should be made known to all those involved in the program—including trainees and upper management. For trainees, the results of evaluations can enhance motivation and learning. For upper management, the results may be the basis for making decisions about the training program itself.

绩效评估

8-8 Performance Appraisal

Learning Objective

8-8 Discuss performance appraisal techniques and performance feedback.

Performance appraisal is the evaluation of employees' performance to allow managers to make unbiased human resources decisions. For many firms, these appraisals occur once a year, but more organizations are beginning to drop the annual performance review in favor of more frequent feedback sessions that account for changing priorities and situations. The financial services firm Deloitte, for example, has employees check in with supervisors every other week about their performance progress, challenges, successes, and career aspirations.[22] Some companies call this approach *performance management* because it is ongoing and helps employees be their best.

Regardless of frequency, the appraisal process has three main objectives. First, managers use performance appraisals to let workers know how well they are doing and how they can improve. Second, a performance appraisal provides an effective basis for distributing rewards, such as pay raises and promotions. Third, performance appraisal analysis helps the organization monitor its employee selection, training, and development activities. If large numbers of employees continually perform below expectations, the firm may need to revise its selection process or strengthen its training and development activities. Most performance appraisal processes include a written document. An example appears in Figure 8-3.

常用的评估技术

8-8a Common Evaluation Techniques

The techniques and methods for appraising employee performance are either objective or judgmental in nature.

Objective Methods Objective appraisal methods use some measurable quantity as the basis for assessing performance. Units of output, dollar volume of sales, number of defective products, and number of insurance claims processed are all objective, measurable quantities. Thus, an employee who processes an average of 26 insurance claims per week is given a higher evaluation than one whose average is 19 claims per week.

Such objective measures may require adjustment depending on the work environment. Suppose that the first of our insurance claims processor works in New York City and the second works in rural Iowa. Both must visit each client because they are processing homeowners' insurance claims. The difference in their average weekly output may be entirely because of the long distances the Iowan must travel to visit clients. In this case, the two workers may very well be equally competent and motivated. Thus, a manager must take into account circumstances that may be hidden by a purely statistical measurement.

Judgmental Methods Judgmental appraisal methods are used much more frequently than objective methods. They require that the supervisor judge or estimate the employee's performance level. These methods are based on

绩效评估

performance appraisal the evaluation of employees' performance to allow managers to make objective human resources decisions

Figure 8-3 Performance Appraisal

3M **Contribution and Development Summary**
FORM 37450 - B

Employee Name	Employee Number	Job Title
Department		Location
Coach/Supervisor(s) Name(s)		Review Period From : To :

Major Job Responsibilities

Goals/Expectations | **Contributions/Results**

Contribution (To be completed by coach/supervisor)

- ☐ Good Level of Contribution for this year
- ☐ Exceptional Level of Contribution for this year
- ☐ Unsatisfactory Level of Contribution for this year

page 3

Development Summary

Areas of Strength	Development Priorities

Career Interests

Next job	Longer Range

Current Mobility

- ☐ 0 - Currently Unable to Relocate
- ☐ 1 - Position In Home Country Only (Use if Home Country is Outside U.S.)
- ☐ 2 - Position Within O.U.S. Region (e: Nordic, SEA...)
- ☐ 3 - Position Within O.U.S. Area (ex: Europe, Asia)
- ☐ 4 - Position In U.S.
- ☐ 5 - Position Anywhere In The World

Development

- ☐ W - Well placed. Development plans achievable in current role for at least the next year
- ☐ C - Ready now for a move to a different job for career broadening experience
- ☐ I - Ready now for a move to a different job involving increased responsibility
- ☐ X - Not well placed. Action required to resolve placement issues.

Comments on Development

Employee Comments

Coach/Supervisor Comments	**Other Supervisor (if applicable) and/or Reviewer**

Signatures

Coach/Supervisor	Date	Other Coach/Supervisor or Reviewer	Date
Employee			Date

page 4

Source: Courtesy of 3M.

employee ranking or rating scales. When ranking is used, the manager ranks subordinates from best to worst. This approach has drawbacks, including the lack of an absolute standard. Use of rating scales is the most popular judgmental appraisal technique. A *rating scale* consists of a number of statements, on which each employee is rated based on the degree to which the statement applies. For example, one statement might be, "This employee always does high-quality work." The supervisor would give the employee a rating, from 5 down to 1, corresponding to gradations ranging from "strongly agree" to "strongly disagree." The ratings on all the statements are added to obtain the employee's total evaluation.

Avoiding Appraisal Errors Managers must be cautious if they are to avoid making mistakes when appraising employees. It is common to overuse one portion of an evaluation instrument, thus risking overemphasizing or underemphasizing issues. Supervisors must guard against allowing an employee's poor performance on one activity to influence their judgment of that subordinate's work on other activities. Similarly, putting too much weight on recent performance can distort an employee's evaluation. For example, if the employee is being rated on performance over the last year, a manager should not permit last month's disappointing performance to overshadow the quality of the work done in the first 11 months of the year. Finally, a manager must guard against discrimination on the basis of race, age, gender, religion, national origin, or sexual orientation.

绩效反馈

8-8b Performance Feedback

Performance feedback can help employees progress within an organization. A business usually evaluates its employees on an annual basis, but sometimes it does so quarterly or even monthly, especially when employees are newly hired. Performance reviews that gather feedback about employees from their peers, subordinates, and supervisors can help them get a realistic view of their strengths and weaknesses.

No matter which appraisal technique is used, managers should discuss the results with the employee soon after completion. The manager should explain the basis for present rewards and let the employee know what can be done to improve. The supervisor can also communicate about opportunities for training and development to help employees overcome any performance deficiencies and develop new skills to advance in their careers. The information provided to an employee in such discussions is called *performance feedback*, and the process is known as a *performance feedback interview*.

There are three major approaches to performance feedback interviews: tell-and-sell, tell-and-listen, and problem solving. In a *tell-and-sell* feedback interview, the superior tells the employee how good or bad the employee's performance has been and attempts to persuade the employee to accept the evaluation. Because the employee has no input into the evaluation, the tell-and-sell interview can lead to defensiveness, resentment, and frustration on the part of the subordinate.

With the *tell-and-listen* approach, the supervisor tells the employee what the employee has done right and wrong and then gives him or her a chance to respond. The subordinate may simply be given an opportunity to react to the supervisor's statements or may be permitted to offer a full self-appraisal.

In the *problem-solving* approach, employees evaluate their own performance and set their own goals for future performance. The supervisor is more a colleague than a judge and offers comments and advice in a noncritical manner while mutually agreeing with the employee on goals for improvement. This is the method most likely to result in employee commitment to the established goals.

To avoid some of the problems associated with the tell-and-sell interview, supervisors sometimes use a mixed approach. The mixed interview uses the tell-and-sell approach to communicate administrative decisions and the problem-solving approach to discuss employee-development issues and future performance goals.

Another approach that has become popular is called a *360-degree evaluation*. A 360-degree evaluation collects anonymous reviews about employees from their peers, subordinates, and supervisors and compiles them into a feedback report for each employee. Companies that invest significant resources in employee-development efforts are especially likely to use 360-degree evaluations. Employees should not be given a feedback report without first having a one-on-one meeting with their supervisor. To ensure effective implementation, upper-level management should adopt this approach first and coach managers on how to use the feedback to achieve positive performance and behavioral outcomes.

Many managers find it difficult to discuss negative appraisals, leading them to ignore performance feedback. However, it is important for employees to be informed of how they can improve so that they can be their best. Employers should emphasize employee strengths when delivering a negative appraisal. Without feedback, employees may be unaware of their weaknesses and therefore not realize that they need to take steps to address them. Only through tactful, honest communication can the results of an appraisal be fully used.

✓ Concept Check

- What are the main objectives of performance appraisal?
- What methods are used?
- Describe the three approaches to performance feedback interviews.

员工流动

8-9 Employee Turnover

Companies make huge investments in training and development and provide performance appraisals to help reduce employee turnover. **Turnover** occurs when employees leave their jobs—whether they quit, retire, are laid off or fired, or even are promoted to a higher level within the firm. Regardless of why an employee leaves, they likely will have to be replaced or other employees will have to take over the tasks that employee once did. Understaffed firms often require other employees to take up the slack in the form of longer hours and overtime, which can lead to dissatisfaction and even more turnover. High levels of turnover are undesirable because recruiting, selecting, and training new employees is a costly process. Moreover, high turnover can stifle productivity and focus. Finally, high turnover can indicate a problem with morale that should be addressed. Turnover therefore requires careful monitoring by human resources personnel to minimize disruptions, reduce costs, and maximize overall employee satisfaction.

Undesirable turnover is primarily due to **terminations**, which are involuntary separations from a firm. When there is a mismatch between a firm's supply of and demand for human resources or a significant reduction in resources is needed to survive, it may need to consider **downsizing** by eliminating positions. In such cases, a company may implement a hiring freeze, cut back employees' hours and/or benefits, or *lay off* some employees—dismiss them from the workforce until they are needed again. In the case of layoffs, it is the positions that are eliminated rather than the employees holding those positions. In the face of drastically reduced revenues during the COVID-19 pandemic, Airbnb was forced to downsize, laying off about 1,900 employees or 25 percent of its workforce. The travel company offered laid-off employees severance pay, a year's worth of health insurance, and equity in the firm.[23] Perhaps the most compassionate method for making personnel cutbacks is through attrition. *Attrition* is the normal reduction in the workforce that occurs when employees leave a firm due to retirement or finding a new job. *Early retirement* is another option for reducing workforce size. Under early retirement, people who are within a few years of retirement are permitted to retire ahead of schedule with full benefits. *Buyouts* are similar to early retirement in that employees are offered a severance package in order to leave their jobs. Buyouts typically offer a number of weeks of pay for every year an employee has worked plus a specified period of extension of benefits after the employee leaves. As a last resort, unnecessary employees are sometimes simply *fired* if cause can be found, such as failure to measure up to a specified performance standard or the terms of an employment contract. In such cases, companies must take care to document employees' performance and should give them warning that their performance is subpar long before a pink slip is handed out. However, because of its negative impact, this method generally is used only when absolutely necessary.

It is important to recognize that not all turnover is due to such unhappy events. Sometimes current employees are considered for *promotion* to higher-level positions. They may be considered for *transfer* from one position to another at the same level. While promotions and transfers create new openings that must be filled, generally everyone in the organization is happy that they have occurred.

Learning Objective

8-9 List common forms of employee turnover and explain why firms should strive to minimize it.

员工流动
turnover when employees leave their jobs

解雇
terminations involuntary separations

裁员
downsizing eliminating positions

✓ Concept Check

- What is turnover?
- Why is turnover potentially problematic?
- What are common types of turnover?

Discussion Questions 讨论题

1. In general, on what basis is responsibility for HRM divided between line and staff managers?
2. How is a forecast of human resources demand related to a firm's organizational planning?
3. How accurately can managers plan for future human resources needs?
4. What are the major challenges and benefits associated with a diverse workforce?
5. What are the advantages and disadvantages of external recruiting? Of internal recruiting?
6. How is a job analysis used in the process of job evaluation?
7. For some companies, onboarding and orientation are synonymous. How are they different?
8. Suppose that you have just opened a new Ford sales showroom and repair shop. Which of your employees would be paid wages, which would receive salaries, and which would receive commissions?
9. Are employee benefits really necessary? Why?
10. As a manager, what actions would you take if an operations employee with six years of experience on the job refused ongoing training and ignored performance feedback?
11. Why is it so important to provide feedback after a performance appraisal?

Case 8 案例8：塔可贝尔应对大规模招聘

Taco Bell Tackles Large-Scale Recruitment

With intense competition in the fast-food space, Taco Bell has leaned into innovation as a way to stand out with new restaurant concepts, delivery services, creative menu partnerships, and plant-based offerings. The Mexican-inspired fast-food restaurant is not only innovating its restaurant concepts and menu, but it's also finding new ways to enhance the restaurant employee experience with new approaches to recruitment and retention through its "Start With Us, Stay With Us" platform.

Taco Bell is innovating its external recruiting efforts. The restaurant company shows job candidates it's the life of the party by putting on an event of its own: summer hiring parties. During the summer months, Taco Bell recruiting ramps up as it works to match employee supply with forecasted demand. To fill thousands of jobs, the company hosted nearly 600 hiring parties—its take on a career fair—complete with free food, festivities, and on-the-spot job interviews at various restaurant locations. Taco Bell considers this large-scale recruitment effort to be an effective way to give candidates a glimpse of the company's fun-loving culture and the opportunity to interview in a casual environment. Though the primary objective is to recruit seasonal help, the company also hopes some of the new hires will become long-term employees. The company promoted the recruiting event through public relations, in-store signage, and social media.

The career fair events are part of a broader initiative to create new jobs in the United States. Even during the COVID-19 pandemic, when many retailers and restaurants laid off employees, Taco Bell forecasted more team members would be necessary as more consumers chose drive-through dining restaurants. The company committed to hiring more than 30,000 workers to fill traditional team member roles as well as new roles related to enhancing safety measures and social distancing requirements. To effectively hire this large number of workers, Taco Bell conducted virtual and curbside interviews.

Taco Bell's employees will experience a variety of changes as the company invests in new restaurant concepts. For example, Taco Bell's Go Mobile prototype restaurant is built around digital transactions. The stores are much smaller than the restaurant's traditional footprint with a double drive-through lane that features a dedicated pick-up option for app users. Employees will benefit from smart technology in the kitchen that syncs with the Taco Bell app. Taco Bell will also introduce so-called bellhops to streamline the drive-through experience. These employees will utilize handheld tablets to increase efficiency.

Taco Bell has also invested in technology to improve communication with frontline employees. For example, Taco Bell partnered with Crew to rapidly roll out its messaging and scheduling app at 470 corporate locations and more than 4,500 franchise locations. The app made real-time communication to team members a reality and streamlined workflows, syncing the company's various scheduling systems. The Crew app proved to be an asset during the global pandemic as franchisees were able to send critical top-down communications and maintain business continuity amid rapidly shifting safety procedures.

Taco Bell's "Start With Us, Stay With Us" platform is more than a slogan, it's a mentality. The company wants to provide career paths and educational opportunities for team members to contribute to their future success. This approach to recruitment and retention has changed the restaurant employee experience and stands to create employee advocates and attract talent that will be with the company long term.[24]

Questions

1. How has Taco Bell innovated its external recruiting efforts?
2. How has technology improved communication with employees?
3. Describe how Taco Bell devised a course of action for matching employee supply with demand during the summer months.

Chapter 9

Motivating and Satisfying Employees

激励和提高员工的满意度

Why Should You Care?

As you move up into management positions or operate your own business, you will need to understand what motivates others in an organization.

Learning Objectives

Once you complete this chapter, you will be able to:

9-1 Explain motivation and its importance.

9-2 Describe some major historical perspectives on motivation.

9-3 Explore three contemporary views of motivation: equity theory, expectancy theory, and goal-setting theory.

9-4 Discuss the effects of organizational culture on employee performance.

9-5 Explain several techniques for increasing employee motivation.

Inside Business 商业透视：全食超市充分利用工资透明制度

Whole Foods Gives the Whole Picture with Wage Transparency

Corporate America is embracing transparency, from supply chain practices to social responsibility efforts. One subject, however, often remains taboo: wages. Whole Foods takes a different approach. The average pay of the supermarket chain's employees—from team member to store team leader—is available for anyone to see on its website. This practice is called *wage transparency*. Whole Foods CEO John Mackey introduced wage transparency at Whole Foods in 1986, six years after the grocery store was established. The policy is still going strong more than 35 years later.

In the past, employers have attempted to prevent wage information from spreading. This has left professionals feeling that the subject of pay is off-limits even though the law protects an employee's right to share salary information with co-workers. Many executives believe wage transparency has an unpredictable effect on morale. Mackey, on the other hand, says wage transparency motivates employees and helps promote fairness. For example, individuals may be surprised to learn that store team leaders have the potential to make more than $100,000 per year between wages and other benefits. By openly sharing the company's pay structure, it is easier to find, and therefore correct, discrepancies. At the same time, it gives Whole Foods the ability to defend wages when they are called into question.

Despite these benefits, the adoption of wage transparency policies remains low. According to nonprofit World at Work and human resources consulting firm Mercer, only 14 percent of organizations have embraced this concept beyond a moderate level. Whether or not the practice of wage transparency truly increases motivation and improves morale is uncertain, but it's clear Whole Foods' policy is here to stay.[1]

Did You Know?

Whole Foods employs more than 90,000 people.

To achieve its goals, any organization—be it Whole Foods, a local food truck, or a nonprofit organization—must be sure that its employees have more than the right raw materials, adequate facilities, and equipment that works. The organization also must ensure that its employees are *motivated*. A high level of employee motivation derives from effective management practices.

In this chapter, after first explaining what motivation is, we present several studies and views of motivation that have influenced management practices over the years: scientific management, Mayo's Hawthorne Studies, Maslow's hierarchy of needs, Herzberg's motivation–hygiene theory, McGregor's Theory X and Theory Y, Ouchi's Theory Z, and reinforcement theory. Then, turning our attention to contemporary theory, we examine equity, expectancy, and goal-setting theories. Next, we explore organizational culture and how it can influence employee performance. Finally, we discuss specific techniques managers can use to foster employee motivation and satisfaction.

动机
motivation the individual internal process that energizes, directs, and sustains behavior; the personal "force" that causes you or me to behave in a particular way

什么是动机

9-1 What Is Motivation?

Learning Objective

9-1 Explain motivation and its importance.

A *motive* is something that causes a person to act. A successful athlete is said to be "highly motivated." A student who avoids work is said to be "unmotivated." We define **motivation** as the individual internal process that energizes, directs, and sustains behavior. It is the personal "force" that causes you or me to act in a particular way. For example, although job rotation may increase your job satisfaction and your enthusiasm for your work so that you devote more energy to it, it may not have the same impact on someone else.

Morale is an employee's attitude or feelings about the job, about superiors, and about the firm itself. To achieve organizational goals effectively, employees need more than the right raw materials, adequate facilities, and efficient equipment. High morale results mainly from the satisfaction of needs on the job or as a result of doing the job. One need that might be satisfied on the job is the need *to be recognized* as an important contributor to the organization. A need satisfied as a result of the job is the need for *financial security*. High morale leads to dedication, loyalty, and a desire to do the job well. Low morale, however, can lead to shoddy work, absenteeism, and high turnover rates as employees leave to seek more satisfying jobs with other firms. Turnover can be very costly. To minimize it, companies may try to create work environments that increase employee satisfaction. One obvious indicator of satisfaction at a specific organization is whether employees report that they like working there and whether other people want to work there. In a recent list of *Fortune* magazine's "Top 100 Companies to Work For," the top ten best companies to work for were Hilton, Ultimate Software, Wegmans Food Markets, Cisco, Workday, Salesforce, Edward Jones, Stryker, American Express, and Kimpton Hotels & Restaurants.[2] Motivation, morale, and the satisfaction of employees' needs are highly intertwined considerations. Their relationships to business success and productivity have been the subject of much study since the end of the 19th century. We continue our discussion of motivation by outlining some landmarks of the early research.

✓ Concept Check

- What is motivation?
- Why is understanding motivation important?

动机的历史观点

9-2 Historical Perspectives on Motivation

Learning Objective

9-2 Describe some major historical perspectives on motivation.

Researchers often begin a study with a fairly narrow goal in mind, usually to test a specific hypothesis. After they develop an understanding of their subject, however, they sometimes realize that their research has broader applications. This is exactly what happened when early research into productivity grew into the study of employee motivation.

科学管理

9-2a Scientific Management

Toward the end of the 19th century, several engineers became interested in improving the efficiency of individual workers. Industrial engineers Frank and Lillian Gilbreth used filmed motion studies to identify efficiency improvements in work movements that could benefit employee wellbeing and motivation. Frederick W. Taylor, an American mechanical engineer, sought to identify efficiencies due to his own experiences in manufacturing plants. Their studies eventually led to the development of **scientific management**, the application of scientific principles to management of work and workers.

One of Taylor's first jobs was with the Midvale Steel Company in Philadelphia, where he developed a strong distaste for waste and inefficiency. While there, he observed a practice he dubbed "soldiering." Workers "soldiered," or worked slowly, because they feared that if they worked faster, they would run out of work and lose their jobs. Taylor realized that workers could get away with this because managers had no idea what productivity levels *should* be.

After Midvale, Taylor spent several years at Bethlehem Steel. While there, he made his most significant contribution to the field of motivation. He suggested that each job be broken down into separate tasks. Then management should determine (1) the best way to perform each task and (2) the job output to expect when employees performed the tasks properly. Next, management should choose the best person for each job and train that person in doing the job properly. Finally, management should monitor workers to ensure that jobs were performed as planned.

Taylor also developed the idea that most people work only to earn money. He therefore reasoned that pay should be tied directly to output. The more a

士气
morale an employee's feelings about the job, about superiors, and about the firm itself

科学管理
scientific management the application of scientific principles to management of work and workers

worker produces, the more the worker should be paid. This gave rise to the *piece-rate system,* under which employees are paid a certain amount for each unit of output they produce. Under Taylor's piece-rate system, each employee is assigned an output quota. If they exceed the quota, they receive a higher per unit rate for all work produced (refer to Figure 9-1).

When Taylor's system was put into practice at Bethlehem Steel, the results were dramatic. Average earnings per day for steel handlers rose from $1.15 to $1.88. (Do not let the low wages obscure the fact that this was an increase of more than 61 percent!) The average amount of steel handled per day increased from 16 to 57 tons. Today, the piece-rate system is still used by some manufacturers and by farmers who grow crops that are harvested by farm laborers.

The Gilbreths' and Taylor's revolutionary ideas had a profound impact on management practice. However, their views of motivation were soon recognized as overly simplistic and narrow. It is true that most people expect to be paid for their work, but it is also true that people work for a variety of reasons other than pay. Therefore, simply increasing a person's pay may not increase that person's motivation or productivity.

Is anyone happy? **Historically, most businesses in the United States weren't overly concerned about employee satisfaction. This is not the case today. Why do you think attitudes about employee motivation and satisfaction have changed?**

霍桑实验

9-2b The Hawthorne Studies

Between 1927 and 1932, Elton Mayo, an Australian sociologist and organizational theorist, conducted two experiments at the Hawthorne plant of the Western Electric Company in Chicago. The original objective of these studies, now referred to as the *Hawthorne Studies*, was to determine the effects of the work environment on employee productivity.

The first set of experiments tested the effect of lighting levels on productivity. One group of workers was subjected to varying lighting, while a second was not. To the amazement of the researchers, productivity increased for both groups. For the group whose lighting was varied, productivity remained high until the light was reduced to the level of moonlight!

The second set of experiments focused on the effectiveness of the piece-rate system in increasing the output of groups of workers. Researchers expected that

Figure 9-1 Taylor's Piece-Rate System

Workers who exceeded their quotas were rewarded with a higher rate per piece for all the pieces they produced.

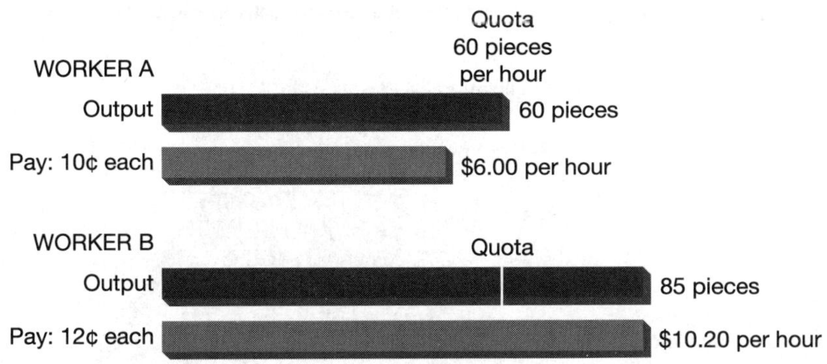

output would increase because faster workers would put pressure on slower workers to produce more. Again, the results were not as expected. Output remained constant irrespective of the "standard" rates management set.

When faced with unexpected outcomes, the researchers concluded that *human factors* were responsible for the results. In the lighting experiments, researchers had given both groups of workers a *sense of involvement* in their jobs merely by asking them to participate in the research. These workers—perhaps for the first time—felt as though they were an important part of the organization. The level of light did not matter. In the piece-rate experiments, each group of workers informally set the acceptable rate of output for the group. To gain or retain the *social acceptance* of the group, each worker felt pressure to produce at the same rate as the group pace.

The Hawthorne Studies showed that such human factors are at least as important to motivation as pay rates. From these and other studies, the *human relations movement* in management was born. **Human relations** is the study of people and groups in the workplace and what motivates them to achieve organizational goals. The premise of the human relations movement was simple: Employees who are happy and satisfied with their work are motivated to perform better. Hence, management is best served by providing a work environment that maximizes employee satisfaction.

马斯洛需要层次理论
9-2c Maslow's Hierarchy of Needs

Abraham Maslow, an American psychologist whose best-known works were published in the 1960s and 1970s, developed a theory of motivation based on a hierarchy of needs. A *need* is a personal requirement. Maslow assumed that humans are "wanting" beings who seek to fulfill a variety of needs, which he argued can be arranged from most basic to most complex in a sequence now known as **Maslow's hierarchy of needs** (refer to Figure 9-2).

At the bottom of the pyramid are *physiological needs,* the things we require to survive. They include food and water, clothing, shelter, and sleep. In the employment context, these needs usually are satisfied through adequate wages.

At the next level are *safety needs,* the things we require for physical and emotional security. Safety needs may be satisfied through job stability, health insurance, pension plans, and safe working conditions. The escalating costs of healthcare in today's work environment threaten some workers' sense of safety. Many firms are switching to more part-time workers for low-wage positions in order to avoid health insurance costs and fees. The move might backfire as employees seek to satisfy their safety needs at more secure jobs. On the other hand, some companies strive to stand out by offering benefits that satisfy safety needs even to part-time employees. One such company is Starbucks, which offers part-time employees healthcare coverage and the opportunity to participate in a 401(k) retirement plan as long as they work

Figure 9-2 Maslow's Hierarchy of Needs

Psychologist Abraham Maslow believed that people act to fulfill five categories of needs.

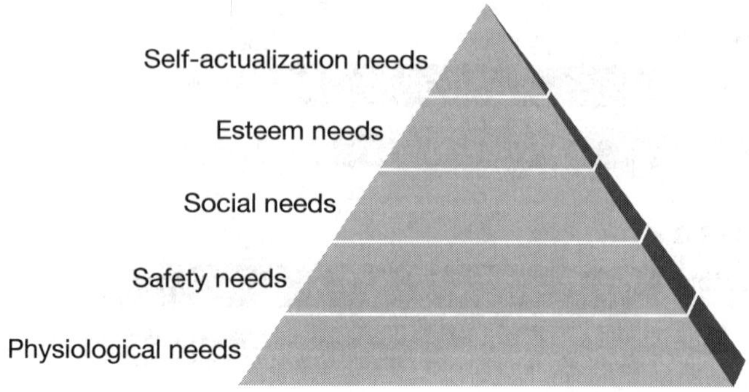

人际关系
human relations the study of people and groups in the workplace and what motivates them to achieve organizational goals

马斯洛的需要层次
Maslow's hierarchy of needs a sequence of human needs in the order of their importance

at least 20 hours per week. The company also offers paid leave, education tuition assistance, transit passes, and, of course, free coffee.[3]

Next are the *social needs,* the human requirements for love and affection and a sense of belonging. These needs are fulfilled in the workplace through the work environment and the informal organization and outside of the workplace by family and friends. At Colorado-based real estate firm East West Partners, for example, employees can join company kickball, softball, and snowshoe-running games and go on trips together.[4] Employers are increasingly offering their workers flexible scheduling options in order to improve their quality of life, which includes time for family and friends. Employees who have flexible work schedules are more likely to be able to attend family events or care for children or aging relatives. Employers can help workers satisfy social needs by providing useful feedback and fostering workplace cooperation and communication through a variety of media.

At the level of *esteem needs,* we require respect and recognition from others and a sense of our own accomplishment and worth (self-esteem). These needs may be satisfied through personal accomplishment, promotion to positions with greater responsibility, various honors and awards, and other forms of recognition.

At the top of the hierarchy are the *self-actualization needs,* which are the need to grow, develop, and become all that we are capable of being. These are the most difficult needs to satisfy, and the means of satisfying them tend to vary with the individual. For some people, learning a new skill, starting a new career after retirement, or trying to become the best at some endeavor may be the way to realize self-actualization. Some companies reimburse employees for continuing education expenses—even another college degree—knowing they get the benefit of employees with more knowledge as well as more satisfied employees who feel supported in their efforts to improve themselves.

Maslow suggested that people work up the hierarchy, satisfying their physiological needs before safety needs, for example. However, needs at one level do not have to be satisfied completely before needs at the next higher level come into play. People can also move up and down the hierarchy. For example, if a person loses a good job, he may find himself trying to satisfy safety needs when he only recently had focused on social needs.

Maslow's hierarchy of needs provides a guide for management and a useful way of viewing employee motivation. By and large, American business has been able to satisfy workers' basic needs, but the higher-order needs present more of a challenge. The means of satisfying these needs varies from one employee to another.

赫茨伯格的双因素理论

9-2d Herzberg's Motivation-Hygiene Theory

Frederick Herzberg, an American psychologist, interviewed approximately 200 accountants and engineers in Pittsburgh in the 1950s to develop his theory of motivation. He asked them to think of a time when they had felt especially good about their jobs and their work and to describe the factor or factors that had caused them to feel that way. Next, he asked them about a time when they had felt especially bad about their work. He was surprised to find that feeling good and feeling bad resulted from entirely different factors. That is, low pay may make a particular person feel bad, but high pay does not necessarily make that same person feel good.

Satisfaction and Dissatisfaction Before Herzberg's interviews, the general assumption was that employee satisfaction and dissatisfaction lay at opposite ends of the same scale. However, Herzberg's interviews convinced him that satisfaction and dissatisfaction are different dimensions altogether. In other words, the opposite of satisfaction is not dissatisfaction. The idea that satisfaction and dissatisfaction are separate and distinct dimensions is referred to as the **motivation-hygiene theory** (refer to Figure 9-3).

双因素理论
motivation-hygiene theory
the idea that satisfaction and dissatisfaction are separate and distinct dimensions

Figure 9-3 Herzberg's Motivation-Hygiene Theory

Herzberg's theory takes into account that there are different dimensions to job satisfaction and dissatisfaction and that these factors do not overlap.

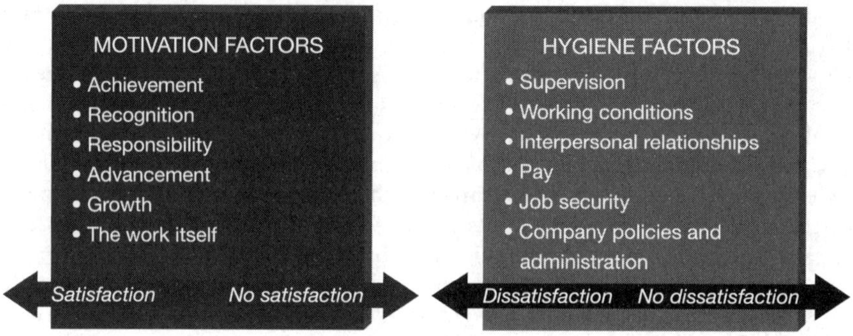

The job factors that Herzberg found most frequently associated with satisfaction were achievement, recognition, responsibility, advancement, growth, and the work itself. These factors generally are referred to as **motivation factors** because their presence increases motivation. However, their absence does not necessarily result in dissatisfaction. When motivation factors are present, they act as *satisfiers*.

Dissatisfaction, on the other hand, is caused by job factors such as supervision, working conditions, interpersonal relationships, pay, job security, company policies, and administration. These factors, called **hygiene factors**, reduce dissatisfaction when they are present to an acceptable degree. However, they do not necessarily result in high levels of motivation. When hygiene factors are absent, they act as *dissatisfiers*.

激励因素
motivation factors job factors that increase motivation, although their absence does not necessarily result in dissatisfaction

保健因素
hygiene factors job factors that reduce dissatisfaction when present to an acceptable degree but that do not necessarily result in high levels of motivation

Using Herzberg's Motivation-Hygiene Theory Herzberg provides explicit guidelines for using the motivation-hygiene theory of employee motivation. He suggests that the hygiene factors must be present to ensure that a worker can function comfortably. He warns, however, that a state of *no dissatisfaction* cannot exist. In any situation, people always will be dissatisfied with something.

According to Herzberg, managers should utilize hygiene factors to make the work environment as positive as possible, but should expect only short-term improvements in motivation. Managers must focus instead on providing those satisfiers that will enhance motivation and long-term effort.

We should note that employee pay has proven to have more effect than Herzberg's theory indicates. He suggests that pay provides only short term, not true, motivation. Yet, in many organizations, pay is a form of recognition and reward for achievement—and recognition and achievement are both motivation factors. The effect of pay may depend on how it is distributed. If a pay increase does not depend on performance (as in across-the-board or cost-of-living raises), it may not motivate people. However, if pay is increased as a form of recognition (as in bonuses or incentives), it can play a role in motivating employees to higher performance.

What satisfies employees? Companies sometimes use travel awards as incentives for better employee performance. According to the motivation-hygiene theory, when an incentive for higher performance is not provided, is that a dissatisfier?

X 理论和 Y 理论
9-2e Theory X and Theory Y

The concepts of Theory X and Theory Y were advanced by Douglas McGregor, an American business professor, in his book, *The Human Side of Enterprise*, in 1960. They represent opposing sets of assumptions that underlie management's attitudes and beliefs regarding workers' behavior.

Theory X is a concept of employee motivation generally consistent with Taylor's ideas about scientific management. Theory X is based on the following assumptions:

1. People dislike work and try to avoid it.
2. Because people dislike work, managers must coerce, control, and frequently threaten employees to achieve organizational goals.
3. People generally must be led because they have little ambition and will not seek responsibility; they are concerned mainly about security.

The logical outcome of such assumptions will be a highly controlled, autocratic work environment—one in which managers make all the decisions and employees take all the orders.

On the other hand, **Theory Y** is a concept of employee motivation generally consistent with the ideas of the human relations movement. Theory Y is based on the following assumptions:

1. People do not naturally dislike work. In fact, work is an important part of all of our lives.
2. People will work toward goals to which they are committed.
3. People become committed to goals when it is clear that accomplishing the goals will bring personal rewards.
4. People often seek out and willingly accept responsibility.
5. Employees have the potential to help accomplish organizational goals.
6. Organizations generally do not make full use of their human resources.

Obviously, Theory Y is much more positive than Theory X. McGregor argued that most managers behave in accordance with Theory X, but he maintained that Theory Y is more appropriate and effective as a guide for managerial action (refer to Table 9-1).

The human relations movement and Theories X and Y increased managers' awareness of the importance of social factors in the workplace during the second half of the 20th century. However, human motivation is a complex and dynamic process to which there is no simple key. It is clear from decades of research that neither money nor social factors alone can provide the answer.

Table 9-1 Theory X and Theory Y Contrasted

Area	Theory X	Theory Y
Attitude toward work	Dislike	Involvement
Control systems	External	Internal
Supervision	Direct	Indirect
Level of commitment	Low	High
Employee potential	Ignored	Identified
Use of human resources	Limited	Not limited

X 理论
Theory X a concept of employee motivation generally consistent with Taylor's scientific management; assumes that employees dislike work and will function only in a highly controlled work environment

Y 理论
Theory Y a concept of employee motivation generally consistent with the ideas of the human relations movement; assumes responsibility and work toward organizational goals, and by doing so employees also achieve personal rewards

Z理论
9-2f Theory Z

William Ouchi, a management professor at UCLA, studied business practices in American and Japanese firms as discussed in his book, *Theory Z: How American Management Can Meet the Japanese Challenge*. He concluded that different types of management systems dominate in these two countries. In Japan, Ouchi found what he calls *type J* firms. They are characterized by lifetime employment, collective (or group) decision making, collective responsibility for the outcomes of decisions, slow evaluation and promotion, implied control mechanisms, nonspecialized career paths, and a holistic concern for employees as people.

American industry is dominated by what Ouchi calls *type A* firms, which follow a different pattern. They emphasize short-term employment, individual decision making, individual responsibility for the outcomes of decisions, rapid evaluation and promotion, explicit control mechanisms, specialized career paths, and a segmented concern for employees only as employees.

A few very successful American firms represent a blend of the type J and type A patterns. These firms, called *type Z* organizations, emphasize long-term employment, collective decision making, individual responsibility for the outcomes of decisions, slow evaluation and promotion, informal control along with some formalized measures, moderately specialized career paths, and a holistic concern for employees.

Ouchi's **Theory Z** posits that some middle ground between his type A and type J practices is best for American business (refer to Figure 9-4). A major part of Theory Z emphasizes participative decision making. The focus is on "we" rather than on "us versus them." Theory Z employees and managers view the organization as a family. This participative spirit fosters cooperation and encourages the dissemination of information and organizational values.

Z理论
Theory Z a concept of management which emphasizes participative decision making, with a holistic concern for employees

强化理论
reinforcement theory a theory of motivation based on the premise that rewarded behavior is likely to be repeated, whereas punished behavior is less likely to recur

强化理论
9-2g Reinforcement Theory

Reinforcement theory is based on the premise that people will repeat behavior that is rewarded and will cease behavior that is punished. A *reinforcement* is an action that follows directly from a particular behavior. It may be a pay raise after a particularly large sale to a new customer or a reprimand for coming late to work.

Figure 9-4 The Features of Theory Z

The best aspects of Japanese and American management theories combine to form the nucleus of Theory Z.

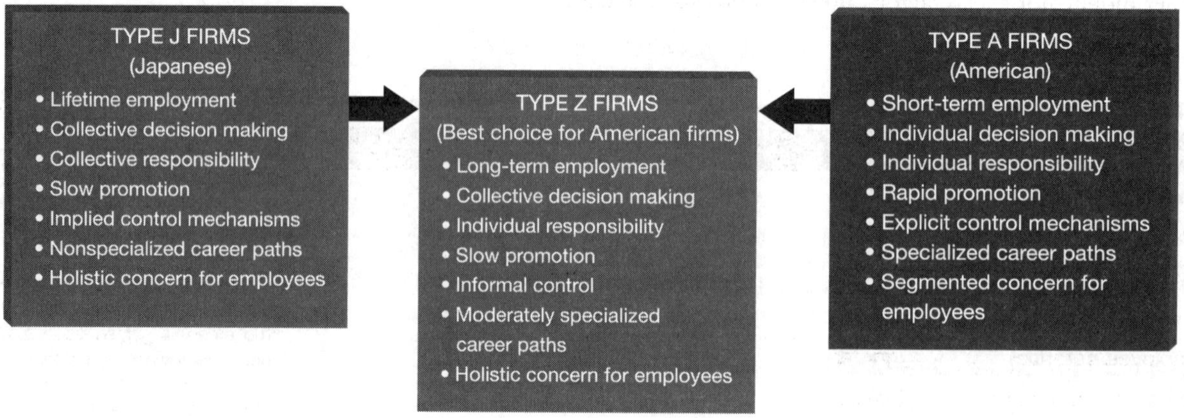

Reinforcements can take a variety of forms and can be used in a number of ways. A *positive reinforcement* is one that strengthens desired behavior by providing a reward, such as praise or recognition from supervisors for a job done well. A reward increases (strengthens) one's willingness to perform well in the future. A *negative reinforcement* strengthens desired behavior by eliminating an undesirable task or situation. Suppose that a machine shop must be cleaned thoroughly every month—a dirty, miserable task. During a month when the workers do a less-than-satisfactory job, the boss requires them to clean the factory themselves, rather than bringing in the usual private maintenance service. The employees will be motivated to work harder the next month to avoid the unpleasant cleanup duty.

Punishment is a consequence of undesirable behavior. Common forms of punishment used in organizations include reprimands, reduced pay, disciplinary layoffs, and termination (firing). Punishment often does more harm than good by creating a negative work environment, fostering worker hostility, and encouraging employees to engage in undesirable behaviors behind the backs of supervisors.

Managers who rely on *extinction* hope to eliminate undesirable behavior by not responding to it with the hope that the behavior will eventually go "extinct." Suppose, for example, that an employee writes memo after memo to his or her manager about insignificant events. If the manager does not respond to any of these memos, the employee probably will stop writing them, and the behavior will stop.

The effectiveness of reinforcement depends on which type is used and how it is timed. Some situations lend themselves to the use of more than one approach. Generally, positive reinforcement is considered the most effective with most employees, and it is recommended when the manager has a choice.

Continual reinforcement can become tedious for both managers and employees, especially when the same behavior is being reinforced over and over again in the same way. At the start, it may be necessary to reinforce a desired behavior every time it occurs. Generally, once a desirable behavior has been more or less established, only occasional reinforcement will be needed.

✓ Concept Check

- What are the major elements of Taylor's "scientific management"?
- What were Elton Mayo's conclusions from the Hawthorne Studies?
- What are the different levels in Maslow's hierarchy of needs?
- What are the major elements of Herzberg's motivation-hygiene theory?
- What are the underlying assumptions of Theory X and Theory Y?

当代动机理论

9-3 Contemporary Views of Motivation

Learning Objective

9-3 Explore three contemporary views of motivation: equity theory, expectancy theory, and goal-setting theory.

Maslow's hierarchy of needs and Herzberg's motivation-hygiene theory are popular and widely known theories of motivation. Each takes a broader view than the narrow focus of scientific management and Theories X and Y. However, they do have a weakness: each attempts to specify *what* motivates people, but neither explains *why* or *how* motivation develops or is sustained over time. More recently, managers have explored three other models that take a more dynamic view of motivation. These are equity theory, expectancy theory, and goal-setting theory.

公平理论

9-3a Equity Theory

The **equity theory** of motivation is based on the premise that people are motivated to obtain and preserve equitable treatment for themselves. As used here, *equity* is the distribution of rewards in direct proportion to each employee's contribution to the organization. Everyone need not receive the same rewards, but the rewards should be in accordance with individual contributions.

According to this theory, we conceive of equity in the following way. First, we develop our own input-to-outcome ratio. *Inputs* are the time, effort, skills, education, experience, and so on that we contribute to the organization. *Outcomes* are the rewards we get from the organization, such as pay, benefits, recognition, and promotions. Next, we compare this ratio to what we perceive as the input-to-outcome ratio for some other person. It might be a co-worker, a friend who works for another firm, or even an average of all the people in our organization. This person is called the *comparison other*.

公平理论
equity theory a theory of motivation based on the premise that people are motivated to obtain and preserve equitable treatment for themselves

Employees want to be treated fairly. Employees compare the amount of effort they put into their jobs and the outcomes they get to that of their co-workers. This is the idea behind equity theory. At sweatshops such as this one, though, all employees are treated unfairly. Does equity theory come into play in this instance?

Note that the important consideration is that we believe our perception to be correct, whether or not it is.

If the two ratios are roughly the same, we feel that the organization is treating us equitably. In this case, we are motivated to leave things as they are. However, if our ratio is the higher of the two, we feel under-rewarded and are motivated to make changes. We may (1) decrease our own inputs by not working as hard, (2) try to increase our outcome by asking for a raise in pay, (3) try to get the comparison other to increase some inputs or receive decreased outcomes, (4) leave the work situation, or (5) conduct a new comparison with a different comparison other.

Equity theory is most relevant to compensation as an outcome. Because compensation is a very real measure of a person's worth to an organization, comparisons involving compensation are a natural part of organizational life. Managers can try to avoid problems arising from inequity by ensuring that rewards are distributed on the basis of performance and that everyone clearly understands the basis for their own pay.

期望理论

9-3b Expectancy Theory

Expectancy theory, developed by Victor Vroom, a Canadian business professor, is a very complex model of motivation based on a simple assumption. According to expectancy theory, motivation depends on how much we want something and on how likely we think we are to get it (refer to Figure 9-5). Consider, for example, the case of three sales representatives who are candidates for promotion to one sales manager's job. Juan has had a very good sales year and always gets positive performance evaluations. However, he is not sure that he wants the job because it involves travel, long working hours, and stress and pressure. Paul wants the job badly, but does not think he has much chance of getting it. He has had a terrible sales year and gets only mediocre performance evaluations from his present boss. Sarah wants the job as much as Paul, and she thinks that she has a pretty good shot. Her sales have improved this past year, and her evaluations are the best in the company. Expectancy theory would predict that Juan and Paul are not very motivated to seek the promotion. Juan does not really want it, and Paul does not think that he has much of a chance of getting it. Sarah, however, is very motivated to seek the promotion because she wants it and thinks that she can get it.

Figure 9-5 Expectancy Theory

Vroom's theory is based on the idea that motivation depends on how much people want something and on how likely they think they are to get it.

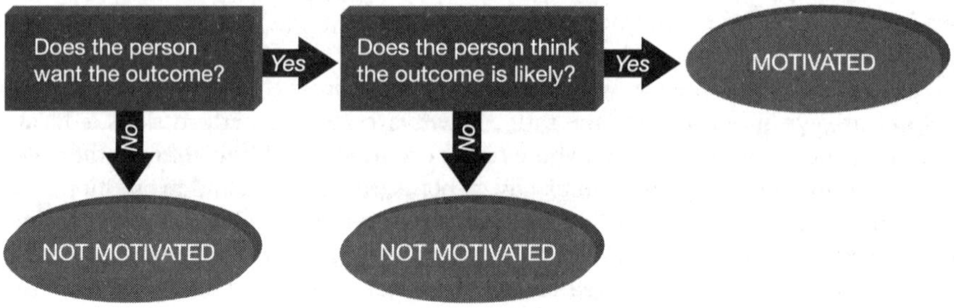

期望理论
expectancy theory a model of motivation based on the assumption that motivation depends on how much we want something and on how likely we think we are to get it

Expectancy theory is complex because each action we take is likely to lead to several outcomes, some of which we want and others we do not. For example, a person who works hard and puts in many extra hours may get a pay raise, be promoted, and gain valuable new job skills. However, that person may also be forced to spend less time with his or her family and to cut back on social activities.

For one person, the promotion may be paramount, the pay raise and new skills fairly important, and the loss of family and social life of negligible importance. For someone else, the family and social life may be most important, the pay raise of moderate importance, the new skills unimportant, and the promotion undesirable because of the additional hours it would require. The first person would be motivated to work hard and put in the extra hours, whereas the second person would not be motivated at all to do so. In other words, it is the bundle of outcomes combined with the individual's perception of each outcome's importance that determines motivation.

What do employees want? That's what their managers need to determine. Different employees are motivated by different rewards. Figuring out which rewards motivate each employee is a key step in goal setting.

Expectancy theory is difficult to apply, but it does provide several useful guidelines for managers. It suggests that managers must recognize that (1) employees work for a variety of reasons, (2) these reasons, or expected outcomes, may change over time, and (3) it is necessary to show employees how they can attain the outcomes they desire.

目标设定理论
9-3c Goal-Setting Theory

Goal-setting theory states that employees are motivated to achieve goals that they and their managers establish together. The goal should be very specific, moderately challenging, and one that the employee will be committed to achieve.[5] Rewards should be tied directly to goal achievement. Using goal-setting theory, a manager can design rewards that fit employee needs, clarify expectations, maintain equity, and provide reinforcement. For example, a manager might discover that one of her employees is very motivated by the occasional day off. Therefore, the manager and the employee may work out a plan that involves a free day as a reward after he completes a project satisfactorily and ahead of schedule, as long as he is up-to-date in his other work. This theory takes into account the goal the employee has to achieve and the rewards that will accrue if the goal is accomplished.

目标设定理论
goal-setting theory a theory of motivation suggesting that employees are motivated to achieve goals that they and their managers establish together

✓ Concept Check

- What is equity theory?
- How do managers use it in order to decide the pay structure of employees?
- What is expectancy theory and how is it different from goal-setting theory?

组织文化
9-4 Organizational Culture

Learning Objective

9-4 Discuss the effects of organizational culture on employee performance.

One factor that plays a significant role in employee motivation is organizational, or corporate, culture. In fact, in a recent survey of 5,000 employees in the United States and Europe, more than half said they viewed corporate culture as more important than salary with regard to job satisfaction.[6] While it has been described in many ways, **organizational culture** can generally be defined as the inner rituals, traditions, processes, and values of a firm. Consider Southwest Airlines, which is known for its fun, friendly, people-first culture. The low-cost airline strives to hire people who share its values, pays them well, treats them fairly, and acknowledges their contributions to its success. In addition to generous compensation and benefits, the airline recognizes employees' efforts and milestones with special awards and celebrations. It also hosts fun companywide and local office festivities such as rallies and chili cook-offs. Southwest

组织文化
organizational culture the inner rituals, traditions, processes, and values of a firm

Organizational culture. Corporate culture can influence whether and how employees celebrate special occasions.

has long recognized that satisfied, happy employees who feel valued will have a "Fun-LUVing Attitude" and deliver "Legendary Customer Service."[7] The company's strong culture helps it succeed in a very competitive industry and land routinely on "Most Admired Company" and "Best Company to Work for" lists.

Organizational culture exists in all organizations whether they are small businesses, large corporations, or nonprofit organizations. It includes both the formal rules and structure of a firm as well as informal and even unwritten norms, stories, rules, dress codes, and so on. While an organizational culture can influence public perception of an organization, it can also have a powerful influence on employee motivation, performance, and choices. Organizational culture also sets the tone for how managers view and treat workers.

When managers develop and nurture a culture that addresses the reasons why people work, employees are more likely to be motivated to work toward the organization's goals. Researchers have identified six core reasons why people want to work: play, purpose, potential, emotional pressure, economic pressure, and inertia. When firms foster a culture that allows employees to have a sense of play, fulfill their purpose, and/or develop their potential, employees are more likely to feel satisfied and therefore motivated to work to achieve organizational goals and satisfy customers. On the other hand, when companies create, purposefully or otherwise, a culture that subjects workers to emotional or economic pressure or allows them to suffer from inertia, performance may suffer

Exploring Careers

职业探索：审视雇主的价值观以避免提前离职

Vet Employer Values to Avoid an Early Exit

Finding the right company to work for can be a matter of finding the right cultural fit for you. Organizational culture provides alignment to the organization's vision, purpose, and goals. Because organizational culture has a powerful influence on an organization's employees, it's important to do your homework and research prospective employers.

When researching a prospective employer, explore the company's benefits such as healthcare, flexible work schedules, and discounts and identify the company's leadership team. A company's website and blog as well as its social media profiles can provide a wealth of information. During the interview, ask if there are different rules for different employees. This can reveal which people and actions the organization values most. If interviewing through a recruiter, ask them if they think you're the right fit. They may have valuable insight into why the individual vacated the role you're about to take. Lastly, request a tour and walk the halls of the potential employer. The way employees interact with a job candidate can be telling.

Employees are less likely to thrive in an incompatible corporate culture. According to a TopResume survey, job seekers say company culture is nearly as important as salary and bonuses when deciding which job offer to accept. Failing to vet employer values can lead to an early exit. Research the company's core mission and find a company with goals that resonate with your interests.

Sources: Based on information in "The Complete Guide to Researching a Company," *Indeed*, January 9, 2021; Joann S. Lublin, "Considering a New Job? Beware a Culture Misfit," *The Wall Street Journal*, January 15, 2020; Natalie Baumgartner, "Build a Culture That Aligns with People's Values," *Harvard Business Review*, April 8, 2020.

because employees are less motivated. Recall Southwest Airlines. When researchers studied the airline industry to measure the total motivation of employees at different airlines (as determined by assessing play, purpose, potential, emotional pressure, economic pressure, and inertia), they found that Southwest Airlines' employees scored very high relative to those of other airlines. Southwest also routinely earns some of the highest customer satisfaction scores in the industry.[8] Firms with strong cultures that motivate employees are likely to recruit better quality job candidates and experience reduced employee turnover and lower absenteeism, which is likely to translate to more satisfied customers and greater profitability.

Professors Robert Quinn and Kim Cameron identified four distinct types of organizational cultures (refer to Figure 9-6) based on two dimensions. They assess organizational cultures as being along a continuum of flexibility and discretion versus stability and control. Some organizations value stability and strive to impose it with strong control measures, while others value flexibility and allow employees discretion to achieve it. Quinn and Cameron also evaluate cultures as to the degree they are focused internally or externally. Based on these dimensions, Quinn and Cameron classify organizations into clan, adhocracy, hierarchy, or market culture types.[9]

The *clan culture* is characterized by a family-like structure that values loyalty, cohesion, and personal relationships within the firm. As we have already seen, Southwest Airlines is an example of a company with a clan structure. This structure is also common in smaller firms where a less formal culture evolves with employees looking out for each other and having a strong emotional investment in the firm and its mission.

The *adhocracy culture* is characterized by its risk-taking, problem-solving nature. Disruptive firms like Uber and Facebook often have adhocracy cultures that can be nimble in responding to changes in the environment and identifying underserved markets. Nike is another company with an adhocracy culture. Its design teams strive to "learn, fail fast, and keep moving" to research and find solutions for all kinds of athletes who want the most from their performance clothing. One such challenge they identified was Muslim women who want to swim and compete in swimming but could not find modest yet competitive swimwear. When Nike targeted this underserved group with a moisture-wicking hijab head covering, it was rewarded with strong sales. Buoyed by that success, Nike then spent several years developing

Figure 9-6 Types of Organizational Cultures

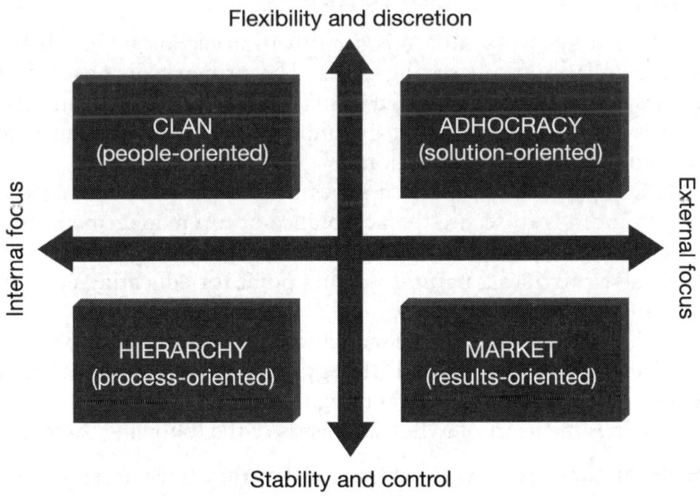

Source: Adapted from Kim S. Cameron and Robert E. Quinn, *Diagnosing and Changing Organizational Culture* (San Francisco: Jossey-Bass, 2006), p. 35.

a modesty swimsuit that provides full coverage as well as full mobility with style and practicality.[10]

The *market culture* is very results-oriented, which makes it well-suited for financial firms. Amazon and Apple also have market cultures. These firms tend to be very competitive and focus strongly on achieving market share and bottom-line objectives. It is worth noting, however, that a strong results orientation can push people into making less desirable choices in an effort to meet organizational goals.

Finally, the *hierarchical culture* is very formal with a traditional chain of command. These bureaucratic cultures value efficiency and stability and have strict rules and boundaries. It should come as no surprise that the hierarchical structure is very common in the military and many government agencies. However, this structure may be less nimble in responding to fast-changing business environments.

Regardless of what type of culture an organization has, managers need to recognize that culture can motivate employees and push them to achieve the organization's goals. They need to model their firms' values, enforce the formal rules, and nurture an environment that supports employees' ability to satisfy their needs and feel that their contributions are valued. A strong culture that satisfies and motivates employees in healthy ways can ensure their loyalty and effort and thereby inspire customer devotion. It is also important to recognize that organizational cultures evolve as companies grow and change. Managers need to monitor, communicate about, and guide these changes to ensure they do not negatively affect employee morale and motivation.

✓ Concept Check

- What is organizational culture?
- How can organizational culture promote employee motivation?
- Explain the four types of organizational cultures.

关键激励技巧

9-5 Key Motivation Techniques

Learning Objective

9-5 Explain several techniques for increasing employee motivation.

As we have seen, it takes more than a generous salary to motivate employees today. In addition to developing and nurturing rewarding organizational cultures, companies are increasingly trying to provide motivation by satisfying employees' less-tangible and changing needs. Businesses may use simple, low- or no-cost, or complex and expensive approaches to motivation. In this section, we discuss several specific techniques that help managers boost employee motivation and job satisfaction. The bottom line is that these approaches may help employees feel satisfied and valued—and thus more likely to remain with the organization.

目标管理

9-5a Management by Objectives

Management by objectives (MBO) is a motivation technique in which managers and employees collaborate in setting goals. The primary purpose of MBO is to clarify the roles employees are expected to play in reaching the organization's goals. MBO increases employee motivation by empowering them with an active role in goal-setting and performance evaluation.

Most MBO programs consist of a series of five steps. The first step in setting up an MBO program is to secure the acceptance of top management. It is essential that top managers endorse and participate in the program if others in the firm are to accept it. This also provides a natural starting point for educating employees about the purposes and mechanics of MBO.

In the second step, top management and other parties must establish preliminary goals that reflect a firm's mission and strategy. The intent of an MBO program is to have these goals filter down through the organization.

The third step is the heart of MBO. It consists of the following three smaller steps:

1. The manager explains to every employee that they have accepted certain goals for the organization, or a group within the organization, and asks them to think about how they can help achieve these goals.

目标管理
management by objectives (MBO) a motivation technique in which managers and employees collaborate in setting goals

2. The manager later meets with each employee individually. Together they establish individual goals for the employee. Whenever possible, the goals should be measurable and should specify the time frame for completion (usually one year).
3. The manager and the employee decide what resources the employee will need to accomplish his or her goals.

As the fourth step, the manager and employees meet periodically to review each employee's progress. They may agree to modify certain goals during these meetings if circumstances have changed. For example, a sales representative accepted a goal of increasing sales by 20 percent. However, an aggressive competitor has since entered the marketplace, making this goal unattainable. In light of this circumstance, the goal is revised down to 10 or 15 percent.

The fifth step in the MBO process is evaluation. At the end of the designated time period, the manager and each employee meet again to determine which of the individual's goals were met and which were not, and why. The employee's reward (in the form of a pay raise, praise, or promotion) is based primarily on the degree of goal attainment.

As with every other management method, MBO has advantages and disadvantages. MBO can motivate employees by involving them actively in the life of the firm. The collaboration on goal setting and performance appraisal improves communication and makes employees feel that they are an important part of the organization. Periodic progress reviews also enhance quality control within an organization. Shortcomings of MBO are that it must have the support of top management, it can result in a lot of paperwork, and managers may not like to work out goals with subordinates.

工作丰富化

9-5b Job Enrichment

Job enrichment is a method of motivating employees by providing them with variety in their tasks while giving them some responsibility for, and control over, their jobs. At the same time, employees gain new skills and acquire a broader perspective about how their individual work contributes to the goals of the organization. Earlier in this chapter, we noted that Herzberg's motivation-hygiene theory is one rationale for the use of job enrichment. That is, the added responsibility and control that job enrichment confers on employees increases their satisfaction and motivation. For example, some employees at Microsoft, Apple, and Google have been allowed to spend a fraction of their time at work on projects of their choosing. This type of enrichment can motivate employees and result in benefits for the company. At times, **job enlargement**, expanding a worker's assignments to include additional but similar tasks, can lead to job enrichment. Job enlargement might mean that a worker on an assembly line who used to connect three wires to components moving down the line now connects five wires. Unfortunately, the added tasks often are just as routine as those the worker performed before the change and may not be an effective motivator over the long term.

Although job enlargement does not really change the routine and monotonous nature of jobs, job enrichment does. Job enrichment results in an increased sense of employee responsibility, increased control over how the job is performed, and new tasks. Job enrichment gives workers more authority and assigns tasks in complete, natural units (rather than breaking it down into the smallest possible task). Employees frequently are given fresh and challenging job assignments. By blending more planning and decision making into jobs, enrichment gives work more depth and complexity.

Job redesign is a type of job enrichment in which work is restructured in ways that cultivate the worker-job match. Job redesign can be achieved by

工作丰富化
job enrichment a motivation technique that provides employees with more variety and responsibility in their jobs

工作扩大化
job enlargement expanding a worker's assignments to include additional but similar tasks

工作再设计
job redesign a type of job enrichment in which work is restructured to cultivate the worker–job match

Job enlargement versus job enrichment. It's no secret. Doing the same task over and over at your job is boring. Being able to do a variety of tasks (job enlargement) helps. Having more responsibility over how you do your job (job enrichment) is even better.

combining tasks, forming work groups, or establishing closer customer relationships. Employees often are more motivated when jobs are combined because the increased variety of tasks presents a more rewarding challenge. Depending on the form it takes, job redesign can give employees a stronger sense of belonging to a team, a clearer image of how their work contributes to the organization as a whole, and a more personal investment in the satisfaction of clients. Furthermore, a job redesign that carefully matches worker to job can prevent stress-related injuries. Employees may play an active role in redesigning their jobs to their liking. If employees recognize opportunities to rework their job in such a way as to improve efficiency or productivity, they may want to approach a superior with the idea.

Job enrichment works best with employees who want more challenging work. Employees must desire personal growth and have the skills and knowledge to perform more complex tasks. Lack of self-confidence, fear of failure, and distrust of management's intentions are likely to lead to ineffective performance on enriched jobs. Some workers prefer routine jobs because they find them satisfying. Job enrichment would not be appealing for these individuals. Companies that use job enrichment as an alternative to specialization also face extra expenses, such as the cost of retraining.

行为矫正

9-5c Behavior Modification

Behavior modification is a systematic program of reinforcement to encourage desirable behavior. Behavior modification involves both rewards to encourage desirable actions and punishments to discourage undesirable actions. Rewards, such as compliments and expressions of appreciation, tend to be much more effective behavior modifiers than punishments, such as reprimands and scorn.

When applied to management, behavior modification strives to encourage desirable organizational behavior. This technique begins with identifying and measuring a *target behavior*—the behavior that is to be changed (e.g., low production levels or a high rate of absenteeism). Next, managers provide positive reinforcement in the form of a reward when employees exhibit the *desired behavior* (e.g., increased production or less absenteeism). The reward might be praise or a more tangible form of recognition, such as a gift, meal, or trip. For example, Apple has a Corporate Gifts and Rewards Program that gives companies the ability to reward their staff or very loyal customers with Apple Watches, iPhones, iPads, Mac computers, or Apple gift cards. Finally, the levels of the target behavior are measured again to determine whether the desired changes have been achieved. If the target behavior has not changed significantly in the desired direction, the reward system must be changed to one that is likely to be more effective. The key is to devise effective rewards that will not only modify employees' behavior in desired ways, but also motivate them. To this end, experts suggest that management should reward quality, loyalty, and productivity.

弹性工作安排

9-5d Flexible Scheduling Options

The needs and lifestyles of today's workforce are changing. Dual-income families make up a much larger share of the workforce than ever before, and women are one of its fastest-growing sectors. In addition to child-rearing duties, a growing number

行为矫正
behavior modification a systematic program of reinforcement to encourage desirable behavior

Entrepreneurial Success

创业成功：如何认可工作出色的员工

How to Recognize Employees for a Job Well Done

Rewarding employees with praise or recognition for a job well done is a form of positive reinforcement. For Generation Z and Millennial employees in particular, positive reinforcement is a major contributor to satisfaction in the workplace. According to a study by daVinci Payments, a payroll solutions firm, many young employees feel dissatisfied with their work but say that more recognition would increase a sense of loyalty to their employer. One way for small businesses to build a culture of recognition is to implement a recognition program.

Recognition should feel meaningful and authentic. To achieve this, employee recognition programs should be tied to specific business objectives, and recognition should be delivered promptly. This can come in the form of gift cards, customized gifts, a free meal, volunteer opportunities, awards, social media accolades, and more. While small businesses may have limited resources to offer financial incentives, an everyday thank-you, such as a handwritten note, can be just as meaningful. To have the greatest impact, employers should link employee achievements with the company's overall success, sharing how employee efforts are helping the organization reach its objectives. Once a program is in place, employers should continually reassess recognition efforts to ensure employee needs are being met.

Implementing recognition programs can help employees better understand how their contributions are connected to the bigger picture. Employee appreciation builds trust, boosts productivity, encourages high performance, increases engagement, decreases turnover, and improves brand reputation.

Sources: Based on information in Bennett Conlin, "19 Creative Ways to Show Employee Appreciation," *Business News Daily*, February 18, 2021; Claire Hastwell, "Creating a Culture of Recognition," *Great Place to Work*, November 24, 2020; Stephen Miller, "Generation Z and Millennials Seek Recognition at Work," *Society for Human Resource Management*, September 12, 2019.

of employees are responsible for the care of older relatives. The U.S. Bureau of Labor Statistics estimates that 40 million Americans are assisting at least one parent 65 years or older with daily living activities,[11] and most of these caretakers are also employees who may have to come in late, leave early, or make other adjustments to care for their family member. Moreover, younger workers are increasingly seeking out employers that offer more flexible work schedules. Recognizing that these changes increase the demand for flexibility during the normal work day, a growing number of employers are offering flexible work schedules to help employees manage their time better and increase employee motivation and job satisfaction.

Flextime is a system in which employees set their own work hours within certain limits determined by employers. Typically, the firm establishes two bands of time: the *core time*, when all employees must be at work, and the *flexible time*, when employees may choose whether to be at work. The only condition is that every employee must work a total of eight hours each day. For example, the hours between 9 and 11 a.m. and 1 and 3 p.m. might be core times, and the hours between 6 and 9 a.m., 11 a.m. and 1 p.m., and 3 and 6 p.m. might be flexible times. This would give employees the option of coming in early and getting off early, coming in later and leaving later, or taking a long lunch break. But flextime also ensures that everyone is present at certain times, when conferences with supervisors and department meetings can be scheduled.

Another flexible scheduling option is the **compressed workweek**, which allows employees to work the same number of hours in a shorter time period. Compressed workweeks are typically defined as 40 hours of work in four days instead of five, although a few companies specify that it is 80 hours of work over a nine-day period. In both situations, workers gain three-day weekends or longer, though they must work longer hours each day to get it. Compressed workweeks are becoming more

弹性工作制
flextime a system in which employees set their own work hours within employer-determined limits

压缩工作周
compressed workweek allows employees to work a 40-hour work week in four days instead of five

popular, particularly outside the United States. When Microsoft Japan experimented with compressed workweeks, it found that not only did productivity rise by 40 percent, but the unit's electricity costs declined by 23 percent. Other companies with compressed workweeks have reported improved productivity, creativity, and employee satisfaction.[12] Of course, compressed workweeks may not be appropriate for all organizations.

Research has found that employees with more flexible schedules experience less stress and burnout and greater job satisfaction; their employers say well-managed flexible scheduling programs can boost employee retention, productivity, diversity, and employee engagement while reducing their need for office space and overall carbon footprint.[13] However, two common problems associated with using flexible schedules are (1) supervisors sometimes find their jobs complicated by having employees who come and go at different times and (2) employees with more conventional work schedules sometimes resent co-workers who have flextime.

While most people still work standard 40-hour weeks, flexible schedules are becoming much more common and easier to manage as improvements in technology allow people to stay connected, no matter where they are or what time it is. The medical and health professions, education and training departments, administrative jobs, and accounting divisions are all likely to offer flexible schedule options. For example, the accounting financial services firm Deloitte has offered flexible scheduling options for decades. The global company has found that this flexibility helps satisfy employees because they have better work–life balance. It also helps Deloitte get closer to its environmental sustainability goals and achieve its gender parity goals by attracting more working parents. Its flexible work policies have helped land Deloitte on *Working Mother* magazine's "100 Best Companies" list for more than 20 years.[14] Flex policies like this help reduce employee burnout and keep turnover low in what can be a stressful industry.

兼职工作
part-time work permanent employment in which individuals work less than a standard work week

工作共享
job sharing an arrangement whereby two people share one full-time position

兼职工作和工作共享

9-5e Part-Time Work and Job Sharing

Part-time work is permanent employment in which individuals work less than a standard work week. The specific number of hours worked varies, but part-time jobs are structured so that all responsibilities can be completed in the number of hours an employee works. Part-time work is of special interest to students and parents who need more time with their children. While some firms, such as Starbucks, REI, Costco, and Trader Joe's, are famous for offering part-time workers benefits, most do not offer this perk. In fact, more companies are switching to part-time workers in order to cut back on the rising cost of offering benefits, especially the health-insurance benefits now required of all companies with more than 50 full-time employees.

Part-time pay, full-time benefits. Many employees want to work part-time but can't afford not to have benefits such as health insurance. Companies known for hiring part-time employees with full benefits include Starbucks, REI, Lands' End, UPS, and Barnes & Noble.

Job sharing (sometimes referred to as *work sharing*) is an arrangement whereby two people share one full-time position. One job sharer may work from 8 a.m. to noon, and the other from 1 to 5 p.m., or they may alternate workdays. Job sharing is different than part-time work because two people share one single position, which is generally more skilled than a part-time position would be. Job sharing can be difficult to orchestrate at the beginning, but may contribute to greater job satisfaction and ease in creating work–life balance. Job sharing can actually lead people to be more productive, as they know that their time at work is limited and that someone else is directly depending on the quality of their work. Job sharing combines the security of a full-time position with the flexibility of a part-time one, which may be especially valuable for working parents. For firms, job sharing provides a unique opportunity to attract highly skilled employees who are not available on a full-time basis. In addition, companies can save on benefits expenses and avoid the disruptions of employee turnover. For employees, opting for the flexibility of job sharing may mean giving up some of the benefits, such as health insurance, received for full-time work. Job sharing is difficult if tasks are not easily divisible or if two people do not work or communicate well with one another.

远程办公

9-5f Telecommuting

A rapidly growing number of companies allow **telecommuting**, working remotely all the time or for a portion of the work week. Technology such as email, cloud computing, smart phones, laptops, tablets, video conferencing, and overnight couriers all make skipping the commute to work at home, a coffee shop, or coworking office easier and more convenient than ever before. Working at home means that individuals can set their own hours and have more time with their families as long as they produce the desired results. Telecommuting has boomed 173 percent since 2005, and now comprises 3.6 percent of the U.S. workforce, excluding the self-employed.[15] Of course, during the COVID-19 pandemic, telecommuting and working at home became even more prevalent, and some organizations have said their employees can continue to telecommute as long as they desire. Telecommuting can be especially beneficial for employees with disabilities, working parents, and employees taking care of family members who are older or disabled, though in fact, telecommuters include all demographic groups.

远程办公
telecommuting working remotely all the time or for a portion of the work week

Technology and Innovation

技术与创新：居家办工革命走向高科技

The Work-From-Home Revolution Goes High-Tech

During the COVID-19 pandemic, organizations rapidly shifted to telecommuting. Organizations quickly had to find ways to communicate and collaborate. This led to the accelerated adoption of cloud-based videoconferencing platforms such as Zoom and collaboration software such as Microsoft Teams. Zoom's daily downloads increased more than 30 times year-over-year with total users reaching more than 200 million. Even as the pandemic subsided, many organizations made the switch to telecommuting permanent.

Historically, businesses hesitated to allow employees to work from home due to productivity concerns, but the forced adoption of a remote workforce proved that working from home could be efficient and effective. As the pandemic continued, some organizations introduced permanent work-from-home policies, from partial telecommuting to fully remote workforces. For example, Facebook, Twitter, Coinbase, Zillow, Shopify, and Microsoft all gave employees the option to work from home ongoing at least part-time.

Existing platforms such as communications software Slack and project management tool Asana welcomed the work-from-home revolution. The movement also gave rise to new platforms such as Microsoft Viva. Viva analyzes employee activity to improve wellbeing and provides a hub for company resources. Managers receive de-identified insights to protect employee privacy. Viva joins an emerging category of employee experience technology that aims to improve work quality and employee satisfaction. Microsoft's investment in this area suggests the digital workforce is here to stay.

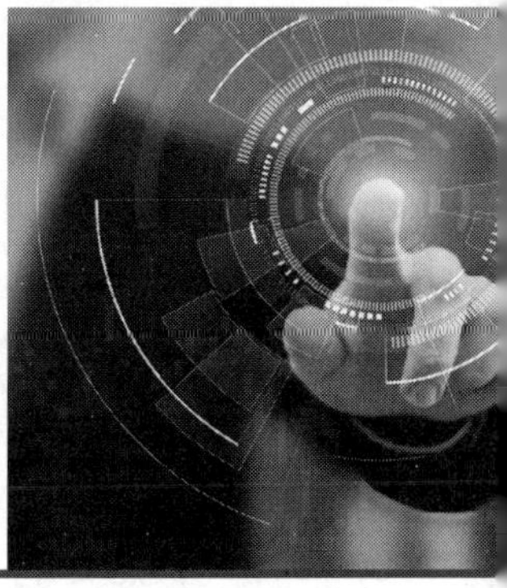

Sources: Based on information in Dain Evans, "How Zoom Became So Popular During Social Distancing," *CNBC*, April 4, 2020; Gillian Friedman and Kellen Browning, "July Is the New January: More Companies Delay Return to the Office," *The New York Times*, October 13, 2020; Todd Bishop, "Microsoft Unveils 'Viva' on Teams in Bid To Shake up $300B Employee Experience Technology Market," *GeekWire*, February 4, 2021.

Office space—at home. Some companies are finding it cost-effective to allow employees to work at home. Working at home means that parents can spend more time with their children. Telecommuting arrangements such as this can be a win–win situation for both employees and their firms.

A growing body of research indicates that telecommuters are actually more effective than their in-office counterparts. Numerous research studies have found that telecommuting employees generally perform better and faster than their peers who work in the office. Additionally, they are more likely to continue working even when they are sick. Finally, remote workers generally report higher levels of happiness and personal satisfaction with their work.[16]

In addition to increased productivity, companies that allow occasional telecommuting have lower real estate and travel expenses, improved morale, and the flexibility to access larger labor pools. Telecommuting also reduces fossil fuel emissions from putting fewer cars on the road, and employees who do not have to commute report lower levels of stress. When Chinese travel website Ctrip allowed half of its employees to telecommute, the company saved $1,900 per employee in furniture and space costs over nine months. Moreover, the telecommuting employees were so efficient that they effectively netted the company an extra day of work per week. The telecommuters used fewer sick days, quit at a much lower rate, and reported much higher job satisfaction.[17]

Among the disadvantages of telecommuting are feelings of isolation, putting in long hours, and being distracted by family or household responsibilities. The stigma also remains, in spite of evidence to the contrary, that telecommuters are less productive than office-based staff. In addition, some supervisors have difficulty monitoring the productivity of remote workers.

员工授权

9-5g Employee Empowerment

Many companies are increasing employee motivation and satisfaction through the use of empowerment. **Empowerment** means making employees more involved in their jobs and in the operations of the organization by increasing their participation in decision making. With empowerment, control no longer flows exclusively from the top level of the organization downward. Empowered employees have a voice in what they do and how and when they do it. In some organizations, employees' input is restricted to individual choices, such as when to take breaks. In other companies, their responsibilities may encompass more far-reaching issues. Successful companies treat their employees like assets, empowering them to fully utilize their talents. Technology clearly plays a role in empowering employees. Allowing employees access to information, such as reports, performance data, and communications, can empower them and make them feel more satisfied with their jobs.

For empowerment to work effectively, management must be involved. Managers should set expectations, communicate standards, institute periodic evaluations, and guarantee follow-up. If effectively implemented, empowerment can lead to increased job satisfaction, improved job performance, higher self-esteem, and increased organizational commitment. Obstacles to empowerment include resistance on the part of management, distrust of management on the part of workers, inadequate training of employees, and poor communication between levels of the organization.

授权
empowerment making employees more involved in their jobs by increasing their participation in decision making

Ethics and Social Responsibility

商业伦理与社会责任：惠普永远为员工授权

HP Empowers Employees for Good

Empowering employees to make decisions, solve problems, and innovate can contribute to motivation and satisfaction. Some employers are taking this concept and applying it to sustainability and social responsibility. Hewlett-Packard (HP) believes that empowering individuals is key to the success of its sustainable impact strategy.

The human, economic, and environmental impacts of sustainability issues can feel too immense to tackle for any one individual, but HP hopes to change that by offering employees the agency to set their own sustainability and social responsibility goals. Employees can support closed-loop recycling, help customers transition to a circular economy, or join the HP Racial Equality and Social Justice Task Force to identify opportunities to improve racial equality within HP, just to name a few examples. Employees are given training and support to sync initiatives with their individual roles and job responsibilities, giving them a greater sense of control and purpose in their work. This, in turn, supports HP's corporate vision and strategy and creates lasting, transformative change at scale.

HP creates more than just PCs, printers, and mobile solutions; it also creates change. The company is fueling purpose, passion, and ingenuity for employees across every job function, and, as HP sees it, it is effectively empowering a 55,000-person worldwide sustainable impact team. By turning employee interests into action, the technology company demonstrates that sustainability and social responsibility are core to HP's culture.

Sources: Based on information in Ellen Jackowski, "Empowering a Cultural Shift to Accelerate a More Sustainable and Just Future," *CSR Wire*, January 27, 2021; HP, "HP Racial Equality and Social Justice".

员工持股

9-5h Employee Ownership

Some organizations have discovered that an effective technique for motivating employees is **employee ownership**—that is, employees own the company they work for by virtue of being stockholders. Employee-owned businesses directly reward employees for success. When the company enjoys increased sales or lower costs, employees benefit directly. The National Center for Employee Ownership, an organization that studies employee-owned American businesses, reports that employee stock ownership plans (ESOPs) provide considerable employee incentive and increase employee involvement and commitment. In the United States today, an estimated 14 million employees participate in 6,416 ESOPs.[18] Employees in an ESOP may own all or part of a company's stock. In the United States, employee-owned companies include Publix Super Markets, Harpoon Brewing, Bob's Red Mill Natural Foods, and Davey Tree. ESOPs have also become more popular in Europe.

As a means to motivate executives and managers to feel invested in the company as they work long days, some firms provide stock options as part of the employee compensation package. An option is simply the right to buy shares of the firm within a prescribed time at a set price. If the firm does well and its stock price rises past the set price (presumably because of all the work being done by the employee), the employee can exercise the option and sell the stock to cash in on the company's success. However, not all companies choose to engage in ESOPs because they can be complex and expensive for the firm. This is particularly true of smaller organizations that may not have the means to manage such a program.

✓ Concept Check

- What are the five steps of most MBO programs?
- How can companies use job enrichment as a method for motivating employees?
- What is behavior modification and how is it used in organizations?
- What benefits does a company receive when using flextime, job sharing, and telecommuting?
- How do employee ownership and employee empowerment help in increasing employee motivation and satisfaction?

员工持股

employee ownership a situation in which employees own the company they work for by virtue of being stockholders

Discussion Questions 讨论题

1. How did the results of the Hawthorne Studies influence researchers' thinking about employee motivation?
2. What are the five levels of needs in Maslow's hierarchy? How are a person's needs related to motivation?
3. What are the two dimensions in Herzberg's theory? What kinds of elements affect each dimension?
4. According to equity theory, how do employees determine whether they are being treated equitably?
5. According to expectancy theory, what two variables determine motivation?
6. How can managers nurture organizational cultures that motivate employees?
7. Which type of organizational culture do you think would best motivate employees? Least motivate?
8. What are the objectives of the MBO? What do you think might be its disadvantage?
9. How do flexible scheduling strategies and telecommuting increase motivation?
10. How can employee empowerment and ownership increase motivation?
11. What combination of motivational techniques do you think would result in the best overall motivation and reward system?

Case 9 案例9：谷歌的员工福利令人满意

Google's Employee Perks Satisfy

Google is continually recognized for its employee-centric culture and is considered one of the best companies to work for. This is due in large part to Google's wide array of employee benefits. Bicycles and scooters to get across campus, complimentary meals, healthcare, on-site physicians, gaming rooms, and nap pods are just a few of the things that individuals enjoy at Google.

Google's workplace culture is built on data. Every decision Google makes hinges on qualitative and quantitative data. It's no surprise, then, that the company's human resources (HR) department, called People Operations, uses data analytics to glean insights about employee behavior. As an example, the company measures total waiting time for employees at lunch to improve the flow of the cafeterias. Using internal data offers a way for the tech giant to increase happiness and satisfaction. For example, when the company uncovered high turnover rates among employees who were pregnant, Google introduced an enhanced paid parental leave policy.

Google's culture fosters fun and creativity. Ping pong, billiards, and foosball tables as well as arcade-style video games are found throughout Google's buildings. Free meals add to the appeal of working at Google's offices. Instead of confining employees to cubicles, they are encouraged to make use of a variety of community areas including breakout zones, coffee bars, lounges, and cafeterias. Google's headquarters, called the Googleplex, was designed by South African architect Clive Wilkinson who kept teamwork and creativity top of mind when creating the facility. The Googleplex's features were intended to boost productivity and improve employee satisfaction. Workspaces are designed to accommodate three to four people, which is said to be effective for sharing ideas without distracting the rest of the office. Employees are encouraged to share ideas and engage in discussion with co-workers because it can lead to unexpected, innovative results.

Google takes a decentralized approach to empowering its employees. It's said that employees are often allowed to use 20 percent of their time for independent side projects to promote and inspire creativity. This side project mindset gave birth to many of Google's most successful products such as Gmail, AdSense, and Google News. One of Google's pillars for innovation is to strive for continual innovation rather than instant perfection. For example, the initial version of AdWords released in 1999 was a flop. But, after many iterations and experiments, Google reached the Google Ads model that exists today. Extending its 20-percent-time concept even further, Google introduced the Google.org Fellowship that allows its employees to work full-time for nonprofit partners for up to six months. Collectively, Google aims for 50,000 hours of pro bono work annually through the program. The program allows Google to have a lasting impact in the areas of education, criminal justice, and economic opportunity while allowing its employees to grow and gain outside experience and inspiration.

Looking to the future, one challenge Google faces is maintaining its fun, creative culture as the workforce becomes increasingly remote. This presented itself during the COVID-19 pandemic when Google ordered employees to stay home for more than a year, affecting nearly all of the company's full-time and contract employees. Google employees were told they could not expense food or gym costs while working from home in an updated policy. Employees went as far as to say their productivity declined due to the lack of free coffee and food. Google will likely have more and more remote employees in the long run and will need to identify ways to engage remote team members.

As a global leader in the tech space, Google has high demands and standards for its employees. By building a culture of happiness and supporting employees' creative endeavors, Google can not only attract and retain top talent but also improve productivity and fuel innovation. This innovative work environment is one of the reasons Google is so successful.[19]

Questions

1. How does Google promote creativity and innovation?
2. How is data analytics used to inform Google's benefits?
3. What perks could Google offer to engage remote employees?

PART 5
Marketing
市场营销

The business activities that make up a firm's marketing efforts are those more directly concerned with satisfying customers' needs. In this part, we explore these activities in some detail. Initially, we discuss markets, marketing mixes, marketing environment forces, marketing plans, and buying behavior. Then, we discuss the four elements that together make up a marketing mix: product, price, distribution, and promotion.

Chapter

10

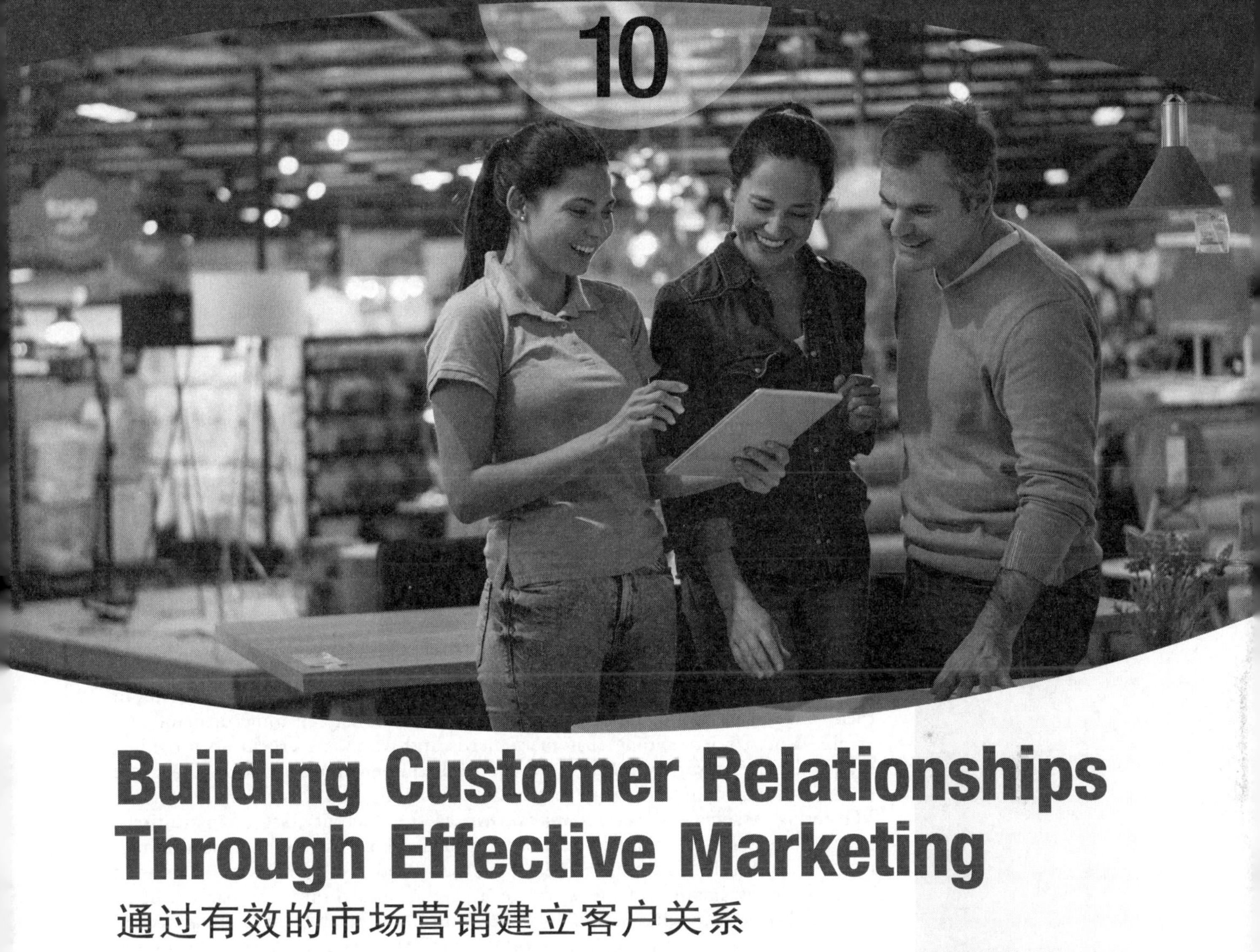

Building Customer Relationships Through Effective Marketing

通过有效的市场营销建立客户关系

Learning Objectives

Once you complete this chapter, you will be able to:

10-1 Describe the meaning of *marketing* and the importance of managing customer relationships.

10-2 Explain how marketing adds value by creating several forms of utility.

10-3 Discuss the development of the marketing concept and how it is implemented.

10-4 Define what markets are and classify them.

10-5 Describe the two major components of a marketing strategy—target market and marketing mix.

10-6 Explain how the marketing environment affects strategic market planning.

10-7 Examine the major components of a marketing plan.

10-8 Describe how market measurement and sales forecasting are used.

10-9 Explain how marketers collect and analyze information useful for marketing decision making.

10-10 Identify the major steps in the consumer buying decision process and the sets of factors that may influence this process.

Why Should You Care?

Marketers are concerned about building long-term customer relationships. To develop competitive product offerings, business people must identify acceptable target customer groups and understand their behaviors.

Inside Business 商业透视：Netflix 在客户保留率方面领先于竞争对手

Netflix Tops the Competition in Customer Retention

Netflix, the world's largest subscription-based streaming service, is deep in the trenches of the streaming war. Competitors such as Amazon Prime Video, Hulu, Disney+, HBO Max, Peacock, and Apple TV+ crowd the market, and Netflix's first-mover advantage is quickly fading. Netflix must continue to adapt and innovate to stay ahead.

One data point, however, suggests that Netflix has a strong hold on its top spot: churn rate. *Churn rate* refers to the percentage of subscribers who do not renew their subscriptions during a given time frame. As competition heats up, one would expect Netflix's churn rate to suffer, but so far that hasn't been the case. The company's churn is between 2 and 3 percent, which is below all of its rivals. Subscription services HBO and Showtime often see their churn rates spike following a popular series finale, underscoring one of Netflix's key strengths: its extensive content library. The data indicate that customers see value in Netflix beyond a single television show.

Netflix further adds value to its product through personalization, an area where other streaming services lag behind. By investing in exclusive shows and movies, as well as page personalization, search algorithms, and personalized messaging and marketing, Netflix satisfies its customers' needs for content and a quality browsing experience. The homepage not only recommends content a subscriber is likely to enjoy, but it also goes as far as to personalize the artwork for each show and movie to an image the individual is more likely to select. The company uses machine learning, text analytics, and collaborative filtering to power its search function. All of these elements contribute to Netflix's high customer retention and demonstrate that the company has a firm grasp on the marketing concept.[1]

Did You Know?

Netflix has more than 200 million subscribers.

Like Netflix, organizations use marketing activities to inform customers about their range of products and how these products can satisfy customer demand and create value. Understanding customers' needs and wants are crucial to providing the products that satisfy them. Although marketing encompasses a diverse set of decisions and activities, it always begins and ends with the customer. The American Marketing Association defines **marketing** as the "activity, set of institutions, and processes for creating, communicating, delivering, and exchanging offerings that have value for customers, clients, partners, and society at large."[2] **Value** is a customer's estimation of the worth of a product based on a comparison of its costs and benefits, including quality, relative to other products. For some people, value means the lowest price, but for others it might mean products that cost more but last a long time. The marketing process involves eight major functions and numerous related activities, all of which are essential to the marketing process (refer to Table 10-1).

In this chapter, we examine how marketing activities add value to products. We begin by exploring how organizations seek to maintain positive relationships with customers through marketing activities and develop products that create utility. We trace the evolution of the marketing concept and describe how organizations practice it. Next, we shift our focus to classifying markets and developing marketing strategy by targeting an appropriate marketing mix at a target market. We also examine the uncontrollable factors in the marketing environment and the major components of a marketing plan. Then we consider tools for strategic market planning, including market measurement, sales forecasts, marketing analytics, and marketing research. Finally, we look at the forces that influence consumer and organizational buying behavior.

市场营销
marketing the activity, set of institutions, and processes for creating, communicating, delivering, and exchanging offerings that have value for customers, clients, partners, and society at large

价值
value a customer's estimation of the worth of a product based on a comparison of its costs and benefits, including quality, relative to other products

Table 10-1 **Eight Major Marketing Functions**

Exchange functions: All companies—manufacturers, wholesalers, and retailers—buy and sell to market their merchandise.
1. **Buying** includes obtaining raw materials to make products, knowing how much merchandise to keep on hand, and selecting suppliers.
2. **Selling** creates possession utility by transferring the title of a product from seller to customer.
Physical distribution functions: These functions involve the flow of goods from producers to customers.
3. **Transporting** involves selecting a mode of transport that provides an acceptable delivery schedule at an acceptable price.
4. **Storing** goods is often necessary to sell them at the optimal selling time.
Facilitating functions: These functions help the other functions to take place.
5. **Financing** helps at all stages of marketing. To buy raw materials, manufacturers often borrow from banks or receive credit from suppliers. Wholesalers may be financed by manufacturers, and retailers may receive financing from the wholesaler or manufacturer. Finally, retailers often provide financing to customers.
6. **Standardizing** sets uniform specifications for products or services. Grading classifies products by size and quality, usually through a sorting process. Together, standardizing and grading facilitate production, transportation, storage, and selling.
7. **Risk taking**—even though competent management and insurance can minimize risks—is a constant reality of marketing because of such losses as bad-debt expense, obsolescence of products, theft by employees, and product-liability lawsuits.
8. **Gathering** market information is necessary for making all marketing decisions.

客户关系管理

10-1 Managing Customer Relationships

Learning Objective

10-1 Describe the meaning of *marketing* and the importance of managing customer relationships.

Without relationships with customers, businesses would not be successful. Therefore, maintaining positive relationships with customers is an important goal for marketers. The term **relationship marketing** refers to marketing decisions and activities focused on achieving long-term, satisfying relationships with customers. Relationship marketing deepens and reinforces the buyer's trust in the company, which, as the customer's loyalty grows, increases a company's understanding of the customer's needs and desires. Successful marketers respond to customers' needs and strive to increase value to buyers continually over time. Eventually, this interaction becomes a solid relationship that fosters cooperation and mutual trust. The internet has expanded and improved relationship marketing options for many firms by making targeted communication faster, cheaper, and easier. Digital technologies allow firms to connect to consumers and interact with them in real time. This not only improves the speed at which firms can innovate, but also makes consumers feel more satisfied because they feel the firm is listening to them.

To build long-term customer relationships, marketers rely on marketing research and information technology. **Customer relationship management (CRM)** focuses on using information about customers to create marketing strategies that develop and sustain desirable customer relationships. By increasing customer value over time, organizations try to retain and increase long-term profitability through customer loyalty. Because CRM is such an important part of creating and building customer loyalty, many companies have developed high-tech tools aimed at helping them to identify their more profitable customers and to manage relations with them over the long term. Starbucks, for example, rewards regular customers through an app that records their purchase history and offers them free food or drink on their birthday or after accruing points.

关系营销
relationship marketing establishing long-term, mutually satisfying buyer–seller relationships

客户关系管理
customer relationship management (CRM) using information about customers to create marketing strategies that develop and sustain desirable customer relationships

Developing long-term customer relationships. Many companies spend a considerable amount of money on marketing programs to develop and maintain long-term relationships with their customers—especially the valuable ones. Often it's more profitable to retain these customers by offering them big rewards than to attract new customers who may never develop the same loyalty.

The data accumulated from the app, along with store sales data and information about weather, holidays, and special events helps Starbucks understand customers' ordering habits so that it can personalize their experience and make astute recommendations according to time of day and weather—even if they normally frequent a different store. With nearly 20 million users, the Starbucks app helps the company build long-term relationships.[3] The accessibility of technology has contributed to a more even playing field for firms of all sizes.

Managing customer relationships requires identifying patterns of buying behavior and using this information to focus on the most promising and profitable customers. Companies must be sensitive to customers' requirements and desires and establish communication to build customers' trust and loyalty. In some instances, it may be more profitable for a company to focus on satisfying a valuable existing customer than to attempt to attract a new one who may never develop the same level of loyalty. This involves determining how much customers will spend over their lifetime. The **customer lifetime value (CLV)** is a measure

Sustaining the Planet

保护地球：客户反馈促使 Native 走向无塑料化

Customer Feedback Pushes Native to Go Plastic-Free

Native, a personal care company, understands the importance of developing long-term, satisfying relationships with its customers. The direct-to-consumer company, best known for its cult-favorite aluminum-free deodorant, enjoys a dedicated and loyal fan base. When its customers asked Native to reconsider its plastic packaging, the company listened and then introduced paper-based applicators for its all-natural products.

With an influx of customer requests for sustainable packaging, Native gathered and analyzed the feedback from a variety of sources including social media, customer service phone calls, and surveys. This marketing research revealed that customer communication related to environmentally conscious packaging had increased by more than 900 percent. After developing a prototype for the new packaging, Native sold 200 units, collected feedback, and analyzed the data. Based on input from the early adopters, Native made final tweaks before initiating a full rollout. The product innovation team is now considering ways to switch to 100 percent plastic-free packaging across its entire product mix.

Native has long relied on brand advocates to spread the word about the company's products. For example, Native leverages the 15,000 five-star reviews it has collected from customers to promote its deodorant, body wash, bar soap, and toothpaste. In the company's early years, Native knew it was onto something special when its repeat purchase rate reached 50 percent. By engaging with these loyal customers, Native can better understand their wants and needs, build a sense of trust, and deepen relationships.

Sources: Based on information in Kathryn Lundstrom, "Customer Feedback Inspired Native's New Plastic-Free Paper Packaging for Its Deodorant," *AdWeek*, July 20, 2020; Eric Bandholz, "Native Deodorant Founder on Scaling to $100 Million in 2 Years," *Practical Ecommerce*, October 9, 2020; Madge Maril, "Native's Cult-Favorite Deodorant Now Comes In Plastic-Free Packaging," *The Zoe Report*, June 24, 2020.

of a customer's worth (sales minus costs) to a business during one's lifetime.[4] CLV also includes the intangible benefits of retaining lifetime-value customers, such as their ability to provide feedback to a company and refer new customers of similar value, and these are important considerations as well. The amount of money a company is willing to spend to retain such customers is also a factor. In general, when marketers focus on customers chosen for their lifetime value, they earn higher profits in future periods than when they focus on customers selected for other reasons.[5] It is a fairly straightforward task to calculate CLV. In fact, businesses can utilize reliable free online tools to calculate CLV. Because the loss of a potential lifetime customer can result in lower profits, managing customer relationships has become a major focus of marketers.

✓ Concept Check

- Why is managing customer relationships important?
- How can technology help to build long-term customer relationships?
- What are the benefits of retaining customers?

效用：通过营销增加价值

10-2 Utility: The Value Added by Marketing

Learning Objective

10-2 Explain how marketing adds value by creating several forms of utility.

Utility is the ability of a good or service to satisfy a human need. The latest Xbox, Nike Air Jordan athletic shoes, or Mercedes Benz luxury car all satisfy human needs. Thus, each possesses utility. There are four kinds of utility (refer to Figure 10-1).

Form utility is created by converting production inputs into finished products. Marketing efforts may influence form utility indirectly because the data gathered as part of marketing research are frequently used to determine the size, shape, and features of a product.

The three kinds of utility that are created directly by marketing are place, time, and possession utility. **Place utility** is created by making a product available at a location where customers wish to purchase it. A pair of shoes is given place utility when it is shipped from a factory to a department store or made available for sale at Zappos.com.

Time utility is created by making a product available when customers wish to purchase it. For example, Halloween costumes may be manufactured in April but not displayed until September, when consumers start buying them. By storing the costumes until there is a demand, the manufacturer or retailer provides time utility.

Possession utility is created by transferring title (or ownership) of a product to a buyer. For a product as simple as a pair of shoes, ownership usually is transferred by means of a sales slip or receipt. For such products as automobiles and homes, the transfer of title is a more complex process. Along with the title to products, the seller transfers the right to use that product.

Figure 10-1 Types of Utility

Form utility is created by the production process, but marketing creates place, time, and possession utility.

客户终身价值
customer lifetime value (CLV) a measure of a customer's worth (sales minus costs) to a business over one's lifetime

效用
utility the ability of a good or service to satisfy a human need

形式效用
form utility utility created by converting production inputs into finished products

地点效用
place utility utility created by making a product available at a location where customers wish to purchase it

时间效用
time utility utility created by making a product available when customers wish to purchase it

拥有效用
possession utility utility created by transferring title (or ownership) of a product to a buyer

Place, time, and possession utility have real value in terms of both money and convenience. This value is created and added to goods and services through a wide variety of marketing activities—from research suggesting desired features to advertising those features to product warranties ensuring that customers get what they pay for. Overall, these marketing activities account for about half of every dollar spent by consumers. When they are part of an integrated marketing program that delivers maximum utility to the customer, many would agree that they are worth the cost.

✓ Concept Check

- Explain the four kinds of utility.
- Provide an example of each.

营销理念

10-3 The Marketing Concept

Learning Objective

10-3 Discuss the development of the marketing concept and how it is implemented.

营销理念

marketing concept a business philosophy that a firm should provide goods and services that satisfy customers' needs through a coordinated set of activities that allow the firm to achieve its objectives.

The **marketing concept** is a business philosophy that a firm should provide goods and services that satisfy customers' needs through a coordinated set of activities that allow the firm to achieve its objectives. Initially, the firm communicates with potential customers to assess their product needs. Then, the firm develops a good or service to satisfy those needs. Finally, the firm continues to seek ways to provide customer satisfaction. This process is an application of the marketing concept or marketing orientation. Consider the century-old Nordstrom department store chain. Long renowned for its customer service, the company continues to innovate by developing and acquiring technology to improve its customer experience both in stores and online. It also satisfies regular customers with a rewards program and curbside pickup. Through partnerships, the company has brought in many new products to appeal to diverse consumers, especially Millennials. While other retailers are faltering and shuttering stores, Nordstrom is experimenting with new store concepts, like its inventory-free Nordstrom Local stores where customers can try on products, pick up Style Board orders that have been curated for them, and more. These efforts help Nordstrom learn what customers want now so that it can satisfy them and keep them coming back.[6] It is important to recognize that all functional areas—research and development, production, finance, human resources, and, of course, marketing—play a role in providing customer satisfaction.

Putting products at the customer's fingertips. Firms try to provide customers with products when and where they need them.

营销理念的演变

10-3a Evolution of the Marketing Concept

From the start of the Industrial Revolution until the early 20th century, business effort was directed mainly toward the production of goods. Consumer demand for manufactured products was so great that manufacturers could almost bank on selling everything they produced. Business had a strong *production orientation,* which placed an emphasis on increased output and production efficiency. Marketing activities were limited to taking orders and distributing finished goods.

In the 1920s, production caught up with and began to exceed demand. Producers had to direct their efforts toward selling goods rather than just producing them. This new *sales orientation* was characterized by increased advertising, enlarged sales forces, and, occasionally, high-pressure selling techniques. Manufacturers produced the goods they expected consumers to want, and marketing consisted primarily of promoting products through personal selling and advertising, taking orders, and delivering goods.

During the 1950s, however, businesspeople started to realize that even enormous advertising expenditures and proven sales techniques were not sufficient to gain a competitive edge. It was then that business managers recognized that they were not primarily producers or sellers, but were in the business of satisfying customers' needs. Marketers realized that the best approach was to adopt a *customer orientation*—in other words, the organization had to first determine what customers need and then develop goods and services to fill those particular needs (refer to Table 10-2).

The marketing concept is dynamic and has continued to evolve. In the late 1990s, marketers increasingly focused their efforts on building and maintaining long-term relationships with customers. This *relationship orientation* adopted customer relationship management tools and technology to try to retain and increase long-term profitability through customer loyalty. In today's digital world where consumers can find just about anything they want at the touch of a smartphone button, the marketing concept continues to evolve to include social media and mobile technology. As an example, Zappos, the online shoe store renowned for its customer service, uses social media to respond to consumer queries, resolve issues, elicit consumer feedback, and highlight customers, all of which help it refine its marketing strategies.[7] Marketers also must adopt multiple distribution channels to reach customers wherever and whenever they might choose to shop—in stores, online, and through smart device apps. Nonetheless, all marketers still must focus on providing products that satisfy customers' needs and wants as well as their own objectives.

Tell us what you *really* think. Customer satisfaction is a major element of the marketing concept. Many businesses attempt to measure customer satisfaction through surveys. Surveys can be conducted in a variety of ways: in person, by mail or phone, or online. Online surveys have made it very inexpensive for firms to gather customer feedback.

营销理念的实施

10-3b Implementing the Marketing Concept

To implement the marketing concept, a firm first must obtain information about its present and potential customers. The firm must determine not only what customers' needs are, but also how well these needs are satisfied by products currently in the market—both its own products and those of competitors. It must ascertain how its products might be improved and what opinions customers have about the firm and its marketing efforts.

The firm then must use this information to pinpoint the specific needs and potential customers toward which it will direct its marketing activities and resources.

Table 10-2 Evolution of Customer Orientation

Business managers recognized that they were not primarily producers or sellers, but were in the business of satisfying customers' wants.

Production Orientation	Sales Orientation	Customer Orientation	Relationship Orientation
Take orders	Increase advertising	Determine customer needs	Use all possible media to build relationships
Distribute goods	Enlarge sales force	Develop products to fill those needs	Increase value to customer over time
	Intensify sales techniques	Achieve the organization's goals	Gain customer loyalty and increase long-term profitability

Next, the firm must mobilize its marketing resources to (1) provide a product that will satisfy its customers, (2) price the product at a level that is acceptable to buyers and will yield a profit, (3) promote the product so that potential customers will be aware of its existence and its ability to satisfy their needs, and (4) ensure that the product is distributed so that it is available to customers where and when it is needed.

Finally, the firm must again obtain marketing information—this time regarding the effectiveness of its efforts. Can the product be improved? Is it being promoted effectively? Is it being distributed efficiently? Is the price too high or too low? The firm must be ready to modify any or all of its marketing activities based on information about its customers and competitors. Consider Zara, the fashion retailer owned by Spain-based Inditex, which employs a strategy of quickly designing, manufacturing, and stocking small quantities of fashion items—in as little as two weeks—and then nimbly updating inventories in response to customer reaction and requests. The firm's strategy and strong customer focus allow it to maintain fresh and exciting product assortments that keep customers happy.[8]

✓ Concept Check

- Identify the major components of the marketing concept.
- How did the customer orientation evolve?
- What steps are involved when implementing the marketing concept?

市场及其分类

10-4 Markets and Their Classification

Learning Objective

10-4 Define what markets are and classify them.

A **market** is a group of individuals or organizations, or both, that need products in a given category and that have the ability, willingness, and authority to purchase them. Markets are broadly classified as consumer or business-to-business, and marketing efforts vary depending on the intended market. Marketers should understand the general characteristics of these two groups.

Consumer markets consist of purchasers and/or household members who intend to consume or benefit from the purchased products and who do not buy products to make profits. *Business-to-business (B2B) markets,* also called *industrial markets,* are grouped broadly into producer, reseller, governmental, and institutional categories. These markets purchase specific kinds of products for use in making other products for resale or for day-to-day operations. *Producer markets* consist of individuals and business organizations that buy certain products to use in the manufacture of other products. *Reseller markets* include intermediaries, such as wholesalers and retailers, that buy finished products and sell them for a profit. *Government markets* consist of federal, state, county, and local governments that buy goods and services to maintain internal operations and to provide citizens with such products as highways, education, water, energy, and national defense. Government purchases total billions of dollars each year. *Institutional markets* include churches, not-for-profit private schools and hospitals, civic clubs, fraternities and sororities, charitable organizations, and foundations. Their goals are different from the typical business goals of profit, market share, or return on investment.

✓ Concept Check

- What is a market?
- Identify and describe the major types of markets.

制定营销策略

10-5 Developing Marketing Strategies

Learning Objective

10-5 Describe the two major components of a marketing strategy—target market and marketing mix.

市场
market a group of individuals or organizations, or both, that need products in a given category and that have the ability, willingness, and authority to purchase them

A **marketing strategy** is a plan that will enable an organization to make the best use of its resources and advantages to meet its objectives. A marketing strategy consists of (1) the selection and analysis of a target market and (2) the creation and maintenance of an appropriate **marketing mix**, a combination of product, price, distribution, and promotion developed to satisfy a particular target market.

目标市场的选择和评估

10-5a Target Market Selection and Evaluation

A **target market** is a group of individuals or organizations, or both, for which a firm develops and maintains a marketing mix suitable for the specific needs and preferences of that group. In selecting a target market, marketing managers examine potential markets for their possible effects on the firm's sales, costs, and profits. The managers attempt to determine whether the organization has the resources to produce a marketing mix that meets the needs of a particular target market and whether satisfying these needs is consistent with the firm's overall objectives. They also analyze the strengths and number of competitors already marketing to the target market. A target market can range in size from millions of people to only a few, depending on the product and the marketer's objectives. Consider Zipcar, a car-sharing company that targets people who live in cities and do not want to own a car, as well as those who cannot afford a car or only need one occasionally. Its target market treats cars as a sustainable option for getting around, not as a status symbol.[9] On the other hand, Rolls-Royce targets its automobiles toward a small, very exclusive market: wealthy people who want the ultimate in prestige in an automobile. Some companies target multiple markets with different products, prices, distribution systems, and promotions for each one. Some high-end clothing designers, for instance, target multiple markets when they introduce more affordable lines distributed at mass market retail outlets, such as Target and Walmart. This strategy allows designers to reach customers with varying needs and levels of disposable income. Target has partnered with such high-end designers as Victoria Beckham, Marimekko, and Lily Pulitzer to offer affordable versions of high-end products.[10] The strategy has introduced the normally elite brands to a much larger market, enhancing Target's stylish image.

Reaching the right market segments. The market for fragrances is segmented based on gender. Some fragrances are aimed at men while others, such as the perfume in this photo, are aimed at women.

Undifferentiated Approach A company that designs a single marketing mix and directs it at the entire market for a particular product is using an **undifferentiated approach** (refer to Figure 10-2). This approach assumes that individual customers in the target market for a specific kind of product have similar needs and that the organization can satisfy most customers with a single marketing mix, which consists of one type of product with little or no variation, one price, one promotional program aimed at everyone, and one distribution system to reach all customers in the total market. Products that can be marketed successfully with the undifferentiated approach include staple food items, such as sugar and salt, and some produce. An undifferentiated approach is useful in only a limited number of situations because buyers have varying needs for most product categories, which requires the market segmentation approach.

Market Segmentation Approach Market segmentation is required because different consumers have different needs. A firm that markets 40-foot yachts would not direct its marketing effort toward every person in the total boat market, for instance, because not all boat buyers have the same needs. Marketing efforts directed at the wrong target market are wasted.

Instead, the firm should direct its attention toward a particular portion, or segment, of the total market for boats. A **market segment** is a group of individuals or organizations within a market that shares one or more common characteristics. The process of dividing a market into segments is called **market segmentation**. As shown in Figure 10-2, there are two market segmentation approaches: concentrated and differentiated. When an organization uses *concentrated* market segmentation, a single marketing mix is directed at a single market segment. Pair Eyewear, for example, targets its direct-to-consumer eyeglasses at children (and their parents) with fun colors and patterns, along with a child-friendly home tryout process.[11]

营销策略
marketing strategy a plan that will enable an organization to make the best use of its resources and advantages to meet its objectives

营销组合
marketing mix a combination of product, price, distribution, and promotion developed to satisfy a particular target market

目标市场
target market a group of individuals or organizations, or both, for which a firm develops and maintains a marketing mix suitable for the specific needs and preferences of that group

无差别方法
undifferentiated approach directing a single marketing mix at the entire market for a particular product

细分市场
market segment a group of individuals or organizations within a market that shares one or more common characteristics

市场细分
market segmentation the process of dividing a market into segments and directing a marketing mix at a particular segment or segments rather than at the total market

Figure 10-2 General Approaches for Selecting Target Markets

The undifferentiated approach assumes that individual customers have similar needs and that most customers can be satisfied with a single marketing mix. When customers' needs vary, the market segmentation approach—either concentrated or differentiated—should be used.

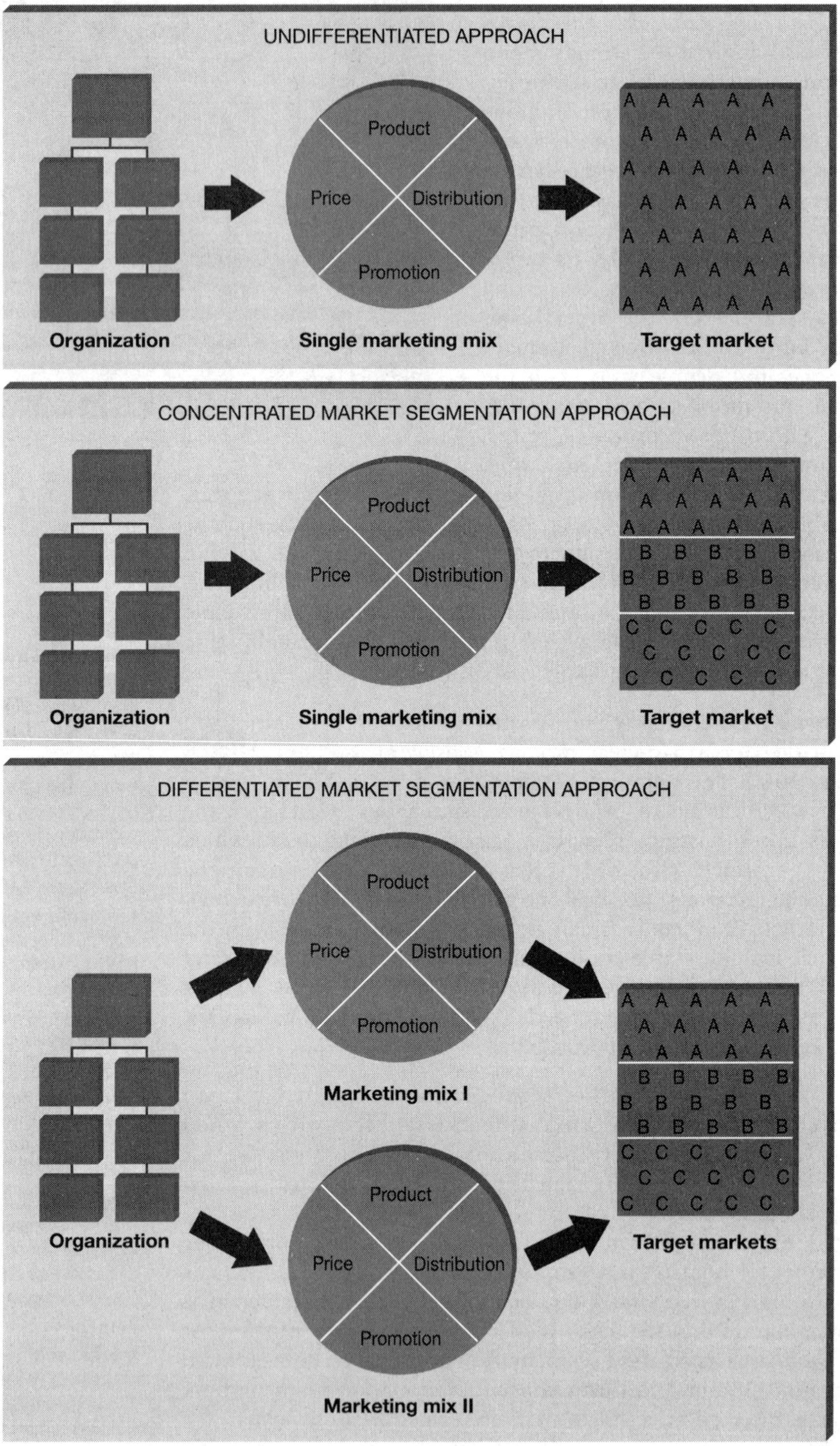

Note: The letters in each target market represent potential customers. Customers that have the same letters have similar characteristics and similar product needs.

If *differentiated* market segmentation is used, multiple marketing mixes are focused on multiple market segments. Kellogg's employs a differentiated approach; for instance, it targets health-conscious consumers with Special K and Smart Start cereals, and parents of young children with Apple Jacks and Fruit Loops cereals and Pop-Tarts.

In our boat example, one common characteristic, or *basis*, for segmentation might be end use of a boat. The firm would be interested primarily in the market segment whose uses for a boat could lead to the purchase of a 40-foot yacht. Other bases for segmentation might be income or geographic location. Variables can affect the type of boat an individual might purchase. When choosing a basis for segmentation, it is important to select a characteristic that relates to differences in customers' needs for a product. The yacht producer, for example, would not use religion to segment the boat market because people's needs for boats do not vary based on religion.

Differentiated targeting strategy. Gillette employs a differentiated targeting strategy for its razors. The company uses multiple marketing mixes and aims them at multiple target markets. As shown here, Gillette aims its razor on the left at men and its razor on the right at women.

Marketers use a wide variety of segmentation bases. Those most commonly applied to consumer markets are shown in Table 10-3. Each may be used as a single basis for market segmentation or in combination with other bases. For example, Honda and Toyota use gender and family life cycle as bases for marketing their respective minivans, the Odyssey and the Sienna, with features and advertising designed to appeal to parents.

创建营销组合

10-5b Creating a Marketing Mix

A business controls four important elements of marketing that it combines in a way that reaches the firm's target market. These are the *product* itself, the *price* of the product, the means chosen for its *distribution*, and the *promotion* of the product. When combined, these four elements form a marketing mix (refer to Figure 10-3). A firm can vary its marketing mix by changing any one or more of the ingredients. Thus, a firm may use one marketing mix to reach one target market and another

Table 10-3 Common Bases of Market Segmentation

Demographic	Psychographic	Geographic	Behavioristic
Age	Personality attributes	Region	Volume usage
Gender	Motives	Urban, suburban, rural	End use
Race	Lifestyles	Market density	Benefit expectations
Ethnicity		Climate	Brand loyalty
Income		Terrain	Price sensitivity
Education		City size	
Occupation		County size	
Family size		State size	
Family life cycle			
Religion			
Social class			

Figure 10-3 The Marketing Mix and the Marketing Environment

The marketing mix consists of elements that the firm controls—product, price, distribution, and promotion. The firm generally has no control over forces in the marketing environment.

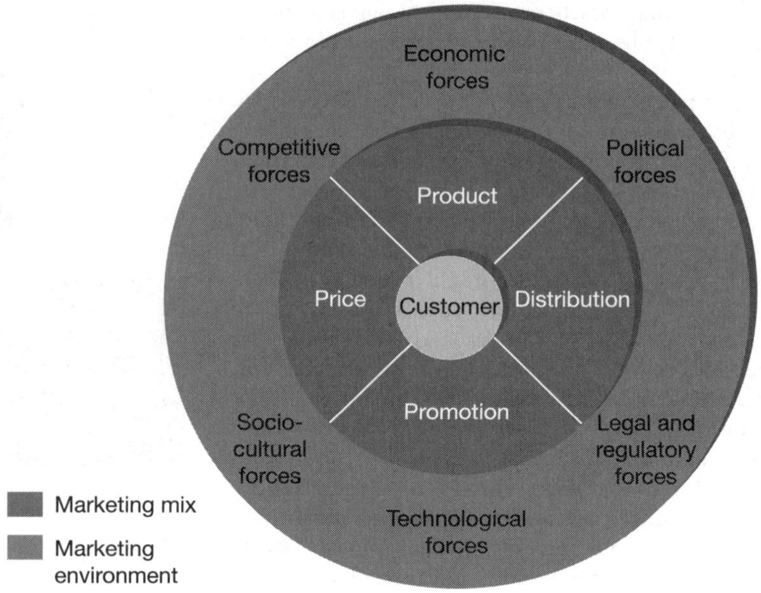

marketing mix to reach a different target market. For example, most automakers produce several different types and models of vehicles and aim them at different market segments based on the potential customers' age, income, family life-cycle stage, and other factors.

The most visible ingredient of the marketing mix is obviously the *product*. Product decisions typically relate to the product's design, functions, features, brand name, packaging, and warranties. When McDonald's decides on new menu items, brand names, package designs, sizes of orders, flavors of sauces, and recipes, these choices are all part of the product ingredient.

The *pricing* ingredient is concerned with both base prices and discounts. Consider the Samsung Galaxy Fold Z2 smartphone, which is priced at $2,000.[12] Pricing decisions are intended to achieve particular goals, such as to maximize profit or to make room for new models. The rebates offered by automobile manufacturers are a pricing strategy developed to boost low auto sales. Product and pricing are discussed in more detail in Chapter 11.

The *distribution* ingredient involves not only transportation and storage, but also intermediaries. How many levels of intermediaries are appropriate in the distribution of a particular product and

Developing the right marketing mix. Firms have little control over the marketing environment. However, they *can* control the marketing mixes for their products—that is, the nature of the products themselves and how they are priced, distributed, and promoted. Marketers at PepsiCo have developed a specific marketing mix for regular Pepsi.

should it be distributed as widely as possible or restricted to specialized outlets? Companies may have to alter the distribution ingredient over time. For example, as customers' consumption habits shift, retailers are adapting their distribution to include online and mobile sales. Retailers are increasingly developing their own apps to have greater control over their customer experience and to allow customers to order products whenever and wherever they might think about it. Sephora customers, for example, can use its app to shop for products and see their past purchases so they can reorder just the right shade. The app also lets shoppers "try on" various facial products so they can find the ideal products.[13]

The *promotion* ingredient focuses on providing information to target markets. The major forms of promotion are advertising, personal selling, sales promotion, and public relations. Careful planning and implementation of promotional tools is crucial to ensure their effectiveness. Distribution and promotion are discussed in more detail in Chapter 12.

These ingredients of the marketing mix are controllable elements. A firm can vary each of them to suit its organizational and marketing goals and target market needs. For instance, it can add new features to a product or reduce its price to reach a particular segment or to boost its *market share*—the percentage of a market that actually buys a specific product from a particular company. Microsoft, for example, added Microsoft Editor, Teams for Consumers, and greater cloud storage to its Microsoft 365 subscription office software suite for personal use.[14] As we extend our discussion of marketing strategy, we will see that the marketing environment includes a number of *uncontrollable* elements as well.

✓ Concept Check

- What are the major components of a marketing strategy?
- Describe the major approaches used in target market selection.
- Identify the four elements of the marketing mix.

营销策略与营销环境

10-6 Marketing Strategy and the Marketing Environment

Learning Objective

10-6 Explain how the marketing environment affects strategic market planning.

The marketing mix consists of elements that a firm controls and uses to reach its target market. The firm also has control of organizational resources, such as finances and data, which can be utilized to accomplish marketing goals and refine the marketing mix. All of a firm's marketing activities can be affected by external forces, which are generally uncontrollable. As Figure 10-3 illustrates, the following forces make up the external *marketing environment:*

- *Economic forces*—the effects of economic conditions on customers' ability and willingness to buy;
- *Sociocultural forces*—influences in a society and its culture that result in changes in attitudes, beliefs, norms, customs, and lifestyles;
- *Political forces*—influences that arise through the actions of political figures;
- *Competitive forces*—the actions of competitors, who are in the process of implementing their own marketing plans;
- *Legal and regulatory forces*—laws that protect consumers and competition and government regulations that affect marketing; and
- *Technological forces*—technological changes that can create new marketing opportunities or cause products to become obsolete rapidly.

These forces influence decisions about marketing mix ingredients. Changes in the environment can affect existing marketing strategies. Consider the challenges faced by marketers during the COVID-19 pandemic and the resulting economic downturn. While many Americans slashed their spending after losing their jobs, many others began to work from home. Consumers bought more laptops, desk

✓ Concept Check

- Describe the environmental forces that affect a firm's marketing decisions and activities.
- How are marketing decisions affected by environmental forces?

chairs, and baking supplies, but spent less on gasoline and cosmetics. All consumers spent more on cleaning supplies and pantry staples, but stopped going to movie theaters and gyms. Marketers had to shift gears to ensure they were offering the products consumers were willing to buy, pricing and promoting them appropriately, and distributing far more of them via online outlets, while navigating supply chain challenges and a shifting regulatory environment. In addition, changes in environmental forces may lead to dramatic shifts in customers' needs or wants. Consider the effect technological forces have had on printed newspapers. Years ago, very few people would have predicted that consumers would one day read the news on their phone, yet most people now do exactly that.

制订营销计划

10-7 Developing a Marketing Plan

Learning Objective

10-7 Examine the major components of a marketing plan.

营销计划

marketing plan a written document that specifies an organization's resources, objectives, strategy, and implementation and control efforts to be used in marketing a specific product or product group

A **marketing plan** is a written document that specifies an organization's resources, objectives, marketing strategy, and implementation and control efforts to be used in marketing a specific product or product group. The marketing plan describes the firm's current position or situation, establishes marketing objectives for the product, and specifies how the organization will attempt to achieve these objectives. Marketing plans vary with respect to the time period involved. Short-range plans are for one year or less, medium-range plans cover from over one year to five years, and long-range plans cover periods of more than five years.

Although time-consuming, developing a clear, well-written marketing plan is important. The plan helps establish a unified vision for an organization and is used for communication among the firm's employees. It covers responsibilities, tasks, and schedules for implementation, specifies how resources are to be allocated to achieve marketing objectives, and helps marketing managers monitor and evaluate

Table 10-4 Components of the Marketing Plan

Plan Component	Component Summary	Highlights
Executive summary	One- to two-page synopsis of the entire marketing plan	1. Stress key points 2. Include one to three key points that make the company unique
Environmental analysis	Information about the company's current situation with respect to the marketing environment	1. Assessment of marketing environment factors 2. Assessment of target market(s) 3. Assessment of current marketing objectives and performance
SWOT analysis	Assessment of the organization's strengths, weaknesses, opportunities, and threats	1. Strengths of the company 2. Weaknesses of the company 3. Opportunities in the environment and industry 4. Threats in the environment and industry
Marketing objectives	Specification of the firm's marketing objectives	1. Qualitative measures of what is to be accomplished 2. Quantitative measures of what is to be accomplished
Marketing strategies	Outline of how the firm will achieve its objectives	1. Target market(s) 2. Marketing mix
Marketing implementation	Outline of how the firm will implement its marketing strategies	1. Marketing organization 2. Activities and responsibilities 3. Implementation timetable
Performance evaluation	Explanation of how the firm will measure and evaluate the results of the implemented plan	1. Performance standards 2. Financial controls 3. Monitoring procedures (audits)

the performance of the marketing strategy. Because the forces of the marketing environment are subject to change, marketing plans have to be updated frequently. Consider Coca-Cola's Powerade sports drink brand, which has experienced lagging sales in recent years as exercise patterns shifted and consumers turned to other options like coconut water and enhanced waters after exercise. The company responded by adjusting its marketing mix to introduce new products, such as Power Water, a line of electrolyte-enhanced flavored water targeted at casual exercisers, and Powerade Ultra, targeted at more serious athletes with 50 percent more electrolytes and creatine, to compete.[15] Such changes in strategy will likely be reflected in the firm's marketing plan.

The major components of a marketing plan are shown in Table 10-4.

✓ Concept Check

- What are the major components of a marketing plan?
- Why is developing a well-written marketing plan important?

市场评估和销售预测

10-8 Market Measurement and Sales Forecasting

Learning Objective

10-8 Describe how market measurement and sales forecasting are used.

Measuring the sales potential of specific market segments can help an organization make important decisions. An accurate measure of a market segment can help a firm to determine the feasibility of entering new segments and how best to allocate marketing resources and activities among market segments in which it is already active. All such estimates should identify the relevant time frame. As with marketing plans, these plans may be short-range for periods of less than one year, medium-range for one to five years, or long-range for more than five years. The estimates should also define the geographic boundaries of the forecast, such as a city, county, state, or group of nations. Finally, analysts should indicate whether their estimates are for a specific product item, a product line, or an entire product category.

A **sales forecast** is an estimate of the amount of a product that an organization expects to sell during a certain period of time based on a specified level of marketing effort. Managers may rely on sales forecasts when they purchase raw materials, schedule production, secure financial resources, consider plant or equipment purchases, hire personnel, and plan inventory levels. Because the accuracy of a sales forecast is so important, organizations often use several forecasting methods, including executive judgments, surveys of buyers or sales personnel, time-series analyses, correlation analyses, and market tests. The specific methods used depend on the costs involved, type of product, characteristics of the market, time span of the forecast, purposes for which the forecast is used, stability of historical sales data, availability of the required information, and expertise and experience of forecasters. To assist with complicated predictions, many companies utilize sales forecasting software.

✓ Concept Check

- Why is sales forecasting important?
- What methods do businesses use to forecast sales?

营销信息

10-9 Marketing Information

Learning Objective

10-9 Explain how marketers collect and analyze information useful for marketing decision making.

Developing effective marketing strategies requires understanding target markets. Marketers therefore require accurate and timely information about customers' needs and desires, new marketing opportunities, and changing customer attitudes and purchase patterns, as well as changes in the forces of the marketing environment. The availability and analysis of marketing information improve a firm's ability to make informed decisions and respond to a changing environment, which can lead to better performance. Thanks to the proliferation of information-gathering technology, marketers can obtain a wealth of data to support decision making.

收集和分析营销信息

10-9a Collecting and Analyzing Marketing Information

Marketers have greater access to reliable data and tools for analyzing them than ever before. They often use the term *big data* to refer to the massive amounts of data that come from a variety of sources. Data from *internal* sources include sales figures,

销售预测
sales forecast an estimate of the amount of a product that an organization expects to sell during a certain period of time based on a specified level of marketing effort

Exploring Careers

职业探索：趋势提醒——市场研究分析师需求量很大

Trend Alert: Market Research Analysts Are in High Demand

Data analysis and analytical reasoning are two of the most in-demand skills in the job market. Big data analytics—mining insights from large amounts of data to identify trends—has given rise to the market research analyst role in the United States. According to the U.S. Bureau of Labor Statistics, this role is projected to grow 18 percent within the next 10 years, significantly faster than the 4 percent average growth for all occupations.

Big data can come in the form of social media comments, online product reviews, transaction data, and much more. Marketers have a vast amount of data at their fingertips, but it's not always easy to know what to do with it or how to use it effectively. Analysts will be needed to identify customer needs and wants, establish key performance indicators (KPIs), monitor the impact of marketing strategies, and more. Problem-solving, identifying new opportunities, and monitoring and forecasting trends using statistical software and internal systems are just a few of the duties at the core of the market research analyst job.

Analytical skills, communication skills, critical thinking skills, and a detail-oriented mindset are important soft skills for data analysts. Analysts must be able to digest large amounts of data as well as have strong interpersonal skills to communicate their findings. A variety of employers such as marketing agencies, financial institutions, universities, and government agencies will seek out professionals matching this skill set as the market research analyst role becomes increasingly important.

Sources: Based on information in Mara Leighton, "5 Skills LinkedIn Say Will Help You Get Hired in 2020 - and Where to Learn Them," *World Economic Forum*, September 3, 2020; U.S. Bureau of Labor Statistics, "Market Research Analysts".

product and marketing costs, inventory levels, and activities of the sales force. The savviest marketers also collect data from following every move consumers make on their websites and their social media interactions. Data from *external* sources relate to the organization's suppliers, intermediaries, and customers. It can also come from competitors' marketing activities and economic conditions.

Typically, these data are stored in one or more databases that allow marketers to access both internal and external sources. Many marketers also subscribe to commercial databases, such as LEXISNEXIS and Dun & Bradstreet's Data Cloud, to obtain information for marketing decisions. A great deal of information that used to be attainable only for a high price from companies specializing in producing commercial databases is now available via the internet.

Information provided by a single firm on household demographics, purchases, television-viewing and online behavior, and responses to promotions such as coupons and free samples is called *single-source data*. Consumers often use multiple devices to view shows and movies, including televisions, smartphones, and computers, making it difficult for companies to track media consumption habits and needs. To solve this problem, Nielsen has formed partnerships with Facebook, Twitter, and Instagram to compile accurate single-source data about what and how people are watching shows and when, as well as when they are talking about shows in social media. The partnerships represent a step forward in helping marketers track consumer media consumption over multiple devices.[16]

The internet, of course, is a powerful communication medium that links customers and organizations around the world and provides affordable data to help better understand customers. Companies like Lands' End and Paula's Choice that sell online accumulate data by tracking customers' purchases as well as the items they browse. By collecting and analyzing this data, the marketing information system helps the company track the buying habits of its most valued customers and informs decision making in response to these changes.

Businesses increasingly are using **marketing analytics**, the collection, organization, and interpretation of data about marketing performance, to mine useful insights from the huge amounts of data they collect. Marketing analytics begins with collecting and organizing the massive amounts of data obtained from customer contacts, retailer scanning, inventory management, and production. For instance, frequent-user programs like Marriott's Bonvoy not only collect data about customers' usage patterns by time of day, week, month, and year, but they can also ask loyal customers to participate in surveys about their needs and desires. Supermarkets and other retailers may offer store discount cards, which allow them to gain data on purchases through checkout scanners. These can be combined with other information a firm can acquire such as industry forecasts, business trends, and search data. The size and complexity of the diverse data requires sophisticated computer programs to store, organize, and analyze it. Many firms use customer relationship management (CRM) technologies and cloud computing to network technologies and organize the marketing data available to them.

Marketing analytics can allow marketers to look at patterns of purchase and consumption to discover trends that predict future buying behaviors. Not all of these patterns would be as visible through traditional marketing research methods. Identifying these trends and patterns can result in more precise adjustments to marketing strategies or entirely new ones. Consider the Coca-Cola Company, which crunches numbers not only from sales but also from social media, vending machines, and self-serve soft drink fountains that permit customers to mix their own drinks. Analysis of these data identified that the most popular combination mixed at fountains was Sprite with cherry shots, so the company introduced Cherry Sprite as a new flavor of soft drink. The company has also installed some vending machines with artificial intelligence that can adapt to their location and personalize customer

营销分析
marketing analytics the collection, organization, and interpretation of data about marketing performance

Technology and Innovation

技术与创新：抖音使用人工智能和大数据留住用户

TikTok Uses AI and Big Data to Keep Users Coming Back for More

China-based TikTok, an app for sharing short-form videos, is one of the world's fastest-growing social networking platforms. With a reported 500 million active global users, TikTok knows a thing or two about keeping its users engaged. TikTok's parent company, ByteDance, is a multinational technology company that works with artificial intelligence (AI) algorithm development and big data analysis to understand and impact user behavior.

TikTok videos, which range from 5 to 60 seconds long, cater to a short attention span. The app defaults to the "For You" tab, a curated, seemingly never-ending feed of lip-syncing, storytelling, memes, makeup tutorials, cooking instructions, dancing, and more. Videos play automatically, quickly sucking users in. Users can easily swipe up to load new videos. The algorithm learns from user engagement—from watch time and likes to shares and comments—to personalize video recommendations in real time, getting better and better as time goes on. The average user opens the app eight times a day, consuming 46 minutes of content.

These personalization algorithms are at the heart of the app's technology. TikTok found that when app users are shown previews and given a choice of what to watch, such as on the YouTube app, they often disengage from the platform, overwhelmed by determining what to watch next. By delivering a hyper-personalized feed that immediately immerses users, TikTok answers the user's question of "What should I watch?" for them and better satisfies users with a frictionless experience.

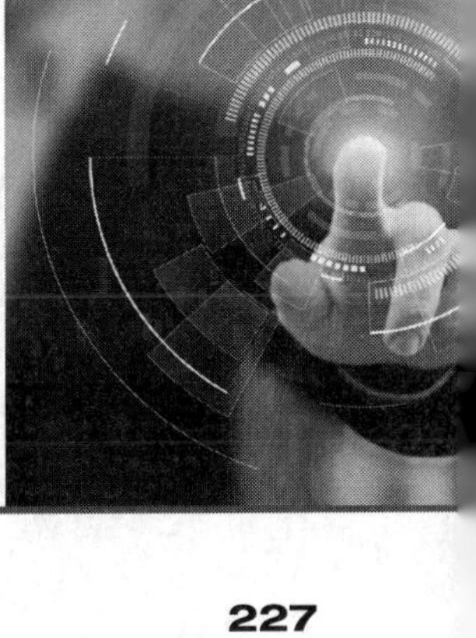

Sources: "Explaining TikTok's Machine Learning Algorithm," *Jumpstart Mag*, June 22, 2020; Katie Sehl, "20 Important TikTok Stats Marketers Need to Know in 2020," *Hootsuite*, May 7, 2020; "How Cutting-Edge AI Is Making China's TikTok the Talk of Town," *Medium*, November 15, 2018.

selections as well as report sales data back to the company.[17] Marketing analytics provides new understanding of customer behavior that has the potential to help firms create competitive advantage.

市场调研

10-9b Marketing Research

Although analyzing marketing information yields useful insights, it does not always provide specific information to solve a problem or refine a strategy, in which case research may be called for. **Marketing research** is the process of systematically gathering, recording, and analyzing data concerning a particular marketing problem. Marketing research is an important step of the marketing process because it involves collecting and analyzing data on what consumers want and need, their consumption habits, trends, and changes in the marketing environment. Information obtained from research increases marketers' ability to respond to those changes. For instance, many marketers would be interested in recent research that found that consumers are more likely to trust product recommendations from a family member, friend, or social media influencer than from brands on social media.[18] Such research can point marketers to new marketing channels for reaching particular target market segments.

Marketers collect *primary data* directly from consumers when they conduct mail, telephone, personal interview, online, focus group, or social networking surveys or conduct direct observation of consumer behavior. For example, focus groups are often used to test actual consumer reactions to advertisements, product modifications, and even movie endings. Marketers use *secondary data* from sources compiled inside or outside of the firm to help support marketing research initiatives. These sources often include commercial and government reports as well as internal databases. Marketing researchers are increasingly monitoring blogs and social networks to discover what consumers are saying about their products—both positive and negative. Many companies use social media outlets to solicit feedback from customers on their existing or upcoming products. While there is always a risk that customers will give a company or its products bad reviews online, most firms deem the risk worthwhile to conduct the low-cost research they need to be successful. If handled correctly, consumer complaints can be an important source of data on how to improve products and services. Indeed, the internet has made marketing research easier and cheaper than ever. Social media sites such as Facebook and Twitter can help small firms gauge potential market demand and try out product ideas for little or no cost. The internet also offers numerous databases and other sources of valuable information on competitors, target markets, and the marketing environment.

市场调研
marketing research the process of systematically gathering, recording, and analyzing data concerning a particular marketing problem

Focus groups. Many business organizations use focus groups as one method of doing marketing research. A variety of different types of information can be collected through focus groups.

Table 10-5 lists a variety of useful resources for secondary information, which is existing information that has been gathered by other organizations. As can be seen in Table 10-5, secondary information can come from a variety of sources, including governments, trade associations, general publications and news outlets, and corporate information.

Table 10-6 outlines a six-step procedure for conducting marketing research. It is particularly well suited to test new products, determine various characteristics of consumer markets, and evaluate promotional activities. Even when marketers outsource marketing research to external firms such as IQVIA, Nielsen, and IRI, these firms generally apply this process.

Table 10-5 Sources of Secondary Information

Government Sources	
U.S. Census	https://www.census.gov/
International Trade Administration—country market research	https://www.trade.gov/research-country
National Technical Information Services	https://www.ntis.gov/
Canadian trade	https://strategis.ic.gc.ca/
Trade Associations and Shows	
Center for Association Leadership	https://www.asaecenter.org/
Directory of Associations	https://directoryofassociations.com/
Trade Show News Network	https://www.tsnn.com/
U.S. Chamber of Commerce	https://www.uschamber.com/
Magazines, Newspapers, Video, and Audio News Programming	
Google Video Search	https://www.google.com/videohp?hl=en
Google News Directory	https://news.google.com/
Yahoo! Video Search	https://video.search.yahoo.com/
Corporate Information	
The Public Register Online—corporate annual reports	http://www.publicregister.com/
Bitpipe	https://www.bitpipe.com/
Business Wire—press releases	https://www.businesswire.com/
PR Newswire—press releases	https://www.prnewswire.com/

Source: Adapted and updated from "Data Collection: Low-Cost Secondary Research," KnowThis.com.

✓ Concept Check

- How can marketing analytics improve marketing decisions?
- What are the major reasons for conducting marketing research?
- Identify and describe the six steps of the marketing research process.

Table 10-6 The Six Steps of Marketing Research

1. Define the problem.	The problem is stated clearly and accurately, as it will determine the research issues and approaches, the right questions to ask, and the types of solutions that are acceptable. This is a crucial step that should not be rushed.
2. Make a preliminary investigation.	The preliminary investigation aims to develop a sharper definition of the problem and a set of tentative answers, which are developed by examining internal information and published data and by talking with persons who have experience with the problem. These answers will be tested by further research.
3. Plan the research.	At this stage, researchers know what facts are needed to resolve the identified problem and what facts are available. They make plans on how to gather needed but missing data.
4. Gather factual information.	Once a plan is in place, researchers can collect primary data from surveys and/or observation, and get secondary data from commercial or government data sources. The choice depends on the plan and the available sources of information.
5. Interpret the information.	Facts by themselves do not always provide a sound solution to a marketing problem. They must be interpreted and analyzed to determine the choices available to management.
6. Reach a conclusion.	Once the data have been evaluated, researchers seek to draw conclusions and make recommendations. These may be obvious or not, depending on intangible factors and whether data used were complete. When there are gaps in the data, it is important for researchers to state this.

Ethics and Social Responsibility

商业伦理与社会责任：营销人员必须遵守数据伦理

Marketers Must Embrace Data Ethics

Privacy and data collection have become increasingly important issues, yet less than half of major brands have data ethics policies in place. Research from the World Federation of Advertisers (WFA) revealed that data ethics is a priority for marketers, but major gaps still exist between what companies should be doing to protect data versus what they are currently doing. The WFA hopes its findings will encourage businesses to be more proactive in their data practices and establish their own ethics policies.

Many companies have been criticized for the way they collect, store, and use customer data. The possibility of racial bias in artificial intelligence (AI), for example, raises ethical concerns. Humans are susceptible to bias, which can lead to the unintentional creation of discriminatory algorithms. IBM shut down its facial recognition programs due to concerns the AI-enabled algorithms would be used for mass surveillance, racial profiling, and human rights violations.

Individuals entrust businesses with vast amounts of personal information, from credit card data and mailing addresses to Social Security numbers and shopping preferences. Organizations should take the utmost care to protect consumer data with proper data handling and security measures to fend off breaches. Breaches can quickly erode consumer trust. Ancestry.com, a family history search company, faced a leak that exposed sensitive data belonging to 60,000 customers. Unlike other countries, the United States lacks general consumer data privacy laws, leaving businesses to self-regulate. According to the WFA, respect, fairness, accountability, and transparency should be at the center of data ethics policies.

Sources: Based on information in Rebecca Stewart, "CMOs Accept Data Ethics Falls on Their Shoulders, but Brands' Policies Are Lacking," *The Drum*, June 1, 2020; Eugene Bekker, "2020 Data Breaches | The Most Significant Breaches of the Year," Identity Force, January 3, 2020; "IBM Abandons 'Biased' Facial Recognition," BBC, June 9, 2020.

购买行为的类型

10-10 Types of Buying Behavior

Learning Objective

10-10 Identify the major steps in the consumer buying decision process and the sets of factors that may influence this process.

Buying behavior may be defined as the decisions and actions of people involved in buying and using products. **Consumer buying behavior** refers to the purchasing of products for personal or household use, not for business purposes. **Business buying behavior** is the purchasing of products by producers, resellers, governmental units, and institutions. Because a firm's success depends in large part on buyers' reactions to a marketing strategy, it is important to understand buying behavior. Marketing managers are better able to predict customer responses to marketing strategies and to develop a satisfying marketing mix if they are aware of the factors that affect buying behavior.

购买行为
buying behavior the decisions and actions of people involved in buying and using products

消费者购买行为
consumer buying behavior the purchasing of products for personal or household use, not for business purposes

企业购买行为
business buying behavior the purchasing of products by producers, resellers, governmental units, and institutions

消费者购买行为

10-10a Consumer Buying Behavior

Consumers' buying behaviors differ for different types of products. For frequently purchased low-cost items, a consumer uses *routine decision making* which involves very little search or decision-making effort. The buyer uses *limited decision making* for purchases made occasionally, or when they need more information about an unknown product in a well-known product category. When buying an unfamiliar or expensive item, or one that is seldom purchased, the consumer engages in *extended decision making*. Consumers have become empowered by information available on the internet that allows them to compare prices and features and read reviews about goods and services without stepping into a store. Increasingly, buyers feel sufficiently informed by their online research to proceed with buying decisions without the help of a salesperson. In this environment, marketing and customer service are increasingly important.

A person deciding on a purchase goes through some or all of the steps shown in Figure 11-4. First, the consumer recognizes that a problem exists that might be solved by a good or service. The "problem" might be something the person desires but does not possess, like the latest iPhone or Xbox. Second, the buyer looks for information, which may include brand names, product characteristics, warranties, and other features, as well as product reviews. Next, the buyer weighs the various alternatives, makes a choice, and acquires the item. In the after-purchase stage, the consumer evaluates the suitability of the product, which will affect future purchases. Consider the Geico advertisement, which highlights the fact that its product can solve the problem of paying too much for insurance. The ad further informs potential consumers of the benefits of Geico's customer service in addition to saving them money on insurance products. As Figure 10-4 depicts, the buying process is influenced by situational factors (physical surroundings, social surroundings, time, purchase reason, and buyer's mood and condition), psychological factors (perception, motivation, learning, attitudes, personality, and lifestyle), and social factors (family, roles, reference groups, digital influences, social class, culture, and subculture).

Consumer buying behavior is also affected by the ability to buy, called one's *buying power*, which is largely determined by income. As every taxpayer

Problem recognition. This Geico advertisement attempts to stimulate problem recognition. What's the problem? How can I save money on my insurance?

Figure 10-4 **Consumer Buying Decision Process and Possible Influences on the Process**

A buyer goes through some or all of these steps when making a purchase.

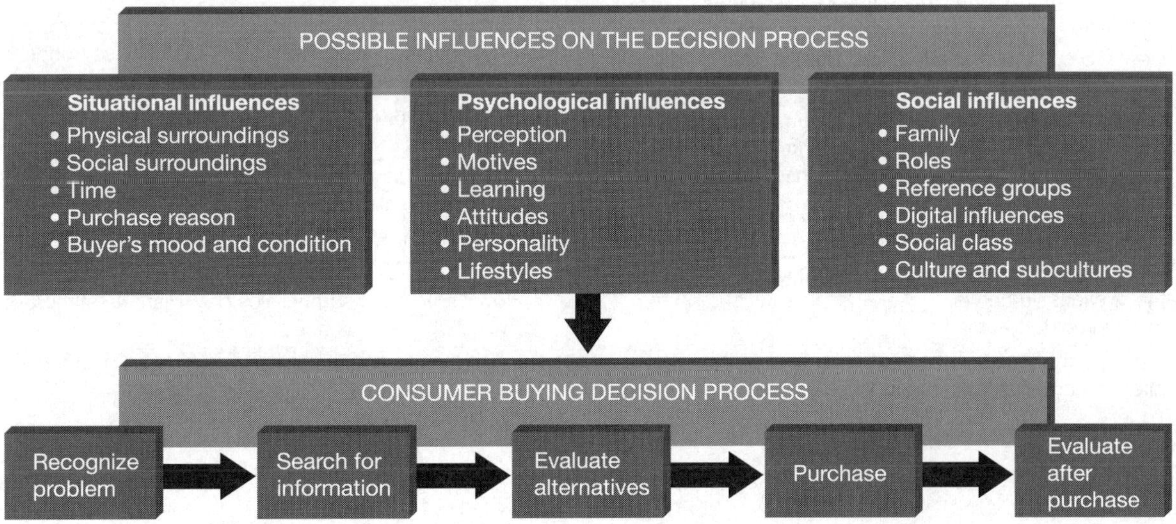

knows, not all income is available for spending. For this reason, marketers consider income in three different ways. **Personal income** is the income an individual receives from all sources. **Disposable income** is personal income *less* all personal taxes. These taxes include income, estate, gift, and property taxes levied by local, state, and federal governments. **Discretionary income** is disposable income *less* savings and expenditures on food, clothing, and housing. Discretionary income is of particular interest to marketers because consumers have the most choice in spending it. Consumers use their discretionary income to purchase a wide variety of items ranging from automobiles and vacations to movies and pet food. In China, for example, a growing middle class with rising discretionary income is more interested than ever in Western brands. To capitalize on this demand, Walmart plans to open 14 more Sam's Club membership stores in China, bringing its total stores there to more than 40, all stocking popular Western brands alongside store branded Chinese products. It also plans to invest hundreds of millions of dollars in renovating existing stores and improving its supply chain there.[19]

✓ Concept Check

- Why is it important to understand buying behavior?
- How does a customer's decision-making time vary with the type of product?
- What are the five stages of the consumer buying decision process?
- What are the possible influences on this process?
- What is the difference between disposable income and discretionary income?

个人收入
personal income the income an individual receives from all sources

可支配收入
disposable income personal income *less* all personal taxes

可自由支配收入
discretionary income disposable income *less* savings and expenditures on food, clothing, and housing

企业购买行为

10-10b Business Buying Behavior

The business buying decision process is similar to the consumer process, but business buyers are generally better informed than consumers and consider a product's quality, its price, and the service provided by suppliers. Business purchases can be large, and a committee or a group of people, rather than just one person, often decides on purchases. Committee members must consider the organization's objectives, purchasing policies, resources, and personnel. The process of business buying is different than consumer buying. It occurs through description, inspection, sampling, or negotiation. Because business transactions can be more complicated and orders tend to be larger, obtaining complete and correct information on buyers and sellers is important.

Discussion Questions 讨论题

1. Define marketing in your own words.
2. Why are companies so interested in relationship marketing?
3. How is a customer-oriented firm different from a production-oriented firm or a sales-oriented firm?
4. What are the major requirements for a group of individuals and organizations to be a market? How does a consumer market differ from a business-to-business market?
5. What are the major components of a marketing strategy?
6. What is the purpose of market segmentation? What is the relationship between market segmentation and the selection of target markets?
7. Describe the forces in the marketing environment that affect an organization's marketing decisions.
8. What is a marketing plan, and what are its major components?
9. What new information technologies are changing the ways that marketers keep track of business trends and customers?
10. Why do marketers need to understand buying behavior?
11. Is it a good strategy to focus most marketing efforts on the most profitable customers?
12. How might adoption of the marketing concept benefit a firm? How might it benefit the firm's customers?
13. How can marketing analytics help marketers improve marketing performance?
14. How does the marketing environment affect a firm's marketing strategy?

Case 10 案例 10：星巴克“酿造”客户满意度

Starbucks Brews Customer Satisfaction

With more than 32,000 stores across more than 80 markets, Starbucks is the world's largest coffeehouse chain. In 50 years of business, the company grew from a single coffee shop in Seattle to a booming $80 billion business that holds a 57 percent share of the U.S. café market. Zev Siegl, Jerry Baldwin, and Gordon Bowker opened the first Starbucks location in Seattle's historic Pike Place Market in 1971 under the guidance of Alfred Peet, the founder of Peet's Coffee. Starbucks faced many challenges on its way to the top, including overexpansion and shifting consumer preferences.

Interestingly, the first Starbucks locations didn't serve coffee, selling whole and ground beans exclusively. At the time, Starbucks enticed consumers who were more accustomed to instant or canned coffee by offering high-quality beans. It wasn't until Howard Schultz joined Starbucks in the 1980s as director of retail operations and marketing that Starbucks evolved. After visiting Italy, Schultz had a vision of recreating the Italian coffeehouse concept in the United States. In 1984, the company opened its first downtown Seattle café and served the first Starbucks Caffè Latte.

The concept proved to be a success. Schultz worked with investors in 1987 to buy Starbucks for $3.8 million and pursued an aggressive expansion strategy. When the company went public in 1992, it had 265 stores. By the time Schultz left Starbucks in 2000, it had more than 2,000 locations, a number that quadrupled by 2007. At the height of its growth, it seemed there was a Starbucks on nearly every corner in densely populated urban areas. This clustering strategy proved to be a misstep that resulted in fewer transactions at individual locations. After the Great Recession began in 2007, Starbucks realized its mistake. Though people loved their daily Starbucks fix, the financial crisis caused consumers to tighten their purse strings.

With Starbucks' stock price plummeting, Schultz returned to the helm. He slowed expansion in the United States, closing redundant locations and focusing more on international growth and enhancing the customer experience. For one day, Schultz closed all U.S. stores to retrain baristas in the art of espresso to improve quality. The stores reintroduced in-house coffee grinding to bring back the café ambiance. Schultz's strategy worked, and same-store sales rebounded. It wasn't until 2012 that the company set its sights on domestic expansion once again.

Now, Starbucks is focusing on adjusting its product mix to accommodate changing consumer preferences. The Frappuccino, for example, was one of the company's most popular beverages, but a sharp drop in sales reflected the fact that consumers have become more health-conscious, moving away from sugary drinks. Starbucks has since focused on drinks such as its Refreshers and cold brew to adapt to changing consumer preferences.

Starbucks is also investing in delivery as an avenue for growth, entering into partnerships in the United States with Brightloom and Uber Eats. Online orders, especially delivery orders, tend to result in higher checks, which could be good news for Starbucks. Another major undertaking is the opening of upscale Starbucks Reserve Roastery stores. These 20,000-square foot stores, located in Shanghai, Tokyo, Manhattan, Chicago, Seattle, New York, and Milan, are designed to be tourist destinations. The roasteries serve a wide array of coffee and experiment with coffee beverages. The high-end experiential stores contribute to the so-called halo effect, which elevates Starbucks in the minds of consumers.

Under the leadership of Starbucks' current CEO Kevin Johnson, the company opened a 20,000-square foot facility called the Tryer Center at its headquarters in Seattle where employees test new concepts using rapid prototyping. Employees quickly test new concepts and deploy ideas in just a matter of months. For example, a single-cup brewing prototype was created with the lab's 3D printer and deployed a month later. Starbucks employees from every level of the business submit ideas. The innovation lab makes Starbucks more agile in developing, testing, and releasing new products and systems.

Starbucks has tackled challenges head-on on its path to the top, demonstrating its ability to identify and adapt to changes in the market. With a heightened focus on innovation, Starbucks can refine the customer experience, improve its systems and processes, and introduce new, relevant products.[20]

Questions

1. Discuss the result of Starbucks' aggressive expansion strategy.
2. In what ways has Starbucks created products that satisfy consumer wants and needs?
3. How does Starbucks support innovation?

Chapter

11

Creating and Pricing Products That Satisfy Customers

创造和定价让客户满意的产品

Learning Objectives

Once you complete this chapter, you will be able to:

11-1 Explain what a product is and how products are classified.

11-2 Describe the product life cycle and how it leads to new-product development.

11-3 Define product line and product mix and distinguish between the two.

11-4 Identify the methods available for managing a product mix.

11-5 Examine the uses and importance of branding, packaging, and labeling.

11-6 Describe the economic basis of pricing and the means by which sellers can control prices and buyers' perceptions of prices.

11-7 Specify the major pricing objectives used by businesses.

11-8 Compare the three major pricing methods that businesses employ.

11-9 Explain the different strategies available to companies for setting prices.

11-10 Recognize three major types of pricing associated with business products.

Why Should You Care?

To be successful, a businessperson must understand how to develop and manage a mix of appropriately priced products and to change the mix of products as customers' needs change.

Inside Business 商业透视：Petco的品牌重塑专注于宠物健康

Petco Rebrand Focuses on Pet Health and Wellness

In a push to center itself as a leading pet health and wellness company, Petco rebranded itself from Petco Animal Supplies to Petco, The Health + Wellness Co. This is part of a greater strategy to stand out from the competition and fend off online retailer Chewy's impressive growth. Petco competes with Chewy as well as other traditional retailers such as PetSmart, Pet Supermarket, Walmart, and a growing number of independent healthy pet stores.

A significant element of the rebranding is the expansion of its in-store veterinary hospitals. The company's 100 veterinary hospitals are integrated with PetCoach, its digital pet medical advice service. To increase revenue from this side of its business, Petco introduced Vital Care, a vet service membership program with perks such as unlimited nail trims and teeth-brushing for dogs. To further support its image as a pet health and wellness company, Petco announced it would stop selling shock collars, a controversial product category that is worth $10 million a year. This follows a $100 million decision to eliminate food with artificial ingredients.

Petco's pivot into health and wellness demonstrates that pet food and basic pet supplies have become commoditized, which means the products are just one more in a sea of similar products. This happens when customers begin to perceive competing products as offering roughly the same benefits. This makes price increasingly important, which is bad news for pet supply retailers. In this reality, Petco's growth must come from other product categories, such as its veterinary services and fresh and frozen pet food offerings.

By shifting into pet health and wellness, Petco is following the money. U.S. consumers spend approximately $30 billion per year on vet care and products alone, according to the American Pet Products Association. Because online retailers like Chewy and Amazon don't have brick-and-mortar locations to offer vet services, Petco believes this is the perfect area for growth.[1]

Did You Know?

Petco operates more than 1,500 stores in the United States, Mexico, and Puerto Rico.

Brands, like Petco, are an important way that consumers recognize products. A **product**, like Twisted Mango Diet Coke, has everything one receives in an exchange, including all tangible and intangible attributes and expected benefits. A car includes tangible benefits, such as comfortable seats, a warranty, and Apple CarPlay or Android Auto interface, as well as intangible attributes, such as status and the memories generated from road trips. Developing and managing products effectively, including these tangible and intangible benefits, are crucial to an organization's ability to maintain successful marketing mixes.

A product can be a good, a service, or an idea. A *good* is a real, physical thing that we can touch, such as an Oreo cookie. A *service* is the result of applying human or mechanical effort to a person or thing. A service is a change we pay others to make for us. A real estate agent's services result in a change in the ownership of real property. A hair stylist's services result in a change in your hairstyle. An *idea* may take the form of philosophies, lessons, concepts, or advice. Often ideas are bundled with a good or service. Thus, we might buy a book (a good) that provides ideas on how to lose weight. Alternatively, we might join Weight Watchers for ideas on how to lose weight and for help (service) in doing so.

产品
product everything one receives in an exchange, including all tangible and intangible attributes and expected benefits; it may be a good, a service, or an idea

In this chapter, we first look at the different aspects of products. We examine product classifications and describe the four stages of the product life cycle through which every product progresses. Next, we examine how companies manage products by modifying or deleting existing ones and developing new products. We also discuss branding, packaging, and labeling. Then our focus shifts to pricing. We explain competitive factors that influence sellers' pricing decisions and explore buyers' perceptions of prices. After considering organizational objectives that can be accomplished through pricing, we outline several methods for setting prices. Finally, we describe pricing strategies by which sellers can reach target markets successfully.

产品分类

11-1 Classification of Products

Different classes of products are directed at different target markets according to their varying needs and wants. A product's classification largely determines what kinds of distribution, promotion, and pricing are appropriate in marketing it.

Learning Objective

11-1 Explain what a product is and how products are classified.

Products can be grouped into two general categories: consumer and business (also called *business-to-business* or *industrial products*). A product purchased to satisfy personal and family needs is a **consumer product**. A product bought by a business for resale, for making other products, or for use in a firm's operations is a **business product**. The same item can be both a consumer and a business product, depending on the buyer's end use. LED light bulbs are a consumer product when you use them in your home, but are a business product if you purchase them for use in an office.

消费品的分类

11-1a Consumer Product Classifications

The traditional and most widely accepted system of classifying consumer products consists of four categories: convenience, shopping, specialty, and unsought products. These groupings are based primarily on characteristics of buyers' purchasing behavior.

A **convenience product** is a relatively inexpensive, frequently purchased item for which buyers want to exert only minimal effort to procure. Examples include bread, gasoline, newspapers, soft drinks, and chewing gum. The buyer spends little time in planning the purchase of a convenience item or in comparing available brands or sellers.

A **shopping product** is an item for which buyers are willing to expend considerably more effort on planning and purchasing. Shopping products cost more than convenience products and buyers allocate ample time for comparing prices, product features, qualities, services, and warranties between different stores and brands. Appliances, upholstered furniture, men's suits, bicycles, and mobile phones are examples of shopping products. These products are expected to last for a fairly long time and thus are purchased less frequently than convenience items.

A **specialty product** possesses one or more unique characteristics for which a group of buyers is willing to expend considerable purchasing effort. Buyers know exactly what they want and will not accept a substitute. When seeking out specialty products, purchasers do not compare alternatives. Examples include unique sports cars, a rare imported beer, or original artwork.

Unsought products are those that people do not plan on purchasing, such as products that address a sudden problem or that customers are unaware of until they see them in a store or online. Emergency medical services and automobile repairs are examples of products needed quickly and suddenly to solve a problem. A consumer who is sick or injured has little time to plan to go to an emergency medical center or hospital and will find the closest location to receive service. In such cases, speed of problem resolution is more important than price or other features a buyer might normally consider if there were more time for making a decision.

消费品

consumer product a product purchased to satisfy personal and family needs

工业品

business product a product bought for resale, for making other products, or for use in a firm's operations

便利产品

convenience product a relatively inexpensive, frequently purchased item for which buyers want to exert only minimal effort

选购产品

shopping product an item for which buyers are willing to expend considerable effort on planning and making the purchase

特色产品

specialty product an item that possesses one or more unique characteristics for which a significant group of buyers is willing to expend considerable purchasing effort

非求购产品

unsought product an item that people do not plan on purchasing, such as one that addresses a sudden problem or that customers are unaware of until they see it in a store or online

Consumer products can be classified into convenience, shopping, and specialty. Cheetos, a convenience product, is an item you are likely to grab off the shelf without much thought as you walk through the snack aisle of a supermarket. By contrast, people may spend a considerable amount of time and effort engaged in comparison shopping behavior when buying a shopping product, like a pair of Nike shoes.

工业品的分类

11-1b Business Product Classifications

Based on their characteristics and intended uses, business products can be classified into the following categories: raw materials, major equipment, accessory equipment, component parts, process materials, supplies, and services.

A **raw material** is a basic material that becomes part of a physical product. It usually comes from mines, forests, oceans, or recycled solid wastes. Raw materials are generally bought and sold according to grades and specifications.

Major equipment includes large tools and machines used for production purposes. Examples of major equipment are lathes, cranes, and stamping machines. Some major equipment is custom-made for a particular organization, but other items are standardized products that perform one or several tasks for many types of organizations.

Accessory equipment is standardized equipment used in a firm's production or office activities. Examples include hand tools, photocopiers, fractional horsepower motors, and calculators. Compared with major equipment, accessory items are usually less expensive and are purchased routinely with less negotiation.

A **component part** becomes part of a physical product and is either a finished item ready for assembly or a product that needs little processing prior to assembly. Although it becomes an element of a larger product, a component part can often be identified easily. Clocks, tires, computer chips, and switches are examples of component parts.

A **process material** is used directly in the production of another product. Unlike a component part, a process material is not readily identifiable in the finished product. Like raw materials, process materials are purchased according to industry standards or to the specifications of the individual purchaser. Examples include industrial glue and food preservatives.

A **supply** facilitates production and operations but does not become part of a finished product. Paper, pencils, oils, and cleaning agents are examples.

A **business service** is an intangible product that an organization uses in its operations. Examples include financial, legal, online, janitorial, and marketing research services. Purchasers must decide whether to provide their own services internally or to hire a contractor from outside the organization.

原材料
raw material a basic material that becomes part of a physical product; usually comes from mines, forests, oceans, or recycled solid wastes

主要设备
major equipment large tools and machines used for production purposes

附属设备
accessory equipment standardized equipment used in a firm's production or office activities

零部件
component part an item that becomes part of a physical product and is either a finished item ready for assembly or a product that needs little processing before assembly

工艺材料
process material a material that is used directly in the production of another product but is not readily identifiable in the finished product

供应品
supply an item that facilitates production and operations but does not become part of a finished product

✓ Concept Check

- Identify the general categories of products.
- Describe the classifications of consumer products.
- Based on their characteristics, business products can be classified into what categories?

产品生命周期

11-2 The Product Life Cycle

In a way, products are like people. They are born, they live, and they die. Every product progresses through a **product life cycle**, a series of stages in which a product's sales revenue and profit increase, reach a peak, and then decline. A firm must be able to launch, modify, and delete products from its offering in response to changes in product life cycles. Otherwise, the company's profits will disappear, and the firm will fail. Depending on the product, life-cycle stages vary in length. In this section, we discuss the stages of the life cycle and how marketers can use this information.

Learning Objective

11-2 Describe the product life cycle and how it leads to new-product development.

产品生命周期的各阶段

11-2a Stages of the Product Life Cycle

Generally, the product life cycle is composed of four stages—introduction, growth, maturity, and decline—as shown in Figure 11-1. Some products progress through these stages rapidly, in a few weeks or months, while others can take years. The Koosh Ball, popular in the late 1980s, had a short life cycle. In contrast, Parker Brothers' Monopoly game, which was introduced nearly a century ago, is still going strong.

Introduction In the *introduction stage*, customer awareness and acceptance of the new product are low. Sales rise gradually as a result of promotion and distribution activities. There are no competitors at this stage. High development and marketing costs result in low profit, or even in a loss, initially. The price can be high as the company recoups research and development expenses and ramps up production. Customers are primarily people who want to be at the forefront of owning the new product. Examples of products in the introductory stage include self-driving cars and smart glasses such as Amazon's Echo frames. The marketing challenge at this stage is to make potential customers aware of the product's existence and its features, benefits, and uses. Marketers may make the product available to social media influencers so that they will share information about the product with their followers.

Figure 11-1 Product Life Cycle

The graph shows sales volume and profits during the life cycle of a product.

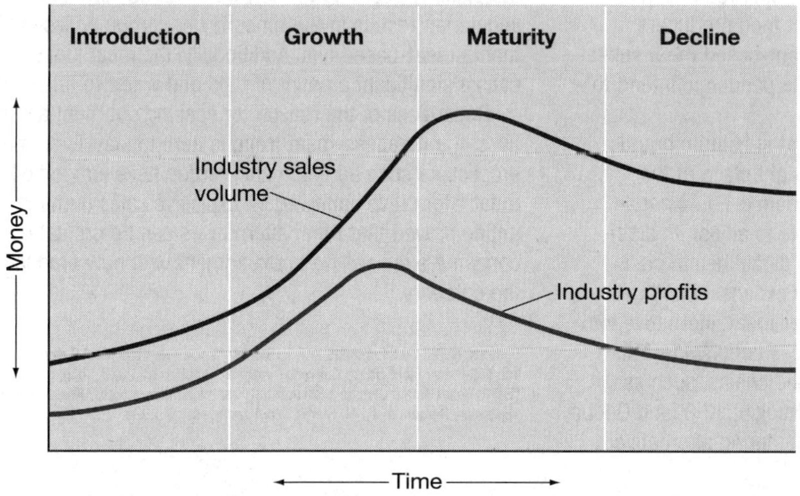

商业服务
business service an intangible product that an organization uses in its operations

产品生命周期
product life cycle a series of stages in which a product's sales revenue and profit increase, reach a peak, and then decline

A new product is seldom an immediate success. Marketers must monitor early buying patterns and be prepared to modify the product promptly if necessary. The company should attempt to price the product to attract the market segment that has the greatest desire and ability to purchase it. Plans for distribution and promotion should suit the targeted market segment. All ingredients of the marketing mix may need to be adjusted quickly to maintain sales growth during the introduction stage.

Growth In the *growth stage*, sales increase rapidly as consumers gain awareness of the product. Other companies have begun to market competing products. The competition and decreased unit costs (owing to mass production) result in a lower price, which reduces the profit per unit. Industry profits reach a peak and begin to decline during this stage. To meet the needs of the growing market, the originating firm offers modified versions of the product and expands distribution. Virtual reality headsets, esports, and products with CBD are currently in the growth stage.

Marketers' goal in the growth stage is to stabilize and strengthen the product's position by encouraging brand loyalty. To beat the competition, the company may further improve the product or expand the product line to appeal to additional market segments. For example, to compete with the Amazon Echo smart speaker with Alexa the voice assistant, Google and Apple introduced their own smart speakers with voice assistants aimed at capturing different market segments and gaining market share in the growing industry.

A firm also may compete by lowering prices if increased production efficiency has resulted in sufficient savings. As the product becomes more widely accepted,

Sustaining the Planet 保护地球：消费者选择肉食替代品而成为弹性素食者

Consumers Go Flexitarian with Fake Meat

The alternative protein category has experienced skyrocketing growth in recent years with the widespread availability of brands such as Beyond Meat and Impossible Foods. Supply chain disruptions during the COVID-19 pandemic led many consumers to try so-called fake meat products for the first time in the face of meat shortages. According to research from Archer Daniels Midland, one of the world's largest food producers, 97 percent of people who tried plant-based meat substitutes for the first time during the pandemic intend to purchase them again.

Many plant-based meat substitute brands found themselves in the right place at the right time during the pandemic. For example, Impossible Foods was able to adjust its distribution strategy when the global health crisis struck, speeding up retail expansion and getting its plant-based burger meat alternative into thousands of grocery stores nationwide. This was paired with major food chains, such as Starbucks, Burger King, Dunkin', KFC, and Qdoba, introducing menu items featuring alternative meats.

Though Americans aren't becoming full-fledged vegetarians in large numbers, there is a significant trend toward a flexitarian diet, which is a veggie-centric way of eating. Consumers often cite health, safety, and convenience as top reasons for eating meat alternatives, while others believe that eating a plant-based diet is better for the planet. According to the Vegetarian Society, eating vegetarian results in 2.5 times fewer carbon emissions than a meat-based diet. Additionally, the meat industry uses a significant amount of land and water to raise cattle.

Regardless of the reason for seeking out meat alternatives, the meatless-meat trend is here to stay. Even meat processors such as Tyson and Perdue have jumped on the meat alternative bandwagon. Explosive sales during quarantine proved that meat alternatives can be profitable, and consumers are willing to experiment with new products in the category.

Sources: Based on information in T. L. Stanley, "Lockdown Fake Meat Buyers Turned Into Full-Blown Plant-Based Converts," *Adweek*, October 30, 2020; Vegetarian Society, "Eat to Beat Climate Change"; Rhian Hunt, "Can't Find Burger Meat? Kroger Stocks Impossible Burgers in 1,700 Stores," *USA Today*, May 6, 2020.

marketers may be able to broaden the network of distributors. Marketers can also emphasize customer service and prompt credit for defective products. During this period, promotional efforts attempt to build brand loyalty among customers.

Maturity Sales are still increasing at the beginning of the *maturity stage*, but the rate of increase has slowed. Later, the sales curve peaks and begins to decline, as do industry profits. Product lines are simplified, markets are segmented more carefully, and price competition increases, which forces weaker competitors to leave the industry. Marketers continue to introduce refinements and extensions of the original product to the market, like Samsung's folding Galaxy smartphone. Yes, smartphones have entered the maturity stage.

During a product's maturity stage, its market share may be strengthened by redesigned packaging or style changes. As an example, J.M. Smucker Company introduced Jif peanut butter in squeezable upright pouches to give consumers more flexibility when using the product. The new package lets consumers spread the product without a knife, measure precise amounts for recipes, or facilitate children serving themselves.[2] Redesigned packaging may convince consumers to use the product more often or in new ways, improving flagging sales.

Pricing strategies are flexible during the maturity stage. Markdowns and price incentives are not uncommon, although price increases may work to offset production and distribution costs. Marketers may offer incentives and assistance of various kinds to dealers to encourage them to support mature products, especially in the face of competition from private-label brands. New promotional efforts and aggressive personal selling may be necessary during this period of intense competition.

Decline During the *decline stage*, sales volume decreases sharply, and profits continue to fall. The number of competing firms declines, and the only survivors in the marketplace are businesses that specialize in marketing the product. Production and marketing costs become the most important determinant of profit. Mp3 players and landlines are examples of declining products.

When a product adds to the success of the overall product line, the company may retain it. Otherwise, marketers must determine when to eliminate it. A product usually declines because of technological advances, environmental factors, or consumers switching to alternative products. Therefore, few changes are made in the product itself during this stage. Instead, managers may raise the price to cover costs, reprice to maintain market share, or lower the price to reduce inventory. They will narrow distribution to the most profitable existing markets. During this period, the company probably will not spend heavily on promotion, although it may use some advertising and sales incentives to slow the product's decline. The company may choose to eliminate less-profitable versions of the product from the product line or may decide to drop the product entirely. Coca-Cola, for example, discontinued its Tab diet soft drink as part of a companywide strategic culling of underperforming products and brands. The nearly 60-year-old Tab brand languished after the introduction of Diet Coke, which went on to become one of Coca-Cola's best-selling soft drinks.[3]

Saying "goodbye" to the pay telephone. The pay telephone is in the decline stage of the product life cycle. Do you recall seeing one? If so, when and where? You might have a hard time remembering.

产品生命周期的运用

11-2b Using the Product Life Cycle

When making marketing strategy decisions, managers must be aware of the life-cycle stage of each product for which they are responsible and to estimate how long the product is expected to remain in that stage. For example, if a product is expected to remain in the maturity stage for a long time, there is no rush to develop a replacement product. A company risks speeding the decline of an existing product by releasing a replacement before the earlier product has reached the decline stage. Even so, a firm will be willing to take that risk in some cases. In other situations, a company will attempt to extend a product's life cycle. Extending its life can be an important tool in maintaining a product's profitability. A condiment staple since its introduction more than 140 years ago, Heinz Ketchup has extended its life through packaging innovations, such as squeeze bottles and single-serving containers, releasing different flavors like balsamic and sriracha, and even experimenting with purple and green-colored ketchup.

✓ Concept Check

- Explain the four stages of the product life cycle.
- How does knowledge of the product life cycle relate to the introduction of new products?

产品线和产品组合

11-3 Product Line and Product Mix

Learning Objective

11-3 Define *product line* and *product mix* and distinguish between the two.

A **product line** is a group of similar products that differ only in relatively minor characteristics. Generally, the products within a product line are related to each other in the way they are produced, marketed, or used. Procter & Gamble, for example, manufactures and markets several shampoos, including Pantene, Head & Shoulders, and Herbal Essences.

While organizations may start a new product line, many opt to introduce new products within existing product lines. It is less costly than starting a new product line and permits them to apply the experience and knowledge they have acquired to the production and marketing of new products. FritoLay, for example, regularly introduces new flavors of its popular potato chips, such as Flamin' Hot and Kettle Cooked Jalapeno.

An organization's **product mix** consists of all the products the firm offers for sale. For example, Procter & Gamble has about 60 brands—some of which are well known, like Gillette and Febreze, and others that are less familiar in the United States, such as Lenor and Ariel—that fall into several product lines.[4] Two "dimensions" are often applied to a firm's product mix. The *width* of the mix is the number of product lines it contains. The *depth* of the mix is the average number of individual products within each line. These measures are general—no exact numbers correspond to these categories. Some organizations offer a broad product mix as a means of trying to be competitive in many different categories.

✓ Concept Check

- How does a product line differ from a product mix?
- Can a product line be a product mix?

产品组合的管理

11-4 Managing the Product Mix

Learning Objective

11-4 Identify the methods available for managing a product mix.

To provide products that satisfy people in a firm's target market or markets and that also achieve the organization's objectives, a marketer must develop, adjust, and maintain an effective product mix. The same product mix is rarely effective for long. As customers' product preferences and attitudes change, their desire for a product may diminish or grow. A company may also need to alter its product mix to adapt to changes in the competition. For example, a marketer may have to introduce a new product, modify an existing one, or eliminate a product from the mix because one or more competitors have grown more dominant in the market segment. A marketer may also expand the firm's product mix to take advantage of excess marketing and production capacity. Panera, for instance, introduced three flavors of flatbread pizzas to help bring customers into its casual dining restaurants at dinnertime.[5] A company must be careful when altering the product mix that the

产品线
product line a group of similar products that differ only in relatively minor characteristics

产品组合
product mix all the products a firm offers for sale

changes made bring about improvements in the mix. There are three major ways to improve a product mix: change an existing product, delete a product, or develop a new product.

Part of a product line. These products are part of Lay's potato chip product line.

现有产品的管理

11-4a Managing Existing Products

A product mix can be changed by deriving additional products from existing ones. This can be accomplished through product modifications and by line extensions.

Product Modifications **Product modification** refers to changing one or more of a product's characteristics. For this approach to be effective, several conditions must be met. First, the product must be modifiable. Second, existing customers must be able to perceive that a modification has been made, assuming that the modified item is still directed at the same target market. Third, the modification should make the product more consistent with customers' desires so that it provides greater satisfaction. For example, after being acquired by Ferrero Group, Keebler reformulated a number of its cookies to capitalize on the growing consumer demand for "cleaner" foods. The company replaced high-fructose corn syrup and artificial vanilla with more natural ingredients. It also redesigned the packaging to improve freshness, highlight the ingredient changes, and unify designs across the Keebler brand.[6]

Existing products can be altered in three primary ways: in quality, function, and aesthetics. *Quality modifications* are changes that relate to a product's dependability and durability and are usually achieved by alterations in the materials or production process. *Functional modifications* affect a product's versatility, effectiveness, convenience, or safety. They usually require redesign of the product. Typical product categories that have undergone extensive functional modifications include home appliances, office and farm equipment, and consumer electronics. *Aesthetic modifications* change the sensory appeal of a product by altering its taste, texture, sound, smell, or visual characteristics. Because a buyer's purchasing decision is affected by sensory stimuli, an aesthetic modification may impact purchases. Through aesthetic modifications, a company can differentiate its product from competing brands and gain market share if customers find the modified product more appealing.

产品改进
product modification the process of changing one or more of a product's characteristics

产品线延伸
line extension development of a new product that is closely related to one or more products in the existing product line but designed specifically to meet somewhat different customer needs

Line Extensions A **line extension** is the development of a product closely related to one or more products in the existing product line but designed specifically to meet somewhat different customer needs. For example, Hostess Brands introduced new flavors of its perennial snack cakes, including caramel-filled Ding Dongs and mixed berry Twinkies, as well as several holiday themed versions of Twinkies, Hostess CupCakes, SnoBalls, and Donettes.[7]

Many of the so-called new products introduced each year are in fact line extensions. Line extensions are more common than new products because they are a less-expensive, lower-risk alternative for increasing sales. A line extension may focus on a different market segment or be an attempt to increase sales within the same market segment by more precisely satisfying that segment's needs, hopefully taking away market share from competitors.

Line extensions help companies to be more competitive and to maintain or increase their market shares. There are 40 flavors of Oreos in the United States, and more than 85 worldwide. Each flavor is a line extension derived from the original product.

Exploring Careers

职业探索：您准备好从事产品管理工作了吗

Are You Ready for a Career in Product Management?

Product managers are responsible for coordinating activities related to understanding customers' needs, the development of products, and product design. While product managers are not necessarily charged with product development specifically, they guide decision making across teams by communicating customer pain points and helping identify solutions. Product managers may come from a variety of backgrounds, which creates many types of product management.

Customer-focused product managers often have a background in sales or customer support and are focused on how to best serve the needs of customers. These product managers ask questions such as "Who is the customer?" "What is the customer problem or opportunity?" and "What does the customer experience look like?" On the other end of the spectrum is business-focused product management. These managers usually have a sales background and focus on how to develop, fund, and improve products and how the products will affect the business.

Technical product managers come from the areas of information technology and software engineering and focus on how a product is developed. These managers work on technical products such as Software-as-a-Service (SaaS, a software licensing and delivery model) products. Lastly, design-focused product managers focus on elements such as packaging, labeling, and functionality. Many more types of product managers exist, and more often than not, these types of product management blend together. Apple, for instance, hires product managers to drive design and work with engineering to differentiate its customer-centric products.

There is no "one size fits all" career path to becoming a product manager, so there are several ways to enter the field. Regardless of their background, a product manager must be a team player with a creative mind and excellent communication, organization, problem-solving, interpersonal, and technical skills. Technical skills, such as the ability to develop product strategies, are learned along the way.

Sources: Based on information in Kristen Baker, "How to Start Your Career in Product Management," *Hubspot,* November 6, 2019; Karthik Sankar, "How to Do Customer-Focused Product Management," *Products That Count,* April 13, 2020; Roi Lavan, "Are You an Apple-Like or Google-Like Product Manager," *Medium,* February 22, 2017.

淘汰产品

11-4b Deleting Products

To maintain an effective product mix, an organization often has to eliminate some products. This is called **product deletion**. A weak and unprofitable product costs a company time, money, and resources that could be used to modify other products or develop new ones. A weak product's unfavorable image can negatively affect the customer perception and sales of other products sold by the firm.

Most organizations find it difficult to delete a product because of the costs associated with bringing the product to market or for more emotional reasons. Some companies drop weak products only after they have become severe financial burdens. A better approach is to conduct a systematic review of the product's impact on the overall effectiveness of a firm's product mix. Such a review should analyze a product's contribution to a company's sales for a given period and should include estimates of future sales, costs, and profits. This review should help a firm to determine whether changes in the marketing strategy might improve the product's performance.

A product-deletion program can improve a company's performance. The Canadian aircraft maker Bombardier surprised the aviation world when it announced that it would stop selling Learjet small private aircraft, which have seen declines in demand and profits in recent years. Celebrities and wealthy customers have been turning away from the 60-year-old brand in recent years in favor of larger, more long-range aircraft. Discontinuing Learjet will allow the company to cut costs and

产品淘汰
product deletion the elimination of one or more products from a product line

improve cash flow, which the company will channel into its more lucrative, larger business jet aircraft.[8]

开发新产品

11-4c Developing New Products

Developing and introducing new products is frequently time consuming, expensive, and risky. Joby Aviation, for example, has spent a decade and more than $100 million developing a fast, electric air taxi that it hopes one day will compete with Uber and Lyft for short trips.[9] Thousands of new products are introduced annually. For most firms, more than half of new products will fail. Although developing new products is risky, failing to introduce new products can be just as hazardous. Successful new products can produce benefits for an organization, including survival, profits, a sustainable competitive advantage, and a favorable public image.

New products are generally grouped into three categories on the basis of their degree of similarity to existing products. *Imitations* are products designed to compete with existing products of other companies. The success of Mark Anthony Brand's White Claw hard seltzer, for instance, spawned many competitors such as Truly (Boston Beer), Bud Light Seltzer (Anheuser-Busch InBev), and Vizzy (Molson Coors). *Adaptations* are variations of existing products that are intended for an established market. Product refinements and line extensions are the adaptations considered most often, although imitative products may also include some refinement and extension. *Innovations* are entirely new products. They may give rise to a new industry or disrupt an existing one, like Chime's no-fee, app-based financial service did for the banking industry. Innovative products take considerable time, effort, and money to develop. They are by far the riskiest new product to develop and launch and are therefore less common than adaptations and imitations. While other companies market basic hair straighteners that cost $13–$200, the $500 Dyson Corrale flat iron uses proprietary technology and design that makes it operate cooler and safer, easier to use, and less damaging to hair. Dyson spent seven years and $43 million dollars developing the new product.[10] As shown in Figure 11-2, the process of developing a new product consists of seven phases.

Figure 11-2 Phases of New-Product Development

Generally, marketers follow these seven steps to develop a new product.

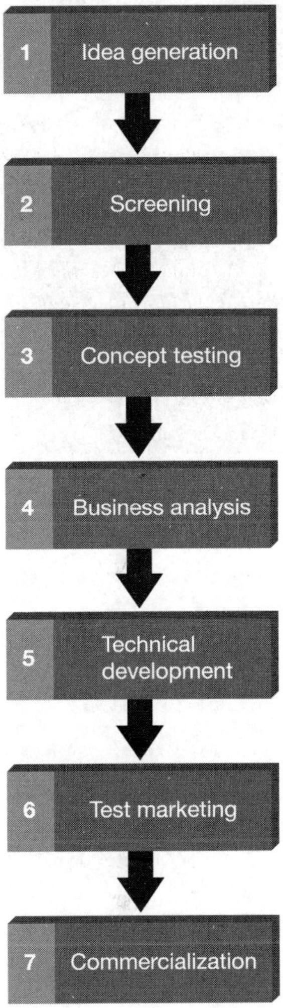

Idea Generation Idea generation involves looking for product ideas that will help a firm achieve its objectives. Although some organizations get their ideas almost by chance, companies trying to maximize product-mix effectiveness develop systematic approaches for generating new-product ideas. Ideas may come from virtually any stakeholder associated with the firm, including managers, employees, researchers, engineers, competitors, advertising agencies, management consultants, private research organizations, customers, salespersons, or top executives. Sometimes, large companies with superior experience and resources may mentor small firms and help them generate ideas to help their businesses grow. Business incubators exist all over the country that pair new businesses with established ones so that the new business can learn about marketing and branding from experts. Goldman Sachs, Walmart, Chase Bank, and Staples have all hosted events and programs to counsel start-ups. Jim Koch of Boston Beer Company, maker of Sam Adams, partners with the small business lender, Accion, for the Brewing the American Dream program, which offers speed coaching sessions and loans to small businesses.[11]

Screening During screening, ideas that do not match organizational resources and objectives are rejected. In this phase, a firm's managers consider whether the organization has the financial resources and personnel with the correct expertise to develop and market the proposed product. Additionally, the company will assess whether the idea can address some need or want of buyers. Marketers may reject a good idea because the company lacks the necessary skills and abilities to make the product a success or because there is no apparent market for the product. The largest number of product ideas is rejected during the screening phase.

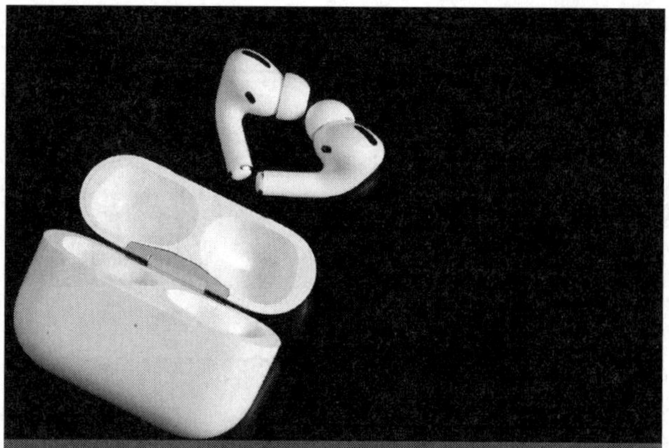

New product. Apple AirPods Pro are a new product that allow users to connect wirelessly to their cell phones through Bluetooth technology. There are also different levels of noise cancellation that now allow you to be fully in tune with your music, podcasts, and calls whenever and wherever you desire.

Concept Testing Concept testing is a phase in which a product idea is presented to a sample of potential buyers through a written or oral description (and perhaps drawings) to determine their attitudes and initial buying intentions. An organization may test one or several concepts when developing a product idea. Concept testing is a low-cost means for an organization to determine consumers' initial reactions to an idea before investing considerable resources in product research and development (R&D). Product development personnel use the results of concept testing to make product attributes and benefits reflect the characteristics and features most important to potential customers. The questions asked vary considerably depending on the type of product idea being tested. The following are typical:

- Which benefits of the proposed product are especially attractive to you?
- Which features are of little or no interest to you?
- What are the primary advantages of the proposed product over the one you currently use?
- If this product were available at an appropriate price, how often would you buy it?
- How could this proposed product be improved?

Business Analysis Business analysis generates tentative ideas about a potential product's financial performance, including profitability. During this stage, the firm considers how the new product, if it were introduced, would affect the firm's overall sales, costs, and profits. Marketing personnel usually work up preliminary sales and cost projections at this point, with the help of R&D and production managers.

Technical Development In the technical development phase, the company must determine whether it is technically feasible to produce the product and if the product can be made at a low enough cost for the company to generate a profit. If a product idea makes it to this point, it is transformed into a working model, or *prototype*. Often, this step is time consuming and expensive for the organization. When James Dyson was working to invent his first cyclonic, bagless vacuum cleaner, he went through more than 5,000 prototypes before he found the right one; his company continues to go through many prototypes throughout the research and development process of creating new products that solve problems.[12] If a product moves through this step successfully, then it is ready for test marketing.

Test Marketing Test marketing is the limited introduction of a product in several towns or cities that are representative of the intended target market. Its aim is to determine buyers' probable reactions. Marketers experiment with advertising, pricing, and packaging in different test markets and measure the extent of brand awareness, brand switching, and repeat purchases that result from alterations in the marketing mix. As an example, Chick-fil-A, test marketed a new Honey Pepper Pimento Chicken sandwich in restaurants in some cities in North and South Carolina. The fast-food chain has been testing new chicken sandwich flavors to broaden its appeal and compete with new chicken sandwich offerings from Popeyes, KFC, and even McDonald's.[13]

Commercialization During commercialization, the organization completes plans for full-scale manufacturing and marketing and prepares project budgets. In the

Technology and Innovation

技术与创新：高科技就是高级时尚

High-Tech Is High Fashion

By and large, the fashion industry is incredibly unsustainable. Fast fashion—mass-producing low-priced, trendy clothing at a low cost—in particular, comes at an extraordinary environmental cost. According to the World Economic Forum (WEF), the fashion industry emits more carbon than international flights and maritime shipping combined. Improvements driven by new technologies, however, have the power to turn the industry around.

Major brands are pledging to make sustainability a greater priority. Zara, one of the largest fast-fashion brands, pledged to use only organic, sustainable, or recycled cotton, linen, and polyester by 2025. By the same year, Nike said its plants will be powered by 100 percent renewable energy. Other companies, such as Wrangler, have developed new processes that reduce or eliminate water waste.

Many of these changes are enabled by advances in technology. Consumers are demanding that fashion brands become more transparent with their supply chains. They want to know where and how clothing is made. To achieve this, some brands have begun using blockchain technology to track their supply chains. For example, H&M partnered with VeChain to provide consumers with detailed supply chain tracing data. With just a click, consumers can view the suppliers and factories that contributed to a particular piece of clothing. With blockchain technology, the ledger creates permanent, time-stamped records of each step in a product's journey.

It can be challenging for companies to measure their social and environmental impact, but the growing demand for social accounting has given rise to new technology that will make it easier. Google Cloud partnered with designer Stella McCartney to create a tool powered by data analytics and machine learning to help do just that. The tool will give companies better insights into the environmental impact of their production processes.

Sustainability is the future of fashion. Circular business models, which aim to reduce waste through the continual use of resources, as well as supply chain tracing will become mainstream in the long run as technology accelerates. Consumers increasingly demand transparency, sustainability, and accountability across industries, and fashion is no exception.

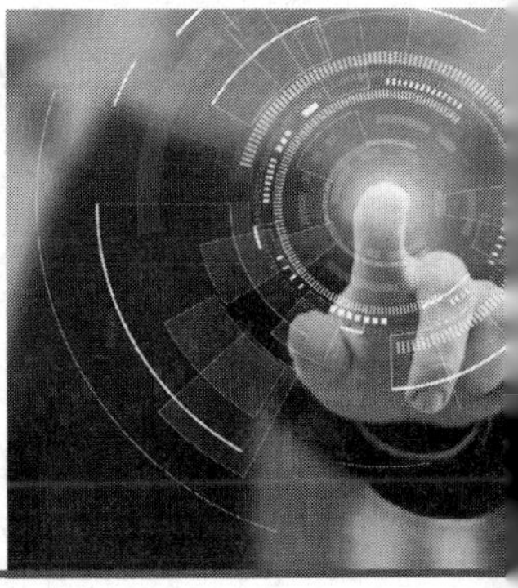

Sources: Based on information in Nell Lewis and Max Burnell, "Look and Feel Good: How Tech Could Save the Fashion Industry," *CNN*, September 30, 2019; Morgan McFall-Johnsen, "These Facts Show How Unsustainable the Fashion Industry Is," *World Economic Forum*, January 31, 2020; "H&M Head of Sustainability Praises VeChain's Traceability Solution," *Crypto News Flash*, September 1, 2020.

early part of the commercialization phase, marketing management analyzes the results of test marketing to determine necessary changes in the marketing mix. Test marketing may reveal, for example, that marketers need to change the product's physical attributes, modify the distribution plan, alter promotional efforts, or change the price. Most new products are marketed in stages, beginning in selected geographic areas and expanding into adjacent areas over a period of time.

为什么产品会失败

11-4d **Why Do Products Fail?**

Despite this rigorous process for developing product ideas, most new products end up as failures. In fact, many well-known companies have produced market failures (refer to Table 11-1).

Why does a new product fail? Mainly because the product and its marketing program are not planned and tested as thoroughly as they should be. For example, Samsung's Galaxy Note S7 phablet—a supersized smartphone—failed because some of the phones' batteries caught on fire. After the phones were banned from domestic flights, Samsung recalled the phones and ultimately opted to discontinue the model rather than lose more money on its investment.[14] To save on development costs, a firm may market-test a product before the kinks are worked out, or may not test its entire marketing mix. Or, when problems show up in the testing stage, a

Table 11-1 Examples of Product Failures

Company	Product
Microsoft	Zune (2006)
Apple	Newton (1993)
Amazon	Fire Phone (2014)
Coca-Cola	New Coke (1985)
Frito-Lay	WOW! Chips (1998)

Sources: Adapted from: "When Corporate Innovation Goes Bad—The 160 Biggest Product Failures of All Time," *CBInsights*, April 7, 2020; Ben Gilbert, "25 of the Biggest Failed Product from the World's Biggest Companies," *Business Insider*, October 17, 2019.

Concept Check

- What are some ways to improve a product mix? Describe two approaches to use existing products to strengthen a product mix.
- Why is it important to delete certain products? The largest number of product ideas are rejected during which stage?
- What is the aim of test marketing?
- Describe the seven phases of new-product development.

company may try to recover its product development costs by pushing ahead with full-scale marketing anyway. Finally, some companies try to market new products with inadequate financing.

品牌、包装和标签

11-5 Branding, Packaging, and Labeling

Learning Objective

11-5 Examine the uses and importance of branding, packaging, and labeling.

Three important features of a product (particularly a consumer product) are its brand, package, and label. These features may be used to associate a product with a successful product line or to distinguish it from existing products. They may be designed to attract customers at the point of sale or to provide information to potential buyers. Because the brand, package, and label are integral elements of the product, they deserve careful attention during product planning.

什么是品牌

11-5a What Is a Brand?

A **brand** is a name, term, symbol, design, or any combination that identifies a seller's products and distinguishes it from other sellers' products. A **brand name** is the part of a brand that can be spoken. It may include letters, words, numbers, or pronounceable symbols, such as the ampersand in *Procter & Gamble*. A **brand mark**, on the other hand, is the part of a brand that is a symbol or distinctive design, such as the Nike "swoosh." A **trademark** is a brand name or brand mark that is registered with the U.S. Patent and Trademark Office and thus is legally protected from use by anyone except its owner. A **trade name** is the complete and legal name of an organization, such as Pizza Hut or Cengage (the publisher of this text).

品牌的类型

11-5b Types of Brands

Brands are often classified according to who owns them: manufacturers or stores. A **manufacturer (or producer) brand**, as the name implies, is a brand that is owned by the manufacturer. Many foods (Kellogg's Frosted Flakes), major appliances (Whirlpool), gasolines (Chevron), automobiles (Honda), and clothing (American Eagle) are sold as manufacturers' brands. Some consumers prefer manufacturer brands because they are usually nationally known, offer consistent quality, and are widely available.

A **store (or private) brand** is a brand that is owned by an individual wholesaler or retailer. Among the better-known store brands are Cat & Jack (Target), Kirkland Signature (Costco), and Trader Joe's. Owners of store brands claim that they can offer lower prices, earn greater profits, and improve customer loyalty by offering their own brands. Target, the first company to have ten billion-dollar store brands, uses them to help distinguish itself from rivals and to build loyalty among customers.[15]

品牌
brand a name, term, symbol, design, or any combination of these that identifies a seller's products as distinct from those of other sellers

品牌名称
brand name the part of a brand that can be spoken

品牌标志
brand mark the part of a brand that is a symbol or distinctive design

商标
trademark a brand name or brand mark that is registered with the U.S. Patent and Trademark Office and thus is legally protected from use by anyone except its owner

经营名称
trade name the complete and legal name of an organization

制造商（或生产商）品牌
manufacturer (or producer) brand a brand that is owned by a manufacturer

商店（或私人）品牌
store (or private) brand a brand that is owned by an individual wholesaler or retailer

Some companies that manufacture private brands also produce their own manufacturer brands. They often find such operations profitable because they can use excess capacity and avoid most marketing costs. Many private-branded grocery products are produced by companies that specialize in making private-label products. Most supermarkets rely heavily on their store brands. In the United States, store brands account for about 18 percent of all consumer packaged goods sales, and these private brand sales are rising faster than large manufacturer brand sales.[16]

A **generic product** (sometimes called a **generic brand**) is a product with no brand at all. Its plain package carries only the name of the product—applesauce, peanut butter, or potato chips. Generic products, available in supermarkets since 1977, are sometimes made by the major producers that manufacture name brands.

You can easily recognize a manufacturer's brand because it is not sold by just one retailer. This brand was initiated by the manufacturer and is owned and supported by the manufacturer. Pop-Tarts are sold in many supermarkets.

品牌化的好处
11-5c Benefits of Branding

Consumer confidence is the most important element in the success of a branded product, whether the brand is owned by a producer or by a retailer. Because branding identifies each product, customers can easily repurchase products that provide satisfaction, performance, and quality. Moreover, they can just as easily avoid or ignore unsatisfactory products. In supermarkets, the products most likely to keep their shelf space are the brands with large market shares and strong customer loyalty.

Both buyers and sellers benefit from branding. Because brands are easily recognizable, they reduce the amount of time buyers spend on shopping, as they can quickly identify the brands they prefer. Choosing particular brands, such as Chanel, Polo, Patagonia, or Nike, can be a way of expressing oneself and identifying with certain lifestyle characteristics and values. Brands also help reduce the perceived risk of purchase. Finally, customers may receive a psychological reward from owning a brand that symbolizes status. The Lexus brand is an example.

Branding helps a firm introduce a new product that carries a familiar brand name because buyers already know the brand. Branding aids sellers in their promotional efforts because promotion of each branded product indirectly promotes other products of the same brand. H.J. Heinz, for example, markets many products with the Heinz brand name, such as ketchup, vinegar, gravies, barbecue sauce, and steak sauce.

One chief benefit of branding is the creation of **brand loyalty**, the extent to which a customer is favorable toward buying a specific brand. The stronger the brand loyalty, the greater is the likelihood that buyers will consistently choose the brand. There are three levels of brand loyalty: recognition, preference, and insistence. *Brand recognition* is the level of loyalty at which customers are aware that the brand exists and will purchase it if their preferred or familiar brands are unavailable. This is the weakest form of brand loyalty. *Brand preference* is the level of brand loyalty at which a customer prefers one brand over competing brands. However, if the preferred brand is unavailable, the customer is willing to substitute another brand. *Brand insistence* is the strongest and least common level of brand loyalty. Brand-insistent customers will not buy substitutes. Apple is a brand known for having brand-insistent customers. Every time Apple releases a new product, customers will stand in line for hours, even days, just to be among the first to purchase it. Brand loyalty in general seems to be declining, partly due to marketers' increased dependence on discounted prices, coupons, and other short-term promotions, and partly because of the enormous array of new products with similar characteristics. It is also easier than ever to comparison shop for products that meet customers' needs at the lowest possible price.

一般产品（或通用品牌）
generic product (or **generic brand)** a product with no brand at all

品牌忠诚度
brand loyalty extent to which a customer is favorable toward buying a specific brand

Table 11-2 Top Ten Most Valuable Brands in the World

Brand	Brand Value (billion $)
1. Apple	323.0
2. Amazon	200.7
3. Microsoft	166.0
4. Google	165.4
5. Samsung	62.3
6. Coca-Cola	56.9
7. Toyota	51.6
8. Mercedes-Benz	49.3
9. McDonald's	42.8
10. Disney	40.8

Source: "Best Global Brands Rankings," *Interbrand.*

Brand equity is the marketing and financial value associated with a brand's strength in a market. Although difficult to measure, brand equity represents the value of a brand to an organization. The top ten most valuable brands in the world are shown in Table 11-2. The four major factors that contribute to brand equity are brand awareness, brand associations, perceived brand quality, and brand loyalty. Brand awareness leads to brand familiarity—buyers are more likely to select a familiar brand. The symbolic associations of a brand connect it to a personality type or lifestyle. For example, customers associate Michelin tires with protecting family members, Nike products with pushing yourself athletically ("Just Do It"), and Dr Pepper with a unique taste. When consumers are unable to judge for themselves the quality of a product, they may rely on a brand's perceived level of quality. Finally, brand loyalty is a valued element of brand equity because it reduces both a brand's vulnerability to competitors and the need to spend tremendous resources to attract new customers. Loyalty also increases brand visibility and encourages retailers to carry the brand. Sometimes, large firms opt to purchase a well-known brand to diversify or complement their existing brands. As an example, Mohawk Group, a consumer products conglomerate, acquired the Spiralizer, PurSteam, and Pohl Schmitt brands in order to diversify its portfolio of brands with small appliance options.[17]

选择和保护品牌

11-5d Choosing and Protecting a Brand

A number of issues should be considered when selecting a brand name. The name should be easy for customers to say, spell, and recall. Short, one-syllable names such as *Tide* often satisfy this requirement. Words, numbers, and letters can be combined to yield brand names such as Samsung's Galaxy S21 Ultra phone or BMW's Z4 Roadster. The brand name should suggest, in a positive way, the product's uses, special characteristics, and major benefits, and should be distinctive enough to set it apart from competing brands.

It is important that a company select a brand that can be protected through registration, reserving it for exclusive use by that firm. Some brands, because of their designs, are infringed on more easily than others. Registration protects trademarks domestically for ten years and can be renewed indefinitely. To protect its exclusive right to the brand, the company must ensure that the selected brand will not be considered an infringement on any existing brand already registered with the U.S. Patent and Trademark Office. This task may be complicated by the fact that courts determine infringement and base their decisions on whether a brand causes consumers to be confused, mistaken, or deceived about the source of the product. McDonald's is one company that is known for aggressively protecting its trademarks against infringement. It has brought charges against a number of companies with *Mc* names because of concerns that the use of the prefix might give consumers the impression that these companies are associated with or owned by McDonald's.

A business does not want a brand name to become a generic term that refers to a general product category. Generic terms cannot be legally protected as exclusive brand names. For example, names such as *yo-yo, aspirin, escalator,* and *thermos*—all exclusively brand names at one time—eventually were declared generic terms that refer to product categories. As such, they can no longer be protected. To ensure that a brand name does not become a generic term, the firm should spell the name with a capital letter and use it as an adjective to modify the name of the general product class, as in Jell-O Brand Gelatin. An organization can deal directly with this problem by advertising that its brand is a trademark and should not be used generically. Firms also can use the registered trademark symbol® to indicate that the brand is trademarked.

品牌资产

brand equity marketing and financial value associated with a brand's strength in a market

品牌战略

11-5e Branding Strategies

The basic branding decision for any firm is how to brand its products. A producer may market its products under its own brands, private brands, or both. A retail store may carry only producer brands, its own brands, or both. Once either type of firm decides to brand, it chooses one of two branding strategies: individual branding or family branding.

Individual branding is the strategy in which a firm uses a different brand for each of its products. For example, Procter & Gamble uses individual branding for its line of bar soaps, which includes Ivory, Safeguard, and Olay. Individual branding offers two major advantages: a problem with one product will not affect the good name of the firm's other products and the different brands can be directed toward different market segments.

Family branding is the strategy in which a firm uses the same brand for all or most of its products. Sony, Dell, IBM, and Xerox use family branding for their product mixes. A major advantage of family branding is that successful promotion for any one item that carries the family brand can help all other products with the same brand name. In addition, a new product has a head start when its brand name is already known and accepted by customers. As an example, when Anheuser-Busch InBev introduced a new seltzer product to compete with White Claw, it called the line Bud Light Seltzer to capitalize on the name recognition of its Bud Light brand.[18]

品牌延伸

11-5f Brand Extensions

A **brand extension** occurs when an organization uses one of its existing brands to brand a new product in a different product category. The French fashion house Louis Vuitton, for example, extended its brand when it opened an LV branded chocolate shop and café in a new glass tower in Ginza in Tokyo.[19] A brand extension should not be confused with a line extension. A *line extension* refers to using an existing brand on a new product in the same product category, such as a new flavor or new sizes. Pringles engages in line extension when releasing a new flavor, such as Nashville Hot Chicken flavor. Marketers must be careful not to extend a brand too many times or extend too far outside the original product category. Either action may weaken the brand.

包装

11-5g Packaging

Packaging consists of all the activities involved in developing and providing a container with graphics for a product. The package is a vital part of the product. It can make the product more versatile, safer, or easier to use. Through its shape, size, appearance, and printed message, a package can influence purchasing decisions.

Packaging Functions Effective packaging is a combination of function and aesthetics. The basic function of packaging materials is to protect the product and maintain its functional form. Fluids such as milk, orange juice, and hair spray need packages that preserve and protect the product inside. Packaging should prevent damage that would affect the product's usefulness and increase costs. Because product tampering has become a problem for marketers of many types of goods, packaging techniques have been developed to counter this danger. Some packages are also designed to foil shoplifting.

独立品牌
individual branding the strategy in which a firm uses a different brand for each of its products

家族品牌
family branding the strategy in which a firm uses the same brand for all or most of its products

品牌延伸
brand extension using an existing brand to brand a new product in a different product category

包装
packaging all the activities involved in developing and providing a container with graphics for a product

Another function of packaging is to offer consumer convenience. For example, individual-serving boxes or plastic bags that contain liquids and do not require refrigeration appeal strongly to parents of small children and to young adults with active lifestyles. The size or shape of a package may relate to the product's storage, convenience of use, or replacement rate. Small, single-serving cans of vegetables, for instance, may prevent waste and make storage easier.

A third function of packaging is to promote a product by communicating its features, uses, benefits, and image. Sometimes a firm develops a reusable package to make its product more desirable. For example, CleanPath multi-surface cleaners employ Replenish technology which allows them to be sold as cleaner concentrate in pods that screw onto the bottom of a spray bottle. Consumers purchase the bottle once, add water, and the pod releases the correct amount of cleaner concentrate. The system saves on plastic and water waste and is cheaper than many competitors' products.[20]

Package Design Considerations Many factors must be weighed when developing packages. Obviously, one major consideration is cost. Expensive packaging can affect the final cost of a product.

Marketers must also decide whether to package the product in single or multiple units. Multiple-unit packaging can increase demand by increasing the amount of the product available at the point of consumption (in the home, for example). Multiple-unit packaging does not work for infrequently used products because buyers generally prefer not to have an excess supply or to store products for a long time. However, multiple-unit packaging can make storage and handling easier (as in the case of twelve-packs used for soft drinks). It can also facilitate special price offers, such as two-for-one sales. Multiple-unit packaging may encourage customers to try a product several times, but it may also backfire and deter them from trying the product if they cannot purchase just one.

Marketers should consider how much consistency is desirable among an organization's package designs. To promote an overall company image, a firm may decide that all packages must be similar or include a distinct design element. This approach, called *family packaging* is often used only for lines of products, as with Campbell's soups, Weight Watchers foods, and Planters nuts. The best policy is sometimes no consistency, especially if a firm's various products are unrelated or aimed at different target markets.

Packages also play an important promotional role. Through verbal and nonverbal symbols, the package informs potential buyers about the product's content, uses, features, advantages, and hazards. Businesses can create desirable images and associations by choosing particular colors, designs, shapes, and textures. Many cosmetics manufacturers, for example, design their packages to create impressions of richness, luxury, and exclusivity. The package performs another promotional function when it is designed to be safer or more convenient to use than competitors'.

Packaging also must meet the needs of intermediaries. Wholesalers and retailers consider whether a package is easy to transport, handle, and store. Resellers may refuse to carry certain products if their packages are too cumbersome.

Finally, firms must consider the issue of environmental responsibility when developing packages. Companies must balance consumers' desires for convenience against the need to preserve the environment. Reducing packaging will help with global waste problems because about one-half of all garbage consists of plastic packaging. As part of its long-term World Without Waste initiative, Coca-Cola introduced a new soft drink bottle made from 100 percent recycled plastic. It first rolled out the new 13.2-ounce bottles for Coke, Diet Coke, and Fanta in some areas, gradually expanding the geographic distribution and number of brands using the new recycled bottles. The new bottles are part of Coke's goal of making 100 percent of its packaging recyclable by 2025 and to use 50 percent recycled content by 2030.[21]

标签
labeling the presentation of information on a product or its package

质量保证书
express warranty a written explanation of the producer's responsibilities in the event that a product is found to be defective or otherwise unsatisfactory

标签

11-5h Labeling

Heinz turns the ketchup bottle on its head. The original design of the ketchup bottle made it difficult for customers to get the ketchup out. To solve this problem, Heinz put the cap on the bottom of the bottle and made the opening larger. In addition, Heinz made the bottle squeezable.

Labeling is the presentation of information on a product or its package. The *label* is the part of a package that contains information, including the brand name and mark, the registered trademark symbol®, the package size and contents, product claims, directions for use and safety precautions, ingredients, the name and address of the manufacturer, and the Universal Product Code (UPC) symbol, which is used for automated checkout and inventory control. Labels are significant during the consumer buying decision process. Researchers have found that 60 percent of consumers will bypass a product when its label fails to present sufficient details, and 33 percent will reject a product if they don't like the design of the label.[22]

A number of federal regulations specify information that *must* be included in the labeling for certain products:

- Garments must be labeled with the name of the manufacturer, country of manufacture, fabric content, and cleaning instructions.
- Food labels must contain the most common term for ingredients and indicate whether the item contains common allergens.
- Any food product for which a nutritional claim is made must have nutrition labeling that follows a standard format.
- Food product labels must state the number of servings per container, the serving size, the number of calories per serving, the number of calories derived from fat, and the amounts of specific nutrients.
- Nonedible items such as shampoos and detergents must carry safety precautions and instructions for use.

Such regulations are aimed at protecting customers from misleading product claims and the improper (and thus unsafe) use of products. Food manufacturers are not allowed to make misleading health claims about their products.

Labels also may carry the details of written, or express, warranties. An **express warranty** is a written explanation of the producer's responsibilities in the event that a product is found to be defective or otherwise unsatisfactory.

✓ Concept Check

- Describe the major types of brands.
- How do brands help customers in product selection? How do brands help companies introduce new products? Explain the three levels of brand loyalty.
- Define brand equity and describe the four major factors that contribute toward brand equity. What issues must be considered while choosing a brand name?
- What are the major functions of packaging?

产品定价

11-6 Pricing Products

Learning Objective

11-6 Describe the economic basis of pricing and the means by which sellers can control prices and buyers' perceptions of prices.

A product is a set of attributes and benefits that has been designed to satisfy its market while earning a profit for its seller. Pricing is an integral part of this equation. Each product has a price at which consumers' desires and expectations are balanced with a firm's need to make a profit. We will now look more closely at how businesses go about determining a product's price.

价格的含义和用途

11-6a The Meaning and Use of Price

The **price** of a product is the amount of money a seller is willing to accept in exchange for the product at a given time and under given circumstances. At times, the price results from negotiations between buyer and seller. In many business situations, however, the price is fixed by the seller. Suppose that a seller

价格

price the amount of money a seller is willing to accept in exchange for a product at a given time and under given circumstances sets a price of $10 for a product. The seller is saying, "Anyone who wants this product can have it here and now in exchange for $10." Each interested buyer then makes a personal judgment regarding the product's utility, often in terms of a dollar value. People who feel that they will get at least $10 worth of want satisfaction (or value) from the product are likely to buy it. If they believe they can get more want satisfaction by spending $10 in some other way, they will not buy the product.

Price thus serves the function of *allocator*. First, it allocates goods and services among those who are willing and able to buy them. (The answer to the economic question "For whom to produce?" depends primarily on prices.) Second, price allocates financial resources (sales revenue) among producers according to how well they satisfy customers' needs. Third, price helps customers allocate their own financial resources among various want-satisfying products.

价格竞争和非价格竞争
11-6b Price and Non-Price Competition

Before a product's price can be set, an organization must determine whether it will compete on the basis of price alone, or on a combination of factors. The choice influences pricing decisions as well as other marketing-mix variables.

价格竞争
price competition an emphasis on setting a price equal to or lower than competitors' prices to gain sales or market share

非价格竞争
non-price competition competition based on factors other than price

产品差异化
product differentiation the process of developing and promoting differences between one's product and all similar products

Price competition occurs when a seller emphasizes a product's low price and sets a price that equals or beats competitors' prices. Planet Fitness, for example, experienced dramatic growth by offering $10/month gym memberships when other sport club memberships average $50 a month. Although Planet Fitness offers fewer amenities, its lower price is appealing to consumers who don't use most gym amenities—or simply forget to cancel.[23] To use this approach most effectively, a seller must have the flexibility to change prices often, rapidly, and aggressively in response to competitors' price changes. Price competition allows a marketer to set prices based on product demand or in response to changes in the firm's finances. Competitors can do likewise, however, which is a major drawback of price competition. If circumstances force a seller to raise prices, competing firms may be able to maintain their lower prices. The internet has made it more difficult than ever for sellers to compete on the basis of price, as consumers can quickly and easily conduct comparison-shopping online.

How low can you go? Price competition is fierce among fast-food restaurants. Value pricing has been used by some fast-food organizations for more than 20 years.

Non-price competition is competition based on factors other than price. It is used most effectively when a seller can make its product stand out through distinctive product quality, customer service, promotion, packaging, or other features. Buyers must be able to perceive these characteristics and consider them desirable. Once customers have chosen a brand for non-price reasons, they may not be as attracted to competing businesses and brands. In this way, a seller can build customer loyalty to its brand. A method of non-price competition, **product differentiation**, is the process of developing and promoting differences between one's product and all similar products. Consider the direct-to-consumer hair care company Prose, which creates customized shampoo and conditioner formulas for each customer, based on hair texture, local weather and water conditions, and what styling treatments they use. Although the products are offered at prices considerably higher than mass shampoos sold in stores, customers do not seem to mind paying more for products personalized just for them.[24]

Ethics and Social Responsibility

商业伦理与社会责任：企业为了对种族和文化更加敏感而重塑品牌

Companies Rebrand to Be More Sensitive

Over the years, critics have called for brands that use symbols that perpetuate racial stereotypes or are culturally insensitive to abandon them or remake them to convey more positive images. In recent years, social unrest and heightened calls for racial justice sparked a new national conversation about race in America. Many companies saw this as an opportunity to support people of color by ending brand imagery with insensitive connotations.

PepsiCo, the parent company for Quaker Oats, announced that it would rebrand its 130-year-old Aunt Jemima syrup brand, including the name and symbol. Although the Aunt Jemima brand mark had evolved over the decades, the company acknowledged in its statement that "Aunt Jemima's origins are based on a racial stereotype." The line of pancake mixes and syrups was reintroduced a year later as the Pearl Milling Company. Mars, Inc., which owns the Uncle Ben's brand of rice products, quickly followed with its own announcement, renaming the brand to Ben's Original.

The owners of other brands, including Cream of Wheat and Mrs. Butterworth, also pledged to examine their products and packaging for racially and culturally insensitive symbols. Land O'Lakes redesigned its packaging and dropped the Native American "butter maiden." Likewise, Dreyer's Grand Ice Cream announced that it would rebrand the century-old Eskimo Pie chocolate-covered ice cream and discontinue its Eskimo character symbols. Changing a brand, including its name and symbols, can be very expensive, but these companies recognize that rebranding positions them as being part of the solution to racial inequality.

Sources: Based on information in Maria Cramer, "After Aunt Jemima, Reviews Underway for Uncle Ben, Mrs. Butterworth and Cream of Wheat," *The New York Times*, June 17, 2020; Maria Cramer, "Maker of Eskimo Pie Ice Cream Will Retire 'Inappropriate' Name," *The New York Times*, June 20, 2020; Ben Kesslen, "Aunt Jemima Brand to Change Name, Remove Image that Quaker Says Is 'Based on a Racial Stereotype,'" *NBCNews*, June 17, 2020.

购买者对价格的看法

11-6c Buyers' Perceptions of Price

In setting prices, managers should consider the price sensitivity of the target market. Members of one market segment may be more influenced by price than members of another. Consumer price sensitivity can also vary between products. For example, buyers may be more sensitive to price when purchasing gasoline than when purchasing running shoes.

Buyers will tolerate a narrow range of prices for certain items and a wider range for others. Consider the varying prices of soft drinks—from 15 cents per ounce at the movies down to 1.5 cents per ounce on sale at the grocery store. Managers should be aware of consumers' price limits and the products to which they apply. The company also should take note of buyers' perceptions of a given product relative to competing products. A premium price may be appropriate if a product is considered superior to others in its category, or if the product has inspired strong brand loyalty. On the other hand, a lower price may be necessary if buyers have even a slightly negative product perception.

Sometimes buyers equate price and quality. Managers involved in pricing decisions should determine whether this outlook is widespread in the target market. If it is, a higher price may improve a product's image, making it more desirable.

✓ Concept Check

- What factors must be considered when pricing products?
- How does a change in price affect the demand and supply of a product?
- Differentiate price competition and non-price competition.
- Why is it important to consider the buyer's sensitivity to price when pricing products?

定价目标

11-7 Pricing Objectives

Learning Objective

11-7 Specify the major pricing objectives used by businesses.

Before setting prices for a firm's products, marketers must establish pricing objectives that are aligned with organizational and marketing objectives. Of course,

What does a product's price communicate to you? How buyers perceive a product is often determined by its price. High prices communicate quality and status—which is why the makers of luxury goods such as Chanel handbags are often reluctant to sell them at a discount. The producers of these goods don't want to "cheapen" their brands for a quick sales boost because it could hurt the image of the brand.

one objective of pricing is to make a profit, but this may not be a firm's primary objective. One or more of the following factors may be just as important.

基于生存目标

11-7a Survival

A firm may have to price its products to survive—either as an organization or as a player in a particular market. This usually means that the company will cut its price to attract customers, even if it must operate at a loss for a while. Obviously, such a goal cannot be pursued on a long-term basis, for consistent losses would cause the business to fail.

基于利润最大化目标

11-7b Profit Maximization

Many businesses may state that their goal is to maximize profit, but this goal is impossible to define (and thus impossible to achieve). What, exactly, is the *maximum* profit? How does a company know when it has been reached? Firms that wish to set profit goals should express them as either specific dollar amounts, or percentage increases, over previous profits.

基于投资回报率目标

11-7c Target Return on Investment

The *return on investment* (ROI) is the amount earned as a result of a financial investment. Some businesses set an annual percentage ROI as a quantifiable means to gauge the success of their pricing goal.

基于市场份额目标

11-7d Market-Share Goals

A firm's *market share* is its proportion of total industry sales. Some companies attempt, through pricing, to maintain or increase their market shares. Both U.S. cola giants, Coke and Pepsi, continually try to gain market share through aggressive pricing and other marketing efforts.

为了维持现状而定价

11-7e Status-Quo Pricing

In pricing their products, some businesses are guided by a desire to maintain the status quo. This is especially true in industries that depend on price stability. If such a firm can maintain its profit or market share simply by matching the competition—charging about the same price as competitors for similar products—then it will do so.

✓ Concept Check

- Explain the various types of pricing objectives.
- Which ones will usually result in a firm having lower prices?

定价方法

11-8 Pricing Methods

Learning Objective

11-8 Compare the three major pricing methods that businesses employ.

Once a firm has developed its pricing objectives, it must select a pricing method to reach that goal. Two factors are important to every company engaged in setting prices. The first is recognition that the market, and not the firm's costs, ultimately determines the price at which a product will sell. The second is awareness that costs and expected sales can be used only to establish a *price floor,* the minimum price at which the firm can sell its product without incurring a loss. In this section, we look at three kinds of pricing methods: cost-based, demand-based, and competition-based pricing.

成本导向定价

11-8a Cost-Based Pricing

Using the simplest method of pricing, *cost-based pricing*, the seller first determines the total cost of producing (or purchasing) one unit of the product. The seller then adds an amount to cover additional costs (such as insurance or interest) and profit. The amount that is added is called the **markup**. The total of the cost plus the markup is the product's selling price.

Marketers can calculate markup as a percentage of total costs. Suppose, for example, that the total cost of manufacturing and marketing 1,000 headsets is $100,000, or $100 per unit. If the manufacturer wants a markup that is 20 percent above costs, the selling price will be $100 plus 20 percent of $100, or $120 per unit.

Markup pricing is easy to apply and is used by many businesses (mostly retailers and wholesalers). However, it has two major flaws. The first is the difficulty of determining the best markup percentage. If the percentage is too high, the product may be overpriced for its market and too few units will be sold to cover the cost of producing and marketing it. If the markup percentage is too low, the seller forgoes profit it could have earned by assigning a higher price.

The second problem with markup pricing is that it separates pricing from other business functions. The product is priced *after* production quantities are determined, *after* costs are incurred, and almost without regard for the market or the marketing mix. To be most effective, the cost of various business functions should be integrated. *Each* should have an impact on all marketing decisions.

Cost-based pricing can also be calculated through breakeven analysis. For any product, the **breakeven quantity** is the number of units that must be sold for the total revenue (from all units sold) to equal the total cost (of all units sold). **Total revenue** is the total amount received from the sales of a product. We estimate projected total revenue as the selling price multiplied by the number of units expected to be sold.

The costs involved in operating a business can be broadly classified as either fixed or variable. A **fixed cost** is a cost incurred no matter how many units of a product are produced or sold. Rent, for example, is a fixed cost because it remains the same whether 1 or 1,000 units are produced. A **variable cost** is a cost that depends on the number of units produced. The cost of fabricating parts for a stereo receiver is a variable cost. The more units produced, the more efficient production will be and the per-unit cost of the parts will go down. The **total cost** of producing a certain number of units is the sum of the fixed costs and the variable costs attributed to those units.

If we assume a particular selling price, we can find the breakeven quantity either graphically or by using a formula. Figure 11-3 graphs the total revenue earned and the total cost incurred by the sale of various quantities of a hypothetical product. With fixed costs of $40,000, variable costs of $60 per unit, and a selling price of $120, the breakeven quantity is 667 units (represented in Figure 11-3 as the intersection of the total revenue and total cost curves). To find the breakeven quantity, first deduct the variable cost from the selling price to determine how much money the sale of

加价
markup the amount a seller adds to the cost of a product to determine its basic selling price

盈亏平衡量
breakeven quantity the number of units that must be sold for the total revenue (from all units sold) to equal the total cost (of all units sold)

总收入
total revenue the total amount received from the sales of a product

固定成本
fixed cost a cost incurred no matter how many units of a product are produced or sold

可变成本
variable cost a cost that depends on the number of units produced

总成本
total cost the sum of the fixed costs and the variable costs attributed to a product

Figure 11-3 Breakeven Analysis

Breakeven analysis answers the question: What is the lowest level of production and sales at which a company can break even on a particular product?

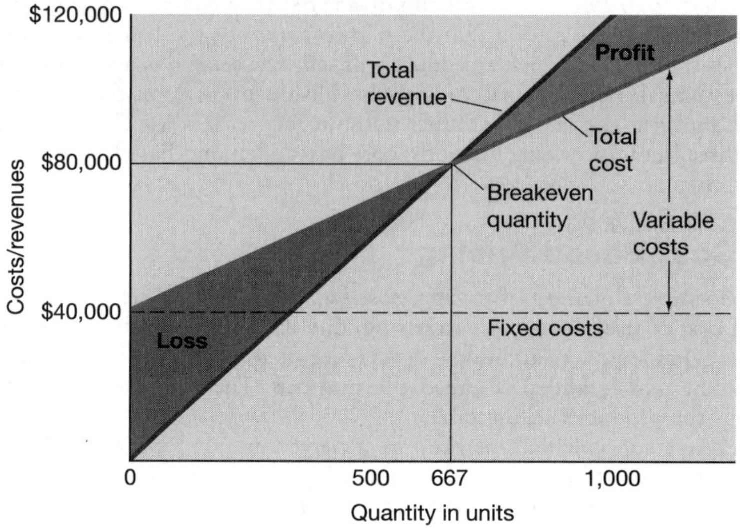

one unit contributes toward offsetting fixed costs. Divide that contribution into the total fixed costs to arrive at the breakeven quantity. If the firm sells more than 667 units at $120 each, it will earn a profit. If it sells fewer units, it will suffer a loss.

需求导向定价

11-8b Demand-Based Pricing

Rather than basing the price of a product on its cost, companies sometimes use a pricing method based on the level of demand for the product: *demand-based pricing*. This method results in a higher price when product demand is strong and a lower price when demand is weak. To use this method, a marketer estimates the amount of a product that customers will demand at different prices and then chooses the price that should generate the highest total revenue. Obviously, the effectiveness of this method depends on the firm's ability to estimate demand accurately.

Did you pay twice as much for your plane ticket as the person sitting next to you? Airlines use demand-based pricing. The sophisticated software the companies use constantly re-prices seats based on historical data, as well as how many customers are purchasing tickets at any given time on a specific flight.

A company may favor a demand-based pricing method called *price differentiation* if it wants to use more than one price in the marketing of a specific product. Price differentiation can be based on such considerations as time of the purchase, type of customer, or type of distribution channel. The use of so-called *dynamic pricing*—which raises prices during periods of high demand—is growing, especially for services such as car ride-hailing apps like Uber and Lyft as well as restaurants looking for a more even flow of customers throughout the day. For instance, all tickets for Los Angeles Dodgers' baseball games are sold using dynamic pricing. Ticket prices are adjusted based on real-time market conditions that include seat location, the popularity of time and day, as well as whether there are special promotions like bobblehead giveaways.[25] For price differentiation to work, the company must be able to segment a market on the basis of different strengths of demand. The company must then be able to keep the segments separate enough so that those who buy at lower prices cannot sell to buyers in segments that are charged a higher price. This isolation can be accomplished, for example, by selling to geographically separated segments. However, the internet has made price differentiation for products more difficult.

Compared with cost-based pricing, demand-based pricing places a firm in a better position to attain higher profit levels, assuming that buyers value the product at levels sufficiently above the product's cost. To use demand-based pricing, however, management must be able to estimate demand at different price levels, which may be difficult to assess accurately.

竞争导向定价

11-8c Competition-Based Pricing

In using *competition-based pricing*, an organization considers costs and revenue secondary to competitors' prices. The importance of this method increases if competing products are similar and the organization is serving markets in which price is the crucial variable of the marketing strategy. A firm that uses competition-based pricing may choose to sell below competitors' prices, slightly above competitors' prices, or at the same level. The price that your bookstore paid to the publishing company of this text was determined using competition-based pricing. Competition-based pricing can help to attain a pricing objective to increase sales or market share. Competition-based pricing may also be combined with other cost approaches to arrive at a profitable level.

✓ Concept Check

- List and explain the three kinds of pricing methods.
- Give an advantage and a disadvantage for each method.

定价策略

11-9 Pricing Strategies

A *pricing strategy* is a course of action designed to achieve pricing objectives. The extent to which a business uses any of the following strategies depends on its pricing and marketing objectives, the markets for its products, the degree of product differentiation, the product's life-cycle stage, and other factors. Figure 11-4 is a list of the major types of pricing strategies. We discuss these strategies in the remainder of this section.

Learning Objective

11-9 Explain the different strategies available to companies for setting prices.

新产品定价

11-9a New-Product Pricing

The two primary types of new-product pricing strategies are price skimming and penetration pricing. An organization can use either one, or even both, over a period of time.

Figure 11-4 Types of Pricing Strategies

Companies have a variety of pricing strategies available to them.

Price Skimming Some consumers are willing to pay a high price for an innovative product, either because of its novelty or because of the prestige or status that ownership confers. **Price skimming** is the strategy of charging the highest possible price for a product during the introduction stage of its life cycle. This strategy helps to recover the high costs of R&D quickly. In addition, a skimming policy may hold down demand for the product, which is helpful if the firm's production capacity is limited during the introduction stage. A danger is that a price-skimming strategy may make the product appear more lucrative than it actually is to potential competitors, encouraging more competitors to enter the market.

Penetration Pricing At the opposite extreme, **penetration pricing** is the strategy of setting a low price for a new product to build market share quickly. The seller hopes that building a large market share will discourage competitors from entering the market. If the low price stimulates sales, the business may also be able to order longer production runs, which usually results in lower production costs per unit. A disadvantage of penetration pricing is that it places a firm in a less flexible position on pricing. It is more difficult to raise prices significantly than it is to lower them.

差别定价

11-9b Differential Pricing

An important issue in pricing decisions is whether to use a single price or different prices for the same product. *Differential pricing* means charging different prices to different buyers for the same quality and quantity of product. For example, many theaters offer discounted tickets for daytime matinee performances, and airlines have different pricing tiers for airline seats depending on whether customers paid extra to board early or other perks. For differential pricing to be effective, the market must consist of multiple segments with different price sensitivities. When this method is employed, caution should be used to avoid confusing or antagonizing customers. Differential pricing can take several forms, including negotiated pricing, secondary-market pricing, periodic discounting, and random discounting.

Negotiated Pricing **Negotiated pricing** occurs when the final price is established through bargaining between the seller and the customer. Negotiated pricing occurs at all levels of distribution and is common in a variety of industries. Even when there is a predetermined stated price or a price list, manufacturers, wholesalers, and retailers may negotiate to establish the final sales price. Consumers commonly negotiate prices for houses, cars, and used equipment.

Secondary-Market Pricing **Secondary-market pricing** means setting one price for the primary target market and a different price for another market. The price charged in the secondary market is often, but not always, lower. Examples of secondary markets include a geographically isolated domestic market, a market in a foreign country, and a segment willing to purchase a product during off-peak times (such as "early bird" dinners at restaurants and matinee showings at movie theaters).

Periodic Discounting **Periodic discounting** is the temporary reduction of prices on a patterned or systematic basis. For example, many retailers have annual holiday sales, and apparel stores have seasonal sales. From the marketer's point of view, a problem with periodic discounting is that customers can predict when the reductions will occur and may delay their purchases until they can take advantage of the lower prices.

Random Discounting To alleviate the problem of customers holding off on purchases until a discount period, some organizations employ **random discounting**. That is, they reduce their prices temporarily on a nonsystematic basis. When price

撇脂定价
price skimming the strategy of charging the highest possible price for a product during the introduction stage of its life cycle

渗透定价
penetration pricing the strategy of setting a low price for a new product to build market share quickly

协议定价
negotiated pricing establishing a final price through bargaining

二级市场定价
secondary-market pricing setting one price for the primary target market and a different price for another market

定期折扣
periodic discounting temporary reduction of prices on a patterned or systematic basis

随机折扣
random discounting temporary reduction of prices on an unsystematic basis

reductions of a product occur randomly, current users of that brand are not able to predict when reductions will occur. They therefore will not delay their purchases in anticipation of purchasing the product at a lower price. Marketers also use random discounting to attract new customers.

心理定价
11-9c Psychological Pricing

Psychological pricing strategies encourage purchases based on emotional responses rather than on economically rational ones. These strategies are used primarily for consumer products rather than business products.

Odd-Number Pricing Many retailers believe that consumers respond more positively to odd-number prices such as $4.99 than to whole-dollar prices such as $5. **Odd-number pricing** is the strategy of setting prices using odd numbers that are slightly below whole-dollar amounts. Nine and five are the most popular ending figures for odd-number prices.

Multiple-Unit Pricing Many retailers (supermarkets in particular) practice **multiple-unit pricing**, setting a single price for two or more units, such as two cans for 99 cents, rather than 50 cents per can. Especially for frequently purchased products, this strategy can increase the amount of an item that is sold. Customers who see the single price and who expect eventually to use more than one unit of the product will purchase multiple units to save money.

Reference Pricing **Reference pricing** means pricing a product at a moderate level and positioning it next to a more expensive model or brand in the hope that the customer will use the higher price as a reference price (i.e., a comparison price). Because of the comparison, the customer is expected to view the moderate price favorably.

Bundle Pricing **Bundle pricing** is the packaging together of two or more products, usually of a complementary nature, to be sold for a single price. To be attractive to customers, the single price usually is considerably less than the sum of the prices of the individual products. Because the products are complementary, such as shampoo and conditioner, the customer will also find convenience value from purchasing them together. The firm may find bundling to be a valuable strategy because, by bundling slow-moving products with more popular ones, an organization can stimulate sales and increase revenues. Selling products as a package rather than individually also may result in cost savings for the organization. It is common for telecommunications providers to sell service bundles of cable, internet, and phone service for one price.

Everyday Low Prices (EDLPs) To reduce or eliminate frequent short-term price reductions, some organizations use an approach referred to as **everyday low prices (EDLPs)**. When EDLPs are used, a marketer sets a low price for its products on a consistent basis, rather than setting high prices and frequently discounting them. EDLPs, though not deeply discounted, are set far enough below competitors' prices to make customers feel confident that they are receiving a good deal. EDLPs are employed by retailers such as Walmart and by manufacturers such as Procter & Gamble. A company that uses EDLPs benefits from reduced promotional costs, reduced losses from frequent markdowns, and more stability in sales. However, customers may not trust the EDLP and assume the deal is merely a marketing gimmick.

Customary Pricing In **customary pricing**, certain goods are priced primarily on the basis of tradition. It is not as common as it once was, but examples of customary, or traditional, prices are those set for candy bars and chewing gum.

奇数定价
odd-number pricing the strategy of setting prices using odd numbers that are slightly below whole-dollar amounts

多单位定价
multiple-unit pricing the strategy of setting a single price for two or more units

参考定价
reference pricing pricing a product at a moderate level and positioning it next to a more expensive model or brand

捆绑定价
bundle pricing packaging together two or more complementary products and selling them for a single price

每日低价
everyday low prices (EDLPs) setting a low price for products on a consistent basis

习惯性定价
customary pricing pricing on the basis of tradition

产品线定价
11-9d Product-Line Pricing

Rather than considering products on an item-by-item basis when determining pricing strategies, some marketers employ product-line pricing. *Product-line pricing* means establishing and adjusting the prices of multiple products within a product line. Product-line pricing can provide marketers with flexibility in price setting. For example, marketers can set prices high so that one product is highly profitable, whereas another has a low price to increase market share.

When marketers employ product-line pricing, they have several strategies from which to choose. These include captive pricing, premium pricing, and price lining.

Captive Pricing When **captive pricing** is used, the basic product in a product line is priced low, but the price on the items required to operate or enhance it are higher. Two common examples of captive pricing are razor blades and printer ink. The razor handle and the printer are generally priced quite low, but the razor blades and the printer ink replacement cartridges are usually very expensive.

Premium Pricing **Premium pricing** occurs when the highest-quality product or the most-versatile version of similar products in a product line is assigned the highest price. Other products in the line are priced to appeal to more price-sensitive shoppers, or to those seeking product-specific features. Marketers that employ premium pricing often realize a significant portion of profits from the premium-priced products. Examples of product categories in which premium pricing is common are small kitchen appliances, beer, ice cream, and television cable service.

Price Lining **Price lining** is the strategy of selling goods only at certain predetermined prices that reflect definite price breaks. For example, a shop may sell men's ties only at $22 and $37. This strategy is used in clothing and accessory stores. It eliminates minor price differences from the buying decision—both for customers and for managers who buy merchandise to sell in these stores.

促销价
11-9e Promotional Pricing

Price, as an ingredient in the marketing mix, often is coordinated with promotions. The two variables sometimes are so interrelated that the pricing policy is promotion-oriented. Examples of promotional pricing include price leaders, special-event pricing, and comparison discounting.

Price Leaders Sometimes, a firm prices a few products below the usual markup, near cost, or below cost, which results in **price leaders**. This type of pricing is used most often in supermarkets and restaurants to attract customers by giving them especially low prices on a few items. Management hopes that customers will purchase regularly priced items as well, which will offset the reduced revenues from the price leaders.

Special-Event Pricing To increase sales volume, many organizations coordinate price with advertising or sales promotions for seasonal or special occasions. **Special-event pricing** involves advertised sales or price cutting linked to a holiday, season, or event. If the pricing objective is survival, then special sales events may be designed to generate the necessary operating capital.

Comparison Discounting **Comparison discounting** sets the price of a product at a specific level and compares it with a higher price. The higher price may be the product's previous price, the price of a competing brand, the product's price at another retail outlet, or a manufacturer's suggested retail price. Comparison discounting can significantly influence customers' decisions. Because this pricing

附属产品定价
captive pricing pricing the basic product in a product line low, but pricing related items at a higher level

溢价定价
premium pricing pricing the highest-quality or most-versatile products higher than other models in the product line

分级定价
price lining the strategy of selling goods only at certain predetermined prices that reflect definite price breaks

价格领导者
price leaders products priced below the usual markup, near cost, or below cost

特殊事件定价
special-event pricing advertised sales or price cutting linked to a holiday, season, or event

比较折扣
comparison discounting setting a price at a specific level and comparing it with a higher price

strategy can lead to deceptive pricing practices, the Federal Trade Commission (FTC) has established guidelines for comparison discounting. If the higher price against which the comparison is made is the price formerly charged for the product, sellers must have made the previous price available to customers for a reasonable period of time. If sellers present the higher price as the one charged by other retailers in the same trade area, they must be able to demonstrate the veracity of the claim. When they present the higher price as the manufacturer's suggested retail price, then the higher price must be similar to the price at which a reasonable proportion of the product was sold.

> **✓ Concept Check**
> - Identify the five categories of pricing strategies.
> - Describe two specific pricing strategies in each category.

工业品定价

11-10 Pricing Business Products

> **Learning Objective**
> **11-10** Recognize three major types of pricing associated with business products.

Many of the pricing issues discussed thus far in this chapter deal with pricing in general. However, setting prices for business products is different from setting prices for consumer products because of factors such as the size of purchases, transportation considerations, and geographic issues. We examine three types of pricing associated with business products: geographic pricing, transfer pricing, and discounting.

地理定价

11-10a Geographic Pricing

Geographic pricing strategies deal with delivery costs. The pricing strategy that requires the buyer to pay the delivery costs is called *FOB origin pricing*. This stands for "free on board at the point of origin," which means that the price does not include freight charges. Thus, the buyer must pay the transportation costs from the seller's warehouse to the buyer's place of business. *FOB destination* indicates that the price does include freight charges, and thus the seller pays these charges.

转让定价

11-10b Transfer Pricing

When one unit within an organization sells a product to another unit, **transfer pricing** occurs. The price is determined by calculating the cost of the product. A transfer price can vary depending on the types of costs included in the calculations. The choice of the costs to include depends on the company's management strategy and the nature of the units' interactions. An organization also must ensure that transfer pricing is fair to all units involved in the purchases.

转让定价
transfer pricing prices charged in sales between an organization's units

折扣
discount a deduction from the price of an item

折扣

11-10c Discounting

A **discount** is a deduction from an item's price. Producers and sellers may offer a wide variety of discounts to their customers, including trade, quantity, cash, and seasonal discounts and allowances. *Trade discounts* are reductions taken off the list prices that are offered to marketing intermediaries, or middlemen. *Quantity discounts* are discounts given to customers who buy in large quantities, which makes the seller's per-unit selling cost lower for larger purchases. *Cash discounts* are concessions offered for prompt payment. A seller may offer a discount of "2/10, net 30," meaning that the buyer receives a 2 percent discount if full payment occurs within ten days; otherwise, payment in full is due within 30 days. A *seasonal discount* is a price reduction to buyers that purchase out of season. This discount encourages off-season sales and ensures steady production throughout the year. An *allowance* is a reduction in price to achieve a desired goal. Trade-in allowances, for example, are price reductions granted for turning in used equipment when purchasing new equipment. Table 11-3 describes some of the reasons for using these discounting techniques and some examples.

> **✓ Concept Check**
> - Describe the three types of pricing associated with business products.
> - Differentiate between FOB origin and FOB destination pricing.
> - Explain the five types of discounts for business products.

Table 11-3 Discounts Used for Business Markets

Type	Reasons for Use	Examples
Trade (functional)	To attract and retain effective resellers by compensating them for performing certain functions, such as transportation, warehousing, selling, and providing credit.	A college bookstore pays about one-third less for a new textbook than the retail price a student pays.
Quantity	To encourage customers to buy large quantities when making purchases and, in the case of cumulative discounts, to encourage customer loyalty.	Large department store chains purchase some women's apparel at lower prices than do individually owned specialty stores.
Cash	To reduce expenses associated with accounts receivable and collection by encouraging prompt payment of accounts.	Numerous companies serving business markets allow a 2 percent discount if an account is paid within ten days.
Seasonal	To allow a marketer to use resources more efficiently by stimulating sales during off-peak periods.	Florida hotels provide companies, holding national and regional sales meetings, with deeply discounted accommodations during the summer months.
Allowance	In the case of a trade-in allowance, to assist the buyer in making the purchase and potentially earn a profit on the resale of used equipment. In the case of a promotional allowance, to ensure that dealers participate in advertising and sales support programs.	A farm equipment dealer takes a farmer's used tractor as a trade-in on a new one. Nabisco pays a promotional allowance to a supermarket for setting up and maintaining a large end-of-aisle display for a two-week period.

Discussion Questions 讨论题

1. What major factor determines whether a product is a consumer or a business product?
2. What are the four stages of the product life cycle? How can a firm determine which stage a particular product is in?
3. Under what conditions does product modification work best?
4. Some companies do not delete products until they become financially threatening. What problems may result from this practice?
5. Why should businesses introduce new products?
6. What is the difference between manufacturer brands and store brands? Between family branding and individual branding?
7. What is the difference between a line extension and a brand extension?
8. For what purposes is labeling used?
9. Compare and contrast the characteristics of price and non-price competition. Under what conditions would a firm be most likely to use non-price competition?
10. How might buyers' perceptions of price influence pricing decisions?
11. What are the five major categories of pricing strategies? Give at least two examples of specific strategies that fall into each category.
12. Identify and describe the main types of discounts that are used in the pricing of business products.
13. Under what conditions would a business most likely decide to employ one of the differential pricing strategies?
14. For what types of products are psychological pricing strategies most likely to be used?

Case 11　案例 11：值得关注的 Shinola

Shinola Is One to Watch

Shinola Watch Company is a luxury design brand that sells timepieces, leather goods, jewelry, and more. The Shinola brand dates back to 1877 when it was a shoe polish company in Rochester, New York. It operated for nearly 100 years before going out of business in 1960. Tom Kartsotis, the founder of Fossil Group, a multi-billion-dollar watch company, decided to create Shinola Watch Company in 2011 with investment group Bedrock Manufacturing. Kartsotis's goal was to create a high-quality American watch brand that could compete with Swiss watchmakers at a lower price point. The company introduced its first watch in 2013, producing 2,500 watches and selling them for $550 each. The watches sold out in two weeks. Shinola was creating timepieces in a way that hadn't been done in the United States since the 1960s.

The company's watch and leather factory is located in Detroit, Michigan. Inside, artisans assemble Shinola's timepieces and other products by hand. The company employs more than 500 people and is committed to delivering the highest quality products. Shinola creates opportunities for its employees with extensive training. Employees meticulously assemble watches by hand. The Shinola team assembles between 500 and 700 watches per day and cuts and sews up to 550 leather watch straps per day. From start to finish, each watch may touch the hands of more than 30 people.

A commitment to quality is at the core of Shinola Watch Company. For example, its watches and leather straps that are produced in-house are done so using labor-intensive methods and custom Italian machinery. For its other leather goods, Shinola partnered with hand-selected manufacturers to scale production. The watchmaker creates products that last and stands behind its craftsmanship with industry-leading guarantees. Shinola offers a limited lifetime warranty of its core watch styles and a best-in-class three-year-limited warranty on its Detrola Watch Collection.

Shinola has promoted itself as an American-made brand and a supporter of Detroit. Its watches are even labeled "Detroit." However, the company's American pride was called into question when the Federal Trade Commission (FTC) discovered that some of its watches were made almost entirely out of foreign parts. The FTC is charged with protecting consumers from deceptive advertising. In response, Shinola changed its labeling to read "built in Detroit" and "Swiss & imported parts."

The company has also been criticized for using Detroit as a marketing tool and exploiting the city's hardships to sell watches. Supporters of the company say this is not the case and highlight the fact that Shinola has supported the local economy by adding jobs and helping to make Detroit a cleaner and safer place. However, recently, the company laid off several employees and announced plans to outsource leather design and product development to keep costs down, remain competitive in the watch industry, and clear a path to profitable growth.

Shinola's customers are its top supporters. Notable customers include former Michigan governor Rick Snyder, Oscar-winning director Peter Farrelly, and former presidents Bill Clinton and Barack Obama. Today, Shinola continues to match its high-quality timepieces along with a variety of other luxury goods. The company operates boutiques in 14 cities in the United States, Canada, and the United Kingdom along with its own boutique hotel in downtown Detroit.[26]

Questions

1. How does Shinola Watch Company back up its commitment to quality?
2. What measures has Shinola taken to keep its prices lower than Swiss competitors?
3. Why do you think Shinola advertises itself as being an American brand?

Chapter

12

Distributing and Promoting Products

产品分销和产品促销

Learning Objectives

Once you complete this chapter, you will be able to:

12-1 Examine the various distribution channels and market coverage of products.

12-2 Explain how supply chain management facilitates partnering among channel members.

12-3 Describe the types of wholesalers and the services they provide.

12-4 Distinguish among the major types of retailers and shopping centers.

12-5 Identify the five most important logistics activities.

12-6 Define integrated marketing communications.

12-7 List the basic elements of the promotion mix.

12-8 Examine advertising, including types of advertising, the advertising campaign, and social and legal considerations.

12-9 Explore personal selling, including the types of salespersons, the personal-selling process, and major sales management tasks.

12-10 Identify sales promotion objectives and methods.

12-11 Describe the types and uses of public relations.

Why Should You Care?

Not only is it important to create and maintain a mix of products that satisfies customers but also to make these products available at the *right place* and *time* and to communicate with customers effectively.

Inside Business 商业透视：沃尔玛整合了采购团队

Walmart Brings Its Buying Teams Together

To increase e-commerce profits and streamline in-store and online operations, Walmart combined its online and store product-buying teams. Before the merger, product manufacturers that wanted the retail giant to carry their products both on Walmart.com and in stores had to pitch their goods to two separate buying teams. Not only were these two functions split, but also the teams worked in different offices. E-commerce teams worked in Arkansas and store teams worked in California and New Jersey.

This inefficiency often created conflict between the units related to pricing. Having separate buying teams became a more prominent issue as Walmart started to use stores to facilitate online home delivery sales. In about 4,700 U.S. locations, Walmart offers a service that allows its customers to buy online and pickup orders from the store parking lot. Additionally, 1,600 currently offer online grocery delivery. The company has been hard at work figuring out how to blend online and in-store inventory and make hard-to-manage categories, such as apparel, available both in-store and online. Bringing its buying teams together follows a move to combine its online and store supply chains and finance teams.

In the new structure, Walmart created six category teams (e.g., food, consumables, apparel, and entertainment) that are each managed by an executive. Restructuring and centralizing merchandising added to the company's product assortment online and made prices as well as the shopper experience more consistent. Walmart's expansion of its online-meets-in-store strategy facilitates its ability to offer a seamless experience on mobile, desktop, or traditional retail spaces. If Walmart can perfect this omnichannel strategy, it will have a major leg up on e-commerce competitor Amazon.[1]

Did you know?

There are approximately 10,500 Walmart stores in 24 countries.

Successful companies like Walmart use multiple avenues of distribution, which helps give them a sustainable competitive advantage. Nearly 2 million firms in the United States help to move products from producers to consumers. Store chains such as Dollar General, Starbucks, Forever 21, and Target operate retail outlets where consumers make purchases. Some retailers, such as Avon Products and Arbonne, send their salespeople to the homes of customers. Other retailers, such as Lands' End and REI, sell in stores, online, through catalogs, or a combination of the three. Still others, such as Amazon, sell primarily online.

In this chapter, we first examine the various distribution channels through which products move as they progress from producer to ultimate user as well as supply chain management. Then we discuss wholesalers, including their types and the services they provide. Next, we focus on retailers, including online retailing, retail stores, shopping centers, and nonstore retailing. We then explore the logistics function and the major modes of transportation that are used to move goods. We then turn our attention to integrated marketing communication and the elements of the promotion mix. Finally, we discuss each element of the promotion mix: advertising, personal selling, sales promotion, and public relations.

分销渠道及市场覆盖

12-1 Distribution Channels and Market Coverage

A **distribution channel** (or **marketing channel**) is a sequence of marketing organizations that directs a product from the producer to the ultimate user. Every marketing channel begins with the producer and ends with either the consumer or the business user. A marketing organization that links a producer and user within a marketing channel is called a **middleman** (or **marketing intermediary**). For the most part, middlemen are concerned with the transfer of *ownership* of products along their journey from producer to customer. In many cases, intermediaries handle the product, including its ownership, and add their own value as they move it along the distribution channel. Let's take a closer look at these channels and intermediaries.

Learning Objective

12-1 Examine the various distribution channels and market coverage of products.

常用分销渠道

12-1a Commonly Used Distribution Channels

Different channels of distribution generally are used to move consumer and business products. Figure 12-1 illustrates the most common distribution channels for consumer and business products.

Producer to Consumer This channel, often called the *direct channel*, has no marketing intermediaries. Most services and a few consumer goods are distributed through a direct channel. If you buy a laptop directly from Apple's or Dell's website, you are using a direct channel. Direct marketing via the internet has become a critically important part of many companies' distribution strategies, often as a complement to selling products in retail stores. A growing number of companies have disrupted their industries by selling directly to consumers online using a *direct-to-consumer (D2C)* strategy, including Warby Parker, Casper, Bonobos, and Glossier.

Producers sell directly to consumers for several reasons. They can better control the quality and price of their products. They can maintain closer relationships with customers and better understand their needs. Also, they do not have to pay (through discounts) for the services of intermediaries.

分销渠道（或营销渠道）
distribution channel (or **marketing channel**) a sequence of marketing organizations that directs a product from the producer to the ultimate user

中间商（或营销中介）
middleman (or **marketing intermediary**) a marketing organization that links a producer and user within a marketing channel

Figure 12-1 Distribution Channels

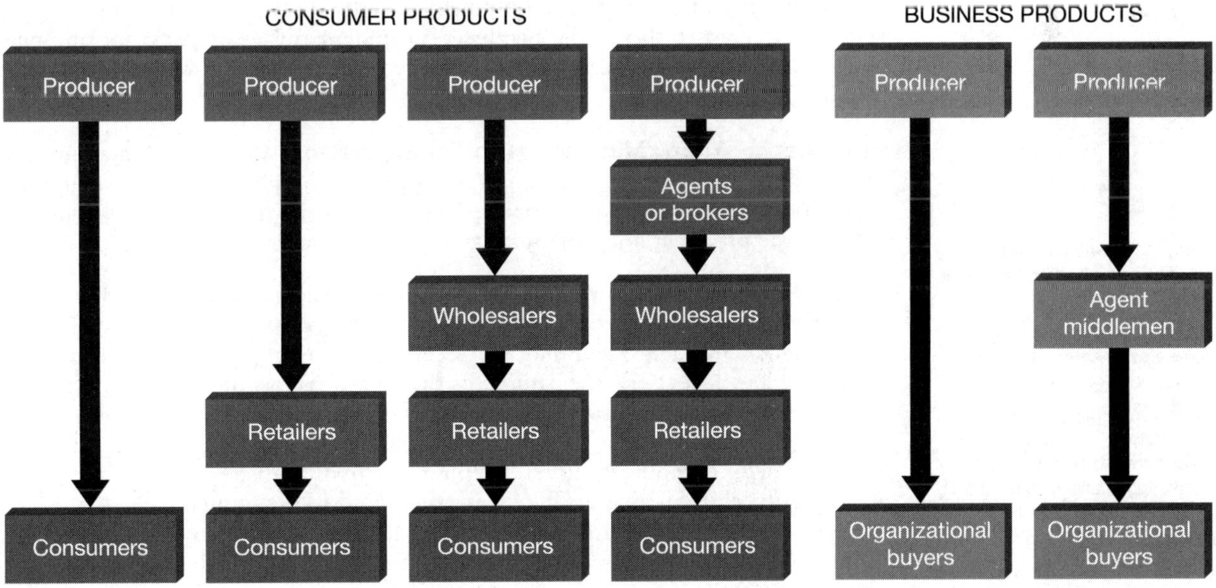

Using multiple marketing channels. Sometimes, companies use multiple marketing channels rather than just one. College textbook publishers often sell their products through multiple marketing channels. This textbook can be purchased directly from the publisher. It can also be purchased at a campus bookstore, or through Amazon.

Producer to Retailer to Consumer A **retailer** is an intermediary that buys from producers or other middlemen and sells to consumers. Producers sell directly to retailers when the retailers are large enough to buy in large quantities. This channel is used most often for products that are bulky, such as furniture and automobiles, for which additional handling would increase marketing costs. It is also the usual channel for perishable products, such as fruits and vegetables, and for clothing.

Producer to Wholesaler to Retailer to Consumer This channel is known as the *traditional channel* because many consumer goods (especially convenience goods) pass through wholesalers to retailers. A **wholesaler** is an intermediary that sells products to other firms. These businesses may be retailers, industrial users, or other wholesalers. A producer uses wholesalers when its products are carried by so many retailers that the producer cannot manage and distribute all of them. For example, chewing gum and candy manufacturers often use this type of channel.

Producer to Agent to Wholesaler to Retailer to Consumer Producers can use agents to reach wholesalers. Agents are functional middlemen that do not take title to products and are compensated by commissions paid by producers. Often the products with which agents deal are inexpensive, frequently purchased items. For example, to reach a large number of potential customers, a small manufacturer of gas-powered lawn trimmers might choose to use agents to market them to wholesalers. The wholesalers then sell the product to a large network of retailers. This channel is also used for seasonal products (such as Christmas decorations) and by producers that do not have in-house sales forces.

Producer to Organizational Buyer In this direct channel, the manufacturer's own sales force sells directly to organizational buyers, or business users. Heavy machinery, aircraft, and major equipment usually are distributed in this way. The very short channel allows the producer to understand customers' specific needs and to provide them with expert and timely services, such as delivery, machinery installation, and repairs.

Producer to Agent Middleman to Organizational Buyer Manufacturers use this channel to distribute such items as operating supplies, accessory equipment, small tools, and standardized parts. The agent is an independent intermediary between the producer and the user. Agents generally represent sellers.

Using Multiple Channels Often a manufacturer uses different distribution channels to reach different market segments. For example, candy bars may be sold through channels containing wholesalers and retailers, as well as channels in which the producer sells them directly through large retailers. Today, businesses are likely to engage in **multichannel (**or **omnichannel) distribution**—the use of a variety of marketing channels to ensure maximum distribution. Dell, for example, sells computers direct, through its own website, as well as through strategically chosen retailers like Best Buy. Multiple channels are also used to increase sales or to capture a larger share of the market with the goal of selling as much merchandise as possible. Some products forgo physical distribution altogether: **Digital distribution** involves delivering content through the internet to a computer or other device. For example, when you stream content on Netflix

零售商
retailer an intermediary that buys from producers or other middlemen and sells to consumers

批发商
wholesaler an intermediary that sells products to other firms

多渠道（或全渠道）分销
multichannel (or **omnichannel) distribution** the use of a variety of marketing channels to ensure maximum distribution

数字分销
digital distribution delivering content through the internet to a computer or other device

or Spotify, subscribe to Office 365 software, or book a rental through Airbnb, you are making use of a digital distribution channel.

市场覆盖水平
12-1b Level of Market Coverage

As with other marketing decisions, producers must analyze all relevant factors when deciding which distribution channels and intermediaries to use. Marketers should weigh the firm's production capabilities and marketing resources, the target market and buying patterns of potential customers, and the product itself. After evaluating these factors, the producer chooses the appropriate level of *intensity of market coverage*. Then the producer selects channels and intermediaries to implement that coverage.

Intensive distribution is the use of all available outlets for a product. It gives a product the widest possible exposure in the marketplace. The manufacturer reaches the market by selling to any intermediary of good financial standing that is willing to stock and sell the product. For the consumer, intensive distribution means being able to shop at a convenient store and spend minimum time selecting and buying the product. Many convenience goods, including candy, gum, and soft drinks, are distributed intensively.

Selective distribution is the use of only a portion of the available outlets for a product in each geographic area. Manufacturers of goods such as furniture, major home appliances, and clothing typically prefer selective distribution. For instance, you may prefer Hanes brand socks, which are distributed through retailers such as Target and Kohl's.

Exclusive distribution is the use of only a single retail outlet for a product in a large geographic area. Exclusive distribution usually is limited to prestigious products. It is appropriate, for instance, for specialty goods such as grand pianos, fine china, and expensive jewelry. The producer usually places many requirements (such as inventory levels, sales training, service quality, and warranty procedures) on exclusive dealers. For example, Patek Philippe watches, which may sell for $500,000 or more, are available in only a few select locations.

✓ Concept Check

- How do the different types of intermediaries link a producer to a user within a marketing channel?
- Describe the six distribution channels. Give an example of each.
- Explain the three intensities of market coverage. Which types of products are generally associated with each of the different intensity levels?

通过供应链管理建立伙伴关系
12-2 Partnering Through Supply Chain Management

Learning Objective

12-2 Explain how supply chain management facilitates partnering among channel members.

Supply chain management refers to the coordination of all marketing channel activities associated with the flow and transformation of supplies, products, and information throughout the supply chain to the ultimate consumer. It requires cooperation throughout the entire marketing channel, including manufacturing, research, sales, advertising, and shipping. Supply chains focus not only on producers, wholesalers, retailers, and customers, but also on component-parts suppliers, shipping companies, communication companies, and other organizations that participate in product distribution. Suppliers strongly influence what items retail stores carry.

Supply chain management encourages cooperation in reducing the costs of inventory, transportation, administration, and handling. It also accelerates order-cycle times and increases profits for all channel members. When buyers, sellers, marketing intermediaries, and facilitating agencies work together, customers' needs regarding delivery, scheduling, packaging, and other requirements are better met. As an example, Procter & Gamble developed new packaging for its leading laundry brands to make them easier to ship to customers who order them from online retailers. The new packaging for Tide laundry detergent concentrates the liquid in a sealed bag with a dripless spout inside of a shoe-box sized container, which Amazon and other online retailers can ship without additional packaging. The new designs are environmentally friendlier and provide greater value for retailers, shippers, and customers.[2]

密集分销
intensive distribution the use of all available outlets for a product

选择性分销
selective distribution the use of only a portion of the available outlets for a product in each geographic area

独家经销
exclusive distribution the use of only a single retail outlet for a product in a large geographic area

供应链管理
supply chain management the coordination of all marketing channel activities associated with the flow and transformation of supplies, products, and information throughout the supply chain to the ultimate consumer

Sustaining the Planet

保护地球：千禧一代青睐符合伦理的钻石

Millennials Take a Shining to Ethically Sourced Diamonds

Diamonds are thought to be synonymous with love, but it's love for planet Earth that's leading to their downfall. Diamonds, which are mined from the earth, are inherently unsustainable. A new wave of jewelry makers is using lab-grown and recycled diamonds as well as recycled metals to appeal to Millennials. De Beers, an international diamond mining company, popularized the diamond engagement ring in the 1940s, a time when the company controlled 90 percent of the diamond market. Millennials often see through marketing ploys and are more focused on ethics, social responsibility, and sustainability than prior generations, a trend that seems likely to continue with Generation Z.

Man-made diamonds are chemically the same as natural diamonds. They both have the same crystal structure and are assigned the same grades based on the four Cs: carat, cut, clarity, and color. Plus, lab-grown diamonds tend to be more affordable than diamonds that are mined from the earth. The Diamond Producers Association implied that lab-grown diamonds are not real in its "Real Is Rare, Real Is a Diamond" smear campaign, but the Federal Trade Commission responded by issuing new guidelines that established lab-grown diamonds are in fact "real."

This new crop of sustainable jewelry makers is forcing old-school jewelry companies to adapt. Though retailers initially attempted to discredit and disparage lab-grown diamonds, the tactic flopped. Kay Jewelers and Jared, for example, now offer lab-created diamond jewelry as well. Despite the rise in sustainable diamond sales, the jewelry industry as a whole is grappling with declining consumer demand. Every segment (mass, premium, and luxury) has been affected. Eco-friendly jewelry companies and traditional jewelers alike have been negatively affected by declining marriage rates. Traditional jewelers are now on board with the eco-friendly alternative because it could spark more excitement and attract a new generation of customers.

Sources: Based on information in Pamela N. Danziger, "Lab-Grown and Natural Diamond Industries End Hostilities, as Declining Jewelry Demand Threatens All," *Forbes*, July 19, 2020; Lane Florsheim, "For Engagement Rings, Are Natural Diamonds on the Way Out?" *The Wall Street Journal*, September 25, 2020; Stephanie Osmanski, "Why You Should Consider Ethical and Sustainable Diamonds," *Green Matters*, May 20, 2019.

Technology has enhanced the implementation of supply chain management significantly. Through computerized integrated information sharing, channel members reduce costs and improve customer service. Additionally, technologies such as blockchain, artificial intelligence (AI), and robotics can help improve efficiency, responsiveness, and transparency throughout the supply chain. DHL, for example, has invested more than $300 million in AI and robotics technologies for the benefits of its customers. AI helps the shipping company analyze its supply chain to identify areas for improvement, while specialized robots have increased the company's productivity and safety by reducing mistakes and shortening the time required for routine or physically demanding activities.[3] As many major industries transform their processes, the end result is increased productivity by reducing inventory, shortening cycle time, and reducing wasted human effort.

✓ Concept Check

- How does supply chain management encourage cooperation between buyers and sellers?
- How has technology enhanced the implementation of supply-chain management?

营销中介：批发商

12-3 Marketing Intermediaries: Wholesalers

Learning Objective

12-3 Describe the types of wholesalers and the services they provide.

Wholesalers are possibly the most misunderstood of marketing intermediaries. Producers sometimes try to cut out wholesalers in favor of dealing directly with retailers or consumers. However, wholesalers increase distribution efficiency. The marketing activities performed by wholesalers *must* be performed by other channel members if wholesalers are eliminated, which means that cutting out wholesalers may not reduce distribution costs.

Wholesalers facilitate trade by connecting manufacturers with retailers. A general-merchandise wholesaler buys many types of products from a broad range of manufacturers, warehouses the products, and then sells them to retailers. So, instead of having to contact hundreds of different manufacturers to stock their shelves, retailers need to contact only a small number of wholesalers.

批发商向零售商和制造商提供服务
12-3a Wholesalers Provide Services to Retailers and Manufacturers

Wholesalers help retailers by:

- Buying in large quantities and selling to retailers in smaller quantities and delivering goods to retailers.
- Stocking in one place the variety of goods that retailers otherwise would have to buy from many producers.
- Providing assistance in other vital areas, including promotion, market information, and financial aid.

Wholesalers help manufacturers by:

- Performing functions similar to those provided to retailers.
- Providing a sales force, reducing inventory costs, assuming credit risks, and furnishing market information.

批发商的类型
12-3b Types of Wholesalers

Wholesalers generally fall into two categories: merchant wholesalers, and agents and brokers. Of these, merchant wholesalers constitute the largest portion. They account for about four-fifths of all wholesale establishments and employees.

Merchant Wholesalers A **merchant wholesaler** is an intermediary that purchases goods in large quantities and sells them to other wholesalers or retailers and to institutional, farm, government, professional, or industrial users.

Merchant wholesalers have the following characteristics:

- They usually operate one or more warehouses at which they receive, take title to, and store goods. These wholesalers are sometimes called *distributors* or *jobbers*.
- Most merchant wholesalers are businesses composed of salespeople, order takers, receiving and shipping clerks, inventory managers, and office personnel.
- The successful merchant wholesaler must analyze available products and market needs. It must be able to adapt the type, variety, and quality of its products to changing market conditions.
- Merchant wholesalers may be classified as full-service or limited-service wholesalers depending on the number of services they provide. A **full-service wholesaler** performs the entire range of wholesaler functions. These functions

批发销售商
merchant wholesaler an intermediary that purchases goods in large quantities and sells them to other wholesalers or retailers and to institutional, farm, government, professional, or industrial users

全方位服务批发商
full-service wholesaler an intermediary that performs the entire range of wholesaler functions

include delivering goods, supplying warehousing, arranging for credit, supporting promotional activities, and providing general customer assistance.

A full-service wholesaler can be of the following three different types:

- A **general-merchandise wholesaler** deals in a wide variety of products, such as over-the-counter medications, hardware, nonperishable foods, cosmetics, detergents, and tobacco.
- A **limited-line wholesaler** stocks only a few product lines but carries numerous product items within each line.
- A **specialty wholesaler** carries a select group of products within a single line. Food delicacies, such as shellfish, represent a product handled by this type of wholesaler. One type of specialty wholesaler you may encounter is a *rack jobber,* which owns and stocks display racks in supermarkets, drugstores, and discount and variety stores.

一般商品批发商
general-merchandise wholesaler an intermediary that deals in a wide variety of products

有限产品线批发商
limited-line wholesaler an intermediary that stocks only a few product lines but carries numerous product items within each line

专业批发商
specialty wholesaler an intermediary that carries a select group of products within a single line

代理人
agent an intermediary that expedites exchanges, represents a buyer or a seller, and often is hired permanently on a commission basis

经纪人
broker an intermediary that specializes in a particular commodity, represents either a buyer or a seller, and is likely to be hired on a temporary basis

Agents and Brokers Agents and brokers perform a small number of marketing activities and are paid a commission that is a percentage of the sales price. They do not take ownership of the products they carry.

An **agent** is an intermediary that expedites exchanges, represents a buyer or a seller, and often is hired permanently on a commission basis. When agents represent producers, they are known as *sales agents* or *manufacturer's agents*. As long as the products represented do not compete, a sales agent may represent one or several manufacturers on a commission basis. The agent solicits orders for the manufacturers within a specific territory. As a rule, the manufacturers ship the merchandise and bill the customers directly. The manufacturers also set the prices and other conditions of the sales. The sales agent provides immediate entry into a territory, regular calls on customers, selling experience, and a known, predetermined selling expense (a commission that is a percentage of sales revenue).

A **broker** is an intermediary that specializes in a particular commodity, represents either a buyer or a seller, and is likely to be hired on a temporary basis. Food brokers that sell grocery products to resellers are the exception to this rule. They generally have long-term relationships with clients. Brokers may perform only the selling function or both buying and selling using their established contacts and specialized knowledge of their fields.

✓ Concept Check

- What services do wholesalers provide to producers and to retailers?
- Identify and describe the various types of wholesalers.

营销中介：零售商

12-4 Marketing Intermediaries: Retailers

线上零售
online retailing retailing that makes products available to buyers through computer or mobile connections

Learning Objective

12-4 Distinguish among the major types of retailers and shopping centers.

Retailers are the final link between producers and consumers. Retailers may buy from either wholesalers or producers. They can sell goods, services (such as auto repairs or haircuts), or both. Home Depot, for instance, sells consumer goods, financial services, and installation and repair services for home appliances purchased at Home Depot.

The U.S. Bureau of Labor Statistics reports that the United States has about 1 million retail establishments ringing up total sales of more than $4 trillion.[4] Most retailers are small, with annual revenues well under $1 million. However, some retailers are quite large, with hundreds or even thousands of stores. Table 12-1 lists the ten largest retail organizations in the United States, their sales revenues, and number of stores. In recent years, conventional retail stores have faced numerous challenges, including changing consumer habits, the growth of online shopping, and the COVID-19 pandemic.

线上和多渠道零售

12-4a Online and Multichannel Retailing

As you probably know from firsthand experience, **online retailing** makes products available to buyers through computer or mobile connections. Online retailing is a rapidly growing segment with sales expected to exceed $1 trillion by 2023;

Table 12-1 The Ten Largest U.S. Retailers

Rank	Company	Sales (in billions)	# of Stores
1	Walmart	$524.0	5,355
2	Amazon	$250.5	564
3	Costco	$152.7	542
4	Walgreens Boots Alliance	$136.9	9,168
5	Kroger	$122.3	3,003
6	Home Depot	$110.5	1,973
7	CVS Health	$88.5	9,909
8	Target	$77.1	1,868
9	Lowe's	$72.2	1,727
10	Albertsons	$62.4	2,258

Source: National Retail Federation, "Top 100 Retailers 2020 List".

online purchases now account for 19 percent of all retail sales and are expected to grow to 33 percent by 2030.[5] Business and consumer spending on sites like Amazon, Alibaba, and Jet have come at the expense of conventional stores. To remain competitive, most retailers today have websites to sell products, provide information about their company, and offer incentives. Nordstrom, for example, gets more than one-half of its sales online, and its online presence supports its conventional stores.[6] Larger retailers like Starbucks, Best Buy, and Kohl's also have their own apps for customers to carry out retailing activities on their tablets or smartphones wherever they may be. Starbucks' app, for example, allows customers to order and pay right from their phone as well as accumulate loyalty reward points, while Target's app lets customers shop online and arrange for pickup or delivery or to find products in the store and identify coupons and other savings.

Many retailers today actually engage in **multichannel retailing** by employing multiple types of retailing. These retailers integrate a particular combination of brick-and-mortar stores, websites, apps, catalogs, direct-response marketing, telemarketing, and even vending so that a customer can research a product and purchase it from home, work, or in the car. D2C mattress retailer Casper, for example, has opened brick-and-mortar stores where customers can try out its mattresses before they buy. The company also has partnerships with retailers such as Sam's Club and Ashley HomeStore so that consumers can try out mattresses. These stores complement Casper's online efforts by opening more avenues for interacting with customers wherever they want to shop.[7]

多渠道零售
multichannel retailing employing multiple types of retailing

独立零售商
independent retailer a firm that operates only one retail outlet

连锁零售商
chain retailer a company that operates more than one retail outlet

零售店的类型
12-4b Types of Retail Stores

One way to classify retailers is by the number of stores owned and operated by the firm.

1. An **independent retailer** is a firm that operates only one retail outlet. Most retailers are independent, one-store operators that generally provide personal service and a convenient location.
2. A **chain retailer** is a company that operates more than one retail outlet. By adding outlets, chain retailers reach new geographic markets. As sales increase, chains usually buy merchandise in larger

Utilizing multiple retail approaches. Many retailers use multichannel retailing to reach potential customers. IKEA operates more than 455 retail stores in 52 countries. It also engages in direct marketing through online retailing.

Accessing customers through different types of retailers. When people are asked to name a retailer, they often think of brick-and-mortar establishments like the one shown in this photo. However, retailing goes on in all kinds of places, including in people's homes and workplaces, online, over the phone and on TV, and even on the streets.

quantities and thus take advantage of quantity discounts. They also wield more power in their dealings with suppliers. There are many fewer chain retail organizations than independent retailers.

Another way to classify retail stores is by store size and the kind and number of products carried. We will now take a closer look at store types based on these dimensions.

Department Stores These large retail establishments consist of several sections, or departments, that sell a wide assortment of products. The U.S. Census Bureau defines a **department store** as a retail store that (1) employs 25 or more persons and (2) sells at least home furnishings, appliances, family apparel, and household linens and dry goods, each in a different part of the store. Macy's, Kohl's, Selfridges, and Printemps are examples of large, international, department stores. Traditionally, department stores have been service-oriented. Along with the goods they sell, these retailers provide credit, personal assistance, liberal return policies, and pleasant shopping atmospheres.

Discount Stores A **discount store** is a self-service general-merchandise outlet that sells products at lower-than-usual prices. Stores like Target and Walmart operate on smaller markups and higher merchandise turnover than other retailers and offer minimal customer services. There has been a rise of extreme-value stores like Dollar General and Dollar Tree, which are a fraction of the size of conventional discount stores and typically offer very low prices on smaller-size name-brand nonperishable household items.

Warehouse Showrooms A **warehouse showroom** is a retail facility with five basic characteristics: (1) a large, low-cost building, (2) warehouse materials-handling technology, (3) vertical merchandise displays, (4) a large, on-premises inventory, and (5) minimal service. Some of the best-known showrooms are operated by big furniture retailers, including IKEA. These operations employ few personnel and offer few services. Most customers carry away purchases in the manufacturer's carton and assemble the products themselves, although some warehouse showrooms will deliver for a fee.

Convenience Stores A **convenience store** is a small food store that sells a limited variety of products but remains open well beyond normal business hours. Because convenience stores are common, most patrons of a particular store live within a mile of it. 7-Eleven, Circle K, Turkey Hill, and Open Pantry stores, for example, are convenience stores found either regionally or nationally in the United States. Limited product mixes and higher prices keep convenience stores from threatening the business of other grocery retailers. There are more than 150,000 convenience stores in the United States.[8]

Supermarkets A **supermarket** is a large self-service store that sells primarily food and household products. It stocks fresh, canned, frozen, and processed foods, paper products, and cleaning supplies. Sometimes called grocery stores, supermarkets also may sell such items as housewares, toiletries, toys and games, pharmacy products, stationery, books and magazines, plants and flowers, and a few clothing items. Supermarkets like Kroger, Albertsons, and H-E-B are large-scale operations that emphasize low prices and one-stop shopping for household needs.

Superstores A **superstore** is a large retail store that carries not only food and nonfood products ordinarily found in supermarkets, but also additional product lines

百货商店
department store a retail store that (1) employs 25 or more persons and (2) sells at least home furnishings, appliances, family apparel, and household linens and dry goods, each in a different part of the store

折扣店
discount store a self-service general-merchandise outlet that sells products at lower-than-usual prices

仓储式展厅
warehouse showroom a retail facility in a large, low-cost building with a large on-premises inventory and minimal service

便利店
convenience store a small food store that sells a limited variety of products but remains open well beyond normal business hours

超市
supermarket a large self-service store that sells primarily food and household products

大型超级商场
superstore a large retail store that carries not only food and nonfood products ordinarily found in supermarkets but also additional product lines

such as housewares, hardware, small appliances, clothing, personal-care products, garden products, and automotive merchandise. Superstores also provide services, including automotive repair, snack bars and restaurants, photo printing, and banking. Target, Walmart, and H-E-B operate some superstores.

Warehouse Clubs The **warehouse club** is a large-scale members-only establishment that combines features of cash-and-carry wholesaling with discount retailing. For an annual fee, small retailers or individuals may become members and purchase products at low prices for business use, for resale, or for personal use. Because their product lines are shallow and sales volumes are high, warehouse clubs like Sam's Club and Costco can offer a broad range of merchandise, including perishable and nonperishable foods, beverages, books, appliances, housewares, automotive parts, hardware, and furniture.

Killing the competition? Or not? Home Depot is an example of a category killer. Category killers aren't likely to annihilate all of the competition though. Small retailers with less product variety and higher prices have found it difficult to compete against category killers. However, small retailers that carry a smaller inventory of products that are different from those stocked by category killers and compete on the basis of service, rather than price, can survive.

Traditional Specialty Stores A **traditional specialty store** carries a narrow product mix with deep product lines. Traditional specialty stores are sometimes called *limited-line retailers*. If they have depth in one product category, such as baked goods or jewelry, they may be called *single-line retailers*. Specialty stores usually offer deeper product mixes than department stores. They attract customers by emphasizing service, atmosphere, and location. Consumers who are dissatisfied with the impersonal atmosphere of large retailers often find the attention offered by specialty stores appealing. Specialty stores include chains such as the Gap, Bath and Body Works, and Foot Locker, as well as many independent stores.

Off-Price Retailers An **off-price retailer** is a store that buys manufacturers' seconds, overruns, returns, and off-season merchandise at below-wholesale prices and sells them to consumers at deep discounts. Off-price retailers sell limited lines of national-brand and designer merchandise, usually clothing, shoes, or housewares. Off-price retailers include T.J. Maxx, Burlington, and Ross. Off-price stores charge up to 50 percent less than department stores for comparable merchandise but offer few customer services. They often include community dressing rooms and central checkout counters. Some off-price retailers have a no-returns, no-exchanges policy.

Category Killers A **category killer** is a very large specialty store that concentrates on a single product line and competes by offering low prices and an enormous number of products. These stores are called *category killers* because they take business away from smaller, higher-priced retail stores. Category killers such as PetSmart and Office Depot are seeing increased competition from online retailing. The cost of maintaining such large stores can drain a company of its profits.

购物中心的类型
12-4c Types of Shopping Centers

There are several different types of shopping centers where retailers can choose to locate. A *planned shopping center* is a self-contained retail facility operated by independent owners and consisting of various stores. Shopping centers are designed and promoted to serve diverse groups of customers with widely differing needs. The management of a shopping center strives for a coordinated mix of stores, a comfortable atmosphere, adequate parking, pleasant landscaping, and special events to attract customers. The convenience of shopping for most family and household

仓储会员店
warehouse club a large-scale members-only establishment that combines features of cash-and-carry wholesaling with discount retailing

传统专卖店
traditional specialty store a store that carries a narrow product mix with deep product lines

低价零售店
off-price retailer a store that buys manufacturers' seconds, overruns, returns, and off-season merchandise for resale to consumers at deep discounts

品类杀手
category killer a very large specialty store that concentrates on a single product line and competes on the basis of low prices and product availability

Lifestyle shopping center. Lifestyle shopping centers include specialty retailers, restaurants, and areas for cultural activities in an open-air setting.

needs in a single location is an important element of shopping-center appeal. There are several types of shopping centers: lifestyle, neighborhood, community, or regional.

A **lifestyle shopping center** is a shopping center that has an open-air configuration and is occupied primarily by upscale national chain specialty stores. The lifestyle shopping center model is popular because it combines shopping with the feel of strolling along Main Street. Some lifestyle shopping centers, like The Domain in Austin, Texas, include residences and offices above the stores, as well as activities and culture in their design in order to attract a wide variety of people.

A **neighborhood shopping center**, also called a *strip mall,* typically consists of several small convenience and specialty stores. Businesses in neighborhood shopping centers might include small grocery stores, drugstores, gas stations, and fast-food restaurants. These retailers serve consumers who live less than ten minutes away, usually within a two- to three-mile radius. Unlike in a lifestyle shopping center, most purchases in the neighborhood shopping center are based on convenience or personal contact. These retailers generally make only limited efforts to coordinate their promotional activities.

A **community shopping center** includes one or two department stores and some specialty stores, along with convenience stores. It attracts consumers from a wider geographic area who will drive longer distances to find products and specialty items unavailable in neighborhood shopping centers. Community shopping centers, which are carefully planned and coordinated, generate traffic with special events such as art exhibits, automobile shows, and sidewalk sales. The management of a community shopping center maintains a mix of tenants so that the center offers wide product mixes and deep product lines.

A **regional shopping center** usually has large department stores, numerous specialty stores, restaurants, movie theaters, and sometimes even hotels. It carries a similar mix of merchandise to that available in a downtown shopping district. Regional shopping centers carefully coordinate management and marketing activities to reach the 150,000 or more customers in their target market. These large centers usually advertise, hold special events, and may even provide transportation for customers. National chain stores can gain leases in regional shopping centers more easily than small independent stores because they are better able to meet the centers' financial requirements.

In addition to these types of shopping centers, outlet malls feature discount and factory outlet stores carrying traditional manufacturer brands, such as Polo Ralph Lauren, Nike, Guess, and Sunglass Hut. Some outlet centers feature upscale products from last season, discounted for quick sale. Manufacturers own these stores and make a special effort to avoid conflict with traditional retailers of their products. Manufacturers place these stores in noncompetitive locations, often outside of metropolitan areas. Factory outlet centers attract value-conscious customers seeking quality and major brand names. They operate in much the same way as regional shopping centers, but usually draw customers, some of whom may be tourists, from a larger shopping radius.

生活方式购物中心
lifestyle shopping center an open-air-environment shopping center with upscale chain specialty stores

邻里购物中心
neighborhood shopping center a planned shopping center consisting of several small convenience and specialty stores

社区购物中心
community shopping center a planned shopping center that includes one or two department stores and some specialty stores, along with convenience stores

区域性购物中心
regional shopping center a planned shopping center containing large department stores, numerous specialty stores, restaurants, movie theaters, and sometimes even hotels

无店铺零售
nonstore retailing selling that does not take place in conventional store facilities

无店铺零售
12-4d Nonstore Retailing

Nonstore retailing is selling that does not take place in conventional store facilities. Consumers may purchase products without ever visiting a store. This form of retailing accounts for an increasing percentage of total retail sales. Nonstore retailers use direct selling, direct marketing, and vending.

Direct Selling **Direct selling** is the marketing of products to customers through face-to-face sales presentations at home or in the workplace. Traditionally called *door-to-door selling,* direct selling in the United States began with peddlers more than a century ago and is now a major industry with $35 billion in U.S. sales annually.[9] Instead of the door-to-door approach, many companies today—such as Mary Kay, Amway, and Avon—use other approaches. They can identify customers by mail, telephone, or the internet and then set up appointments. Direct selling sometimes involves the "party plan," which can occur in the customer's home or workplace. Direct selling through the party plan requires effective salespeople who identify potential hosts and provide encouragement and incentives for them to organize a gathering. Companies that commonly use the party plan are Tupperware, Cutco, and Pampered Chef.

Direct Marketing **Direct marketing** is the use of the telephone, internet, and nonpersonal media to communicate product and organizational information to customers, who then can purchase products via mail, telephone, or the internet. Direct marketing can occur online (discussed earlier) and through catalog marketing, direct-response marketing, telemarketing, and television home shopping.

In **catalog marketing**, an organization provides a catalog from which customers make selections and place orders by mail, telephone, or the internet. Catalog marketing began in 1872 when Montgomery Ward issued its first catalog to rural families. There are thousands of catalog marketing companies in the United States, many of which publish online. Some catalog marketers sell products spread over multiple product lines, while others are more specialized. Catalog companies, such as Burpee (seeds and plants) and Coldwater Creek (women's apparel), offer considerable depth in only one major product line. The advantages of catalog marketing include efficiency and convenience for customers because they do not have to visit a store. The retailer benefits by being able to locate in remote, low-cost areas, save on expensive store fixtures, and reduce both personal selling and store operating expenses. Disadvantages are that catalog marketing is inflexible, provides limited service, and is most effective for only a selected set of products.

Direct-response marketing occurs when a retailer advertises a product and makes it available through mail, telephone, or online orders. This marketing method has resulted in some products gaining widespread popularity. You may have heard of the Shamwow, Snuggie, and Magic Bullet—all of which became popular through direct response television marketing campaigns. Direct-response marketing can also be conducted by sending letters, samples, brochures, or booklets to prospects on a mailing list.

Telemarketing is the performance of marketing-related activities by telephone. Some organizations use a prescreened list of prospective clients. Telemarketing has many advantages, such as generating sales leads, improving customer service, speeding up payments on past-due accounts, raising funds for nonprofit organizations, and gathering market data. However, many consumers do not like being contacted by marketers via the phone and increasingly restrictive telemarketing laws have made it a less appealing marketing method. In 2003, U.S. Congress implemented a national do-not-call registry, which lists more than 241 million people who wish to opt out of telemarketing calls. Companies that make telemarketing phone calls must pay for access to the do-not-call registry and must obtain updated numbers from the registry at least every three days. The Federal Trade Commission (FTC) enforces violations, and companies are subject to fines of up to $16,000 for each call made to numbers on the list. The Federal Communications Commission (FCC) further outlaws prerecorded calls—"robocalls"—from companies for marketing purposes. However, new technologies mean that some unscrupulous firms are increasingly ignoring the National Do Not Call Registry and using robocalls for telemarketing purposes.[10]

Television home shopping presents products to television viewers, encouraging them to order through toll-free numbers and pay with credit cards.

直销
direct selling the marketing of products to customers through face-to-face sales presentations at home or in the workplace

直接营销
direct marketing the use of the telephone, internet, and nonpersonal media to introduce products to customers, who then can purchase them via mail, telephone, or the internet

目录营销
catalog marketing a type of marketing in which an organization provides a catalog from which customers make selections and place orders by mail, telephone, or the internet

直复营销
direct-response marketing a type of marketing in which a retailer advertises a product and makes it available through mail, telephone, or online orders

电话营销
telemarketing the performance of marketing-related activities by telephone

电视家庭购物
television home shopping a form of selling in which products are presented to television viewers, who can buy them by calling a toll-free number and paying with a credit card

> **✓ Concept Check**
> - Describe the major types of retail stores. Give an example of each.
> - What are the most common types of shopping centers, and what types of store does each typically contain?
> - How does nonstore retailing occur?

Home Shopping Network (HSN) originated and popularized this format. Most homes in the United States receive at least one home shopping channel.

Vending **Vending** is the use of machines to dispense products. Vending, which accounts for less than 2 percent of all retail sales, is one of the most impersonal forms of retailing. Small, standardized, routinely purchased products can be sold in machines because they do not readily spoil and consumers appreciate the convenience. Customers can now find a wide variety of products dispensed via vending machine, even high-end items such as gold bars, cars, and iPods as well as cosmetics and food.

物流

12-5 Logistics

Learning Objective

12-5 Identify the five most important logistics activities.

自动售货机
vending the use of machines to dispense products

物流
logistics all those activities concerned with the efficient flow and storage of products from the producer to the ultimate user

Logistics, also known as physical distribution, is all those activities concerned with the efficient flow and storage of products from the producer to the ultimate user. Logistics, therefore, is the movement of the products themselves—both goods and services—through their channels of distribution. The annual cost of business logistics in the United States is tremendous, at $1.63 trillion. To put this in perspective, logistics costs are 7.6 percent of gross domestic product (GDP).[11] It combines several interrelated business functions, the most important of which are inventory management, order processing, warehousing, materials handling, and transportation. Because these functions and their costs are highly interrelated, marketers view logistics as an integrated effort that supports other marketing activities. The overall goal of logistics is to get the right product to the right place at the right time and at minimal total cost.

Technology and Innovation

技术与创新：开启无人机送货时代

Drone Delivery Takes Off

Drones, which have grown rapidly in popularity, have many potential applications for business such as inventory management, package delivery, surveillance, and aerial photography. While commercial deployment has been slow due to regulation issues, society has begun to realize, thanks to the COVID-19 pandemic, that the utility of these unmanned aerial vehicles may outweigh potential risks.

During the pandemic, when social distancing was an imperative, drone delivery pilot programs experienced a surge. For example, Wing, operated by Alphabet, has been working on making drone delivery a reality since 2012. It doubled deployment rates during the global health crisis, working with FedEx and Walgreens to deliver household goods and select food items from a local bakery in Christiansburg, Virginia. This afforded customers greater access to necessities. Likewise, JD.com, the largest retailer in China, made deliveries to rural villages and semi-isolated islands. The crisis drove changes in policy because drones were seen as a way to reduce human contact during the pandemic. For delivery programs to become widespread, regulations need to advance even further.

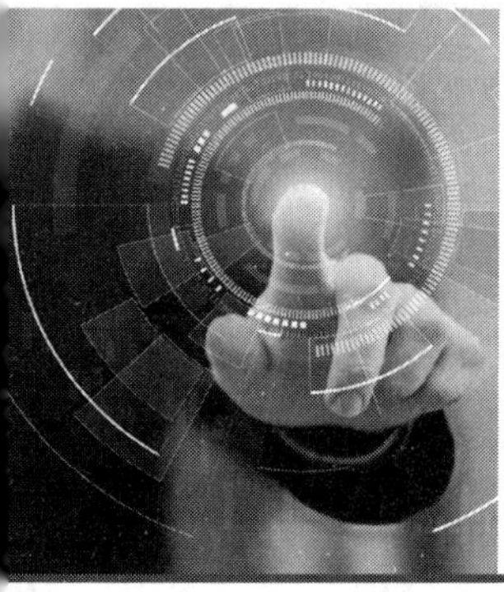

The Federal Aviation Administration (FAA) pushed the commercial drone market forward by creating a regulatory framework with its consumer drone registry. The pace of adoption has been slow because until recently, operators who wanted to fly a drone over people or at night needed a waiver. Drones must still be flown within the visual line of sight unless the FAA says otherwise. Wing was the first drone service to receive permission from the FAA to allow multiple pilots to operate multiple drones making deliveries simultaneously to the public. As we enter the Golden Age of drone delivery, commercial drone operators will have to work together to demonstrate to the public as well as regulators how drones benefit society.

Sources: Based on information in Harrison Wolf, "We're About to See the Golden Age of Drone Delivery – Here's Why," *World Economic Forum*, July 6, 2020; "Drone Technology Uses and Applications for Commercial, Industrial and Military Drones in 2021 and the Future," *Business Insider*, January 12, 2021; "FAA Outlines New Rules for Drones and Their Operators," *Los Angeles Times*, December 30, 2020.

库存管理
12-5a Inventory Management

We define **inventory management** as the process of managing inventories in such a way as to minimize inventory costs, including both holding costs and potential stock-out costs. *Holding costs* are the expenses of storing products until they are purchased or shipped to customers. *Stock-out costs* are sales lost when items are not in inventory. Marketers seek to balance these two costs so that the company always has sufficient inventory to satisfy customer demand, but with little surplus because storing unsold products can be very expensive.

Holding costs include the money invested in inventory, the cost of storage space, insurance costs, and inventory taxes. Often even a relatively small reduction in inventory can generate a large increase in available working capital. Sometimes firms discover that risking some stockout costs can be cheaper than having too much inventory. Generally speaking, inventory management software helps companies maintain the correct levels of inventory and know when to place orders.

订单处理
12-5b Order Processing

Order processing consists of activities involved in receiving and filling customers' purchase orders. It may include not only the means by which customers order products but also procedures for billing and granting credit.

Fast, efficient order processing can provide a dramatic competitive edge. Those in charge of purchasing goods for intermediaries are especially concerned with their suppliers' promptness and reliability in order processing. To them, promptness and reliability mean minimal inventory costs as well as the ability to order goods when they are needed rather than weeks in advance. The internet is providing new opportunities for improving services associated with order processing.

仓储
12-5c Warehousing

Warehousing is the set of activities involved in receiving and storing goods and preparing them for reshipment. Goods are stored to create time utility, meaning they are held until they are needed for use or sale. Warehousing includes the following activities:

- *Receiving goods.* The warehouse accepts delivered goods and assumes responsibility for them.
- *Identifying goods.* Records are made of the quantity of each item received. Items may be marked, coded, or tagged for identification.
- *Sorting goods.* Delivered goods may have to be sorted before being stored.
- *Dispatching goods to storage.* Items must be moved to storage areas, where they can be found later.
- *Holding goods.* The goods are protected in storage until needed.
- *Recalling, picking, and assembling goods.* Items that are to leave the warehouse must be selected from storage and assembled efficiently.
- *Dispatching shipments.* Each shipment is packaged and directed to the proper transport vehicle. Shipping and accounting documents are prepared.

A firm may use its own private warehouses or rent space in public warehouses. A *private warehouse,* owned and operated by a particular firm, can be designed to serve the firm's specific needs. However, the organization must take on the task of financing the facility and determining the best location for it.

Public warehouses are open to all individuals and firms. Most are located on the outskirts of cities, where rail and truck transportation is easily available. They provide storage facilities, areas for sorting and assembling shipments, and office and display spaces for wholesalers and retailers. Public warehouses also will hold—and issue receipts for—goods used as collateral for borrowed funds.

库存管理
inventory management the process of managing inventories in such a way as to minimize inventory costs, including both holding costs and potential stock-out costs

订单处理
order processing activities involved in receiving and filling customers' purchase orders

仓储
warehousing the set of activities involved in receiving and storing goods and preparing them for reshipment

物料搬运

12-5d Materials Handling

Materials handling is the actual physical handling of goods—in warehouses as well as during transportation. Proper materials-handling procedures and techniques can increase the efficiency and capacity of a firm's warehouse and transportation system, as well as reduce product breakage and spoilage. Increasingly, companies use technology such as robotics and *radio frequency identification (RFID)*—a system of tags and readers that use radio waves to identify and track materials tagged with special microchips—to facilitate efficient handling.

Materials handling attempts to reduce the number of times a product is handled. One method is called *unit loading*. Several smaller cartons, barrels, or boxes are combined into a single standard-size load that can be moved efficiently by forklift, conveyer, robot, or truck. Another is *containerization*, which involves consolidating many items into single, large containers that are sealed at their point of origin and opened at their destination. Their uniform size means they can be stacked and shipped via train, barge, or ship.

运输

12-5e Transportation

As a part of logistics, **transportation** is simply the shipment of products to customers. Transportation in the United States costs $1.06 trillion a year, 65 percent of total logistics activities' costs.[12] The greater the distance between seller and purchaser, the more important is the choice of the mode of transportation and the particular carrier. In recent years, the internet has emerged as a mode of transportation for digital products like streamed entertainment products such as songs and TV shows and downloadable products such as software.

A firm that offers transportation services is called a **carrier**. A *common carrier* is a transportation firm whose services are available to all shippers. Railroads, airlines, and most long-distance trucking firms are common carriers. A *contract carrier* is available for hire by one or several shippers. Contract carriers do not serve the general public and the number of firms they can handle at a time is limited by law. A *private carrier* is owned and operated by the shipper.

There are six major criteria that marketers use for selecting transportation modes: cost, speed, dependability, load flexibility, accessibility, and frequency. Table 12-2 compares these.

Obviously, the *cost* of a transportation mode is an important consideration. However, it is not the only one. Higher-cost modes of transportation can convey important benefits. *Speed* is measured by the total time that a carrier possesses the products, including time

物料搬运
materials handling the actual physical handling of goods, in warehouses as well as during transportation

运输
transportation the shipment of products to customers

承运商
carrier a firm that offers transportation services

Table 12-2 Characteristics of Transportation Modes

Selection Criteria	Railroads	Trucks	Pipelines	Waterways	Airplanes	Internet
Cost	Moderate	High	Low	Very low	Very high	Very low
Speed	Average	Fast	Slow	Very slow	Very fast	Very fast
Dependability	Average	High	High	Average	High	High
Load flexibility	High	Average	Very low	Very high	Low	Low
Accessibility	High	Very high	Very limited	Limited	Average	Very high
Frequency	Low	High	Very high	Very low	Average	Very high
Products carried	Coal, grain, lumber, heavy equipment, paper and pulp products, chemicals	Clothing, computers, books, groceries and produce, livestock	Oil, processed coal, natural gas, wood chips	Chemicals, bauxite, grain, motor vehicles, agricultural implements	Flowers, food (highly perishable), technical instruments, emergency parts and equipment, overnight mail	Information, songs, TV shows, movies, software, services

required for pickup and delivery, handling, and movement between point of origin and destination. Usually there is a direct relationship between cost and speed, meaning faster modes of transportation are more expensive. A transportation mode's *dependability* is determined by its consistency of service. *Load flexibility* is the degree to which a transportation mode can be adapted for moving different kinds of products with varying requirements, such as controlled temperatures or humidity levels. *Accessibility* refers to a transportation mode's ability to move goods over a specific route or network. *Frequency* refers to how frequently a marketer can ship products by a specific transportation mode. While pipelines provide continuous shipments, railroads and waterways follow specific schedules for moving products from one location to another. Table 12-2 compares each transportation mode according to these six selection criteria.

Railroads Shipping by railroad remains one of the most important modes of transportation in the United States. Rail is also the least expensive mode for many products. Almost all railroads are common carriers, although a few coal-mining companies operate their own lines. Many commodities carried by railroads could not be transported easily by any other means.

Trucks The trucking industry consists of common, contract, and private carriers. Trucks are a very popular transportation mode because they have the advantage of being able to move goods to areas not served by railroads. They can handle freight quickly and economically, and they can carry a wide range of shipments. Many shippers favor this mode because it offers door-to-door service, less stringent packaging requirements than ships and airplanes, and flexible delivery schedules. Railroad and truck carriers sometimes team up to provide a form of transportation called *piggyback*, wherein truck trailers are loaded onto railroad flatcars for much of the distance and then pulled by trucks to the final destination.

Airplanes Air transport is the fastest, but most expensive, means of transportation. All certified airlines are common carriers. Supplemental or charter lines are contract carriers. Because of the high cost, uneven geographic distribution of airports, and reliance on weather conditions, airlines carry only a tiny fraction of intercity freight. Usually, only high-value, perishable items or goods that are needed immediately are shipped by air.

Waterways Cargo ships and barges offer the least expensive, but slowest, form of transportation. They are used mainly for bulky, nonperishable goods such as iron ore, bulk wheat, motor vehicles, and agricultural implements. Of course, shipment by water is limited to ports and cities located on navigable waterways. Many international distributors will combine this mode with a land mode to transport products to their destination.

Pipelines Pipelines are a highly specialized mode of transportation. They are used primarily to carry petroleum and natural gas. Such products as semiliquid coal and wood chips also can be shipped through pipelines, although their use can be controversial when they cut across animal migratory pathways or spring a leak in remote areas.

Internet In recent years, the internet has emerged as a mode of transportation for digital products. Examples include streamed entertainment products such as songs and TV shows and downloadable products such as software.

✓ Concept Check

- How is inventory management a balancing act between stockout costs and holding costs?
- Explain the seven major warehousing activities.
- What is the goal of materials handling?
- Describe the major characteristics of the primary transportation modes.

什么是整合营销传播

12-6 What Is Integrated Marketing Communications?

整合营销传播
integrated marketing communications coordination of promotion efforts to ensure maximal informational and persuasive impact on customers

Learning Objective

12-6 Define integrated marketing communications.

Integrated marketing communications is the coordination of promotion efforts to ensure maximum informational and persuasive impact on customers. A major goal of integrated marketing communications is to send a consistent message to customers. Unilever's Dove brand, for example, ran the successful Dove Campaign for Real Beauty, which employed variations on the message in advertising on billboards, television, and online for more than a decade, with some ads being watched and shared millions of times. The brand also paired the Real Beauty messaging with its Dove Self-Esteem Project used by parents and educators to help promote confidence in children. The integrated campaign helped increase the brand's sales by $1.5 billion over ten years.[13]

Integrated marketing communications helps organizations coordinate and manage promotions in order to convey a consistent message. This approach fosters long-term customer relationships as well as the efficient use of promotional resources. The concept of integrated marketing communications has been increasingly accepted for several reasons. Mass-media advertising, a very popular promotional method in the past, is used less today because of its high costs and variable audience sizes. Marketers now take advantage of highly targeted promotional tools, such as social media, cable TV, direct mail, DVDs, the internet, special-interest magazines, and podcasts. These vehicles let marketers be more precise in targeting individual customers. As an example, affordable beauty firm e.l.f. Cosmetics uses TikTok and Instagram to reach its diverse customer base with fun and creative messaging that reinforces its brand and depicts ways customers use its products.[14]

Because the overall costs of marketing communications are significant, managers demand systematic evaluations of communications efforts to ensure that promotional resources are being used efficiently. Although the fundamental role of promotion has not changed, the specific communication vehicles employed and the precision with which they are used are evolving.

✓ Concept Check

- What is the major goal of integrated marketing communications?
- Why are integrated marketing communications being increasingly accepted?

促销组合：概述

12-7 The Promotion Mix: An Overview

Learning Objective

12-7 List the basic elements of the promotion mix.

Promotion is communication about an organization and its products that is intended to inform, persuade, or remind target-market members. Promotion is not limited to business. Charities use promotion to inform us about their cause or issue, to persuade us to donate, and to remind us to do so. Even the Internal Revenue Service uses promotion (in the form of publicity) to remind us of the mid-April deadline for filing tax returns.

A **promotion mix** (sometimes called a *marketing-communications mix*) is the particular combination of promotion methods a firm uses to reach a target market. The makeup of a mix depends on many factors, including the firm's promotional resources and objectives, the nature of the target market, the product characteristics, and the feasibility of the various promotional methods. The four elements of the promotion mix are advertising, personal selling, sales promotion, and public relations, as illustrated in Figure 12-2.

Advertising is a paid nonpersonal message communicated to a select audience through a mass medium. Advertising is flexible and can reach a very large or a small, carefully chosen target group. **Personal selling** is personal communication aimed at

促销
promotion communication about an organization and its products that is intended to inform, persuade, or remind target-market members

促销组合
promotion mix the particular combination of promotion methods a firm uses to reach a target market

广告
advertising a paid nonpersonal message communicated to a select audience through a mass medium

人员推销
personal selling personal communication aimed at informing customers and persuading them to buy a firm's products

Figure 12-2 Possible Elements of a Promotion Mix

Depending on the type of product and target market involved, one or more of these ingredients are used in a promotion mix.

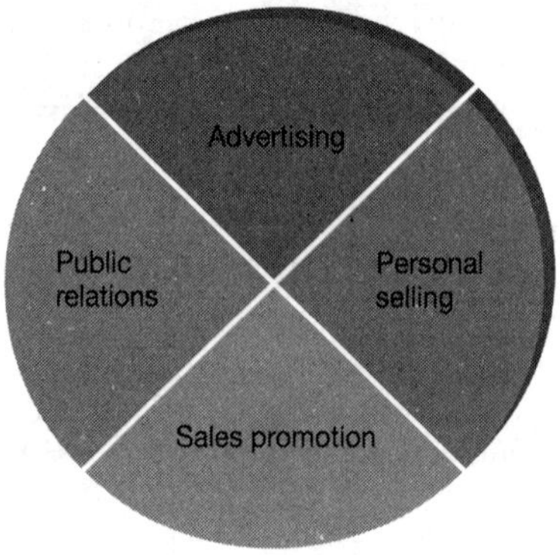

informing customers and persuading them to buy a firm's products. It is more expensive to reach a consumer through personal selling than through advertising, but this method provides immediate feedback and often is more persuasive than advertising. **Sales promotion** is the use of activities or materials as direct inducements to customers or salespersons, which can add value to the product and increase the customer's incentive to make a purchase. **Public relations** is a broad set of communication activities used to create and maintain favorable relationships between an organization and various public groups, both internal and external. Public relations activities are numerous and varied and can be a very effective form of promotion.

In addition to deciding which combination of promotional methods is most appropriate for a marketing strategy, marketers must decide whether to use a push or pull strategy. With a *push policy,* a producer promotes the product only to the next organization down the marketing channel, and each channel member in turn promotes to the next. In a marketing channel with wholesalers and retailers, the producer promotes to the wholesaler because, in this case, the wholesaler is the channel member just below the producer. As an example, a paper wholesaler might offer an office-supply store $3 off every box of paper purchased for sale in the store; an appliance manufacturer's sales representatives might use personal selling to encourage retailers to carry a new model. Indeed, a push policy normally stresses personal selling. With a *pull policy,* however, a marketer promotes directly to consumers to spur strong consumer demand for its products. It does so primarily through advertising and sales promotion. Because consumers are persuaded to seek the products in retail stores, retailers in turn go to wholesalers or the producers to buy the products. An example of a pull policy is the Apple iPhone. Apple uses advertising to tease each new iPhone or Apple Watch, which creates demand through word-of-mouth. Consumers hear about Apple's new product and are encouraged to seek out more information. Push and pull policies are not mutually exclusive. At times, an organization uses both simultaneously.

While it is possible for a marketer to only use one ingredient of the promotion mix, it is more likely that two, three, or even all four of these ingredients will be used, depending on the type of product and target market involved.

✓ Concept Check

- What are the major elements of a promotion mix?
- How can each element help a firm reach a target market?
- How does a push strategy differ from a pull strategy?

销售促销
sales promotion the use of activities or materials as direct inducements to customers or salespersons

广告

12-8 Advertising

Learning Objective

12-8 Examine advertising, including the types of advertising, the advertising campaign, and social and legal considerations.

Advertising is a very important element of the promotion mix. Organizations currently spend around $169.9 billion annually on advertising in the United States.[15] In this section, we discuss the types of advertising and how to develop an advertising campaign.

按目的划分的广告类型

12-8a Types of Advertising by Purpose

Depending on its purpose and message, advertising may be classified into one of three groups: primary demand, selective demand, or institutional.

Primary-Demand Advertising **Primary-demand advertising** is advertising aimed at increasing the demand for all brands of a product within a specific industry. Trade and industry associations, such as the National Pork Producers Council and the California Milk Processor Board, use primary-demand advertising. To reach out to a new generation of potential home buyers, the National Association of Realtors launched a multimedia campaign, "That's Who We R," to highlight stories of professional realtors helping all kinds of families buy homes and start businesses.[16]

Selective-Demand Advertising **Selective-demand** (or **brand) advertising** is advertising that is used to sell a particular brand of product. It is by far the most common type of advertising, and it accounts for the majority of advertising expenditures. As an example, Burger King used radio ads to introduce its Impossible Whopper, humorously highlighting the confusion people experience eating a plant-based burger that tastes just like a Whopper made with beef.[17]

公共关系
public relations communication activities used to create and maintain favorable relationships between an organization and various public groups, both internal and external

基本需求广告
primary-demand advertising advertising whose purpose is to increase the demand for *all* brands of a product within a specific industry

选择性需求（或品牌）广告
selective-demand (or **brand) advertising** advertising that is used to sell a particular brand of product

Harnessing the power of social media. Social media allows a business to reach out to customers in a context that is familiar and comfortable to them. Firms attempt to measure the effectiveness of their social media efforts by gathering statistics on the number of followers and fans they have, traffic to their websites, and mentions of their products on social networking sites.

Selective-demand advertising that aims at persuading consumers to make purchases within a short time is called *immediate-response advertising*. Most local advertising is of this type. Often local advertisers promote products with immediate appeal. Selective advertising aimed at keeping the public aware of a firm's name or product is called *reminder advertising*. *Comparative advertising* compares the sponsored brand with one or more identified competing brands. The association shows the sponsored brand to be as good as or better than the other identified competing brands. Marketers must be careful when using this technique to present information truthfully and not to obscure or distort facts.

Institutional Advertising **Institutional advertising** is advertising designed to enhance a firm's image or reputation. Some large firms allocate a portion of advertising dollars to build goodwill, rather than to stimulate sales directly. As an example, McDonald's ran commercials thanking healthcare workers, firefighters, and other first responders for their service during the COVID-19 pandemic. The fast-food chain also gave away "Thank You Meals" that included a thank you note to first responders.[18] A positive public image helps an organization to attract customers, employees, and investors.

开展广告活动的主要步骤

12-8b Major Steps in Developing an Advertising Campaign

An advertising campaign is developed in several stages, which can vary in the order in which they are implemented. Factors affecting a campaign include the company's resources, products, and target audiences. The development of a campaign in any organization includes the following steps in some form:

1. Identify and Analyze the Target Audience The target audience is the group toward which a firm's advertisements are directed. To pinpoint the organization's target audience and develop an effective campaign, marketers analyze various factors, such as the geographic distribution of potential customers, their age, gender, race, income, and education, and their attitudes toward the product, the nature of the competition, and the product's features. It is crucial to identify the target market correctly because all subsequent efforts will fail if not directed at the right audience.

2. Define the Advertising Objectives The goals of an advertising campaign should be stated precisely and in quantifiable terms. Objectives should give specific details about the actual and desired position of the company and how it will arrive there, including a timetable for achieving goals. For example, advertising objectives that focus on sales will stress increasing sales by a certain percentage or dollar amount, or expanding the firm's market share by a specific amount.

3. Create the Advertising Platform An advertising platform includes the important selling points, or features, that an advertiser will incorporate into the advertising campaign. These should be features that are lacking in competitors' products and that are important to customers. Although research into what consumers view as important issues is expensive, it is the most productive way to determine what to include in an advertising platform.

4. Determine the Advertising Appropriation The advertising appropriation is the total amount of money designated for advertising in a given time period. Developing an acceptable advertising appropriation is critical—too little and promotional efforts will not meet demand, too much will waste resources and

商誉广告
institutional advertising
advertising designed to enhance a firm's image or reputation

reduce the funds available for other activities. Advertising appropriations may be based on historical or forecasted sales, what competitors spend on advertising, or executive judgment. Companies that spend the most on advertising in the United States include Amazon, Procter & Gamble, L'Oréal, Samsung, and Unilever.[19]

5. Develop the Media Plan A media plan includes media selection and media scheduling. This involves deciding which media vehicles to use: internet and mobile, television, radio, out of home, magazines, newspapers, or some combination. Although cost-effectiveness is not easy to measure, the primary concern of the media planner is to reach the largest proportion of the target audience possible for each dollar spent. Media planners must also consider the location and demographics of the target market, the content of the message, and the characteristics of the audiences reached by various media. The media planner begins with general media decisions, selects subclasses within each medium, and chooses specific media vehicles for the campaign. The advantages and disadvantages of the major media classes are shown in Table 12-3.

Table 12-3 Advantages and Disadvantages of Major Media Classes

	Advantages	Disadvantages
Internet/Digital Media	Immediate response, potential to reach a precisely targeted audience, ability to track customers and build databases, highly interactive medium, real-time analytics	Costs of precise targeting can be high, inappropriate ad placement, effects difficult to measure, concerns about security and privacy
Social Media	Target, interact, and connect more personally with customers, receive real-time feedback, direct messages to specific individuals, effectively reach target market/followers	Restricted number of contacts per message because of highly targeted nature, new media—unsure of best applications and how to calculate ROI, large time commitment to monitor
Television	Reaches large audiences, high frequency available, dual impact of audio and video, highly visible, high prestige, geographic and demographic selectivity, difficult to ignore, on-demand capabilities	Very expensive, highly perishable message, size of audience not guaranteed, amount of prime time limited, lack of selectivity in target market
Radio	Reaches a large proportion of consumers, mobile and flexible, low relative costs, ad can be changed quickly, high level of geographic and demographic selectivity, encourages use of imagination	Lacks visual imagery, short life of message, listeners' attention limited, market fragmentation, difficult buying procedures, limited media and audience research
Out of Home	Allows for frequent repetition, low cost, message can be placed close to point of sale, geographic selectivity, operable 24 hours a day, high creativity	Message must be short and simple, no demographic selectivity, seldom attracts readers' full attention, criticized as traffic hazard and blight on landscape, much wasted coverage, limited capabilities
Magazines	Demographic selectivity, good reproduction, long life, prestige, geographic selectivity when regional issues available	High costs, 30- to 90-day average lead time, high level of competition, limited reach, communicates less frequently
Newspapers	Reaches large audience, purchased to be read, geographic flexibility, short lead time, frequent publication, favorable for cooperative advertising	Not selective for socioeconomic groups or target market, short life, limited reproduction capabilities, large advertising volume limits exposure
Direct Mail	Little wasted circulation, highly selective, circulation controlled by advertiser, few distractions, personal, stimulates actions, easy to measure performance, hidden from competitors	Very expensive, lacks editorial content to attract readers, often thrown away unread as junk mail, criticized as invasion of privacy, consumers must choose to read the ad

Sources: Adapted from William F. Arens and Michael Weigold, *Contemporary Advertising & Integrated Communications,* 16th ed. (Burr Ridge, IL: Irwin/McGraw-Hill, 2021); George E. Belch and Michael Belch, *Advertising and Promotion: An Integrated Marketing Communications Perspective,* 12th ed. (Burr Ridge, IL: Irwin/McGraw-Hill, 2021).

6. Create the Advertising Message The content and form of a message are influenced by the product's features, the characteristics of the target audience, the objectives of the campaign, and the choice of media. An advertiser must consider these factors to choose words and illustrations that will be meaningful and appealing to the target audience. The copy, or words, of an advertisement will vary depending on the media choice, but attempt to engage the audience and move them through attention, interest, desire, and action. Artwork and visuals should complement copy by being visually attractive and communicating an idea quickly.

7. Execute the Campaign Execution of an advertising campaign requires extensive planning, scheduling, and coordinating because the tasks are carried out by many people and organizations and must be completed on time. Production companies, research organizations, media firms, printers, photoengravers, and commercial artists are just a few of the potential contributors to a campaign. Advertising managers must constantly assess the quality of the work and take corrective action when necessary. In some instances, advertisers must make changes in the middle of the campaign to meet objectives.

8. Evaluate Advertising Effectiveness A campaign's success should be compared against original objectives at regular intervals before, during, and after campaign launch. An advertiser should be able to track the impact of the campaign on sales and market share, as well as changes in customer attitudes and brand awareness. Data from past and current sales and responses to coupon offers and customer surveys administered by research organizations are some of the ways in which advertising effectiveness can be evaluated. Table 12-4 shows the five advertisers with the most effective campaigns according to the Effie Effectiveness Index, a global ranking system for advertising effectiveness. This ranking takes into account factors such as ROI, sales growth, and brand awareness in relation to money spent on promotional activities.

广告公司

12-8c Advertising Agencies

Advertisers can plan and produce their own advertising with help from in-house media personnel, or they can hire advertising agencies. An **advertising agency** is an independent firm that plans, produces, and places advertising for clients. Many large

广告公司
advertising agency an independent firm that plans, produces, and places advertising for its clients

Table 12-4 Most Effective Advertisers

Ranking	Advertiser
1	Unilever
2	Coca-Cola
3	Nestlé
4	AB InBev
5	PepsiCo

Source: Effie Worldwide, "2020 Effie Effectiveness Index: Overview".

Exploring Careers

职业探索：如何在广告公司找到工作

How to Land a Job in an Advertising Agency

Advertising, personal selling, sales promotion, and public relations are the four elements of the promotion mix. Advertising alone is a multibillion-dollar industry in the United States and offers exciting career opportunities. Instead of working for an individual company, many people seek employment at advertising agencies, independent firms that plan, produce, and place advertising for their clients. Some of the largest advertising agencies include BBDO, Deloitte Digital, Dentsu, Ogilvy, and TBWA Worldwide.

An early step toward starting a career in advertising is seeking a degree in a related field such as business, marketing, or communications. Some universities specifically offer a bachelor's degree in advertising that focuses on the principles of advertising, communication theory and analysis, creative strategy, media planning, ad sales, and more. Beyond college, one way to get a foot in the door of an agency is to apply for an internship. Internships provide valuable, hands-on experience in the fast-paced world of advertising. Many internships end with a job offer for an entry-level position.

Jobs in advertising include account coordination, copywriting, media buying, and more. To build a portfolio of work, freelancing can be an effective way to break into copywriting and graphic design in particular. In addition to traditional person-to-person networking, websites like Fiverr and Upwork can help individuals land clients. Even without engaging in freelancing, job seekers can hone their skills by creating spec ads by either reimagining existing print, digital, mobile, outdoor, or radio advertisements or conceptualizing an original campaign from the ground up. The important element is to show an understanding of the brand or product being promoted and demonstrate creativity and effective communication.

Though print advertising is in decline, the advertising industry as a whole is flourishing as companies invest in digital and mobile. Digital advertising will continue to grow at a greater rate than traditional media, accounting for more than 50 percent of ad spending. The changing landscape of advertising makes this career path both exciting and lucrative.

Sources: Based on information in Apryl Duncan, "How to Work for an Advertising Agency," *The Balance Careers*, January 4, 2020; "US Digital Ad Spending Will Surpass Traditional in 2019," *eMarketer*, February 19, 2019; "How to Get Into Advertising: Step-by-Step Career Guide," *Masterclass*, November 8, 2020.

ad agencies also help with sales promotion and public relations. The cost of using an advertising agency can be moderate, especially for large campaigns. It is usually around 15 percent commission. Some firms opt to use a combination of in-house advertising talent and outside specialists.

广告中的社会和法律因素
12-8d **Social and Legal Considerations in Advertising**

Critics of U.S. advertising have two main complaints—that it is wasteful and that it can be deceptive. Although advertising (like any other activity) can be performed inefficiently, evidence shows that it is not wasteful:

- Advertising is the most effective and least expensive means of communicating product information to a large number of individuals and organizations.
- Advertising encourages competition. It thus leads to the development of new and improved products, wider product choices, and lower prices.
- Advertising revenues support mass-communication media—internet, television, newspapers, magazines, and radio, effectively paying for news coverage and entertainment programming.
- Advertising provides job opportunities in fields ranging from sales to film production.

✓ Concept Check

- Describe the major types of advertising by purpose.
- Explain the eight major steps in developing an advertising campaign.

A number of government and private agencies scrutinize advertising for false or misleading claims or offers that might harm consumers. At the national level, the Federal Trade Commission (FTC), the Food and Drug Administration (FDA), and the Federal Communications Commission (FCC) oversee advertising practices. Advertising also may be monitored by state and local agencies, better business bureaus, and industry associations.

订单开发者
order getter a salesperson who is responsible for selling a firm's products to new customers and increasing sales to current customers

人员推销

12-9 Personal Selling

Learning Objective

12-9 Explore personal selling, including the types of salespersons, the personal-selling process, and major sales management tasks.

Personal selling is the most adaptable of all promotional methods because the person presenting the message can modify it to suit the individual buyer. However, it is also the most expensive method because it involves salespeople communicating with customers one at a time or in small groups. Many selling situations demand the face-to-face contact and adaptability of personal selling. This is especially true of industrial sales, in which a single purchase may amount to millions of dollars. Obviously, sales of that size must be based on carefully planned presentations, personal contact with customers, and thorough negotiations.

创造性销售
creative selling selling products to new customers and increasing sales to current customers

订单接单员
order taker a salesperson who handles repeat sales in ways that maintain positive relationships with customers

销售支持人员
sales support personnel employees who aid in selling but are more involved in locating prospects, educating customers, building goodwill for the firm, and providing follow-up service

销售人员的种类

12-9a Kinds of Salespersons

Because most businesses employ different salespersons to perform different functions, marketing managers need to select the kinds of sales personnel that will be most effective in selling the firm's products. Salespersons may be identified as order getters, order takers, and support personnel. A single individual can, and often does, perform all three functions.

Order Getters An **order getter** is responsible for what is sometimes called **creative selling**—selling a firm's products to new customers and increasing sales to current customers. An order getter must be able to perceive buyers' needs, supply customers with information about the product, and persuade them to buy it.

The pros and cons of personal selling. Personal selling is sometimes more effective than advertising. It's easy to ignore an advertisement. Saying "no" to a salesperson is much harder. The main drawback of personal selling is that it's expensive, which is why it's generally used to sell high-dollar goods and services.

Order Takers An **order taker** handles repeat sales and customer demands to maintain positive relationships. *Inside order takers* receive incoming mail, online, and telephone orders for businesses. Salespersons in retail stores are also inside order takers. *Outside* (or *field*) *order takers* travel to customers. Often the buyer and the field salesperson develop a mutually beneficial relationship of placing, receiving, and delivering orders. Both inside and outside order takers are active salespersons and produce a large proportion of their companies' sales.

Support Personnel **Sales support personnel** aid in selling but are more involved in locating prospects (likely first-time customers), educating customers, building goodwill for the firm, and providing follow-up service. The most common categories of support personnel are missionary, trade, and technical salespersons.

A **missionary salesperson**, who usually works for a manufacturer, visits retailers to persuade them to buy the manufacturer's products. If the retailers agree, they buy the products from wholesalers, who are the manufacturer's actual customers.

A **trade salesperson**, who generally works for a food producer or processor, assists customers in promoting products, especially in retail stores. A trade salesperson may obtain additional shelf space for the products, restock shelves, set up displays, and distribute samples. Because trade salespersons usually are order takers as well, they are not strictly support personnel.

A **technical salesperson** assists a company's current customers in technical matters. Technical salespeople may explain how to use a product, how it is made, how to install it, or how a system is designed. They should have degrees in science or engineering.

Firms usually need to employ sales personnel from several of these categories. Factors that affect which sales personnel are hired include the number of customers and their characteristics; the product's attributes, complexity, and price; the distribution channels used by the company; and the company's approach to advertising.

人员推销过程

12-9b The Personal-Selling Process

No two selling situations are exactly alike, and no two salespeople perform their jobs in exactly the same way. Most salespeople, however, follow the six-step procedure illustrated in Figure 12-3.

Prospecting The first step in personal selling is to research potential buyers and choose the most likely customers, or prospects. Business associates and customers, social media contacts, public records, telephone and trade-association directories, and company files can all be good sources of new prospects. The salesperson also assesses whether prospects have the financial resources, willingness, and authority to buy the product, a process known as *qualifying*.

Approaching the Prospect First impressions are often lasting. Therefore, a salesperson's first contact with a prospect is crucial to successful selling. A salesperson should be friendly and knowledgeable about the product, the prospect's needs, and how the product can meet those needs. Those salespeople who demonstrate an understanding of and sensitivity to a customer's situation are more likely to make a good first impression and make a sale.

Making the Presentation The next step is actual delivery of the sales presentation, which often includes a product demonstration. The salesperson points out the product's features, its benefits, and how it is superior to competitors' merchandise. The salesperson may list other clients (if given permission) during the presentation.

During a demonstration, the salesperson may suggest that the prospect try out the product personally. The demonstration and product trial should underscore specific points made during the presentation.

Answering Objections The prospect may raise objections or ask questions at any time during the process. This is the salesperson's chance to eliminate objections that could prevent a sale, to point out additional features, or to mention special services the company offers.

Closing the Sale To close the sale, the salesperson asks the prospect to buy the product. This is the critical point in the selling process. Many experienced salespeople employ a *trial closing,* in which they ask questions before the actual close in a tone that assumes a successful sale. Typical questions are: "When would you want delivery?" and "Do you want the standard model or the one with the special options package?" They allow the salesperson to gauge the likelihood and imminence of a sale.

Following Up The salesperson's job does not end with a sale. They must follow up to ensure that the product is delivered on time, in the right quantity, and in proper

Figure 12-3 The Six Steps of the Personal-Selling Process

Personal selling is not only the most adaptable of all promotional methods but also the most expensive.

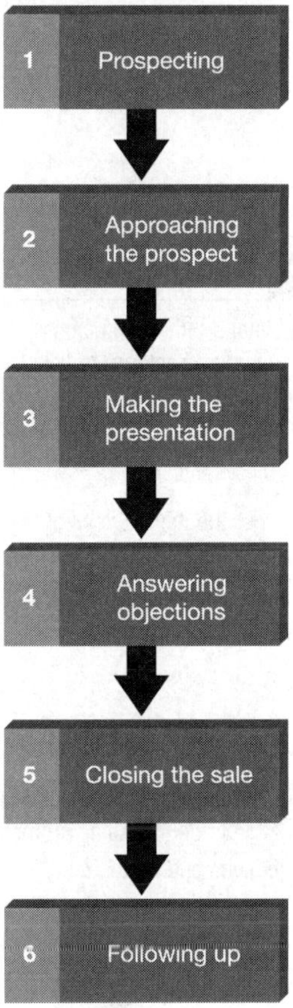

推销式销售人员
missionary salesperson a salesperson—generally employed by a manufacturer—who visits retailers to persuade them to buy the manufacturer's products

快消品销售人员
trade salesperson a salesperson—generally employed by a food producer or processor—who assists customers in promoting products, especially in retail stores

技术销售人员
technical salesperson a salesperson who assists a company's current customers in technical matters

operating condition. During follow-up, salespeople should also make it clear that they are available in case problems develop. Follow-up is essential to the selling process because it leaves a good impression and helps to increase the likelihood of future sales.

主要的销售管理工作

12-9c Major Sales Management Tasks

A firm's success often hinges on the competent management of its sales force. Although some companies operate efficiently without one, most firms rely on a strong sales force—and the revenue it brings in—for their success.

Sales managers must:

- Set sales objectives in concrete, quantifiable terms and specify a period of time and geographic area;
- Adjust the size of the sales force to meet changes in the firm's marketing plan and the marketing environment;
- Attract and hire effective salespersons;
- Develop a training program and decide where, when, how, and for whom to conduct the training;
- Formulate a fair and adequate compensation plan to retain qualified employees;
- Motivate salespersons to keep their productivity high;
- Define sales territories and determine scheduling and routing of the sales force; and
- Evaluate the operation holistically, through sales reports, communications with customers, and invoices.

✓ Concept Check

- What are the advantages and disadvantages of using personal selling?
- Identify the three types of salespersons.
- Describe the six steps of the personal-selling process.

销售促销

12-10 Sales Promotion

Learning Objective

12-10 Identify sales promotion objectives and methods.

Sales promotion consists of activities or materials that are direct inducements to customers or salespersons. Receiving a free sample at the supermarket or using a frequent flier program are examples of sales promotions. Sales promotion techniques can significantly affect sales and are often used to enhance and supplement other promotional methods. Firms have dramatically increased spending on sales promotions as they increase their importance as part of the promotion mix.

促销目标

12-10a Sales Promotion Objectives

Sales promotion activities may be used singly or in combination to achieve one goal or a set of goals. Marketers use sales promotion activities and materials for a number of purposes, including:

1. To attract new customers;
2. To encourage trial of a new product;
3. To invigorate the sales of a mature brand;
4. To boost sales to current customers;
5. To reinforce advertising;
6. To increase traffic in retail stores;
7. To smooth out customer demand;
8. To build up reseller inventories;
9. To neutralize the competition's promotional efforts; and
10. To increase the attractiveness of shelf placement and displays.

Sales promotion objectives should be consistent with the organization's general goals and with its marketing and promotional objectives.

促销方法

12-10b Sales Promotion Methods

Do you use coupons? Companies give away coupons to increase the sales of their products and encourage consumers who are unfamiliar with their products to give them a try.

Most sales promotion methods can be classified as promotional techniques for either consumer sales or trade sales.

A **consumer sales promotion method** attracts consumers to particular retail stores and motivates them to purchase certain new or established products. A **trade sales promotion method** encourages wholesalers and retailers to stock and actively promote a manufacturer's product. Incentives such as money, merchandise, marketing assistance, and gifts may provide incentives to resellers to purchase products or support a firm in other ways. Of the combined dollars spent on sales promotion and advertising, about one-half is spent on trade promotions, one-fourth on consumer promotions, and one-fourth on advertising.

Rebates A **rebate** is a return of part of the purchase price of a product. Usually the rebate is offered by the producer to consumers who submit proof of purchase and perhaps other documents. Rebating is a relatively low-cost promotional method, but consumers may not be attracted by it because they view it to be too complicated or time consuming.

Coupons A **coupon** reduces the retail price of a particular item by a stated amount at the time of purchase. Coupons may be worth anywhere from a few cents to a few dollars. Customers can find coupons online, through apps, and in newspapers, magazines, direct mail, and shelf dispensers in stores. After declining throughout the 1990s, the popularity of coupons has rebounded, largely because consumers can visit coupon websites, and companies send coupons via email or smartphone to loyal customers. Target, for instance, offers customers customized coupons and more via its Target app. RetailMeNot gives consumers access to digital coupon offers and promo codes from 70,000 stores and restaurants via a website or smartphone app.[20]

Samples A **sample** is a free product given to customers to encourage trial and purchase. Marketers utilize samples to increase awareness of a product, which can increase sales volume in the early stages of a product's life cycle and improve distribution. Samples may be offered via online coupons or direct mail or in stores. It is the most expensive sales promotion technique. Established brands, such as cosmetics companies, may use free samples to attract customers and renew interest in a brand. Club Demonstration Services, which operates sampling tables for Costco, reported that its sampling of a frozen pizza product at many retailers boosted sales by an average of 600 percent.[21] Organizations must consider such factors as seasonal demand for the product, market characteristics, and prior advertising when designing a free sample campaign.

Premiums A **premium** is a gift that a producer offers a customer in return for buying its product. It is used to attract competitors' customers, introduce different sizes of established products, add variety to other promotional efforts, and stimulate consumer loyalty. Creativity is essential when using premiums. To stand out and achieve a significant number of redemptions, the premium must suit the target audience and the brand's image. The premium must also be recognizable and desirable to customers. Premiums are generally placed on or inside packages.

Frequent-User Incentives A **frequent-user incentive** is a program developed to reward customers who engage in repeat (frequent) purchases. These are often called customer loyalty programs, and increasingly, they are app-based. Such programs are used commonly by service businesses such as airlines, hotels, auto

消费者促销法
consumer sales promotion method a sales promotion method designed to attract consumers to particular retail stores and to motivate them to purchase certain new or established products

贸易促销法
trade sales promotion method a sales promotion method designed to encourage wholesalers and retailers to stock and actively promote a manufacturer's product

回扣
rebate a return of part of the purchase price of a product

优惠券
coupon reduces the retail price of a particular item by a stated amount at the time of purchase

样品
sample a free product given to customers to encourage trial and purchase

赠品
premium a gift that a producer offers a customer in return for buying its product

常客激励
frequent-user incentive a program developed to reward customers who engage in repeat (frequent) purchases

购买点展台
point-of-purchase display promotional material placed within a retail store

行业展会
trade show an industry-wide exhibit at which many sellers display their products

购买折让
buying allowance a temporary price reduction to resellers for purchasing specified quantities of a product

合作广告
cooperative advertising an arrangement whereby a manufacturer agrees to pay a certain amount of a retailer's media cost for advertising the manufacturer's products

rental agencies, and coffee shops. Frequent-user incentives foster customer loyalty because the customer is given an additional reason to continue patronizing the company or group of companies. A well-structured program can also generate significant data about customer usage and preferences that companies can use to refine their marketing strategies.

Point-of-Purchase Displays A **point-of-purchase display** is promotional material placed within a retail store. The display is usually located near the product being promoted. It may hold merchandise or information and encouragements to buy the product. Most point-of-purchase displays are prepared and set up by manufacturers and wholesalers.

Trade Shows A **trade show** is an industry-wide exhibit at which many sellers display their products. Many trade shows are organized exclusively for dealers—to permit manufacturers and wholesalers to show their latest lines to retailers. Others are promotions designed to stimulate consumer awareness and interest, such as annual home or bridal shows.

Buying Allowances A **buying allowance** is a temporary price reduction to resellers for purchasing specified quantities of a product. A laundry detergent manufacturer might give retailers $1 for each case of detergent purchased. A buying allowance is an incentive to resellers to handle new products and may stimulate purchase of items in large quantities. A shortcoming of buying allowances is that competitors can counter quickly with their own buying allowances.

Cooperative Advertising **Cooperative advertising** is an arrangement whereby a manufacturer agrees to pay a certain amount of a retailer's media cost for advertising the manufacturer's products. To be reimbursed, a retailer must show proof that the advertisements did appear. Not all retailers take advantage of available cooperative advertising offers, either because they cannot afford to advertise or choose not to.

促销方式的选择
12-10c Selection of Sales Promotion Methods

Several factors affect a marketer's choice of sales promotion methods, including:

1. The objectives of the promotional effort;
2. Product characteristics—size, weight, cost, durability, uses, features, and hazards;
3. Target-market profiles—age, gender, income, location, density, usage rate, and buying patterns;
4. Distribution channels and availability of appropriate resellers; and
5. The competitive and regulatory forces in the environment.

✓ Concept Check

- Why do marketers use sales promotion?
- What are the two classifications of sales promotion methods?
- What factors affect the choice of sales promotion used?

公共关系
12-11 Public Relations

Learning Objective

12-11 Describe the types and uses of public relations.

As noted earlier, public relations is a broad set of communication activities used to create and maintain favorable relationships between an organization and various public groups, both internal and external. These groups may include customers, employees, stockholders, suppliers, educators, the media, government officials, and society in general.

公共关系工具的类型
12-11a Types of Public Relations Tools

Organizations use a variety of public relations tools to convey messages and to create images. Public relations professionals prepare written materials such as brochures,

Entrepreneurial Success

创业成功：BODEN是一家屡获殊荣的拉美裔所有的公关公司

Inside BODEN, an Award-Winning, Latina-Owned PR Company

BODEN is an independent communications agency in Miami, Florida, which was founded by Honduran native Natalie Boden. Boden has received numerous accolades for her agency's successes, including being inducted into PRWeek's "Hall of Femme." She also serves on the board of directors for the Culture Marketing Council.

Boden started with a single client, the Miami Parking Authority. After building a small set of retainer clients (clients who pay a fee in advance for services over an extended period of time), Boden hired her first employee. Not long after, the agency landed its first Fortune 500 clients, Target and McDonald's. The company has been recognized by the Hispanic Public Relations Association as "PR Agency of the Year" and by PR News as being one of the "Best Places to Work."

Boden says that her public relations agency's competitive advantage is its independence. BODEN can offer the creativity and quick turnaround of a boutique agency while upholding the standards of a global agency. The agency, which includes communicators, strategists, creatives, and digital and social experts, focuses on building trust with multicultural and Hispanic communities. Rather than turning to paid media (i.e., advertising), BODEN's approach centers around earned media (i.e., public relations). The PR agency has built relationships with influencers, organizations, community leaders, and the media to generate publicity.

Boden discourages her clients from using clichéd tactics such as hiring Hispanic celebrities or developing a Spanish advertisement. To stand out to Hispanic audiences, BODEN's mission is to "help global brands lead with culture." This means standing out with bold, culturally strategic communications that are both authentic and inspiring. The agency stands behind long-term, purpose-driven strategies that will leave a legacy.

Sources: Based on information in Court Stroud, "How One Latina Entrepreneur Founded an Award-Winning, Female-Led PR Company," *Forbes*, April 29, 2020; Steve Barrett, "Cafecito Break with Boden PR's Natalie Boden," *PR Week*, October 14, 2020; BODEN, "About Us".

newsletters, company magazines, annual reports, and news releases. They also create corporate-identity materials such as logos, business cards, signs, and stationery. Speeches, YouTube videos, and social media accounts at TikTok, Twitter, Instagram, and Facebook are additional public-relations tools through which companies can communicate information and ideas, interact with customers and other brands, or respond to negative information about the firm. Consider the San Diego Zoo, which has nearly 2 million followers on TikTok and uses the platform to post humorous animal videos that keep the nonprofit organization on the public's mind.[22]

Another public relations tool is event sponsorship, in which a company pays for all or part of a special event such as a concert, sports competition, festival, or play. Sponsoring special events is an effective way for organizations to increase brand recognition and receive media coverage, sometimes with relatively little investment. The energy drink brand Red Bull, for example, underscores its reputation for giving consumers energy through sponsoring athletes and teams, acts of daring, concerts, and festivals such as Coachella.

Event sponsorships are intended to promote a positive image of a firm. Event sponsorships are a public relations tool. They are often used in conjunction with advertising, personal selling, and sales promotions.

Publicity is an important part of public relations, as it increases public awareness of a firm or brand through mass media communications at no cost to the business. **Publicity** is communication in news-story form about an organization, its products, or both. Organizations use publicity to provide information about products; to

宣传

publicity communication in news-story form about an organization, its products, or both

新闻稿
news release a typed page of about 300 words provided by an organization to the media as a form of publicity

专题文章
feature article a piece (of up to 3,000 words) prepared by an organization for inclusion in a particular publication

带说明的照片
captioned photograph a picture accompanied by a brief explanation

新闻发布会
press conference a meeting at which invited media personnel hear important news announcements and receive supplementary textual materials and photographs

announce new product launches, expansions, or research; and to strengthen the company's image. Public relations personnel sometimes organize events, such as grand openings with prizes and celebrities, to generate news coverage of a company.

The most widely used tool of publicity is the **news release**. It is generally one typed page of about 300 words provided by an organization to the media as a form of publicity. The release includes the firm's name, address, phone number, and contact person. A **feature article**, which may run as long as 3,000 words, is usually written for inclusion in a particular publication. For example, a software firm might send an article about its new product to a computer magazine. A **captioned photograph**, a picture accompanied by a brief explanation, is an effective way to illustrate a new or improved product. A **press conference** allows invited media personnel to hear important news announcements and to receive supplementary materials and photographs. Finally, letters to the editor, special newspaper or magazine editorials, and videos may be prepared and distributed to appropriate media for possible use in news stories.

公共关系的运用
12-11b Uses of Public Relations

Public relations can be used to promote many things, including people, places, activities, and ideas. Public relations focuses on enhancing the reputation of the total organization by increasing public awareness of a company's products, brands, or activities and by fostering desirable company images, such as that of innovativeness, dependability, or social responsibility. By getting the media to report on a firm's accomplishments, public relations helps a company to maintain public visibility. Effective management of public relations efforts also can reduce the amount of unfavorable coverage surrounding negative events. For example, after KFC UK suffered negative publicity when it was unable to receive chicken supplies due to a delivery snafu, the company launched a mischievous campaign that included full-page ads and irreverent tweets to apologize and update British customers in a humorous way on when restaurants would resume normal operations.[23]

✓ Concept Check

- What are the common tools of public relations?
- What is publicity, and why do organizations use it?
- What are the four common types of publicity?

Discussion Questions 讨论题

1. What are the most common marketing channels for consumer products? For industrial products?
2. What are the levels of market coverage? What types of products are each used for?
3. What services are performed by wholesalers for producers and for retailers?
4. Identify three kinds of full-service wholesalers. What factors are used to classify wholesalers into one of these categories?
5. Differentiate among the types of retailers.
6. What can nonstore retailers offer their customers that in-store retailers cannot?
7. What is logistics? Which major functions does it include?
8. Can a middleman be eliminated from a marketing channel? Explain.
9. What is integrated marketing communications, and why is it becoming increasingly accepted?
10. Identify and describe the major ingredients of a promotion mix.
11. Identify and give examples of the three major types of salespersons.
12. What are the major tasks involved in managing a sales force?
13. What is the difference between publicity and public relations? What is the purpose of each?
14. Why do firms use event sponsorship?

Case 12 案例 12：在箱子里思考的 Casper

Casper Thinks Inside the Box

Known for its "bed-in-a-box" concept, Casper Sleep Inc. was created in 2014 with the simple idea of selling a mattress online. The company's goal was to create an affordable foam mattress that could be shipped in a box. The direct-to-consumer (D2C) mattress company wanted to bypass traditional mattress showrooms and deliver mattresses direct to its customer's doors.

Investors initially turned their nose up at Casper's concept. They thought no one would ever purchase a mattress online and didn't see a path for Casper to disrupt the $14 billion mattress market. The founders charged tens of thousands of dollars to their credit cards to bring the brand to life. Eventually, they caught the eye of an investor who had experience with other D2C brands. When Casper launched, it sold out of inventory on day one. The company expected to make $1.8 million in its first year, but it ended up hitting that goal within two months. The online mattress market is now crowded with competitors such as Leesa, Purple, and Tuft & Needle.

Excitement around the brand ramped up quickly, attracting the attention of celebrity investors such as actor Ashton Kutcher and rapper Nas. Casper became known for its quirky advertising, such as puzzles on subway ads, but its social media mentions, both paid and organic, became the company's bread and butter. Happy customers were excited to spread the word about Casper online. Casper implemented a referral program to capitalize on this word-of-mouth communication. The program took off, leading to a wave of unboxing videos on YouTube.

The popular mattress brand has run into its fair share of challenges. The company was initially considered a "unicorn" leading up to its initial public offering (IPO), meaning the privately held company was valued at more than $1 billion. This made Casper seem like a good investment, but things took a turn when Casper reduced its IPO price from $17 to $12. Shortly after the IPO, investors filed a lawsuit against the company for allegedly misleading them and not disclosing material information prior to the IPO. While Casper's revenue was up, so were losses. Additionally, the company spent more than $400 million in less than three years on marketing alone to maintain its edge over the competition. The bigger issue was that Casper was worth much less than $1 billion.

Some say Casper intentionally mislead investors, reporting steadily increasing profits when the reality was more dismal. Additionally, although Casper's registration statement detailed growth efforts with the introduction of retail stores in 20 countries, the company stated shortly after the IPO that it would reduce the size of its global operations and wind-down its European operations. This led to a reduction of its workforce by 21 percent. Lastly, Casper also failed to disclose that it was unloading large amounts of old inventory to customers at steep discounts.

Despite these challenges, the CEO and co-founder of Casper, Philip Krim, continues to be enthusiastic about the company's future. Krim says that by opening more stores and initiating more retail partnerships, the company could spend less on sales and marketing.[24]

Questions

1. How does Casper's distribution strategy differ from traditional mattress companies?
2. Casper disrupted the mattress industry. Why do you think investors were initially hesitant to back Casper?
3. Describe Casper's promotion mix.

PART 6
Information, Accounting, and Finance
信息、会计和理财

In this part of Foundations of Business, we focus on how social media and e-business are changing the world of business. We also examine how management information, accounting, and financial management are used to ensure that money is available when needed, that it is obtained at the lowest possible cost, and that it is used as efficiently as possible.

Chapter

13

Exploring Social Media and e-Business

探索社交媒体和电子商业

Learning Objectives

Once you complete this chapter, you will be able to:

13-1 Examine why it is important for a business to use social media.

13-2 Discuss how businesses use social media tools.

13-3 Explain the business objectives for using social media.

13-4 Describe how businesses develop a social media plan.

13-5 Explain the meaning of e-business.

13-6 Define the fundamental models of e-business.

13-7 Identify the factors that will affect the future of the internet, social media, and e-business.

Why Should You Care?

Question: How important are social media and e-business for a business today? Answer: Today, more and more businesses are using social media and e-business to reach new customers and increase sales and profits.

Inside Business 商业透视：Netflix 在客户保留率方面领先于竞争对手

Netflix Tops the Competition in Customer Retention

Netflix, the world's largest subscription-based streaming service, is deep in the trenches of the streaming war. Although it may have been the first successful entertainment company to stream programming, Netflix's advantage is quickly fading because of new competitors, including Amazon Prime Video, Hulu, Disney+, HBO Max, Apple TV+, and Peacock. In order to maintain its standing as the largest streaming service, Netflix must continue to build its content library, provide exceptional customer service, create original programming, retain existing customers, and add new subscribers to stay ahead of competitors.

While Netflix faces stiff competition, one measurement—churn rate—indicates that Netflix is likely to remain the leader in streaming services. Churn rate refers to the percentage of subscribers who do not renew their subscriptions during a given time frame. As competition heats up, one would expect Netflix's churn rate to increase because subscribers have more choices, but that hasn't been the case. The company's churn rate is between 2 and 3 percent, which is below the same measurement for all of its rivals. Competitors like HBO and Showtime often see a temporary increase in subscribers because viewers want to watch a new series that has been heavily marketed to build subscriber interest. Once subscribers see the series finale, streaming companies often experience a churn rate spike because they don't have additional content subscribers want. On the other hand, Netflix is able to retain customers because of its extensive content library that enables subscribers to always find something interesting that they want to watch.

Netflix also adds value to its service through personalization, an area where other streaming competitors lag behind. By considering the viewer's previous content choices and investing in search site algorithms, text analytics, and filtering to power its search function, Netflix is able to improve the subscriber's browsing experience and help viewers choose the content they will enjoy.

Is Netflix winning the war for subscribers? With 200 million subscribers worldwide and year-over-year subscriber growth rates in the double digits, it is beating the competition—for now. Still, Netflix knows the war is far from over. To maintain its number one position, Netflix knows it must retain existing customers and find ways to reach new customers. It must also continue to innovate and to build on the business and marketing practices that enabled it to become the leader in the subscription-based streaming service market.[1]

Did You Know?

Netflix has more than 200 million subscribers.

Take a moment to think about how social media and e-business affect your own life. In just a few short years, it has changed the way we communicate with each other, it has changed the way we meet people, and it has changed the way we shop. It has also changed the way we watch television. Netflix, the company profiled in the Inside Business feature for this chapter, is the leader in subscription streaming services. And yet, Netflix has big-name competitors that want a share of this market. The fact there are so many companies competing for a share of a large global market is evidence of how important streaming services (and e-business) have become. In this chapter, we explore how these trends affect both individuals and businesses.

We begin this chapter by examining why social media is important for both individuals and business firms. Next, we discuss how companies can use social media to build relationships with customers, the objectives for social media, the steps to build a social media plan, and ways to measure the effectiveness of a firm's social media activities. In the last part of this chapter, we take a close look at how firms use e-business and technology to conduct business using computers and the internet and what growth opportunities and challenges affect both social media and e-businesses.

为什么社交媒体很重要

13-1 Why Is Social Media Important?

Next time you go to lunch at your favorite restaurant or go to a ball game or the shopping mall, take a look at the number of people using their smartphones or even a tablet *and* social media to communicate with friends and relatives. In fact, if you are under the age of 40, you know exactly what social media is because you have grown up with computers and technology and are comfortable sharing information about yourself. If you are anyone else, social media seems like a strange (but exciting) phenomenon where millions of people freely share, create, vote, and connect with other people effortlessly using internet-based technologies.

Learning Objective

13-1 Examine why it is important for a business to use social media.

什么是社交媒体，它有多受欢迎

13-1a What Is Social Media and How Popular Is It?

Today, there are many definitions of social media because it is still developing and continually changing. For our purposes, **social media** represents the online interactions that allow people and businesses to communicate and share ideas, personal information, and information about products and services. Simply put, social media is about people. It is about a culture of participation, meaning that people can now discuss, vote, create, connect, and advocate much easier than ever before. For example, you can post your plans for a weekend trip on Facebook. Then you can share a travel itinerary and chronicle your trip through videos, photos, and ratings on Facebook, Snapchat, Pinterest, Twitter, and other social media sites. While it's hard to imagine, many popular social media sites like Facebook and Google were only created in the past 25 years (refer to Figure 13-1). Because early social media sites were so successful, more sites were developed. For example, TikTok was launched in 2016 and had more than 675 million monthly users at the beginning of 2021.

So, how popular are social media sites? A recent Pew Internet Research study found that 70 percent of Facebook users visit the site each day as part of their daily routine. Other sites including Instagram (59 percent), Snapchat (59 percent), YouTube (54 percent), and Twitter (46 percent) also have a large percentage of users that visit each site every day.[2] Among the most popular worldwide social media sites are Facebook, which has approximately 2.7 billion users, YouTube, which has more than 2 billion users, and Instagram, which has more than 1 billion users.[3] These numbers increase daily as people log onto social media from home, from work, and from smartphones to stay in touch with family and friends, reconnect with old friends or classmates, share photos and videos, and obtain information available on the internet.

社交媒体

social media the online interactions that allow people and businesses to communicate and share ideas, personal information, and information about products and services

企业为什么要使用社交媒体

13-1b Why Businesses Use Social Media

Social media has completely changed the business environment. Just the sheer number of people using social media makes using social media a top priority for many business firms. Today, a business can use social media to:

- Connect with its customers and stakeholders;
- Provide information that is valuable to customers; and
- Provide another means of customer service.

Now many companies, large and small, are using social media to learn about customers' likes and dislikes, seek public input about products and marketing, and promote specific products. Macy's, for example, is active on Facebook, Twitter, Pinterest, YouTube, and a blog designed

The leader! When it comes to social media, Facebook is the most popular site in the world and has more than 2.7 billion users. For many people, Facebook is the go-to site to keep up with friends and relatives or reconnect with people they haven't talked to in years. Other people just want to see what's happening in someone else's life.

Figure 13-1 Timeline for Many Popular Social Media Sites

Ever wonder when your favorite social media site was created? To answer that question, look at the timeline below.

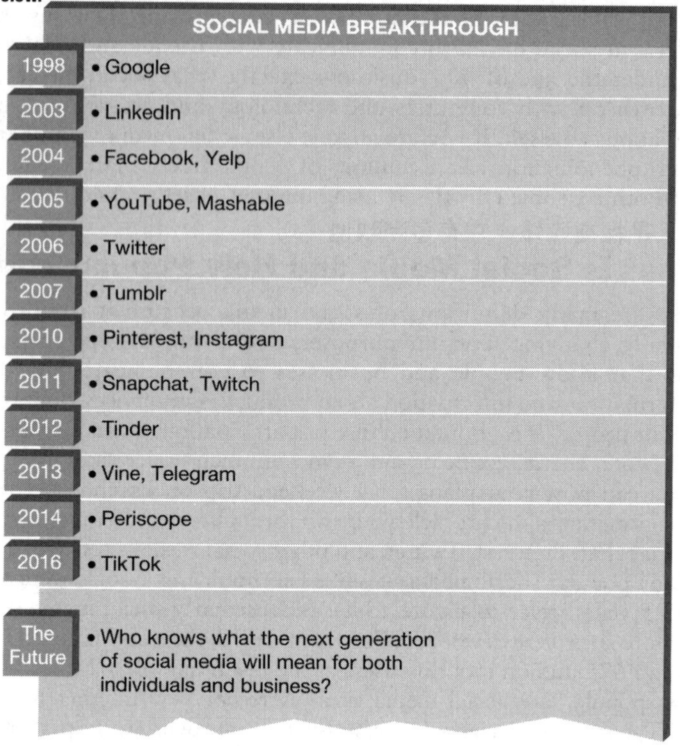

Note: Although there have been fewer internet and social media startups since 2016, they are usually small and when successful are often acquired by larger companies—many of the same companies listed in this figure.

to be read on mobile screens. The company uses its Facebook site, for example, to provide fashion tips and news about new products and special events to communicate with its 14.6 million-plus Facebook fans. Often it uses the Twitter hashtag #Macys to highlight special in-store events and announce discounts and clearance sales. A **hashtag** is either a word or a short phrase, preceded by the pound sign (#), to identify different topics. On Pinterest, Macy's lets pictures do the talking with "pinned" images of the latest in beauty products, fashions, bridal registry items, and home decor. Its YouTube channel includes Macy's commercials, coverage of the annual Thanksgiving Day Parade, behind-the-scenes designer interviews, and videos about fashion trends.

The fact that so many people are actively sharing information about themselves and their likes and dislikes online for all to see was a driving force for many companies to develop a social media presence. Unlike social media, traditional marketing and advertising messages were top-down because companies used television, newspapers, and magazine ads to promote their product to a large audience without any opportunity for feedback. With social media, customers can and do provide feedback. If people have bad experiences with a product or service, they tend to let the world know by writing about it on a blog, mentioning it on Facebook, or tweeting about it. A recent survey by Customer Care Measurement and Consulting found that 66 percent of households experienced a problem with a product or service in the last 12 months, and many of the survey respondents used social media to complain. In addition, the survey also discovered that 55 percent of the respondents expect a response to a complaint posted on social media and nearly half of the same respondents got no response. Seventeen percent of customers who experience poor customer service tell their friends and neighbors to raise public awareness of their experience.[4] While companies no longer have much

话题标签
hashtag a word or a short phrase, preceded by the pound sign (#), to identify different topics

Figure 13-2 The Six Most Important Benefits for a Business That Uses Social Media

While there are many reasons a business uses social media, the number one reason is that social media generates increased exposure for a business.

Source: Michael A. Stelzner, "2020 Social Media Marketing Industry Report," The Social Media Examiner.

control over what is said about their products or services, many still respond to negative comments about the company and its products or services made by their customers. Even if the company's response doesn't completely resolve the issue, customers appreciate the company's effort to improve customer service.

In addition to complaints, companies often use social media to respond to questions and positive customer feedback to provide additional information and build customer goodwill. The bottom line: If businesses aren't using social media to see what customers are saying about their products or services, they are missing an opportunity to increase sales and profits. For more information about why businesses use social media (and the benefits for a business), refer to Figure 13-2.

✓ Concept Check

- According to material in this section, what are the reasons why people use social media?
- How has social media changed the environment for business firms?

商用社交媒体工具

13-2 Social Media Tools for Business Use

Learning Objective

13-2 Discuss how businesses use social media tools.

For a business, part of what makes social media so challenging is the sheer number of ways to interact with other businesses and existing and potential customers. For example, companies can use **social content sites** to create and share information about their products. Commercials, for example, can go viral on social media, especially when linked to major sporting events like the Super Bowl or the World Cup. Jeep, Doritos, and Facebook used social media to generate millions of online views for their Super Bowl commercials both before and after the game.[5] For businesses selling to other businesses, social content sites can also include webinars and online promotional materials. In addition to social content sites, businesses can use blogs, photos, videos, podcasts, and social media ratings to increase customer awareness of their products and services.

博客的商业用途

13-2a Business Use of Blogs

A **blog** is a website that allows a company to share information to increase customers' knowledge about its products and services, as well as to build trust. Once a story or information is posted, customers can provide feedback through comments, which is one of the most important ways of creating a conversation with customers, not just as existing or potential customers, but as people.

Blogs are effective at developing better relationships with customers, attracting new customers, telling stories about the company's products or services, and providing an active forum for testing new ideas. For example, the Brooklyn-based online crafts marketplace Etsy uses its blogs to communicate with both buyers and

社交内容网站
social content sites websites which allow companies to create and share information about their products and services

博客
blog a website that allows a company to share information to increase the customer's knowledge about its products and services, and to build trust

Exploring Careers

职业探索：HBO Max 实习生玩转抖音

HBO Max Interns Rock TikTok

Social media is an ever-changing landscape, making it challenging for companies to keep up with emerging trends and platforms. To bring in a fresh perspective, HBO Max hired five interns, Ashley Xu, Gray Fagan, Preeti Singh, Conor Driscoll, and Paravi Das, to create TikTok videos to promote the HBO Max subscription video on demand service. While each video was tied to HBO Max and its entertainment content, they were also created to entertain and make viewers laugh and at the same time increase HBO Max's TikTok following. The move paid off. Because of the videos created by the interns, HBO Max's TikTok following increased from 29,000 to more than 728,000 followers at the time of publication of your text.

TikTok is a short-form mobile video platform known for viral memes, dancing, educational content, challenges, and comedic sketches. The key for businesses like HBO Max to succeed on TikTok is to create content that feels in line with the app's culture and target viewers. While there are exceptions, the majority of TikTok viewers are Gen Z (people born after 1997) and Millennials (people born between 1981 and 1996). To reach the target audience, the five interns began by creating a makeup challenge video to promote the HBO Max show *Euphoria*. The video went viral, receiving more than 3 million views. Their first video was topped by another of their videos that got more than 32 million views.

HBO Max's competitive paid internship program is immersive and hands-on. While someone doesn't need a degree in business or marketing to work in social media, a wide variety of skills are valuable in this arena. For example, Fagan was a film production major, Driscoll was a business administration major, and Singh was a public relations and advertising major. The interns pooled their knowledge of public relations, advertising, business, film production, and, of course, social media to produce 60-second TikTok skits to engage users on the platform. Their creativity and ability to tell stories made them an asset to the company. Though their internship was set to end, the students successfully pitched a proposal to HBO Max leadership to extend their stay. And, in typical fashion, the five made a TikTok video to go along with their proposal. End result: Their internship was extended for another three months.

Sources: Based on information in Sarah Whitten, "HBO Max Activations Double to 17.2 Million in Fourth Quarter," *CNBC*, January 27, 2021; Kelsey Sutton, "HBO Max's Secret to Viral TikToks: Letting Their Interns Run the Account," *Adweek*, October 12, 2020; Michelle Anguka, "Savvy Storytelling, TikTok Skills Lead Chapman Film Students to HBO Max Internships," *Chapman University Newsroom*, October 7, 2020.

媒体共享网站
media sharing sites websites which allow users to upload photos, videos, and podcasts

sellers. Its blog posts, some written by artisans and some by Etsy personnel, profile online shops, highlight new fashion trends, teach do-it-yourself craft techniques, and showcase unusual and unique items for sale. Etsy also maintains a "Seller Handbook" blog to help sellers succeed on Etsy.

照片、视频和播客

13-2b Photos, Videos, and Podcasts

In addition to blogs, another tool for social content is **media sharing sites**, which allow users to upload photos, videos, and podcasts. Before creating a media sharing site, managers and employees should consider the following three factors:

- Who will create the photos, videos, and podcasts that will be used?
- How will the content be distributed to interested businesses and consumers?
- How much will it cost to create and distribute the material?

One increasingly popular form of media is photo sharing. Today, photo sharing provides a method for a company to tell a compelling story about its products or services through postings on either the company's website or a social media site. Target, Gap, and many other retailers, for example, post photos of clothing available in their stores or online on their Pinterest sites.

Videos have also gained popularity because of their ability to tell stories. Companies know that YouTube and other sites are useful because they are already recognized by other businesses and consumers as a source of both entertainment and information. For example, entertainment companies, like Disney and MGM, use YouTube to showcase movie trailers. Home Depot and Lowe's have also posted great do-it-yourself videos on their YouTube channels. For example, Martha Stewart has teamed up with Home Depot to create livestream videos that describe how you can create home décor. Other uses of livestream videos include online classes, interviews, and question and answer sessions with a social media influencer. An **influencer** is a person known on social media who has an influence over a large number of followers.

Podcasts are digital audio or video files that people listen to or watch online on tablets, computers, smartphones, or other mobile devices. Think of podcasts as programs that are distributed through various means and not linked to scheduled time periods. The great thing about podcasts is that they are available for download at any time. Shopify—an e-commerce site that provides e-commerce software and other management tools to help business start-ups and existing businesses—uses a series of podcasts to provide entrepreneurs with information that can be used to grow their businesses.

How do you find the best restaurant in town? Answer: Read the ratings social media users post on Yelp. While known for its restaurant reviews, the Yelp site also has ratings for shopping, automotive repairs, home services, and even nightlife. More than 175 million people visit the Yelp website each month to find out what other people think about local businesses.

大咖
influencer a person known on social media who has an influence over a large number of followers

播客
podcasts digital audio or video files that people listen to or watch online on tablets, computers, smartphones, or other mobile devices

社交媒体评级
13-2c Social Media Ratings

Social media enables shoppers to access ratings, reviews, opinions, recommendations, and referrals from others who have bought a product or service. Sites for reviews and ratings are based on the idea that consumers trust the opinions of others when it comes to purchasing products and services. According to a recent survey by BrightLocal, a marketing research company with locations in the United States and three other countries, 93 percent of consumers used the internet to find a local business in the last year.[6] Based on the early work of Amazon, eBay, Google, and Yelp, consumers can rate local businesses or compare products and services. In addition, individual businesses that range from retailers like Home Depot and Target to travel services like Priceline and Trip Advisor provide a way for consumers to share information about products and services.

According to consumers, the most important review factors are the overall star rating, if the review seems to be legitimate, if the reviews are current, and the number of reviews.[7] Consumer reviews are especially influential in certain purchase situations. For example, retailers, restaurants, medical services, repair services, and travel are types of businesses where ratings make a difference in consumer buying decisions. Knowing this, Wyndham Hotel Group puts the ratings of consumers who use TripAdvisor directly on its websites so travelers can see what others say about each individual hotel. By examining the reviews, Wyndham can get a good sense of its online reputation and identify specific areas for improvement.[8]

✓ Concept Check

- What is a blog? How can a business use a blog to develop relationships with customers?
- What types of content can be used on a media sharing site? What factors should be considered when developing content for a media sharing site?
- How important are social media ratings for consumers? For businesses?

通过社交媒体实现商业目标

13-3 Achieving Business Objectives Through Social Media

Learning Objective

13-3 Explain the business objectives for using social media.

Although social media is a recent phenomenon, many businesses are already using it to achieve important objectives. Some of these goals are long term— such as building brand awareness and brand reputation—while others are more short term—such as increasing website traffic or generating sales leads. Regardless of how social media is used, there are a lot of business opportunities. In this section, we explore a few ways that companies have used social media effectively to achieve business objectives.

社交媒体社区

13-3a Social Media Communities

Social media communities are groups of people who share common interests and who want to use technology and the internet to connect with people with similar interests. People who are part of the communities can share information and even develop profiles. Individuals in a community can be called friends, fans, followers, or connections. Popular social networking sites include Facebook (the largest), LinkedIn (for professionals), Twitter, YouTube, Pinterest, and many others. To see how many businesses use the top six social media community sites, refer to Figure 13-3.

There are social communities for every interest, ethnic group, and lifestyle. Different types of social communities include forums and wikis. A **forum** is an interactive version of a community bulletin board that focuses on threaded discussions. These are particularly popular with people who share a common interest such as animal protection, health issues, or the latest movies. One of the most popular internet forums is Reddit, which is a massive collection of forums where people can share news and content and comment on other people's posts. Reddit is further broken down into subreddits, which are forums dedicated to specific topics. For example, there are subreddit communities for gaming, sports, television, travel, health and fitness, fashion, and many others. In reality, there are thousands of subreddits, and the number of subreddits continues to increase as more people with special interests interact on the Reddit site.

Another community based on social media is a wiki. A **wiki** is a collaborative online working space that enables members to contribute content that can be shared with other people. With wikis, members of the community are the editors and gatekeepers ensuring that the content is correct and updated. Wikipedia—the free online encyclopedia—is the best example of a wiki.

Figure 13-3 The Top Six Social Media Networking Sites Used by Businesses

For businesses using social media, the most popular social networking sites are Facebook and Instagram.

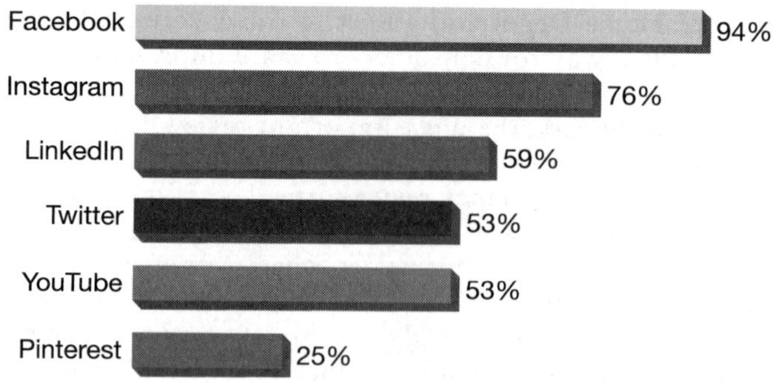

Source: Michael A. Stelzner, "2020 Social Media Marketing Industry Report," The Social Media Examiner.

社交媒体社区
social media communities groups of people who share common interests and who want to use technology and the internet to connect with people with similar interests

论坛
forum an interactive version of a community bulletin board that focuses on threaded discussions

维基
wiki a collaborative online working space that enables members to contribute content that can be shared with other people

Today, many companies and nonprofit organizations are using social media to build communities to achieve important objectives. For a business, developing social media communities is a way to interact with customers. Coca-Cola uses many different types of social media to build a community for people who want more information about Coca-Cola products and stories about Coke's involvement in the community. Because companies like Coca-Cola recognize the value of this type of social media, the largest companies now have a team of professionals to develop and monitor their social media activities led by a social media community manager. A **social media community manager** is a high-level executive who is responsible for all of a company's social media activities. Nonprofit organizations also use social media to promote and fund their programs. The nonprofit organization Kiva has helped build communities around the globe by matching lenders and struggling would-be entrepreneurs. Using Kiva to identify potential borrowers, anyone who can lend $25 (or more) can loan money to people who need a bit of cash to go into business or keep a business running. To date, there are 1.9 million Kiva lenders that have funded loans of more than $1.6 billion to people in 77 different countries.[9]

危机与声誉管理

13-3b Crisis and Reputation Management

One of the most important reasons for listening to stakeholders is to determine whether there is a crisis brewing. Crises happen more often than most managers, employees, and customers realize. A recent survey by accounting firm PricewaterhouseCoopers (PWC) found that almost 70 percent of corporate managers have experienced a crisis in the last five years.[10] For example, consider the effect of the COVID-19 pandemic on businesses throughout the world. The pandemic quickly made its way to regions including Europe, South America, and North America. Businesses in the United States were especially hit hard when non-essential businesses were in lockdown during spring 2020. Then the virus made a resurgence toward the end of the year. In many cases, social media was used to let customers know if businesses were open and what precautions they were using to keep both customers and employees safe during the pandemic. For example:

- Many businesses, including Home Depot, Lowe's, and Ace Hardware, were open, but strict requirements for masks, social distancing, and reduced operating hours were announced on their social media sites.
- Restaurants including Saltgrass Steakhouses, the Olive Garden, Red Lobster, and other national chains used social media to inform people of their operating hours and if they were open for food pick-up, delivery, or if dine-in was an option at some of their locations.
- Many manufacturers used social media to communicate with their customers—wholesalers, distributors, and retailers—about plant closures, product availability, and expected delivery dates.

Although the previous examples highlight how companies used social media to inform customers, employees, and stakeholders of the steps they were taking to fight a pandemic, often they will use social media to respond to negative reviews about the company's products or services. The following illustrates how Jet Blue Airlines handled a negative Twitter post.[11]

Customer – *My view during all the flight (4 hours). No movies, no TV. First complaint to one of my favorite airlines. [Followed by an image of a blank TV screen]*
Jet Blue Response – *Oh no! That's not what we like to hear! Were all the TVs out on the plane or is it just yours?*
Customer – *Just my TV. The ones I saw next to me, everything was working.*
Jet Blue Response – *We always hate it when that happens. Send us a direct message with your confirmation code to get you a credit for the non-working TV.*

社交媒体社区经理
social media community manager a high-level executive who is responsible for all of a company's social media activities

The Jet Blue Twitter team did a great job responding to this customer's complaint. First, they quickly acknowledged the problem, and then they asked for more information. Finally, they apologized and offered a credit for the non-working TV.

Although most companies spend more time responding to negative reviews, they also respond to positive complements about their product or service. In either case, the goal is to build customer goodwill, increase customer retention, and ultimately increase sales. Even though businesses can't anticipate when and what type of crisis will occur or when they will receive negative reviews, planning should begin before a problem situation develops. Employees should already be trained in social media etiquette and be monitoring social media sites to see what is said about the company and its products. During a crisis, companies can use social media to answer questions with carefully worded posts, reassure the public, and present positive information to help rebuild their reputations.

听取利益相关者的意见

13-3c Listening to Stakeholders

Listening to people, whether they are customers or not, is always an important aspect of a company's social media plan. Indeed, listening is often the first step when developing a social media strategy. By monitoring Facebook, Twitter, or other social media sites, companies can determine what customers think about their products or services. If a company receives negative comments, it's important to respond

Technology and Innovation

技术与创新：大众在愚人节的恶作剧适得其反

VW's April Fools' Day Prank Backfires

While social media is a valuable tool to help brands recover in the wake of a reputational crisis, it can also be a threat to an organization's reputation. If a crisis is handled poorly, social media can amplify damage rather than restoring faith in the brand. Additionally, because of the viral nature of social media, news can quickly spread, putting a company in the global spotlight before a company even has time to respond to negative comments. Consider what happened with an April Fool's Day prank orchestrated by automaker Volkswagen.

April Fool's Day pranks often cause a stir on social media. VW discovered that's not always a good thing. The company leaked a phony press release saying it would change its name to Voltswagen to bring attention to its $86 billion push into the electric vehicle market. The company tweeted, "We know, 66 is an unusual age to change your name, but we've always been young at heart. Introducing Voltswagen. Similar to Volkswagen, but with a renewed focus on electric driving."

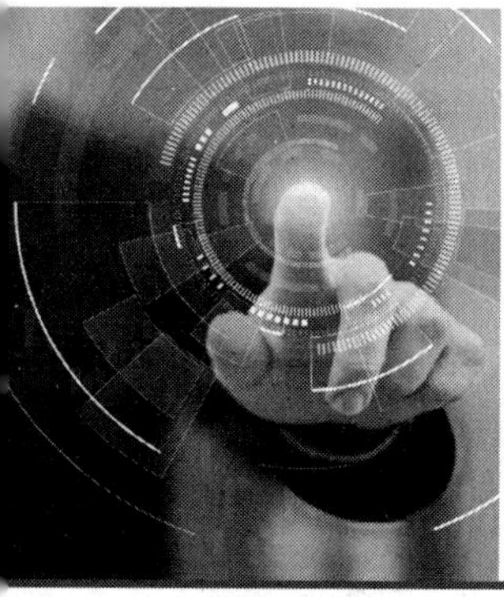

Unfortunately, many people, including reporters, did not realize it was a joke because it seemed authentic and was posted days ahead of April Fool's Day. The announcement was shared as a real news story on *USA Today*, *The Associated Press*, the *BBC*, *The Verge*, and dozens of other outlets. Social media users speculated about the press release for days before VW finally declared the announcement was a prank.

"What began as an April Fool's effort got the whole world buzzing," VW tweeted. "Turns out people are as passionate about our heritage as they are about our electric future. So, whether it's Voltswagen or Volkswagen, people talking about electric driving and our ID.4 can only be a good thing." (Note: ID.4 is VW's new electric SUV.) Consumers and the media did not agree, and the stunt was widely slammed.

The automaker, which was at the center of a previous emissions scandal where it lied to the public and regulators in 2015, has worked for years to repair its reputation. The April Fool's misstep dredged up memories of its unethical past. In fact, many media experts believe Volkswagen undermined its own efforts to move on from the emission scandal and eroded the company's trust and credibility.

Sources: Based on information in Aaron Gold, "How Volkswagen's 'Voltswagen' April Fools' Prank Backfired," *Motortrend*, April 5, 2021; Sean O'Kane, "Volkswagen of America Lied about Rebranding to 'Voltswagen'," *The Verge*, March 30, 2021; Volkswagen [@VW], *Twitter*, March 31, 2021; @RationalEtienne, *Twitter*, March 31, 2021.

quickly. A personal response either on social media or a personal contact often will help resolve a complaint and at the same time restore customer goodwill. It also helps if the customer feels that the company will take action to correct the problem. For example, many companies encourage customers to complete quick surveys about products or services. Brinker International—parent company of Chili's and Maggiano's restaurants—provides customers with a link to a short survey on the bottom of their receipt. Customers are free to provide both positive and negative comments about their dining experience. Those comments are then used to fine-tune restaurant operations. In some cases, when negative reviews are justified, customers receive a personal note, a phone call, or an email reply that may be accompanied with a gift card to encourage customers to become return customers.

目标客户
13-3d Targeting Customers

Many companies are using social media to increase awareness and build their brand among customers. It is especially valuable to target people based on their age. Common population age groups are often referred to as generations. For example, Generation Z (people born after 1997) is America's largest generation and accounts for 27 percent of the U.S. population.[12] Other generations in the U.S. population include:

- Millennials—people born between 1981 to 1996 and represent 25 percent;
- Generation X—people born between 1965 to 1980 and represent 20 percent;
- Baby Boomers—people born between 1946 to 1964 and represent 21 percent;
- The Silent Generation—people born between 1928 to 1945 and represent 7 percent; and
- The Greatest Generation—people born before 1928 and represent less than 1 percent.

To reach people who are included in each generation, it helps to identify who the customer is and what characteristics make the customer unique. For example, many people in Generation Z are now teenagers and represent younger consumers compared to people in the other generations. People in Generation Z grew up with technology, the internet, and social media. Facebook, Instagram, Snapchat, and YouTube are popular social media sites for people in this age group. In fact, Generation Z is quickly surpassing Millennials as a key target group of customers for retailers and manufacturers. For example, Nike—one of the most well-known brands in the world recognizes Generation Z as one of the most important groups to reach on social media. In fact, Nike uses Instagram, Facebook, Twitter, YouTube, and Pinterest to reach out to people in each generation.[13] Each of these social media sites is used to promote Nike athletic footwear, clothing, and other items with many posts, photos, and social media activities directed to specific age groups in different generations. As a result of social media and other promotion activities, the Nike swoosh and its marketing phrase "Just Do It" are known throughout the world. And yet, the real story is that the brand isn't using social media to just sell a specific product; Nike is selling the benefits and image of its products that literally become part of a person's lifestyle.[14] For the company, the investment in social media has increased brand awareness, but more importantly increased sales and profits.

社交媒体营销
social media marketing the utilization of software, computer technology, and the internet to provide information about a firm's products and services, increase sales revenues, and improve customer service

面向消费者的社交媒体营销
13-3e Social Media Marketing for Consumers

Social media marketing is the utilization of software, computer technology, and the internet to provide information about a firm's products and services, increase sales revenues, and improve customer service.

As companies become more comfortable with social media, we can expect even more companies to use social media to market products and services to their customers. Already, research indicates that companies are shifting their advertising money from traditional marketing (like television and magazines) to digital marketing (like internet search engines and social media). Experts now predict that companies will shift more marketing dollars to digital marketing over the next few years. And by 2024, some experts expect that spending on digital marketing will account for more than 50 percent of the marketing budget for many firms.[15] The primary reason is simple: People are spending more time on social media sites. Often the first step for a business that wants to use social media is to go to Facebook, Twitter, Snapchat, YouTube, LinkedIn, or some other popular social media site. As you can see from the information in Figure 13-4, companies like Snapchat make using their technology as easy as possible to connect with potential or existing customers.

其他业务的社交媒体营销

13-3f Social Media Marketing for Other Businesses

集客式营销

inbound marketing a marketing term that describes new ways of gaining attention, and ultimately customers, by creating content on a website that pulls customers in

Today, many companies have been quite successful using social media marketing not only to develop customer awareness, but also to obtain sales leads and increase actual sales to other businesses. HubSpot, for example, is a software company that helps companies develop inbound marketing programs. **Inbound marketing** is a marketing term that describes new ways of gaining attention, and ultimately customers, by

Figure 13-4 Snapchat's Marketing Solutions for Businesses

Like many social media sites, Snap's marketing tools help businesses connect with customers all over the globe. By using Snapchat, Domino's Pizza strengthened its brand awareness and surpassed both the company's and Snapchat's "success" benchmarks after a recent promotional campaign in Norway.

Source: Snapchat, https://forbusiness.snapchat.com/inspiration/dominos-strengthened-their-appeal-through-successful-campaign-on-snapchat, March 24, 2021.

creating content on a website that pulls customers in. Tools used for inbound marketing programs include search engine optimization, emails, blogging, videos, and social media. In order to market its software products, HubSpot shunned traditional advertising and began to practice what it preached. First, the company developed its own inbound marketing program by creating valuable content and marketing information that was then distributed through social media and search engine websites. Companies interested in HubSpot's software were required to enter contact information (name, phone number, and email address) in order to view the information because they believed the company's software could help them improve their marketing activities. As a result of HubSpot's inbound marketing program, the cost of generating new sales leads was reduced, the number of customers increased, and sales increased.

Companies also use social media marketing to sell goods and services, invite customer feedback, and reinforce a positive brand image. For General Electric (GE), social media marketing sets the stage for global sales of turbines, jet engines, and medical devices, among other products. GE is a social media innovator with award-winning videos, striking Instagram and Pinterest photos of its industrial products, followers on Facebook and Twitter, and a popular YouTube channel.

As important as social media marketing is, it is only one aspect of digital marketing. Indeed, digital marketing (sometimes referred to as online marketing) is comprised of several areas and also includes:

- *Search engine optimization*—using keywords in a company's website in order to rank higher in search engine results;
- *Search engine marketing*—buying advertising on sites like Google Ads to increase traffic to a company's website;
- *Display advertising*—buying banner ads; and
- *Email marketing*—targeting customers through opt-in email campaigns.

众包
crowdsourcing outsourcing tasks to a group of people in order to tap into the ideas of the crowd

From an ethical perspective, all company employees should identify themselves during social media interactions with customers and be transparent about their role in digital marketing. For example, Intel, which makes computer chips, is one of many businesses that require disclosure of ties to the company when employees participate in different types of digital marketing.

产生新产品创意

13-3g Generating New Product Ideas

Companies can use social media to conduct much of their consumer-based research. Using insight gained from Facebook or Twitter, for example, allows a company to modify existing products and services and develop new ones. Another method, **crowdsourcing** involves outsourcing tasks to a group of people in order to tap into the ideas of the crowd. In some cases, valuable information can be obtained by crowd voting. Frito-Lay, for example, has used crowd voting to determine which television commercials to advertise its popular Doritos brand. The company has also used crowdsourcing for product development. And in 2020, Frito-Lay used crowdsourcing to honor ordinary people who do extraordinary things to create joy in their communities. Family and friends were able to nominate someone who goes to great lengths to inspire joy. Once the crowd—a national sample of 5,000 adults—chose the winners, Frito-Lay then redesigned its famous potato chip bags to feature the smiles of the winners.[16]

The power of the crowd. LEGO—the Danish toymaker—uses crowdsourcing to generate new product ideas. Here's how it works. Customers can post and vote on ideas at https://ideas.lego.com. Ideas that get at least 10,000 votes are submitted to the company's review board. Then LEGO makes a final selection of promising ideas that begin the production process. For LEGO, the benefits include a new way to generate new product ideas and to build customer loyalty.

Companies can even build communities for specific brands in order to obtain information and new ideas from consumers. The Danish toymaker LEGO has created an online site called LEGO Ideas (https://ideas.lego.com) where brand enthusiasts can post and vote on new product ideas. LEGO benefits from its customers' creativity and the goodwill generated by seeking the community's input. Just as important, the creators receive credit for their ideas plus a small royalty from product sales.[17]

✓ Concept Check

- In your own words, describe how social media can help businesses to connect with other businesses and consumers.
- For a business, why are crisis and reputation management, listening to stakeholders, and targeting specific types of customers important activities?
- How can social media be used to market a firm's products or services to consumers and other businesses?
- How can social media help a firm generate new product ideas and recruit employees?

招聘员工

13-3h Recruiting Employees

For years, companies have used current employees to recruit new employees based on the theory that "birds of a feather flock together." The concept is simple: Current employees' friends and family may prove to be good job candidates. Social media takes that concept to a whole new level. LinkedIn, the largest social network for professionals, has been used quite effectively by large corporations, small businesses, nonprofit organizations, and government agencies that want to recruit new employees. Because LinkedIn hosts more than 750 million registered members, employers using the site can save time, reduce their recruiting costs, and see more information about individual candidates.[18] Companies like 3M, Coca-Cola, Four Seasons Hotels and Resorts, Hewlett Packard, IBM, Microsoft, Procter & Gamble, and many others have all had recruiting success with LinkedIn. Many other social media sites, including Glassdoor, Facebook, Instagram, and YouTube, can also be used for networking and to learn about a company where you might want to work.

制订社交媒体计划

13-4 Developing a Social Media Plan

Learning Objective

13-4 Describe how businesses develop a social media plan.

Before developing a plan to use social media, it is important to determine how social media can improve the organization's overall performance and how it "fits" with a company's objectives and other promotional activities. For example, if a social media plan attempts to improve customer service, it needs to link to the company's other efforts to improve customer service.

制订社交媒体计划的步骤

13-4a Steps to Build a Social Media Plan

Once it is determined how social media links to the company's other activities, there are several steps that should be considered.

Step 1: Listen to Determine Opportunities As pointed out earlier in this chapter, social media is often used to "listen" to what customers like and don't like about a company's products or services. For example, reading comments on social media sites can yield some insight into how consumers are reacting to a price increase for an existing product or service. Monitoring social media sites also allows managers and employees to not only listen but also to enter the conversation and tell the company's side of the story. In addition, companies can monitor social media sites to gather information about competitors as well as what is being said about the industry.

Step 2: Establish Social Media Objectives After listening to customers and analyzing the information obtained from social media sites, it is important to use that information to develop specific objectives. For social media, an objective is a statement about what a social media plan should accomplish. Each objective should be specific, measurable, achievable, realistic, and oriented toward the future. In addition, all objectives need to be linked to specific actions that can be used to accomplish each objective.

For most companies, the most popular objectives are:[19]

- Improving customer service
- Increasing brand awareness

- Building brand presence
- Acquiring new customers
- Developing loyalty programs

Other objectives that are often important for many firms include introducing new products, improving search engine ranking, and increasing the number of people who visit the company's social media sites.

Step 3: Segment and Target the Social Media Customer Ideally, a company will have developed a customer profile that describes a typical customer in terms of age, income, gender, ethnicity, etc. When segmenting or targeting customers, it also helps to know how they think, how they spend their time, how much they buy, and how often they buy. Additionally, it is important to really understand how customers use social media.

- Do they create content like photos, videos, blog posts, etc.?
- Do they use social media for information, ratings, and reviews?
- Do they spend a lot of time using social media?

More information about potential customers will help you develop a social media plan to achieve a company's objectives. Lack of information about customers can lead to wasted time and money and the inability to successfully achieve the firm's social media objectives. For example, most companies feel that they must use Facebook, Instagram, and Twitter. But if their core customer does not use these social media sites, then it does not make sense to use them. Some of the information that can help you target just the "right" social media customer is illustrated in Figure 13-5.

Figure 13-5 Types of Information That Can Help Target Different Social Media Customers

The more information you have about customers, the easier it is to develop a social media plan that targets the "right" customer.

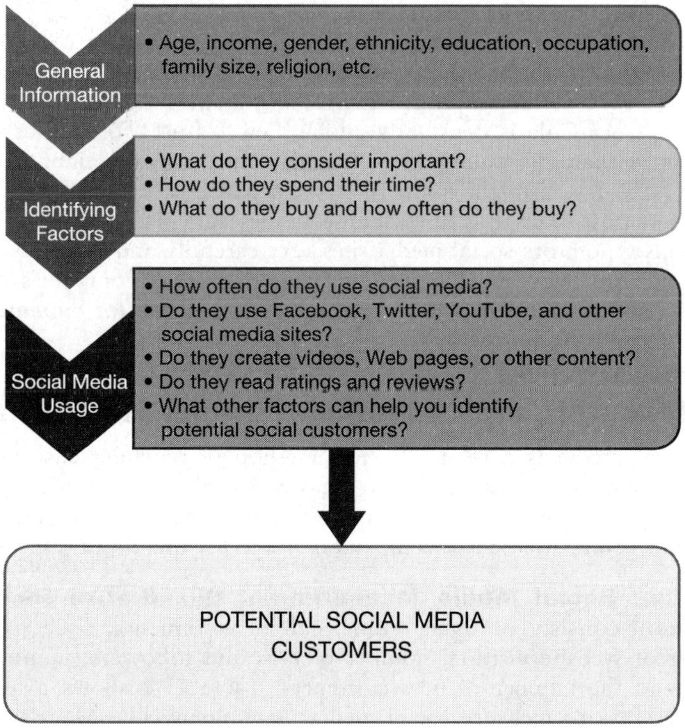

Step 4: Select Social Media Tools The search for the right social media tool(s) usually begins with the company's social media objectives, outlined in Step 2. It also helps to review the target customer or segment of the market the company is trying to reach (Step 3). With this information, the next step is to choose the right social media tools to reach the right customers. A company can use social media content sites, blogs, photos, videos, podcasts, or crowdsourcing to reach potential or existing customers. For example, if the goal is to recruit college graduates for sales positions for a large pharmaceutical company, LinkedIn may be a good choice. Remember, it is not necessary (or even advisable) to use all of the above tools. It is also possible for a business to build a social media community—especially when the objective is to fund business start-ups. Often money for worthwhile projects is obtained through crowdfunding. **Crowdfunding** is a method of raising money to fund a project for a business, a nonprofit organization, or an individual. The money raised can be an investment, a loan, or a donation. For example, a young startup company, Oculus VR, used Kickstarter—a crowdfunding site to raise $250,000. The money (along with later funding from venture capitalists) was used to build a virtual-reality headset, Oculus Rift, that puts players into their favorite games. Oculus VR was so successful that later Facebook bought the company for $2 billion.[20]

Step 5: Implement and Integrate the Plan Once social media tools have been identified, a company can implement and integrate the social media plan. Because a social media plan doesn't necessarily have a start and stop date, it is different from traditional advertising campaigns. Some social media activities continue and have a life of their own. For example, Zappos, a very successful online retailer, is a company that is always "on" in terms of its social media. Indeed, they do very little traditional advertising and instead rely on the company's website and social media to promote products, monitor customer service, and enhance the company's reputation. If a customer uses social media to complain, their customer service representatives will often contact the customer and try to resolve any problems the customer has experienced. This customer-focused approach often leads to increased customer satisfaction and increased sales.

Some companies, on the other hand, feel that it is important to have a mix of short- and long-term social media promotion. In this case, it's important to key the content to each social media site and to coordinate the timing of promotions. For example, Coca-Cola is constantly adding new features to its Facebook page, which has more than 105 million likes. One day, the company might post its latest video. The next day, it might invite visitors to participate in a survey. Knowing that customers post thousands of social media messages about its brand every day, Coca-Cola also monitors social media sites very carefully and responds quickly to questions and comments. Finally, like a growing number of companies, Coca-Cola integrates its social media and traditional marketing efforts for maximum impact and to get "more bang for the buck."

衡量和调整社交媒体计划

13-4b Measuring and Adapting a Social Media Plan

Because social media is a relatively new method of reaching customers, many companies struggle when attempting to measure social media. Generally, there are two types of social media measurement. While both quantitative and qualitative measurements can be used, most companies tend to use quantitative measurements.

Quantitative Social Media Measurement **Quantitative social media measurement** consists of using numerical measurements, such as counting the number of website visitors, number of fans and followers, number of leads generated, and the number of new customers. Table 13-1 shows a few popular quantitative ways to measure social media. A company like Macy's counts not

众筹
crowdfunding a method of raising money to fund a project for a business, a nonprofit organization, or an individual

量化社交媒体测量
quantitative social media measurement using numerical measurements, such as counting the number of website visitors, number of fans and followers, number of leads generated, and the number of new customers

Table 13-1 Quantitative Measurements for Selected Social Media Websites

Type of Social Media	Typical Measurements
Blogs	• Unique visitors • Number of views • Ratio of visitors to posted comments
Twitter	• Number of followers • Number of tweets and retweets • Click through rate (CTR) of tweeted links • Visits to website from tweeted links
Facebook	• Number of likes • Number of comments and responses • Visits to websites from Facebook links
YouTube	• Number of videos • Number of visitors • Ratio of comments to the number of videos • Watch time

only the number of social media likes and followers but also the number of times the company is mentioned each day. Although such measures help the company gauge brand awareness, determining how social media affects actual purchases of consumer products, like clothing and jewelry, can be difficult. Business-to-business marketers frequently set additional goals to track how social media activities lead to sales contacts and then to purchases. SAP North America, which markets software and technology services to corporations, uses social media to generate leads and facilitate the sales process. For example, SAP sponsors special events, workshops, and presentations that showcase the firm's software products. Both current and prospective customers often find out about these programs by accessing the firm's social media sites. To attend many of these events, people must register and provide basic contact information. Later, the person's contact information is used to initiate future sales calls.[21] By tracking such contacts, SAP can determine the effect of its programs on the company's sales revenues.

A number of companies are also using key performance indicators to measure their social media activities. **Key performance indicators (KPIs)** are measurements that define and measure the progress of an organization toward achieving its objectives. Generally, KPIs are *quantitative* (based on numbers like the number of YouTube views).

If measuring the success or failure of social media activities with KPIs, the first step is to connect KPIs with objectives. The second step is to set a benchmark—a number that shows what success should look like. Assume Mercedes-Benz sets a benchmark of 750,000 views for a new YouTube video that introduces a new S-Class model automobile. If at the end of a specified time period, 840,000 people have viewed the video, it would indicate the company's video campaign was successful.

Qualitative Social Media Measurement **Qualitative social media measurement** is the process of accessing the opinions and beliefs about a brand. This process primarily uses sentiment analysis to categorize what is being said about a company. **Sentiment analysis** is a measurement that uses technology to detect the mood,

关键绩效指标
key performance indicators (KPIs) measurements that define and measure the progress of an organization toward achieving its objectives

定性社交媒体测量
qualitative social media measurement the process of accessing the opinions and beliefs about a brand

情感分析
sentiment analysis a measurement that uses technology to detect the mood, attitudes, or emotions of people who experience a social media activity

Quantitative or qualitative measurements—Which one is best? That's a hard question to answer. Both methods can be used to measure the effectiveness of a company's social media plan. Quantitative measurements are numerical, like the number of visitors to a site. Qualitative measurements analyze a customer's sentiments, like what people think about a company's customer service. Sometimes just asking customers to check a box if they like a product or service or not is all it takes.

attitudes, or emotions of people who experience a social media activity. Other measurements for determining customer sentiment include:

- *Customer satisfaction score*—the relative satisfaction of customers;
- *Issue resolution rate*—the percentage of customer service inquiries resolved satisfactorily using social media; and
- *Resolution time*—the amount of time taken to resolve customer service issues.

When compared to quantitative measurement, it should be noted that many of these qualitative social media measurements are more subjective in nature.

维护社交媒体计划的成本
13-4c The Cost of Maintaining a Social Media Plan

Basic assumption: Social media is not free and can be quite expensive. Because social media costs both time and money, it is important to measure the success of a social media plan and make adjustments and changes if needed. Based on quantitative and qualitative measurements, the company may also try to determine if it is getting a positive return on its investment in social media.

After reviewing results for social media activities against pre-established benchmarks, it may be necessary to make changes and update the plan to increase the effectiveness of the social media plan. A social media plan, for example, must provide current and up-to-date information in order to keep customers coming back to see what's new. Without updates, customers lose interest and the number of returning customers can drop dramatically. After all, one of the major objectives of social media activities is to provide customers and stakeholders with current and useful information about the company and its products or services. Once it is determined that updates and changes are needed, many of the same steps described in this section may be used to improve a firm's social media plan. It is also important to create future social media plans based on what worked and what didn't work in previous plans.

Social media is particularly important to businesses that use computers and the internet to sell their products and services online. In the next section, we take a close look at how e-business firms are organized, satisfy needs online, and earn profits.

✓ Concept Check

- What are the steps required to develop a social media plan?
- What is the difference between quantitative and qualitative measurements? Which type of measurement do you think is the most reliable when measuring the effectiveness of a company's social media plan?

电子商业的定义
13-5 Defining e-Business

Learning Objective

13-5 Explain the meaning of e-business.

We define *business* as the organized effort of individuals to produce and sell, for a profit, the goods and services that satisfy society's needs. Working from this original definition, then, **e-business (or electronic business)**, can be defined as the organized effort of individuals to produce and sell, for a profit, the goods and services that satisfy society's needs *through the facilities available on the internet*. Sometimes people use the term *e-commerce* instead of *e-business*. In a strict sense, e-business is used when you're talking about all business activities and practices conducted on the internet by an individual firm or industry. On the other hand, **e-commerce** is a part of e-business and usually refers only to buying and selling activities conducted online. Although actual statistics vary depending on the source, U.S. e-commerce retail sales already account for approximately $432 billion a year and are expected to increase to $563 billion by 2025.[22]

With the popularity of smartphones and tablet computers, many companies are also using **mobile marketing** to communicate with and sell to customers through mobile devices. Mobile marketing covers a range of activities, from optimizing websites for viewing on smartphones and tablets to delivering promotional messages and discounts via mobile devices. Because mobile devices are used in over 40 percent of online transactions, many businesses are investing more heavily in mobile marketing.[23] A growing number of companies have *apps* to make mobile

电子商业
e-business (or **electronic business)** the organized effort of individuals to produce and sell, for a profit, the goods and services that satisfy society's needs through the facilities available on the internet

电子商务
e-commerce a part of e-business and usually refers only to buying and selling activities conducted online

移动营销
mobile marketing communicating with and selling to customers through mobile devices

transactions faster and more convenient for customers. For example, Starbucks offers an easy-to-use app for customers to pay for their lattes or espressos directly from a smartphone or tablet.

组织电子商业资源
13-5a Organizing e-Business Resources

To be organized, a business must combine *human, material, informational,* and *financial resources.* This is true of e-business, too (refer to Figure 13-6), but in this case, the resources may be more specialized than in a typical business. For example, people who can design, create, and maintain websites are only a fraction of the specialized human resources required by e-businesses. Material resources often include customized computers and high-speed internet connections. Computer software programs that track the number of visitors who view a firm's website and customers who make online purchases are generally among the specialized informational resources required. Financial resources, the money required to start and maintain the firm and allow it to grow, usually reflect greater participation by individual entrepreneurs, venture capitalists, and investors willing to invest in a high-tech firm instead of conventional financial sources such as banks.

In an effort to reduce the cost of specialized resources that are used in e-business, many firms have turned to outsourcing. **Outsourcing** is the process of finding outside vendors and suppliers that provide professional help, parts, or materials at a lower cost. For example, a firm that needs computer programmers and specialized software to complete a project may turn to an outside firm located in another part of the United States, India, or an Eastern European country.

满足线上需求
13-5b Satisfying Needs Online

The internet has created some new customer needs that did not exist before its creation. Consider what happened during the second quarter (April, May, and June) of 2020. e-Commerce sales grew an average of 45 percent when compared to the same period the previous year.[24] The growth was the result of the COVID-19 pandemic. Because of a shutdown of non-essential businesses and fear for the health of not only themselves but also their families, customers turned to online shopping to obtain the products they needed. For the remainder of the year, the growth rate for e-commerce continued to rise to record levels. For example, 44 percent more

Figure 13-6 Combining e-Business Resources

While all businesses use four resources (human, material, informational, and financial), these resources are typically more specialized when used in an e-business.

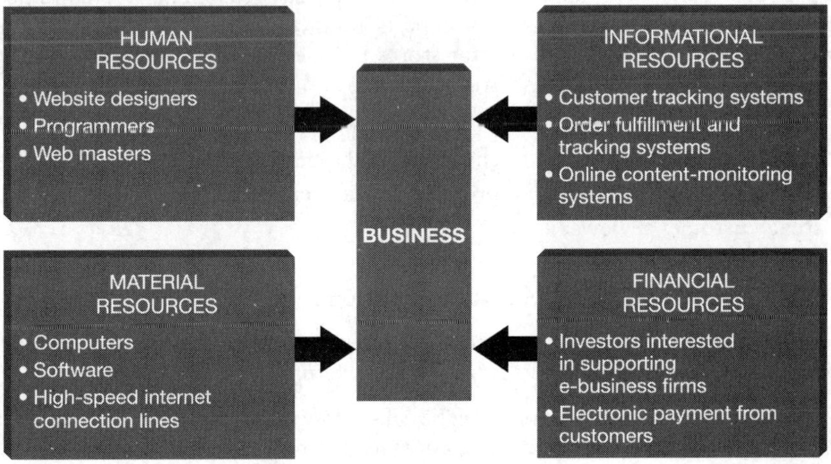

外包
outsourcing the process of finding outside vendors and suppliers that provide professional help, parts, or materials at a lower cost

Entrepreneurial Success

创业成功：为什么小企业喜欢 Shopify

Why Small Businesses Like Shopify

In 2004, Tobias Lütke, Daniel Weinand, and Scott Lake came up with the idea for Shopify, a Canadian e-commerce platform, while opening a small online business for snowboarding equipment called Snowdevil. The three entrepreneurs were dissatisfied with existing e-commerce sites, so Lütke, a computer programmer, decided to build his own. Two years later, the platform hosting Snowdevil was launched as Shopify.

Now, more than 1 million businesses in 175 countries use Shopify to sell merchandise. One of the keys to Shopify's success is that instead of positioning itself as a traditional e-commerce platform, it markets itself as a one-stop-shop for business owners to start, run, and grow their businesses. Small business owners that use Shopify typically use a variety of services, including email marketing, website hosting, logistics management, and point-of-sale software. This all-in-one approach is attractive for small business owners who have limited time, resources, and technical expertise because it eliminates the need to deal with third parties to get the tools that they need to operate their businesses. For example, its customizable themes and drag-and-drop store builder tool eliminate the need for design skills. Another attractive feature allows Shopify users to sync online and in-store sales using its point-of-sales software. According to many users, Shopify offers solutions, tools, and services that were previously unavailable for many small business owners for a relatively small monthly fee.

Shopify was already growing steadily when the COVID-19 pandemic struck. With lockdown restrictions in place for many nonessential businesses and an increasing number of customers shopping online, many small business owners scrambled to get their businesses online. Shopify enticed new users by extending its 14-day free trial to 90 days for a limited time on select plans. Extending the free trial gave customers more time to determine if Shopify was the right e-commerce platform for them. As a result, Shopify experienced rapid growth.

Small business owners aren't the only ones enjoying everything Shopify has to offer. Major brands such as Pepsi, Heinz, and Staples also use the Shopify e-commerce platform. While it faces a variety of e-commerce competitors, including Adobe's Commerce, BigCommerce, WooCommerce, Wix, and even Amazon, Shopify stands out from the competition because of its ability to meet the needs of its small-business customers.

Sources: Based on information in Lauren Debter, "During Pandemic, Shopify Woos A Wave Of Small Businesses Eager To Get Online," *Forbes*, May 8, 2020; Matt Grossman and Kimberly Chin, "Shopify's Revenue Nearly Doubles as Covid-19 Pushes Shopping Online," *The Wall Street Journal*, July 30, 2020; Laura Forman, "Shopify's Business Sells Itself, for Now," *The Wall Street Journal*, July 29, 2020.

people made purchases online during the Thanksgiving to Cyber Monday period in 2020 when compared to the previous year.[25] This increase was caused by people avoiding crowded stores that are typical of this holiday season. Now even as people return to more normal times, many experts predict online sales will continue to increase and sales in brick-and-mortar stores will decline in the future. While there are many reasons for the increase in e-commerce and online shopping, major reasons include the ability to:

- Save time when compared to shopping at the mall or store;
- Compare prices for the same product on different websites;
- Read customer reviews;
- Avoid checkout lines; and
- Have products delivered without leaving home.

In addition to purchasing products, the internet can be used by both individuals and business firms to obtain information. For example:

- Internet users can access newspapers, magazines, radio, and television programming at a time and place convenient to them.

- The internet provides the opportunity for two-way interaction between an internet firm and the customer. For example, many new-car dealers have a "chat" option on their websites for customers who can ask specific questions or want more information about their automobiles or service.
- Finally, the internet allows customers to choose the content they are offered. For the advertiser, knowing that its advertisements are being directed to the most likely customers represents a better way to spend advertising dollars.

Who is the largest retailer in the world? Walmart is number one when you measure total sales from brick-and-mortar stores *and* e-commerce. And yet, if you *measure just e-commerce sales*, Amazon is larger. One of the reasons why Amazon is the leader in online retailing is that it is easy to purchase just about anything you want and have it delivered in a few days or even the same day in some locations. Now that's fast.

创造电子商业利润
13-5c Creating e-Business Profit

Business firms can increase profits either by increasing sales revenue or by reducing expenses through a variety of e-business activities.

Increasing Sales Revenue Each source of sales revenue flowing into a firm is referred to as a **revenue stream**. Today, there are many different ways to use the internet and technology to increase sales revenue. Because the opportunity to shop on the internet is virtually unrestricted, traditional retailers like Target (www.target.com) and Walmart (www.walmart.com) can obtain additional revenue by selling to a global customer base 24 hours a day, seven days a week. However, shifting revenues earned from customers inside a real store to revenues earned from these same customers online does not create any real new revenue for a firm. The goal is to find *new customers* that shop online and generate *new sales* so that *total revenues are increased.*

Intelligent information systems also can help to generate sales revenue for internet firms such as Amazon (www.amazon.com). Such systems store information about each customer's purchases, along with a variety of other information about the buyer's preferences. Using this information, the system can assist customers the next time they visit the website. For example, if the customer has bought a Carrie Underwood CD in the past, the system might suggest CDs by similar artists who have won awards from the Academy of Country Music.

Many internet firms generate revenue from commissions earned from sellers of products linked to their internet sites. For example, both Amazon and eBay earn revenue by providing a website where vendors can sell merchandise to buyers who may be located any place in the world.

Although some customers may not make a purchase online, the existence of the firm's website and the services and information it provides may lead to increased sales in the firm's physical stores. For example, Honda's website (www.honda.com) can provide basic comparative information for shoppers so that they are better prepared for their visit to an automobile showroom.

In addition to selling products or services online, e-business revenue streams are created by advertising placed on web pages and by subscription fees charged for access to online services and information. For example, Dun & Bradstreet (www.dnb.com/), a comprehensive source for company and industry information, makes some of its online content free for anyone who visits the site, but more detailed information is available only by paid subscription.

Reducing Expenses Reducing expenses is the second major way in which e-businesses can help to increase profitability. Providing online access to information

收入流
revenue stream a source of revenue flowing into a firm

✓ Concept Check

- What are the four major factors contained in the definition of e-business?
- How does e-business satisfy needs online?
- How do e-businesses generate revenue streams, reduce expenses, and earn a profit?

that customers want can reduce the cost of dealing with customers. T-Mobile, for instance, is just one company that maintains an extensive website where potential customers can learn more about products and services, and where current customers can access personal account information, send questions to customer service, and purchase additional products or services. With such extensive online services, T-Mobile does not have to maintain as many physical store locations as it would without these online services. We examine more examples of how e-business contributes to profitability throughout this chapter, especially as we focus on some of the business models for activity on the internet.

电子商业的基本模式

13-6 Fundamental Models of e-Business

Learning Objective

13-6 Define the fundamental models of e-business.

A **business model** represents a group of common characteristics and methods of doing business to generate sales revenues and reduce expenses. Each of the models discussed in the following text represents a primary e-business model. Regardless of the type of business model, planning often depends on if the e-business is a new firm or an existing firm adding an online presence—refer to Figure 13-7. It also helps to keep in mind that in order to generate sales revenues and profits, a business—especially an e-business—must meet the needs of its customers.

企业对企业（B2B）模式

13-6a Business-to-Business (B2B) Model

Some firms use the internet mainly to conduct business with other businesses. These firms are generally referred to as having a **business-to-business** (or **B2B**) **model.**

Figure 13-7 Planning for a New Internet Business or Building an Online Presence for an Existing Business

The approach taken to creating an e-business plan will depend on whether you are establishing a new Internet business or adding an online component to an existing business.

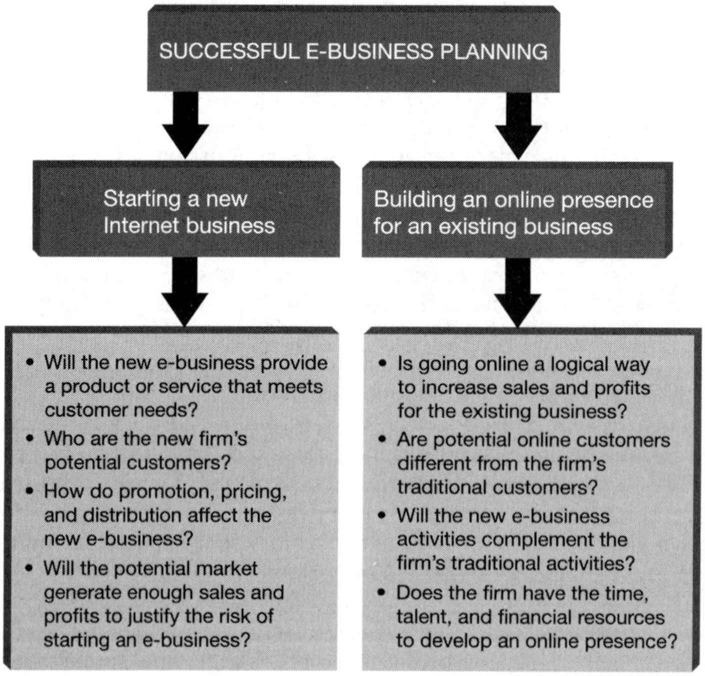

商业模式
business model a model that represents a group of common characteristics and methods of doing business to generate sales revenues and reduce expenses

企业对企业（或 B2B）模式
business-to-business (or **B2B**) **model** a model used by firms that conduct business with other businesses

When examining B2B firms, two clear types emerge. In the first type, the focus is facilitating sales transactions between businesses. For example, Dell manufactures computers to specifications that customers enter on the Dell website (www.dell.com). A large portion of Dell's online orders are from corporate clients who are well informed about the products they need and are looking for fairly priced, high-quality computer products that will be delivered quickly. By dealing directly with Dell, customers eliminate costs associated with wholesalers and retailers, thereby helping to reduce the price they pay for equipment.

A second, more complex type of B2B model involves a company and its suppliers. Today, suppliers use the internet to bid on products and services they wish to sell to a business customer and learn about the customer's rules and procedures that must be followed. For example, Ford, General Motors, and Chrysler have developed a B2B model to link thousands of suppliers that sell the automobile makers parts, supplies, and raw materials worth millions of dollars each year. Although the B2B site is expensive to start and maintain, there are significant savings for all three automakers. Given the potential savings, it is no wonder that many other manufacturers and their suppliers are beginning to use the same kind of B2B systems that are used by the automakers.

Tired of standing in the checkout line at the grocery store? Then shop online. Many supermarket chains are experiencing an uptick in the number of consumers who are using their e-commerce sites to buy groceries. For consumers, the process is simple: Order your merchandise online, pay online, and then either pick up your groceries at the store's customer pickup location or have your purchases delivered to your home.

企业对消费者（B2C）模式

13-6b Business-to-Consumer (B2C) Model

In contrast with the B2B model, firms such as Amazon (www.amazon.com), Walmart (www.walmart.com), and Dick's Sporting Goods clearly are focused on individual consumers. These companies are referred to as having a **business-to-consumer (or B2C) model**. In a B2C situation, understanding how consumers behave online is critical to a firm's success. Typically, a business firm that uses a B2C model must answer the following questions:

- What sorts of products and services are best suited for online consumer shopping?
- Will consumers use websites to simplify and speed up comparison shopping?
- Will consumers purchase services and products online or end up buying at a traditional retail store?
- Are consumers willing to wait for purchases to be delivered, will they pay for next-day delivery, or will they collect online purchases from a convenient pickup site?

In addition to providing round-the-clock global access to all kinds of products and services, B2C firms often attempt to build long-term relationships with their customers. Often, firms will make a special effort to make sure that the customer is satisfied and that problems, if any, are solved quickly. Most B2C firms, for example, have liberal return policies and often pay for returning merchandise that the customer does not like. Specialized software can also help build good customer relationships. Tracking the decisions and buying preferences when customers shop online, for instance, helps a B2C business provide suggestions for additional merchandise or services the customer may want to consider. In essence, this is Orbitz's (www.orbitz.com) online selling

企业对消费者（或 B2C）模式
business-to-consumer (or B2C) model a model used by firms that focus on conducting business with individual consumers

Table 13-2 Other Business Models That Perform Specialized e-Business Activities

Although modified versions of B2B or B2C, these business models perform specialized e-business activities to generate revenues.

Advertising e-business model	Advertisements that are displayed on a firm's website in return for a fee. Examples include pop-up and banner advertisements on search engines and other popular internet and social media sites.
Brokerage e-business model	Online marketplaces where buyers and sellers are brought together to facilitate an exchange of goods and services. One example is 1stDIBS (www.1stdibs.com), which provides a site for buying and selling furniture, lighting, home décor, antiques, jewelry, and fashion items.
Consumer-to-consumer model	Peer-to-peer software that allows individuals to share information over the internet. For example, Craigslist is a site where users can buy and sell all kinds of items.
Consumer to business model	Social media influencers, bloggers, or paid reviewers create content that promotes a company's products or services. In turn, the business pays either a predetermined dollar amount or a percentage of revenue for the promotion or information provided.
Subscription and pay-per-view e-business models	While some information may be free, detailed content is available only to users who pay a fee to gain access to a website. Examples include investment information provided by Morningstar (www.morningstar.com) and business research provided by Forrester Research, Inc. (www.forrester.com).

✓ Concept Check

- What are the two-fundamental e-business models?
- Assume that you are the owner of a small company that produces outdoor-living furniture. Describe how you could use the B2C business model to sell your products to consumers.

approach. By tracking and analyzing customer data, the online travel company can provide individualized service to its customers. Although a "little special attention" may increase the cost of doing business for a B2C firm, the customer's repeated purchases will repay the investment many times over.

Today, B2B and B2C models are the most popular business models for e-business. And yet, there are other business models that perform specialized e-business activities to generate revenues. Most of the business models described in Table 13-2 are modified versions of the B2B and B2C models.

互联网、社交媒体和电子商业的未来

13-7 The Future of the Internet, Social Media, and e-Business

Learning Objective

13-7 Identify the factors that will affect the future of the internet, social media, and e-business.

Since the beginning of commercial activity on the internet, developments in computer technology, social media, and e-business have been rapid, with spectacular successes such as Facebook, Amazon, Google, eBay, and Pinterest. However, success is not guaranteed just because it is a "technology" firm. Even firms with a promising idea must develop a business plan to turn the idea into a reality—and a successful business. Today, most firms involved in the internet, social media, and e-business use a very intelligent approach to the initial start-up phase and expansion and development. The long-term view held by the vast majority of analysts is that the internet, social media, and e-business will continue to expand to meet the needs of businesses and consumers.

互联网的增长潜力

13-7a Internet Growth Potential

To date, only about 65 percent of the global population uses the internet. In late 2020, estimates suggest that about 5.1 billion of the 7.9 billion people in the world use the internet.[26] In the United States, 297 million, or about 90 percent of the nation's population use the internet. With approximately 90 percent of the U.S. population already using the internet, potential growth in the United States is limited.[27] On the other hand, the number of internet users in the world's developing countries is expected to increase dramatically.

Although the number of global internet users is expected to increase, that's only part of the story. Perhaps the more important question is why people are using the internet. Primary reasons for using the internet include the ability to connect with other people, to obtain information, or to purchase a firm's products or services. Of particular interest to business firms is the growth of social media. For example, Facebook now has approximately 2.7 billion users worldwide. And because only about 34 percent of the world population currently uses Facebook, the number of Facebook users is expected to continue to increase for years to come.[28] In fact, the number of users for other social media sites, like TikTok, YouTube, Twitter, Instagram, and Pinterest, is also expected to increase.

Experts also predict that the number of companies using e-business to increase sales and reduce expenses will continue to increase. Firms that adapt existing business models to an online environment will continue to dominate development. Although products or services will continue to be sold in the traditional way, more and more products will be sold online.

Even small businesses can sell merchandise online. While big retailers like Macy's, Walgreens, and Home Depot are increasing sales revenue from online sales, small businesses can also sell merchandise online. In fact, if a small business doesn't have a website, it's missing an opportunity to sell its products and services—especially unique or one-of-a-kind items.

伦理和法律问题

13-7b Ethical and Legal Concerns

The social and legal concerns for the internet, social media, and e-business extend beyond those shared by all businesses. Essentially, the internet is a new "frontier" without borders and with little control by governments or other organizations.

Ethics and Social Responsibility Socially responsible and ethical behavior by individuals and businesses on the internet are major concerns. For example, an ethically questionable practice in cyberspace is the unauthorized use of information discovered through computerized tracking of users once they are connected to the internet. Essentially, a user may visit a website and unknowingly receive a small piece of software code called a **cookie**. This cookie can track where the user goes on the internet and measure how long the user stays at any particular website. Although this type of software may produce valuable customer information, it also can be viewed as an invasion of privacy, especially since users may not even be aware that their movements are being monitored. AT&T, Verizon, and other cell phone service providers use cookies to track an individual's browsing on mobile devices for advertising purposes. Shoppers with smartphones and a retailer's app on their smartphones may even be tracked when they enter a store. Once the store knows your location in the store, it can send texts or posts about discounts and merchandise that is on sale. Unlike the situation with cookies, however, shoppers must download the app to be tracked—but in exchange, they benefit by receiving personalized discounts.

Some firms also practice data mining. **Data mining** refers to the practice of searching through data records looking for useful information. Customer registration forms typically require a variety of information before a user is given access to a site. Based on an individual's information, data mining analysis can then provide what might be considered private and confidential information about individuals. For instance, assume an individual frequents a website that provides information about a life-threatening disease. If this information is sent to an insurance company, the

网络跟踪软件
cookie a small piece of software sent by a website that tracks an individual's internet use

数据挖掘
data mining the practice of searching through data records looking for useful information

The hackers are coming! Today it's hard to turn on your computer or read an email without worrying if you will get a computer virus that will enable hackers to steal your personal and financial information and then use it for their own personal gain. In fact, identity and computer security is such a big problem that it has created a whole new industry—the software security industry.

company might refuse to insure this individual, thinking that there is a higher risk associated with someone who wants more information about this disease.

Besides the unauthorized use of cookies and tracking your location and your online behavior, there are several other threats to users' privacy and confidentiality. Monitoring an employee's computer usage may be intended to help employers police unauthorized internet use on company time. However, the same records can also give a firm the opportunity to observe what otherwise might be considered private and confidential information. A recent survey of over 300 employers by the American Management Association and the ePolicy Institute found that two thirds of employers monitor employee usage.[29] Today, legal experts suggest that, at the very least, employers need to disclose the level of surveillance to their employees and consider the corporate motivation for monitoring employees' behavior.

Ethics and Social Responsibility

商业伦理与社会责任：加州加大隐私保护力度

California Ups the Ante on Privacy Protection

Data privacy is a major legal and ethical issue. In fact, 85 percent of U.S. internet users are concerned about how much information advertisers have collected about them. Even so, there is no comprehensive federal law that governs data privacy in the United States. Personal information, such as postal addresses, credit card numbers, email addresses, and browsing history, is a valuable marketing tool for companies, but the same information can open the door for identity thieves if it is not handled properly.

California took matters into its own hands with the California Consumer Privacy Act (CCPA). The act gave consumers more control over how their data is collected and used by businesses. The CCPA secured privacy rights for Californians, including the right to know what data is being collected and how it is used and shared, the right to have companies delete personal information (with some exceptions), the right to opt-out of having their personal information sold by one company to another, and the right to non-discrimination for exercising their CCPA rights.

California voters have also amended CCPA with the California Privacy Rights Act (CPRA). The CPRA amendment raised the privacy bar even higher. The original provisions put the burden on individuals to become aware of and protect their data instead of changing the way businesses collect, store, and use the data. The CPRA amendment created new requirements for businesses, such as limiting data retention, protecting data security, and minimizing data collection. It also strengthens accountability measures by requiring companies to conduct privacy risk assessments and cybersecurity audits.

Although the law was enacted in California, the importance of these laws goes beyond the state's boundaries because of the number of businesses that do business with California consumers. Also, the laws impact how marketers and ad publishers such as Facebook and Google personalize digital advertising. Finally, compliance will affect businesses financially when they hire data protection officers, implement new policies and procedures, train employees, modify processes, and monitor compliance.

Experts predict that California's privacy laws could become the national standard for data privacy, whether a federal law is created or not. Even if Congress enacts a national privacy law, it could face stiff opposition from Californians if the federal law does not meet or exceed the protections provided by the existing California law. The bottom line: Companies will need to find ways to help prevent identity theft and improve data protection now more than ever.

Sources: Based on information in Cameron F. Kerry and Caitlin Chin, "By Passing Proposition 24, California Voters up the Ante on Federal Privacy Law," *Brookings*, November 17, 2020; Yory Wurmser, "Election Impact: Why the Passing of California's Prop 24 Matters for Marketers and What to Expect in 2021," *Business Insider*, November 4, 2020; State of California Department of Justice, "California Consumer Privacy Act (CCPA)".

Internet Crime Because the internet is often regarded as an unregulated frontier, both individuals and business users must be particularly aware of online risks and dangers. For example, a general term that describes software designed to infiltrate a computer system without the user's consent is **malware**. Malware is often based on the creator's criminal or malicious intent and can include computer viruses, spyware, deceptive adware, and other software capable of criminal activities. According to TechJury, more than 30,000 websites are hacked each day.[30] In fact, the increase in internet crime and the devastating effects of both malware and computer viruses have given rise to a software security industry.

In addition to the risk of computer viruses and hackers, identity theft is one of the most common computer crimes that impacts both individuals and business users. A recent report by the United States Federal Trade Commission (FTC) determined that more than 1.4 million Americans reported identity theft in one year.[31] In recent years, major government entities including the United States government and many businesses such as Microsoft, MGM Resorts, Walgreens, T-Mobile, and many others have been hacked by thieves who stole sensitive data from tens of millions of people.[32]

Most consumers are also concerned about fraud. Because the internet allows easy creation of websites, access from anywhere in the world, and anonymity for the creator, it is almost impossible to know with certainty that the website, organization, or individuals that you believe you are interacting with are what they seem. As always, caveat emptor ("let the buyer beware") is a good suggestion to follow whether on the internet or not.

计算机技术、社交媒体和电子商业的未来挑战
13-7c Future Challenges for Computer Technology, Social Media, and e-Business

Today, more information and technology is available than ever before. Although individuals and business users may think we are at the point of information overload, the amount of information will only increase in the future. In order to obtain more information in the future, both business users and individuals must consider the cost of obtaining additional information and computer technology. In an effort to reduce expenses and improve accessibility, some companies and individuals are now using cloud computing. **Cloud computing** is a type of computer usage in which services stored on the internet are provided to users on a temporary basis. When cloud computing is used, a third party makes processing power, software applications, databases, and storage available for on-demand use from anywhere. Instead of running software and storing data on their employer's computer network or their individual computers, employees log onto the third party's system and use (and pay for) only the applications and data storage they actually need. Amazon Web Services (AWS), Microsoft, Google, IBM, Oracle, and many other firms in the technology industry offer cloud services. In addition to just cost, there are a number of external and internal factors that a business must consider.

Although the demands for a business are complex, it is useful to think of them as either *internal* or *external* forces that affect how a business uses computer technology. Internal forces are those that are closely associated with the actions and decisions taking place within a firm. As shown in Figure 13-8, typical internal forces include a firm's planning activities, organizational structure, human resources, management decisions, information database, and available financing. A shortage of skilled employees needed for a specialized project, for instance, can undermine a firm's ability to sell its services to clients. Unlike the external environmental forces affecting the firm, internal forces, such as this one, are more likely to be under the direct control of management. In this case, management can either hire the needed staff or choose to pass over a prospective project or outsource some of the work that is needed. In addition to the obvious internal factors that affect how a company operates, a growing number of firms are concerned about how their use of technology affects the environment. The term **green IT** is now used to describe all of a firm's activities to support a healthy environment

恶意软件
malware software designed to infiltrate a computer system without the user's consent

云计算
cloud computing a type of computer usage in which services stored on the internet are provided to users on a temporary basis

绿色 IT
green IT a term used to describe all of a firm's activities to support a healthy environment and sustain the planet

Figure 13-8 Internal and External Forces That Affect an e-Business

Today, managers and employees of an e-business must respond to internal forces within the organization and external forces outside the organization.

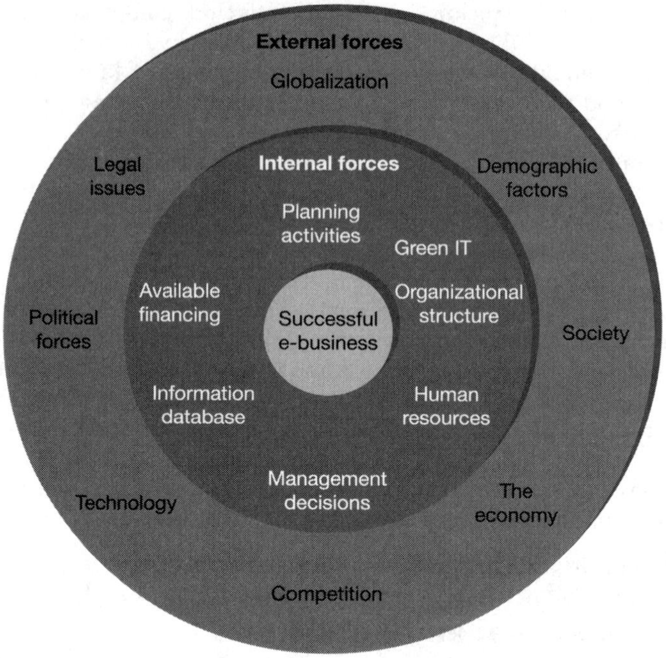

✓ Concept Check

- Experts predict that the internet will continue to expand along with related technologies. What effect will this expansion have on society, business, and individuals in the future?
- Give an example of an unethical use of computer technology by a business.
- What is the difference between internal and external forces that affect an e-business?

and sustain the planet. Many offices, for example, are reducing the amount of paper they use by storing data and information on computers.

In contrast, external forces affect a company's use of technology and originate outside the organization. These forces are unlikely to be controllable by a company. Instead, managers and employees of a company generally will react to these forces, attempting to shield the organization from any negative effects and finding ways to take advantage of opportunities in an ever-changing technology environment. The primary external forces affecting a company's use of technology include globalization, demographic, societal, economic, competitive, technological, and political and legal forces.

In this chapter, we have explored how both individuals and businesses use social media. We also examined how e-business and e-commerce are changing the way that firms do business. In Chapter 14, we examine a business firm's need for information and why accounting is a major source of information for business.

Discussion Questions 讨论题

1. Given the fast pace of everyday life, most people often feel there is not enough time to do everything that needs to be done. Yet, people do find time to post text messages and personal information, photos, etc., on Facebook, Twitter, blogs, and other social media sites. Why do you think people are so fascinated with social media?
2. How can a small cosmetics wholesaler located in Jacksonville, Florida, use social media and e-business to increase its customer base, increase revenues, and reduce expenses?
3. Is outsourcing good for an e-business firm? The firm's employees? Explain your answers.
4. What distinguishes a B2B from a B2C e-business model?
5. Experts predict that the internet, social media, and e-business will continue to expand along with related computer technologies. What effect will this expansion have on how businesses (1) market and sell merchandise, (2) get paid for merchandise, and (3) deliver merchandise to customers?

Case 13 案例 13：Target 在数字领域的大赌注

Target's Big Bet on Digital

When Target's CEO Brian Cornell announced the company would spend $7 billion for capital improvements and $1 billion more per year for operating costs to modernize operations for the digital age, investors weren't sold. "I had people shaking their heads," Cornell said. "You could see it." Target's stock price plummeted the day the announcement was made. Looking back now, Cornell knows the company made the right decision.

Target, one of the largest retailers in the United States, has spent billions on its stores and technology infrastructure. The company reimagined its stores, built new, smaller stores in urban areas, and invested in technology and fulfillment capabilities. According to the CEO, the investment is paying off. All of these elements have worked together to drive growth, increase market share, and boost in-store and online traffic.

One of the most important initiatives was focused on remodeling existing stores and opening new small-format stores. In Target's smaller stores, the company reduced the amount of inventory and adopted a just-in-time approach to inventory management. The goal was simple: Deliver what the stores need, when they need it.

Target also invested in its supply chain in order to meet the needs of the "new" Target. For example, the company now utilizes artificial intelligence and robotics to support its warehouse teams. And, Target invested in creating backroom shipping and packaging centers in retail stores that act as distribution centers for online orders. Using its own retail stores as distribution centers gives it a significant advantage over Amazon. In-store and curbside pickup, for example, cost 90 percent less on average than fulfilling orders from a warehouse and then delivering the merchandise.

Target's $550 million acquisition of Shipt has also paid off. Shipt—a company known for offering same-day and next-day delivery—enables Target to go head-to-head against Amazon and other e-commerce retailers. It also acquired technology assets from Deliv—a same day delivery startup in California. Target is even testing the use of sort centers in areas with high delivery volume. The centers will be smaller and less expensive than Target's usual retail footprint and will be closer to customers. Target hopes that the use of sort centers will eliminate the need to sort packages at the store level and reduce its overall shipping costs.

These and other improvements have helped Target support in-store pickup, curbside delivery, and home delivery of online orders. In fact, it is now possible for "guests," as Target often calls its customers, throughout the United States and other countries to shop for all major product cat-egories available from Target 24 hours a day, seven days a week. As an added bonus, technology has reduced the number of out-of-stock items and ultimately improved the customer's overall shopping experience.

Target's investments were well-timed. As a result of the COVID-19 pandemic and stay-at home mandates, Target's online business surged as shoppers turned to e-commerce to make purchases. In the first quarter of 2020, Target fulfilled more curbside deliveries than it did in the entire year of 2019. The company has also found that when customers shop online and use more of its delivery options, they ultimately spend more both online and in-store.

By investing in these new distribution strategies, Target is now able to compete against some big e-commerce companies. Although Target is now one of the top ten e-commerce businesses in the United States, the company has a long way to go to capture more market share. Amazon controls nearly 40 percent of U.S. retail e-commerce sales. Target, which has 1.2 percent market share, lags behind not only Amazon, but also Walmart, eBay, Apple, Home Depot, Wayfair, and Best Buy. While Target has taken some giant steps to increase sales online and in its brick-and-mortar stores, there's still room for growth as more and more customers shop online. Looking forward, Target executives will need to remember the old phrase—Where there's a will, there's a way.[33]

Questions

1. Why do you think Target's plan to spend $7 billion for capital improvements and an additional $1 billion more per year for operating costs initially worried investors? What do you believe investors think now?
2. Although many people think of Target as a big discount store that competes with Walmart, it has opened new, smaller stores that carry less inventory. What do you think is the driving force behind Target's smaller store concept?
3. Much of the information in this case describes Target's efforts to improve its supply chain. In your own words describe what the term "supply chain" means. How important is a firm's supply chain for a retailer like Target that has both in-store and online sales?

Chapter

14

Using Management and Accounting Information

利用管理和会计信息

Learning Objectives

Once you complete this chapter, you will be able to:

14-1 Examine how information can reduce risk when making a decision.

14-2 Discuss management's information requirements.

14-3 Outline the five functions of an information system.

14-4 Explain why accurate accounting information and audited financial statements are important.

14-5 Interpret a balance sheet.

14-6 Interpret an income statement.

14-7 Describe business activities that affect a firm's cash flow.

14-8 Summarize how managers evaluate the financial health of a business.

Why Should You Care?

Question: How important is management and accounting information for a successful business?
Answer: It would be extremely difficult to manage even a small business without management and accounting information.

Inside Business 商业透视：在四大会计师事务所工作是什么体验

What It's Like to Work for the Big Four

The four largest accounting firms in the world, referred to as the "Big Four," are Deloitte, Ernst & Young (EY), PricewaterhouseCoopers (PwC), and Klynveld Peat Marwick Goerdeler (KPMG). These organizations audit most of the companies in the S&P 500, a stock market index of 500 large companies in the United States. In addition to auditing services, the Big Four offer legal, tax, advisory, and consulting services, among others. They each earn billions in revenue each year and offer significant employment opportunities for accountants.

Working for a Big Four accounting firm can be an attractive career option. Employees must be prepared for the demands of a high-performance work culture to excel at a Big Four firm. Even landing a job at a Big Four accounting firm is competitive because these prestigious firms provide individuals with above average salaries, a variety of work experiences, education and training programs, and leadership development opportunities. KPMG International, for example, has several programs to help employees with professional development such as global short-term assignments, office relocations, and job rotation. The Big Four also offer competitive benefits packages, including generous parental leave policies, good health care, and gym reimbursement. At PwC, for example, employees can accrue between three weeks and one month of vacation time each year in addition to 15 paid holidays. Some firms even offer flexible schedules to support better work-life balance.

There are also drawbacks for employees at the Big Four accounting firms. For instance, tax season, which runs from January to April, can be demanding, with some individuals reporting 80-hour workweeks. Other tax filing deadlines throughout the year can also lead to working overtime. According to a survey by Vault, a career advice and company review website, Big Four employees often say firms are understaffed and compensation could be better, which can both lead to burnout and low morale. For these firms, long work hours, heavy workloads, and high stress can lead to high employee turnover.[1]

Did You Know?

Collectively, the Big Four firms employ more than 1 million people worldwide.

Information and accounting—that's what this chapter is all about! We begin this chapter with information about how employees in each of the Big Four accounting firms help clients obtain the information they need to operate a business and improve management decisions. Because employees at a Big Four firm are responsible for generating and reporting the information and accounting reports their clients need, working conditions are sometimes stressful and hours may be long. On the other hand, employees at the Big Four are paid above average salaries and enjoy competitive benefits packages. Working for a Big Four accounting firm is just one option in the information and accounting industries. There are other career options where employees can help businesses, nonprofit organizations, and government entities use information and accounting to improve decision making.

In this chapter, we begin by describing why employees need information. The first three major sections in this chapter answer the following questions:

- How can information reduce risk when making a decision?
- What is a management information system?
- How do employees use a management information system?

Next, we look at why accounting information is important and careers in the accounting industry. Then we examine the basic accounting equation and the three most important financial statements: the balance sheet, the income statement, and the statement of cash flows. Finally, we take a look at how managers evaluate the firm's financial health.

信息如何降低决策风险

14-1 How Can Information Reduce Risk When Making a Decision?

Learning Objective

14-1 Examine how information can reduce risk when making a decision.

Think back for a moment about the COVID-19 pandemic. For most people, one of the frustrations they faced was the inability to get information from reliable sources. While some information was based on facts, other information was based on opinions and conjecture without valid research to back up the statements some "experts" and politicians were making. Unfortunately, the lack of reliable information just added to the uncertainty of the pandemic and increased the risk of making poor decisions for both individuals and businesses.

As we know, information is one of the four major resources (along with material, human, and financial resources) managers must have to operate a business. Although a successful business uses all four resources efficiently, it is information that helps managers reduce risk when making a decision.

信息和风险

14-1a Information and Risk

To improve the decision-making process, the information used by individuals and business firms must be relevant. Using relevant information results in better decisions.

Relevant information → Better intelligence and knowledge → Better decisions

For businesses, better intelligence and knowledge that lead to better decisions are especially important because they can provide a *competitive edge* over competitors and improve a firm's *profits*.

Theoretically, with accurate and complete information, there is no risk whatsoever. On the other hand, a decision made without any information is a gamble. These two extreme situations are rare in business. For the most part, business decision makers see themselves located someplace between the extremes. As illustrated in Figure 14-1, when the amount of available information is high, there is less risk; when the amount of available information is low, there is more risk.

Think for a moment about Tesla's plan to produce a new all-electric sports car called the Model R. To make very important decisions, executives at Tesla relied on information. Without any information, Tesla executives might as well have made the decision by flipping a coin—heads we make the new Model R or tails we don't. For a decision this important that could impact both sales and profits for the entire company, executives began by gathering information from customers. Simply put: Did customers think a new all-electric, high performance roadster was a good idea? Customers also provided Tesla with additional information about the price that they were willing to pay for the car and about features and options they would like on a new vehicle. Information was also obtained from Tesla's own product engineers, production employees, marketing employees, and key executives. Only after all of the information was obtained and analyzed did Tesla make the decision to produce and market the Model R. Thus, information, when understood properly, produces knowledge and empowers managers and employees to make better decisions while also reducing the risk of making bad decisions.

Figure 14-1 The Relationship Between Information and Risk

When the amount of available information is high, managers tend to make better decisions. On the other hand, when the amount of information is low, there is a high risk of making a poor decision.

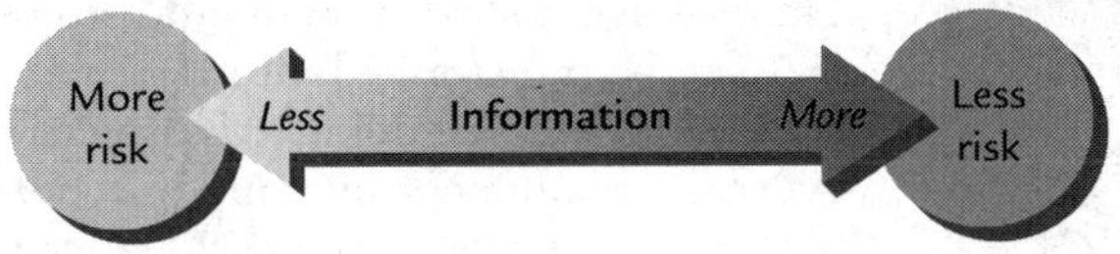

信息规则

14-1b Information Rules

Marketing research continues to show that discounts influence people when buying consumer products. Simply put, if manufacturers and retailers lower prices on their products or services, their sales will increase. For example, if Best Buy lowers its price for a new Vizio 75-inch LED television from $1,699 to $1,499, the retailer will sell more televisions. This relationship between buyer behavior and price can be thought of as an information rule that will usually guide the marketing manager correctly. An information rule emerges when research confirms the same results each time that it studies the same or a similar set of circumstances.

Because of the volume of information they receive each day and their need to make decisions on a daily basis, businesspeople try to accumulate information rules to shorten the time they spend analyzing choices. Information rules are the "great simplifiers" for all decision makers. Managers and employees are continuously looking for new rules that can be put to good use and looking to discredit old ones that are no longer valid. This ongoing process is necessary because business conditions rarely stay the same for very long.

数据和信息的区别

14-1c The Difference Between Data and Information

Many people use the terms *data* and *information* interchangeably, but the two differ in important ways. **Data** are numerical or verbal descriptions that usually result from some sort of measurement. Your current wage level, the amount of last year's after-tax profit for Google, and the current retail prices of Dell computers are all data. Most people think of data as being numerical only, but they can be nonnumerical as well. A description of an individual as a "tall, athletic person with short, dark hair" certainly would qualify as data.

数据
data numerical or verbal descriptions that usually result from some sort of measurement

信息
information data presented in a form that is useful for a specific purpose

Information is data presented in a form that is useful for a specific purpose. For example, Apple has earned a reputation as one of the best employers in the nation based on employee satisfaction, employee diversity and company culture, and its efforts to promote equal pay when female and male employees perform the same duties in the workplace. To verify that all employees receive the same pay for the same job, Apple has analyzed the salaries and bonuses that employees received over the last few years. To complete the analysis, human resources managers begin with data reported in computer printouts listing each worker employed by the firm, job classification, and each worker's current wages. Such printouts consist of data rather than information.

Numbers and charts and more numbers and charts. In today's business world, there's so much data available that many managers and employees often believe they are looking for a needle in a haystack. To find just the right information, they often must dig deeper and use computers and graphics programs to process large amounts of data into the information they need to make informed decisions.

Now suppose that the manager uses a computer to graph the average wages paid to men and to women for each job classification. The result is information because the manager can use it to compare wages paid to women with those paid to men. If a gap exists, based on the information presented in the graph, management can address the problem. For a manager, information presented in a practical, useful form, such as a graph, simplifies the decision-making process.

知识管理

14-1d Knowledge Management

The average company maintains a great deal of data that can be transformed into information. Typical data include records pertaining to personnel, inventory, sales, expenses, manufacturing, and accounting. Often each type of data is stored in individual departments within

Technology and Innovation

技术与创新：美国国税局利用人工智能和技术来改善税收

The IRS Uses Artificial Intelligence and Technology to Improve Tax Collection

Data scientists at the IRS are using artificial intelligence (often referred to as AI) and increased technology to detect tax evasion, accounting fraud, and more. By translating tax regulations into source code and software, a group of computer scientists from the Massachusetts Institute of Technology was able to demonstrate how algorithms can detect tax evasion. Tax evasion occurs when an individual or business does not report income, takes more deductions than they are entitled, or are not paying taxes on income.

With a tight budget, the IRS has been slow to update its technology over the years. However, investing in AI and technology to fight tax evasion and accounting fraud may pay off since taxes are the primary source of income for the federal and state governments. As a result of the renewed interest in AI and technology, there are a number of ways the IRS is increasing the amount of taxes collected from tax cheaters. For example, the IRS is creating a tool for auditors that will spot questionable activities when auditing suspicious tax returns. Technology is also used to analyze internal and external data to identify people and businesses that are not filing tax returns. AI is even used to analyze the methods—letters, formal notices, or audits—that are most likely to convince taxpayers to pay back taxes and penalties.

AI is not without risks. Algorithmic "bias" in AI systems can exist when inaccurate data and information are used to build the algorithm. For example, an AI-powered auditing tool could provide inaccurate recommendations for auditing specific returns based on race, gender, or geographic location. It is also limited in that tax laws often have gray areas that are open to human interpretation, which could be challenging for machine intelligence to handle. Finally, U.S. taxpayers often find dealing with the IRS becomes even more impersonal when AI and technology are used.

At the same time the IRS is using AI and technology to fight tax fraud, tax preparers and accounting firms are using the same technology to boost tax refunds and minimize tax bills. In fact, all of the Big Four accounting firms (Deloitte, EY, PwC, and KPMG) use artificial intelligence tools for advising clients. The bottom line: AI and technology are already changing how taxes are collected and how individuals and businesses do tax planning.

Sources: Based on information in Richard Rubin, "AI Comes to the Tax Code," *The Wall Street Journal*, February 26, 2020; Naveen Joshi, "How AI And Robotics Can Change Taxation," *Forbes*, January 9, 2020; Lynnley Browning, "Computer Scientists Wield Artificial Intelligence to Battle Tax Evasion," *The New York Times*, October 9, 2015.

an organization. However, the data can be used more effectively when they are organized into a database. A **database** is a single collection of data and information stored in one place that can be used by people throughout an organization to make decisions. Although databases are important, the way the data and information are used is even more important—and more valuable to the firm. As a result, management information experts now use the term **knowledge management (KM)** to describe a firm's procedures for generating, using, and sharing important data and information.

数据库
database a single collection of data and information stored in one place that can be used by people throughout an organization to make decisions

知识管理
knowledge management (KM) a firm's procedures for generating, using, and sharing important data and information

决策支持系统
decision-support system (DSS) a type of software program that provides relevant data and information to help a firm's employees make decisions

Making Smart Decisions How do managers and employees sort out relevant and useful information from spam, junk mail, and useless data? Today, different software applications can actually help to improve and speed the decision-making process for people at different levels within an organization. For example, a **decision-support system (DSS)** is a type of software program that provides relevant data and information to help a firm's employees make decisions. It also can be used to determine the effect of changing different variables and answer "what if"-type questions. For example, managers at D.R. Horton, one of the largest home builders

Table 14-1 Current Business Application Software Used to Improve Productivity

Word processing	Users can prepare and edit written documents and store them in the computer or on a memory device.
Desktop publishing	Users can combine text and graphics in professional reports, newsletters, and pamphlets.
Accounting	Users can record routine financial transactions and prepare financial reports at the end of the accounting period.
Database management	Users can electronically store large amounts of data and transform the data into information.
Graphics	Users can display and print pictures, drawings, charts, and diagrams.
Spreadsheets	Users can organize numerical data into a grid of rows and columns.

in the United States, can use a DSS to determine prices for new homes built in an upscale, luxury subdivision. By entering the number of homes that will be built along with different costs associated with land, labor, building materials, building permits, promotional costs, and all other costs, a DSS can help determine a base price for each new home. When a DSS is used, it is also possible to revise home prices if building costs change. For example, if the cost of materials or labor increases, a DSS can determine new home prices for each set of assumptions.

Another type of software program is an expert system that uses computers, software, data, and information to mimic the thinking of employees. Simply put, an **expert system** is a type of computer program that uses artificial intelligence to imitate a human's ability to think. Using a set of rules determined by employees, an expert system can analyze available data and information about a particular activity or problem. Based on the information supplied, the expert system then provides recommendations or suggests specific actions in order to help make decisions. Expert systems, for example, have been used to schedule manufacturing tasks, diagnose illnesses, determine credit limits for credit card customers, evaluate loan applications, and develop electronic games.

Concept Check

- In your own words, describe how information reduces risk when you make a personal or work-related decision.
- What are information rules? How do they simplify the process of making decisions?
- What is the difference between data and information? Give an example of accounting data and accounting information.
- Describe how decision support systems, expert systems, and business application software can help improve employee productivity.

Business Application Software In addition to decision support and expert systems, a number of business software applications can improve both employee decision making and productivity. Early business application software typically performed a single function. Today, however, *integrated* software combines many functions in a single package. Integrated packages allow for the easy linking of text, numerical data, graphs, photographs, and even audiovisual clips. A business report prepared using the Microsoft Office package, for instance, can include all these components. From a career standpoint, you should realize that employers will assume that you possess, or will possess after training, a high degree of working comfort with several of the software applications described in Table 14-1.

Typically, data, information, databases, knowledge management, and computer software all become important parts of a firm's management information system.

专家系统
expert system a type of computer program that uses artificial intelligence to imitate a human's ability to think

管理信息系统
management information system (MIS) a system that provides managers and employees with the information they need to perform their jobs as effectively as possible

什么是管理信息系统

14-2 What Is a Management Information System?

Learning Objective

14-2 Discuss management's information requirements.

A **management information system (MIS)** is a system that provides managers and employees with the information they need to perform their jobs as effectively as possible. The purpose of an MIS (sometimes referred to as an information technology system or simply an IT system) is to distribute timely and useful information from both internal and external sources to the managers and employees who need it.

Figure 14-2 Management Information System (MIS)

After an MIS is installed, employees and managers can get information directly from the MIS without having to go through other people in the organization.

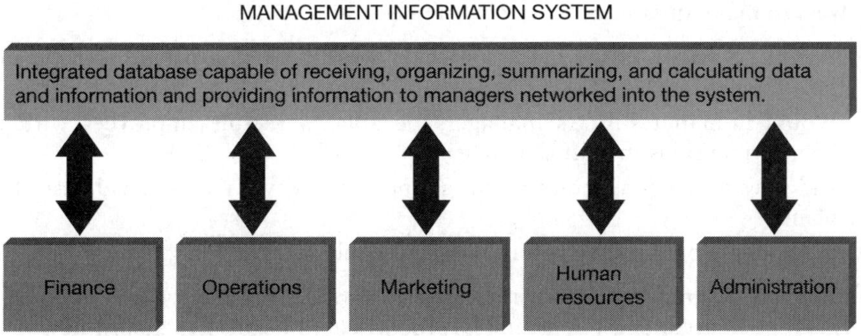

企业的信息需求

14-2a A Firm's Information Requirements

Employees and managers have to plan for the future, implement their plans in the present, and evaluate results against what has been accomplished in the past. Of course, the specific types of information they need depend on their work area and on their level within the firm.

Today, many firms are organized into five areas of management: *finance, operations, marketing, human resources,* and *administration.* Managers in each of these areas need specific information in order to make decisions (refer to Figure 14-2).

- *Financial managers* are obviously most concerned with a firm's finances. They must ensure that the firm's managers and employees, lenders and suppliers, stockholders and potential investors, and government agencies have the information they need to measure the financial health of the firm.
- *Operations managers* are concerned with present and future sales levels; current inventory levels of resources, work in process, and finished goods; and the availability and cost of the resources required to produce goods and services.
- *Marketing managers* need to have detailed information about a firm's products and services and those offered by competitors. Such information includes sales projections, promotion and pricing strategies, products that competitors are test marketing, information concerning the firm's customers, and new and pending product legislation that may impact future sales.
- *Human resources managers* must be aware of anything that pertains to a firm's employees. Key examples include current wage levels and benefits packages both within the firm and in firms that compete for valuable employees and current legislation and court decisions that affect employment practices.
- *Administrative managers* are responsible for the overall management of the organization. Thus, they are concerned with the coordination of information—just as they are concerned with the coordination of material, human, and financial resources.

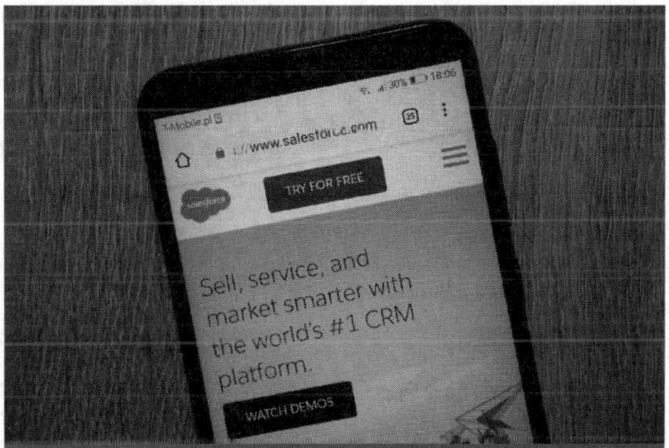

Question: What is customer relationship management (CRM) software? **The quick answer is that customer relationship management software is designed to enable a company and its salesforce to use data and information to track all interactions with potential and existing customers to increase sales and profits. While there are many companies that can provide CRM software, the world's leading source for help improving customer satisfaction and building customer loyalty is Salesforce.com located in San Francisco, California.**

Administrative managers must ensure information is used in a consistent manner throughout the firm. For example, in 2018, Airbus began constructing a new $300 million plant in Mobile, Alabama, to produce A220 passenger airplanes. In the initial planning stages, Airbus' administrative managers and employees wanted answers to many questions:

- Was the capacity of the plant consistent with marketing plans based on sales projections?
- Would human resources managers be able to recruit employees with the appropriate skills to staff the plant?
- Did sales projections indicate enough income to cover the expected cost of the plant?
- How long would it take before the plant could start building planes?

After much planning and construction, the production facility was completed, workers were hired, and the assembly process could begin. Eventually, new A220 aircraft were sold to Delta, JetBlue, Air Canada, and other airlines.

Also, administrative managers must make sure all managers and employees are able to use the information technology that is available. Certainly, this requires that all employees receive the skills training required to access the information. Finally, administrative managers must commit to the costs of updating the firm's MIS and providing additional training when necessary.

管理信息系统的成本和限制

14-2b Costs and Limits of the System

Can employees, managers, and executives have too much information? The answer is yes. The truth is that each group needs relevant information that helps them make better decisions. And yet, too much information can lead to information overload. Another problem is the amount of worthless information, junk emails, and advertising that contribute to information overload. Unfortunately, there are many misuses of information technology that do nothing but rob employees of time that could be devoted to more productive activities.

In addition to lower employee productivity, the cost of computers, software, and related equipment can be staggering. One of the main goals of a firm's information technology officer (or IT department) is to make sure that a firm has the equipment necessary to provide information the employees need to make effective decisions—*at a reasonable cost.*

In reality, an MIS must be tailored to the needs of the organization it serves. In some firms, a tendency to save on initial costs may result in a system that is too small or overly simple. Such a system generally ends up serving only one or two management levels or a single department. Managers in other departments "give up" on the system as soon as they find that it cannot process their data, is unreliable, or is too slow to meet their information needs.

Almost as bad is an MIS that is too large or too complex for the organization. Unused capacity and complexity do nothing but increase the cost of owning and operating the system. In addition, a system that is difficult to use probably will not be used at all.

✓ Concept Check

- How do the information requirements of managers differ by management area?
- What happens if a business has a management information system that is too large?
- What happens if a business has a management information system that is too small?

员工如何使用管理信息系统

14-3 How Do Employees Use a Management Information System?

Learning Objective

14-3 Outline the five functions of an information system.

To provide information, an MIS must perform five specific functions. It must (1) collect data, (2) store the data, (3) update the data, (4) process the data into information, and (5) present the information to users (refer to Figure 14-3).

步骤 1：收集数据

14-3a **Step 1: Collecting Data**

A firm's employees, with the help of an MIS system, must gather the data and information needed to establish the firm's *database*. The database should include all past and current data that may be useful in managing the firm. Clearly, the data entered into the system must be *relevant* to the needs of the firm's employees. And perhaps most important, the data must be *accurate*. Irrelevant data are simply useless; inaccurate data can be disastrous. There are two data sources: *internal* and *external*.

Typically, most of the data gathered for an MIS come from internal sources. The most common internal sources of information are managers and employees, company records and reports, accounting data, and minutes of meetings.

External sources of data include customers, suppliers, banks, trade and business publications, industry conferences, online computer services, lawyers, government sources, and firms that specialize in gathering marketing research for organizations.

Whether the source of the data is internal or external, always remember the following two cautions:

1. The cost of obtaining data from some external sources, such as marketing research firms, can be quite high.
2. Although computers generally do not make mistakes, the people who use them can make or cause errors. When data (or information) and your judgment disagree, always check the data.

Figure 14-3 Five Management Information System Functions

Every MIS must be tailored to the organization it serves and must perform the following five functions.

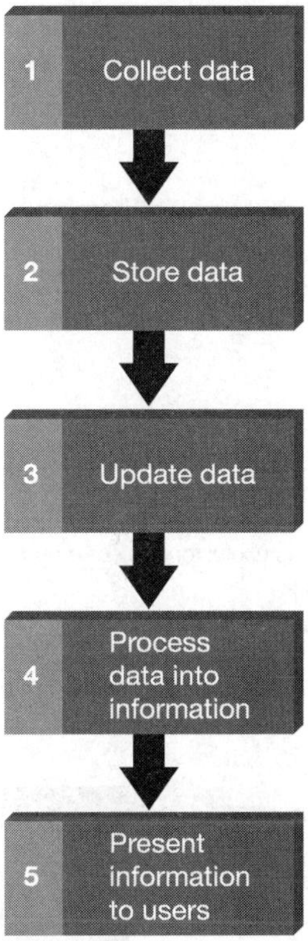

步骤 2：存储数据

14-3b **Step 2: Storing Data**

An MIS must be capable of storing data until they are needed. Typically, the method chosen to store data depends on the size and needs of the organization. Small businesses may enter data and then store them directly on an employee's computer. Generally, medium-sized to large businesses store data in a larger computer system and provide access to employees through a management information system.

步骤 3：更新数据

14-3c **Step 3: Updating Data**

Today, an MIS must be able to update stored data regularly to ensure that the information presented to managers and employees is accurate, complete, and up-to-date. The frequency with which the data are updated depends on how fast they change and how often they are used. When it is vital to have current data, updating may occur as soon as the new data are available. For example, Macy's, a national retailer that sells a wide range of merchandise including apparel, cosmetics, home furnishings, and other consumer goods, has cash registers that automatically transmit data on each item sold in each store and online to a central computer. The computer adjusts the store's inventory records accordingly. In addition to maintaining accurate inventory records, sales representatives can tell customers where they can obtain merchandise if the store where they are shopping is out of the merchandise they want or if the merchandise can be purchased online. Data may also be entered into a firm's data bank at certain intervals—every 24 hours, weekly, or monthly.

步骤 4：处理数据
14-3d Step 4: Processing Data

Some data are used in the form in which they are stored, whereas other data require processing to extract, highlight, or summarize the information they contain. **Data processing** is the transformation of data into a form that is useful for a specific purpose.

For verbal data, this processing consists mainly of extracting the pertinent material from storage and combining it into a report. Most financial data, however, are in the form of numbers—large groups of numbers, such as daily sales totals or production costs for a specific product. Fortunately, computer software can process large volumes of numbers quickly, and their contents can be summarized through the use of statistics. A **statistic** is a measure that summarizes a particular characteristic of an entire group of numbers.

步骤 5：信息呈现
14-3e Step 5: Presenting Information

An MIS must be capable of presenting information in a usable form. That is, the method of presentation—reports, graphs, charts, or tables, for example—must be appropriate for the information itself and for its intended use.

Business Reports Verbal information may be presented in list or paragraph form. Employees often are asked to prepare formal business reports. A typical business report includes:

- An introduction
- The body of the report
- The conclusions
- The recommendations

数据处理
data processing the transformation of data into a form that is useful for a specific purpose

统计
statistic a measure that summarizes a particular characteristic of an entire group of numbers

The *introduction,* which sets the stage for the remainder of the report, describes the problem to be studied in the report, identifies the research techniques that were used, and previews the material that will be presented in the report. The *body* of the report should objectively describe the facts that were discovered in the process of completing the report. The *conclusions* are statements of fact that describe the findings contained in the report. The *recommendations* section presents suggestions on how the problem might be solved. Like the conclusions, the recommendations should be specific, practical, and based on the evidence contained in the report.

With the right information and a computer, preparing a report may be easier than you think! The decision makers in a successful business need information that is relevant, accurate, up-to-date, *and* accessible. To make information more accessible, employees are often asked to prepare a report that summarizes information in a more concise form. This same information may even be easier to understand if the report contains graphs, charts, or tables—all features that are easily created using computer software.

Visual Displays and Tables A visual display can also be used to present information and may be a diagram that represents several items of information in a manner that makes comparison easier. Figure 14-4 illustrates examples of visual displays including graphs, bar charts, and pie charts generated by a computer.

A tabular display is used to present verbal or numerical information in columns and rows. It is most useful in presenting information about two or more related variables. A table, for example, can be used to illustrate the number of salespeople in each region of the country, sales for different types of products, and total sales for all products

Figure 14-4 Typical Visual Displays Used in Business Presentations

Visual displays help businesspeople present information in a form that can be understood easily.

GRAPH

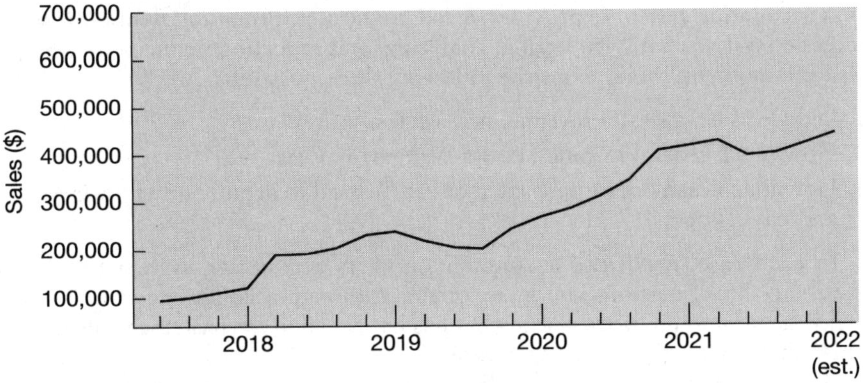

BAR CHART

Profits for the period 2017–2022 in millions

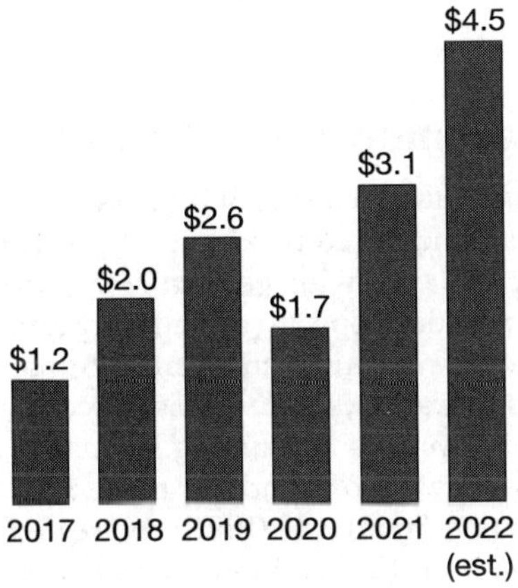

PIE CHART

Sales figures for selected products of Martin Manufacturing

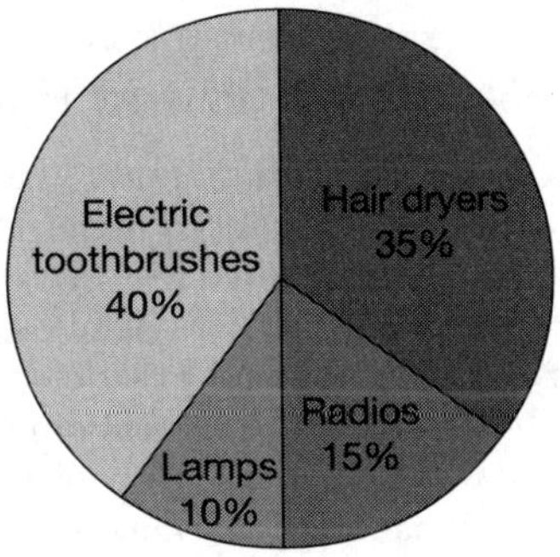

(refer to Table 14-2). Tabular displays generally have less impact than visual displays. However, displaying the information that could be contained in a multicolumn table such as the one shown in Table 14-2 would require several bar or pie charts.

Table 14-2 Typical Four-Column Table Used in Business Presentations

Tables are most useful for displaying information about two or more variables. All-Star Technology Projected Sales

Section of the Country	Number of Salespeople	Consumer Electronic Products ($)	Industrial Electronic Components ($)
Eastern territory	15	1,500,000	3,500,000
Midwestern territory	20	2,000,000	5,000,000
Western territory	10	1,000,000	4,000,000
TOTAL	45	4,500,000	12,500,000

✓ Concept Check

- List the five functions of an MIS.
- What are the components of a typical business report?
- What types of information could be illustrated in a visual display? In a tabular display?

为什么会计信息很重要
14-4 Why Accounting Information Is Important

Learning Objective

14-4 Explain why accurate accounting information and audited financial statements are important.

In order to obtain needed information, firms use an MIS like the one described in the first part of this chapter. Executives, managers, and employees also rely on the firm's accounting system to provide needed financial information. **Accounting** is the process of systematically collecting, analyzing, and reporting financial information. Just for a moment, think about the following three questions:

1. Did Coca-Cola's sales revenue increase last year?
2. How much federal income tax did Walmart pay last year?
3. How much cash does Intel have that can be used to acquire other business firms and pay its debts?

In each case, the firm's accountants and its accounting system provide the answers to these questions and many others. Although accounting information can be used to answer questions about what has happened in the past, it can also be used to help make decisions about the future.

Because the information provided by a firm's accountants and its accounting system is so important, managers and employees, investors, financial analysts, lenders, suppliers, government agencies, and other interested groups must be able to "trust the numbers." To improve the accuracy of a firm's accounting information and its financial statements, businesses rely on audits conducted by accountants employed by public accounting firms.

为什么审计过的财务报表很重要
14-4a Why Audited Financial Statements Are Important

An **audit** is an examination of a company's financial statements and the accounting practices that produced them. The purpose of an audit is to make sure that a firm's financial statements have been prepared in accordance with **generally accepted accounting principles (GAAPs)**. GAAPs have been developed to provide an accepted set of guidelines and practices for U.S. companies reporting financial information and the accounting profession. At the time of publication, the Financial Accounting Standards Board (FASB), which establishes and improves accounting standards for U.S. companies, is working toward establishing a new set of standards that combines GAAPs with the International Financial Reporting Standards (IFRS) to create one set of accounting standards that can be used by both U.S. and multinational firms. For multinational firms like Johnson & Johnson, Royal Dutch Shell, ExxonMobil, Walmart, and Toyota, the benefits of global accounting standards are huge because preparing financial statements and accounting records that meet global standards saves both time and money.

If accountants determine that a firm's financial statements present financial information fairly and conform to GAAPs, then they will issue the following statement:

> *In our opinion, the financial statements ... present fairly, in all material respects the financial position of the company ... in conformity with generally accepted accounting principles.*

Although an audit and the resulting report do not *guarantee* that a company has not "cooked" the books, it does imply that, on the whole, the company has followed GAAPs. Also, it should be noted that without the audit function and GAAPs, there would be very little oversight or supervision. The reliability of a firm's financial statements and its accounting records would drop quickly, and firms would find it difficult to obtain debt financing, use credit to purchase goods and services from suppliers, find investor financing, or prepare documents requested by government agencies.

会计
accounting the process of systematically collecting, analyzing, and reporting financial information

审计
audit an examination of a company's financial statements and the accounting practices that produced them

一般公认会计原则
generally accepted accounting principles (GAAPs) an accepted set of guidelines and practices for U.S. companies reporting financial information and for the accounting profession

Ethics and Social Responsibility

商业伦理与社会责任：毕马威深陷欺诈丑闻

KPMG Caught in Widespread Cheating Scandal

KPMG, one of the Big Four accounting firms, was caught engaging in a series of unethical behaviors. First, KPMG stole regulatory information to cheat on audit inspections. The company, which employs more than 219,000 individuals worldwide and earns more than $29 billion annually, improperly received inspection information from the Public Company Accounting Oversight Board (PCAOB). Allegedly, KPMG obtained information about which of its audits the PCAOB would review from a former PCAOB staff member it hired. This behavior continued as other PCAOB staffers sought employment at KPMG. This resulted in $50 million in fines.

Then, during the Securities and Exchange Commission (SEC) investigation of this scandal, it was uncovered that KPMG auditors, including some senior partners responsible for public company audits, engaged in sharing questions and answers for internal exams related to mandatory ethics, integrity, and compliance training. As part of a settlement with the SEC, three former KPMG audit partners were suspended from accounting activities, including financial reporting and auditing for public companies. As a result of the cheating scandal, KPMG took steps to strengthen its governance and compliance program.

Ethics and compliance programs alone are not enough to ensure misconduct will not occur. Employee training, behavior monitoring, and ongoing reevaluation of the ethics program and business practices are also required. Additionally, management is responsible for setting the tone at the top of the organization and creating an ethical atmosphere. The fact that executives and senior partners were involved in these scandals suggests KPMG could have a more widespread culture problem on its hands.

Sources: Based on information in KPMG, "KPMG Fast Facts," March 18, 2021; Francine McKenna, "The KPMG Cheating Scandal Was Much More Widespread Than Originally Thought," *Market Watch*, June 18, 2019; Aaron Nicodemus, "KPMG Audit Partners Settle Test Cheating Allegations," *Compliance Week*, May 19, 2020.

会计欺诈、伦理行为和改革

14-4b Accounting Fraud, Ethical Behavior, and Reform

Question: Why did Celadon, one of the largest trucking companies in the United States, file for bankruptcy?

Answer: While there are other factors, accounting fraud was a major factor behind the bankruptcy filing.[2]

Celadon's problems began when the company used a complex accounting scheme to inflate the values for older trucking equipment. The Securities and Exchange Commission (SEC) charged Celadon, the president and chief operating officer, and the chief financial officer with violating various antifraud provisions of the federal securities laws, lying to auditors, and "cooking" the books to inflate the amounts reported for income and earnings per share. Eventually, Celadon agreed to pay a $42.2 million fine to settle the SEC case. Because of the accounting problems, the SEC lawsuit, and a downturn in the trucking industry, the company eventually filed bankruptcy in December 2019. On March 31, 2021—15 months after the initial bankruptcy filing—the Celadon case was finally closed.

Unfortunately, the ones hurt when companies (and their executives and accountants) report inaccurate or misleading accounting information often are not the high-paid corporate executives. In many cases, it's the employees who lose their jobs, as well as the money they invested in the company's retirement program, if the company files for bankruptcy. In addition, investors, lenders, and suppliers who relied on fraudulent accounting information in order to make a decision to invest in or lend money to the company also usually experience a loss.

Today, much of the pressure on corporate executives to "cook" the books is driven by the desire to look good to Wall Street analysts and investors. Recently, the SEC charged Illinois-based Power Solutions, and its former CEO and two other

Ouch—an audit! The word audit only contains five letters, but this word often provokes a deep fear in most people including business executives and employees. The audit process for a business is to make sure the company has followed generally accepted accounting principles (GAAPs) when it prepared its financial statements and accounting information. While an audit does not guarantee a company hasn't "cooked" the books, it does provide assurance it has used GAAPs to report financial information.

former executives with inflating financial results by almost $25 million. All three executives were charged with securities fraud by the SEC and the Department of Justice. The company agreed to pay $1.7 million to settle the SEC charges. The motivation behind the accounting fraud was to meet sales and revenue projections.[3] If a company reports sales and profit figures that are higher than expected, the company's stock value can increase dramatically. On the other hand, if a company, like Power Solutions, reports sales and revenue that are lower than expected, its stock can drop. Greed—especially when executive salaries and bonuses are tied to a company's stock value—is another factor that can lead some corporate executives to use unethical accounting methods to inflate a firm's sales revenues and profit amount.

To help ensure that corporate financial information is accurate and to prevent the type of accounting scandals that have occurred in the past, Congress enacted the Sarbanes-Oxley Act. Key components include the following:[4]

- The SEC is required to establish a full-time five-member public company accounting oversight board.
- Executive and financial officers are responsible for accuracy, documentation, and submission of financial reports and are liable for intentional violations of securities reporting requirements.
- Accounting firms are prohibited from providing many types of non-audit and consulting services to the companies they audit.
- Auditors or accountants must maintain financial documents and audit work papers. The time period is usually five to seven years depending on the type of document.
- Auditors, accountants, and employees can be imprisoned for up to 20 years and subject to fines for destroying financial documents and for willful violations of the securities laws.
- A public corporation must change its lead auditing firm every five years.
- There is added protection for whistle-blowers who report violations of the Sarbanes-Oxley Act.

Although most people welcome the Sarbanes-Oxley Act, complex rules make compliance more expensive and time-consuming for corporate management and more difficult for accounting firms. Yet, most people agree that the cost of compliance is justified.

会计的不同类型

14-4c Different Types of Accounting

Although many people think that all accountants do the same tasks, there are special areas of expertise within the accounting industry. In fact, accounting is usually broken down into two broad categories: managerial and financial.

管理会计
managerial accounting provides managers and employees with the information needed to make decisions about a firm's financing, investing, marketing, and operating activities

Managerial accounting provides managers and employees within the organization with the information needed to make decisions about a firm's financing, investing, marketing, and operating activities. By using managerial accounting information, both managers and employees can evaluate how well they have done in the past and what they can expect in the future.

Financial accounting, on the other hand, generates financial statements and reports for interested people outside of an organization. Typically, investors, financial analysts, bankers, lenders, suppliers, government agencies, and other interested groups use the information provided by financial accounting to determine how well a business firm has achieved its goals. In addition to managerial and financial accounting, additional special areas of accounting include the following:

- *Cost accounting*—determining the cost of producing specific products or services
- *Tax accounting*—planning tax strategy and preparing tax returns for firms or individuals
- *Government accounting*—providing basic accounting services to ensure that tax revenues are collected and used to meet the goals of state, local, and federal agencies
- *Not-for-profit accounting*—helping not-for-profit organizations to account for all donations and expenditures

Ever wonder what an accountant does during a typical workday? While activities vary, there is a good chance an accountant is preparing information about the items listed in this photo that can be reported to the people who need it—employees, managers, business owners, and individuals—to improve their financial decisions.

会计职业

14-4d Careers in Accounting

Accounting can be an exciting and rewarding career. To be successful in the accounting industry, employees must:

- be responsible, honest, and ethical;
- have a strong background in financial management;
- know how to use a computer and software to process data into accounting information; and
- be able to communicate with people who need accounting information.

According to the *Occupational Outlook Handbook*, published by the Department of Labor, job opportunities for accountants, as well as auditors in the accounting area, are expected to experience a 4 percent increase by the year 2029.[5] And more good news: Salaries for employees in the accounting industry are often higher than the salaries for other industries.

What is the typical day like for accountants? While each day may be different than the next and depending on if they are self-employed, work for a business, or work for an accounting firm, accountants typically:

- assist employees, managers, and owners to improve financial decisions;
- suggest ways to reduce costs, increase revenues, and improve profits;
- ensure the business is using generally accepted accounting procedures;
- prepare financial statements at the end of an accounting period;
- calculate the amount of taxes owed, prepare tax returns, and ensure that taxes are paid properly and on time; and
- organize and maintain financial records and make sure the firm's bills are paid on time.

Today, accountants generally are classified as either private accountants or public accountants. A *private accountant* is employed by a specific organization. On the other hand, a *public accountant* works on a fee basis for clients and may be self-employed or be the employee of an accounting firm. Accounting firms range

财务会计
financial accounting generates financial statements and reports for interested people outside an organization

Exploring Careers

职业探索：法务会计正在兴起

Forensic Accounting Is on the Rise

Why do people become forensic accountants? The answer: It is an exciting career path that is growing and combines accounting, auditing, and investigative skills to analyze financial documents in search of fraudulent activities and financial misconduct. Simply put, forensic accountants function as detectives. Their findings and analysis are often used in legal proceedings to prosecute people guilty of accounting fraud or even criminal activities. The origins of forensic accounting date back to the 1930s with the publishing of *Principles of Criminology*, which described the so-called fraud triangle. The triangle outlines how opportunity, incentive, and rationalization contribute to the risk of fraud.

Today, the demand for forensic accounting is on the rise. To comply with current auditing standards and laws such as the Sarbanes-Oxley Act, many accounting and auditing firms are expanding their fraud-detection services. Additionally, several federal government agencies use forensic accountants to tackle complex investigative work related to corporate fraud, healthcare fraud, securities fraud, and more.

The analysis provided by forensic accountants can even be applied to areas such as cybercrime, public corruption, and counterterrorism. For example, the Federal Bureau of Investigation (FBI) hires forensic accountants to follow money trails of criminal activity and national security threats by acquiring, organizing, analyzing, and reporting financial data.

The duties of a forensic accountant can include gathering evidence, investigating financial documents, examining business records, working alongside law enforcement, and testifying in court. These duties require strong analytical and reasoning skills, the ability to effectively communicate, and a skeptical mind. The Association of Certified Fraud Examiners (ACFE), which is the world's largest anti-fraud organization, certifies accounting professionals as certified fraud examiners (CFEs). ACFE has grown to more than 90,000 members with the goal of reducing business fraud around the world and improving public confidence within the profession of accounting.

Sources: Based on information in Association of Certified Fraud Examiners, "About ACFE," March 16, 2021; FBI Jobs, "Forensic Accountants," March 15, 2021; Yigal Rechtman, "The Past, Present, and Future of Forensic Accounting," *The CPA Journal*, April 2020.

in size from one-person operations to huge international firms with hundreds of accounting partners and thousands of employees.

Typically, public accounting firms include on their staffs at least one **certified public accountant (CPA)**, an individual who has met state requirements for accounting education and experience and has passed a rigorous accounting examination. More information about general requirements and the CPA profession can be obtained by contacting the American Institute of CPAs (AICPA) at www.aicpa.org. Be sure and click on the tab "Career Guidance" for information about how to become a CPA.

✓ Concept Check

- What purpose do audits and GAAPs serve in today's business world?
- How do the major provisions of the Sarbanes-Oxley Act affect a public company's audit procedures?
- Based on the information in this section, would you choose accounting as a career?

会计恒等式和资产负债表

14-5 The Accounting Equation and the Balance Sheet

Learning Objective

14-5 Interpret a balance sheet.

At the beginning of this chapter, *information* was defined as data presented in a form that is useful for a specific purpose. Now, we examine how financial *data* are transformed into financial *information* and reported on three very important financial statements—the balance sheet, income statement, and statement of cash flows. We begin by describing why the fundamental accounting equation is the basis for a firm's balance sheet.

会计恒等式

14-5a The Accounting Equation

The accounting equation is a simple statement that forms the basis for the accounting process. This equation shows the relationship between a firm's assets, liabilities, and owners' equity.

- **Assets** are the resources a business owns—cash, inventory, equipment, and real estate.
- **Liabilities** are the firm's debts—borrowed money it owes to others that must be repaid.
- **Owners' equity** is the difference between total assets and total liabilities—what would be left for the owners if the firm's assets were sold and the money used to pay off its liabilities.

The relationship between assets, liabilities, and owners' equity is shown by the following **accounting equation**:

Assets = Liabilities + Owners' equity

Whether a business is a small corner grocery store or a global giant like Procter & Gamble or Amazon, the total dollar amount for assets must equal the sum of its liabilities and owners' equity. To use this equation, a firm's accountants must record raw data—that is, the firm's day-to-day financial transactions—using the double-entry system of bookkeeping. The **double-entry bookkeeping system** is a system in which each financial transaction is recorded as two separate accounting entries to maintain the balance shown in the accounting equation. At the end of a specific accounting period, all of the financial transactions can now be summarized in the firm's financial statements. The form of the financial statements is pretty much the same for all businesses, from a neighborhood video store or small dry cleaner to giant corporations such as Home Depot, Boeing, and FedEx. A firm's financial statements are prepared at least once a year and included in the firm's annual report. An **annual report** is a report distributed to stockholders and other interested parties that describes a firm's operating activities and its financial condition. Because the information contained in financial statements can help executives and employees manage a business and plan for the future, most firms also have financial statements prepared semiannually, quarterly, or monthly.

资产负债表

14-5b The Balance Sheet

Question: *Where could you find the total amount of assets, liabilities, and owners' equity for The Hershey Company?*

Answer: The firm's balance sheet.

A **balance sheet** (sometimes referred to as a **statement of financial position**) is a summary of the dollar amounts of a firm's assets, liabilities, and owners' equity accounts at the end of a specific accounting period. The balance sheet must demonstrate that assets are equal to liabilities plus owners' equity, and the accounting equation is still in balance. Most people think of a balance sheet as a statement that reports the financial condition of a business firm such as The Hershey Company, but balance sheets apply to individuals, too. For example, Marty Campbell graduated from college three years ago and now is employed as a sales representative for a medical supply firm. After going to work, he established a checking and savings account and purchased an automobile, stereo, television, and furniture for his apartment. Marty paid cash for some purchases, but he had to borrow money to pay for the larger ones. Figure 14-5 shows Marty's current personal balance sheet. Marty Campbell's assets total \$26,500, and his liabilities amount to \$10,000. Although the difference between total assets and total liabilities is referred to as *owners' equity* or

注册会计师
certified public accountant (CPA) an individual who has met state requirements for accounting education and experience and has passed a rigorous accounting examination

资产
assets the resources that a business owns

负债
liabilities a firm's debts and obligations

所有者权益
owners' equity the difference between a firm's assets and its liabilities

会计恒等式
accounting equation the basis for the accounting process: *Assets = Liabilities + Owners' equity*

复式簿记系统
double-entry bookkeeping system a system in which each financial transaction is recorded as two separate accounting entries to maintain the balance shown in the accounting equation

年度报告
annual report a report distributed to stockholders and other interested parties that describes the firm's operating activities and its financial condition

资产负债表（或财务状况表）
balance sheet (or **statement of financial position)** a summary of the dollar amounts of a firm's assets, liabilities, and owners' equity accounts at the end of a specific accounting period

Figure 14-5 Personal Balance Sheet

Often, individuals determine their net worth by subtracting the value of their liabilities from the value of their assets.

Marty Campbell
Personal Balance Sheet
December 31, 20XX

ASSETS			LIABILITIES		
Cash	$ 2,500		Automobile loan	$ 9,500	
Savings account	5,000		Credit card balance	500	
Automobile	15,000		TOTAL LIABILITIES		$10,000
Stereo	1,000				
Television	500				
Furniture	2,500		NET WORTH (Owners' Equity)		16,500
TOTAL ASSETS		$26,500	TOTAL LIABILITIES AND NET WORTH		$26,500

stockholders' equity for a business, it is normally called *net worth* for an individual. As reported on Marty's personal balance sheet, net worth is $16,500. The total assets ($26,500) and the total liabilities *plus* net worth ($26,500) are equal. Thus, the accounting equation (Assets = Liabilities + Owners' equity) is still in balance.

Figure 14-6 shows the balance sheet for Northeast Art Supply, a small wholesale business that sells picture frames, paints, canvases, and other artists' supplies

Figure 14-6 Business Balance Sheet

A balance sheet (sometimes referred to as a statement of financial position) summarizes a firm's assets, liabilities, and owners' equity. Note that assets ($340,000) equal liabilities plus owners' equity ($340,000) and the accounting equation is still in balance.

NORTHEAST ART SUPPLY, INC.

Balance Sheet
December 31, 20XX

ASSETS			
Current assets			
Cash		$ 59,000	
Marketable securities		10,000	
Accounts receivable	$ 40,000		
Less allowance for doubtful accounts	2,000	38,000	
Notes receivable		32,000	
Merchandise inventory		41,000	
Prepaid expenses		2,000	
Total current assets			$182,000
Fixed assets			
Delivery equipment	$110,000		
Less accumulated depreciation	20,000	$ 90,000	
Furniture and store equipment	$62,000		
Less accumulated depreciation	15,000	47,000	
Total fixed assets			137,000
Intangible assets			
Patents		$ 21,000	
Total intangible assets			21,000
TOTAL ASSETS			$340,000

LIABILITIES AND STOCKHOLDERS' EQUITY			
Current liabilities			
Accounts payable	$ 35,000		
Notes payable	25,675		
Salaries payable	4,000		
Taxes payable	5,325		
Total current liabilities		$ 70,000	
Long-term liabilities			
Mortgage payable on store equipment	$ 40,000		
Total long-term liabilities		$ 40,000	
TOTAL LIABILITIES			$110,000
Stockholders' equity			
Common stock (25,000×$6)		$ 150,000	
Retained earnings		80,000	
TOTAL OWNERS' EQUITY			230,000
TOTAL LIABILITIES AND OWNERS' EQUITY			$340,000

to retailers in New England. Let's work through the different accounts in Figure 14-6.

资产

14-5c Assets

On a balance sheet, assets are listed in order from the *most liquid* to the *least liquid*. The **liquidity** of an asset is the ease with which it can be converted into cash.

Current Assets **Current assets** are assets that can be converted quickly into cash or that will be used in one year or less. Because cash is the most liquid asset, it is listed first. Next are *marketable securities*—stocks, bonds, and other investments—that can be converted into cash in a matter of days.

Next are the firm's receivables. Its *accounts receivable,* which result from allowing customers to make credit purchases, generally are paid within 30 to 60 days. However, the firm expects that some of these debts will not be collected. Thus, it has reduced its accounts receivables by a 5 percent *allowance for doubtful accounts*. The firm's *notes receivable* are receivables for which customers have signed promissory notes. They generally are repaid over a longer period of time than the firm's accounts receivable.

Northeast's *merchandise inventory* represents the value of goods on hand for sale to customers. Since Northeast Art Supply is a wholesale business, the inventory listed in Figure 14-6 represents finished goods ready for sale to retailers. For a manufacturing firm, inventory also may represent raw materials or work that has been partially completed but requires further processing.

Northeast Art's last current asset is *prepaid expenses,* which are assets that have been paid for in advance but have not yet been used. An example is insurance premiums. They are usually paid at the beginning of the policy year. The unused portion (say, for the last four months of the time period covered by the policy) is a prepaid expense. For Northeast Art, all current assets total $182,000.

This Caterpillar bulldozer is no toy. While the child is wondering if he could drive this monster, this bulldozer is a necessary piece of equipment that costs thousands of dollars for a construction company. Like all other assets, the value of this bulldozer and other heavy construction equipment would be listed as a fixed asset on the construction firm's balance sheet.

Fixed Assets **Fixed assets** are assets that will be held or used for a period longer than one year. They generally include land, buildings, and equipment used in the continuing operation of the business. Although Northeast Art owns no land or buildings, it does own delivery equipment that originally cost $110,000. It also owns furniture and store equipment that originally cost $62,000.

Note that the values of both fixed assets are decreased by their *accumulated depreciation*. **Depreciation** is the process of apportioning the cost of a fixed asset over the period during which it will be used. The depreciation amount allotted to each year is an expense for that year, and the value of the asset must be reduced by the amount of depreciation expense. For example, $20,000 of Northeast's delivery equipment value has been depreciated since it was purchased. Its value at this time is $110,000 less $20,000, or $90,000. For Northeast Art, all fixed assets total $137,000.

流动性
liquidity the ease with which an asset can be converted into cash

流动资产
current assets assets that can be converted quickly into cash or that will be used in one year or less

固定资产
fixed assets assets that will be held or used for a period longer than one year

折旧
depreciation the process of apportioning the cost of a fixed asset over the period during which it will be used

Intangible Assets **Intangible assets** are assets that do not exist physically but that have a value based on the rights or privileges they confer on a firm. They include patents, copyrights, trademarks and brands, and goodwill. By their nature, intangible assets are long-term assets—they are of value to the firm for a number of years.

Northeast Art Supply lists a *patent* for a special oil paint that the company purchased from the inventor. The firm's accountants estimate that the patent has a current market value of $21,000. The firm's intangible assets total $21,000. Now it is possible to add the total amounts for current assets ($182,000), fixed assets ($137,000), and intangible assets ($21,000) to calculate total assets for Northeast Art. As shown in Figure 14-6, total assets are $340,000.

负债和所有者权益
14-5d Liabilities and Owners' Equity

The liabilities and the owners' equity accounts complete the balance sheet. The firm's liabilities are separated into two categories—current and long-term liabilities.

Current Liabilities A firm's **current liabilities** are debts that will be repaid in one year or less. Northeast Art Supply purchased merchandise from its suppliers on credit. Thus, its balance sheet includes an entry for accounts payable. *Accounts payable* are short-term obligations that arise as a result of a firm making credit purchases.

Notes payable are obligations that have been secured with promissory notes. They are usually short-term obligations, but they may extend beyond one year. Only those that must be paid within the year are listed under current liabilities.

Northeast Art also lists *salaries payable* and *taxes payable* as current liabilities. These are both expenses that have been incurred during the current accounting period but will be paid in the next accounting period. For Northeast Art, current liabilities total $70,000.

Long-Term Liabilities **Long-term liabilities** are debts that need not be repaid for at least one year. Northeast Art lists only one long-term liability—a $40,000 *mortgage payable* for store equipment. As you can see in Figure 14-6, Northeast Art's current and long-term liabilities total $110,000.

Owners' or Stockholders' Equity For a sole proprietorship or partnership, the owners' equity is shown as the difference between assets and liabilities. In a partnership, each partner's share of the ownership is reported separately in each owner's name. For a corporation, the owners' equity usually is referred to as *stockholders' equity*. The dollar amount reported on the balance sheet is the total value of stock plus retained earnings that have accumulated to date. **Retained earnings** are the portion of a business's profits not distributed to stockholders.

The original investment by the owners of Northeast Art Supply was $150,000 and was obtained by selling 25,000 shares at $6 per share. In addition, $80,000 of Northeast Art's earnings have been reinvested in the business since it was founded. Thus, owners' equity totals $230,000. Now it is possible to add the total for liabilities ($110,000) and owners' equity ($230,000) to calculate the total for liabilities and owners' equity. As shown in Figure 14-6, the sum of total liabilities and owners' equity is $340,000.

As the two grand totals in Figure 14-6 show, Northeast Art's assets and the sum of its liabilities and owners' equity are equal—at $340,000. The accounting equation (Assets = Liabilities + Owners' equity) is still in balance.

无形资产
intangible assets assets that do not exist physically but that have a value based on the rights or privileges they confer on a firm

流动负债
current liabilities debts that will be repaid in one year or less

长期负债
long-term liabilities debts that need not be repaid for at least one year

留存收益
retained earnings the portion of a business's profits not distributed to stockholders

✓ Concept Check

- How are current assets distinguished from fixed assets?
- Why are fixed assets depreciated on a firm's balance sheet?
- How do you determine the dollar amount of owners' equity for a sole proprietorship, a partnership, or a corporation?
- If a business firm has assets worth $170,000 and liabilities that total $40,000, what is the value of the owners' equity?

Sustaining the Planet

保护地球：会计师越来越关注社会和环境问题

Accountants Grow Concerned About Social and Environmental Issues

To measure the effect a business has on society and the environment, many businesses use social accounting to take a look at the bigger picture. This type of accounting considers how the organization creates value for various stakeholders and attempts to demonstrate how organizations are providing not only economic value, but also how businesses impact society and the environment. Even though many companies issue annual social responsibility audits and sustainability reports along with their financial reports, they are often separate, which makes it difficult to make connections between financial performance and the impact a firm has on society.

According to a survey by the Association of Chartered Certified Accountants (ACCA), accountants are worried about environmental and social issues. In fact, 90 percent of those surveyed believe businesses can make a more positive impact on society and the environment. Ninety-five percent of the accountants surveyed also agreed that accountants and finance managers have a role to play in building a more socially inclusive and environmentally protected world in the future. Already, accountants in many businesses are beginning to track the results and costs of a firm's social impact and sustainability activities. However, experts are quick to point out that an organization's social responsibility and environmental initiatives should not be judged solely on the financial cost.

Conclusion: Even though more and more accountants recognize the need for businesses to better address social inequalities and environmental issues, there are still some barriers that discourage more robust social accounting activities. Potential costs, lack of buy-in from upper management, and misaligned financial priorities can hinder efforts to improve the current situation. Still, it is important to effectively measure an organization's social and environmental impact to prove that these activities provide value. And combining financial data with social and environmental data can strengthen the case for businesses to invest further in these types of initiatives.

Sources: Based on information in Carleton Centre for Community Innovation, "Accounting for Social Impact," March 10, 2021; Michael Cohn, "Accountants Worried About Environmental and Social Issues," *Accounting Today*, October 13, 2020; George Spencer, "5 Steps for Reliable ESG Reporting Amid Growing Demand," *Journal of Accountancy*, February 5, 2021.

损益表

14-6 The Income Statement

Learning Objective

14-6 Interpret an income statement.

Question: *Where can you find the profit amount for Apple, Inc.?*

Answer: The firm's income statement.

An **income statement** is a summary of a firm's revenues and expenses during a specified accounting period—one month, three months, six months, or a year. The income statement is sometimes called the *earnings statement* or *the statement of income and expenses*. Let's begin our discussion by constructing a personal income statement for Marty Campbell. Having worked as a sales representative for a medical supply firm for the past three years, Marty now earns $45,000 a year, or $3,750 a month. After deductions, his take-home pay is $2,625 a month. As illustrated in Figure 14-7, Marty's typical monthly expenses include payments for an automobile loan, credit card payments, apartment rent, utilities, food, clothing, and recreation and entertainment.

损益表

income statement a summary of a firm's revenues and expenses during a specified accounting period

Although the difference between income and expenses is referred to as *profit* or *loss* for a business, it is normally referred to as a *cash surplus* or *cash deficit* for

Figure 14-7 Personal Income Statement

By subtracting expenses from income, you can construct a personal income statement and determine if you have a surplus or deficit at the end of each month.

Marty Campbell
Personal Income Statement
For the month ended December 31, 20XX

INCOME (Take-home pay)		$2,625
LESS MONTHLY EXPENSES		
Automobile loan	$ 350	
Credit card payment	100	
Apartment rent	900	
Utilities	200	
Food	325	
Clothing	100	
Recreation & entertainment	250	
TOTAL MONTHLY EXPENSES		2,225
CASH SURPLUS (or profit)		$ 400

an individual. Fortunately for Marty, he has a surplus of $400 at the end of each month. He can use this surplus for savings, investing, or paying off debts. It is also possible to use the information from a personal income statement to construct a personal budget. A *personal budget* is a specific plan for spending your income—over the next month or a specified time period.

Figure 14-8 shows the income statement for Northeast Art Supply. For a business,

Revenues *less* → Cost of goods sold *less* → Operating expenses equals → Net income

收入
14-6a Revenues

Revenues are the dollar amounts earned by a firm from selling goods, providing services, or performing business activities. Like most businesses, Northeast Art Supply obtains its revenues solely from the sale of its products or services. The revenues section of its income statement begins with gross sales. **Gross sales** are the total dollar amount of all goods and services sold during the accounting period. Deductions made from this amount are:

- *sales returns*—merchandise returned to the firm by its customers;
- *sales allowances*—price reductions offered to customers who accept slightly damaged or soiled merchandise; and
- *sales discounts*—price reductions offered to customers who pay their bills promptly.

The remainder is the firm's net sales. **Net sales** are the actual dollar amounts received by the firm for the goods and services it has sold after adjustment for returns, allowances, and discounts. For Northeast Art, net sales are $451,000.

收入
revenues the dollar amounts earned by a firm from selling goods, providing services, or performing business activities

销售总额
gross sales the total dollar amount of all goods and services sold during the accounting period

净销售收入
net sales the actual dollar amounts received by a firm for the goods and services it has sold after adjustment for returns, allowances, and discounts

Figure 14-8 Business Income Statement

An income statement summarizes a firm's revenues and expenses during a specified accounting period. For Northeast Art Supply, net income after taxes is $28,045.

NORTHEAST ART SUPPLY, INC.		Income Statement for the Year Ended December 31, 20XX	
Revenues			
Gross sales		$465,000	
Less sales returns and allowances	$ 9,500		
Less sales discounts	4,500	14,000	
Net sales			$451,000
Cost of goods sold			
Beginning inventory, January 1, 20XX		$ 40,000	
Purchases	$346,000		
Less purchase discounts	11,000		
Net purchases		335,000	
Cost of goods available for sale		$375,000	
Less ending inventory December 31, 20XX		41,000	
Cost of goods sold			334,000
Gross profit			$117,000
Operating expenses			
Selling expenses			
Sales salaries	$ 22,000		
Advertising	4,000		
Sales promotion	2,500		
Depreciation—store equipment	3,000		
Depreciation—delivery equipment	4,000		
Miscellaneous selling expenses	1,500		
Total selling expenses		$ 37,000	
General expenses			
Office salaries	$ 28,500		
Rent	8,500		
Depreciation—furniture	1,500		
Utilities expense	2,500		
Insurance expense	1,000		
Miscellaneous expense	500		
Total general expense		42,500	
Total operating expenses			79,500
Net income from operations			$ 37,500
Less interest expense			2,000
NET INCOME BEFORE TAXES			$ 35,500
Less federal income taxes			7,455
NET INCOME AFTER TAXES			$ 28,045

销货成本

14-6b Cost of Goods Sold

The standard method of determining the **cost of goods sold** by a retailing or a wholesaling firm can be summarized as follows:

Cost of goods sold = Beginning inventory + Net purchases – Ending inventory

According to Figure 14-8, Northeast Art Supply began its accounting period on January 1 with a merchandise inventory that cost $40,000. During the next 12 months, the firm purchased merchandise valued at $346,000. After deducting *purchase discounts,* however, it paid only $335,000 for this merchandise. Thus, during the year, Northeast had total *goods available for sale* valued at beginning inventory ($40,000) plus net purchases ($335,000), for a total of cost of goods available for sale ($375,000).

Twelve months later, at the end of the accounting period on December 31, Northeast still had inventory valued at $41,000. For Northeast, the cost of goods available for sale ($375,000) less ending inventory ($41,000) equals the firm's total of cost of goods sold ($334,000). It is now possible to calculate gross profit.

销货成本
cost of goods sold the dollar amount equal to beginning inventory *plus* net purchases *less* ending inventory

If you want to know if a company is profitable or not, look at its income statement. An income statement is the "go-to" source for executives, managers, employees, and investors who want to know if a firm is earning a profit or operating at a loss. This same statement also contains information about its costs of goods sold, operating expenses, finance costs, and the amount of taxes it must pay.

The firm's **gross profit** is net sales ($451,000) *less* cost of goods sold ($334,000), for a $117,000 gross profit.

营业费用

14-6c Operating Expenses

A firm's **operating expenses** are all business costs other than the cost of goods sold. Total operating expenses generally are divided into two categories: selling expenses and general expenses.

Selling expenses are costs related to the firm's marketing activities. For Northeast Art Supply, selling expenses total $37,000. *General expenses* are costs incurred in operating a business, in this case, a total of $42,500. Now it is possible to total both selling and general expenses. As Figure 14-8 shows, total operating expenses for the accounting period are $79,500.

净收益

14-6d Net Income

When revenues exceed expenses, the difference is called **net income**. When expenses exceed revenues, the difference is called **net loss**.

Profit or Loss = Revenues − Expenses

As Figure 14-8 shows, Northeast Art's *net income from operations* is computed as gross profit ($117,000) less total operating expenses ($79,500). For Northeast Art, net income from operations is $37,500. From this amount, *interest expense* of $2,000 is deducted to obtain a *net income before taxes* of $35,500. The interest expense is deducted in this section of the income statement because it is not an operating expense. Rather, it is an expense that results from financing the business.

Northeast Art's *federal income taxes* are $7,455. Although these taxes may or may not be payable immediately, they are definitely an expense that must be deducted from income. This leaves Northeast Art with a *net income after taxes* of $28,045. This amount may be used to pay a dividend to stockholders, it may be retained or reinvested in the firm, it may be used to reduce the firm's debts, or all three.

✓ Concept Check

- What is the difference between a balance sheet and an income statement?
- Explain how a retailing firm would determine the cost of goods sold during an accounting period.
- If a retailer has revenues of $700,000, cost of goods sold that total $270,000, and operating expenses that total $200,000, what is its net income before taxes?

Learning Objective

14-7 Describe business activities that affect a firm's cash flow.

现金流量表

14-7 The Statement of Cash Flows

Cash is vital to any business. Both the Securities and Exchange Commission and the Financial Accounting Standards Board require all publicly traded companies to include a statement of cash flows, along with their balance sheet and income statement, in their annual report. The **statement of cash flows** illustrates how the company's operating, investing, and financing activities affect cash during an accounting period. While a firm's balance sheet reports dollar values for assets, liabilities, and owners' equity and an income statement reports the firm's dollar amount of profit or loss, the statement of cash flows focuses on how much cash is on hand to pay the firm's bills. Also, the information on the statement of cash flows can be used to evaluate decisions related to a firm's future investments and financing needs. Investors, lenders, and suppliers are also interested in a firm's statement of cash flows. Investors want to know if a firm can pay dividends. Before extending credit to a firm, lenders and suppliers often use the information on the statement of cash flows to evaluate the firm's ability to repay its debts.

毛利润
gross profit a firm's net sales *less* the cost of goods sold

营业费用
operating expenses all business costs other than the cost of goods sold

净收益
net income occurs when revenues exceed expenses

净亏损
net loss occurs when expenses exceed revenues

A statement of cash flows for Northeast Art Supply is illustrated in Figure 14-9. It provides information concerning the company's cash receipts and cash payments and is organized around three different activities: operating, investing, and financing.

- *Cash flows from operating activities.* This is the first section of a statement of cash flows. It addresses the firm's primary revenue source—providing goods and services. Typical adjustments include adding the amount of depreciation to a firm's net income. Other adjustments that increase or decrease the amounts for accounts receivable, inventory, accounts payable, and income taxes payable are also required to reflect a true picture of cash flows from operating activities.
- *Cash flows from investing activities.* The second section of the statement is concerned with cash flow from investments. This includes the purchase and sale of equipment, land, and other assets and investments.
- *Cash flows from financing activities.* The third and final section deals with the cash flow from all financing activities. It reports changes in debt obligation and owners' equity accounts. This includes loans and repayments, the sale and repurchase of the company's own stock, and cash dividends.

The totals of all three activities are added to the beginning cash balance to determine the ending cash balance. For Northeast Art Supply, the ending cash

现金流量表
statement of cash flows a statement that illustrates how the company's operating, investing, and financing activities affect cash during an accounting period

Figure 14-9 Statement of Cash Flows

A statement of cash flows summarizes how a firm's operating, investing, and financing activities affect its cash during a specified accounting period. For Northeast Art Supply, the amount of cash at the end of the year reported on the statement of cash flows is $59,000—the same amount reported for the cash account on the firm's balance sheet.

NORTHEAST ART SUPPLY, INC.		Statement of Cash Flows for the Year Ended December 31, 20XX
Cash flows from operating activities		
Net Income		$28,045
Adjustments to reconcile net income to net cash flows		
Depreciation	$ 8,500	
Decrease in accounts receivable	1,000	
Increase in inventory	(5,000)	
Increase in accounts payable	6,000	
Increase in income taxes payable	3,000	13,500
Net cash provided by operating activities		$41,545
Cash flows from investing activities		
Purchase of equipment	$ (2,000)	
Purchase of investments	(10,000)	
Sale of investments	20,000	
Net cash provided by investing activities		8,000
Cash flows from financing activities		
Payments on debt	$(23,000)	
Payment of dividends	(5,000)	
Net cash provided by financing activities		(28,000)
NET INCREASE IN CASH		$21,545
Cash at beginning of year		37,455
CASH AT END OF YEAR		$59,000

✓ Concept Check

- What is the purpose of the statement of cash flows?
- In a statement of cash flows, what is included in the operating activities section? In the investing activities section? In the financial activities section?

balance is $59,000. Note that this is the same amount reported for the cash account on the firm's balance sheet. Together, the statement of cash flows, balance sheet, and income statement illustrate the results of past business decisions and reflect the firm's ability to pay debts and dividends and to finance new growth.

评估财务报表
14-8 Evaluating Financial Statements

Learning Objective

14-8 Summarize how managers evaluate the financial health of a business.

All three financial statements—the balance sheet, the income statement, and the statement of cash flows—can provide answers to a variety of questions about a firm's ability to do business and stay in business, its profitability, and its value as an investment. Even more information about a firm's financial health can be obtained by comparing its financial information with the same information for competing firms, with industry averages, and with its financial information over recent accounting periods.

比较财务数据
14-8a Comparing Financial Data

Comparisons of a firm's financial and accounting information are possible as long as accountants follow GAAPs to prepare the firm's financial statements. Except for minor differences in format and terms, a balance sheet, income statement, and statement of cash flows for Lowe's, for example, will be similar to the financial statements for Home Depot because both companies are in the home improvement industry. Comparisons among firms give executives, managers, and employees a general idea of a firm's standing within the industry. Competitors' financial information can be obtained from their annual reports, information filed with the SEC, and investment sites like Bloomberg and Yahoo! Finance—if they are public corporations. Industry averages are published by reporting services such as Dun & Bradstreet (D&B) and BizMiner, as well as by some industry trade associations.

Today, most corporations include in their annual reports comparisons of the important elements of their financial statements for recent years. For example, Figure 14-10 shows comparisons—of revenue, research and development (R&D) costs, operating income, and sales and marketing expenses—for Microsoft Corporation, a world leader in the computer software industry. By examining this information, a manager in the research and development division can tell whether R&D expenditures have been increasing or decreasing over the past three years. The vice president of marketing can determine if the total amount of sales and marketing expenses is changing. Stockholders and potential investors, on the other hand, may be more concerned with increases or decreases in Microsoft's revenues and operating income over the same time period. Still another type of analysis of a firm's financial health involves computation of financial ratios.

财务比率
14-8b Financial Ratios

A **financial ratio** is a number that shows the relationship between two elements of a firm's financial statements. While it is possible to calculate many different financial ratios, we'll only discuss three different ratios that are used to measure a firm's profitability, its ability to pay its debts, and how often it sells its inventory. Like the individual elements in financial statements, these ratios can be compared with those of competitors, with industry averages, and with the firm's past ratios from previous accounting periods. The information required

财务比率
financial ratio a number that shows the relationship between two elements of a firm's financial statements

Figure 14-10 Comparisons of Present and Past Financial Statements for Microsoft Corporation

Most corporations include in their annual reports comparisons of the important elements of their financial statements for recent years.

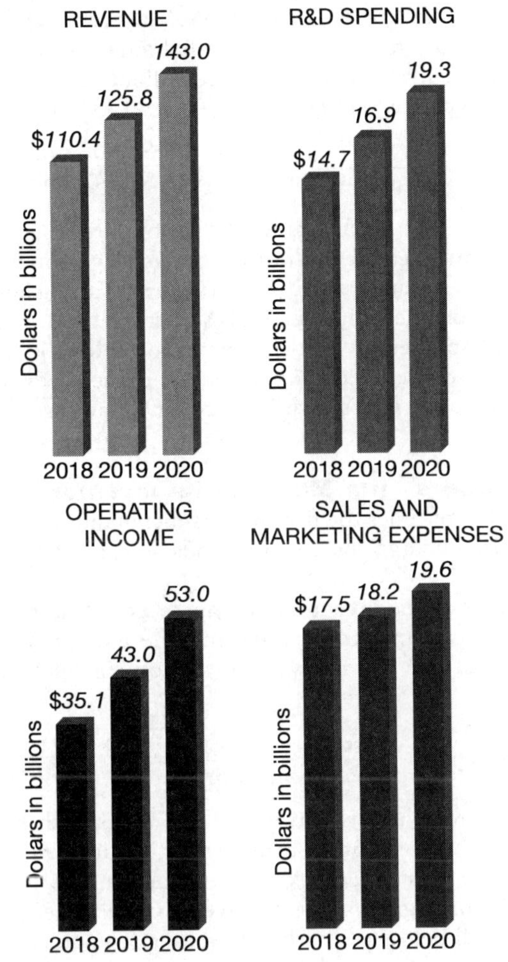

Source: Adapted from the Microsoft Corporation 2020 Annual Report.

to form these ratios is found in a firm's balance sheet, income statement, and statement of cash flows.

Measuring a Firm's Ability to Earn Profits A firm's net income after taxes indicates whether the firm is profitable. It does not, however, indicate how effectively the firm's resources are being used. For this latter purpose, a net profit margin can be computed. **Net profit margin** (sometimes called **return on sales**) is a financial ratio calculated by dividing net income after taxes by net sales. For Starbucks—a company known for world class coffee—its net profit margin is 4.8 as calculated below.

$$\text{Net profit margin} = \frac{\text{Net income after taxes}}{\text{Net sales}} = \frac{\$\ 928 \text{ million}}{\$\ 19{,}165 \text{ million}}$$

$$= 0.048 = 4.8 \text{ percent}$$

净利润率（或销售利润率）
net profit margin (or **return on sales**) a financial ratio calculated by dividing net income after taxes by net sales

A higher return on sales is better than a low one. Today, the average net profit margin for all business firms is between 4 and 5 percent. With a return on sales of 4.8 percent, Starbucks is toward the high end of the average. A low return on sales can be increased by reducing expenses and increasing sales.

Measuring a Firm's Ability to Pay Its Debts A current ratio can be used to evaluate a firm's ability to pay its current liabilities. A firm's **current ratio** is computed by dividing current assets by current liabilities. The current ratio for Starbucks is 1.06 as calculated below.

$$\text{Current ratio} = \frac{\text{Current assets}}{\text{Current liabilities}} = \frac{\$7{,}806 \text{ million}}{\$7{,}347 \text{ million}} = 1.06$$

This ratio indicates that Starbucks has $1.06 of current assets for every $1 of current liabilities. The average for this ratio varies greatly from industry to industry, but many financial experts suggest that a firm's current ratio should range between 1.2 and 2 depending on the industry. A high current ratio indicates that a firm can pay its current liabilities. A low current ratio (below 1.2) can be improved by repaying current liabilities, reducing expenses, reducing dividend payments to stockholders to increase the firm's cash balance, or obtaining additional cash from investors.

Measuring How Well a Firm Manages Its Inventory A firm's **inventory turnover** is the number of times the firm sells its merchandise inventory in one year. It is approximated by dividing the cost of goods sold in one year by the average value of the inventory.

The average value of the inventory for one accounting period can be found by adding the beginning inventory value and the ending inventory value and dividing the sum by 2. The inventory turnover for Starbucks is 5 as calculated below.

$$\text{Inventory turnover} = \frac{\text{Cost of goods sold}}{\text{Average inventory}} = \frac{\$7{,}695 \text{ million}}{\$1{,}540 \text{ million}} = 5$$

Starbucks sells its merchandise inventory five times each year, or about once every 73 days. The average inventory turnover for all firms ranges between 5 and 10 depending on the industry. For example, supermarkets may have inventory turnover rates of 20 or higher, whereas inventory turnover rates for furniture stores are generally well below the national average. The quickest way to improve inventory turnover is to order merchandise in smaller quantities at more frequent intervals.

Like the three ratios described in this section, the calculations for other financial ratios, including return on owners' equity, earnings per share, working capital, and debt-to-equity, are based on the information contained in a firm's balance sheet, income statement, and statement of cash flows. For more detailed information on ratio analysis, you may want to read more on the topic in an accounting or finance textbook or use an internet search engine.

In this chapter we have discussed the importance of information and accounting information. In Chapter 15, we examine how information can help improve a firm's financial planning. We also examine why firms need financing, how they obtain it, and how they ensure that funds are used effectively in keeping with the organization's goals.

流动比率
current ratio a financial ratio computed by dividing current assets by current liabilities

存货周转率
inventory turnover a financial ratio calculated by dividing the cost of goods sold in one year by the average value of the inventory

✓ Concept Check

- What are the benefits of comparing a firm's current financial information with information for previous accounting periods, with industry averages, and with financial information for competitors?
- Explain the calculation procedures for and significance of each of the following:
  a. Net profit margin
  b. Current ratio
  c. Inventory turnover

Discussion Questions 讨论题

1. Do managers really need all the kinds of information discussed in this chapter? If not, which kinds can they do without?
2. How can confidential data and information (such as the wages of individual employees) be kept confidential and yet still be available to managers who need them?
3. Bankers usually insist that prospective business borrowers submit audited financial statements along with a loan application. Why should financial statements be audited by a CPA?
4. Do the balance sheet, income statement, and statement of cash flows contain all the information you might want as a potential lender or investor? What other information would you like to examine?
5. Of the three financial ratios discussed in this chapter, which do you think is the most important financial ratio? Why?

Case 14 案例 14：拉里·埃里森和甲骨文公司计划如何赢得云计算战争

How Larry Ellison and Oracle Plan to Win the Cloud Wars

Larry Ellison is an American businessperson and is one of the wealthiest people in the world. He is chairperson, chief technology officer, and co-founder of Oracle, an integrated cloud applications and platform services company based in Austin, Texas. The company sells cloud-based tools to store and analyze data and information as well as software, hardware, and other technology applications. The company was founded in 1977 after Ellison discovered there was a growing need for database management systems. Just two years later, the company introduced its own database management system, finally answering the question of how technology could help companies manage large amounts of data and information.

Oracle has always had a reputation for introducing new products before competitors. It developed the first client-server database, the first media server to support video on demand, and the first internet development suite, among others. The company's goal has always been to help its business customers collect, store, update, process, and present data—the five management information system functions described in this chapter. Now, according to Ellison, Oracle's databases manage most of the world's data with more than 430,000 customers in 175 countries. "We are the dominant database supplier on the planet Earth," Ellison said on a recent earning's call. He went on to say, "we're bigger than IBM and Microsoft combined" when it comes to total database revenues.

Oracle competes with companies such as technology giants IBM, Microsoft, and Amazon Web Service (AWS), which offer similar cloud databases and other cloud-based services. Though Oracle admittedly took longer than its competitors to take its database to the cloud, Ellison believes its systems are now more secure and more affordable than other available systems. In fact, Ellison plans to win the cloud wars by competing on price, quality, and security.

Lower pricing for Oracle's products that are recognized for quality helps Oracle win new customers. According to Oracle, its cloud infrastructure, for example, is consistently less expensive than Amazon Web Services. The method used to price some products also helps Oracle win new customers. Customers who use Oracle's FastConnect infrastructure, which transfers information from customer data centers to the cloud through private connections, pay fixed monthly charges. The fixed charge means that their customers have a predictable monthly bill compared to AWS customers who are billed based on data transfer activity.

To keep a leg up on the competition, Oracle invests heavily in research and development (R&D), which generates world-class technologies. The company has spent $56 billion on R&D since 2012 and an additional $80 billion on acquisitions of companies that had promising ideas or products that fit with Oracle's product mix. Its R&D activities are constantly finding ways to introduce new or improve existing products that can satisfy customer needs. For instance, Oracle created the world's first autonomous database. The product, Oracle Autonomous Linux, serves to reduce maintenance and downtime and at the same time increase security. Before Oracle's new product was introduced, companies that attempted to take their large workloads to the cloud experienced high costs and security concerns. When Oracle Autonomous Linux was introduced, the company had thousands of customers waiting in the wings for the product to be deployed in addition to thousands more who signed up for product demonstrations.

The company has also made significant investments in security all the way down to the chip level to reduce concerns of advanced and persistent threats that use sophisticated hacking techniques to steal data. Its products have layered security defenses and controls such as security zones, data encryption, and firewalls. This security-first approach builds trust among Oracle customers. One of the major selling points of its autonomous database is that it eliminates human error while improving cybersecurity.

A culture of innovation has fueled Oracle since day one. Ellison is competitive by nature and will do what it takes to build the best cloud management system and technology products possible. Introducing new and innovative products that are recognized for their quality, pricing its products competitively, and taking a security-first approach make Oracle a leader in cloud computing.[6]

Discussion Questions

1. While Oracle is a recognized giant in the technology world, it competes with other successful companies including IBM, Microsoft, and Amazon Web Services. Describe the three factors that Larry Ellison plans to use to win the technology wars.
2. Although Oracle is successful, it continues to invest in research and development and acquire other companies that have promising ideas or products that complement Oracle's product mix. Explain why you think continued research and development and acquisitions are important for Oracle's future growth.
3. How important is protection from hackers and computer security for a technology company like Oracle? What steps is Oracle taking to protect information stored in its cloud-based database and technology products?

Chapter

15

Mastering Financial Management

掌握财务管理

Learning Objectives

Once you complete this chapter, you will be able to:

15-1 Explain why financial management is important in today's competitive economy.

15-2 Identify a firm's short- and long-term financial needs.

15-3 Summarize the process of planning for financial management.

15-4 Identify the services provided by banks and financial institutions for their business customers.

15-5 Describe the advantages and disadvantages of different methods of short-term debt financing.

15-6 Evaluate the advantages and disadvantages of equity financing.

15-7 Evaluate the advantages and disadvantages of long-term debt financing.

Why Should You Care?

The old saying goes, "Money makes the world go around." For business firms, this is true. It's hard to operate a business without money. In this chapter, we discuss how financial management is used to obtain money and ensure that it is used effectively.

Inside Business 商业透视：疫情期间西南航空公司的财务管理

Southwest Navigates Financial Management During Pandemic

Southwest Airlines, the world's largest low-cost airline, carries more than 130 million passengers each year, earning more than $2.3 billion in income. *Until the COVID-19 pandemic, that is.* The pandemic, which was responsible for travel restrictions, flight cancellations, and limited seating capacity, left the company with a $3.5 billion annual loss in 2020, its first annual loss since 1972. While many airlines tried to minimize short-term losses during the pandemic, Southwest was able to focus on expanding its long-term competitive advantage because of aggressive financial management and its healthy balance sheet. These same factors enabled the air carrier to continue to operate during the pandemic and manage the economic problems caused by the downturn in air travel.

At one point during the pandemic, Southwest was able to fill only 8 percent of available seats with paying customers. Eventually the number of ticket sales began to increase, but recovery for most airlines was slow because of travel restrictions, and travelers were afraid to leave their homes and travel for business or pleasure. However, Southwest experienced a quicker recovery than many of its competitors. Unlike other major airlines that reduced flight schedules and eliminated less popular travel destinations, Southwest kept providing service to established destinations and was able to accommodate the customers that needed to travel in the initial stages of recovery. In fact, Southwest even launched service to six new destinations in 2020 with plans to begin service to at least eight more the following year. To further encourage passengers to choose Southwest, it left middle seats open for the majority of 2020 to allow for greater social distancing in addition to implementing other health and safety protocols.

Southwest's management team also had to consider the effect of the pandemic on employees and developed a plan with different options for employees who didn't feel that it was safe to work during the pandemic. In addition to implementing other health and safety protocols described above, Southwest offered its workforce a variety of voluntary severance packages rather than laying off or furloughing employees. Options included early retirement or extended leave of up to 18 months at half of their base pay. About 27 percent of Southwest's employees took one of these options. Though it cost the company $1.7 billion, these options helped increase employee loyalty and at the same time let employees know it was concerned about both their customers *and* their employees.

No one can argue that the travel and tourism industries were greatly impacted by the global pandemic. The financial management decisions that Southwest's executives made during the pandemic were "make or break" decisions and cost millions of dollars. And yet, these decisions enabled the airline to not only survive the pandemic but even build for the future.[1]

Did you know?

Southwest flies to 101 destinations across the United States and 10 additional countries.

A company like Southwest Airlines can't survive without money! Even though Southwest lost $3.5 billion during the COVID-19 pandemic, its financial management team was able to guide the company to recovery. Financial managers were also able to fund expansion and provide service to new destinations because Southwest had built a strong balance sheet and substantial cash reserves just in case of a downturn in air travel for any reason, including a pandemic.

Without money, employees don't get paychecks, creditors and lenders can't be paid, and the business may close its doors and cease to exist. On the other hand, when a company—like Southwest Airlines, Facebook, Citibank, or a small neighborhood business—manages its finances it can not only pay its bills and employees, but can also meet the needs of its customers and society and even grow and expand.

In this chapter we examine why financial management is important. Then, we discuss how firms find the financing required to start a business and keep it going and then how they manage that money effectively. We also look at how firms develop financial plans and evaluate financial performance. Finally, we examine typical banking services and compare various methods of obtaining short- and long-term financing.

为什么要进行财务管理

15-1 Why Financial Management?

Learning Objective

15-1 Explain why financial management is important in today's competitive economy.

Many businesses realized how planning coupled with effective financial management could increase their ability to meet the needs of customers, increase sales, and keep the doors open during the COVID-19 pandemic. For example, financial managers for each of the firms listed below had to compare the cost of each action with the potential increase in sales revenue before making a recommendation to implement the following changes:

- Red Roof Hotels offered special rates for rooms to provide a quiet, private space for workers who couldn't work at the office or home.
- Best Buy increased its focus on virtual support, technology repair, and promoted its e-commerce site as a way for customers to purchase computers and electronic gear without leaving their home.
- Kroger turned some locations into fulfillment centers designed to speed delivery of merchandise to an increasing number of customers who ordered online.
- Walgreens began offering delivery of personal care products and food items to customers.[2]

While the goals of each of these companies were to meet the needs of customers and increase sales, each action required executives and managers to make important financial decisions to turn the ideas into a reality.

Managers and employees must find the money needed to keep a business operating and fund all the goals and objectives that a successful business wants to achieve. A business that cannot pay its bills may have to close its doors and even be forced to file for bankruptcy protection. As shown in Figure 15-1, the number of business firms filing for bankruptcy varies from one year to the next. However, financial experts agree that the number of business bankruptcies increases or decreases depending on the stage of the business cycle the nation's economy may be in at a specific time. A nation's business cycle was compared to a roller coaster ride with periods of prosperity or high points and troughs or low points. A pandemic, political unrest, world economic problems, terrorist threats and wars, interest rates, and other factors can also lead to an increase

Figure 15-1 Business Bankruptcies in the United States

The nation's economy and other factors can affect the number of businesses that file for bankruptcy. (Note: At the time of publication, 2020 was the most recent year for which complete statistics were available.)

Source: Based on the American Bankruptcy Institute website.

in business bankruptcies. Despite the COVID-19 pandemic, the number of businesses filing for bankruptcy in 2020 actually decreased when compared to the number of bankruptcy cases for the previous four years.

Poor financial management can lead to bankruptcy. While business owners don't plan to fail, sometimes poor financial management, low sales revenues, poor location, uncontrolled expenses, and a lot of other factors including the nation's economy can cause a business to fail. In thousands of cases each year, bankruptcy may be the only solution for a business that cannot pay its creditors.

财务管理的必要性
15-1a The Need for Financial Management

Financial management consists of all the activities concerned with obtaining money and using it effectively. To some extent, financial management can be viewed as a two-sided problem. On one side, the uses of funds often dictate the type or types of financing needed by a business. On the other side, the activities a business can undertake are determined by the types of financing available. Financial managers must ensure that funds are available when needed both now and in the future, that they are obtained at the lowest possible cost, and that they are used as efficiently as possible. In addition, proper financial management must also ensure that:

- Financing priorities are established in line with organizational goals and objectives;
- Spending is planned and controlled;
- A firm's credit customers pay their bills on time, and the number of past due accounts is reduced;
- Bills are paid promptly to protect the firm's credit rating and its ability to borrow money;
- The funds required for paying the firm's taxes are available when needed to meet tax deadlines; and
- Excess cash is invested in certificates of deposit (CDs), government securities, or conservative, marketable securities.

To encourage more responsible financial management, political leaders, the Securities and Exchange Commission (SEC), self-regulatory organizations like the Financial Industry Regulatory Authority (FINRA), and companies in the banking and financial industry often enact regulations and create guidelines that encourage legal and ethical behavior. Many security laws date back to the 1930s and were enacted to curb the abuses and practices that led to the Great Depression in 1929. Through the years more laws have been passed to strengthen regulation of the banking and finance industry. One of the more important laws enacted is the Dodd-Frank Wall Street Reform and Consumer Protection Act, which was designed to create a sound economic foundation that would encourage job growth, rein in Wall Street and prohibit some speculative techniques, end financial bailouts, and prevent future financial crises. The Dodd-Frank Act also provided new regulations to protect American families from unfair and abusive financial and banking practices.

Even with the new regulations, some experts and politicians still argue current laws do not go far enough and there is a need for additional regulations and increased government oversight. For business firms, the impact of new laws could increase the time and cost of obtaining both short- and long-term financing.

财务管理
financial management all the activities concerned with obtaining money and using it effectively

Ethics and Social Responsibility

商业伦理与社会责任：高盛因海外贿赂被罚款数十亿美元

Goldman Sachs Fined Billions for Foreign Bribery

Goldman Sachs Group Inc., a leader in global investment banking, securities, and investment management, and its Malaysian subsidiary admitted to conspiring to violate the anti-bribery provisions of the Foreign Corrupt Practices Act (FCPA). It was discovered that over a period of five years the company engaged in bribery by offering financial incentives to influence high-level government officials. Goldman Sachs agreed to pay more than $2.9 billion in U.S. fines as well an additional $3.9 billion to settle with the Malaysian government.

Goldman Sachs engaged in a scheme to pay more than $1 billion in bribes to government officials in Malaysia in exchange for approval to sell bonds to raise $6.5 billion that had been earmarked to help the people of Malaysia. Government approval enabled Goldman Sachs to earn profits for selling the bonds, but most of the money from the sale of the bonds benefited the country's leaders and their associates.

Several current and former top executives were implicated in the scandal. These individuals were required to return more than $174 million in pay and bonuses from prior years. Repayments like this are often referred to as a clawback. Tim Leissner, Goldman Sachs' former Southeast Asia chairman, pleaded guilty to conspiracy to violate the FCPA and conspiracy to commit money laundering. Ng Chong Hwa (also known as Roger Ng), former head of investment banking for Goldman Sachs Malaysia, was also charged with conspiracy to violate the FCPA and conspiracy to commit money laundering. Ng was extradited from Malaysia to face trial in the United States.

The scandal negatively impacted not only Goldman Sachs' reputation but also the reputation of other American financial institutions operating abroad. Experts also point out that this type of unethical behavior, which involves high-level executives, suggests a culture problem exists and undermines public confidence in American business in the United States and abroad.

Sources: Based on information in United States Department of Justice, "Goldman Sachs Resolves Foreign Bribery Case And Agrees To Pay Over $2.9 Billion," October 22, 2020; "Goldman to Pay Nearly $3 Billion Fine Following Foreign Bribes Probe," *CBS News*, October 23, 2020; Matthew Goldstein and Emily Flitter, "Goldman Sachs Malaysia Arm Pleads Guilty in 1MDB Fraud," *The New York Times*, October 22, 2020.

金融职业

15-1b Careers in Finance

A career in finance can be rewarding. As an added bonus, the Bureau of Labor Statistics projects there will be a 15 percent increase in the number of jobs in the financial sector of the economy between now and 2029.[3] People in finance must have certain traits and skills. One of the most important priorities for someone interested in a finance career is honesty. Be warned: Investors, lenders, government regulators, and other corporate executives expect financial managers to be above reproach. In addition to honesty, managers and employees in the finance area must:

1. Have a strong background in finance, accounting, or mathematics.
2. Know how to use a computer to analyze data.
3. Be an expert at both written and oral communication.

Careers in the financial services industry are on the rise! Between now and 2029, jobs in finance are expected to increase 15 percent—that's much faster than the average growth for other industries. As an added bonus, employees enjoy higher salaries and increased benefits when compared to careers in other industries. You can find more information for this career and other options by exploring the information available in the Occupational Outlook Handbook.

Today, there are many different types of positions in finance. Typical job titles include chief financial officer, vice president of finance, bank officer, consumer credit officer, financial analyst, financial

✓ Concept Check

- For a business firm, what type of activities does financial management involve?
- To be successful, what traits and skills does an employee in the finance industry need?

Learning Objective

15-2 Identify a firm's short- and long-term financial needs.

planner, loan officer, insurance analyst, and investment account executive. Depending on qualifications, work experience, and education, salaries generally are higher in the financial industry when compared with careers in other industries. Many employees also have excellent benefits and other perks that make a career in financial management attractive.

融资需求

15-2 The Need for Financing

Money is needed both to start a business and to keep it going. The original investment of the owners, along with money they may have borrowed, should be enough to open the doors. After that, ideally sales revenues should be used to pay the firm's expenses and provide a profit as well.

This is exactly what happens in a successful firm—over the long run. However, income and expenses may vary from month to month or from year to year. Short-term financing may be needed when sales are low and expenses are high. For example, many businesses experienced lower sales during the COVID-19 pandemic, but still had expenses and bills that had to be paid. On the other hand, long-term financing may be needed to open new retail locations, to purchase equipment, or to build a new plant. For example, management at Cincinnati-based Graeter's Ice Cream—the company profiled in the end-of-part cases for this text—recognized they needed long-term financing to build a new plant and buy out an existing franchisee. To see how management financed both opportunities, read the case in the "Running a Business" section in Part 6.

短期融资

15-2a Short-Term Financing

Short-term financing is money that will be used for one year or less. As illustrated in Table 15-1, there are many short-term financing needs, but three deserve special attention. First, certain business practices may affect a firm's cash flow and create a need for short-term financing. **Cash flow** is the movement of money into and out of an organization. The goal is to have sufficient money coming into the firm in any period to cover the firm's expenses during that period. This goal, however, is not always achieved. For example, California-based Callaway Golf offers credit to retailers that carry the firm's golf clubs, balls, clothing, and golf accessories. Credit purchases made by Callaway's retailers generally are not paid until 30 to 60 days (or more) after the transaction. Callaway therefore may need short-term financing to solve its cash flow problem and to pay its bills until its customers have paid theirs.

A second need for short-term financing is speculative production. **Speculative production** refers to the production of goods which is followed by a time lag before the actual sale of those goods. Consider what happens when a firm such as Connecticut-based Stanley Black & Decker begins to manufacture power and small hand tools for sale during the Christmas season. Manufacturing begins in March, April, and May, and the firm negotiates short-term financing to buy materials and

Table 15-1 Comparison of Short- and Long-Term Financing

Whether a business seeks short- or long-term financing depends on what the money will be used for.

Short-Term Financing Needs	Long-Term Financing Needs
Cash-flow problems	Business start-up costs
Speculative production	Mergers and acquisitions
Current inventory needs	New product development
Monthly expenses	Long-term marketing activities
Short-term promotional needs	Replacement of equipment
Unexpected emergencies	Expansion of facilities

短期融资
short-term financing money that will be used for one year or less

现金流
cash flow the movement of money into and out of an organization

投机性生产
speculative production the production of goods which is followed by a time lag before the actual sale of those goods

Figure 15-2 Cash Flow for a Manufacturing Business

Manufacturers such as Stanley Black & Decker often use short-term financing to pay expenses during the production process. Once goods are shipped to retailers and wholesalers and payment is received, sales revenues are used to repay short-term financing.

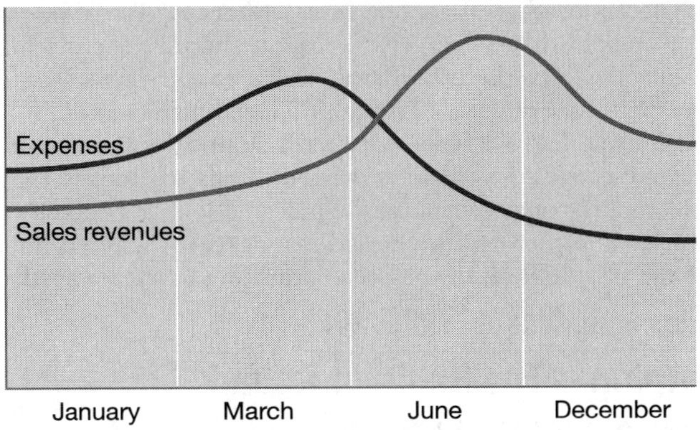

supplies, to pay wages and rent, and to cover inventory costs until its products eventually are sold to wholesalers and retailers later in the year. Take a look at Figure 15-2. Although Stanley Black & Decker manufactures and sells finished products all during the year, expenses peak during the first part of the year. During this same period, sales revenues are low. Once the firm's finished products are shipped to retailers and wholesalers and payment is received (usually within 30 to 60 days), sales revenues are used to repay short-term financing.

A third need for short-term financing is to increase inventory. Retailers that range in size from Walmart to the neighborhood drugstore need short-term financing to build up their inventories before peak selling periods. For example, Dallas-based Bruce Miller Nurseries must increase the number of shrubs, trees, and flowering plants that it makes available for sale during the spring and summer growing seasons. To enable Bruce Miller to obtain the merchandise inventory it needs, growers and wholesalers extend the repayment period. Then once the merchandise is sold, Bruce Miller repays the growers and wholesalers.

长期融资

15-2b Long-Term Financing

Long-term financing is money that will be used for longer than one year. Long-term financing obviously is needed to start a new business. As Table 15-1 shows, it is also needed for business mergers and acquisitions, new product development, long-term marketing activities, replacement of equipment that has become obsolete, and expansion of facilities.

长期融资
long-term financing money that will be used for longer than one year

The amounts of long-term financing needed by large firms can seem almost unreal. Intel—a leader in the technology industry with a long history of investing in research and development—spent over $13.5 billion in 2020 to develop new technology that is used to produce state-of-the art electronic devices.[4]

风险回报比率

15-2c The Risk–Return Ratio

According to financial experts, business firms will find it more difficult to raise both short- and long-term financing in the future for two reasons. First, financial reform and increased government regulations

✓ Concept Check

- How does short-term financing differ from long-term financing? Give two business uses for each type of financing.
- What is speculative production? How is it related to a firm's cash-flow problems?
- As an employee in the finance department of a large company, how would you explain the risk–return ratio to an investor?

will lengthen the process required to obtain financing. Second, both investors and lenders are more cautious about who receives financing. As a result of these two factors, financial managers must develop a strong financial plan that describes how the money will be used and how it will be repaid. When developing a financial plan for a business, a financial manager must also consider the risk–return ratio when making decisions that affect the firm's finances. The **risk–return ratio** is based on the principle that a high-risk decision should generate higher financial returns for a business. On the other hand, more conservative decisions (with less risk) often generate lesser returns. Although financial managers want higher returns, they often must strive for a balance between risk and return. For example, Ohio-based American Electric Power is investing billions of dollars to fund research into renewable energy sources including wind and solar technology. Yet, financial managers (along with other executives and managers throughout the organization) must evaluate the potential return before committing to such a costly project.

计划——健全财务管理的基础

15-3 Planning—The Basis of Sound Financial Management

Learning Objective

15-3 Summarize the process of planning for financial management.

In Chapter 5, we defined a *plan* as an outline of the actions by which an organization intends to accomplish its goals and objectives. A **financial plan**, then, is a plan for obtaining and using the money needed to implement an organization's goals and objectives.

制订财务计划

15-3a Developing the Financial Plan

Financial planning (like all planning) begins with establishing a set of valid goals and objectives. Financial managers must then determine how much money is needed to accomplish each goal and objective. Finally, financial managers must identify available sources of financing and decide which to use. The three steps involved in financial planning are illustrated in Figure 15-3.

Figure 15-3 The Three Steps of Financial Planning

After a financial plan has been developed, it must be monitored continually to ensure that it actually fulfills the firm's goals and objectives.

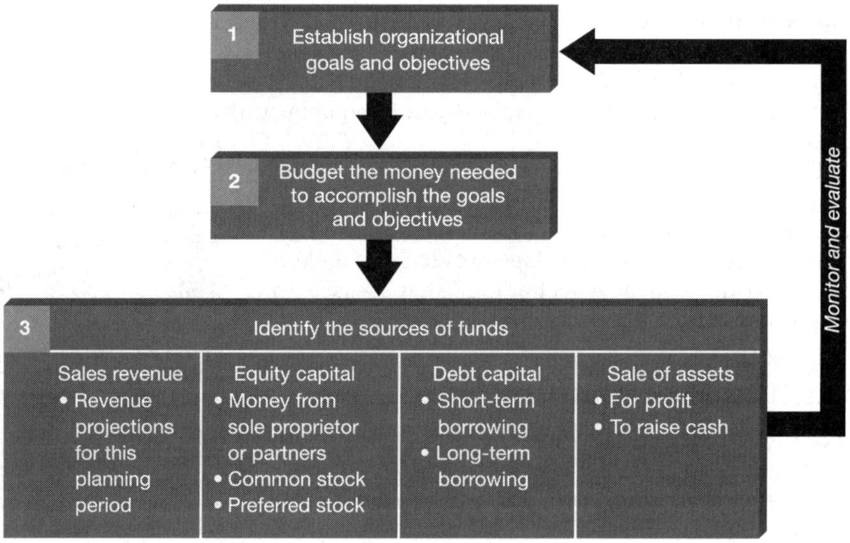

风险回报比率

risk–return ratio a ratio based on the principle that a high-risk decision should generate higher financial returns for a business and more conservative decisions often generate lower returns

财务计划

financial plan a plan for obtaining and using the money needed to implement an organization's goals and objectives

Establishing Organizational Goals and Objectives As pointed out in Chapter 5, a *goal* is an end result that an organization expects to achieve over a one- to ten-year period. An *objective* was defined in Chapter 5 as a specific statement detailing what an organization intends to accomplish over a shorter period of time. If goals and objectives are not specific and measurable, they cannot be translated into dollar costs, and financial planning cannot proceed. For large corporations, both goals and objectives can be expensive. For example, have you ever wondered how much McDonald's spends on advertising? Well, to reach almost 70 million customers that it serves each day, the world's most famous fast-food restaurant chain spends over $600 million each year.[5]

Do you have a budget? After establishing goals and objectives, a successful business takes the next step and constructs a budget to project revenues, expenses, or both for a specified period of time. You, just like a business, can do the same thing and build a budget to help you manage your personal finances and achieve your short- and long-term goals.

Budgeting for Financial Needs Once planners know what the firm's goals and objectives are for a specific period—say, the next calendar year—they can construct a budget that projects the costs the firm will incur and the sales revenues it will receive. Specifically, a **budget** is a financial statement that projects income, expenditures, or both over a specified future period.

Usually, the budgeting process begins with the construction of departmental budgets for sales and various types of expenses. Financial managers can easily combine each department's budget for sales and expenses into a company-wide cash budget. A **cash budget** estimates cash receipts and cash expenditures over a specified period. Notice in the cash budget for Stars and Stripes Clothing, shown in Figure 15-4, cash sales and collections are listed at the top for each calendar quarter. Payments for purchases and routine expenses are listed in the middle section. Using this information, it is possible to calculate the anticipated cash gain or loss at the end of each quarter for this retail clothing store.

Most firms today use one of two approaches to budgeting. In the *traditional* approach, each new budget is based on the dollar amounts contained in the budget for the preceding year. These amounts are modified to reflect any revised goals,

预算
budget a financial statement that projects income, expenditures, or both over a specified future period

现金预算
cash budget a financial statement that estimates cash receipts and cash expenditures over a specified period

Figure 15-4 Cash Budget for Stars and Stripes Clothing

A company-wide cash budget projects cash sales, collections, purchases, and expenses over a specified period to anticipate cash gains and losses.

STARS AND STRIPES CLOTHING
Cash Budget
From January 1, 20xx to December 31, 20xx

	First Quarter ($)	Second Quarter ($)	Third Quarter ($)	Fourth Quarter ($)	Total ($)
Cash sales and collections	150,000	160,000	150,000	185,000	645,000
Less payments					
Purchases	110,000	80,000	90,000	60,000	340,000
Wages/salaries	25,000	20,000	25,000	30,000	100,000
Rent	10,000	10,000	12,000	12,000	44,000
Other expenses	4,000	4,000	5,000	6,000	19,000
Taxes	8,000	8,000	10,000	10,000	36,000
Total payments	157,000	122,000	142,000	118,000	539,000
Cash gain or (loss)	(7,000)	38,000	8,000	67,000	106,000

and managers are required to justify only new expenditures. The problem with this approach is that it leaves room for padding budget items to protect the (sometimes selfish) interests of managers or their department. This problem is essentially eliminated through zero-base budgeting. **Zero-base budgeting** is a budgeting approach in which every expense in every budget must be justified.

To develop a plan for long-term financing needs, managers often construct a capital budget. A **capital budget** estimates a firm's expenditures for major assets, including new product development, expansion of facilities, replacement of obsolete equipment, and mergers and acquisitions. For example, Uber—a company known for providing consumers with ride services and food delivery—acquired Postmates—a food delivery competitor. Uber constructed a capital budget to determine if it should pay cash or offer stock to pay for the smaller company. Uber chose to use the stock option and no cash outlay was required.[6]

零基预算
zero-base budgeting a budgeting approach in which every expense in every budget must be justified

资本预算
capital budget a financial statement that estimates a firm's expenditures for major assets and its long-term financing needs

Identifying Sources of Funds The four primary sources of funds, listed in Figure 15-3, are sales revenue, equity capital, debt capital, and proceeds from the sale of assets. Future sales revenue generally provides the greatest part of a firm's financing. Figure 15-4 shows that for Stars and Stripes Clothing, sales for the year are expected to cover all expenses and to provide a cash gain of $106,000. However, Stars and Stripes has a problem in the first quarter, when sales are expected to fall short of expenses by $7,000. In fact, one of the primary reasons for financial planning is to provide management with adequate lead time to solve this type of cash-flow problem.

Exploring Careers

职业探索：如何成为首席财务官

How to Become a CFO

A chief financial officer (CFO) is a senior-level executive that manages a company's finances. As the overseer of the finance and accounting divisions, the CFO is responsible for planning how to finance the firm's activities, borrowing money when needed, managing cash flow, ensuring financial statements and tax returns are accurate, and even paying bills to protect the firm's credit rating. In addition to making important financial decisions, a CFO must help other high-level managers make decisions that could often make or break the business.

There is not just one route to becoming a CFO. Previous job titles often include senior financial controller, director of finance, or treasurer. To be successful, CFOs must have a working knowledge of accounting, financial analysis, risk management, regulatory compliance, investments, and budgeting. A broad understanding of business management, operations management, and retailing is also helpful.

For many CFOs, preparation begins with college courses in accounting or finance that eventually lead to a bachelor's or master's degree in business administration, accounting, or finance. A working knowledge of computers, software, and technology can also help process the data and information a CFO needs to make important decisions. In addition to these skills, the ability to communicate and work with people and to use critical thinking skills to solve problems are valuable skills for a CFO executive.

Following the CFO career path can be both rewarding and challenging. The average base salary for a CFO is more than $136,000, but salaries can be much higher in large corporations. Executives at this level also have excellent benefits and retirement packages. While this is a highly-paid position, it also comes with great responsibility. This important role is reserved for professionals with established track records, broad business experience, and a deep understanding of finance.

Sources: Based on information in "How to Become a CFO – 7 Steps to Guide Your Career Path," *Robert Half*, March 2020; Mitchell Grant, "Chief Financial Officer (CFO)," *Investopedia*, February 28, 2021; "Average Chief Financial Officer (CFO) Salary," *PayScale*, March 18, 2021.

A second type of funding is **equity capital**. For a sole proprietorship or partnership, equity capital is provided by the owner or owners of the business. For a corporation, equity capital is money obtained from the sale of shares of ownership in the business. Equity capital is used almost exclusively for long-term financing.

A third type of funding is **debt capital**, which is borrowed money. Debt capital may be borrowed for either short- or long-term use—and a short-term loan seems made to order for Stars and Stripes Clothing's shortfall problem. The firm probably would borrow the needed $7,000 (or perhaps a bit more) at some point during the first quarter and repay it from second-quarter sales revenue.

Proceeds from the sale of assets are the fourth type of funding. Selling assets is often a drastic step. However, it may be a reasonable last resort when sales revenues are declining, and equity capital or debt capital cannot be found. Assets also may be sold to increase a firm's cash balance or when they are no longer needed or do not "fit" with the company's core business. Berkshire Hathaway sold its newspaper holdings to Lee Enterprises for $140 million. Berkshire Hathaway—a corporate giant—can use the proceeds of the sale to acquire other companies with more potential.[7]

监督和评估财务绩效

15-3b Monitoring and Evaluating Financial Performance

It is important to ensure that financial plans are implemented properly and to catch potential problems before they become major ones. Despite efforts to raise additional financing, reduce expenses, and increase sales to become profitable, retailer JCPenney filed for bankruptcy in 2020 and closed over 150 stores or about 15 percent of its retail locations.[8] To prevent such problems, financial managers should establish a means of monitoring financial performance. Interim budgets (weekly, monthly, or quarterly) may be prepared for comparison purposes. These comparisons highlight areas that require additional or revised planning—or at least areas calling for a more careful investigation. Budget comparisons can also be used to improve the firm's future budgets.

✓ Concept Check

- What is the function of a cash budget? A capital budget?
- What is the difference between equity capital and debt capital?
- Describe the four sources of funds for a business.
- How does a financial manager monitor and evaluate a firm's financing?

银行和其他金融机构提供的金融服务

15-4 Financial Services Provided by Banks and Other Financial Institutions

For a business owner, it helps to know your banker. Banking services can be divided into three broad categories: traditional services, electronic banking services, and international services.

Learning Objective

15-4 Identify the services provided by banks and financial institutions for their business customers.

为商业客户提供的传统银行服务

15-4a Traditional Banking Services for Business Clients

Traditional services provided by banks and other financial institutions include savings and checking accounts, loans, processing credit card and debit card transactions, and providing professional advice.

Savings and Checking Accounts Savings accounts provide a safe place to store money a business doesn't immediately need. The usual *passbook savings account* earns between 0.05 and 0.25 percent in most financial institutions. A business with excess cash it is willing to leave on deposit with a bank for a set period of time can earn a higher rate of interest. To do so, the business firm buys a certificate of deposit. A **certificate of deposit (CD)** is a document stating that the bank will pay the depositor a guaranteed interest rate on money left on deposit for a specified period of time. At the time of publication, one-year CDs were paying between 0.25 and 1.10 percent. The rate can vary depending on the financial institution and the amount of time until maturity.

权益资本
equity capital money received from the owners or from the sale of shares of ownership in a business

债务资本
debt capital borrowed money obtained through loans of various types

存单
certificate of deposit (CD) a document stating that the bank will pay the depositor a guaranteed interest rate on money left on deposit for a specified period of time

For a business, a relationship with a banker can mean the difference between success and failure. Although JP Morgan Chase—often referred to as Chase—is the largest bank in the United States, it still must meet the needs of its customers. Like many competitors, Chase offers the services a business (or an individual) needs to manage their finances, including savings and checking accounts, short- and long-term loans, credit and debit card processing, and financial advice.

Business firms (and individuals) also deposit money in checking accounts so that they can write checks to pay for purchases. For businesses, monthly charges are based on the average daily balance in the checking account and/or the number of checks written.

Business Loans Banks, savings and loan associations, credit unions, and other financial institutions provide short- and long-term loans to businesses. *Short-term business loans* must be repaid within one year or less. To help ensure that short-term money will be available when needed, many firms establish a line of credit. A **line of credit** is a loan that is approved before the money is actually needed. Because all the necessary paperwork is already completed and the loan is preapproved, the business can obtain the money later without delay, as soon as it is required. Even with a line of credit, a firm may not be able to borrow money if the bank does not have sufficient funds available. For this reason, some firms prefer a **revolving credit agreement**, which is a guaranteed line of credit. Under this type of agreement, the bank guarantees that the money will be available when the borrower needs it. In return for the guarantee, the bank may charge a commitment fee. Typical commitment fees range from 0.25 to 1.0 percent of the *unused* portion of the revolving credit agreement. The usual interest rate is charged for the portion that *is* borrowed.

Long-term business loans are repaid over a period of years. The average length of a long-term business loan is generally 3 to 7 years but sometimes as long as 15 to 20 years. Loans to purchase real estate may even be as long as 30 years. Most lenders require some type of collateral for long-term loans. **Collateral** is real estate or property (e.g., stocks, bonds, equipment, or any other asset of value) pledged as security for a loan.

Repayment terms and interest rates for both short- and long-term loans are arranged between the lender and the borrower. For businesses, repayment terms may include monthly, quarterly, semiannual, or annual payments.

The Basics of Getting a Loan According to many financial experts, preparation is the key when applying for a business loan. To begin the process, you should get to know potential lenders before requesting a loan. Although there may be many potential lenders that can provide the money you need, the logical place to borrow money is where your business does its banking. Before applying for a loan, you may also want to check your firm's credit rating with a national credit bureau such as Dun & Bradstreet (sometimes referred to as D&B). Typically, business owners will be asked to fill out a loan application. In addition to the loan application, the lender will also want to see your current business plan. Be sure to explain how much funding you require to accomplish your goals and how the loan will be repaid. Most lenders insist that you submit current financial statements that have been prepared by an independent certified public accountant. Then compile a list of references that includes your suppliers, other lenders, or the professionals with whom you are associated. You may also be asked to discuss the loan request with a loan officer. Hopefully, your loan request will be approved. If not, try to determine why your loan request was rejected. Think back over the loan process and determine what you could do to improve your chances of getting a loan the next time you apply.

信用额度
line of credit a loan that is approved before the money is actually needed

循环信贷协议
revolving credit agreement a guaranteed line of credit

抵押品
collateral real estate or property pledged as security for a loan

Technology and Innovation

技术与创新：万事达卡推进其开放银行战略

Mastercard Advances Its Open Banking Strategy

Though Mastercard is often thought of as simply a credit card company, this multinational corporation is actually a technology company that specializes in financial services and global payment solutions. The company's consumer payment products include credit, debit, and prepaid cards. For businesses, Mastercard offers a variety of products and payment solutions such as secure payment systems that protect customers and merchants, co-branded cards, business-to-business (B2B) payment services, and more. It is also a leader in developing open banking.

The concept of open banking refers to sharing financial information electronically and securely with other businesses. To strengthen its open banking platform, Mastercard acquired Finicity for $825 million. Finicity is a company that has a history of helping consumers and organizations use financial data and technology to make better decisions. For Mastercard, the acquisition is another way to use a competitive edge over competitors like Visa, American Express, and Discover. At the same time, financial information gathered by Finicity will help connect consumers with companies—especially lenders—that need accurate, real time data to approve or reject credit applications. To illustrate how open banking can speed the loan approval process, consider the following example. A couple wants to buy a home, but they need financing. They apply for a loan from a lender like Rocket Mortgage. By accessing real-time data from Finicity, Rocket Mortgage obtains the financial data it needs to evaluate the couple's ability to repay the loan without having to go to multiple sources. Because of open banking, the time required to approve or reject a loan request can be reduced, which is an advantage for both the borrower and the lender.

Mastercard—the parent company of Finicity—believes that open banking platforms that use technology will become even more important as the financial industry continues to innovate and use technology to provide improved service to both consumers and merchants around the globe. Although open banking on a global scale can be challenging because every country has its own set of financial rules and regulations, Mastercard has already developed plans to expand its open banking solutions outside of the United States and Europe.

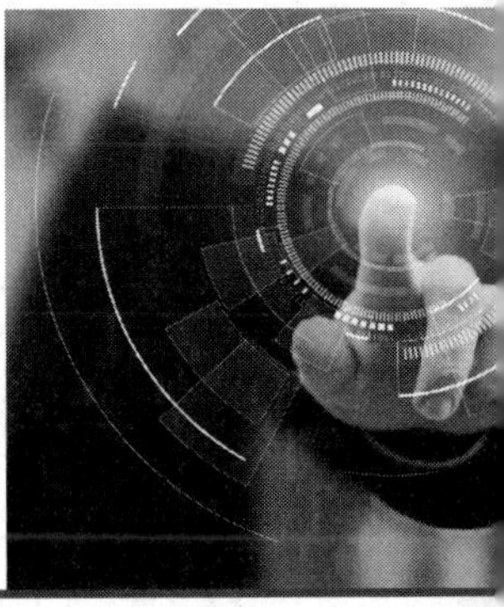

Sources: Based on information in Anna Hrushka, "Mastercard Deal Brings Finicity to Global Stage, CEO Says," *Banking Dive*, July 17, 2020; Mastercard, "Mastercard Extends Open Banking Efforts with Close of Finicity Acquisition," November 19, 2020; "DOJ Approves Mastercard's $825M Acquisition Of Finicity," *PYMNTS*, November 16, 2020.

借记卡交易、信用卡交易和移动支付

15-4b Debit and Credit Card Transactions and Mobile Pay

Today, customers have multiple ways to pay for merchandise and services. According to a recent Federal Reserve System survey that tracked payments made by more than 3,000 individuals over a three-day period, debit cards were used most often to pay for purchases followed by cash, credit cards, electronic payments, and checks—refer to Table 15-2.[9] Each of the payment options requires a business to set up procedures and work with banks and other financial institutions in order to process payments for merchandise and services. A **debit card** is a card that electronically subtracts the amount of the purchase from a customer's bank account at the moment the purchase is made. For example, when you use a debit card to pay for lunch at Olive Garden, the restaurant must use electronic equipment to process the debit card transaction before funds are deposited in the restaurant's account. Note: Don't confuse debit cards with credit cards. Although they may look alike, there are important differences. A debit card electronically subtracts the amount of a customer's purchase from a bank account at the moment the purchase is made. If you use a credit card to pay for your purchase, the credit card company extends short-term financing, and you do not make payment until you receive your next statement.

借记卡

debit card a card that electronically subtracts the amount of a purchase from a customer's bank account at the moment the purchase is made

Table 15-2 Consumer Payment Options

Although there are many ways to pay for merchandise and services, most people prefer using debit cards.

Payment Option	Percentage of People Who Prefer This Option
Debit cards	30 Percent
Cash	26 percent
Credit cards	24 percent
Electronic payments	11 percent
Checks	5 percent

Source: Laura Kim, Raynil Kumar, and Shaun O'Brien, "2020 Findings from the Diary of Consumer Payment Choice," Federal Reserve Bank of San Francisco.

Consumers also use credit cards to pay for everything from tickets on American Airlines to Zebco fishing gear. Recent statistics published by CardRates.com indicate that 61 percent of Americans have at least one credit card. And on average Americans have four cards. More importantly, 75 percent of consumers with credit cards carry an average balance of more than $6,200.[10] Still, merchants accept and even encourage customers to use credit cards to pay for their purchases. The reason is simple: Often consumers that don't have the cash to make a purchase will use a credit card to make the purchase. For example, many consumers used their credit cards to purchase everyday necessities in the spring of 2020 when the number of unemployed workers increased to record levels as a result of the temporary closure of nonessential businesses during the first phase of the COVID-19 pandemic.

By depositing credit transaction slips in a bank or other financial institution, the merchant can convert card sales into cash. In return for processing the merchant's card transactions, the financial institution charges a fee that generally ranges between 1 and 3.5 percent. The number of card transactions, the total dollar amount of debit and credit sales, and how well the merchant can negotiate the fees the financial institution charges determine actual fees. Typically, small, independent businesses pay more than larger stores or chain stores.

In addition to debit and credit cards, mobile payments are now accepted by many businesses. **Mobile payments** allow customers to use an electronic device or app to pay for a product or service. The most common electronic devices used to complete mobile payments are cell phones or tablets. Examples of mobile payment systems are Apple Pay, PayPal, and Google Pay. For merchants, processing a mobile payment is similar to processing debit card transactions. For customers, mobile pay is convenient and often safer than carrying plastic debit or credit cards. Most experts agree that mobile payments and other electronic payment methods will become even more popular in the future.

电子银行服务
15-4c Electronic Banking Services

An **electronic funds transfer (EFT) system** is a means of performing financial transactions through a computer terminal. The following four EFT applications are changing how banks and financial institutions help firms do business:

1. *Automated teller machines (ATMs)*. An ATM is an electronic bank teller—a machine that provides many of the same services a human teller can provide. Once the customer is properly identified, the machine dispenses cash from the customer's checking or savings account or makes a cash advance charged to a credit card. Customers have access to ATMs at all times of the day or night. There may be a fee for each transaction.
2. *Automated clearinghouses (ACHs)*. Designed to reduce the number of paper checks, automated clearinghouses process checks, direct deposits, recurring

移动支付
mobile payment payment for a product or service which is made using an electronic device or an app

电子资金转账系统
electronic funds transfer (EFT) system a means of performing financial transactions through a computer terminal

bill payments, Social Security benefits, and employee salaries. For example, large companies use the ACH network to transfer salaries directly into their employees' bank accounts, thus eliminating the need to make out individual paychecks.

3. *Point-of-sale (POS) terminals.* A POS terminal is a computerized cash register located in a retail store. Assume you want to pay for purchases at a Walmart Supercenter. You begin the process by pulling your credit or debit card through a magnetic card reader or inserting your card into the chip reader. A central processing center notifies a computer at your bank that you want to make a purchase. The bank's computer immediately adds the amount to your credit card account for a credit transaction. In a similar process, the bank's computer deducts the amount of the purchase from your bank checking account if you use a debit card. Finally, the amount of your purchase is added to the store's account. The Walmart store then is notified that the transaction is complete, and the cash register prints out your receipt. A POS system can also collect customer information for a marketing database and provide sales information for a firm's inventory system.
4. *Electronic check conversion (ECC).* Electronic check conversion is a process used to convert information from a paper check into an electronic payment for merchandise, services, or bills. When you give your completed check to a store cashier at a Best Buy store, the check is processed through an electronic system that captures your banking information and the dollar amount of the check. Once the check is processed, the funds to pay for your transaction are transferred into the business firm's account. Finally, you are asked to sign a receipt, and you get a voided (canceled) check back for your records. ECC also can be used for checks you mail to pay for a purchase or to pay on an account.

EFTs are fast, and they eliminate the costly processing of paper checks. However, some customers are reluctant or afraid to use online banking or EFT systems because they fear the computer will garble their accounts. Others are afraid someone will steal their account information. Early on, Congress responded to such fears by passing the Fair Credit Billing Act and the Electronic Funds Transfer Act, which protect the customer in case the bank makes an error or the customer's credit or debit card is stolen.

国际银行服务

15-4d International Banking Services

For international businesses, banking services are extremely important. Depending on the needs of an international firm, a bank can help by providing a letter of credit or a banker's acceptance.

A **letter of credit** is a legal document issued by a bank or other financial institution guaranteeing to pay a seller a stated amount for a specified period of time if certain conditions or requirements are met. In most cases, a letter of credit is valid for 30 to 60 days. With a letter of credit, certain conditions or requirements, such as proof of shipment or delivery of the merchandise, may be specified before payment is made.

A **banker's acceptance** is a written order for a bank to pay a third party a stated amount of money on a specific date. With a banker's acceptance, no conditions or requirements are specified. It is simply an order to pay without any strings attached.

Both a letter of credit and a banker's acceptance are popular methods of paying for import and export transactions. Imagine that you are a business owner in the United States who wants to purchase some leather products from a small business in Florence, Italy. You offer to pay for the merchandise with your company's check drawn on an American bank, but the Italian business owner is worried about payment. To solve the problem, your bank can issue either a letter

信用证
letter of credit a legal document issued by a bank or other financial institution guaranteeing to pay a seller a stated amount for a specified period of time if certain conditions or requirements are met

银行承兑汇票
banker's acceptance a written order for a bank to pay a third party a stated amount of money on a specific date

✓ Concept Check

- Describe the traditional banking services provided by financial institutions.
- What are the major advantages of electronic banking services?
- How can a bank or other financial institution help American businesses to compete in the global marketplace?

of credit or a banker's acceptance to guarantee that payment will be made. In addition to a letter of credit and a banker's acceptance, banks also can use EFT technology to speed international banking transactions.

One other international banking service should be noted. Banks and other financial institutions provide for currency exchange. If you place an order with a Japanese manufacturer for merchandise valued at $50,000, how do you pay for the order? Do you use U.S. dollars or Japanese yen? To solve this problem, you can use the bank's currency-exchange service. To make payment, you can use either currency, and if necessary, the bank will exchange one currency for the other to complete your transaction.

短期债务融资来源

15-5 Sources of Short-Term Debt Financing

Learning Objective

15-5 Describe the advantages and disadvantages of different methods of short-term debt financing.

The decision to borrow money does not necessarily mean that a firm is in financial trouble. On the contrary, astute financial management often means regular, responsible borrowing of many different kinds to meet different needs. In this section, we examine the sources of *short-term debt financing* available to businesses. In the next two sections, we look at long-term financing options: equity capital and debt capital.

无担保短期融资来源

15-5a Sources of Unsecured Short-Term Financing

Short-term debt financing is usually easier to obtain than long-term debt financing for three reasons:

1. For the lender, the shorter repayment period means less risk of nonpayment.
2. The dollar amounts of short-term loans are usually smaller than those of long-term loans.
3. A close working relationship normally exists between the short-term borrower and the lender.

Most lenders do not require collateral for short-term financing. Remember in the last section that *collateral* was defined as real estate or property pledged as security for a loan. If they do require collateral, it is usually because they are concerned about the size of a particular loan, the borrowing firm's poor credit rating, or the general prospects of repayment.

Unsecured financing is financing that is not backed by collateral. A company seeking unsecured short-term financing has several options.

Trade Credit Manufacturers and wholesalers often provide financial aid to their customers by allowing them 30 to 60 days (or more) in which to pay for merchandise. This delayed payment, known as **trade credit**, is a type of short-term financing extended by a seller who does not require immediate payment after delivery of merchandise. It is the most popular form of short-term financing because most manufacturers and wholesalers do not charge interest for trade credit. In fact, from 70 to 90 percent of all transactions between businesses involve some trade credit.

Assume that Walmart receives a shipment of clothing from a manufacturer. Along with the merchandise, the manufacturer sends an invoice that states the terms of payment. Walmart now has two options for payment. First, it may pay the invoice promptly and take advantage of any cash discount the manufacturer offers. Cash-discount terms are specified on the invoice. For instance, "2/10, net 30" means that the customer—Walmart—may take a 2 percent discount if it pays the invoice within 10 days of the invoice date.

A second option is to wait until the end of the credit period before making payment. If payment is made between 11 and 30 days after the date of the invoice,

无担保融资
unsecured financing financing that is not backed by collateral

商业信用
trade credit a type of short-term financing extended by a seller who does not require immediate payment after delivery of merchandise

Walmart must pay the entire amount. As long as payment is made before the end of the credit period, the business maintains the ability to purchase additional merchandise from the seller using the trade-credit arrangement.

In 1950, Sam Walton opened a dime store called Walton's in Bentonville Arkansas. Then, in 1962, Mr. Walton opened the first Walmart Discount store in Rogers, Arkansas. Today, Walmart is the largest retailer in the world. A great deal of the retailer's success is built on its relationship with more than 2,800 suppliers that allow Walmart to use trade credit to purchase merchandise and then pay for it 30 to 60 days or more after the merchandise is sold in its stores.

Promissory Notes Issued to Suppliers A **promissory note** is a written pledge by a borrower to pay a certain sum of money to a creditor at a specified future date. Suppliers uneasy about extending trade credit may be less reluctant to offer credit to customers who sign promissory notes. Unlike trade credit, however, promissory notes usually require the borrower to pay interest. Although repayment periods may extend to one year, most short-term promissory notes are repaid in 60 to 180 days.

A promissory note offers two important advantages to the firm extending the credit.

1. A promissory note is legally binding and an enforceable contract.
2. A promissory note is a negotiable instrument.

Because a promissory note is negotiable, the manufacturer, wholesaler, or company extending credit may be able to discount, or sell, the note to its own bank (or another business). If the note is discounted, the dollar amount received by the company extending credit is slightly less than the maturity value because the bank charges a fee for the service. The company extending credit recoups most of its money immediately, and the bank collects the entire amount when the note matures.

Unsecured Bank Loans Banks and other financial institutions offer unsecured short-term loans to businesses at interest rates that vary with each borrower's credit rating. The **prime interest rate** is the lowest rate charged by a bank for a short-term loan. Figure 15-5 traces the fluctuations in the average prime rate

Figure 15-5 Average Prime Interest Rate Paid by U.S. Businesses, 1990–March 2021

The prime rate is the interest rate charged by U.S. banks when businesses with the "best" credit ratings borrow money. All other businesses pay higher interest rates than the prime rate.

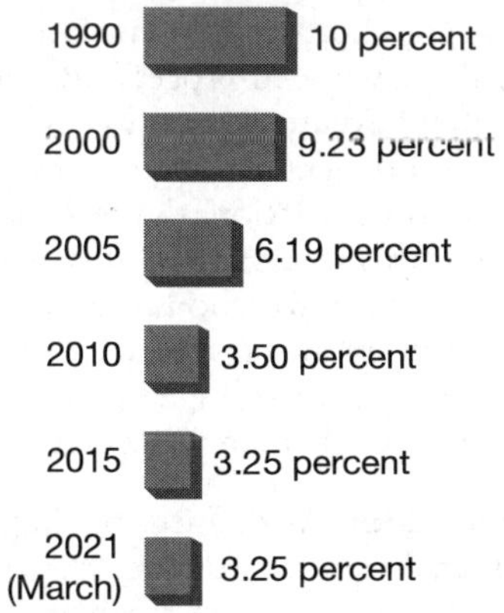

Source: Federal Reserve Bank.

期票
promissory note a written pledge by a borrower to pay a certain sum of money to a creditor at a specified future date

最优惠利率
prime interest rate the lowest rate charged by a bank for a short-term loan

charged by U.S. banks from 1990 to March 2021. This lowest rate generally is reserved for large corporations with excellent credit ratings. Organizations with good to high credit ratings may pay the prime rate plus 2 percent. Firms with questionable credit ratings may have to pay the prime rate plus 4 percent. Of course, if the banker believes that loan repayment may be a problem, the borrower's loan application may be rejected.

When a business obtains a short-term bank loan, interest rates and repayment terms may be negotiated. As a condition of the loan, a bank may require that a *compensating balance* be kept on deposit at the bank. Compensating balances, if required, are typically 10 to 20 percent of the borrowed funds. The bank may also require that every commercial borrower pay off its short-term loans at least once each year and not use short-term borrowing again for a period of 30 to 60 days.

Commercial Paper Large firms with excellent credit reputations like Microsoft, Procter & Gamble, and General Motors Acceptance Corporation can raise large sums of money quickly by issuing commercial paper. **Commercial paper** is a short-term promissory note issued by a large corporation. The maturity date for commercial paper is normally 270 days or less.

Commercial paper is secured only by the reputation of the issuing firm; no collateral is involved. The interest rate a corporation pays when it sells commercial paper is tied to its credit rating and its ability to repay the commercial paper. In most cases, corporations selling commercial paper pay interest rates below the interest rates charged by banks for short-term loans. Thus, selling commercial paper is cheaper than getting short-term financing from a bank.

Although it is possible to purchase commercial paper in smaller denominations, larger amounts—$100,000 or more—are quite common. Money obtained by selling commercial paper is most often used to purchase inventory, finance a firm's accounts receivables, pay salaries and other necessary expenses, and solve cash-flow problems.

有担保的短期融资来源

15-5b Sources of Secured Short-Term Financing

If a business cannot obtain enough money through unsecured financing, it must put up collateral to obtain additional short-term financing. Almost any asset can serve as collateral. However, *inventories* and *accounts receivable* are the assets most commonly pledged for short-term financing. Even when it is willing to pledge collateral to back up a loan, a firm that is financially weak may have difficulty obtaining short-term financing or its loan request may be rejected.

Loans Secured by Inventory Normally, manufacturers, wholesalers, and retailers have large amounts of money invested in finished goods. In addition, manufacturers carry raw materials and work-in-process inventories. All three types of inventory may be pledged as collateral for short-term loans. However, lenders prefer finished merchandise to raw materials or work-in-process inventories.

A lender may require that inventory used as collateral be stored in a public warehouse. Because of this requirement, this type of financing is sometimes referred to as warehouse financing. In this situation, the receipt issued by the warehouse is retained by the lender. Without this receipt, the public warehouse will not release the merchandise. The lender releases the warehouse receipt—and the merchandise—to the borrower when the borrowed money is repaid. In addition to paying the interest on the loan, the borrower must pay for storage in the public warehouse. As a result, this type of loan is more expensive than an unsecured short-term loan.

Loans Secured by Receivables As defined in Chapter 14, *accounts receivable* are amounts owed to a firm by its customers. A firm can pledge its accounts receivable as collateral to obtain short-term financing. A lender may advance 70 to 80 percent of the dollar amount of the receivables. First, however, it conducts

商业票据
commercial paper a short-term promissory note issued by a large corporation

Table 15-3 Comparison of Short-Term Financing Methods

Type of Financing	Cost	Repayment Period	Businesses That May Use It	Comments
Trade credit	Low, if any	30–60 days	All businesses with good credit	Usually no finance charge
Promissory note issued to suppliers	Moderate	One year or less	All businesses	Usually unsecured but requires legal document
Unsecured bank loan	Moderate	One year or less	All businesses	Promissory note is required and compensating balance may be required
Commercial paper	Moderate	270 days or less	Large corporations with high credit ratings	Usually available only to large firms
Secured loan	High	One year or less	Firms with questionable credit ratings	Inventory or accounts receivable often used as collateral
Factoring	High	None	Firms that have large numbers of credit customers	Accounts receivable sold to a factor

a thorough investigation to determine the *quality* of the receivables. (The quality of the receivables is the creditworthiness of the firm's customers, coupled with the customers' ability to repay their credit obligations when they are due.) If a favorable determination is made, the loan is approved. Like most business loans, the borrower and the lender negotiate interest rates and repayment terms.

应收账款保理

15-5c Factoring Accounts Receivable

Accounts receivable may be used in one other way to help raise short-term financing: They can be sold to a factoring company (or factor). A **factor** is a firm that specializes in buying other firms' accounts receivable. The factor buys the accounts receivable for less than their maturity value; however, it collects the full maturity value when each account matures. The factor's profit is the difference between the maturity value of the accounts receivable and the amount the factor has paid for them. Generally, the amount of profit the factor receives is based on the risk the factor assumes. Risk, in this case, is the probability that the accounts receivable will not be repaid when they mature.

Even though the firm selling its accounts receivable gets less than face value, it does receive needed cash immediately. Moreover, it has shifted both the task of collecting and the risk of nonpayment to the factor, which now owns the accounts receivable. Generally, customers whose accounts receivable have been factored are given instructions to make their payments directly to the factor.

成本比较

15-5d Cost Comparisons

Table 15-3 compares the various types of short-term financing. As you can see, trade credit is the least expensive. Secured loans and factoring of accounts receivable are typically the highest-cost methods shown.

股权融资来源

15-6 Sources of Equity Financing

Sources of long-term financing vary with the size and type of business. As mentioned earlier, a sole proprietorship or partnership acquires equity capital (sometimes referred to as *owners' equity*) when the owner or partners invest money in the business. For corporations, equity-financing options include the sale of stock and the use of profits not distributed to owners. All three types of businesses can also

✓ Concept Check

- How important is trade credit as a source of short-term financing?
- Why would a supplier require a customer to sign a promissory note?
- What is the prime rate? Who gets the prime rate?
- Explain how factoring works. Of what benefit is factoring to a firm that sells its receivables?

保理公司
factor a firm that specializes in buying other firms' accounts receivable

Learning Objective

15-6 Evaluate the advantages and disadvantages of equity financing.

obtain venture capital and use long-term debt capital (borrowed money) to meet their financial needs.

出售股票
15-6a Selling Stock

Some equity capital is used to start every business—sole proprietorship, partnership, or corporation. In the case of corporations, stockholders who buy shares in the company provide equity capital.

Initial Public Offering and the Primary Market An **initial public offering (IPO)** occurs when a corporation sells common stock to the general public for the first time. McAfee—a corporation known as a leader in protecting consumers, businesses, and governments from cyberattacks—used an IPO to raise $740 million in late 2020. At the time of publication of this text, there are more companies that plan to use IPOs to raise capital as the economy begins to stabilize after the COVID-19 pandemic. As illustrated in Figure 15-6, the largest IPOs for U.S. companies—Visa, Facebook, General Motors, AT&T Wireless, and Kraft Foods—involve companies from a number of different industries.

Established companies that plan to raise capital by selling subsidiaries to the public can also use IPOs. In 2020, global biotech giant GenScript completed an IPO valued at over $400 million by spinning off Legend BioTech—a company that engages in the discovery and development of drug therapies for different kinds of cancer treatments. Monies from the IPO will be used to increase the parent company's cash balance and provide funding for growth and expansion.[11] In addition to using an IPO to increase the cash balance for the parent company, corporations often sell shares in a subsidiary when shares can be sold at a profit or when the subsidiary no longer fits with its current business plan. Finally, some corporations will sell a subsidiary that is growing more slowly than the rest of the company's operating divisions.

When a corporation uses an IPO to raise capital, the stock is sold in the primary market. The **primary market** is a market in which an investor purchases financial securities (via an investment bank) directly from the issuer of the securities. An **investment banking firm** is an organization that assists corporations in raising funds, usually by helping to sell new issues of stocks, bonds, or other financial securities.

Although a corporation can have only one IPO, it can sell additional stock after the IPO, assuming that there is a market for the company's stock. Even though the cost of selling stock (often referred to as *flotation costs*) is high, the *ongoing* costs

首次公开募股
initial public offering (IPO) occurs when a corporation sells common stock to the general public for the first time

一级市场
primary market a market in which an investor purchases financial securities (via an investment bank) directly from the issuer of those securities

投资银行
investment banking firm an organization that assists corporations in raising funds, usually by helping to sell new issues of stocks, bonds, or other financial securities

Figure 15-6 The All-Time Largest Initial Public Offerings for U.S. Companies

These five U.S. corporations raised billions of dollars by selling stock. Visa—the record holder for companies in the United States—raised $17.9 billion when it sold stock for the first time in 2008.

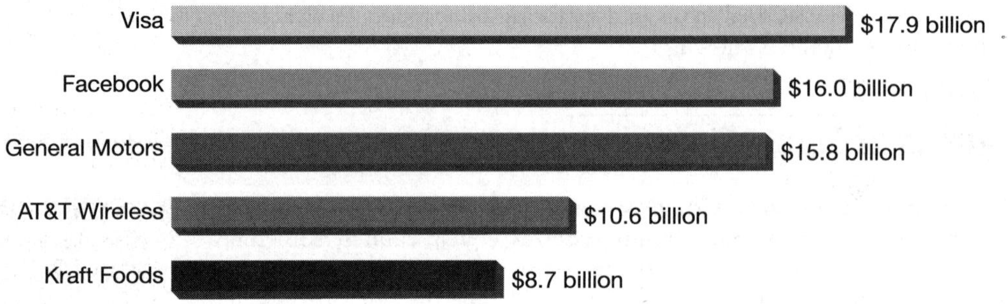

Source: "All-Time Largest U.S. IPOs," Renaissance Capital, Greenwich, CT.

associated with this type of equity financing are low for two reasons. First, the corporation does not have to repay money obtained from the sale of stock because the corporation is under no legal obligation to do so. If you purchase corporate stock and later decide to sell your stock, you may sell it to another investor—not the corporation.

A second advantage of selling stock is that a corporation is under no legal obligation to pay dividends to stockholders. As noted in Chapter 3, a *dividend* is a distribution of earnings to the stockholders of a corporation. For any reason (e.g., if a company has a bad year), the board of directors can vote to omit dividend payments. Earnings then are retained for use in funding business operations. Of course, corporate management may hear from unhappy stockholders if expected dividends are omitted too frequently.

The Secondary Market Although a share of corporate stock is only sold one time in the primary market, the stock can be sold again and again in the secondary market. The **secondary market** is a market for existing financial securities that are traded between investors. Although a corporation does not receive money each time its stock is bought or sold in the secondary market, the ability to obtain cash by selling stock investments is one reason why investors purchase corporate stock. Without the secondary market, investors would not purchase stock in the primary market because there would be no way to sell shares to other investors. Usually, secondary-market transactions are completed through a securities exchange or the over-the-counter (OTC) market.

A **securities exchange** is a marketplace where member brokers meet to buy and sell securities. Generally, securities issued by larger corporations are traded at the New York Stock Exchange (NYSE) or at regional exchanges located in different parts of the country. The securities of very large corporations may be traded at more than one of these exchanges. Securities of firms also may be listed on foreign securities exchanges—in Tokyo or London, for example.

Stocks issued by several thousand companies are traded in the OTC market. The **over-the-counter (OTC) market** is a network of dealers who buy and sell the stocks of corporations that are not listed on a securities exchange. The term *over-the-counter* was coined more than 100 years ago when securities actually were sold "over the counter" in stores and banks. Many stocks are traded through an *electronic* exchange called the Nasdaq (pronounced "nazzdack"). The Nasdaq is now one of the largest securities markets in the world. Today, the Nasdaq is known for its forward-looking, innovative, growth companies, including Intel, Microsoft, Cisco Systems, and Apple Computer.

There are two types of stock: common and preferred. Each type has advantages and drawbacks as a means of long-term financing.

Common Stock A share of **common stock** represents the most basic form of corporate ownership. In return for the financing provided by selling common stock, management must make certain concessions to stockholders that may restrict or change corporate policies. For example, every corporation must hold an annual meeting, at which the holders of common stock may vote for the board of directors. Often, stockholders are also asked to approve or disapprove of major corporate actions.

二级市场
secondary market a market for existing financial securities that are traded between investors

证券交易所
securities exchange a marketplace where member brokers meet to buy and sell securities

场外交易市场
over-the-counter (OTC) market a network of dealers who buy and sell the stocks of corporations that are not listed on a securities exchange

普通股
common stock the most basic form of corporate ownership and whose owners may vote on corporate policies

The NYSE: The largest stock exchange in the world. Most investors think of the New York Stock Exchange—often referred to as the NYSE—as the securities exchange where stocks for well-established, stable companies are traded. On the other hand, Nasdaq—the second largest securities market in the world—is where stocks for many innovative and technology companies are traded. The bottom line: Both the NYSE and Nasdaq are necessary components that enable investors to buy and sell stocks.

Few investors will buy common stock unless they believe that their investment will increase in value. As already mentioned, stockholders may receive dividends if the corporation's board of directors approves a dividend distribution. Also, stockholders can profit from their investment if a corporate stock increases in value.

Preferred Stock As noted in Chapter 3, the owners of *preferred stock* must receive their dividends before holders of common stock receive theirs. And, preferred stockholders know the dollar amount of their dividend because it is stated on the stock certificate. When compared to common stockholders, preferred stockholders also have first claim (after creditors) on assets if the corporation is dissolved or declares bankruptcy. Even so, as with common stock, the board of directors must approve dividends on preferred stock, and this type of financing does not represent a debt that must be legally repaid. In return for preferential treatment, preferred stockholders generally give up the right to vote at a corporation's annual meeting.

留存收益
15-6b Retained Earnings

Most large corporations distribute only a portion of their after-tax earnings to stockholders. The portion of a corporation's profits *not* distributed to stockholders is called **retained earnings**. Because they are undistributed profits, retained earnings are considered a form of equity financing.

The amount of retained earnings in any year is determined by corporate management and approved by the board of directors. Most small or growing corporations pay no cash dividend—or a very small dividend—to their stockholders. All or most earnings are reinvested in the business for research and development, expansion, or the funding of major projects. Reinvestment tends to increase the value of the firm's stock while it provides essentially cost-free financing for the business. More mature corporations may distribute 40 to 60 percent of their after-tax profits as dividends. Utility companies and other corporations with very stable earnings often pay out as much as 80 to 90 percent of what they earn. For a large corporation, retained earnings can amount to a hefty bit of financing. For example, as reported in its last annual report, the total amount of retained earnings for Procter & Gamble was over $100.2 billion.[12]

风险投资、天使投资人和私募
15-6c Venture Capital, Angel Investors, and Private Placements

To establish a new business or expand an existing one, an entrepreneur may try to obtain venture capital. In Chapter 4, we defined *venture capital* as money invested in small (and sometimes struggling) firms that have the potential to become very successful. Most venture capital firms do not invest in the typical small business—a neighborhood convenience store or a local dry cleaner—but in firms that have the potential to become extremely profitable. For example, Google, Apple, Facebook, and Uber all received venture capital before they became large, successful companies.

Generally, a venture capital firm consists of a pool of investors, a partnership established by a wealthy family, or corporations with money to invest. In return for financing, these investors generally receive an equity or ownership position in the business and share in its profits. Although venture capital firms are willing to take chances, they have also become more selective about where they invest their money. Often, venture capitalists prefer to invest in companies that have passed the initial start-up phase and show potential for rapid growth, increased sales and profits, and expansion.

留存收益
retained earnings the portion of a corporation's profits not distributed to stockholders

Another source of capital for a start-up business is an angel investor. An **angel investor** is often a wealthy investor who provides financial backing for small business start-ups or entrepreneurs. Often, an angel investor may be an entrepreneur's family member or a friend that provides the financial support needed to start a business. Unlike venture capitalists, angel investors are often more focused on helping a business or an entrepreneur succeed rather than earning huge profits. Some angel investors even become more involved in the business and become mentors for entrepreneurs to help them grow and expand the business. Angel investors may provide more favorable financial terms when compared with venture capitalists, bankers, and other financial institutions. In return for providing needed financing, angel investors can become an owner with equity in the firm. In other cases, angel investors loan money to a small business much like a bank or other financial institution.

Another method of raising capital is through a private placement. A **private placement** occurs when stock and other corporate securities are sold directly to wealthy investors, banks and financial firms, insurance companies, pension funds, large institutional investors, or mutual funds. When compared with selling stocks and other corporate securities to the public, there are often fewer government regulations and the cost is generally less when the securities are sold through a private placement. Typically, terms between the buyer and seller are negotiated when a private placement is used to raise capital.

天使投资人
angel investor a wealthy investor who provides financial backing for small business start-ups or entrepreneurs

私募
private placement occurs when stock and other corporate securities are sold directly to wealthy investors, banks and financial firms, insurance companies, pension funds, large institutional investors, or mutual funds

✓ Concept Check

- What are the advantages of financing through the sale of stock?
- From a corporation's point of view, how does preferred stock differ from common stock?
- What is venture capital? An angel investor? A private placement?

Entrepreneurial Success

创业成功：小企业如何获得融资

How Can Small Businesses Secure Financing?

To start a small business and keep it running smoothly, owners must provide or obtain money, and there are a variety of financing options for small businesses. Selecting the right type of financing often depends on a variety of factors such as the business's financial needs, the business owner's financial resources, and the owner's willingness to share control of the business.

To start the search for financing, small business owners should determine what the money will be used for and how much money is needed. For example, money is often needed to purchase equipment; retail, manufacturing, or office space; inventory; marketing and advertising; computers and software; web services; and more. When small business owners do not have enough money to purchase the resources needed to open or grow their business, they must look to other sources to secure additional financing.

To retain control of the business, owners can apply for a loan. Applicants are expected to share their business plan, financial projections to demonstrate how much money is needed, how long it will take to repay the loan, and the type of collateral (if any) that will secure the loan. There are many types of loans small business owners can apply for, including business lines of credit, invoice financing available from suppliers, long-term loans, and loans from the Small Business Administration. It is even possible to apply for a microloan, which are offered by nonprofits and mission-based lenders to help small business owners start a business in disadvantaged communities. The most popular microloan source is Kiva (kiva.org).

To avoid involving investors and financial institutions, business owners can also use crowdfunding to raise small amounts of money from many individuals. The most popular sites for crowdfunding are Kickstarter, Indiegogo, and Patreon. Because people that contribute to crowdfunding projects do not receive a share of ownership in the companies they support, they are not considered investors or lenders.

One additional way business owners can secure funding is to seek venture capital. Venture capital is a form of private equity that provides businesses with money in exchange for an ownership share or an active role in the company. It is also considered a form of long-term financing. Venture capitalists typically focus on high-growth companies that have the potential to become extremely profitable. In return for higher returns, they are willing to accept the higher risk often associated with high-growth companies.

Sources: Based on information in U.S. Small Business Administration, "Fund Your Business," March 11, 2021; Steve Nicastro, "Types of Business Loans: Compare Your Financing Options," *Nerd Wallet*, December 23, 2020; Chloe Goodshore, "Best Small-Business Funding Options 2021," December 17, 2020.

长期债务融资来源

15-7 Sources of Long-Term Debt Financing

Learning Objective

15-7 Evaluate the advantages and disadvantages of long-term debt financing.

As pointed out earlier in this chapter, businesses borrow money on a short-term basis for many valid reasons other than desperation. There are equally valid reasons for long-term borrowing. In addition to using borrowed money to meet the long-term needs listed in Table 15-1, successful businesses often use the financial leverage it creates to improve their financial performance. **Financial leverage** is the use of borrowed funds to increase the return on owners' equity. To understand how financial leverage can increase a firm's return on owners' equity, study the information for Texas-based Cypress Springs Plastics presented in Table 15-4. Pete Johnston, the owner of the firm, is trying to decide how best to finance a $100,000 purchase of new high-tech manufacturing equipment.

- He could borrow $100,000 and pay 7 percent annual interest.
- He could invest an additional $100,000 in the firm.

Assuming that the firm earns $95,000 a year and that annual interest for this loan totals $7,000 ($100,000 × 0.07 = $7,000), the return on owners' equity for Cypress Springs Plastics would be higher if the firm borrowed the additional financing. Return on owners' equity is determined by dividing a firm's profit by the dollar amount of owners' equity. Based on the calculations illustrated in Table 15-4, Cypress Springs Plastics' return on owners' equity equals 17.6 percent if Johnston borrows the additional $100,000. The firm's return on owners' equity would decrease to 15.8 percent if Johnston invests an additional $100,000 in the business.

The most obvious danger when using financial leverage is that the firm's earnings may be lower than expected. If this situation occurs, the fixed interest charge actually works to reduce or eliminate the return on owners' equity. Of course, borrowed money eventually must be repaid.

For a small business, long-term debt financing is generally limited to loans. Large corporations have the additional option of issuing corporate bonds.

长期贷款

15-7a Long-Term Loans

财务杠杆

financial leverage the use of borrowed funds to increase the return on owners' equity

Many businesses satisfy their long-term financing needs, such as those listed in Table 15-1, with loans from banks and other financial institutions. Manufacturers and suppliers of heavy machinery or equipment may also provide long-term debt financing.

Table 15-4 Analysis of the Effect of Additional Capital from Debt or Equity

Additional Debt		Additional Equity	
Owners' equity	$500,000	Owners' equity	$500,000
Additional equity	+0	Additional equity	+100,000
Total owner's equity	$500,000	Total owner's equity	$600,000
Loan (@ 7%)	+100,000	No loan	+0
Total capital	$600,000	Total capital	$600,000
Year-End Earnings			
Gross profit	$95,000	Gross profit	$95,000
Less loan interest	−7,000	No interest	+0
Profit	$88,000	Profit	$95,000
Return on owners' equity	17.6%	Return on owners' equity	15.8%
($88,000 ÷ $500,000 = 17.6%)		($95,000 ÷ $600,000 = 15.8%)	

Term-Loan Agreements A **term-loan agreement** is a promissory note that requires a borrower to repay a loan in monthly, quarterly, semiannual, or annual installments. As discussed earlier in this chapter, repayment may be as long as 15 to 20 years, but long-term business loans normally are repaid in 3 to 7 years. Loans where real estate serves as collateral may be as long as 30 years.

Assume that Pete Johnston, the owner of Cypress Springs Plastics, decides to borrow $100,000 and take advantage of the principle of financial leverage illustrated in Table 15-4. Although the firm's return on owners' equity does increase, interest must be paid each year and, eventually, the loan must be repaid. To pay off a $100,000 loan over a three-year period with annual payments, Cypress Springs Plastics must pay $33,333 on the loan balance plus $7,000 annual interest, or a total of $40,333 the first year. Although the amount of interest decreases each year because of the previous year's payment on the loan balance, annual payments of this amount are still a large commitment for a small firm such as Cypress Springs Plastics.

Loan approval 101. Before you ask for a loan, you should get to know your banker (or lender). Make sure your banker understands your business, your future plans, and how the loan will be repaid. Then, you will be asked to complete a loan application and interview with a loan officer or even a loan committee before a decision to approve or reject a loan request is made.

The interest rate and repayment terms for term loans often are based on factors such as the reasons for borrowing, the borrowing firm's credit rating, and the value of collateral. Although long-term loans occasionally may be unsecured, the lender usually requires some type of collateral. Acceptable collateral includes real estate, stocks, bonds, equipment, or any asset with value. Lenders may also require that borrowers maintain a minimum amount of working capital.

公司债券
15-7b Corporate Bonds

In addition to loans, large corporations may choose to issue bonds in denominations of $1,000 to $50,000. Although the usual face value for corporate bonds is $1,000, the total face value of all the bonds in an issue usually amounts to millions of dollars. In fact, one of the reasons why corporations issue bonds is because they can sell bonds to a lot of different bondholders and raise larger amounts of money than could be borrowed from one lender. Also, the interest rate for corporate bonds is often lower than the interest rate for a long-term loan from a bank or other financial institution. A **corporate bond** is a corporation's written pledge that it will repay a specified amount of money with interest. Interest rates for corporate bonds vary with the financial health of the company issuing the bond. Specific factors that increase or decrease the interest rate that a corporation must pay when it issues bonds include:

- The corporation's ability to pay interest each year until maturity; and
- The corporation's ability to repay the bond at maturity.

For bond investors, the interest rate on corporate bonds is an example of the risk–return ratio discussed earlier in this chapter. Simply put: Investors expect a higher return when they purchase high-risk, speculative bond issues—refer to Figure 15-7.

Today, most corporate bonds are registered bonds. A **registered bond** is a bond registered in the owner's name by the issuing company. Many corporations do not issue actual bonds. Instead, the bonds are recorded electronically, and the specific details regarding the bond issue, along with the current owner's name and address, are maintained by computer. Computer entries are safer because they cannot be stolen, misplaced, or destroyed, and make it easier to transfer when a bond is sold.

定期贷款协议
term-loan agreement a promissory note that requires a borrower to repay a loan in monthly, quarterly, semiannual, or annual installments

公司债券
corporate bond a corporation's written pledge that it will repay a specified amount of money with interest

记名（公司）债券
registered bond a bond registered in the owner's name by the issuing company

Figure 15-7 The Risk–Return Ratio for Corporate Bond Investors

High-quality corporate bonds pay less interest when compared to bonds that are more speculative.

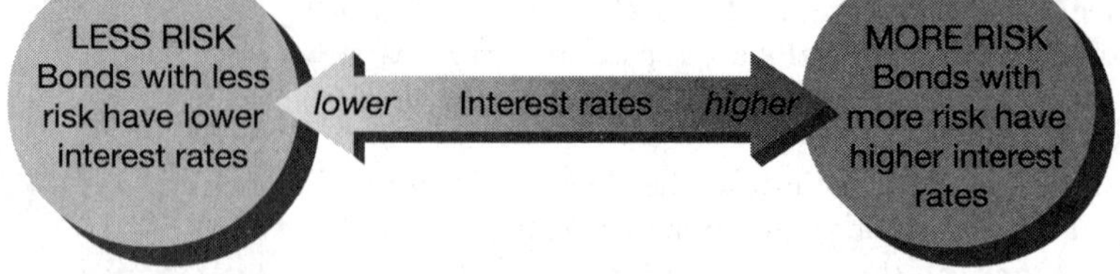

The **maturity date** is the date on which the corporation is to repay the borrowed money. Until a bond's maturity, a corporation pays interest to the bond owner at the stated rate. For example, owners of Dollar Tree bonds that mature in 2028 receive 4.20 percent interest per year for each bond they own. For each $1,000 bond issued, the corporation must pay bondholders $42 ($1,000 × 0.0420 = $42) each year. Because interest for corporate bonds is usually paid semiannually, the owner of a Dollar Tree bond will receive a $21 payment every six months for each bond they own. On the maturity date, a registered owner will receive cash equaling the face value of the bond.

Types of Bonds Corporate bonds are generally classified as debentures, mortgage bonds, or convertible bonds. Most corporate bonds are debenture bonds. A **debenture bond** is a bond backed only by the reputation of the issuing corporation. To make its bonds more appealing to investors, a corporation may issue mortgage bonds. A **mortgage bond** is a corporate bond secured by various assets of the issuing firm. The corporation can also issue convertible bonds. A **convertible bond** can be exchanged, at the owner's option, for a specified number of shares of the corporation's common stock. For example, Southwest Airlines—a passenger airline that provides scheduled flights in both the United States and nearby international locations—has issued convertible bonds that mature in 2025. Each bond can be converted to 25.9909 shares of Southwest Airlines common stock, which means investors could convert each $1,000 bond if the price of a share of the stock increases to $38.48 ($1,000 ÷ 25.9909 = $38.48) a share or higher. A corporation can gain in three ways by issuing convertible bonds. First, convertibles usually carry a lower interest rate than nonconvertible bonds. Second, the conversion feature attracts investors who are interested in the speculative gain that conversion to common stock may provide. Third, if the bondholder converts to common stock, the corporation no longer has to redeem the bond at maturity.

Repayment Provisions for Corporate Bonds Maturity dates for bonds generally range from one to 30 years after the date of issue. Some bonds are callable before the maturity date; that is, a corporation can buy back, or redeem, them. For these bonds, the corporation may pay the bond owner a call premium. The amount of the call premium, if any, is specified, along with other provisions, in the bond indenture. The **bond indenture** is a legal document that details all the conditions relating to a bond issue.

A corporation may use one of three methods to ensure that it has sufficient funds available to redeem a bond issue. First, it can issue the bonds as **serial bonds**, which are bonds of a single issue that mature on different dates. Second, the corporation can establish a sinking fund. A **sinking fund** is a sum of money to which deposits are made each year for the purpose of redeeming a bond issue. When Union Pacific Corporation sold a $275 million bond issue, the company agreed to contribute to a sinking fund until the bond's maturity in the year 2025. Third, a corporation can pay off an old bond issue by selling new bonds.

A corporation that issues bonds must also appoint a **trustee**, an individual or an independent firm that acts as the bond owners' representative. A trustee's duties

到期日
maturity date the date on which a corporation is to repay borrowed money

信用债券
debenture bond a bond backed only by the reputation of the issuing corporation

抵押债券
mortgage bond a corporate bond secured by various assets of the issuing firm

可转换债券
convertible bond a bond that can be exchanged, at the owner's option, for a specified number of shares of the corporation's common stock

债券契约
bond indenture a legal document that details all the conditions relating to a bond issue

分期偿还债券
serial bonds bonds of a single issue that mature on different dates

偿债基金
sinking fund a sum of money to which deposits are made each year for the purpose of redeeming a bond issue

受托人
trustee an individual or an independent firm that acts as the bond owners' representative

Table 15-5 Comparison of Long-Term Financing Methods

Type of Financing	Repayment	Repayment Period	Cost/Dividends/Interest	Businesses That May Use It
Equity				
Common stock	No	None	High initial cost; low ongoing costs because dividends not required	All corporations that sell stock to investors
Preferred stock	No	None	Dividends not required but must be paid before common stockholders receive any dividends	Large corporations that have an established investor base of common stockholders
Debt				
Long-term loan	Yes	Usually 3–7 years	Interest rates between 3 and 12 percent depending on economic conditions, the financial stability of the company requesting the loan, and the amount of the loan	All firms that can meet the lender's repayment and collateral requirements
Corporate bond	Yes	Usually 1–30 years	Interest rates between 1.25 and 8 percent depending on the financial stability of the company issuing the bonds and economic conditions	Large corporations that are financially healthy

are handled most often by a commercial bank or other large financial institution. The corporation must report to the trustee periodically regarding its ability to make interest payments and eventually redeem the bonds at maturity. In turn, the trustee transmits this information to the bond owners, along with its own evaluation of the corporation's ability to pay.

成本比较

15-7c **Cost Comparisons**

Table 15-5 compares some of the methods that can be used to obtain long-term equity *and* debt financing. Although the initial flotation cost of issuing stock is high, selling common stock is generally a popular option for most financial managers. Once the stock is sold and upfront, flotation costs are paid, the *ongoing* costs of using stock to finance a business are low. The type of long-term financing that generally has the highest *ongoing* costs is a long-term loan (debt).

To a great extent, businesses are financed through the investments of individuals—money that people have deposited in banks or have used to purchase stocks, mutual funds, and bonds.

✓ Concept Check

- Describe how financial leverage can increase return on owners' equity.
- For a corporation, what are the advantages of corporate bonds over long-term loans?
- What is a debenture? A mortgage bond? A convertible bond?
- Describe the three methods used to ensure that funds are available to redeem corporate bonds at maturity.

Discussion Questions 讨论题

1. Many small business owners find it is difficult to obtain debt financing. What can small business owners do to improve their chances of getting a loan from a bank or other financial institutions?
2. If you were the financial manager of Stars and Stripes Clothing, what would you do with the excess cash that the firm expects in the second, third, and fourth quarters? (Refer to Figure 16-4.)
3. Develop a *personal* cash budget for the next six months. Explain what you would do if there are budget shortfalls or excess cash amounts at the end of any month during the six-month period.
4. Why would a lender offer unsecured short-term loans when it could demand collateral?
5. How can a business owner or corporate manager use financial leverage to improve the firm's profits and return on owners' equity? Is there a potential danger of using financial leverage?
6. In what circumstances might a large corporation sell stock rather than bonds to obtain long-term financing? In what circumstances would it sell bonds rather than stock?

Case 15 案例 15：DoorDash 完成了首次公开募股

DoorDash Delivers an IPO

After its initial public offering (IPO), DoorDash started trading publicly on the New York Stock Exchange (NYSE) in December 2020. An IPO occurs when a corporation sells stock to the general public for the first time. The DoorDash IPO raised over $3 billion when investors purchased its stock on the first day of trading. Notable investors in DoorDash include SoftBank and venture capital firms CRV and Kleiner Perkins. SoftBank, which is known for investing in ByteDance, Fanatics, and Slack, is now the largest shareholder in DoorDash with a 20 percent ownership share after the IPO. The money from this IPO could be used to pay down corporate debt, expansion of services, or any legal business expense.

DoorDash offered three different classes of stock. While all three classes of stock are the same as far as profit distributions are concerned, they have different voting rights. Class A has one vote per share, Class B has 20 votes, and Class C has no voting rights. Offering multiple classes of stock that give different voting rights to different groups of investors has become a common practice in Silicon Valley. As a result of a voting agreement between co-founders Tony Xu, Andy Fang, and Stanley Tang, Xu, who is the company's CEO, will have significant influence over actions requiring the approval of DoorDash's stockholders. These actions, for example, can include electing individuals to the board of directors, making changes to the corporate charter, and approving mergers or acquisitions.

Because of a potential increase in its user base and encouraging projections for future revenues and profits, investors were anxious to purchase shares in DoorDash's IPO. To understand the "why" behind the investor frenzy to get DoorDash stock, it helps to look at how the delivery company earns revenue. A substantial amount of its revenue comes from fees paid by customers and commissions and fees charged to merchants—usually restaurants and grocery stores—for orders completed through the DoorDash marketplace. In addition, the company's DashPass program, which costs a flat monthly delivery fee of $9.99, also generates revenue for DoorDash.

Another factor that encouraged investors was the effect of the COVID-19 pandemic on revenues for food delivery services. DoorDash, which is the leading food delivery app with a 50 percent market share and more than 18 million customers, benefited from an uptick in deliveries during the pandemic. Even after the temporary shelter-in-place orders were lifted, the surge in demand for food delivery continued. DoorDash quickly surpassed its competitors Uber Eats and Grubhub to become the number one food delivery service. To strengthen its position in the industry, DoorDash acquired on-demand food delivery and catering business Caviar in a deal worth $410 million. While these facts are good news for investors, DoorDash has warned that it may not be able to grow at the same pace that it did during the pandemic.

For investors, risk factors include DoorDash's ability to continue to grow and compete, avoid interruptions in services, and attract and retain dashers (delivery workers). In fact, many experts believe that DoorDash's success depends on the success of the restaurant industry. As a result of the pandemic, a significant percentage of restaurants have closed. At the same time, the availability of food delivery services like DoorDash has given rise to restaurateurs that don't have brick-and-mortar locations. Once food is prepared by the restaurateur in a "ghost kitchen," it is picked up by a food delivery service and is delivered to the consumer.

Over the long-term, DoorDash's growth may also slow as more individuals venture back into dine-in restaurants. Additionally, there is intense competition in the food delivery service. And to make matters worse, there is little differentiation between the big players in food delivery. It's very easy for consumers to switch between food delivery providers, and there is very little brand loyalty. In fact, most people have several food delivery apps downloaded to their phone and will compare prices, merchant selections, and promotions before placing their orders.

Another challenge DoorDash faces is keeping its dashers happy. Like the customers who use food delivery services, there is little loyalty among delivery workers. DoorDash operates in an industry where independent contractors (dashers) provide on-demand services for the company's clients. To maintain an adequate supply of dashers, DoorDash must provide its independent contractors with flexibility, compelling opportunities to earn money, and other incentive programs that meet or exceed those of its competitors.

Despite these challenges, DoorDash is confident that it can become a profitable company. The company continues to innovate and identify trends in the rapidly changing food delivery industry. For example, DoorDash has focused on growing its business in suburban areas, which typically have larger ticket totals and lower costs. So far, the company's strategies have paid off because it now controls a 58 percent market share in suburban areas.

Even though it currently is the recognized leader in the food delivery industry and is experiencing growth in both revenues and its user base, DoorDash will have to continue to innovate to maintain its healthy market share in order to earn a profit for its investors. Like many corporations that use an IPO to raise money, DoorDash can expect that the next few years will be interesting for both management and investors.[13]

Questions

1. For a company like DoorDash, what are the advantages and disadvantages of using an IPO to raise capital?
2. Why do you think DoorDash issued three different classes of stock with different voting rights for each class of stock? As an investor, how important is the right to vote on issues that affect the future of the corporation?
3. Although DoorDash currently has 50 percent of the market for food delivery services and more than 18 million users, it must continue to increase both its number of users and its revenues. What are the challenges and obstacles that could affect DoorDash's plans for future growth?

Endnotes 注释

Chapter 1

1. Based on information in Sara Randazzo, "Purdue Pharma Reaches $8.34 Billion Settlement Over Opioid Probes," *The Wall Street Journal*, October 21, 2020; German Lopez, "Purdue Pharma Admits to Crimes for Its OxyContin Marketing. But No One Is Going to Prison," *Vox*, October 21, 2020; Austin Frakt, "Damage From OxyContin Continues to Be Revealed," *The New York Times*, April 13, 2020; Purdue Pharma, "Purpose Statement and Values".
2. Gwen Aviles, "Kendall Jenner to Pay $90,000 Settlement for Promoting Fyre Festival," *NBCNews*, May 21, 2020; Evan Comen and Thomas C. Frohlich, "The Biggest Corporate Scandals of the Decade," *247wallst.com*, December 20, 2019.
3. Ben Popken, "Chick-fil-A Sues Chicken Producers Alleging Price Fixing on Billions of Dollars of Poultry," *NBC News*, December 7, 2020.
4. "Marketers of Pain Relief Device Settle FTC False Advertising Complaint," press release, U.S. Federal Trade Commission, March 4, 2020.
5. Chris Isadore and Matt Egan, "Robinhood Agrees to Pay a $65 Million Fine for Deceiving Clients," *CNN*, December 17, 2020.
6. Shereen Siewart, "Wausau Woman Sentenced in $700k Embezzlement Case," *Wausau Pilot & Review*, July 29, 2020.
7. Chris Prentice, "Wels Fargo to Pay $3 Billion to U.S., Admits Pressuring Workers in Fake-Account Scandal," *Reuters*, February 21, 2020.
8. Ethics Compliance Initiative, "2020 Report: Global Business Ethics Survey," p. 6.
9. Jonathan Martin, "Plagiarism Costs Degree for Senator John Walsh," *The New York Times*, October 10, 2014.
10. Rob Golum, "Electronic Arts Investors Reject Executive Pay in Rare Rebuke," *Bloomberg News*, August 7, 2020; Stan Choe, "CEO Pay: When Investors Give Thumbs-Down to Soaring Compensation Packages," *Chicago Tribune*, May 24, 2019.
11. Marshall Cohen, "Financial Disclosures Reveal Postmaster General's Business Entanglements and Likely Conflicts of Interest, Experts Say," *CNN*, August 12, 2020, (accessed December 17, 2020); Allison Durkee, "Louis DeJoy Forced to Divest from Former Company that Contracts with Postal Service," *Forbes*, October 15, 2020.
12. Procter & Gamble Company, *Our Worldwide Business Conduct Manual*, p. 51.
13. "False Advertising Consumer Class Actions Related to Coffee Servings Continue with Suit Against Folgers," *The National Law Review*, December 4, 2020.
14. Jared Bryant, Amanda J. Beane, and Jason Howell, "$1 Million Settlement Announced in FTC's 'Made in USA' Enforcement Against Williams-Sonoma," *Consumer Protection Review*, April 24, 2020.
15. O. C. Ferrell and Larry Gresham, "A Contingency Framework for Understanding Ethical Decision Making in Marketing," *Journal of Marketing* 49 (Summer 1985), 89.
16. Starbucks, "Business Ethics and Compliance: Standards of Business Conduct".
17. "Kaiser Foundation Health Plan Will Pay $6.3 Million to Settle Medicare Advantage Fraud Allegations, Whistleblower Will Receive $1.5 Million," December 2, 2020.
18. Michael Josephson, "Can Corporate Ethics Programs Do Any Good," *Josephson Institute blog*, December 27, 2013.
19. "Google, Alphabet, Pledge $14.5 Million to Address Racial Inequity," *Philanthropy News Digest*, June 5, 2020.
20. Procter & Gamble, Tide's Loads of Hope.
21. P. Terry's, https://pterrys.com/giving-back (accessed December 18, 2020).
22. Chris Kempczinski, "McDonald's CEO: How We Are Thinking Differently about Our Role in Society," *CNN*, November 25, 2020.
23. Lieff Cabraser, "11th Circuit Upholds $41 Million Individual Verdict Against RJ Reynolds and Philip Morris in Florida Tobacco Lawsuit," Lieff Cabraser Heimann & Bernstein, blog, March 24, 2020.
24. Isabella Kwai, "Consumer Groups Target Amazon Prime's Cancellation Process," *The New York Times*, January 14, 2021.
25. Larry Light, "Coca-Cola's Brand-Business Rationalization,"

Forbes, August 4, 2020; Toby Howell, "Coca-Cola Cuts 'Zombie Brands' From Its Portfolio," *Morning Brew*, October 8, 2020; "Brands," Coca-Cola Company.

26. Robert Glazer, "CVS Lost $2 Billion with 1 Decision—Here's Why They Were Right," *Forbes*, April 21, 2020.
27. Ryan Luckey, "This Pledge Day, Speak Up Against Distracted Driving," *AT&T*, press release, September 19, 2019.
28. Brittany Baumann, "Midas Hospitality and Boone Center, Inc. Create Hospitality Program," *HospitalityNet*, press release, January 31, 2020.
29. "The 2017 WBI U.S. Workplace Bullying Survey," Workplace Bullying Institute, 2017.
30. Lisa Evans, "Why the Office Bully Is Getting Promoted," *Fast Company*, October 23, 2014.
31. Robin Abcarian, "Just as We Thought: Richie Incognito Bullied Jonathan Martin," *Los Angeles Times*, February 14, 2014.
32. "Sexual Harassment," U.S. Equal Employment Opportunity Commission.
33. Sheryl Estrada, "McDonald's Hit with $500M Sexual Harassment Lawsuit," *HR Dive*, April 15, 2020.
34. "Sexual Harassment Payouts Hit All-Time High in 2019," Fisher Phillips law firm, blog, January 28, 2020.
35. Evans, "Why the Office Bully Is Getting Promoted."
36. United States Courts.
37. Food and Drug Administration, "Food Loss and Waste"; Jennifer Molidor, "Grocery Chains Need to Stop Buying into Food Waste," *Grocery Dive*, November 9, 2020; "Is 'Ugly Produce' the Key to Our Food Waste Problem?" *CBS News*, October 12, 2019.
38. "Company Fined for Ocean Pollution," *The (Kuau'i) Garden Island*, February 11, 2020.
39. Kie Relyea, "EPA Fines Company in Lynden $41,500 for Releasing Pollutants into Fishtrap Creek," *The Bellingham Herald*, June 25, 2020.
40. "Recycle Your Denim with Us," Madewell.
41. "Major Companies Using Green Energy in 2020," *SaveOnEnergy*, May 18, 2020.
42. Chipotle, "Cultivate a Better World: 2019 Sustainability Report Update," April 2020; Peter Adams, "Chipotle Lets Diners Track Environmental Impact of Burritos as Restaurants Prioritize Sustainability," *Marketing Dive*, October 26, 2020.
43. Monica J. Stover, "Environmental Marketing Claims and the FTC's 'Revised Green Guides'," *Michigan Environmental Law Journal*, 37 (Spring 2020).
44. "Environmental, Social and Governance Report, 2019," Citi, p. 114.
45. "Tae Yoo," Cisco.
46. "People Planet Play: Caesar's Entertainment 2019–2020 CSR Report," Caesar's Entertainment.
47. Whole Foods Market, "This Is Whole Trade | Whole Foods Market," *YouTube*, June 20, 2017; Whole Foods Market, "Your Guide to the Whole Trade Guarantee"; Whole Foods Market, "Whole Foods Market History"; Whole Foods Market, "Our Core Values"; Whole Foods Market, "Quality Standards"; Whole Foods Market, "Whole Benefits"; Cale Guthrie Weissman, "Whole Foods Is Becoming 'Whole Paycheck' Once Again," *Fast Company*, February 12, 2019; Andria Cheng, "Two Years After Amazon Deal, Whole Foods Is Still Working To Shed Its 'Whole Paycheck' Image," *Forbes*, August 28, 2019; Karen Weise, "Amazon Wants to Rule the Grocery Aisles, and Not Just at Whole Foods," *The New York Times*, July 28, 2019.

Chapter 2

1. Based on information in Heather Lalley, "International Starbucks Now Outnumber U.S. Units," *Restaurant Business Magazine*, January 11, 2019; Starbucks, "Starbucks Company Profile"; Starbucks, "Company Information"; Kristin Salaky, "Starbucks Will Close 100 Additional U.S. Locations As It Continues To Adapt To Changing Consumer Habits," *Delish*, November 2, 2020; Starbucks, "Starbucks Announces New Roasting Facility in China, Extending Its Global Roasting Network," March 12, 2020.
2. "About the Coca-Cola Company," Coca-Cola Company.
3. "Company Overview," Combustion Associates, Inc..
4. "Liriope Factory," Southern United States Trade Association.
5. U.S. Census Bureau, "U.S. International Trade in Goods and Services, December 2020," February 5, 2021.
6. Ibid.
7. Jefferson Graham, "An iPhone Made in America? Why Building Apple's Smartphone in the USA Is a 'Pipe Dream'," *USA Today*, July 28, 2019.
8. "New Study: Trade Supported Over 40 Million Jobs," *Business Roundtable*, October 5, 2020.
9. "U.S. Trade in Goods and Services—Balance of Payments (BOP) Basis," U.S. Census Bureau.
10. "World Economic Outlook, January 2021," The International Monetary Fund.
11. "Canada – Country Commercial Guide," International Trade Association, August 3, 2020.
12. "Trade in Goods with European Union," U.S. Census Bureau.
13. "Trade in Goods with South and Central America," U.S. Census Bureau.
14. "Trade in Goods with Africa," U.S. Census Bureau.
15. Chuck Cartmill, "Lights and Insights: Streetlight Company Expands into New Solutions," Export Development Canada, blog, November 2, 2020.
16. Szu Ping Chan, "When Pepsi Was Swapped for Soviet

Warships," BBCNews, June 13, 2019.
17. "About Us," Dunkin'.
18. Elizabeth Paton and Sapna Maheshwari, "H&M's Different Kind of Clickbait," *The New York Times*, December 18, 2019; "Supplier List," H&M Group.
19. James Bamford, Gerard Baynham, and David Ernst, "Joint Ventures and Partnerships," *Harvard Business Review*, September–October 2020, pp. 116–124.
20. "GM, Honda Announce North America Car Alliance," *Yahoo Finance*, September 3, 2020.
21. Based on information in Past To Future, "Honda History - How Soichiro Honda Started Company," *YouTube*, February 20, 2019; Honda, "History"; Honda, "Company Overview"; Michael Wayland, "GM, Honda Partner to Develop Two New All-Electric Vehicles," *CNBC*, April 2, 2020; "Honda Accelerates Its 'Electric Vision' Strategy With New 2022 Ambition," *Automotive World*, October 23, 2019; Roberto Baldwin, "Honda Kills Clarity EV, Its Only All-Electric Car in U.S.," *Car and Driver*, March 9, 2020.

Chapter 3

1. Based on information in Darrell Etherington, "Amazon to Acquire Autonomous Driving Startup Zoox," *TechCrunch*, June 26, 2020; Sean O'Kane, "Zoox Unveils a Self-Driving Car That Could Become Amazon's First Robotaxi," *The Verge*, December 14, 2020; Stephen Nellis and Jane Lanhee Lee, "Exclusive: Amazon Plans at Least $100 Million to Keep Zoox Talent After $1.3 Billion Deal," *Reuters*, July 9, 2020.
2. The SC Johnson website.
3. The Procter & Gamble website.
4. The McDonald's website.
5. The Mars Corporate website.
6. The My New Company website.
7. Andrew Willis, "The 10 Biggest IPOs of 2020," the Morningstar website at www.morningstar.com (accessed December 15, 2020).
8. Based on information in SC Johnson, "Fisk Johnson, Current Chairman and CEO of SC Johnson"; SC Johnson, "Samuel Curtis Johnson: The Generous and Determined Founder of a Family Company"; SC Johnson, "Fact Sheet: SC Johnson is a Great Place to Work"; Caitlin Sievers, "SC Johnson Donated $20K a Day for 20 Days in a Row to End 2020; Six Racine-area Organizations Benefit," *The Journal Times*, January 3, 2021; Lauren Anderson, "SC Johnson Doubles Its Commitment to Fight COVID-19 to $10 Million," *BizTimes*, April 9, 2020; SC Johnson, "SC Johnson's Greenlist™ Program: Choosing Product Ingredients to Better Protect Human Health and the Environment," April 19, 2018; "S.C. Johnson Joins with Coke, Walmart, Pepsi and Others to Implement 'Circular Approach' to Plastic Waste," *The Journal Times*, December 20, 2020.

Chapter 4

1. Based on information in "2021 Fastest-Growing Franchises Ranking," *Entrepreneur*; Taco Bell, "Taco Bell History"; Jonathan Maze, "Is the World Ready for Taco Bell?" *Restaurant Business*, May 31, 2019; Lisa Fei, "How Taco Bell Is Becoming the World's Most Innovative Franchise," *Entrepreneur*, February 5, 2021; Danny Klein, "14 Glimpses Into the Fast-Food Restaurant of the Future," *QSR*, January 2021; Crew App, "Taco Bell Keeps the Frontline Connected"; Yum! Brands, "Taco Bell"; Taco Bell, "Taco Bell® Unveils Plans For New, More Experiential Cantina Restaurant Concepts," March 5, 2020.
2. U.S. Small Business Administration, Office of Advocacy, "Frequently Asked Questions," October 2020.
3. "How Much Income Can I Make as a Coffee Shop Owner?" Startmycoffeeshop.com; "Starbucks Reports Q4 Fiscal Year 2020 Results," Starbucks.
4. U.S. Small Business Administration, Office of Advocacy, "Frequently Asked Questions."
5. Ibid.
6. Ibid.
7. Ibid.
8. "Parson's Newly Acquired Braxton Technologies Awarded Tibbitts Innovation Excellence," *ThomasNet*, press release, January 26, 2021.
9. U.S. Small Business Administration, Office of Advocacy, "Frequently Asked Questions."
10. Tina Eaton, "The Bonobos Model: Lessons on Building a $300 MM D2C Brand," Plytix, March 24, 2020; "How Bonobos Went from DNVB Startup to $310M Acquisition Success," *Trade Gecko*, November 13, 2018.
11. "Meet the Winner: Small Businessperson of the Year," Amazon.
12. "About Us—Post Surgery Apparel Store," Renova; "Meet the Winner: Small Business Owner Under 30 of the Year," Amazon.
13. American Express, *The 2019 State of Women-Owned Business Report*.
14. Tom Foster, "This Entrepreneur Hit Rock Bottom Before Building a Billion-Dollar Jewelry Empire (with Only $500)," *Inc.*, Winter 2018/2019.
15. American Express, *The 2019 State of Women-Owned Business Report*.
16. Melody Hahm, "Etsy Seller: '2020 Was One of the Best Years I've Ever Had'," *Yahoo Finance*, December 23, 2020.
17. U.S. Small Business Administration website; SBA Office of Advocacy, "Women-Owned Spotlight Infographic," August 14, 2017.
18. "It All Started with a Bath," Da Bomb, https://dabombfizzers.

com/pages/our-story (accessed February 2, 2021); "Teen Sisters Run a $20 Million Business Sellling Bath Bombs We All Need Right Now," *Inside Edition*, January 16, 2021; "Meet 16 Teen Founders Who Are Building Big Businesses—and Making Big Money," *Entrepreneur*, August 20, 2019.

19. "Jerry Yang," *Forbes*; "Yahoo's Share Price Since Its IPO in 1996," The Atlas.
20. Caleb Watney, "America's Innovation Is Slowing," *The Atlantic*, July 19, 2020; "Billion Dollar Companies Founded by Immigrants," *Immigrant Founders*.
21. U.S. Small Business Administration, Office of Advocacy, "Frequently Asked Questions."
22. Kerry Hannon, "It's a Terrible Time for Small Businesses. Except When It's Not," *The New York Times*, December 14, 2020.
23. U.S. Small Business Administration, Office of Advocacy, "Frequently Asked Questions."
24. Timothy S. Hatten, *Small Business Management: Entrepreneurship and Beyond*, 5th ed., Copyright © 2012 by Cengage Learning. Reprinted with permission.
25. Joseph Pisani, "Amazon Founder Jeff Bezos to Step Down as CEO Later This Year," *KVUE*, February 2, 2021.
26. Dalvin Brown, "Franchises Help African-Americans 'Level the Financial Playing Field'," *USA Today*, February 11, 2020.
27. National Black McDonald's Operators Association.
28. "FAT Brands to Add Three Co-Branded Stores in Kansas," *QSR*, December 2, 2020.
29. "Taco Bell," *Entrepreneur*.
30. Jonathan Maze, "U.S. Franchisees Accuse Tim Hortons of 'Price Gouging'," *Restaurant Business*, February 28, 2020.
31. James Dornbrook, "H&R Block's Latest Filing: A Lawsuit Against an Ex-Franchisee," *Kansas City Business Journal*, February 26, 2020.
32. Aryan Sharma, "Serena Williams Reveals How She Invests Into Companies," *Essentially Sports*, June 6, 2020; "Ignite Change," Serena Ventures.
33. "SBIC Overview," U.S. Small Business Administration Office of Investment and Innovation.
34. Lindsay Blakely, "With Little Cash to Spend, Some Businesses Turn to Zero-Cash Deals," *Inc.*, May 22, 2020.
35. Gerri Detweiler, "Which Type of Crowdfunding Is Best for Your Small Business?" *Forbes*, January 9, 2020.
36. Brandon Gomez, "Latino-Owned Businesses Are Seeing Record Growth. Big Banks Are Still Not Funding Them," *NBC News*, February 5, 2021.
37. Based on information in Billions, "Top 10 Most Successful Entrepreneurs In The World," *YouTube*, August 23, 2020; Ryan Robinson, "8 Surprising Traits of the World's Most Successful Entrepreneurs," *The Balance Small Business*, November 20, 2019; Evan Tarver, "Mark Zuckerberg Success Story: Net Worth, Education, and Influence," *Investopedia*, January 31, 2020; Leah Ginsberg, "How Mark Cuban Started With Just $60 in His Pocket and Became a Billionaire," *CNBC*, July 5, 2017.

Chapter 5

1. Based on information in Georgia Wells, "Twitter's Jack Dorsey Survives Scrutiny From Activist Investor," *The Wall Street Journal*, November 2, 2020; Kirsten Grind and Georgia Wells, "Twitter's Jack Dorsey: A Hands-Off CEO in a Time of Turmoil," *The Wall Street Journal*, October 27, 2020; Lauren Feiner and Alex Sherman, "Twitter CEO Dorsey Keeps His Job After Company Strikes Investment Deal with Elliott Management, Silver Lake," *CNBC*, March 9, 2020.
2. Starbucks, https://www.starbucks.com/about-us/company-information/mission-statement (accessed January 22, 2021).
3. Amazon.com, https://www.aboutamazon.com/about-us (accessed February 2, 2021).
4. Nike, https://about.nike.com (accessed January 22, 2021).
5. Marguerite Ward, "Verizon Unveils New Business Plan with the Goal of Going Carbon Neutral by 2035 and Retraining 500,000 Employees for Emerging Tech Jobs," *Business Insider*, July 14, 2020.
6. Joshua Gans, "Why Elon Musks's New Strategy Makes Sense," *Harvard Business Review*, July 25, 2016; Nathan Furr and Jeff Dyer, "Lessons From Tesla's Approach to Innovation," *Harvard Business Review*, February 12, 2020.
7. Mike Dano, "AT&T Preparing to Unveil Massive, Three-Year Cost-Cutting Plan," *Light Reading*, March 3, 2020.
8. Terri Langford, "How Disaster-Tested H-E-B Navigates the Coronavirus Pandemic," KUT, March 26, 2020.
9. Seth Arenstein, "62% Have Crisis Plans, But Few Update Them or Practice Scenarios," *PRNews*, February 5, 2020.
10. "Cisco: 100 Best Companies to Work For, 2020," *Fortune*; "Benefits and Perks," *Cisco*.
11. Ann Schmidt, "How Mary Barra Led GM Through Its 2014 Recall Scandal and Changed the Company's Culture," *Fox Business*, July 12, 2020; Al Root, "Mary Barra Retooled GM to Keep It Profitable Through the Current Crisis," *Barron's*, June 26, 2020.
12. Ricky Griffin, *Fundamentals of Management*, 9th ed. (Mason, OH: Cengage, 2019), 5.
13. David Yaffe-Bellany, "The New Makers of Plant-Based Meat? Big Meat Companies," *New York Times*, October 14, 2019.
14. Based on information in Visual Capitalist, "The History of Tesla in 5 Minutes," *YouTube*, January 15, 2019; Cadie Thompson and Kristen Lee, "Tesla Celebrates Its 10th Year as a Public Company Today. Here Are the Most Important Moments in Its History," *Business Insider*, June 29, 2020; Andrew Greiner, Ivory Sherman, Tiffany Baker, Allie Schmitz, and Jen Tse, "The History of Tesla and Elon Musk: A Radical

Vision for the Future of Autos," *CNN*, March 22, 2019; Charles Morris, "The Definitive Story of Tesla's Beginnings, Told by Co-Founder Marc Tarpenning," *Evannex*, June 18, 2017; Chuck Squatriglia, "Tesla's Founder Sues Tesla's CEO," *Wired*, June 11, 2009.

Chapter 6

1. Based on information in Dave Sebastian, "Coca-Cola Plans Layoffs, Offers Buyouts to U.S. Staff," *The Wall Street Journal*, August 28, 2020; The Coca Cola Company, "The Coca-Cola Company Announces Strategic Steps to Reorganize its Business for Future Growth," August 28, 2020; Amelia Lucas, "Coca-Cola Will Cut 2,200 Jobs Worldwide as Part of Restructuring Plan," *CNBC*, December 17, 2020; The Coca-Cola Company, "About The Coca-Cola Company," investors.coca-colacompany.com/about.
2. "Structure and Governance," Procter & Gamble.
3. "Annual Report 2019," Toyota.
4. Lawrence A. Cunningham and Stephanie Cuba, "How Warren Buffet Built a $500 Billion Company on the Basis of Trust," *Marker*, January 14, 2020; David Larcker and Brian Tayan, "What It's Like to Be Owned by Berkshire Hathaway," *Harvard Business Review*, December 14, 2015.
5. Shilpa Phadnis, "Infosys to Eliminate Roles to Flatten Organisation," *Times of India*, June 1, 2020.
6. Dana Griffin, "Disadvantages of a Line & Staff Organization Structure," *Small Business*.
7. Ricky W. Griffin, *Fundamentals of Management*, 9th ed. (Boston, MA: Cengage, 2019), 356–357.
8. Benjamin Romano, "Two Pizza Teams and More: Former Amazon Employees Bake Bezos Principles Into Their Startups," *Seattle Times*, November 18, 2019.
9. Based on information in Entrepreneur, "The Origin Story of Sweetgreen," *YouTube*, March 5, 2020; Andrea Kramar and Tom Huddleston Jr., "How These 33-Year-Olds Are Taking Sweetgreen From a Dorm Room Start-up to the 'Starbucks of Salad'," *CNBC*, March 13, 2019; Daniela Galarza, "How Sweetgreen Got to $1 Billion," *Eater*, November 15, 2018; Amy Farley, "The Winner of the Fast-Casual Salad Wars? Sweetgreen, With 91 Restaurants in 8 States, and a Network of 150 Farmers," *Fast Company*, February 19, 2019.

Chapter 7

1. Based on information in Christopher Mims, "Not Even a Pandemic Can Slow Down the Biggest Tech Giants," *The Wall Street Journal*, May 23, 2020; Taylor Soper, "As Shopify Continues To Boom, Amazon Acquires Selz, a Startup That Helps E-Commerce Businesses," *GeekWire*, February 16, 2021; Justin Fox, "Amazon Spends Billions on R&D. Just Don't Call It That," *Bloomberg*, February 11, 2021.
2. The Bureau of Labor Statistics website.
3. Ian Linton, "Five Differences Between Service and Manufacturing Organizations," the *Houston Chronicle* website.
4. The 3M Corporation website.
5. Jill Jusko, "America's New Factory Building Frenzy," *Industry Week* website.
6. "GM Recognizes Suppliers for Delivering World-Class Innovation and Quality," the General Motors website.
7. The Berry Plastics Corporation website.
8. "Everyone Is Part of the Story—AT&T Diversity and Inclusion Annual Report 2019," the AT&T website.
9. "What Makes Six Sigma Work," the iSixSigma website.
10. The International Organization of Standardization (ISO) website.
11. "Productivity Change in the Manufacturing Sector," the Bureau of Labor Statistics website.
12. Ibid.
13. Ibid.
14. "China Is Closing the Gap with the U.S. in R&D Expenditure," the Research America website.
15. "Robotics in Manufacturing: How Robots Play a Role in The Assembly Line," the Robots.Net website.
16. The Sauder website.
17. Based on information in Bloomberg Quicktake, "How Toyota Changed the Way We Make Things," *YouTube*, August 23, 2018; Anjani Trivedi, "Toyota Broke Its Just-in-Time Rule Just in Time for the Chip Shortage," *Bloomberg*, February 15, 2021; Toyota, "Toyota Production System".

Chapter 8

1. Based on information in Aman Kidwai, "Chipotle to Expand Paid Parental Leave, Test Unlimited PTO," *HR Dive*, March 6, 2020; Chipotle, "Chipotle Enhances Paid Parental Leave and Tests Unlimited PTO," March 5, 2020; Chipotle, "Benefits".
2. *Labor Force Characteristics by Race and Ethnicity*, 2019, U.S. Department of Labor, Bureau of Labor Statistics, December 2020; *Women in the Labor Force: A Data Book*, U.S. Department of Labor, Bureau of Labor Statistics, December 2019.
3. *Women in the Labor Force: A Data Book*.
4. Pippa Stevens, "Companies Are Making Bold Promises About Greater Diversity, but There's a Long Way to Go," *CNBC*, June 11, 2020.
5. Chauncey Alcorn, "Target Plans to Increase Its Black Workforce by 20% over the Next Three Years," *CNN*, September 10, 2020.
6. Luz Corona, "Verizon Chief Diversity Officer on Her Unique Role to Shape the Future," *Adweek*, January 25, 2021.

7. "Taco Bell Hiring Parties," Taco Bell.
8. Susan M. Heathfield, "Using Social Media for Recruiting, Screening, and Background Checks," *The Balance Careers*, July 5, 2020.
9. Kate Rockwood, "How to Create an Effective Onboard Program," *SHRM*, May 22, 2020.
10. Alan Murray, "Why PayPal's Dan Schulman Gave Workers Pay Increases, Without the Market Requiring It," September 10, 2020.
11. Nancy Luna, "'Appreciation Bonuses' Coming to McDonald's Corp. Restaurant Workers During Coronavirus Pandemic," *Nation's Restaurant News*, May 7, 2020.
12. Hormel Foods, "Hormel Foods Annual Tradition of Sharing Profits with Its Team Members Continues," press release, November 25, 2020.
13. Jessica Dickler, "Gender Wage Gap Narrows But Shows No Signs of Going Away," *CNBC*, March 5, 2020.
14. Robin Bleiweis, "Quick Facts about the Gender Wage Gap," *Center for American Progress*, March 24, 2020.
15. Monica Langley and Marc Benioff, "How Salesforce Closed the Pay Gap Between Men and Women," *Wired*, October 15, 2019.
16. Elana Lynn Gross, "Tech Companies Are Sharing Gender Pay Data—But Oracle Is Resisting," *Forbes*, November 15, 2019; Stephen Johnson, "'Gender Pay Scorecard' Grades 50 Major Companies," *BigThink*, March 31, 2020.
17. Langley and Benioff, "How Salesforce Closed the Pay Gap."
18. "Employer Costs for Employee Compensation Summary," U.S. Department of Labor, Bureau of Labor Statistics, press release, September 17, 2020.
19. Conor Cawley, "20 Best Companies for Employee Benefits and Perks," *Tech.co*, May 13, 2020.
20. Lori Freifeld, "Dollar General Does It Again!" *Training*, March/April 2020, pp. 22–25; "Dollar General Earns Top Spot on *Training*, Magazine's Top 125 List for Second Consecutive Year," press release, February 25, 2020, via BusinessWire.
21. "2020 Training Industry Report," *Training*, November/December 2020, p. 22.
22. Kathleen Doheny, "Annual Performance Review Bows Out," *Society for Human Resource Management*, January 12, 2021.
23. Christopher Zara, "AirBnB Lays Off 25% of Its Workforce in a Dramatic Retrenchment for the COVID-19 Era," *Fast Company*, May 5, 2020.
24. Based on information in 23 ABC News, "Kern Back in Business: Taco Bell Hiring 250 New Employees," *YouTube*, April 22, 2019; "Taco Bell® Restaurants Hosting Nearly 600 Hiring Parties Across the Country in Time for Summer Hiring," *PR Newswire*, April 4, 2019; Kristin Salaky, "Taco Bell Is Hiring 30,000 Workers This Summer, With Some Newly Created Positions," *Delish*, May 21, 2020; Lisa Fei, "How Taco Bell Is Becoming the World's Most Innovative Franchise," *Entrepreneur*, February 5, 2021; Danny Klein, "14 Glimpses Into the Fast-Food Restaurant of the Future," *QSR*, January 2021; Crew App, "Taco Bell Keeps the Frontline Connected"; Nicole Duncan, "Inside Taco Bell's Innovative Approach to Labor," *QSR*, January 2019.

Chapter 9

1. Based on information in Catherine Clifford, "Whole Foods CEO John Mackey: Store Managers Could Be Making 'Well Over $100,000,' Without a College Degree," *CNBC*, November 5, 2020; Susan Dominus, "Breaking the Salary Sharing Taboo," *The New York Times*, February 19, 2020; "How to Make Pay Transparency Part of HR Strategy: Featuring Starbucks, BBC, Whole Foods, Etc.," *HR Technologist*, March 30, 2020.
2. "100 Best Companies to Work For," *Fortune*, 2020.
3. "12 Companies That Offer Part-Time Jobs with Benefits," Indeed Career Guide, June 1, 2020.
4. Nick Davidson, "The 50 Best Places to Work," *Outside*, November 4, 2019).
5. Ricky W. Griffin, *Fundamentals of Management*, 9th ed. (Mason, OH: Cengage Learning, 2019), 269–270.
6. Natallie Rocha, "Survey Says: Corporate Culture Is Worth More Than a Big Salary," *Fortune*, July 11, 2019.
7. Partially from "Southwest Careers: Culture," Southwest Airlines.
8. Lindsay McGregor and Neel Doshi, "How Company Culture Shapes Employee Motivation," *Harvard Business Review*, November 25, 2015.
9. Kim S. Cameron and Robert E. Quinn, *Diagnosing and Changing Organizational Culture* (San Francisco: Jossey-Bass, 2006).
10. Evan Nicole Brown, "Nike Debuts a Groundbreaking New Modesty Swimsuit," *Fast Company*, December 10, 2019.
11. U.S. Bureau of Labor Statistics, "Unpaid Eldercare in the United States," press release, November 22, 2019.
12. Richard Eisenberg, "The 4-Day Workweek: Has Its Time Come?" *Forbes*, February 6, 2020.
13. Jessica Howington, "How Flexible Work Benefits Companies and Employees," *FlexJobs*, August 20, 2020.
14. "2020 100 Best Companies," *Working Mother*, September 15, 2020; Michelle Parmelee, "Flex Work Is a Frontline Solution—and Not Just in a Crisis," *Forbes*, March 20, 2020.
15. Kate Lister, "Latest Work-At-Home/Telecommuting/Mobile Work/Remote Work Statistics," Global Workplace Analytics, March 2020.
16. Dave Nevogt, "Are Remote Workers More Productive? We've Checked all the Research so You Don't Have To," Hubstaff, August 31, 2020.
17. Nichole Bernier, "The Remote Work Experiment That Upped

Productivity 13%," *BBC*, July 10, 2020; Nicholas Bloom, "To Raise Productivity, Let More Employees Work at Home," *Harvard Business Review*, 92 (January-February 2014), pp. 28-29; Nevogt, "Are Remote Workers More Productive? We've Checked all the Research so You Don't Have To."

18. National Center for Employee Ownership, "Employee Ownership by the Numbers," September 2020.
19. Based on information in The World, "What Perks Does Google Offer Its Employees," *YouTube*, October 24, 2020; Tech Vision, "Inside Google's Massive Headquarters," *YouTube*, November 18, 2020; Rob Copeland and Peter Grant, "Google to Keep Employees Home Until Summer 2021 Amid Coronavirus Pandemic," *The Wall Street Journal*, July 27, 2020; "The Top 10 Reasons to Work at Google," *Investopedia*, September 19, 2020; Susan Wojcicki, "The Eight Pillars of Innovation," *Think with Google*, July 2011; Afdhel Aziz, "How Google.Org Fellows Are Helping Use The Power Of Data For Criminal Justice Reform," *Forbes*, June 16, 2020.

Chapter 10

1. Based on information in Netflix Research, "Personalization & Search"; Jeremy Bowman, "Netflix Is Killing the Competition in This One Key Category," *The Motley Fool*, September 15, 2020; Tara Lachapelle, "Netflix Investors, We Need to Talk About Churn," *Bloomberg*, January 19, 2021.
2. "Definitions of Marketing," American Marketing Association.
3. Bryan Pearson, "12 Ways Starbucks' Loyalty Program Has Impacted the Retail Industry," *Forbes*, December 16, 2020; Bernard Marr, "Starbucks: Using Big Data, Analytics and Artificial Intelligence to Boost Performance," *Forbes*, May 28, 2018.
4. V. Kumar, *Customer Lifetime Value* (Hanover, MA: now Publishers, 2008), p. 5.
5. Rajkumar Venkatesan and V. Kumar, "A Customer Lifetime Value Framework for Customer Selection and Resource Selection and Resource Allocation Strategy," *Journal of Marketing 68* (October 2004), 106–125.
6. Walter Loeb, "Nordstrom's Management Sets a High Target for 2021," *Forbes*, February 8, 2021; Rina Raphael, "Nordstrom Local Expands Its Innovative, Inventory-Free Retail Hubs," *Fast Company*, July 9, 2018.
7. Nikki Gilliland, "30 Brand Strategies with Excellent Social Media Strategies," *Econsultancy*, June 25, 2020; Taylen Peterson, "How Social Media Customer Success Impacts Retention," *Instapage*, January 3, 2020.
8. Hau L. Lee, "How Extreme Agility Put Zara Ahead in Fast Fashion," *Financial Times*, December 9, 2019; "The Secret of Zara's Success: A Culture of Customer Co-Creation," Martin Roll, blog, August 2018.
9. "The Story of Zipcar," Zipcar.
10. "Design Partnerships," Target.
11. Parija Kavilanz, "This Startup Is Making Glasses Kids Will Actually Want to Wear," *CNN*, January 23, 2020; Adam Blair, "Pair Eyewear Focuses on Fun and Fashion to Multiply Sales of Kids' Glasses," *Retail TouchPoints*, February 4, 2020.
12. Jefferson Graham, "Samsung Hits a New Record with the Most Expensive Smartphone: $2,000," *TechExplore*, September 1, 2020.
13. Sephora.com (accessed October 30, 2020); Parija Kavilanz, "No Testers, No Problem: Ulta and Sephora Have a New Take on 'Try Before You Buy'," *CNN*, June 18, 2020.
14. Jacob Krol, "Office 365 Is Becoming Microsoft 365 with New Features for the Same Price," *CNN*, March 30, 2020.
15. Amelia Lucas, "Powerade Is Launching 2 New Product Lines as Consumer Exercise Habits Change," *CNBC*, January 16, 2020.
16. "Social Content Ratings," Nielsen Social.
17. Ritash Pathak, "How Coca-Cola Uses Technology to Stay at the Top," *Analytic Steps*, October 24, 2020.
18. Peter Roeslier, "Consumers Find Influencers More Trustworthy Than Brands During the Pandemic," *Beauty Packaging*, May 26, 2020.
19. Evelyn Cheng, "China's Giant Middle Class Is Still Growing and Companies from Walmart to Startups Are Trying to Cash In," *CNBC*, September 30, 2019.
20. Based on information in CNBC, "How Starbucks Became an $80B Business," YouTube, January 10, 2019; Starbucks, "Starbucks Company Profile"; Starbucks, "Company Information"; Jennifer Warnick, "Five Things to Know About Starbucks (Online) Shareholders Meeting," *Starbucks Stories & News*, March 18, 2020; Kate Rogers, "Starbucks Is Speeding Up Innovation at its Seattle Research Hub," *CNBC*, May 2, 2019; Sarah Whitten and Kate Rogers, "Starbucks Cuts Long-Term Earnings per Share Forecast; Shares Fall," *CNBC*, December 13, 2018.

Chapter 11

1. Based on information in Phil Wahba, "Petco Rebrands, Bans Shock Collars in Health and Wellness Push," *Fortune*, October 7, 2020; Rhian Hunt, "Petco May Be Heading for an IPO as a $6 Billion Company," *The Motley Fool*, September 10, 2020; Petco, "Fact Sheets".
2. Matt Reynolds, "Jif, Skippy Add Flexible, Squeezable Peanut Butter Pack Formats," *Packaging World*, September 11, 2020.
3. Gillian Friedman, "Goodbye Tab: Coca-Cola Will Discontinue the Icononic Soda," *The New York Times*, October 16, 2020.
4. Procter & Gamble, https://us.pg.com/brands/ and https://www.pg.co.uk/brands/ (accessed February 15, 2021).

5. Eric Schroeder, "Panera Debuts Flatbread Pizza," *Food Business News*, October 29, 2020.
6. Monica Watrous, "Inside Ferrara's Transformation of Keebler Cookies," *Food Business News*, July 30, 2020.
7. Eric Schroeder, "Hostess Innovates with New Snack Cake Flavors," *Food Business News*, November 12, 2020.
8. John Bowker, "Bombardier Drops Iconic Learjet to Focus on Luxury Models," *Bloomberg.com*, February 11, 2021.
9. Ashlee Vance and Brad Stone, "Air Taxi Startup Has a Working Prototype and a Fresh $100 Million," *Business Week*, February 1, 2018; Jeff Sloan, "Joby Aviation Acquires Uber Elevate," *Composites World*, December 18, 2020.
10. Mark Wilson, "Dyson's Latest Invention? A $500 Flat Iron That Won't Fry Your Hair," *Fast Company*, March 10, 2020.
11. "Brewing the American Dream," *Samuel Adams Brewing*.
12. "Only a Dyson Works Like a Dyson: The Engineering Behind Dyson Vacuums," *Dyson*.
13. Jonathan Maze, "Chick-Fil-A Is Testing a New Chicken Sandwich," *Restaurant Business*, September 18, 2020.
14. Joe Maring, "Samsung Galaxy Note 7: Everything You Need to Know!," *Android Central*, June 4, 2020.
15. Phil Wahba, "Target's Newish Athletic Line Is Now Its 10th Billion-Dollar Store Brand," *Fortune*, February 8, 2021.
16. Udo Kopka et al, "What Got Us Here Won't Get Us There: A New Model for the Consumer Goods Industry," McKinsey & Company, July 30, 2020.
17. "Mohawk Group Furthers Execution of M&A Strategy Announcing Accretive Acquisition of Mueller, Purstream, Pohl Schmitt and Spiralizer E-Commerce Brands," Globenewswire, press release, December 10, 2020.
18. Emily Price, "Why Bud Light Gave Its New Hard Seltzer the Family Name," *Fortune*, January 29, 2020.
19. Miles Socha, "Louis Vuitton Expands In Tokyo with New Tower, Café—and Chocolate Shop," *WWD*, January 27, 2021.
20. Replenish, https://myreplenish.com/ (accessed February 24, 2021); CleanPath, https://mycleanpath.com/ (accessed February 24, 2021).
21. Stefanie Valentic, "How the Coca-Cola's Recycled Bottle Redesign Is Progressing Sustainability Efforts," *Waste 360*, February 9, 2021.
22. Pamela DeLoatch, "Survey: Packaging, Labeling Determine Whether a Shopper Buys a Product," *FoodDive*, January 4, 2018.
23. Neil Patel, "How Planet Fitness Capitalizes on the Casual Gym-Goer Despite Tough Times," *The Motley Fool*, May 6, 2020; Nathaniel Meyersohn, "Planet Fitness Is Winning by Charging $10 a Month," *CNN*, January 12, 2018.
24. Amy Feldman, "Why One Entrepreneur Thinks Millions of Americans Will Spend $25 on His Personalized Shampoo," *Forbes*, August 18, 2020.
25. Bill Shaikin, "What Does the Dodgers' Dynamic Pricing Schedule Mean for Fans? A Seat That Costs $33 One Day Will Cost $80 Another Day," *Los Angeles Times*, January 26, 2018.
26. Based on information in TimesTicking, "The History of the Shinola Watch Company," *YouTube*, July 16, 2020; Jack Roskopp, "What Is Shinola and Why Did It Get a Shoutout During the Oscars?" *Click Orlando*, February 25, 2019; Shinola, "Our Story"; Randy Wimbley, "Shinola Lays off Employees, Plans to Outsource Some Operations," *Fox 2 Detroit*.

Chapter 12

1. Based on information in Sarah Nassauer, "Walmart to Combine Online and Store Product-Buying Teams," *The Wall Street Journal*, February 25, 2020; Walmart, "About Us"; Ben Unglesbee, "Walmart Cuts Corporate Jobs as It Focuses on Omnichannel Push," *Retail Dive*, July 31, 2020.
2. Pat Reynolds, "P&G Greatly Expands Eco-Box Portfolio," *Packaging World*, April 22, 2020.
3. Blake Morgan, "After a Bruising Year, Logistics and Supply Chains Are Ripe for Technology Disruption," *Tech Exec*, February 22, 2021.
4. Fareeha Ali, "US Ecommerce Grows 44.0% in 2020," *Digital Commerce 360*, January 29, 2021; Bureau of Labor Statistics, "Industries at a Glance".
5. "FTI Consulting Projects U.S. Online Retail Sales Growth to Increase 25% in 2020," FTI Consulting, press release, October 13, 2020.
6. Fareeha Ali, "Nordstrom's Ecommerce Sales Represent 61% of Revenue in Q2," *Digital Commerce 360*, August 31, 2020.
7. Caroline Jansen, "Casper Expands Physical Presence Through Tie-Up with Sam's Club," *Retail Dive*, August 10, 2020.
8. "Fact Sheets," *National Association of Convenience Stores*.
9. "About Direct Selling," *Direct Selling*.
10. *Do Not Call*, "https://www.donotcall.gov" (accessed March 4, 2021); Simon van Zuylen-Wood, "How Robocallers Outwitted the Government and Completely Wrecked the Do Not Call List," *The Washington Post*, January 11, 2018.
11. Dan Gilmore, "State of the Logistics Union 2020," *Supply Chain Digest*, June 25, 2020.
12. Ibid.
13. "Building, Executing, and Measuring an Integrated Marketing Campaign," *Marketing Dive*, April 28, 2020.
14. Jack Neff, "Marketers of the Year No. 7: E.L.F.," *AdAge*, December 7, 2020.
15. "U.S. Measured-Media Spending by Medium in 2019," *Advertising Age Marketing Fact Pack 2021*, December 21, 2020, p. 5.
16. National Association of Realtors, "NAR's 'That's Who We

R' Advertising Campaign Highlights How Realtors® Open Doors to Opportunity for Their Clients and the Communities They Serve," press release, February 16, 2021.
17. Jessica Wohl, "Burger King Brings Humor to These 'Confusing Times' in Impossible Burger Radio Spots," *AdAge*, March 4, 2021.
18. Jessica Wohl, "McDonald's Launches a New Campaign to Promote Free Food for First Responders," *AdAge*, April 21, 2021.
19. "AdAge World's Largest U.S. Advertisers: 25 Biggest Spenders," *AdAge Marketing Fact Pack 2021*, December 21, 2020, p. 6.
20. "We're Disrupting the Way the World Sees Deals," RetailMeNot.
21. Mary Hanbury, "People Are Obsessed with Costco's Free Samples—But It's Actually a Brilliant Business Strategy," *Business Insider*, March 21, 2018.
22. "sandiegozoo," TikTok.
23. Sophie Cole, "How a Strong Brand Tone of Voice Can Help You Recover from Controversy," Stratton Craig, blog, July 10, 2020; Dan Tynan, "How to Survive a Public Brand Scandal and Recover Customers' Trust," Adweek, March 11, 2018.
24. Based on information in CNBC Make It, "How Casper Became A $1 Billion Mattress Start-Up," YouTube, April 9, 2019; "Casper's IPO is Officially a Disaster," *CNN*, February 5, 2020; "Casper, the Mattress Start-Up, Goes Through With Lackluster I.P.O," *The New York Times*, February 6, 2020; Clare Roth, "Mattress Unicorn Casper Accused of Misleading Investors With IPO," *Bloomberg*, June 27, 2020.

Chapter 13

1. Based on information in Netflix Research, "Personalization & Search"; Jeremy Bowman, "Netflix Is Killing the Competition in This One Key Category," *The Motley Fool*, September 15, 2020; Tara Lachapelle, "Netflix Investors, We Need to Talk About Churn," *Bloomberg*, January 19, 2021.
2. Social Media Fact Sheet," Pew Research.
3. Brent Barnhart, "Social Media Demographics to Inform Your Brand's Strategy in 2021," Sprout Social, March 9, 2021.
4. "2020 National Customer Rage Study," Customer Care Measurement and Consulting.
5. "The Top 10 Super Bowl 2020 Commercials by Digital Share of Voice," Ad Age.
6. Rosie Murphy, "Local Consumer Review Survey 2020," BrightLocal.
7. Ibid.
8. The Wyndham Hotel website.
9. Kiva, www.kiva.org (accessed March 13, 2021).
10. "PwC Global Crisis Survey," PricewaterhouseCoopers.
11. Nina Solis, "How to Respond to a Negative Online Review," Broadly.
12. "Generation Z News," *Business Insider*.
13. Kavya Ravi, "6 Ways Nike Built a Strong Brand on Social Media," Unmetric.
14. Ibid.
15. Alexander Santo, "The Ultimate List of Marketing Spend Statistics," Brafton.
16. "More Smiles in 2020: Lay's Kicks Off Search for People Creating Joy Across the Country; Unveils Three New Flavors to Smile About," Frito-Lay.
17. "Lego Ideas," The Lego Group, March 12, 2021.
18. LinkedIn, www.linkedin.com (accessed March 3, 2021).
19. Melissa Barker, Donald Barker, Nicholas Bormann, and Krista E. Neher. *Social Media Marketing: A Strategic Approach* (Mason, OH: Cengage Publishing, 2017).
20. Emily Heaslip, "9 Wildly Successful Crowdfunded Startups," U.S. Chamber of Commerce.
21. SAP, https://www.sap.com/community.html (accessed March 5, 2021).
22. Daniela Coppola, "E-Commerce in the United States—Statistics & Facts," Statista.com.
23. Jullia Andjelic, "47 Mobile Marketing Statistics to Transform Your Business," Smallbizgenius.
24. "Quarterly Retail E-Commerce Sales," *U.S. Census Bureau News*.
25. Natalie Colarossi, "Online Black Friday Shoppers Increase Nearly 45 Percent Amid COVID-19 Pandemic," Newsweek.
26. Internet World Stats, https://www.internetworldstats.com/ (accessed March 16, 2021).
27. Ibid.
28. Brent Barnhart, "Social Media Demographics to Inform Your Brand's Strategy in 2021," Sprout Social.
29. Eugene Lee, "Can My Employer Monitor My Web Surfing or Emails at work? (2020)," California Labor and Employer Law.
30. Jacquelyn Bulao, "How Many Cyber Attacks Happen Per Day in 2020?," TechJury.
31. "Seena Gressin, " Identity Theft Awareness Week Starts Today," Federal Trade Commission.
32. Eugene Bekker, "2020 Data Breaches," IdentityForce.
33. Based on information in Melissa Repko, "Target Aims to Make Its Booming Online Business More Profitable With New Technology, Small Sort Centers," *CNBC*, May 20, 2020; Jackie Crosby, "Target CEO: $7 Billion Investment in Stores and Technology Is Paying Off," *Star Tribune*, March 2, 2019; Shelley E. Kohan, "Target's Big Investments, From Small-Format Stores To Digital, Prove Successful," *Forbes*, March 4, 2020.

Chapter 14

1. Based on information in Derek Loosvelt, "Pros and Cons

of Working for the Big 4 and Other Top Accounting Firms," *Vault*, March 20, 2019; KPMG, "Your Career," March 11, 2021; PwC, "Employee Benefits," March 11, 2021; Will Kenton, "The Big 4," Investopedia, January 7, 2021.

2. Wolf Richter, "Accounting Fraud & Freight Recession Topple Celadon, Largest Truckload-Carrier Bankruptcy In US History," Wolfstreet.
3. Matthew Heller, "Power Solutions Fined for Accounting Fraud," CFO.
4. "Welcome to Sarbanes Oxley 101," Sarbanes Oxley 101.
5. *Occupational Outlook Handbook*, U.S. Bureau of Labor Statistics.
6. Based on information in Oracle, "Oracle Cloud Economics," March 1, 2021; Oracle, "Oracle Security, Identity, and Compliance," March 1, 2021; Oracle, "Oracle Corporate Facts," March 1, 2021; Todd Bishop, "Oracle's Larry Ellison Looks to One-up Amazon, Offering Full Cloud Inside Customer Data Centers," *Geekwire*, July 9, 2020; Bob Evans, "Hello, IBM and Microsoft: Larry Ellison's Big Plans for Oracle Autonomous Database," *Cloud Wars*, September 16, 2019; Fox Business, "Oracle Database, Not Amazon Has Most of the World's Data: Larry Ellison," *YouTube*, October 25, 2018; Oracle, "Oracle Ups the Ante in Cloud with World's First Autonomous Operating System," September 16, 2019; and Silicon Valley Historical Association, "Oracle," 2008.

Chapter 15

1. Based on information in Adam Levine-Weinberg, "Southwest Airlines Takes a Different Path Through the Pandemic," *The Motley Fool*, July 27, 2020; Southwest, "Southwest Corporate Fact Sheet," March 21, 2021; "Southwest Airlines Reports Fourth Quarter and Annual 2020 Results," *PR Newswire*, January 28, 2021.
2. Priya Merchant, "Pivoting During the Pandemic: How These Businesses Succeeded," Entrepreneur.
3. The *Occupational Outlook Handbook*, U.S. Bureau of Labor Statistics.
4. "Income Statement," Intel.
5. S. Lock, "McDonald's: Ad Spend," Statista.com.
6. "Uber Agrees to Buy Food-Delivery Service Postmates for $2.65 Billion in Stock," CNBC.
7. Jonathan Stempel, "Warren Buffett Gives Up on Newspapers; Berkshire Sells Unit to Lee Enterprises," Reuters.
8. Chris Isidore, "As JC Penney Exits Bankruptcy, Its Long-Term Outlook Remains Grim," *CNN.com*.
9. Laura Kim, Raynil Kumar, and Shaun O'Brien, "2020 Findings from the Diary of Consumer Payment Choice," Federal Reserve Bank of San Francisco.
10. John Ulzheimer, "How Many Credit Cards Does the Average American Have?" CardRates.com.
11. Frank Vinluan, "Legend Biotech's Upsized IPO Lands $424M for Multiple Myeloma Drug," Xconomy.
12. Procter & Gamble, https://s1.q4cdn.com/695946674/files/doc_financials/2020/ar/PG-2020-Annual-Report.pdf (accessed March 5, 2021).
13. Based on information in CNBC Television, "DoorDash Releases IPO Filing, Reports $149 Million Loss Through September," *YouTube*, November 13, 2020; Jessica Bursztynsky, "DoorDash Skyrockets in Market Debut, Closes up 85%," *CNBC*, December 9, 2020; Megan Rose Dickey, "DoorDash Is Buying Caviar From Square in a Deal Worth $410 Million," TechCrunch, August 1, 2019.

图书在版编目（CIP）数据

商学导论：第7版：双语教学版：英、汉 /（美）威廉·普赖德，（美）罗伯特·休斯，（美）杰克·卡普尔著；孔小磊译注. -- 北京：商务印书馆，2024.
ISBN 978-7-100-24576-0

Ⅰ. F712

中国国家版本馆CIP数据核字第2024XY1175号

商学导论（第7版，双语教学版）

〔美〕威廉·普赖德　罗伯特·休斯　杰克·卡普尔　著

孔小磊　译注

商 务 印 书 馆 出 版

（北京王府井大街36号　邮政编码100710）

商 务 印 书 馆 发 行

人卫印务（北京）有限公司印刷

ISBN 978-7-100-24576-0

2025年1月第1版　　开本 850×1092　1/16

2025年1月北京第1次印刷　　印张 26¼

定价：128.00元

用心字里行间　雕刻名著经典